The
Life, Passion, Death, & Resurrection
of
JESUS CHRIST

A CHRONICLE
from the Visions of
Anne Catherine Emmerich

BOOK IV

A. C. Emmerick

The
Life, Passion,
Death *&* Resurrection
of
JESUS CHRIST

A Chronicle from the Visions of
Anne Catherine Emmerich

BOOK IV

Lazarus • Land of Three Kings • Last Passover
Passion *&* Death • Ascension *&* Pentecost
Mary after Ascension • Her Death
May AD 32–August AD 44

From the Notes of
CLEMENS BRENTANO

General Editor
James R. Wetmore

Introduction & Chronology
Robert Powell, Ph.D.

First published in the USA
by Angelico Press 2016
Revised Text, New Text, Translations,
and Layout © James R. Wetmore, 2016
Introductory Material and Chronology
© Robert Powell, 2016

For information, address:
Angelico Press
4709 Briar Knoll Dr.
Kettering, OH 45429
www.angelicopress.com

ISBN 978-1-62138-187-7 (pbk)
ISBN 978-1-62138-188-4 (cloth)
ISBN 978-1-62138-189-1 (pbk series)
ISBN 978-1-62138-190-7 (cloth series)

Cover Image:
J. James Tissot (French, 1836–1902)
Nole Me Tangere: Touch Me Not (detail), Brooklyn
Museum, purchased by public subscription: 00.159.335
Reproduced by permission of the Brooklyn Museum
Cover Design: Michael Schrauzer

CONTENTS

CHRONICLE
of the Life, Travels, and Teaching of Jesus
During His Public Ministry

Years 3–4: AD 32–33

MAY 17, AD 32–FEBRUARY 18, AD 33
The Raising of Lazarus • Jesus in the Land of the Three Kings

Jesus in Bethabara and Jericho • Zacchaeus the Publican [1]—Jesus on the Way to Bethany • The Raising of Lazarus [12]—Jesus Begins His Journey into the Land of the Three Holy Kings [18]—Jesus in Kedar [23]—Jesus Goes to Sichar-Kedar and Teaches upon the Mystery of Marriage [27]—(*Jesus Raises a Dead Man to Life* [35])—Jesus Reaches the First Tent City of the Star Worshippers [39]—(*Nocturnal Celebration of the Star Worshippers* [41]—*Jesus Encounters a Pastoral Tribe* [43]—*A Wonderful Globe* [44]—*Abolition of Idol Worship* [46]—*Jesus Continues His Journey to the Tent City of the Kings* [47])—Jesus Ceremoniously Escorted by Mensor to his Tent Castle [50]—Jesus in the Temple of the Kings • Feast of the Apparition of the Star [56]—(*Arrival of the Leader of a Strange Tribe* [62])—Jesus Leaves the Tent City of the Kings and Goes to Visit Azarias, the Nephew of Mensor, in the Settlement of Atom [64]—(*The Wonderful Cure of Two Sick Women* [66])—Jesus Goes to Sikdor, Mozian, and Ur [70]—Jesus Goes to Egypt, Teaches in Heliopolis, and Returns to Judea through the Desert [76]—Jesus in Shechem, Ephron, and Jericho [81]—Jesus Goes to Bethany [89]

THE PASSION
& DEATH OF JESUS CHRIST

FEBRUARY 19–APRIL 1, AD 33
Final Weeks Leading Up to the Passion

The Last Weeks before the Passion • Jesus's Discourse in the Temple [95]—Jesus's Solemn Entrance into Jerusalem [102]—(*Magdalene Repeats*

Her Anointing of Jesus [111]—*Instruction at Lazarus's* • *Peter Receives a Severe Reprimand* [115]—*The Widow's Mite* [116]—*Jesus Speaks of the Destruction of the Temple* [117]—*Jesus in Bethany* [120])—Jesus's Last Discourse in the Temple [121]—Magdalene's Last Anointing [124]

Holy Thursday

APRIL 2–APRIL 3, AD 33
Holy Thursday to Earliest Hours of Good Friday • *Jesus's Arrest*

The Last Passover Supper [129]—The Washing of the Feet [142]—The Institution of the Most Blessed Sacrament [145]—Private Instructions and Consecrations [148]—Jesus on the Mount of Olives [152]—Judas and his Band • The Wood of the Cross [177]—The Arrest of the Lord [181]—Means Taken by Jesus's Enemies for Carrying Out Their Designs [193]—Glance at Jerusalem at this Hour [195]

Good Friday

APRIL 3, AD 33
Early Morning of Good Friday • *Jesus Taken before Annas and Caiaphas, Imprisoned, then Taken to Pilate*

Jesus before Annas [199]—Jesus Led from Annas to Caiaphas [202]—Jesus before Caiaphas [204]—Jesus Mocked and Insulted [210]—Peter's Denial [212]—Mary in the Judgment Hall of Caiaphas [215]—Jesus Imprisoned [218]—Judas at the Judgment Hall [220]—The Morning Trial [220]—The Despair of Judas [222]—Jesus is Taken to Pilate [226]—The Palace of Pilate and its Surroundings [229]

Morning till Noon of Good Friday • *Jesus before Pilate and Herod* • *Seven Falls beneath the Cross* • *Raising of the Cross, and the Crucifixion*

Jesus before Pilate [231]—Origin of the Devotion of the "Holy Way of the Cross" [235]—Pilate and his Wife [237]—Jesus before Herod [239]—Jesus Taken from Herod to Pilate [243]—The Scourging of Jesus [247]—Mary during the Scourging of Jesus [251]—Personal Appearance of Mary and of Magdalene [252]—Jesus Crowned with Thorns and Mocked [253]—"Ecce Homo!" [255]—Jesus Condemned to the Death of the Cross [258]—Jesus Carries his Cross to Golgotha [265]—Jesus's First Fall under the Cross [269]—Jesus, Carrying His Cross, Meets His Most Holy and Afflicted Mother • His Second Fall under the Cross [270]—Simon of

Cyrene • Jesus's Third Fall under the Cross [272]—Veronica and her Veil [273]—The Weeping Daughters of Jerusalem • Jesus's Fourth and Fifth Falls beneath the Cross [277]—Jesus on Golgotha • The Sixth and the Seventh Falls of Jesus • His Imprisonment [278]—Mary and the Holy Women Go to Golgotha [281]—Jesus Stripped for Crucifixion and Drenched with Vinegar [283]—Jesus Nailed to the Cross [285]—The Raising of the Cross [288]—The Crucifixion of the Thieves [289]—The Executioners Cast Lots for Jesus's Garments [293]—Jesus Crucified • The Two Thieves [293]—Jesus Mocked • His First Saying on the Cross [295]

Holy Saturday

APRIL 3–APRIL 4, AD 33
From Noon of Good Friday to Sunset of Holy Saturday • Sayings from the Cross • Death of Jesus • Descent from the Cross • Preparation of the Body • Burial • Descent into Hell

The Sun Obscured • The Second and the Third Sayings of Jesus on the Cross [297]—Fear Felt by the Inhabitants of Jerusalem [299]—Jesus Abandoned • His Fourth Saying on the Cross [300]—The Death of Jesus • Fifth, Sixth, and Seventh Sayings on the Cross [303]—The Earthquake • Apparitions of the Dead in Jerusalem [308]—Joseph of Arimathea Requests the Body of Jesus from Pilate [316]—The Side of Jesus Opened • The Legs of the Thieves Broken [317]—Some Localities of Ancient Jerusalem [320]—Garden and Tomb Belonging to Joseph of Arimathea [322]—The Descent from the Cross [324]—The Body of Jesus Prepared for Burial [329]—The Sepulcher [335]—The Return from the Burial • The Sabbath [337]—The Imprisonment of Joseph of Arimathea • The Holy Sepulcher Guarded [338]—The Friends of Jesus on Holy Saturday [340]—Some Words on Christ's Descent into Hell [344]

RESURRECTION • ASCENSION DESCENT OF THE HOLY SPIRIT

APRIL 4–MAY 31, AD 33
The Resurrection • Love Feasts (Agapes) and Appearances of the Risen One • The Ascension, Pentecost, and Some Early Events in the Community

The Eve of the Holy Resurrection [349]—Joseph of Arimathea Miraculously Set at Large [350]—The Night of Resurrection [351]—The Resurrection of the Lord [353]—The Holy Women at the Sepulcher [355]—The Guards' Statements [361]—The First Love Feast (*Agape*) after the Resurrection [363]—Communion of the Holy Apostles [365]—The Disciples Going to Emmaus • Jesus Appears to the Apostles in the Hall of the Last Supper [366]—The Apostles Preaching the Resurrection [371]—The Second Love Feast (*Agape*) • Thomas Puts his Hand into the Marks of Jesus's Wounds [375]—Jesus Appears to the Holy Apostles at the Sea of Galilee [378]—Jesus Appears to the Five Hundred [387]—Love Feast (*Agape*) in Bethany and in the House of the Last Supper • The Destruction of the Holy Places by the Jews [388]—The Majesty and Dignity of the Blessed Virgin [391]—Increase of the Community [392]—The Days Immediately Preceding the Ascension [395]—Jesus's Ascension into Heaven [398]—The Holy Day of Pentecost [404]—The Church at the Pool of Bethesda [408]—Peter Celebrates the First Holy Mass in the Last Supper Room [411]—First General Communion of the New Converts • Choice of the Seven Deacons [414]

The Life of Mary After Christ's Ascension

JUNE 1, AD 33–AUGUST 15, AD 44

The Life of Mary Following Christ's Ascension, Up Until Her Death and Assumption at Ephesus

The Blessed Virgin Goes with John to the Neighborhood of Ephesus [418]—Mary's "Holy Way of the Cross" near Ephesus • She Visits Jerusalem [423]—The Apostles Arrive to be Present at the Blessed Virgin's Death [425]—Death, Burial, and Assumption of the Blessed Virgin [428]

Maps 437

ILLUSTRATIONS

Portrait with Signature [Frontispiece]—Zaccheus in the Sycamore Awaiting the Passage of Jesus [5]—The Two Blind Men at Jericho [6]—Jesus Traveling Between Towns [94]—The Greeks Ask to See Jesus [109]—The Ointment of Magdalene [110]—Peter and John See the Man Bearing a Pitcher [139]—The Last Supper [140]—You Could Not Watch with Me for One Hour [159]—The Grotto of the Agony [160]—The Guards Falling Backward [183]—The Healing of Malchus [184]—Good Friday Morning: Jesus in Prison [223]—The Morning Judgment [224]—The Judgment on the Gabbatha [261]—Jesus Bearing the Cross [262]—The Raising of the Cross [291]—The Garments Divided by Cast Lots [292]—The Descent from the Cross [325]—The Holy Virgin Kisses the Face of Jesus on the Anointing Stone [326]—Mary Magdalene and the Holy Women at the Tomb [357]—*Noli Me Tangere*: Touch Me Not [358]—The Disbelief of Thomas [379]—The Risen One Appears on the Shore of Lake Tiberias [380]—Feed My Lambs [401]—The Ascension as Seen from Below [402]

YEARS 3–4
Day-by-Day

Chronicle of the Life
Travels, & Teaching of Jesus

The Raising of Lazarus
Jesus in the Land of the Three Kings
May 17, AD 32–February 18, AD 33

Final Weeks Leading Up to the Passion
February 19–April 1, AD 33

Holy Thursday to Early Good Friday
Jesus's Arrest
April 2, AD 30–April 3, AD 33

Good Friday Till Crucifixion
Jesus Taken before Annas & Cleophas,
Imprisoned, then Taken to Pilate • Jesus before
Pilate & Herod • Seven Falls beneath the Cross
Raising the Cross, & the Crucifixion
Morning till Noon, April 3, AD 33

Crucifixion to Holy Saturday
Sayings from the Cross • Death of Jesus
Descent from the Cross • Preparation of the Body
Burial • Descent into Hell
Noon, April 3–Sunset April 4, AD 33

The Resurrection • Love Feasts (*Agapes*) and
Appearances of the Risen One • The Ascension,
Pentecost, & Some Early Events in the Community
April 4–May 31, AD 33

The Life of Mary Following Christ's Ascension
Up Until Her Death & Assumption at Ephesus
June 1, AD 33–August 15, AD 44

The Raising of Lazarus •
Jesus in the Land of the Three Kings

Jesus in Bethabara and Jericho • Zacchaeus the Publican

5/17 WHEN Jesus and the apostles approached Bethabara on **MAP 35**
the Jordan, they found already assembled there an innumerable crowd of
people. The whole country was full, and they were encamping under
sheds and trees. Numbers of mothers with crowds of children of every
age, even infants in the arms, were coming in procession. As they proceeded up the broad street to meet Jesus, the disciples who led the way
wanted, on account of his great fatigue (for he had already blessed a
great many), to repulse the women and children, and that even a little
rudely. But Jesus checked them, and bade them bring the crowd to order.
On one side of the street stood in five long rows children of all ages, one
behind the other, the boys and girls apart, the latter being by far the
more numerous. The mothers with infants in their arms were placed
behind the fifth row. On the other side of the street stood the rest of the
people, who passed in turn from the last rank to the first. Jesus now went
down along the first row of children, laying his hand on their head and
blessing them. He laid his hand on the head of some, on the breast of
others; some he clasped to his breast, and some he held up as models to
the others. He instructed them, exhorted them, encouraged them, and
blessed them. When he had thus passed down one row of children, he
crossed to the opposite side of the street and came up among the grown
people, exhorting and instructing them, and even placing before them
the example of some of the children. Then he went down the next row of
children and came up, as before, among the grown people whose front
ranks had been replaced by those from behind. And so it went on, until
even the infants in the last row had received a loving caress and blessing.
All the children blessed by Jesus received an interior grace, and later on
became Christians. Jesus must have blessed fully a thousand children on
this occasion, for the concourse continued during several days. He
labored constantly, ever grave, mild, and gentle, with a certain secret sadness in his manner very touching to see. He taught now along the streets,
now in some house into which they had pulled him by his robe. He
related many parables, by which he instructed both the wise and the simple, and impressed upon the former the obligation of thankfully returning to God all that they had received from him, as he himself did.

Of the holy women, Veronica, Martha, Magdalene, and Mary Salome
were gone on to Jerusalem. I saw Mary Salome with her sons, John and

James the Greater, coming to Jesus and requesting that they should be allowed to sit, one at his right and the other at his left. Messengers had been sent thither by the Pharisees in Jerusalem, but many of them, being converted, remained; while others, returning in a rage to Jerusalem, repented on the way and later on became Jesus's followers.

5/18 Jesus left Bethabara with the apostles, and on his way he was entreated to visit a house in which lay ten lepers. The apostles, dreading contact with the leprous, went on ahead in a southerly direction, with the intention of waiting for Jesus under a tree. The lepers, enveloped in their mantles and full of sores, lay in a retired part of the house. Jesus commanded them to do something, and it seems to me that he touched one of them and then left them. The lepers one after another were taken by two people to a little pool near the house, and washed in the bathing tubs, after which they were able to present themselves to the priests as cured.

Jesus next went through another building that had a four-cornered courtyard. On either side of the latter was a covered archway, in one of which lay men, sick and crippled, and in the other, afflicted women. The beds were laid in rows of hollow places, scooped out in the ground to receive them. Another covered way on the same line cut through the middle of the house and led to a space in which the cooking and washing were done. Between this middle walk and those in which the sick lay, were grass plots. Jesus again cured several here. As he proceeded on his way, I saw following him one of the lately healed lepers proclaiming his praise. Jesus looked around, and the man fell on his face giving thanks. Further on the route, Jesus blessed many children who had been brought by their mothers to meet him.

5/19 The road traveled by Jesus and the [five] apostles on leaving Bethabara ran on the right past Machaerus and the city of Madian.[†]

5/20 *They did not enter Madian. Instead, they went to a Jewish settlement on the outskirts of the town. Here Jesus taught.*

5/21 They again approached the Jordan, made a circuit of Bethabara, and went by roundabout ways through a desert region toward Jericho.[‡]

5/22 As they proceeded on their journey,[††] the disciples who had been sent out on missions returned to Jesus one after another and related to

[†] On the way, they were joined by four other apostles and several disciples.

[‡] Today Jesus and his traveling companions made their way northward from Madian in the direction of Jericho. They stayed the night with some shepherds.

[††] Not far from the Jordan there was a large house where a shepherd family lived. Jesus went into the house. Here he recounted the parable of the unmerciful servant (Matthew 18:23–35).

him all that they had done. He instructed them in parables, but I remember only these words of his discourse: "They who say they are chaste, but who eat and drink only what pleases their appetite, are like those who try to extinguish a fire with dry wood."

5/23 Jesus and nine apostles and many disciples made their way to Bethjesimoth, where Jesus was awaited by the other apostles (Bartholomew, Judas, and another) and several disciples. With the onset of the sabbath, he taught in the synagogue at Bethjesimoth. He also healed a crippled woman. And again the Pharisees protested against healing on the sabbath.

5/24–27 Jesus remained these four days in Bethjesimoth. The Pharisees tried to prevent him from going into the synagogue, but Jesus walked through them and entered the holy building, where he taught in parables.

5/28 Another parable referred to the future of the twelve apostles. Jesus said: "Now ye cling to me, because ye fare well"; but they did not understand that by these words he meant the peace and beautiful instructions that they then enjoyed. "In the time of need," he continued, "ye will act otherwise. Even they whom I carry about with me like a mantle of love, will cast that mantle off and flee." These words referred to John in the garden of Gethsemane [Mark 14:51–52]. In a little town near the Jordan, I saw a woman entreating Jesus to cure her daughter, who was covered with ulcers. Jesus told her that he would send one of the disciples to her. But she wanted him to go himself, which, however, he did not do. When he was drawing near to Jericho, the woman again approached and begged his aid. She urged that she had now renounced all that he had commanded her. Jesus, however, still repulsed her. Her child was the fruit of sin, and Jesus reproached her with a fault (it appeared to be but a small one) to which she had already clung for several years. He told her that she should not come again to him until she had freed herself from it. Then I saw the woman hurrying past the apostles and disciples toward Jericho.

5/29 Having almost reached the city, four Pharisees sent by their Jerusalem colleagues came and warned him not to enter lest Herod would put him to death. This they did, however, not because they cared for him, but because having heard of his numerous miracles, they were afraid of him. Jesus replied that they should say to Herod, the fox, these words only: "Behold, I cast out devils and do cures today and tomorrow, and the third day I am consummated." Two of these Pharisees were converted and followed Jesus, but the other two returned in a rage to Jerusalem.

Then came to Jesus two brothers belonging to Jericho. They could not agree on the subject of their patrimony; one wanted to remain, the other desired to go away. One proposed that Jesus, so renowned everywhere, should divide the patrimony between them, and they had in consequence come to meet him. But he refused, saying that it was not his business. And when even John remarked to him that it was a good work, and Peter seconded the word, Jesus replied that he was not come to distribute earthly goods, but only heavenly ones. After which he took occasion to deliver a long exhortation before the rapidly increasing crowd. But the disciples as yet did not always understand him rightly. They had not yet received the Holy Spirit and so they went on expecting an earthly kingdom.

Jesus was again met by crowds of women with their children, for whom they implored a blessing. The disciples, disturbed by the recent menaces of the Pharisees and desirous of shunning such excitement, tried to drive the women back, for they were entrusted with the duty of keeping order. But Jesus commanded them to allow the children to come forward. They needed his blessing, he said, in order that they too might become his disciples. Then he blessed many of the infants at the breast and the children of ten and eleven years. Some he did not bless, but later on these again presented themselves.

5/30 Just outside the city, which was surrounded by gardens, pleasure grounds, and villas, Jesus and his followers encountered a dense crowd composed of people from all parts of the country around. They had assembled with their sick, who were lying on litters under sheds and tents. They had been waiting for Jesus, and now they beset him and his disciples on all sides. Zacchaeus, one of the chief publicans, who dwelt outside the city, had stationed himself on the road by which Jesus had to pass. As he was short in stature, he climbed a fig tree in order to be able to see Jesus better in the crowd. Jesus looked up into the tree and said: "Zacchaeus, make haste and come down, for this day I must abide in thy house." Zacchaeus hurried down, bowed humbly to Jesus, and very much touched returned home to make preparations for receiving his honored guest. When Jesus said that he must that day enter into Zacchaeus's house, he meant into his heart, for on that day he went into Jericho itself, and not into the house of Zacchaeus. On arriving at the city gate, Jesus found none of the people assembled to welcome him, for through dread of the Pharisees they were remaining quietly in their homes. The crowd, gathered at some distance from the city, were all strangers come to implore Jesus's assistance in their various needs. He cured a blind man and a deaf mute, but some others he sent away. He blessed the children, especially the babes at the breast, and told the apostles that men must in this way be accustomed to devote their children from earliest youth to him, and that all thus blessed would follow him. Among those sent away was a woman afflicted with an issue of blood.

Zaccheus in the Sycamore Awaiting the Passage of Jesus

The Two Blind Men at Jericho

She had come some days before with the firm resolve to implore Jesus for her cure. I heard Jesus saying to the disciples that whoever does not persevere in prayer, is not in earnest and has no faith.

As the sabbath now began, Jesus went with his apostles and disciples to the synagogue of the city and afterward to the inn. He and the apostles dined in the open refectory, the disciples in the archway. The meal consisted of little rolls, honey, and fruit. They ate standing, Jesus meantime teaching and relating parables. Every three of the apostles drank from one cup, but Jesus had one to himself. The woman that had already been twice repulsed came again to Jesus imploring help for her daughter, but with no better success than before, because she was not sincere. She had been questioning among the Pharisees of Jericho about what was said of Jesus in Jerusalem.

Zacchaeus also here presented himself to Jesus. The new disciples had already taken it ill outside the city that Jesus had accosted the ill-famed publican and even wanted to abide with him, for Zacchaeus in particular was a subject of scandal to them. Some were related to him, and they were ashamed of his remaining a publican so long and up to the present unconverted. Zacchaeus drew near the hall in which the disciples were dining, but no one wanted to have anything to do with him, no one invited him to eat. Then Jesus stepped out into the hall, beckoned Zacchaeus in, and offered him food and drink.

5/31 On the following day, when Jesus went again to the synagogue and told the Pharisees to give place to him, as he intended to read and explain the sabbath lesson, they raised a great contention, but they did not prevail. He inveighed against avarice, and cured an invalid who had been carried on a litter to the door of the synagogue. The sabbath over, Jesus went with his apostles to Zacchaeus's dwelling outside of Jericho. None of the disciples accompanied him. The woman so desirous of help for her daughter again followed Jesus on the road out to Zacchaeus's. He laid his hand on her to free her from her own bad disposition, and told her to return home, for her child was cured. During the meal, which consisted of honey, fruit, and a lamb, Zacchaeus served at table, but whenever Jesus spoke, he listened devoutly. Jesus related the parable of the fig tree in the vineyard which for three years bore no fruit, and for which the vinedresser implored one more year of indulgence. When uttering this parable, Jesus addressed the apostles as the vineyard; of himself he spoke as the owner; and of Zacchaeus as the fig tree. It was now three years since the relatives of the last-named had abandoned their dishonorable calling and followed Jesus, while he all this time had still carried on the same business, on which account he was looked upon with special contempt by the disciples. But Jesus had cast upon him a look of mercy when he called him down from the tree. Jesus spoke also of the sterile trees that produce many leaves, but no fruit. The leaves, he said, are exterior works. They make a great rustling, but soon pass away leaving no seed of good. But the fruits are that interior, efficacious reality in faith and action, with their capability of reproduction, and the prolongation of the tree's life stored away in the kernel. It seems to me that Jesus, in calling Zacchaeus down from the tree, did the same as to engage him to renounce the noise and bustle of the crowd, for Zacchaeus was like the ripe fruit which now detached itself from the tree that for three years had stood unfruitful in the vineyard. Jesus spoke, likewise, of the faithful servants who watched for the coming of their lord, and who suffered no noise that could prevent them from hearing his knock.

6/1–3 *Jesus and the disciples stayed in Jericho.*

6/4 *Today Jesus and his disciples were invited to dine with the Pharisees. During the meal, they accused Jesus of breaking the Law by healing on the sabbath. Jesus replied in words similar to those recorded in Luke 14:1–24. Today, many people in Jericho were baptized by James and Bartholomew.*

6/5 *Jesus taught in the synagogue and on the streets of Jericho. Many tax collectors and sinners came to hear him, and the Pharisees plotted against him (Luke 15:1–2). The disciples were unhappy that Jesus associated with tax collectors and sinners. Because of this, Jesus told them the parables recorded in Luke 15:3–32.*

6/6 *After healing a woman with as issue of blood this morning, Jesus taught concerning repeated and constant prayer. Later, messengers came from Bethany requesting Jesus to go there and heal Lazarus. But Jesus replied that the time was not yet ripe and that he would travel first to Samaria.*

6/7 It appeared as if Jesus was now in Jericho for the last time, and as if he wished to pour out upon it the fullness of his love. He sent the apostles and disciples two by two out into the districts around into which he himself would go no more. In Jericho itself, he went from house to house, taught in the synagogue and on the streets, and everywhere to a great concourse of people.

6/8 Sinners and publicans encompassed him on all sides, and on the roads by which he had to pass lay the sick, sighing and imploring help. He taught and cured without intermission, and was so earnest, so gentle, and so tranquil.†

6/9 The disciples, on the contrary, were anxious and dissatisfied on account of Jesus's so unconcernedly exposing himself to the snares that the

---

† He also sent out the apostles and disciples.

enraged Pharisees, of whom almost a hundred were gathered here from different parts of the country, sought to prepare for him. They sent messengers to Jerusalem to consult as to how they could take him into custody. The apostles too were in a certain dread, as if they thought that Jesus laid himself open to danger and treated with the people rather rashly. Once I saw Jesus surrounded by a great crowd seeking his help, and among them were some sick that had caused themselves to be carried to him. The disciples meanwhile kept at a distance. The palsied woman with the issue of blood whom he had already sent away more than once had caused herself to be carried to the bath of purification, or expiation, with which was connected the forgiveness of sin. She crept afterward to Jesus and touched the hem of his robe. He instantly stood still, looked after her, and healed her. The woman arose, thanked her benefactor, and returned cured to her home in the city. Jesus then taught upon persevering and repeated prayer. He said that one should never desist from his entreaties. I was thinking meantime of the great charity of the good people who had brought the woman so long a distance, carrying her here and there after the Lord, and begging the disciples to inform them whither he was going next, that they might procure for her a good place. Owing to the nature of her sickness, which was regarded as unclean, she could not rest anywhere and everywhere. She had to solicit her cure for eight days long.

6/10 Before Jesus's departure from Jericho, messengers from Bethany brought to the disciples the news of how earnestly Martha and Magdalene were longing for his coming, as Lazarus was very sick. Jesus, however, did not go to Bethany, but to a little village north of Jericho. Here too, a crowd had assembled, and numbers of sick, blind, and crippled were awaiting his arrival. Two blind men, each with two guides, were sitting by the roadside, and when Jesus passed by they cried out after him, begging to be cured. The people tried to silence them with threats, but they followed Jesus, crying after him: "Ah, thou Son of David! Have mercy on us!" Then Jesus turned, commanded them to be led to him, and touched their eyes. They saw and followed him.

6/11 A great tumult arose on account of the cure of these blind men, as well as of those to whom Jesus had restored sight on his entrance into Jericho. The Pharisees instituted an inquiry into the case, and interrogated the father of one of the cured as well as himself. The disciples meantime were very desirous that Jesus should go to Lazarus's, in Bethany, for there they would be in greater peace and less molested. They were in truth a little discontented, but Jesus went on curing numbers. Words cannot express how gentle and forbearing he was under such imputations, attacks, and persecutions, and how sweetly and gravely he smiled when the disciples wanted to divert him from his purpose.

6/12 He next went in the direction of Samaria. Not far from one of the little villages along the highroad, about a hundred paces to one side, there stood a tent in which ten lepers were lying in beds. As Jesus was passing, the lepers came out and cried to him for help. Jesus stood still, but the disciples went on. The lepers, entirely enveloped in their mantles, approached—some quickly, others slowly, as their strength permitted—and stood in a circle around Jesus. He touched each one separately, directed them to present themselves to the priests, and went on his way. One of the lepers, a Samaritan and the most active of the ten, went along the same road with two of the disciples, but the others took different routes. These were not cured all at once; although able to walk, they were not made perfectly clean till about an hour afterward.

Soon after this last encounter, a father from a shepherd village a quarter of an hour to the right of the road came to meet Jesus and begged him to go back with him to the village, for his little daughter was lying dead. Jesus went with him at once, and on the way was overtaken by the cured Samaritan who, touched by his perfect cure, had hurried back to thank his benefactor. He cast himself at the feet of Jesus, who said: "Were not ten made clean? And where are the nine? Is not one found among them to return and give glory to God, but only this stranger? Arise, go thy way! Thy faith hath made thee whole!" This man later on became a disciple. Peter, John, and James the Greater were with Jesus at this time. The little girl, who was about seven years old, was already four days dead. Jesus laid one hand on her head, the other on her breast, and raising his eyes to heaven prayed, whereupon the child rose up alive. Then Jesus told the apostles that even so should they do in his name. The child's father had strong faith, and full of confidence he had awaited Jesus's coming. His wife wanted him to send word to Jesus, but he was full of hope and waited until he came. Soon after, he gave up his business to another and, when his wife died after Jesus's death, he became a disciple and acquired a distinguished name. The little girl restored to life likewise became very pious.

6/13–17 Jesus [and the three apostles] next visited the shepherd huts that lay scattered around, and cured many of the sick in them. He went from hut to hut all along the mountainous country in the direction of Hebron.

6/18 I saw Jesus alone with Peter in one of these abodes, in which a marriage was being celebrated. The bridal couple returned from the nuptial ceremony, which was performed in the school, escorted by their friends and walking under a kind of canopy. A band of little girls adorned with wreaths of colored wool led the way playing on lutes, and gaily dressed boys with similar instruments brought up the rear of the procession. A priest from Jericho was present. When the party entered the house, they were both surprised and delighted to see Jesus, who bade them not to interrupt the wedding festivities lest some might be vexed at it. The guests then drank out of little glasses. The bride retired with the women, and the children played and danced before her. Then I saw the bride-groom and the bride go to Jesus in a room set apart, where he again joined their hands with his own right and blessed their clasped hands, and gave them an instruction upon the indissolubility of marriage and the merit of continency. After that he reclined at table with Peter and the priest, while the bridegroom waited upon them. The priest, however, was angry that the most honorable places had been given to the stranger guests, Jesus and his apostles, and so he soon withdrew from the enter-tainment. I saw too that he hunted up some of the Pharisees, who later on unexpectedly attacked the Lord and called him to account. In the heat of their discussion, one of them pulled his mantle from his shoulder, but Jesus remained calm. As they could neither harm him nor gain a victory over him, they withdrew.

Jesus, with more than ordinary love and kindness, tarried awhile in this shepherd dwelling. The bride's parents and some others of the old shepherds who presented themselves before him, belonged to those that had visited him at the crib on the night of his birth. They began at once, in touching terms, to tell all about that night and to honor Jesus, and the younger ones related what they had heard about it from their deceased parents. They brought to Jesus some aged sick who, on account of the feebleness of old age, could no longer walk, also some sick children, and Jesus cured them all. He told the young married couple to go, after his death, to his apostles, to be baptized and instructed, and to become his followers. During the whole journey, I never saw Jesus so bright and cheerful as he was among these simple people. I saw that all who had honored him in his childhood received the grace to become Christians.

6/19 From this place, Jesus took a more southerly direction into the mountainous district toward Jutta. The wedding guests formed his es-cort. He had with him now six apostles, including Andrew. On the way he cured a number of sick children who were very much swollen and unable to walk. The people of this region were not very good.

6/20 When Jesus reached a little village among the mountains near Jutta, he went straight to the synagogue to teach. The priests forbade it, and went to call assistance, but they were obliged to resign the teacher's chair to Jesus, to whom the people listened with joy.

6/21 The disciples were eager for Jesus now to turn his steps to Nazareth, his native city, since he was always making allusion to his approaching end. But he was desirous that the good among the people here should profit by the time remaining to him, and so he did not go to Nazareth. He taught upon the words: "No man can serve two masters" [Matthew 6:24]

6/22–24 *Jesus taught again in the village. He said that he had come to bring a sword (Matthew 10:34–36). The disciples were confused by this utterance, but Jesus explained to them that he meant the renunciation of all evil.*

6/25 *Jesus sent off most of the apostles and disciples. He left the village and went north to Bethain, where he taught under a tree.*[†]

Jesus on the Way to Bethany • The Raising of Lazarus

7/9 *Jesus stayed at a little village in Samaria. His mother, accompa-* **MAP 36** *nied by her elder sister, Mary Heli, and Mary Heli's daughter, Mary Cleophas, were on their way from Bethany to meet him and urge him to come to Bethany and heal Lazarus.*

7/10 *The three holy women came to Jesus today and told him of Martha and Mary Magdalene's request that he come to Bethany, as Lazarus lay seriously ill (John 11:6).*

7/11–12 *Having talked with Jesus, the three holy women decided to stay in the little village to celebrate the sabbath there. Jesus himself went to another place with a large synagogue. Here he taught and healed and blessed some children.*

7/13–15 *During these days Jesus taught concerning the good Samaritan (Luke 10:30–37) and the lost coin (Luke 15:8–10). He also healed the sick and blessed many children.*

7/16 *Jesus, accompanied by some apostles, returned to the little village where the three holy women were waiting for him. Together they received the news of Lazarus's death. It was here that Jesus spoke the words: "Our friend Lazarus has fallen asleep" (John 11:7–13).*

7/17 As Jesus had been tarrying in a little place near Samaria where too the blessed Virgin and Mary Cleophas were come to spend the sabbath, they had received the news of Lazarus's death. After this event, which happened in Bethany, his sisters left that place and went to their country

---

† Owing to great suffering, at this point Anne Catherine was unable to communicate anything for thirteen days. During this time it is possible that Jesus journeyed northward to Capernaum and was returning back through Samaria when Anne Catherine resumed her account. At first, she was able to communicate only fragments from the period we are now entering that leads up to the raising of Lazarus.

house near Ginea, with the intention of there meeting Jesus and the blessed Virgin.†

7/18 The remains of Lazarus were embalmed and swathed in linen bands, according to the Jewish custom, and then laid in a coffin of woven rods with a convex cover. All the apostles were again united around Jesus. They went in several bands to Ginea, where Jesus taught in the synagogue.

7/19 After the closing exercises of the sabbath, Jesus and the apostles went out to Lazarus's country house. There they found the blessed Virgin, who had gone on before. Magdalene came to meet Jesus and to tell him of her brother's death, adding the words: "Lord, if thou hadst been here, my brother had not died!" Jesus replied that his time was not yet come and that it was well that he had died. Still, he told the two sisters to allow all the effects of their brother to remain at Bethany, for that he himself would go there shortly.

7/20 The holy women, therefore, set out [this morning] for Bethany, while Jesus and the apostles returned to Ginea, from which they went to the inn one hour distant from Bethany. Here another messenger came to him bearing the earnest request of the sisters that he should repair to Bethany, but he still delayed to go.

7/21 *Today, Jesus and the apostles journeyed towards Bethany.*

7/22 *Toward evening they reached the inn of a little place near Bahurim. Here Jesus taught concerning the laborers in the vineyard (Matthew 20:1–16). Mary Salome, the mother of James and John, approached him to request that her two sons be allowed to take a place beside him in his kingdom (Matthew 20:20–21).*

7/23 Jesus rebuked the disciples for their murmuring and impatience at his delaying so long to go to Bethany. He was always like one who could not give an account of his views and actions to them, because they did not understand him. In his instructions to them he was always more desirous of discovering to them their own thoughts and, on account of their earthly-mindedness, of arousing in them distrust of self than of informing them of the reasons of things that they could not comprehend.

7/24 He still taught upon the laborers in the vineyard,‡ and when the mother of James and John heard him speak of the near fulfillment of his mission, she thought it only proper that his own relatives should have

---

† Toward evening, Jesus, accompanied by the three holy women and the apostles, set off for Bethany. They traveled that night by moonlight to Lazarus's country estate near Ginea. Here Martha and Mary Magdalene were waiting for him.

‡ In this little place near Bahurim there were Pharisees who reported back to Jerusalem concerning Jesus.

honorable posts in his kingdom. She consequently approached him with a petition to that effect, but he sternly rebuked her.

7/25 At last Jesus turned his steps to Bethany, continuing all along the way his instructions to the apostles. Lazarus's estate stood partly within the walls surrounding the environs of the city, and partly—that is, a portion of the garden and courtyard—outside those walls, which were now going to ruin.

Lazarus was eight days dead. They had kept him four days in the hope that Jesus would come and raise him to life. His sisters, as I have said, went to the country house near Ginea, to meet Jesus; but when they found that he was still resolved not to go back with them, they had returned to Bethany and buried their brother. Their friends, men and women from the city and from Jerusalem, were now gathered around them, lamenting the dead as was the custom. It seems to me that it was toward evening when Mary Zebedeus[†] went in to Martha,[‡] who was sitting among the women, and said to her softly that the Lord was coming. Martha arose and went out with her into the garden back of the house. There in an arbor was Magdalene sitting alone. Martha told her that Jesus was near, for through love for Magdalene, she wanted her to be the first to meet the Lord. But I did not see Magdalene go to Jesus, for when he was alone with the apostles and disciples he did not allow women easy access to him. It was already growing dusk when Magdalene went back to the women and took Martha's place, who then went out to meet Jesus. He was standing with the apostles and some others on the confines of their garden before an open arbor. Martha spoke to Jesus and then turned back to Magdalene, who also by this time had come up. She threw herself at Jesus's feet, saying: "If thou hadst been here, he would not have died!" All present were in tears. Jesus too mourned and wept, and delivered a discourse of great length upon death. Many of the audience, which was constantly increasing outside the bower, whispered

---

† That is, Mary Salome, wife of Zebedee.

‡ Mary Salome went on ahead, arriving in Bethany toward evening. She went first to Martha to tell her that Jesus was approaching. Mary Magdalene went with Mary Salome to greet him, but she returned without having spoken to him. Then Martha went to meet him. In the exchange that took place between Martha and Jesus, Jesus spoke the words: "I am the resurrection and the life" (John 11:17–27). It was dusk. Martha hurried back and spoke with Mary Magdalene, who went up to Jesus, casting herself at his feet and saying: "Lord, if you had been here, my brother would not have died." Jesus wept (John 11:28–37). Jesus then taught about death late into the night.

to one another and murmured their dissatisfaction at Jesus's not having kept Lazarus alive.

7/26 It seems to me that it was very early in the morning when Jesus went with the apostles to the tomb. Mary, Lazarus's sisters, and others, in all about seven women, were likewise there, as also a crowd of people which was constantly on the increase. Indeed, the throng presented somewhat the appearance of a tumult, as upon the day of Christ's crucifixion. They proceeded along a road upon either side of which was a thick, green hedge, then passed through a gate, after which about a quarter of an hour's distance brought them to the walled-in cemetery of Bethany. From the gate of the cemetery a road led right and left around a hill through which ran a vault. The latter was divided by railings into compartments, and the opening at the end was closed by a grate. One could, from the entrance, see through the whole length of the vault and the green branches of the trees waving outside the opposite end. Light was admitted from openings above.

Lazarus's tomb was the first on the right of the entrance to the vault, down into which some steps led. It was a four-cornered, oblong cave, about three feet in depth, and covered with a flat stone. In it lay the corpse in a lightly woven coffin, and around it in the tomb there was room for one to walk. Jesus with some of the apostles went down into the vault, while the holy women, Magdalene, and Martha remained standing in the doorway. But the crowd pressed around so that many people climbed up on the roof of the vault and the cemetery walls in order to see. Jesus commanded the apostles to raise the stone from the grave. They did so, rested it against the wall, and then removed a light cover or door that closed the tomb below that stone. It was at this point of the proceedings that Martha said: "Lord, by this time he stinketh, for he is now of four days." After that they took the lightly woven cover from the coffin, and disclosed the corpse lying in its winding sheet. At that instant Jesus raised his eyes to heaven, prayed aloud, and called out in a strong voice: "Lazarus, come forth!" At this cry, the corpse arose to a sitting posture. The crowd now pressed with so much violence that Jesus ordered them to be driven outside the walls of the cemetery. The apostles, who were standing in the tomb by the coffin, removed the handkerchief from Lazarus's face, unbound his hands and feet, and drew off the winding sheet. Lazarus, as if waking from lethargy, rose from the coffin and stepped out of the grave, tottering and looking like a phantom. The apostles threw a mantle around him. Like one walking in sleep, he approached the door, passed the Lord and went out to where his sisters and the other women had stepped back in fright as before a ghost.

Without daring to touch him, they fell prostrate on the ground. At the same instant, Jesus stepped after him out of the vault and seized him by both hands, his whole manner full of loving earnestness.

And now all moved on toward Lazarus's house. The throng was great. But a certain fear prevailed among the people; consequently the procession formed by Lazarus and his friends was not impeded in its movements by the crowd that followed. Lazarus moved along more like one floating than walking, and he still had all the appearance of a corpse. Jesus walked by his side, and the rest of the party followed sobbing and weeping around them in silent, frightened amazement. They reached the old gate, and went along the road bordered by verdant hedges to the avenue of trees from which they had started. The Lord entered it with Lazarus and his followers, while the crowd thronged outside, clamoring and shouting.

At this moment Lazarus threw himself prostrate on the earth before Jesus, like one about to be received into a religious order. Jesus spoke some words, and then they went on to the house, about a hundred paces distant.

Jesus, the apostles, and Lazarus were alone in the dining hall. The apostles formed a circle around Jesus and Lazarus, who was kneeling before the Lord. Jesus laid his right hand on his head and breathed upon him seven times. The Lord's breath was luminous. I saw a dark vapor withdrawing as it were from Lazarus, and the devil under the form of a black winged figure, impotent and wrathful, clearing the circle backward and mounting on high. By this ceremony, Jesus consecrated Lazarus to his service, purified him from all connection with the world and sin, and strengthened him with the gifts of the Holy Spirit. He made him a long address in which he told him that he had raised him to life that he might serve him, and that he would have to endure great persecution on the part of the Jews.

Up to this time, Lazarus was in his grave clothes, but now he retired to lay them aside and put on his own garments. It was at this moment that his sisters and friends embraced him for the first time, for before this there was something so corpse-like about him that it inspired terror. I saw meanwhile that Lazarus's soul, during the time of its separation from his body, was in a place peaceful and painless, lighted by only a glimmering twilight, and that while there he related to the just, Joseph, Joachim, Anne, Zechariah, John, etc., how things were going with the Redeemer on earth.

By the Savior's breathing upon him, Lazarus received the seven gifts of the Holy Spirit and was perfectly freed from connection with earthly things. He received those gifts before the apostles, for he had by his death become acquainted with great mysteries, had gazed upon another world. He had actually been dead, and he was now born again. He could therefore receive those gifts. Lazarus comprises in himself a deep significance and a profound mystery.

And now a meal was ready, and all reclined at table, upon which were many dishes and little jugs. A man served. After the meal the women entered, but remained at the lower end of the hall, to hear the teachings of Jesus. Lazarus was sitting next to him. There was a frightful noise around the house, for many had come out from Jerusalem, even the guards, and were now besetting the house. But Jesus sent the apostles out to drive off both people and guards. Jesus continued his instruction till after lamplight, and told the disciples that he was going next morning with two apostles to Jerusalem. When they placed before him the danger attending such a step, he replied that he would not be recognized, that he would not go openly. I saw them afterward taking a little sleep, leaning around against the wall.

7/27 Before daybreak Jesus, accompanied by John and Matthew, who had girded up their garments somewhat differently from their usual custom, started from Bethany for Jerusalem. They went around the city and, taking by-roads, reached the house in which later on the Last Supper was celebrated. There they remained quietly the whole day and the next night, Jesus instructing and confirming his friends of the city. I saw Mary Mark and Veronica in the house, and fully a dozen men. Nicodemus, to whom the house belonged, but who had gladly resigned it for the use of Jesus's friends, was not there. He had on that very day gone to Bethany to see Lazarus.

I saw also a gathering of Pharisees and high priests who had come together to discuss Jesus and Lazarus. Among other things I heard them say that they feared Jesus would raise all the dead, and then what confusion would ensue!

At noon on that day, a great tumult arose in Bethany. If Jesus had been there, they would have stoned him. Lazarus was obliged to hide, and the apostles, to slip away in different directions. All the other friends of Jesus in Bethany were likewise forced to lie in concealment. Minds became calm, however, when people took into consideration that they had no right to take action against Lazarus.

7/28 Jesus passed the whole night till early next morning in the house on Mount Zion. Before day he left Jerusalem with Matthew and John and fled across the Jordan, not by the route he had formerly taken on the side of Bethabara, but by another off to the northeast. It may have been toward noon when he reached the opposite shore of the Jordan. That evening the [six] apostles from Bethany joined him, and they spent the night under a great tree.

7/29 In the morning they started for a little village in the neighborhood, and on their way found a blind man lying on the roadside. He was in charge of two boys, who were not, however, related to him. He was a shepherd from the region of Jericho. He had heard from the apostles that the Lord was coming that way, and he was now crying out to him for a cure. Jesus laid his hand on his head, and the man received his sight. Then he cast off his old rags and, in his undergarment, followed Jesus to the village, where in a hall Jesus taught of following him. He said that they who wanted to do so must, as the blind man did his rags, leave all, to follow him with full use of their sight. A mantle was given to the man cured of blindness. He wanted to join Jesus at once, but he was put off till he should prove his constancy. Jesus taught here until nearly evening. There were about eight apostles with him.

7/30 After that, as he drew near a little city, Jesus was hungry. I could not help smiling at the thought of his being hungry, for Jesus's hunger was very different from that of others. He was hungering after souls. From the last place that he had visited, some people who had not the right dispositions went with him. On the roadside stood a fig tree that bore no fruit. Jesus went up to the tree and cursed it. It withered on the instant, its leaves turning yellow, and the trunk becoming crooked. Jesus taught in the school upon the sterile fig tree. There were some malevolent doctors and Pharisees who invited Jesus to take his departure. A little stream spanned by a bridge ran by this place into the Jordan. The school was built on an eminence. Jesus and his party spent the night at an inn.

Jesus Begins His Journey into the Land of the Three Holy Kings

7/31 NEXT day, when Jesus and his companions left that last place, they took a northeasterly direction through the land of the tribe of Gad. I heard Jesus saying whither he was now about to journey. He told the apostles and disciples that they should separate from him, designated to them where they should and where they should not teach, and where they should again join him. He was now, he said, about to make an extraordinary journey. He would spend the next sabbath in Great Chorazin, then go to Bethsaida, and from there to the south into the region of Machaerus and Midian. Thence he would proceed to where Hagar had exposed Ishmael, and Jacob had set up the stone. Then he would journey to the east around the Dead Sea and on to the place upon which Melchizedek had offered sacrifice before Abraham. On this site there stands today a chapel, in which divine Service is sometimes celebrated. It is built of red stone, and overgrown with moss. Jesus declared his intention of going likewise to Heliopolis in Egypt, where he had once dwelt in childhood. There were some good people there who as children had played with him, and who had not entirely forgotten him. They were constantly asking what had become of him, but they could not believe that he of whom they heard so much was the child of their remembrance. He would return from the other side through Hebron and the valley of Jehosaphat, pass the place at which he had been baptized by John, and through the desert in which he had been tempted. He announced that his absence would be for about three months, and that his followers would be sure to find him at the end of that time at Jacob's well near Sichar, though they might meet him before that, when he would be returning through Judea. He gave them minute instructions in a long discourse, above all as to how they should during his absence conduct themselves in their missionary duties. I remember these words, that wherever they were not well received, they should shake the dust from their shoes. Matthew returned home for awhile. He was a married man. His wife was a very virtuous person and, since Matthew's vocation, they had lived in perfect continency. He was to teach in his own home, and quietly put up with the contempt of his former associates.

8/1 *Jesus wanted to hold the sabbath in the town of Great Chorazin. He dismissed most of the apostles. Then, around noon, he went into the town, accompanied by Andrew, Peter, and Philip. He taught in the synagogue.*

8/2 Toward noon a man from Capernaum, who had been waiting for Jesus, approached him. His son, he said, was sick unto death, and he implored the Lord to go with him and cure him. But Jesus commanded him to return home, for his son was already restored to health. There were many others gathered around Jesus, some belonging to the city, and others from a distance. Some were sick and looking for a cure, others were in search of consolation. He satisfied some at once, but to others he held out the promise of future assistance.

On the evening of that sabbath, Jesus took leave of the inhabitants outside the synagogue and proceeded with several of the apostles up to where the Jordan empties into the sea, in order to cross to the other side. The ferry was higher up, and that made the journey much longer. Here they crossed on a kind of raft formed of beams laid one over another like a grating. In the center, on a raised platform, was an enclosure, like a little half-tub into which the water could not penetrate, and there the baggage of the passengers was deposited. The raft was propelled by means of long poles. The shore of the Jordan was not very high in this place, and it seems to me there were some little islands lying around in this part of the river. I saw the Lord and the three apostles traveling by moonlight. Outside of Bethsaida, as was customary at the entrance to the cities of Palestine, stood a long shed under which travelers used to ungird their garments and brush off the dust of travel before entering the city; generally some people were to be found there to wash their feet. This was the case on the arrival of the Lord and the apostles, after which they repaired to Andrew's, where they partook of a meal of honey, rolls, and grapes. Andrew was married, and his house was by no means a small one. It had a courtyard, was surrounded by walls, and was situated at one side of the city. Peter and Philip accompanied the Lord, but Andrew went on ahead. There were in all twelve men present at the meal, and at the end of it, six women came in to hear Jesus's teaching.

8/3 Next day, as he was leaving Bethsaida with the three apostles, he paused for awhile in a house outside the city in which were all kinds of goods and chattels peculiar to fishing. A great many men were assembled there, and Jesus gave them an instruction.†

8/4 Setting out at last, Jesus and the three apostles journeyed up the shore of the Jordan, crossed the bridge far above the ferry just mentioned, and journeyed for the whole day and night through the region known as Basan, east of the Sea of Galilee.

8/5 I saw in a region beyond the Jordan a district covered with white sand and tiny white pebbles, several disciples in an open shepherd shed awaiting the Lord's coming. They had brought with them three youths, tall and slim. While awaiting Jesus, the disciples had gathered yellow and green berries as large as figs, also little yellow apples that grew some on bushes, others on trees, from which they broke them off with chopping sticks. The road by which Jesus and the three apostles came appeared to be not much frequented, for it was overgrown with long grass, and extended under an avenue of spreading fruit trees whose branches interlaced overhead. The apostles broke off some of the fruit and put it into their pockets, but Jesus took none. He had traveled all night through mountainous districts. The disciples who had been awaiting his coming

---

† On this day Jesus visited another house in Bethsaida. Here some of the holy women had gathered. Later, Jesus and the three apostles left Bethsaida and went to a house north of the town. Here he taught a group of disciples. Then Jesus, accompanied by Andrew, Peter and Philip, traveled further, crossing back across the Jordan.

now went forward to meet him. They pressed around him with words of salutation, but without offering their hands. In front of the shed lay a long, broad, four-cornered log, around which Jesus and the others threw themselves in a reclining posture as at table, and before each was placed a portion of the fruit just gathered. They had brought with them also little jugs containing some kind of beverage. Off in the distance lay a city and behind it rose a mountain chain. I think this region was in the land of the Amorites. From this place the road again took a downward direction. I saw Jesus and his companions journeying the whole day and, in the evening, arriving at a little scattered village. On the roadside stood an inn. The travelers entered and were soon surrounded by a crowd of inquisitive people. They had not heard much of Jesus, but they were for the most part good and simple-hearted. Jesus related to them the parable of the good shepherd, and then traveled on a short distance to another inn, at which he and his followers ate and slept. The Lord told the latter that he intended to go alone with the three youths through Chaldea and the land of Ur, Abraham's birthplace, and thence through Arabia to Egypt. The disciples should scatter here throughout the district and instruct the inhabitants; as for himself, he added, he would teach wherever he went. In fine he again told them that, at the end of three months, they would meet at the well of Jacob near Shechem. I saw Simeon, Cleophas, and Saturnin among the disciples.

8/6 At dawn of day Jesus bade farewell to the apostles and disci- **MAP 37** ples, to each of whom he extended his hand. They were very much troubled at his taking with him only the three youths. These youths were from sixteen to eighteen years old and very different from the Jews. They were more slender and active, and wore long garments. They were like children to Jesus, whom they waited on most affectionately. Whenever they came to water, they washed his feet. They ran off on the road here and there, and came back with little rods, flowers, fruits, and berries. Jesus instructed them most lovingly and explained to them in parables all that had happened up to that time.

The parents of these youths belonged to the family of Mensor. They had come to Palestine with the caravan of the three kings and, at the departure of the same for home, had remained behind among the shepherds in the Valley of the Shepherds. They became Jews, married the daughters of the shepherds, and came into possession of meadowlands between Samaria and Jericho. The youngest of the youths was named Eremenzear and later on was called Hermas. He was the boy whom Jesus, at the prayer of his mother, had cured in the region of Shechem, after his interview with the Samaritan at Jacob's well. The next one was

Sela, or Silas; and the eldest, Eliud, received in baptism the name of Siricius. They were called, also, the secret disciples, and at a later period they were associated with Thomas, John, and Paul. Eremenzear wrote an account of this journey.

On this journey, Jesus wore a brownish tunic, knitted or woven, that fell around him in folds long and full; over that he had a long garment of fine white wool with wide sleeves. It was fastened at the waist by a broad girdle of the same material as the scarf that he wound around his head when sleeping. Jesus was taller than the apostles. Walking or standing, his fair, grave face rose above them. His step was firm, his bearing erect. He was neither thin nor stout, but nobly formed with an appearance of perfect health. His shoulders were broad, and his chest well developed. Exercise and traveling had strengthened his muscles, although they presented no sign of hard labor.

The road taken by Jesus and the youths after parting from the apostles was a constantly ascending one in a direction toward the east, over a white, sandy soil and through cedars and date trees. Opposite arose the mountains of Gilead. Jesus wanted to spend the coming sabbath in the last Jewish city met in this direction. I think it was called Kedar. Jesus and the youths ate on the way the fruits of the trees and berries. The youths carried pouches filled with little rolls, jugs containing some kind of drink, and staves. The Lord sometimes broke off a staff for himself from a tree in passing, and again cast it aside. His feet, otherwise bare, were protected by sandals. In the evening they went to some solitary house occupied by rude, simple people, and there slept for the night. Jesus nowhere made himself known, although he everywhere taught in beautiful parables of all kinds, but principally in those relating to the good shepherd. The people questioned him about Jesus of Nazareth, but he did not tell that it was himself. He in turn put questions to them concerning their work, their business affairs, so that they concluded he was a traveling shepherd looking around after good pasture lands, as was often the case in Jewish countries. I did not see him effect any cure nor work any miracle in these parts.
8/7 Next morning he journeyed on. He may now have still been some miles from Kedar, which was built on rising ground, the mountain chain behind it. Abraham's fatherland was in this direction, but far off toward the northeast; the land of the three kings was toward the southeast.

Some of the disciples had returned to their homes, while others had scattered around the country teaching. Zacchaeus of Jericho accompanied them awhile, after which he returned home, gave up his business, sold all that he had, bestowed the proceeds upon the poor, and went with his wife (with whom he henceforth lived in continency) to another place. The Lord told the disciples that nine weeks would pass before they should join him again.

The excitement in Jerusalem on account of Lazarus was very great. Jesus absented himself during it, that people might lose sight of him, while the conviction of the truth of this miracle disposed many to conversion. When Jesus returned he was very thin. There is no written account of this journey, since no apostle accompanied the Lord on it; perhaps too the apostles did not even know of all the places in which he had been. As well as I remember, I then saw this road for the first time.

8/8 Jesus journeyed on with his three young companions to the southeast, taking byways most frequently, and spending the night, like the preceding one among the shepherds, in a solitary house. The people of these parts were good and artless. They gazed at Jesus in wonder, and loved him at once. He related to them many of the parables he was accustomed to use in Judea, and to them they listened with delight. But he neither healed nor blessed. When they asked him about Jesus of Nazareth, he answered by telling them about those that had quitted all to follow him, and then passed to parables that explained what he had said. The people thought he was a shepherd looking around for herds or meadows.

Jesus in Kedar

JESUS and the youths reached Kedar before the sabbath. They had not traveled by the highroad, but by roundabout ways. As it was too late to enter the city, they passed the night at a large public inn at which other wayfarers had sought shelter. There were open sheds with sleeping accommodations in the enclosure, and the whole was surrounded by a courtyard. A man, the one that superintended the establishment, unlocked the inn, after which he returned to the city. Next morning, he came out again to the inn, and then received a small sum for his services. The travelers went their several ways, but the superintendent took Jesus and his companions back with him to his own house in the city. Kedar was situated at the foot of a mountain, in a valley through which flowed a river. It consisted of an old and a new city separated by the little river, which flowed from the east and off toward Palestine. The shore was very steep, and the river was spanned by two arches very solidly built. On this side the place was poor and insignificant, and inhabited principally by Jewish shepherds who likewise engaged in the manufacture of light huts, and shepherd and stable utensils. On the opposite side Kedar presented a more opulent appearance. There were no Jews there, but only pagans.

The Jewish costume was somewhat modified here, for some of the people wore a pointed cap. In the city this side of the river, there was a synagogue, and upon a square surrounded by grass plots and walks of clean white sand, played a fountain. This was the most beautiful spot in the city.

The Lord and the boys went with their host to the synagogue, and quietly celebrated the sabbath. At the end of the prayers, Jesus asked whether he might venture to relate something to them, and when the good people showed their willingness to listen, he recounted the parable of the prodigal son. They listened attentively, admired him greatly, but knew not who he was. He called himself a shepherd seeking the lost lambs in order to lead them into good pasture. They regarded him as a prophet and, during the rest of the day, conducted him to their houses where too he taught.

8/9–10 The next day he gave an instruction at the fountain. The men and women sat at his feet, and he pressed the children to his breast. He told them about Zacchaeus climbing up the fig tree, of his leaving all and following him; of him who in the temple had said: "I thank God that I am not like the publican"; and lastly, of that other who, striking his breast, said: "Lord, be merciful to me, a poor sinner!" The inhabitants of Kedar became very fond of Jesus and thought no harm of him. They begged him to stay with them till the next sabbath and then teach again in their school, and when they asked him about Jesus of Nazareth, he related to them many things of him and his doctrine.

8/11 *This morning, Jesus was still in Kedar. The people had asked him to remain until the next sabbath and to teach in the synagogue. That evening, he went to a little village east of Kedar to which he had been invited. He stayed there overnight.*

8/12 *This evening, he returned to Kedar.*

8/13 On leaving this place, Jesus and his traveling companions proceeded eastward from Kedar into a country of beautiful meadowlands and palm trees, and thence to Edon. On the way, he visited a house that stood off by itself, and in which both the father and mother of the family had long been bedridden with incurable maladies. Several children were going and coming around the house. All were good. Here also they asked him about Jesus of Nazareth, of whom they had heard diverse reports. Jesus answered them in a beautiful parable of a king and his son, in which he spoke of the one of whom they inquired. He told them that he would be persecuted, and that he would return to his Father's kingdom, which he would share with all those that had followed him. As Jesus spoke I had a vision of his Passion, his Ascension, his throne surrounded by all the angels and set next his Father's, meaning his dominion over the world; and, lastly, I saw the reward portioned out to his followers. I saw likewise the vision of his kingdom and the whole parable that he was relating to the people, and I saw too that he impressed upon their hearts a lasting picture of it. When he asked them whether they believed all he had told them and whether they would follow the good king, and they had protested their belief and their willingness, he promised the two old people that God would reward them by curing them and allowing them to follow him to Edon. And all of a sudden, they were restored to health and, to the astonishment of the beholders, were indeed able to follow Jesus to Edon. The man's name was Benjamin, and he was a direct descendant from Ruth. I think that Titus was either a son or a relative of this couple so suddenly cured. He was at that time between fourteen to sixteen years old. He went to Kedar and to every other place in this region in which Jesus taught, in order to hear him and to listen to others talking about him. Mark, whose birthplace was nearer Judea, was acquainted with this family, and so too was Silas.

8/14 Jesus and the three youths, on leaving that house, went on to Edon through lovely fields and meadows shaded by palm trees. Jesus carried a shepherd's crook in his right hand. In the public feast house, on a large, open square to the left of the entrance to the city, a marriage was being celebrated. The house contained a large hall, at the end of which was the kitchen. All around it were sleeping apartments, in each of which there were three beds that could be separated from one another by an ornamented screen. Although it was clear daylight, a lamp was burning in the hall. The guests, male and female, as also the bride and bridegroom, adorned with flowery wreaths, were all assembled in the same apartment. Boys were singing and playing upon flutes and other instruments. These pious people were awaiting Jesus, whom they looked upon as a prophet. They had heard of his teaching and parables in Kedar and the surrounding district, and had in consequence invited him to their wedding. They received him joyfully and reverently, washed his feet and those of his young companions, and dried them with their own garments. They took from Jesus his staff, placed it in a corner, and prepared for him a table. On it were some little rolls, a honeycomb almost a foot in length, and some red berries from the top of which they detached before eating a little circle of black leaves tipped with white. There were, too, little earthen jugs and cups on the table and some small dishes. The last mentioned looked like glazed earthenware, out of which with little spoons they put something into their drink. The guests reclined at table upon small leaning benches, and to Jesus was given the seat between the bridegroom and the bride. The women sat at the lower end. Jesus blessed the food and drink, of which all then partook.

During the meal, Jesus taught. He told the guests about that man in Judea who, at the marriage of Cana in Galilee, had changed water into wine. When the couple whom the guests had known so long as sick, but who had been restored to health, made their appearance, the amazement was great. They related all that the Lord had told them of the king and his kingdom, declared their belief in it, and said that they were as certain of having a share in that same kingdom as they were now conscious of the fact of having been cured. Jesus repeated to them the parable and told them in plain words that there was still a wall between them and the dominions of that king, but that they could force their way through it if they would overcome themselves. It was morning before the party retired to bed. The Lord and the young boys slept back of the dining hall. Before he lay down, however, he went aside and, kneeling, prayed with uplifted hands to his heavenly Father. I saw streams of light issuing from his mouth, and another stream of light, or an angelic form, descending toward him. This often happened even in full daylight when at any time Jesus retired to a solitary place to pray. I knew this about him even in my childhood, and when I saw him praying thus alone, I tried to imitate him. I saw the blessed Virgin, up to the conception of the Savior, generally standing in prayer, her hands crossed on her breast, and her eyes lowered; but after the most holy Incarnation, she generally knelt, her face raised to heaven, and her hands uplifted.

8/15 Next morning, on account of the great concourse of people, Jesus taught in the open air. He settled many matrimonial affairs, for the people of this place had lost the true conception of the Law on that head. They wanted to espouse two blood relatives in succession, and they questioned Jesus on the matter. He explained to them that it was not allowed by the Mosaic Law, and they promised to refrain from such unions. It was told Jesus also that in one of the neighboring places a certain man was on the point of marrying for the sixth time, his five deceased wives being sisters of the present affianced. Jesus said that he would visit that place. He returned to Kedar for the sabbath, and taught the whole day in the school. He gave decisions upon many questions and doubts concerning the Law and marriage and reconciled some married couples that were at variance.

8/16 *During the day, Jesus taught in the synagogue and, that evening, in the garden next to the synagogue. He spoke again about marriage.*

8/17 *This morning Jesus continued to speak in the synagogue about marriage. A divorced couple came to him. There were two groups: the husband and his relatives and the wife and her relatives. Jesus spoke with each group separately. Then the couple came together, held hands, and Jesus blessed them.*

Jesus Goes to Sichar-Kedar and Teaches upon the Mystery of Marriage

8/18 THIS evening, from Kedar, Jesus, with a numerous escort, wended his way northward, the country everywhere presenting a more level aspect. I saw them reach a shepherd village outside of which were open sheds, long rows of trees with interlacing branches, and huts formed of green boughs and leaves. Under one of the sheds, all partook of figs, grapes, and dates. They were still there, the night being mild and lovely, when the stars shone out in the sky and the dewdrops glittered brightly below.

8/19 When the rest of the party dispersed to their homes, Jesus with the three youths went around the district teaching, and arrived toward evening of the following day at the little city of Sichar-Kedar, built on the declivity of a mountain range. Some people came out to meet him. They conducted him to the public house of the city, which was something like that of Cana in Galilee, and there he found a crowd assembled. Some young married people had lost their parents by a sudden death, and they were now entertaining at this house all those who had followed the remains to the grave. In front of the house was a courtyard enclosed by a railing, and in it an arbor of skillfully woven foliage. In each of the four corners stood a stone cistern full of water out of which grew creeping plants. They were trained up on palings and then allowed to run on arches to the center of the yard, where a carved column of marble supported the verdant roof thus formed. The plants, like reeds or sedges, retained their freshness a long time. This decoration, as well as all the garlands that adorned the house, was of extraordinary beauty. In a hall just off the courtyard, Jesus's feet and those of his companions were washed, and the customary refreshments presented. Then they went to another apartment, in which a meal was in readiness. Jesus insisted upon serving at table. He handed to all the guests bread, fruit, and large pieces of honeycomb, and poured from jugs into the drinking cup of each three kinds of beverage: one was a green juice; another, some kind of yellow drink; and the third, a perfectly white fluid. Jesus taught all the time. Sichar-Kedar was the place of which Jesus had been told at the wedding feast that so many were living there in unlawful marriage relations.

Only the husband of the mourning married couple was present at the funereal feast. He was named Eliud. He had been at the marriage feast at

Edon, and on his return home found that both his parents-in-law had departed this life. They had died suddenly, overcome by grief at the discovery that their daughter, Eliud's wife, was an adulteress. Eliud himself had no intimation of the fact, nor consequently of the cause of the sudden death of his parents-in-law. When the meal spoken of above was over, Jesus allowed himself to be conducted by Eliud to his home. The youths did not go with him. Jesus spoke to the wife in private. She was in great sorrow. She sank at his feet in tears, and confessed her sin. When Jesus left her, Eliud conducted him to his sleeping chamber. I saw the Lord saying some grave and touching words to him and, when Eliud left him, he prayed awhile and then went to rest.

8/20 Early next morning Eliud, with a wash-basin and a green branch, went in to Jesus, who was still lying on the bed supported on his arm. He arose; Eliud washed his feet and dried them in his own garments. Then the Lord told him to conduct him to his chamber, for that he wanted in turn to wash his feet. Eliud would not hear of this. But Jesus told him gravely that if he would not yield, he would instantly leave his house, that it must be, that if he wanted to follow him he must not refuse to obey. On hearing these words, Eliud led Jesus to his bedchamber and brought him a basin of water. Jesus grasped him by the hands, gazed lovingly into his eyes, said a few words on the subject of foot washing, and then informed him that his wife was an adulteress, but penitent, and that he must pardon her. At this information Eliud fell prostrate on the ground, writhing and weeping in an excess of mental agony. Jesus turned away from him and prayed. After a little while, the first bitter struggle being over, Jesus went to him, raised him from the ground, spoke words of consolation to him, and washed his feet. When Eliud had become calm, Jesus commanded him to call his wife. He did so, and she entered the room closely veiled. Jesus took her hand, laid it in that of Eliud, blessed them both, consoled them, and raised the wife's veil. Then he dismissed them with directions to send their children to him, whom when they came he blessed and led back to their parents. From this time forward Eliud and his wife remained faithful to each other, and both made a vow of continency. On that same day, Jesus visited many other homes in order to lead their occupants from the error of their ways. I saw him going from house to house, conversing with the people upon their various affairs and thus winning their confidence.

8/21 On the mountain near this place, Sichar-Kedar, there were whole rows of beehives. The declivity of the mountain was terraced, and on the terraces resting against the mountain stood numerous square, flat-roofed beehives about seven feet in height, the upper part ornamented with knobs. They were placed in several rows, one above the other. They were not rounded in the back, but pointed like a roof, and they could be opened from top to bottom on the shelf side. The whole apiary was enclosed by a fine trellis of woven reeds. Between these stacks of hives there were steps leading up to the terraces, and to the railings on either side bushes bearing white blossoms and berries were trained. One could mount from terrace to terrace, upon each of which were similar arrangements for bees.

When Jesus was asked by the people whence he had come he invariably answered in parables, to which they gave simple-hearted credence. Under the bower of the public house he delivered an instruction, in which he related the parable of the king's son who came to discharge all the debts of his subjects. His hearers took the parable in its literal sense and rejoiced greatly over what it promised. Jesus then turned to the parable of the debtor who, after having obtained a delay for the payment of his own great debt, insisted upon bringing before the judge the man that owed him a trifle. He told them also that his father had given him a vineyard which had to be cultivated and pruned, and that he was looking for laborers to replace the useless, lazy servants whom he was going to chase away, and who were fitting images of the branches they had neglected to prune. Then he explained to them the cutting away of the vinestock, spoke of the quantity of useless wood and foliage, and of the small number of grapes. To this he compared the hurtful elements that had, through sin, entered into man. These, he said, should be cut off and destroyed by the exercise of mortification in order that fruit might be produced. This led to some words on marriage and its precepts, as well as upon the modesty and propriety to be observed in it, after which he returned to the vine and told the people that they too ought to cultivate it. They replied quite innocently that the country was not adapted to vine culture. But Jesus responded that they ought to plant it on that side of the mountain occupied by the apiary, for that was an excellent exposure for it, and then he related a parable treating of bees. The people expressed their readiness to labor in his vineyard, if he would allow them. But he told them that he had to go and discharge the debts, that he had to see that the true vine was put into the wine press, in order to produce a life-giving wine, and to teach others how to cultivate and prepare the same. The simple-hearted people were troubled at the thought of his going away, and implored him to remain with them. But he consoled them by saying that if they believed him, he would send them one who would make them laborers in his vineyard. I saw that the inhabitants of this little place were afterward baptized by Thaddeus, and that all emigrated during a persecution.

Jesus recalled none of the prophecies, performed no miracles in this place. In spite of their moral disorders, these people were simple and childlike. Married couples living apart were again united by Jesus, and he explained to the man who, after having married five sisters was now about to espouse the sixth, that such unions were unlawful.

8/22 This morning Jesus gave another instruction upon marriage. He illustrated his subject by deeply significant similitudes taken from the cultivation of the vine, the care of the vineyard, and the pruning away of the superfluous branches. I was particularly impressed by his remarkable and clearly convincing words to this effect, that wherever discord reigned in the married state and wherever marriage failed to produce good, pure fruit, the fault lay principally on the wife's side. It is for her to endure and to suffer, it is for her to form, to preserve, the fruit of marriage. By her spiritual labors and victories over self, she can perfect her own soul and the fruit of her womb, she can eradicate whatever evil there may be in it, since her whole conduct, all her actions, redound to the blessing or the ruination of her offspring. In marriage there should be no question of sensual gratification, but only of penance and mortification, of constant fear, of constant warfare against sin and sinful desires, and this warfare is best carried on by prayer and self-conquest. Such struggles against self, such victories over self on the mother's part, secure similar victories to her children. All this instruction was given by the Lord in words as wonderful for their significance as for their simplicity. He said many other things, clear and precise, on the same subject. I was so impressed by the truth of what he said and its great necessity that the thought rushed impetuously to my mind: Why is not all this put in writing! Why is there no disciple present who could write it all down, that people far and wide might know it? For in the whole of this vision I was, as it were, present among Jesus's audience, and I followed him here and there. As I was so earnestly revolving that thought, my Lord turned and addressed me in words to this effect: "I rouse charity, I cultivate the vineyard wherever it will best produce fruit. Were these things written down, they would suffer the fate of so many other writings, they would fall into oblivion, or be misinterpreted, or utterly condemned. The words that I have just spoken, as well as innumerable others that have never been written, will become more productive in effects than what has been preserved in writing. It is not the written Law that is obeyed; but they that believe, hope, and love, have everything written in their heart." The way in which Jesus taught all this, the constant use of parables by which he illustrated from the nature of the vine all that he said of marriage and, on the other hand, the borrowing from marriage apt illustrations of the cultivation of the

vine—all was inexpressibly beautiful and convincing. The people questioned the Lord most simply, and he gave them answers that showed still
more clearly how perfectly his similitudes explained his doctrine.

At noon the nuptial ceremony between a poor young couple took
place in front of the synagogue, and at it Jesus assisted. Both were good
and innocent, consequently the Lord was very kind to them. The bridal
procession to the synagogue was headed by little boys of six years with
wreaths on their heads and flutes in their hands, white-robed maidens
carrying little baskets of flowers which they strewed on the ground, and
youths playing on harps, triangles, and other musical instruments now
little known. The bridegroom was dressed almost like a priest. Both he
and the bride were attended by assistants who, during the ceremony, laid
their hands on their shoulders. The marriage was performed by a Jewish
priest, in a hall whose roof had been opened just above the bridal party. It
was near the synagogue. When the stars began to appear in the sky, the
sabbath exercises were celebrated in the synagogue, after which a fast
that lasted until the next evening was begun.

8/23 When that was over, the wedding festivities were held in the public
house used on such occasions, during which Jesus related many parables,
such as that of the prodigal son and the mansions in his Father's house.
The bridegroom had no house of his own. He was to make his home in
that belonging to the mother of his bride. Jesus told him that, until he
should receive a mansion in his Father's house, he should take up his
abode under a tent in the vineyard which he himself was going to lay out
on the mount of the bees.

Then he again taught on marriage, upon which he dwelt for a considerable time. If married people, he said, would live together modestly and
chastely, if they would recognize their state as one of penance, then
would they lead their children in the way of salvation, then would their
state become not a means of diverting souls from their end, but one that
would reap a harvest for those mansions in his Father's house. In this
instruction, Jesus called himself the spouse of a bride in whom all those
that should be gathered, would be born again. He alluded to the marriage
feast of Cana, and told of the changing of water into wine. He always
spoke of himself in the third person, as of that man in Judea whom he
knew so well, who would be so bitterly persecuted, and who would
finally be put to death.

The people heard all this in simple, childlike faith, and the parables
were for them real facts. The bridegroom appeared to be a school
teacher, for Jesus told him how he should teach by his own example.
Jesus made allusion also to Ishmael, for Kedar and the country around

were peopled by his descendants. They were, for the most part, shepherds, and esteemed themselves inferior to the people of Judea, of whom they spoke as of a very great nation, a chosen race. They still clung to the ancient manner of living. The owner of numerous herds lived in a large house surrounded by a moat, and in the midst of the pasture grounds by which it was encompassed stood the houses of the under-shepherds. To the well, which belonged to the head proprietor, only his own herds had a right to go, though those of his neighbors enjoyed the same privilege if there existed an agreement to that effect. Such patriarchal settlements were scattered thickly here and there, though otherwise the place was of little importance.

8/24 Moved thereto by Jesus's words, the people determined to build for the newly-married pair a light habitation on the bee mount where, later on, the vineyard was to be laid out. Every friend in the place constructed for the tent a light wicker wall which was then covered with skins, and afterward coated with something of a viscid nature. When a piece of the work was finished, it was transported to the site for which it was destined. Each one did what was in his power, some more, some less, and they shared with one another whatever was needed. The Lord told them how all was to be done, and they listened in wonder at his knowing so much about such things. He had taught them at the marriage feast that the old and the poor should take the upper places. Jesus went with the people to the little hill in front of the bee mountain in order to choose there the best site for the vineyard. The back of the tent was to rest against the rising ground of the vineyard.

8/25 *Jesus remained in Sichar.*

8/26 As the Feast of the New Moon just now began, all returned with Jesus to the public house. He knew that, when he said that they should build a house for the newly-married pair, many had thought and said to one another: "Perhaps he has no house of his own, no place of abode. Will he, perhaps, take up his residence with these people?" Therefore it was that Jesus now told them that he was not going to stay among them, that he had no abiding place on this earth, that his kingdom was yet to come, that he had to plant his Father's vineyard, and water it with his blood upon Mount Calvary. They could not now comprehend his words, he said, but they would do so after he had watered the vineyard. Then he would come back to them from a dark country. He would send his messengers to call them, and then they would leave this place and follow him. But when he should come again for the third time, he would lead into his Father's kingdom all those who had faithfully labored in the vineyard. Their sojourning here was not to be long, therefore the house they were building was to be a light one, rather a tent that could be easily removed. Jesus next gave a long instruction upon mutual charity. They should, he said, cast their anchor in the heart of their neighbor, that the storms of the world might not separate and destroy them. He spoke again in parables of the vineyard, saying that he would remain only long enough to lay out the vineyard for the newly-married pair and teach them to plant the vines, then he would depart in order to cultivate that belonging to his Father. Jesus taught all these things in language so simple, and yet so nicely adapted to the point in question, that his hearers became more and more convinced of its truth, retaining at the same time their simplicity. He taught them to recognize in all nature, in life itself, a law hidden and holy, though now disfigured by sin. The instruction lasted till late into the night.

8/27 When Jesus wanted to take leave of them, the people detained him. They clasped him in their arms, exclaiming: "Explain it all to us again, that we may understand it better." But he replied that they should practice what he had preached to them, and he promised to send them one who would make it all clear to them. During this assembly they partook of a slight repast, at which all drank out of the same cup.

The young man for whom the Lord had caused the house to be built was named Salathiel, and the bride's name was a word that signified "pretty," or "brunette." With the greater part of the inhabitants of the place, they were baptized by Thaddeus. The Evangelist Mark also was in this region for awhile. Thirty-five years after Christ's Ascension, Salathiel with his wife and three grown-up sons removed to Ephesus. I saw him there in company with the goldsmith Demetrius, who had once raised an insurrection against Paul, but who was afterward converted. Demetrius gave him a long account of Paul, and narrated the history of his conversion. Paul was not then at Ephesus. Salathiel, his three sons, and Demetrius went to join him, while the wife of the first-named remained behind at Ephesus in a house to which many from her own country came and resided with her. Almost all the Jews left Ephesus at this time. Salathiel and his three sons, Demetrius, Silas, and a man named Caius were all in the same ship with Paul when he suffered shipwreck near the island of Malta, and they went with him to the island. From his prison in Rome, Paul assigned to each of the three sons of Salathiel the place in which he was to labor.

8/28 When Jesus went with the men to the bee mount in order to show them how to plant the vines, the site for the tent house was already marked off and an espalier erected. The men told Jesus that grapes raised in those parts were always bitter, to which Jesus responded that that was because they belonged to a poor species. They were of a bad stock, they were allowed to run wild without pruning; consequently they had the appearance only of grapes, without their sweetness. But, he added, those that he was now about to plant would be sweet. The instruction turned again upon marriage which, Jesus said, could produce pure, sweet fruit only when it was guarded by self-command, mortification, and moderation united to pain and labor.

From the young plants that he had ordered to be brought to the spot, Jesus chose five, which he laid in the ground that he had himself previously loosened, and he showed the men how to bind them to the espalier in the form of a cross. All that he said while thus engaged of the nature and training of the vine referred to the mystery of marriage and the sanctification of its fruit. When Jesus continued this instruction in the synagogue, he spoke of the obligation of continency in order to conception and, as a proof of the same, brought forward the depth of corruption into which men had fallen in this particular. Man, he said, might in this respect learn a lesson from the elephant. (There were a few of these animals in that region.) At the close of the instruction Jesus repeated that he must now soon leave them, in order to plant and water the vine on Mount Calvary, but he would send some to teach them all things and to lead them into his Father's vineyard.

8/29 *This evening he went to the synagogue for the sabbath and taught there.*

8/30 When in the synagogue Jesus spoke of the kingdom and the mansions of his Father, the people asked him why he had brought nothing with him from that kingdom and why he went about so poorly clad. Jesus answered that that kingdom was reserved for such as followed him, and that no one would receive it without deserving it. He was, he said, a stranger seeking for faithful servants whom he might call into the vineyard. He had therefore built the bridegroom's house so lightly because the earth was not to be a permanent abode for his posterity and they were not to cling to it. Why should a solid habitation be constructed for the body, since it is itself only a fragile vessel? It should indeed be cared for and purified as the house of the soul, as a sacred temple, but it should not be polluted, or to the prejudice of the soul either overburdened or treated too delicately. From such discourse Jesus turned again to the house of his Father, to the Messiah, and all the signs by which he might be recognized. Among the latter he mentioned the fact that he was to be born of an illustrious race, though of simple, pious parents, and added that, according to the signs of the time, he must have already come. They should, Jesus said, attach themselves to him and observe his teachings.

Jesus next taught on the love of the neighbor and good example. Turning to the bridegroom Salathiel, he told him to allow his house to stand open, to have perfect confidence in what he had said to him, and to live piously; if he did so, God would guard his house for him and nothing would be stolen from him. Salathiel had received for his new house far more than was actually needed, for Jesus had inveighed against selfishness. They must, he said, be willing to sacrifice for God and the neighbor. The communication between Jesus and these people became more and more intimate and, in order to rescue them from the ignorance into which they had fallen, he taught under manifold similitudes upon the chastity, modesty, and self-conquest that should grace the married state. The similitudes referred to the sowing and the harvest.

8/31 He went also to visit two parties who were about to marry notwithstanding their relationship to each other in prohibited degrees. One couple were blood relatives. Jesus summoned them into his presence and told them that their design sprang from the desire of temporal goods, and that it was not lawful. They were terrified on finding that he knew their thoughts, for no one had said anything to him about it; so they relinquished their intention. Here they washed one another's feet, and the bride wiped Jesus's feet with the end of her veil, or the upper part of her mantle. Both the man and the woman recognized Jesus by his teaching as more than a prophet. They were converted and followed him. Jesus next went out to a house in the country, in which lived a stepmother who wanted to marry her stepson, though the latter as yet did not clearly comprehend her design. Jesus made known to the son the danger in which he was, and bade him flee from the place and go labor at Salathiel's, which he obediently did. The Lord washed his feet also. The stepmother, whom Jesus gravely rebuked for her guilt, was greatly exasperated. She did no penance and went to perdition.

The people of this region must have had, through their ancestors, some special relations with the Ark of the Covenant. They asked Jesus what had become of the holy mystery contained in the Ark. He answered that humankind had received so much of it, that it had now passed into them, and that from the fact that it was no longer to be found, they might conclude that the Messiah was born. Many people of this country believed that the Messiah was put to death among the Holy Innocents.

JESUS RAISES A DEAD MAN TO LIFE

9/1 ABOUT one hour to the east of Sichar stood the dwelling of a rich herd proprietor. The house was surrounded by a moat. The owner had died suddenly in a field not far from his house, and his wife and children were in great affliction. The remains were ready for interment, and the family had sent messengers into the city to beg the Lord and some others to come to the funeral. Jesus went, accompanied by his three disciples, Salathiel and his wife, and several others—about thirty in all. The corpse, ready for the grave, was placed in a broad avenue of trees before the house. The man had been struck dead in punishment of his sins, for he had seized upon part of the possessions of some shepherds who, owing to his oppressive treatment, were obliged to leave that section of the country. Shortly after the commission of this sin, he had fallen dead upon the very ground that he had unjustly appropriated. Standing in front of the corpse, Jesus spoke of the deceased. He asked of what advantage was it to him now that he had once pampered and served his body, that house which his soul had now to leave. He had, on account of that body, run his soul into debt which he neither had and which he never could discharge. The wife of the deceased was plunged in grief. She had constantly repeated before Jesus's coming: "If the Jewish king from Nazareth were here, he could raise him from the dead!" In reply to these words, Jesus said: "Yes, the Jewish king can do it. But men will persecute him on that account. They will kill him who gives life, and they will refuse to acknowledge him!" To which those around responded: "If he were among us, we would acknowledge him!"

Jesus resolved to put them to the test. He spoke of faith, and promised that the Jewish king would help them, provided they believed and practiced all that he taught. Then he separated the family of the deceased along with Salathiel and his wife from the rest of the assistants, whom he directed to withdraw, while he spoke with the wife, the daughter, and the son of the dead man. Even before the others had gone out, the wife had addressed these words to Jesus: "Lord, thou speakest as if thou thyself wert the king of the Jews!" But Jesus had motioned her to be silent. When now those others, whom he knew to be weaker in faith, had retired, Jesus told the family that if they would believe in his doctrine, if they would follow him, and if they would keep silence upon the matter, he would raise the dead man to life, for his soul was not yet judged, it was still tarrying in the field, the scene of its injustice as well as of its separation from the body. The family promised with all their heart both obedience and silence, and Jesus went with them to the field in which the man had died. I saw the state in which the soul of the deceased was. I saw it in a circle, in a sphere above the spot upon which he had died. Before it passed pictures of all its transgressions with their temporal consequences, and the sight consumed it with sorrow. I saw too all the punishments it was to undergo, and it was vouchsafed a view of the redemptive

Passion of Jesus. Torn with grief, it was about to enter upon its punishment, when Jesus prayed, and called it back into the body by pronouncing the name Nazor, the name of the deceased. Then turning to the assistants, he said: "When we return, we shall find Nazor sitting up and alive!" I saw the soul at Jesus's call floating toward the body, becoming smaller, and disappearing through the mouth, at which moment Nazor rose to a sitting posture in his coffin. I always see the human soul reposing above the heart from which numerous threads run to the head.

When Jesus and his companions returned to the house they found Nazor, still enveloped in his funereal bands and his hands bound, sitting up in the coffin. His wife unbound his hands and loosened the bands. He stepped forth from the coffin, cast himself at Jesus's feet, and tried to embrace his knees. But the Lord drew back and told him that he should purify himself, should wash, and remain concealed in his chamber, that he should not speak of his resurrection until he himself had left that region. The wife then led her husband into a retired corner of the dwelling, where he washed and clothed himself. Jesus, Salathiel and his wife, and the three disciples took some food and remained at the house. The coffin was placed in the vault. The Lord taught until after nightfall.

9/2 On the following morning Jesus washed the feet of the resuscitated Nazor and exhorted him for the future to think more of his soul than of his body, and to restore the ill-gotten property. After that he called the children to him, spoke of God's mercy which their father had experienced, and exhorted them to the reverence of God; then he blessed them and led them to their parents. The mother, also, Jesus conducted to the father. He presented her to him as to one returned from afar, in order that they might live together in a stricter and more God-fearing manner.

Jesus on that day taught many things relating to marriage, in similitudes. He addressed himself especially to the newly-married couple. To Salathiel he said: "Thou hast allowed thy heart to be moved by the beauty of thy wife! But think how great the beauty of the soul must be, since God sends his Son upon earth to save souls by the sacrifice of his body! Whoever serves the body, serves not the soul. Beauty inflames selfish desire, and such desire corrupts the soul. Incontinence is like a creeping plant that chokes and destroys the wheat and the vines." These last words turned the instruction again upon the subject of vine and wheat culture, and Jesus warned his hearers to keep far from their fields and vineyards two running weeds which he designated by name. At last he announced to them that on the coming sabbath he would teach in the school at Kedar, and on that occasion they would hear what they must do to become his followers and share in his kingdom. He told them, moreover, that he would then depart from that region and journey eastward to Arabia. When they asked him why he was going among those pagans, those star-worshippers, he answered that he had friends among them who had followed a star in order to greet him at his birth. These he wanted to search after, that he might invite them also into the vineyard and the kingdom of his Father, and put them on the straight road to it.

9/3–4 An extraordinarily great multitude assembled in Kedar to meet Jesus, who now began publicly to heal crowds of sick. Sometimes while passing among those that had been brought hither by their friends, he merely pronounced the words: "Arise! Follow me!"—and they rose up cured. The wonder and admiration produced by these miracles reached such a pitch of enthusiasm that had not Jesus himself suppressed it, the whole country would have risen in one sudden transport of joy.

9/5 Salathiel and his wife were among the assembly at Kedar. Jesus once more spoke to them of the duties of the married state, and gave them detailed instructions upon the way in which they should live together in order to become a good vine (that is, one that would produce pure and excellent fruit, such as would become disciples of his apostles, saints, and martyrs). He inculcated the observance of modesty and purity, bade them in all their actions aim at purity of intention, exhorted them to prayer and renunciation, and rigorously commanded perfect continence after the period of conception. He spoke of the mutual confidence that ought to exist between husband and wife, and of the obedience of the latter to the former. The husband should not keep silence when the wife asks him questions. He ought to respect her and be indulgent toward her, since she is the weaker vessel. He should not mistrust her if he sees her talking with others, neither should she be jealous upon beholding him doing the same; still each should be careful not to give to the other cause for vexation. They should suffer no third party to come between them, and should settle their little differences themselves. He told the wife that she should become a pious Abigail, and pointed out to them a region suitable for the cultivation of wheat. They must, he said, raise a hedge around their vineyard, which hedge was to consist of the admonitions he had just given them.

9/6 Before leaving Kedar, Jesus gave in the synagogue another very long instruction, in which he again explained the connection existing between all the points upon which up to that time he had here taught separately. He spoke in simple, childlike allegories of the mysteries of original sin, the impure propagation of the human race, their ever-increasing corruption, the dispositions of God's grace and his guidance of the chosen people from generation to generation down to the blessed Virgin, the mystery of the Incarnation and the regeneration of fallen man from death to eternal life through the Son of the Virgin. Here he introduced the parable of the grain of wheat which had to be buried in the ground before it could spring forth into new fruit, but he was not understood by his hearers. He told them that they should follow him not for a short time only, but on a long journey that would end only at the Judgment. He spoke of the resurrection of the dead and of the Last Judgment, and he bade them watch! Then he related the parable of the slothful servants. Judgment comes like a thief in the night; death strikes at every hour. They, the Ishmaelites, were typified by the servants, and they ought to be faithful. Melchizedek, he said, was a type of himself. His sacrifice consisted of bread and wine, but in him they would be changed into flesh and blood. At last Jesus told them in plain terms that he was the Redeemer. At this revelation, many became timid and fearful, while others grew more ardent and enthusiastic in their adherence to him. He enforced upon them in particular love for one another, compassion, sympathy in joy and sorrow such as the members of the body feel for one another. The pagans from the pagan quarter of Kedar were present at this instruction, to which they listened from a distance. They had been very hostile toward the Jews, but from this time many approached them and questioned them in a friendly manner about Jesus's doctrine and miracles.

9/7–8 Jesus remained in Kedar.

Jesus Reaches the First Tent City of the Star Worshippers

9/9 WHEN Jesus with the three youths left Kedar, Nazor, the ruler of the synagogue (who traced his origin up to Tobias), Salathiel, Eliud, and the youth Titus accompanied him a good part of the way. They crossed the river and passed through the pagan quarter of the city, in which just at that time a pagan feast was being celebrated and sacrifice was being offered in front of the temple. The road ran first eastward and then to the south through a plain that lay between two high mountain ridges, sometimes over heaths, again over yellow or white sand, and sometimes over white pebbles. At last they reached a large, open tract of country covered with verdure, in which stood a great tent among the palm trees, and around it many smaller ones. Here Jesus blessed and took leave of his escort, and then continued his journey awhile longer toward the tent city of the star worshippers. The day was on its decline when he arrived at a beautiful well in a hollow. It was surrounded by a low embankment, and near it was a drinking ladle. The Lord drank, and then sat down by the well. The youths washed his feet and he, in turn, rendered them the same service. All was done with childlike simplicity, and the sight was extremely touching. The plain was covered with palm trees, meadows, and at a considerable distance apart there were groups of tents. A tower, or terraced pyramid of pretty good size, still not higher than an ordinary church, arose in the center of the district. Here and there some people made their appearance and from a distance gazed at Jesus in surprise not unmingled with awe, but no one approached him.

Not far from the well stood the largest of the tent houses. It was surmounted by several spires, and consisted of many stories and apartments connected together by partitions, some grated, others merely of canvas. The upper part was covered with skins. Altogether it was very artistically made and very beautiful. From this tent castle five men came forth bearing branches, and turned their steps in the direction of Jesus. Each carried in his hand a branch of a different kind of fruit: One had little yellow leaves and fruit, another was covered with red berries, a third was a palm branch, one bore a vine branch full of leaves, and the fifth carried a cluster of grapes. From the waist to the knees they wore a kind of woollen tunic slit at the sides, and on the upper part of the body a jacket wide and full, made of some kind of transparent, woollen stuff, with sleeves that reached about halfway to the elbow. They were of fair complexion, had a short, black beard, and long, curling hair. On their head was a sort of spiral cap from which hung many lappets around their temples. They approached Jesus and his companions with a friendly air, saluted them and, while presenting to them the branches they held in their hands, invited them to accompany them back to the tent. The vine branch was presented to Jesus, the one who acted as guide carrying a similar one. On entering the tent Jesus and his companions were made to sit upon cushions trimmed with tassels, and fruit was presented to them. Jesus uttered only a few words. The guests were then led through a tent corridor lined with sleeping chambers containing couch beds, and furnished with high cushions, to that part of the tent in which was the dining hall. In the center of the hall rose the pillar that supported the tent; and around it were twined garlands of leaves and fruits, vine branches, apples, and clusters of grapes—all so natural in appearance that I cannot say whether they really were natural or only painted. Here the attendants drew out a little oval table about as high as a footstool. It was formed of light leaves that could be opened quickly and its feet separated into two supports. They spread under it a colored carpet upon which were representations of men like themselves, and placed upon it cups and other table furniture. The tent was hung with tapestry, so that no part of the canvas itself could be seen.

When Jesus and the young disciples stretched themselves on the carpet around the table, the men in attendance brought cakes, scooped out in the middle, all kinds of fruits, and honey. The attendants themselves sat on low, round folding stools, their legs crossed. Between their feet they stood a little disk supported on a long leg, and on the disk they laid their plate. They served their guests themselves by turns, the servants remaining outside the tent with everything that was necessary. I saw them going to another tent and bringing thence birds, which had been roasted on a spit in the kitchen. This last-named apartment consisted merely of a mud hut in which was an opening in the roof to let out the smoke from the fire on the hearth. The birds were served up in quite a remarkable manner. They were (but I know not how it was done) covered with their feathers, and looked just as if they were alive. The meal over, the guests were escorted by five men to their sleeping rooms, and there the latter were quite amazed at seeing Jesus washing the youths' feet, which service they rendered him in return. Jesus explained to them its signification, and they resolved to practice in future the same act of courtesy.

NOCTURNAL CELEBRATION OF THE STAR WORSHIPPERS

WHEN the five men took leave of Jesus and his young companions, they all left the tent together. They wore mantles longer behind than before, with a broad flap hanging from the back of the neck. They proceeded to a temple which was built in the shape of a large four-cornered pyramid, not of stone but of very light materials such as wood and skins. There was a flight of outside steps from base to summit. It was built in a hollow that rose in terraces and was surrounded by steps and parapets. The circular enclosure was cut through by entrances to the different parts of the temple, and the entrances themselves were screened by light, ornamental hedges. Several hundred people were already assembled in the enclosure. The married women were standing back of the men; the young girls, back of them; and last of all, the children. On the steps of the pyramidal temple were illuminated globes that flashed and twinkled just like the stars of heaven, but I do not know how that was effected. They were regularly arranged, in imitation of certain constellations. The temple was full of people. In the center of the building rose a high column from which beams extended to the walls and up into the summit of the pyramid, bearing the lights by which the exterior globes were lighted. The light inside the temple was very extraordinary. It was like twilight, or rather moonlight. One seemed to be gazing up into a sky full of stars.

The moon likewise could be seen, and far up in the very center of all blazed the sun. It was a most skillfully executed arrangement, and so natural that it produced upon the beholder an impression of awe, especially when he beheld by the dim light of the lower part of the temple the three idols that were placed around that central column. One was like a human being with a bird's head and a great, crooked beak. I saw the people offering to it in sacrifice all kinds of foods. They crammed into its enormous bill birds and similar things which fell down into its body and out again. Another of these idols had a head almost like that of an ox, and was seated like a human being in a squatting posture. They laid birds in its arms, which were outstretched as if to receive an infant. In it was a fire into which, through the holes made for that purpose, the worshippers cast the flesh of animals that had been slaughtered and cut up on the sacrificial table in front of it. The smoke escaped through a pipe sunk in the earth and communicating with the outer air. No flames were to be seen in the temple, but the horrible idols shone with a reddish glare in the dim light. During the ceremony, the multitude around the pyramid chanted in a very remarkable manner. Sometimes a single voice was heard, and then again a powerful chorus, the strains suddenly changing from plaintive to exultant; and when the moon and different stars shone out, they sent up shouts of enthusiastic welcome. I think this idolatrous celebration lasted till sunrise.

9/10 Before taking leave of these people on the following morning, Jesus gave them a few words of instruction. To their questions as to who he was and whither he was journeying, he answered by telling them about his Father's kingdom. He was, he said, seeking friends that had saluted him at his birth. After that he was going down to Egypt, to hunt up some companions of his childhood and to call them to follow him, as he was soon to return to his Father. He spoke to them on the subject of their idolatrous worship, for which they put themselves to so much trouble and slaughtered so many sacrifices. They should adore the Father, the Creator of all things, and instead of sacrificing victims to idols which they themselves had made, they should bestow those gifts upon their poor brethren. The abodes of the women were back of and entirely separate from the tents of the men, each of whom had many wives. They wore long garments, jewels in their ears, and headdresses in the form of a high cap. Jesus commended the separation of the women from the men. It was well, he said, for the former to stand in the background, but against a multiplicity of wives he inveighed strenuously. They should have but one wife, he said, whom they should treat as one that owed submission, though not as a slave. During this instruction, Jesus appeared to them so lovable, so much like a supernatural being, that they implored him to remain with them. They wanted to bring a wise, old priest to converse with him, but Jesus would not allow it. Then they produced some ancient manuscripts which they consulted. They were not rolls of parchment, but thick leaves, which looked as if made of bark, and upon which the writing was deeply imprinted. These leaves were very like thick leather. The pagans insisted upon the Lord's remaining and instructing them, but he refused, saying that they should follow him when he had returned to his Father, and that he would not neglect to call them at the right time.

When about to leave, Jesus wrote for them with a sharp metallic rod on the stone floor of their tent the initials of five members of his race. It looked to me like only the letters, four or five of them, entwined together, and among them I recognized an "M." They were deeply engraven on the stone. The pagans gazed in wonder at the inscription, for which they at once conceived great reverence. Later on they converted the stone upon which it was traced into an altar. I see it now at Rome enclosed in one of the corners of St. Peter's church, nor will the enemies of the church be able to carry it off!

Jesus would not allow any of these pagans to accompany him when he departed. He directed his steps southward with his young disciples through the widely scattered tents and passed the tower of the idols. He remarked to the youths how affectionately he had been received by these pagans for whom he had done nothing, and how maliciously the obstinate, ungrateful Jews had persecuted him, although he had loaded them with benefits. Jesus and his young companions hurried on rapidly the whole of that day. It seems to me that he still had a journey of some days, about fifty miles, before reaching the country of the kings.

JESUS ENCOUNTERS A PASTORAL TRIBE

9/11–12 SHORTLY before the commencement of the sabbath I saw Jesus in the neighborhood of some shepherd tents, where he and his three young companions sat down by a fountain and washed one another's feet. Then he began to celebrate the sabbath, praying with the youths and instructing them in order that even here in a strange land, the Jews' reproaches that he did not sanctify the sabbath day might not be verified. He slept that night with the three youths in the open air by the well. There were no permanent dwellings in this place, and no women among the shepherds. They had only one temporary inn, or caravanserai, near their distant pasture grounds.

9/13 Next morning, the shepherds gathered around Jesus and listened to his words. He asked them whether they had not heard of some people who, three and thirty years before, had been guided by a star to Judea, to salute the newborn king of the Jews. They cried out: "Yes! Yes!" and he went on to tell them that he was now traveling in search of those men. The shepherds exhibited a childlike joy and love for Jesus. On a lovely spot surrounded by palm trees, they made for him a beautiful high seat or throne, up to which led steps covered with sod. They worked so very quickly, cutting and raising the sods with long stone, or bone knives, that the seat was soon finished. The Lord seated himself upon it, and taught in most beautiful parables. The shepherds, about forty in number, listened like little children and afterward prayed with Jesus.

That evening the shepherds took down one of their tents, and uniting it to another, formed thereby one large hall, in which they prepared for the whole party an entertainment consisting of fruit, a kind of thick pap rolled into balls, and camel's milk. When Jesus blessed the food he was about to take, they asked him why he did so, and when he explained the reason, they begged him to bless all the rest of the food, which he did. They wanted him also to leave behind him some blessed food; and when they brought him for that purpose things soft and very perishable, he called for fruits that would not decay. They brought them, and he blessed some white balls made of rice. He told them always to mix a little of the blessed provisions with their other food, which then would never spoil, and the blessing would never be taken away.

The kings already knew through dreams that Jesus was coming to see them.

A WONDERFUL GLOBE

9/14 I SAW Jesus again teaching from the mossy throne. He taught about the creation of the world, the Fall of Man, and the promise of Redemption. Jesus asked whether they preserved the tradition of any Promise. But they knew only a few things connected with Abraham and David, and those were mixed up with fables. They were so simple, just like children in school. Whoever knew anything in answer to a question, said it right out. When Jesus saw how innocent and ignorant they were, he wrought a great miracle in their behalf. I cannot recall exactly what he said, but he appeared to catch with his right hand at a sunbeam from which he drew a ball like a little luminous globe, and let it hang from the palm of the same hand by a ray of light. It seemed to be large enough to contain all things, and all things could be seen in it. The good people and the disciples beheld in it everything just as the Lord related it to them, and they all stood in awe around him. I saw the most holy Trinity in the globe, and when I saw the Son in it, I did not see Jesus any longer upon earth, only an angel hovering by the globe. Once Jesus took the globe upon his hand, and again it seemed as if his hand itself was the globe, in which innumerable pictures unfolded, one from another. I heard something about the number three hundred and sixty-five, as if relating to the days of the year, connected with which also there was something in the pictures formed in the globe.

Jesus taught the shepherds a short prayer, in which occurred words like those of the Lord's Prayer, and he gave them three intentions for which they should alternately recite it. The first was to thank for Creation; the second, for Redemption; and the third, I think, was for the Last Judgment. The whole history of the Creation, the Fall, and the Redemption was unfolded in successive pictures in this globe, along with the means given to man to participate therein. I saw all things in the globe connected by rays of light with the most holy Trinity, out of whom all things proceeded, but from whom many separated miserably. The Lord gave to the shepherds an idea of Creation by the globe which sprang forth from his hand; an idea of the connection of the fallen world with the Godhead and its Redemption by the suspension of the globe from his hand by a thread; and when he held it in his hand, he gave them some idea of Judgment. He taught them likewise about the year and the days that compose it inasmuch as they are figures of this history of Creation, and then he showed by what prayers and good works they ought to sanctify the different seasons.

When the Lord concluded his instruction, the luminous globe with its varied pictures disappeared as it had come. The poor people, quite overcome by the sense of their own profound misery and the godlike dignity of their guest, showed signs of deep affliction and cast themselves, along with the three youths, prostrate on the ground, weeping and adoring. Jesus too became very sad and prostrated on the grassy mound upon which he had been sitting. The youths attempted to raise him; and when at last he arose of himself, the shepherds rose also, and standing around him timidly ventured to ask him the cause of his sadness. Jesus answered that he was mourning with those who mourned. He then took one of the hyacinths that grew wild in that region (but which were far larger and more beautiful than those we have), and asked them whether they knew the properties of that flower. When the sky is troubled, he said, it wilts, it pines as it were, and its color grows pale, and so too a cloud had passed over his own sun. He told them many other remarkable things about these flowers and their signification. I heard him also calling them by an exceedingly strange name which, I was told, corresponded to our name for it, the hyacinth.

ABOLITION OF IDOL WORSHIP

9/15 ALTHOUGH Jesus knew full well, he questioned the shepherds upon the kind of worship they practiced. He was like a good teacher who becomes a child with his children. Thereupon the good people brought to him their gods in the shape of all kinds of animals, sheep, camels, asses—all very skillful imitations of the animals themselves. They appeared to be made of metal, and were covered with skins; and, what was truly amusing, all the idols represented female animals. They were provided with long bags, in imitation of udders, to which were attached reed nipples. These bags they filled with milk, milked them at their feasts, drank, and then danced and leaped about. Everyone selected from his herd the most beautiful, the most excellent cattle, which he raised with care and looked upon as sacred. It was after these holy models that the poor idolaters made their gods, and it was with their milk that they filled the udders. When they celebrated religious services, they brought all their idols together into one tent decorated for the occasion, and then began great carousing as at a carnival. The women and children also were in attendance, and milking and eating, drinking, singing, dancing, and adoring of the idols went on vigorously. It was not the sabbath they were celebrating, but the day after.

While the pagans were relating all this to Jesus and showing him their idols, I saw the whole thing taking shape and being enacted before my eyes. The Lord explained to them what a miserable shadow of true religious service theirs was and, after some more words to that effect, ended by telling them that he himself was the chosen from the herd. He was the Lamb from whom flowed all the milk that was to nourish the soul unto salvation. Then he commanded them to abolish their zoolatry, to drive the living animals back among the herds, and the metal of which the idols were composed to be given to the poor. They should, he said, erect altars, burn upon them incense to the almighty Creator, the heavenly Father, and give thanks to him. They should moreover pray for the coming of the Redeemer, and divide their goods with their poor brethren, for not far off in the desert lived people so poor that they had not even tents to shelter them. Whatever parts of their slaughtered cattle they could not eat ought to be burned as a sacrifice, also the bread that was stale and not intended for the poor. The ashes should be sprinkled upon unproductive ground, which Jesus pointed out to them, in order to attract upon it a blessing. As he prescribed these different points he explained the reasons for observing them. Then he alluded again to the kings that had visited him. The people said, yes, they had heard that thirty-three years before, those kings had journeyed afar in search of the Savior and in the hope of finding along with him everything that could be conducive to happiness and salvation. The kings, they added, had returned to their country and changed something in their religious worship, but that was all they had ever heard about them.

Jesus next went around with these shepherds among their herds and huts, teaching them all kinds of things, even about the different herbs growing there. He promised to send someone to them soon to instruct them. He assured them that he had come on earth not merely for the Jews alone, as they in their humility thought, but for every single human being that sighed for his coming. From the little that they knew of Abraham, this poor shepherd tribe had conceived great esteem for sobriety. The three youths were impressed in a special manner by the late miracle of the luminous globe. Their relations toward the Lord were very different from those of the apostles. They served him in dependence, silence, and child-like simplicity. Unlike the apostles, they never had anything to reply to their Master. The apostles, however, held an office, whereas these youths were like poor, dependent scholars.

JESUS CONTINUES HIS
JOURNEY TO THE TENT CITY OF THE KINGS

9/16–17 WHEN Jesus left the shepherds and pursued his journey to the land of the three kings, about twelve of them bore him company. They appeared to have some kind of a tax to pay for which they were taking with them birds in baskets. This journey was a very lonely one, for on the whole length of the route they did not meet one dwelling house. The road was, however, distinctly marked out, and there was no chance of the traveler's losing his way in the desert. Trees lined the roadside bearing edible fruits the size of figs, and here and there were found berries. At certain points, marking one day's journey, resting places were formed. They consisted of a covered well surrounded by trees, whose tops were drawn together in a large hoop, their hanging branches thus forming an arbor. These resting places were furnished with conveniences for making a fire and passing the night. During the great noonday heat, Jesus and the youths rested at one of these wells and refreshed themselves with some fruit. Each time they thus paused on their journey, Jesus and the youths washed one another's feet. The Lord never permitted any of the others to touch him. The youths, drawn by his goodness, at times treated Jesus with childlike confidence, but again, when they thought of his miracles, his divinity, they cast timid and frightened glances toward him and looked at one another. I saw too that Jesus often appeared to vanish before them, although he did not fail to direct their attention to all that they met on their way and instruct them upon the same.

They journeyed a part of the night. When they paused to rest, the youths struck fire by revolving two pieces of wood together. They had also a lantern at the end of a pole. It was open on top, and its little flame shed around a reddish glare. I do not know of what it consisted. I saw during the night wild animals running furtively about. The road ran sometimes over high mountains, not steep but gently rising. In one field I saw many rows of nut trees, and people filling sacks with the nuts that had fallen. It looked something like a gleaning. There were other trees whose leaves were gone but the fruit was still remaining, peach trees with slender trunks planted on rising ground, and another that looked almost like our laurel. Some of the resting places for travelers were under large juniper bushes whose branches were as thick as the arm of a good-sized man. They were closely grown together overhead, but thinned out below, so as to afford a delightful shelter. The greater part of the journey, however, was through a desert of white sand interspersed with places covered, some with small white pebbles, others with little polished ones like birds' eggs; and there were large beds of black stones, like the remains of fractured pipkins, or pieces of hollow pottery. Some of these fragments were provided with holes like regular rings, or handles, and the people in the country around used to come in search of them in order to utilize them as bowls and other vessels.

9/18 The last mountain the travelers crossed was covered with gray stones only. They found on descending its opposite side a dense hedgerow, behind which flowed a rapid stream around a piece of cultivated land. By the shore lay a ferryboat formed of the trunks of trees woven together with osiers. On this they crossed the stream, and then directed their steps to a row of huts built of sticks woven together and overlaid with moss. They had pointed roofs, and all around the central apartment were sleeping places furnished with mossy seats and couches. The occupants were modestly clothed and wore blankets around them like mantles. At some distance I saw tent buildings, much larger and stronger than any I had hitherto seen. They were raised on a stone foundation and had several stories reached by outside steps. Between the first and the second hut was a well, by which Jesus seated himself. The youths washed his feet, and then he was conducted to a house set apart for strangers. The people here were very good. They who had accompanied Jesus now left him for their homes, taking with them provisions for the way.

This region of moss cabins was of very considerable extent, and numberless dwellings such as described lay around among the meadows, fields, and gardens. The large tent palaces could not be seen from here, for they were still at quite a distance; but they were plainly visible from the descent of the mountain. The whole country was extraordinarily fruitful and charming. On the hills were numerous clusters of balsam trees, which when notched distilled a precious juice. The natives caught it in those stone vessels which looked something like iron pots, and which they found in the desert. I saw also magnificent wheat fields, the stalks as thick as reeds, vines, and roses, flowers as large and round as a child's head; and others remarkable for their great size. There were also little purling brooks clear and rapid, overarched by carefully trimmed hedges whose tops were bound together to form a bower. The flowers of these hedges were gathered with care, and those that fell into the water were caught in nets, spread here and there for that purpose, and thus preserved. At the places at which the blossoms were fished out there were gates in the hedges, which were usually kept closed. The people brought and showed to the Lord all the fruits they had.

When Jesus spoke to them of those men who had followed the star, they told him that on their return from Judea to the place from which they had first noticed the star, they built on the spot a lofty temple in the form of a pyramid. Around it they erected a city of tents in which they dwelt together, although before that they had lived widely apart. They had received the assurance that the Messiah would eventually visit them, and that upon his departure they too would leave the place. Mensor, the eldest, was still alive and well; Theokeno, the second, borne down by the weakness of old age, could no longer walk.† Sair, the third, had died some years previously, and his remains, perfectly preserved, lay in a tomb built in pyramidal form. On the anniversary of his death, his friends visited it, opened it, and performed certain ceremonies over the remains, near which fire was kept constantly burning.

---

† Anne Catherine elsewhere describes Theokeno as the eldest of the three kings, and she speaks of Mensor as the king who brought the gift of gold to the child Jesus. She said that Sair had brought incense and Theokeno myrrh, and that Mary had accepted these gifts with humble gratitude. She added that Mensor and Theokeno were baptized by the apostle Thomas three years after the ascension of Jesus. The two kings then left Chaldea and went to live on the island of Crete.

9/19–20 They enquired of Jesus regarding those of the caravan that had remained behind in Palestine, and sent messengers to the tent city, a couple of hours distant, to inform Mensor that they thought they had among them an envoy of that king of the Jews so much desired by him and his people.

When the hour for the sabbath approached, Jesus asked for one of the unoccupied cabins to be placed at the service of himself and his disciples, and as there were here no lamps of Jewish style, they made one for themselves and celebrated their holy exercises.

Jesus Ceremoniously Escorted by Mensor to his Tent Castle

WHEN the kings received the news of Jesus's arrival, they made great preparations for his reception. Trees were bound together so as to form covered walks, and triumphal arches erected. These latter were adorned with flowers, fruits, ornaments of all kinds, and hung with tapestry. Seven men in white, gold-embroidered mantles, long and training, and with turbans on their heads ornamented with gold and high tufts of feathers, were dispatched to the pastoral region to meet Jesus and bear to him a welcome. Jesus delivered in their presence an instruction in which he spoke of right-minded pagans who, though ignorant, were devout of heart.

The dwelling place of the kings was so commodious and so rich in ornamentation that words cannot describe it. It was more like a delightful pleasure garden than a real tent city. The principal tent looked like a large castle. It consisted of several stories raised upon a stone foundation. The lowest was formed of railings through which the eye could penetrate, and the upper ones contained the various apartments, while all around the immense building ran covered galleries and flights of steps. Similar tent castles stood around, all connected together by walks paved with colored stones ornamented with representations of stars, flowers, and similar devices. These walks, so clean and beautiful, were bordered on either side by grass plots and gardens whose beds, regularly laid out, were full of flowers, slender trees with fine leaves, such as the myrtle and dwarf laurel, and all kinds of berries and aromatic plants. In the center of the city, upon a grassy mound such as described, rose a very high and beautiful fountain of many jets. It was surmounted by a roof supported on an open colonnade around which were placed benches and other seats. The streams from the jets shot far around the central column. Back of this stood the temple, with its surrounding colonnades, containing the vaults of the kings, among which was the tomb of King Sair. This temple was open on one side, but closed on the others by the doors leading to the vaults. It was in shape a four-cornered pyramid, but the roof was not so flat as those that I saw on the early part of the Lord's journey. Spiral steps with railings ran up around the pyramid, whose summit was executed in openwork. I noticed also a tent house in one side of which youths were being educated; and on the other, but entirely separate, girls were instructed in various branches. The dwellings of the females were all together and outside of this enclosure. They lived entirely separate from the men. Words cannot say with what elegance the whole city was laid out, and with what care it was preserved in its beauty, freshness, and neatness. The buildings presented an airy appearance characterized by simplicity of taste. Beautiful gardens with seats for resting were everywhere to be met. I saw an immense cage, more like a large house than a cage, filled from top to bottom with birds; further on, I saw tents and huts in which dwelt smiths and other workmen. I saw also stables and immense meadows full of herds of camels, asses, great sheep with fine wool, also cows with small heads and large horns, very different from those of our country.

I saw no mountain in this region, only gently rising hills, not much higher than our pagan sepulchral mounds. Down through these hills, through pipes inserted for that purpose, borings were made in search of gold. If the boring tube were brought up with gold on its point, the mine was opened in the side of the hill and the gold dug out. It was then smelted in the neighborhood of the mine in furnaces heated not with wood, but with lumps of something brown and clear, which too was dug out of the earth.

9/21 Mensor, who was under the persuasion that it was only an envoy from Jesus who had arrived, set all in motion to give him as solemn a reception as if it were the king of the Jews himself who had come. He deliberated with the other chiefs and priests, and prescribed the various details of his reception. Festal garments and presents were prepared, and the roads by which he was to come magnificently decorated. All was carried forward with joyous earnestness. Mensor, mounted on a richly caparisoned camel which was laden on both sides with small chests, and attended by a retinue of twenty distinguished personages, some of whom had formed part of the caravan to Bethlehem, set out to meet Jesus who, with the three youths and seven messengers, was on his way to the tent castle. Mensor's party chanted, as they went along, a solemn, plaintive melody such as they had nightly sung during their journey to Bethlehem. Mensor, the eldest of the kings, he of the brownish complexion, wore a high, round cap ornamented with some kind of a white puffed border, and a white training mantle embroidered in gold. As a mark of honor, a standard floated at the head of the procession. It looked like a horse's tail fastened to a pole, the top of which was indented with points. The way led through an avenue across lovely meadows carpeted here and there with patches of tender white moss that glanced like dense fungus in the rays of the sun. At last, the procession reached a well covered by a verdant temple of artistically cut foliage. Here Mensor dismounted from his camel and awaited the Lord, who was seen approaching. One of the seven delegated to escort Jesus ran on before and announced his coming. The chests borne by the camels were now opened, and magnificent garments embroidered in gold, golden cups, plates, and dishes of fruit were taken out and deposited upon the carpet that was spread near the well. Mensor, bowed with age, supported by two of his retinue and attended by his train-bearer, went to meet Jesus. His whole demeanor was marked by humility. He carried in his right hand a long staff ornamented with gold and terminating in a scepter-shaped point. At a glance from Jesus he experienced, as formerly at the crib, an interior monition similar to that which had drawn him, first of the three, down upon his knees. Reaching his staff to Jesus, he now prostrated again before him, but Jesus raised him from the ground. Then the old man ordered the gifts to be brought forward and presented to Jesus, who handed them to the disciples, and they were replaced upon the camel. Jesus did indeed accept the splendid garments, though he would not consent to wear them. The camel likewise was presented to him by the old man, but Jesus thanked without accepting.

They now entered the bower. Mensor presented to the Lord fresh water into which he had poured some kind of juice from a small flask, and fruit on little dishes. In a manner inexpressibly humble, childlike, and friendly, Mensor questioned Jesus about the king of the Jews, for he still looked upon him as an envoy, though he could not explain to himself his inward emotion. His companions conversed with the youths and wept for joy when they heard from Eremenzear that he was the son of one of those followers of the kings that had remained behind and settled near Bethlehem. He was a descendant of Abraham by his second wife, Keturah. Mensor wanted Jesus to ride upon his camel when they were again starting for the tent castle, but Jesus insisted on walking, he and the young disciples heading the procession. In about an hour they reached the vast circular enclosure wherein stood Mensor's dwelling and its dependencies, and around which, in lieu of walls, was stretched white tent cloth. Under the triumphal arch before the entrance, Jesus and the disciples were met by a troop of maidens in festive attire. They came forward, two by two, carrying baskets of flowers which they strewed over the way by which he had to pass until it was entirely covered with them. The path led through an avenue of shade trees whose top branches were bound together. The maidens wore under their upper garment, which fell around them in the form of a mantle, wide white pantalets; on their feet, pointed sandals; around their heads, bands of some kind of white fabric; and on their arms and breast and around their necks were wreaths of flowers, wool, and glistening feathers.

They were clothed very modestly, though they wore no veils. The shady avenue ended at a covered bridge which led across the moat, or brook, into the large garden around which the brook ran. In front of the bridge was erected a highly ornamented triumphal arch, under which Jesus was received by five priests in white mantles with long trains. Their robes were richly adorned with lace, and from the right arm of each hung a maniple to the ground. They wore on their head a scalloped crown in the front of which was a little shield in the form of a heart, and from which rose a point. Two of them bore a fire-pan of gold, upon which they sprinkled frankincense from a golden vessel shaped like a boat. They would not allow the trains of their mantles to be held up in Jesus's presence, but tucked them up in a loop behind.

Jesus received all these honors quietly, as he afterward did those of Palm Sunday.

The magnificent garden was watered by many little streams and laid off in triangular flowerbeds by paths beautifully paved with ornamental stones. Through the center of it ran an embowered walk, likewise paved with colored stones in figures, to a second covered bridge. The trees and garden bushes were trained in all kinds of figures. I saw some cut to represent men and animals. The outside row was formed of high trees, but the inner ones were smaller, more delicate, and there were many shady resting places.

The second bridge once crossed, the way led to the middle of a large, circular place that formed the center of the surrounding enclosure. There on a mound entirely surrounded by water stood, over a well, an open edifice, like a little temple. The roof, formed of skins, was raised upon slender pillars. The whole island was one lovely garden, and opposite to it rose the large royal tent.

When Jesus crossed the second bridge, he was received by youths playing on flutes and tambourines. They dwelt near the bridge in low, four-cornered tents which stretched right and left in arches. They must have been a kind of bodyguard, for they carried short swords and stood on guard. They wore caps garnished with something like a feather horn, and they had many kinds of ornaments hanging around them, among them the representation of a large half-moon, in which was a face regularly cut out. The procession halted before the little island of the well. The king dismounted from his camel and led Jesus and the disciples to the fountain, which consisted of a wellspring with many circles of jets one above another, all made of shining metal. When a faucet was turned, the streams of water spouted far around and ran down the mound in channels, through the green hedges, and into the surrounding brook. All around the fountain were seats. The disciples washed Jesus's feet, and he theirs. A covered tent avenue ran over the bridge from the fountain to the other side of the great, circular place and up to Mensor and Theokeno's tent castle. On one side of the tent castle stood, in the spacious enclosure around the fountain island, the temple, a four-cornered pyramid. It was not so high as the tent castle and was surrounded by a colonnade, in which was found the entrance to the vaults of the deceased kings. Around the temple pyramid ran a flight of spiral steps up to the grated summit. Between the temple and the fountain island, the sacred fire was preserved in a pit covered by a metallic dome upon which was a figure with a little flag in its hand. The fire was kept constantly burning. It was a white flame that did not rise above the mouth of the pit. The priests frequently put into it pieces of something that they dug out of the ground.

The tent castle of the kings was several stories high. The lowest, that is, the one next above the solid foundation, was merely grated, so that one could see quite through it. It was full of little bushes and plants, and served as a garden for Theokeno, who could no longer walk. Covered steps and galleries ran around the tent castle from the ground up to the top. Here and there were openings like windows, though not symmetrically placed. The roof of the tent had several gables, all ornamented with flags, stars, and moons.

After a short time spent at the fountain, Jesus was escorted through the covered tent avenue to the castle and into the large octagonal hall. In the center rose a supporting column all around which, one above another, were little circular cavities in which various objects could be placed. The walls were hung with colored tapestry upon which were representations of flowers, and figures of boys holding drinking cups, and the floor was carpeted.

9/22–24 Jesus requested Mensor to conduct him at once to Theokeno, whose rooms were in the trellised basement near the little garden. He was resting on a cushioned couch, and he took part in the meal that was served up in dishes of surpassing beauty. The food dishes were prepared very elegantly. Herbs, fine and delicate, were arranged on the plates to represent little gardens. The cups were of gold. Among the fruits was one particularly remarkable. It was yellow, ribbed, very large, and crowned by a tuft of leaves. The honeycombs were especially fine. Jesus ate only some bread and fruit, and drank from a cup that had never before been used. This was the first time that I saw him eating with pagans. I saw him teaching here whole days at a time, and but seldom taking a mouthful.

He taught during that meal and, at last, told his hosts that he was not an envoy of the Messiah, but the Messiah himself. On hearing this, they fell prostrate on the ground in tears. Mensor especially wept with emotion. He could not contain himself for love and reverence, and was unable to conceive how Jesus could have condescended to come to him. But Jesus told him that he had come for the pagans as well as for the Jews, that he was come for all who believed in him. Then they asked him whether it was not time for them to abandon their country and follow him at once to Galilee, for, as they assured him, they were ready to do so. But Jesus replied that his kingdom was not of this world, and that they would be scandalized, that they would waver in faith if they should see how he would be scorned and maltreated by the Jews. These words they could not comprehend, and they inquired how it could be that things could go so well with the bad while the good had to suffer so much. Jesus then explained to them that they who enjoy on earth have to render an account hereafter, and that this life is one of penance.

The kings had some knowledge of Abraham and David; and when Jesus spoke of his ancestors, they produced some old books and searched in them to see whether they too could not claim descent from the same race. The books were in the form of tablets opening out in a zigzag form, like sample patterns. These pagans were so childlike, so desirous of doing all that they were told. They knew that circumcision had been prescribed to Abraham, and they asked the Lord whether they too should obey this part of the Law. Jesus answered that it was no longer necessary, that they had already circumcised their evil inclinations, and that they would do so still more. Then they told him that they knew something of Melchizedek and his sacrifice of bread and wine, and said that they too had a sacrifice of the same kind, namely, a sacrifice of little leaves and some kind of a green liquor. When they offered it they spoke some words like these: "Whoever eats me and is devout, shall have all kinds of felicity." Jesus told them that Melchizedek's sacrifice was a type of the most holy Sacrifice, and that he himself was the Victim. Thus, though plunged in darkness, these pagans had preserved many forms of truth.

Either the night that preceded Jesus's coming or that which followed,

I cannot now say which, all the paths and avenues to a great distance around the tent castle were brilliantly illuminated. Transparent globes with lights in them were raised on poles, and every globe was surmounted by a little crown that glistened like a star.

Jesus in the Temple of the Kings • Feast of the Apparition of the Star

9/25 THE LORD'S first visit to the temple of the kings took place by day, and he was escorted to it from the tent castle by the priests in solemn procession. They now wore high caps. From one shoulder depended ribbons with numbers of silver shields, and from the opposite arm hung the long maniple. The whole way to the temple was hung with drapery, and the priests walked barefoot. Here and there in the neighborhood of the temple women were sitting, anxious to see the Lord. They had little parasols, little canopies on poles, to shade them from the sun. When Jesus passed in the distance, they arose and bowed low to the ground. In the center of the temple rose a pillar from which chevrons extended to the four walls, and from the highest point was suspended a wheel covered with stars and globes, which was used during the religious ceremonies.

The priests showed Jesus a representation of the crib which, after their return from Bethlehem, they had caused to be made. It was exactly like that which they had seen in the star, entirely of gold, and surrounded by a plate of the same metal in the form of a star. The little child, likewise of gold, was sitting in a crib like that of Bethlehem, on a red cover. Its hands were crossed on its breast up to which from the feet it was swathed. Even the straw of the manger was represented. Behind the child's head was a little white crown, but I do not now know of what it was made. Besides this crib there was no other image in the temple. A long roll, or tablet, was hanging on the wall. It was the sacred writings, and the letters were principally formed of symbolical figures. Between the pillar and the crib stood a little altar with openings in the sides, and they sprinkled water around with a little brush, as we do holy water. I saw also a consecrated branch with which they performed all kinds of ceremonies, some little round loaves, a chalice, and a plate of the flesh of victims sacrificed. As they were showing all these things to Jesus, he enlightened them on the truth and refuted the reasons they advanced for their use.

They took him also to the tombs of King Sair and his family, which lay in the vaults in the covered way that surrounded the pyramidal temple. They looked like couches cut in the wall. The bodies lay in long, white garments, and beautiful covers hung down from their resting places. I saw their half-covered faces and their hands bare and white as snow; but I know not whether it was only their bones or whether they were still covered with dried skin, for I saw that the hands were deeply furrowed. This sepulchral vault was quite habitable, and there was a stool in each of the tombs. The priests brought in fire and burnt incense. All shed tears, especially the aged King Mensor, who wept like a child. Jesus approached the remains and spoke of the dead. Theokeno, speaking to Jesus of Sair, told him that a dove was frequently seen to alight on the branch which, according to their custom, they stuck on the door of his tomb, and he asked what it meant. Jesus in reply asked him what was Sair's belief. To this Theokeno answered: "Lord, his faith was like unto mine. After we began to honor the king of the Jews, Sair up to his death desired that all he thought and did, all that was to befall him, might ever be in accordance with the will of that king."

Thereupon Jesus informed him that the dove on the branch signified that Sair had been baptized with the baptism of desire.

Jesus drew for them on a plate the figure of the lamb resting on the Book with the Seven Seals, a little standard over its shoulder, and he bade them make one on that model and place it on the column opposite the crib.

9/26 Since their return from Bethlehem, the kings had every year celebrated a memorial feast of three days in honor of that upon which, fifteen years before the birth of Christ, they had for the first time seen the star containing the picture of the virgin who held in one hand a scepter, and in the other a balance with an ear of wheat in one dish and a cluster of grapes in the other. The three days were in honor of Jesus, Mary, and Joseph. They reverenced Joseph in a special manner, because he had received them so kindly and graciously. It was now time for this annual festival, but in their humility in presence of the Lord, they wanted to omit the usual religious ceremonies, and begged him to give them an instruction instead. But Jesus told them that they must celebrate their feast, lest the people in their ignorance of what had just taken place might be scandalized at the omission. I saw many things connected with their religion. They had three images in the form of animals standing around outside the temple: one was a dragon with huge jaws; another a dog with a great head; and the third was a bird with legs and neck long, almost like a stork, only that it had a peaked bill. I do not think that these images were adored as gods. They served only as symbols of certain virtues whose practice they inculcated. The dragon represented the bad, the dark principle in man's nature, which he must labor to destroy; the dog, which had reference to some star, signified fidelity, gratitude, and vigilance; and the bird typified filial love. The images embodied besides all kinds of deep, profound mysteries, but I cannot now recall them. I know well however that no idolatry, no abomination was connected with them. They were embodiments of great wisdom and humility, of deep meditation upon the wonderful things of God. They were not made of gold, but of something darker, like those fragments that were used for smelting the ore, or perhaps what remained after that process. Below the figure of the dragon I read five letters, A A S C C or A S C A S, I do not remember exactly which. The dog's name was Sur, but that of the bird I have forgotten.

The four priests delivered discourses in four different places around the temple before the men, the women, the maidens, and the youths. I saw them open the dragon's jaws and I heard them say at the same time: "If, hateful and frightful as he is, he were now alive and about to devour us, who alone could help us but the almighty God?"—and they gave to God some special name that I cannot now recall. Then they caused the wheel to be taken down from its place, put it on the altar in a track formed to receive it, and one of the priests made it revolve. There were several circles one inside the other all hung with hollow golden balls, which glittered and tinkled at every revolution, thus announcing the course of the constellations. This revolving of the wheel was accompanied by singing, the refrain being to this effect: "What would become of the world if God should cease to direct the movement of the stars?" This was followed by the offering of sacrifice before the golden Christ child in the crib, and the burning of incense. Jesus commanded them to do away with those animals for the future, and to teach mercy, love of the neighbor, and the Redemption of the human race; as for the rest, they should admire God in his creatures, give him thanks, and adore him alone. On the evening of the first of these three festivals, the sabbath began for Jesus; therefore, he withdrew with the three youths into a retired apartment of the tent castle to celebrate it. They had with them white garments almost like grave clothes. These they put on, along with a girdle, ornamented with letters and straps, which they crossed like a stole over the breast. On a table covered with red and white stood a lamp with seven burners. When in prayer, Jesus stood between two of the youths, the third behind him. No pagan was present at Jesus's celebration of the sabbath.

9/27 During the whole of the sabbath, the pagans were gathered together in the enclosure around their temple, men, women, youths, and maidens—all had their respective tiers of seats. After Jesus had finished his celebration of the sabbath he went out to the pagans and then I witnessed a wonderful scene. In the center of the women's circle stood the image of the dragon. The women were very differently clothed according to their rank. The poorest wore under their long mantles only a short garment, very simple; but the more distinguished were arrayed like her whom I now saw step in front of the dragon. She was a robust-looking woman of about thirty. Under the long mantle, which she laid aside when seated, she wore a stiff, plaited tunic and a jacket very closely fitting around the neck and breast, and ornamented with glittering jewels and tiny chains. From the shoulder to the elbow hung lappets like open half-sleeves, and the rest of the arms, like the lower limbs, was covered with lace and bracelets. On her head she wore a close-fitting cap that reached down to the eyes, partly concealed the cheeks and chin, and which was formed entirely of rows of curled feathers. Above the middle of the head, bent from the forehead back, arose a kind of roll or pad through which could be seen the hair, braided and ornamented. A great many long ornamental chains hung from the ears down to the breast.

Before the priest began his instruction, the woman, attended by many others, went in front of the dragon, cast herself down and kissed the earth. She performed this action with marked enthusiasm and devotion. At this moment Jesus stepped into the middle of the circle and asked why she did that. She answered that the dragon awoke her every morning before day when she arose, turned toward the quarter in which the image stood, prostrated before her couch, and adored it. Jesus next asked: "Why dost thou cast thyself down before Satan? Thy faith has been taken possession of by Satan. It is true indeed that thou wilt be awakened, but not by Satan. It is an angel that will awake thee. Behold whom thou adorest!" At the same moment, there stood by the woman, and in sight of all present, a spirit in the form of a figure lank and reddish, with a sharp, hideous countenance. The woman shrank back in fright. Jesus, pointing to the spirit, said: "This is he that has been accustomed to awake thee, but every human being has also a good angel. Prostrate before him and follow his advice!" At these words of Jesus, all perceived a beautiful luminous figure hovering near the woman. Tremblingly she prostrated before him. So long as Satan stood beside the woman, the good angel remained behind her, but when he disappeared, the angel came forward. The woman, deeply affected, now returned to her place. She was called Cuppes. She was afterward baptized Serena by Thomas, under which name she was later on martyred and venerated as a saint.

In his instruction to the youths and maidens assembled in the vicinity of the bird, Jesus warned them to observe due measure in their love of both human beings and the lower animals, for there were some among them that almost adored their parents, and others that showed more affection for animals than for their fellow men.

9/28 On the last day of the festival, Jesus desired to deliver a discourse in the temple to the priests and kings and all the people. That the aged King Theokeno also might be among his hearers, Jesus went to him with Mensor, and commanded him to rise and accompany him. He took him by the hand and Theokeno, nothing doubting, rose up at once able to walk. Jesus led him to the temple and from that time forward he retained the use of his limbs. Jesus ordered the doors of the pyramidal temple to be opened, that all the people outside could both see and hear him. He taught sometimes outside among the men and women, the youths, the maidens, and the children, relating to them many of the parables that he had formerly recounted to the Jews. His auditors were privileged to interrupt him in order to ask questions, for he had commanded them to do so. Sometimes also he called upon a certain one to say aloud before all the others the doubts that troubled him, for he knew the thoughts of everyone. Among the questions they asked was this: Why he raised no dead to life, cured no sick, as the king of the Jews had done? Jesus answered that he did not perform such miracles among pagans, but that he would send some men who would work many wonders among them, and that through the bath of baptism they should become clean. They should, he said, until that time take his words on faith.

Jesus then gave an instruction to the priests and kings alone. He told them that whatever in their doctrine bore an appearance of truth, was a mere lie: it had only the semblance, the empty form of truth, and the demon himself gave it that form. As soon as the good angel withdraws, Satan steps forward, corrupts worship, and takes it under his own guardianship. Heretofore, Jesus continued, they had honored all those objects to which they could attach some idea of strength, and of that worship they had omitted many things after their return from Bethlehem. Now, however, he told them they should do away with those figures of animals, should melt them down: and he indicated to them the people to whom their value should be given. All their worship, all their knowledge, he said, valued nothing. They should inculcate love and mercy without the aid of those images, and thank the Father in heaven that he had so mercifully called them to the knowledge of himself. Jesus promised them that he would send one who would more fully instruct them, and he directed them to remove the wheel with its starry representations. It was as large as a carriage wheel of moderate size and had seven concentric rims, on the uppermost and the lowest of which were fastened globes from which streamed rays. The central point consisted of a larger globe, which represented the earth. On the circumference of the wheel were twelve stars, in which were as many different pictures, splendid and glittering. I saw among them one of a virgin with rays of light flashing from her eyes and playing around her mouth, while on her forehead sparkled precious stones; and another of an animal with something in its mouth that emitted sparks. But I could not see all distinctly, because the wheel was constantly revolving. The figures were not all visible at the same time, for at intervals some were hidden.

Jesus desired to leave them some bread and wine blessed by himself. The priests had, in obedience to his directions, prepared some very fine white bread like little cakes, and a small jug of some kind of red liquor. Jesus specified the shape of the vessel in which all was to be preserved. It was like a large mortar. It had two ears, a cover with a knob, and was divided into two compartments. The bread was deposited in the upper one; and in the lower one, in which there was a small door, the little jug of liquor was placed. The outside shone like quicksilver, but the inside was yellow. Jesus placed the bread and the wine on the little altar, prayed, and blessed, while the priests and the two kings knelt before him, their hands crossed on their breast. Jesus prayed over them, laid his hands on their shoulders, and instructed them how they should renew the bread, which he cut for them crosswise, giving them the words and the ceremony of benediction. This bread and wine were to be for them a symbol of Holy Communion. The kings had some knowledge of Melchizedek, and they questioned Jesus concerning his sacrifice. When he blessed the bread for them, he gave them some idea of his Passion and of the Last Supper. They should, he told them, make use of the bread and wine for the first time on the anniversary of their adoration at the crib, and after that three times in the year, or every three months, I cannot recall it exactly.

9/29 Next day Jesus again taught in the temple wherein all were gathered. He went in and out, leaving one crowd to go to another. He allowed the women and children also to come and speak to him, and he instructed the mothers how to rear their children and teach them to pray. This was the first time that I saw many children gathered together here. The boys wore only a short tunic, and the little girls, mantles. The children of the converted lady were present. She was a person of distinction and her spouse, a tall man, was near King Mensor. She had fully ten children with her. Jesus blessed them, laying his hand not on the head as he did to the children of Judea, but on the shoulder.

He instructed the people upon his mission and his approaching end, and told them that his journey into their country was unknown to the Jews. He had, he said, brought with him as companions youths that would take no scandal at what they saw and heard, and who were docile to all his words. The Jews would have taken his life, had he not made his escape. But apart from all that, he was desirous of visiting them because they had visited him, had believed in him, hoped in him, and loved him. He admonished them to thank God for not allowing them to be entirely blinded by idolatry and for giving them the true belief in himself and the grace to keep his commandments. If I do not mistake, he spoke to them also of the time of his return to his heavenly Father, when he would send to them his disciples. He told them too that he was going down into Egypt where as a child he had been with his mother, for there were some people there who had known him in his childhood. He would, however, remain quite unknown, as there were Jews there who would willingly seize him and deliver him to his enemies, but his time was not yet come.

The pagans could not understand the human foresight of Jesus. In their childlike simplicity, they mentally asked themselves: "How could they do such things to him, since he is truly God?" Jesus answered their thoughts by telling them that he was man also, that the Father had sent him to lead back all the scattered, that as a man, he could suffer and be persecuted by men when his hour would have come, and because he was a man, he could be thus intimate with them.

He warned them again to renounce all kinds of idolatry and to love one another. In speaking of his own Passion, he touched upon true compassion. They should, he said, desist from their excessive care of sick animals, and turn their love toward their fellow beings both as regards body and soul; and if there were in their neighborhood none that stood in need of assistance, they should seek at a distance for such as did, and pray for all their destitute brethren. He told them also that what they did for the needy, they did for him, and he made them understand that they were not to treat the lower animals with cruelty. They had entire tents filled with sick animals of all kinds, which they even provided with little beds. They were especially fond of dogs, of which I saw many large ones with enormous heads.

ARRIVAL OF THE LEADER OF A STRANGE TRIBE

JESUS had already taught these pagans for some time, when I saw approaching a caravan on camels. It paused and remained standing at some distance while an old man, a stranger and the leader of the tribe, dismounted and drew near. He was attended by an aged servant whom he very highly respected, and both stood still at a little distance from the assembly. No one noticed them until the Lord's discourse was ended and he, with the disciples, had retired to the tent to take some refreshment. Then the stranger was received by Mensor, and shown to a tent. He afterward went with his old servant to the priests and told them that he could not believe Jesus to be the promised king of the Jews, because he treated with them so familiarly. The Jews had as he well knew, he continued, an Ark wherein was their God, and to it no one dare approach, consequently this man could not be their God. The old servant also gave utterance to some erroneous conceptions of Mary; still both he and his master were good people. This king too had seen the wonderful star, but he had not followed it. He spoke much of his gods, whom he held in high esteem, and told how gracious they were to him, and that they brought him all kinds of good luck. He related also an incident that happened during a war which he had lately waged, and in which his gods had helped him and his old servant had brought him a certain piece of news. This king was of lighter complexion than Mensor, his clothing was shorter, and the turban round his head not so large. He was very much attached to his idols, one of which he always carried about with him on a camel. It was a figure with many arms, and with holes in its body in which could be placed the sacrifices offered it. He had some women in his caravan, which consisted of about thirty persons. As for himself, he was a very simple-minded man. He looked upon his old servant as an oracle, indeed he honored him even as a prophet. The latter had induced his master to make this journey, that he might show him, as he said, the greatest of all the gods, but Jesus did not appear to answer his expectations. What the Lord said of compassion and beneficence pleased him greatly, for he was himself very charitable. He declared that he looked upon it as the greatest crime to neglect human beings for the sake of the lower animals. A meal was afterward prepared for the stranger, but at which Jesus was not present. I did not see him even conversing with him. The king's name sounded like Acicus. The old servant was an astrologer. He was clothed like a prophet in a long robe with a girdle that had many knots around it. His turban had numerous white cords and knots pendent from it. They looked as if made of cotton, and he wore a long beard. The royal stranger and his followers were of fairer complexion than the natives of these parts, among whom they were going to sojourn for some time. The women and their other followers they had left behind near the women's tents. They had come a two days' journey. I did not see Jesus conversing with them, but I heard him say that they would come to the knowledge of the truth, and he praised the king's compassion for men. I heard names that sounded like Ormuzd and Zorosdat.

The husband of Cuppes was a son of Mensor's brother. He had, when a youth, accompanied his uncle to Bethlehem. He and Cuppes were of a yellowish-brown complexion, and both were descendants of Job.

Jesus still taught after nightfall in and around the temple. The whole place was brilliantly illuminated, the temple itself a blaze of light. The inhabitants of the whole region were gathered together, old and young, men and women. Upon the first command of Jesus, they had removed the idols. But I now saw something in the temple that I had not before noticed. Up in the roof I saw a whole firmament of shining stars, and in between were reflected little gardens and brooks and bushes, which were placed up high in the temple and illumined with lights. It was a most wonderful contrivance, and I cannot imagine how it was done.

Jesus Leaves the Tent City of the Kings and Goes to Visit Azarias, the Nephew of Mensor, in the Settlement of Atom

9/30 JESUS left the tent city of the kings before daybreak when the lamps were still burning. They had arranged for him a festive escort such as had welcomed him, but he declined the attention and would not even accept a camel. The disciples took with them only some bread and some kind of liquor in flasks. The aged Mensor earnestly entreated Jesus to remain longer with them. He laid the crown that he wore on his turban at Jesus's feet, and offered him all that he possessed. His treasures were deposited under a grating in the floor of his tent, as in a cellar. They lay there in bars, lumps, and little heaps of grains. Mensor wept like a child. The tears rolled like pearls down his brownish-yellow cheeks. His ancestor Job had the same complexion. It was a very delicate, shining brown, not so dark as that of the people near the Ganges. All wept and sobbed on parting.

Jesus left the city by the side upon which stood the temple, and passed the magnificent tent of the converted Cuppes, who ran forward with her children to meet him. Jesus drew the children to himself and spoke to the mother, who cast herself prostrate at his feet in tears. Mensor, the priests, and many others escorted Jesus, walking at his side two by two in turn. Jesus and the disciples carried staves. When Mensor and the priests reached home, it was already dark. Lamps were burning everywhere and all the people were gathered in and around the temple, kneeling in prayer or prostrate on the ground. Mensor announced to them that everyone who was not willing to live according to the Law of Jesus, and who did not believe in his doctrine, should leave his dominions. There were people here of a complexion still darker than Mensor. His tent city, with its temple and the burial place of the kings, was the metropolis of the star worshippers, but at some hours' distance in the surrounding district there were other tent settlements.

Jesus journeyed eastward. He took up his first night quarters in a shepherd village belonging to Mensor's tribe and at about twelve hours from his tent castle. He slept with his disciples in a circular tent, whose sleeping places were separated from one another by movable screens.

10/1 Next morning Jesus left before the inhabitants were awake. I saw him arrive at a stream that was too wide to ford, in consequence of which he turned his steps northward along its banks until he came to a spot that could be easily crossed. Toward evening he arrived at some huts, built either of moss or earth, near which was an uncovered well surrounded by a rampart. Here he and his companions washed their feet and, without a reception from anyone, turned into a hut made of leafy branches and there slept during the night. This hut was round with a pointed roof. It was open on all sides and appeared to be formed of twisted branches and moss; around it was a closely woven hedge to keep off wild animals.

This region was very fruitful. I saw most beautiful fields bordered by rows of thick, shady trees, and at the corners where the trees met were dwellings, not tents like Mensor's, but round huts woven of branches. The inhabitants of this region were of a sunburnt complexion; their skin was not so rich a brown as Mensor's. They were clad very much like the first star worshippers whom Jesus had met on this journey. The women wore wide pantalets and over them a mantle. The people appeared to be engaged in weaving. From tree to tree, far apart from each other, were stretched pieces of stuff and thread, and many were busy working upon them at the same time. The whole length of the fields, the trees were trimmed in ornamental form, and seats were arranged up in the branches.

10/2 At the first dawn of morning, when the stars were still to be seen in the sky, several people went to the hut, but when they saw Jesus and the disciples still upon their couches, they drew back full of awe and prostrated on the ground. They had toward morning received through a courier from Mensor the news of Jesus's coming, but they did not know that he was already among them. Jesus arose, girded his white undergarment, threw on the mantle which the disciples used to carry in a bundle on their journeys, and after he had prayed with the youths and they had washed his feet, he stepped out of the hut to where the people were lying prostrate on their faces, and bade them not to be frightened at him. Then he went with them to their temple, a great, oblong building with a flat roof upon which one could walk. It had two railings on the roof, and by them

I saw some people gazing at the sky through tubes. In front of the temple was the closed fountain, esteemed sacred by the natives, and a pan of coals. The latter was raised a little above the ground, so that one could see under it. All around the temple were places for the people, separated from one another by bars. The priests that I saw wore long, white garments, trimmed from top to bottom with many-colored laces, and a broad girdle with a long end upon which were glittering stones and an inscription in letters. From their shoulders hung strips of leather, to which little shields were attached. When Jesus reached the temple, he called one of the priests down from the roof where he was observing the stars. The lord of this pastoral settlement, a paternal nephew of Mensor, came forth from the temple to greet Jesus and hand to him the peace branch. Jesus took it and passed it to Eremenzear, who handed it to Silas who, in turn, gave it to Eliud. Eremenzear again received it and bore it into the temple, followed by Jesus and the rest of the party. Here they found a little round altar upon which stood a cup without a handle, something like a mortar. In it was a yellowish pap, into which Eremenzear stuck the branch. This latter was either dried or artificial. It had leaves on both sides, and it seems to me that Jesus said it would become green. The images in the temple were enveloped as with a covering, or mask of very light, stiff material. A teacher's chair had been erected in the enclosure of the temple, and there Jesus taught. He questioned his hearers, as if they were children, upon all that he said. The women stood far in the background. The people were very childlike and accepted everything willingly. Jesus spent the greater part of the day in teaching, and that night accepted hospitality from the lord of the settlement, whose dwelling consisted of several stories. It was a circular edifice with outside steps running around it. Above the door was fastened an oval shield of yellow metal, upon which were inscribed the words, "Azarias of Atom." Azarias had not been able to live upon good terms with Mensor, and hence the latter had divided with him the pasture grounds; but after Jesus's visit, he changed for the better. The interior of his dwelling was very beautiful, fitted up with fine colored carpets and tapestry, and communicating by a covered tent corridor with the apartments of his wife.

When the sabbath began, Jesus withdrew with his disciples in order to celebrate it as he had done in the tent city of the kings.

THE WONDERFUL CURE OF TWO SICK WOMEN

10/3 WHILE Jesus was celebrating the sabbath with the disciples in the open hut in which he had passed the first night, I saw the sick wife of

Azarias seeking her cure before an idol. The lady had many children, and I saw in her apartments several other women, maidservants perhaps. Back from the fireplace and in a corner between the apartments stood a slab, or table, supported on columns. On it was a beautiful pedestal pierced on all sides with holes and covered with a little ornamental roof of leaves and foliage. The pedestal supported an idol in the form of a sitting dog with a thick, flat head. It was resting upon some written pages which were fastened together with cords in the form of a book, one of its forepaws raised over it as if drawing attention to it. Above this idol arose another, a scandalous-looking figure with many arms. I saw priests bringing in fire from the pan near the temple and pouring it under the hollow figure of the sitting dog, whose eyes began to sparkle, and from his mouth and nose immediately issued fire and smoke. Two women conducted Azarias's wife (who was afflicted with an issue of blood) up to the idol and placed her upon cushions and rugs before it. Azarias himself was present. The priests prayed, burnt incense, and offered sacrifice before the idol, but all to no purpose. Flames shot forth from it, and in the dense black smoke issued horrible dog-like figures that disappeared in the air. The sick woman became perfectly miserable. She sank down faint and exhausted like one in a dying state, saying "These idols cannot help me! They are wicked spirits! They cannot longer remain here, they are fleeing from the prophet, the king of the Jews, who is amongst us. We have seen his star and have followed him! The prophet alone can help me!" After uttering these words, she fell back immovable and, to all appearances, lifeless.

The bystanders were filled with terror. They had been under the impression that Jesus was only an envoy of the king of the Jews. They went immediately to the retired hut in which he and the disciples were celebrating the sabbath, and respectfully begged him to go to the sick woman. They told him that she had cried out that he alone could help her, and they informed him likewise of the impotence of their idols.

Jesus was still in his sabbatic robes, the disciples also, when they went to the sick woman, who was lying like one at the point of death. In earnest, vehement words, Jesus inveighed against idols and their worship. They were, he said, the servants of Satan, and all in them was bad. He reproached Azarias for this, that after his return from Bethlehem, whither as a youth he had accompanied the kings, he had again sunk so deep into the abominations of idolatry. He concluded by saying that if they would believe in his doctrine, would obey the commandments of God, and would allow themselves to be baptized, he would in three years send his apostle to them, and he would now help the lady. Then he questioned the latter, and she answered: "Yes, I do believe in thee!" All the by-standers gave him the same assurance.

The screens had been removed from around the tent, and a crowd of people were standing by. Jesus asked for a basin of water, but bade them not to bring it from their sacred fountain. He wanted only ordinary water, nor would he use their holy water sprinkler. They had to bring him a fresh branch with fine, narrow leaves. They had likewise to cover their idols, which they did with fine, white tapestry embroidered in gold. Jesus placed the water on the altar. The three disciples stood around him, one at either side, right and left, and the third behind him. One of them handed him a metal box from the wallet that they always carried with them. Several such boxes of oil and cotton were placed one above the other.

In that which the disciple handed to Jesus, there was a fine, white powder, which appeared to me to be salt. Jesus sprinkled some of it on the water, and bent low over it. He prayed, blessed it with his hand, dipped the branch into it, sprinkled the water over all around him, and extended his hand to the woman with the command to arise. She obeyed instantly, and rose up cured. She threw herself on her knees and wanted to embrace his feet, but he would not suffer her to touch him.

This cure effected, Jesus proclaimed to the crowd that there was another lady present who was much more indisposed than the first and who, notwithstanding, did not ask his help. She adored not an idol, but a man. This lady, by name Ratimiris, was married. Her malady consisted in this, that at the sight, the name, or even the thought of a certain youth, she fell into a sort of fever and became ill unto death. The youth, meanwhile, was perfectly ignorant of her state. Ratimiris, at the call of Jesus, stepped forward greatly confused. Jesus took her aside, laid before her all the circumstances both of her sickness and her sins, all which she freely acknowledged. The youth was one of the temple servers, and whenever she brought her offerings, which he was charged to receive, she fell into that sad state. After Jesus had spoken awhile with her alone, he led her again before the people, and asked her whether she believed in him and whether she would be baptized when he would send his apostle hither. When she, deeply repentant, answered that she did believe and that she would be baptized, Jesus drove the devil out of her. The evil one departed in the form of a spiral column of black vapor.

The youth's name was Caisar, and there was something of John in his appearance. He was pure and chaste, a descendant of Keturah and a relative of Eremenzear, who also was from this place. It was for this reason that on their reception Jesus had given to him the peace branch first.

Caisar spoke with the disciples, for he had long had secret presentiments of salvation. He told them several dreams he had had, among others one in which he dreamed that he had carried a great many people through water. The disciples thought that it signified perhaps that he would convert many. I saw that he accompanied Jesus on his departure. Three years after Christ's Ascension, when Thomas baptized in these parts, he returned with Thaddeus. Later on he was sent by Thomas to the bishop of a certain place where, though innocent, he was, to the great joy of his soul, crucified as a robber and criminal.

Jesus taught here until day dawned and the burning lamps went out. He commanded the people to destroy their images of the devil, and reproached them for adoring woman under a diabolical figure, and yet treating their women worse than dogs, which animals they held sacred. Toward morning Jesus retired again into the solitary house in order to celebrate the sabbath.

I was told why Jesus kept this journey so secret. I remember that he said to his apostles and disciples that he would go away for a little while only, in order that the public might lose sight of him, but they knew nothing of the journey. He had taken with him those innocent boys because they would not be scandalized at his dealings with the pagans, and would not remark things too closely. He had likewise strictly forbidden them to speak of the journey, on which account one of them said in all simplicity: "The blind man whom thou didst forbid to speak of his cure, did not remain silent, and yet thou didst not punish him!" Jesus replied: "That happened for the glory of God, but this would bear fruits of scandal." I think the Jews, and even the apostles themselves, would have been somewhat scandalized had they known that Jesus had been among the pagans.

10/4 When the sabbath was over, the Lord called all together again and instructed them. He blessed some water for them and directed them to prepare for him a chalice like that used by Mensor. Here too as in the former place, he blessed for them bread and the red liquor. In the cup into which Eremenzear upon his arrival had stuck the branch in order to keep it fresh, there was a yellowish-green substance, something like pap, which consisted of the pulp of a plant from which the juice had been expressed. This juice the natives drank as something holy. I saw Jesus the whole night between Saturday and Sunday teaching in front of the temple. He himself helped to smash the idols, and he told the pagans how they should distribute the value of the metal. I saw him also, as in Mensor's land, imposing hands upon the shoulders of the priests, teaching them how to divide the blessed bread, and here as there preparing the beverage. The vessel used here, however, was larger.

Azarias later on became a priest and martyr. The two women also whom Jesus cured here were afterward martyred like Cuppes. The Lord spoke against a multiplicity of wives, and gave instructions on the married state. The wife of Azarias, as well as Ratimiris, wanted Jesus to baptize them right away. He replied that he could indeed do so, but that it would be inopportune. He must first return to the Father and send the Consoler, after which his apostles would come and baptize them. They should, he said, live in the desire of baptism and submission to his will, and such dispositions would, to those that might die in the interim, serve as baptism. Ratimiris was in fact baptized under the name of Emily by Thomas when, three years after Christ's Ascension, he visited this country accompanied by Thaddeus and Caisar. They came in a direction more from the south than did Jesus, and it was then that the kings and their people were baptized.

Jesus Goes to Sikdor, Mozian, and Ur

10/5 FROM Atom, Jesus went first toward the south, then eastwardly through a very fertile region cut up by rivers and canals and planted with fruit trees of various kinds, especially peaches, which grew in long rows. I heard the names Euphrates, Tigris, Chaldar, and I think Ur, the land of Abraham, and that place at which Thaddeus suffered martyrdom were not far distant. Toward evening, Jesus reached a row of flat-roofed houses occupied by Chaldeans. I heard Sikdor as the name of the place in which were established two schools, one for the priests of the country and the other for young girls. The people were not so fully clothed as those of the royal tent city. They wore only blankets over their cinctures, but they were good, and so lowly minded that they thought the Jews alone were the chosen for salvation. They had on a hill a pyramid surrounded by galleries, seats, and immense tubes pointed on high through which they observed the stars. They also predicted future events from the course of animals, and interpreted dreams. Their temple with its forecourt and fountain was oval in form, and occupied the center of the place. It contained numerous metal statues of exquisite workmanship. The principal object of note was a triangular column upon which rested three idols. The first had many feet and arms, the former not in human shape, but like the paws of animals. In its hands it held a globe, a circle, a large ribbed apple on a stem, and bunches of herbs. The face of the figure was like a sun, and its name was Mytor, or Mithras. The second was a unicorn, and it was called Asphas, or Aspax. This animal was represented in the act of using its horn in a struggle against a wild beast that was standing on the third side of the column. It had the head of an owl, a hooked beak, four legs with talons, two wings, and a tail, which last appendage ended like that of a scorpion.

Above these two animals, namely, the unicorn and the wild beast, and projecting from one of the sharp edges of the column, stood another figure, which represented the mother of all the gods. Her name was Woman, or Alpha. She was the most powerful of all their divinities, and whoever desired to obtain anything from the supreme god was obliged to plead for it through her. They called her, likewise, the Granary. Out of the figure issued a large sheaf of wheat, apparently growing, which she clasped with both hands. The head was bowed, and on the neck, bent low between the shoulders, rested a vessel of wine. Above the figure hung a crown, and above the crown were inscribed on the column two letters, or symbols, that looked to me like an "O" or a "W." The lesson taught by these images was that the wheat was to become bread and that the wine was to inebriate all humankind.

There was besides in the temple a brazen altar, and what was my astonishment to see upon it, under a revolving dome, a little circular garden railed in with gold wire like a bird cage, and above it the image of a young virgin! In the center of the garden and roofed in by a little temple was a fountain with several sealed basins one above the other. In front of the fountain rose a green vine with a cluster of red grapes, which drooped over a press whose form reminded me of a cross. From the upper end of a tall stem projected a funnel-shaped, self-opening, leathern pouch with two movable arms, through which the juice of the grapes put into it could be pressed out and allowed to flow down below upon the stem. The little garden was about five or six feet in diameter. It was planted with delicate green bushes and little trees, which like the vine and its grapes looked perfectly natural. They owed this symbol to their star gazing, and they had many others that bespoke their presentiments of the blessed Mother of God. They sacrificed animals, but had a special horror of blood, which they always allowed to run off into the earth. They had likewise their sacred fire and water, their chalice of vegetable juice, and their little loaves, like the people of Atom. Jesus reproved them for their idolatry and for mixing up heavenly predictions and prognostics with Satanic errors. Their symbols, he said, had in them indeed some notions of truth, but they were discordant and filled with Satan. He explained to them the symbol of the garden enclosed. He told them that he himself was the vine whose sap, whose blood, was to quicken the world, that he himself was the grain of wheat which was to be buried in the earth thence to rise again. Jesus spoke here much more freely, much more significantly than among the Jews, for these people were humble. He comforted them by telling them that he had come for all humankind, and he commanded them to break up their idols and give their value to the poor. They showed signs of deep feeling when he was about leaving them, and threw themselves at his feet across the path in order to prevent his departure.

10/6 Some time after, I saw Jesus with the four disciples resting under a great tree that was surrounded by a hedge. It was in front of a house, from which they had been supplied with the bread and honey that they were eating. They journeyed on the whole of the night. I saw them on a plain walking sometimes over white stones, sometimes over meadows carpeted with white blossoms. On their way, they came across numbers of slender peach trees. At times the Lord paused, pointed around, and said something to the disciples. The country was intersected by numerous streams and canals. As a general thing, Jesus journeyed with extraordinary rapidity. He sometimes traveled twenty hours without interruption. His way back to Judea described a very great curve. I am always under the impression that Eremenzear wrote some details of this journey, though only a few fragments of his account escaped the fire that destroyed the rest.

10/7 On the evening of the second day of their departure from Sikdor, I saw Jesus and the disciples drawing near to a city outside of which rose a hill covered with circular gardens. Most of them had a fountain in the center and were planted with fine ornamental trees and shrubbery. The way taken by the Lord ran toward the south: Babylon lay to the north. It seemed as if one would have to descend a mountainous country to reach Babylon, which lay far below. The city was built on the river Tigris, which flowed through it. Jesus entered quietly and without pausing at the gates. It was evening, but few of the inhabitants were to be seen, and no one troubled himself about him. Soon, however, I saw several men in long garments, like those worn by Abraham, and with scarfs wound round their head, coming to meet him and inclining low before him. One of them extended toward him a short, crooked staff. It was made of reed, something like that afterward presented to Christ in derision, and was called the staff of peace. The others, two by two, held across the street a strip of carpet upon which Jesus walked. When he stepped from the first to the second, the former was raised and spread before the latter to be again in readiness for use, and so on. In this way they reached a courtyard, over whose grated entrance with its idols waved a standard upon which was represented the figure of a man holding a crooked staff like that presented to Jesus. The standard was the standard of peace.

They led the Lord through a building from whose gallery floated another standard. It appeared to be the temple, for all around the interior stood veiled idols and in the center was another veiled in the same way, the veil being gathered above it to form a crown. The Lord did not pause here, but proceeded through a corridor, on either side of which were sleeping apartments. At last he and his attendants reached a little enclosed garden planted with delicate bushes and aromatic shrubs, its walks paved in ornamental figures with different kinds of colored stone. In the center rose a fountain under a little temple open on all sides, and here the Lord and the disciples sat down. In answer to Jesus's request, the idolaters brought some water in a basin. The Lord first blessed it, as if to annul the pagan benediction, and then the disciples washed his feet and he theirs, after which they poured what remained into the fountain. The pagans then conducted the Lord into an open hall adjoining, in which a meal had been prepared: large yellow, ribbed apples and other kinds of fruit; honeycombs; bread in the form of thin cakes, like waffles; and something else in little, square morsels. The table upon which they were spread was very low. The guests ate standing. Jesus's coming had been announced to these people by the priests of the neighboring city. They had in consequence expected him the whole day and at last received him with so much solemnity. Abraham also had received a staff of welcome such as had been presented to Jesus.

10/8 The name of this city was Mozin, or Mozian. It was a sacerdotal city, but sunk deep in idolatry. Jesus did not enter the temple. I saw him teaching a crowd of people on a graded hill surrounded by a wall. It was in front of the temple and near a fountain. He reproved them severely for having fallen into idolatry even more deeply than their neighbors, showed them the abominations of their worship, and told them that they had abandoned the Law. I heard him referring to the destruction of the temple in the time of their forefathers, and speaking of Nebuchadnezzar and Daniel. He said that they should separate the believing from the spiritually blind, for there were some good souls among them, and to these he indicated whither they should go. Many of the others were stiff-necked. There was one point that they would not understand, and that was the necessity for abolishing polygamy. The women dwelt in a street to themselves at the extreme end of the city, to which, however, there was communication by shaded walks. They seemed to be held in great contempt, and after a certain age the young girls dared not appear in public. No woman of this place saw Jesus. Only the boys were present with the men.

Jesus used severe words toward these people. They were, he said, so blinded, so obstinate, that when the apostle that he was going to send would make his appearance, he would find them unprepared for baptism. Jesus would not remain longer with them. As he was leaving the city, a procession of young girls met him at the gate, chanting hymns of praise in his honor. They wore white pantalets, had garlands around their arms and necks, and flowers in their hands.

From Mozian, Jesus went with his companions across a large field to a village of pastoral tents. He sat down near the fountain, the disciples washed his feet, and some men of the place approached with the branch of welcome and gave him a glad reception. They were clad in long garments, more like Abraham than any others I had yet seen, and they possessed an astronomical pyramid. I saw no idols. These people appeared to be pure star worshippers and to belong to that race of whom some had accompanied the kings to Bethlehem. They appeared to me to be only a little band of shepherds, of whom the superior alone had a permanent dwelling. Jesus ate bread and fruit in his house standing, and drank out of a special vessel. He afterward taught at the well. When he was leaving them, the people threw themselves across his path and entreated him to remain with them.

10/9 On departing from this place, Jesus traveled throughout the whole of that night and the following day. Once I saw him with the disciples taking a little rest by a fountain under a large shade tree. It was a public resting place for travelers, and there Jesus ate some bread and took a drink.

10/10 The city to which he was going was thirty hours to the south of Mozian, but still on the Tigris. It was called Ur, or Urhi. Jesus reached it on that evening before the commencement of the sabbath. Abraham was from this region. Jesus went to a well outside the city which was surrounded by large shade trees and stone benches. Here the disciples washed the Lord's feet and then their own, lowered their girded garments, and entered the city, whose architecture struck me as different from any other I had seen in these parts. The men and women did not appear to live so much apart. There were many towers provided with galleries and tubes for observing the stars, and to them led steps both inside and outside. The people knew from the stars of the Lord's coming, consequently they had expected him and taken every stranger for him. When, therefore, Jesus's entrance into the city was noticed by some, they hurried to a large flat-roofed house which stood in a large open space, in order to give notice of his arrival. From this house, which appeared to be a school and from which waved a flag, there now issued several men in long garments of one single color, and proceeded to meet Jesus. They were girded with cinctures whose ends hung long and loose, and they wore round caps bordered by a roll of wool, or little feathers, whose strips met on top and formed a plume. The hair could be seen through them. The men prostrated before Jesus, and then led him and his companions back to the school, which consisted of one immense hall. To it flocked crowds of people. Jesus taught for a short time from an elevated seat at the top of a flight of steps, after which he was conducted to another house in which a meal had been prepared. But Jesus took only a few mouthfuls standing, and then went alone with the disciples into a retired apartment where they celebrated the sabbath.

10/11 Next day he taught near a fountain on an open place upon which was a stone seat used for teaching. All the women of the place were present, and so enveloped in their narrow garments that they could scarcely walk. Their caps were like cowls, from which hung two lappets. Jesus spoke of Abraham, and made some severe remarks on the fact of their being sunk in idolatry. There were idolatrous temples here, but the idols were veiled. The Lord did not go into any of them. Thomas did not baptize these people at his first visit to them.

10/12 When Jesus left Ur, the people accompanied him, strewing branches in his way. He journeyed toward the west for a long time, over a beautiful plain which toward the end became sandy, and lastly was covered with underbrush. About noon they reached a well by which they sat down to rest. The remainder of the journey was made through a wood and over cultivated land, until toward evening they arrived at a great, round building encircled by a courtyard and moat. All around stood heavy-looking houses with flat roofs. That of the great building was covered with verdure and even trees, while in the massive wall of the courtyard were the abodes of some poor people. At the fountain in the courtyard Jesus and the disciples washed their feet, as usual. And now, from the round house came forth two men in long garments profusely trimmed with laces and ribbons, and wearing feather caps on their heads. The elder of the two carried a green branch and a little bunch of berries, which he presented to Jesus, who with the disciples followed him into the building. In the center of the house was a hall, lighted from the roof, whose fireplace was reached by steps. From this circular apartment they proceeded around through irregularly shaped rooms opening one into the other, and whose end wall, concave in form, was hung with tapestry, behind which all sorts of utensils were kept. The floor was level, and like the walls covered with thick carpets. In one of these apartments Jesus and his companions took a frugal repast and drank something from vessels never before used. What the beverage was, I do not know.

After the meal, the master of the house took Jesus all around and showed him everything. The whole castle was filled with beautifully wrought idols. There were figures of all sizes, large and small, some with a head like that of an ox, others like that of a dog, and a serpent's body. One of them had many arms and heads, and into its jaws could be put all kinds of things. There were also some figures of swathed infants. Under the trees in the courtyard stood idols in the form of animals, for instance, birds looking upward, and other animals standing around. These people sacrificed animals, but they had a horror of blood, which they always allowed to run off into the earth. They had, also, the custom of distributing bread, of which the more distinguished among them received a larger portion.

Jesus taught at the fountain in the courtyard, and strongly inveighed against their diabolical worship, though his words were not taken in good part. I saw that their chief was particularly obstinate in his errors. He was irritated at Jesus, and even contradicted him. Thereupon I heard Jesus telling the people that, as a proof of the truth of his words, on the night of the anniversary of the star's appearing to the kings, the idols would fall to pieces, those that represented oxen would bellow, the dogs would bark, and the birds would scream. They listened to his predictions disdainfully and incredulously. This was what Jesus had told all whom he had visited on this journey. In all places at which he stopped on his way into the land of the pagans, he predicted that this would happen. On the holy night of Christmas, I had a vision of this whole journey from the pagan city near Kedar to the tent city of the three kings, and thence to this last pagan castle; and everywhere I saw the idols going to pieces, and heard bellowing and barking and screaming from those that represented animals. The kings I saw at prayer in their temple. Numerous lights burned around the little crib, and it seems to me there was now the figure of an ass standing by it. They, it is true, no longer revered their idols; but those in the form of animals bellowed as a sign that Jesus was really the one to whom the star had led them, a fact still doubted perhaps by some weak in faith.

Jesus Goes to Egypt, Teaches in Heliopolis, and Returns to Judea through the Desert

10/13– FROM the castle of the idols, Jesus's route now lay toward the **12/30** west. He traveled quickly with his four companions, pausing nowhere, but ever hurrying on. First, they crossed a sandy desert, toiled slowly up a steep mountain ridge, pursued their way over a country covered with vegetation, then through low bushes like juniper bushes, whose branches, meeting overhead, formed a covered walk. After that they came to a stony region overrun with ivy, thence through meadows and woods until they reached a river, not rapid, but deep, over which they crossed on a raft of beams.†

12/31 It was still night when they arrived at a city built either on both sides of the river, or on one of its branches, or on a canal. It was the first Egyptian city on their route. Here, unobserved by anyone, Jesus and his companions retired under the porch of a temple, where were some sleeping places for travelers. The city appeared to me very much gone to ruin. I saw great, thick walls, massive stone houses, and many poor people. I had an interior perception that Jesus had journeyed hither by the same side of the desert by which the children of Israel had come.

1/1 Next morning, as Jesus and the disciples were leaving the city, children ran after them crying out: "There go holy people!" The inhabitants were very much excited, inasmuch as great disturbances had happened the night before. Many of the idols had fallen from their places, and the children had been dreaming and uttering prophetic words about certain "holy people" that had entered the city.

Jesus and the disciples departed hurriedly, and plunged into the deep ravines that traversed the sandy region. That evening I saw them, not far from a city, resting and taking food at the source of a brook, the disciples having washed Jesus's feet. Nearby on a great round stone was stretched the figure of a dog in a lying posture. It had a human head, the expression of the face quite friendly. It wore a cap, like that worn by the people of the country, a band with hanging lappets notched at the ends. The figure was as large as a cow. Under a tree outside the city stood an idol whose head was like that of an ox. It had holes pierced in its body and several arms. Five streets led from the gate into the great city, and Jesus took the first to the right. It ran along the city wall, which was like a rampart on top of which were gardens and a carriage way. In the lower part

† Today Jesus and the four youths set off on the long journey to Egypt, traveling westward through the Arabian desert. They traveled rapidly. In the course of this journey, which lasted some two and one-half months until the end of the year AD 32. Later, Anne Catherine saw them coming from the Arabian desert and approaching Egypt; they crossed the Sinai desert. finally arriving in a land with more green. She saw the journey of Jesus through Chaldea, from Kedar to the tent city of the kings, to Atom, Sikdor, Mozian, Ur, and the last Chaldean settlement. Everywhere, she saw idols broken and animal idols crying out. Historically (in AD 32) this was probably the night of December 7/8, the anniversary of the immaculate conception of the Virgin Mary, on which night the three kings had first seen the star, fifteen years before the birth of Jesus.

of the walls were dwellings shut in by light doors of wickerwork. Jesus and his disciples passed through the city by night without speaking to anyone, or being remarked by anyone. Here too there were several idolatrous temples, and many massive buildings gone to ruins in whose walls people lived.

1/2 At a good distance from this city, the way led over an immense stone bridge across the broadest river (the Nile) that I saw on this journey. It flowed from south to north, and divided into many branches that ran in different directions. The country was low and level, and off in the distance I saw some very high buildings in form like the temples of the star worshippers, though built of stone and much higher. The soil was exceedingly fruitful, but only along the river.

About one hour's distance from that city in which Jesus as a child had dwelt with his mother (Heliopolis), he took the same road by which, with Mary and Joseph, he had entered it. It was situated on the first arm of the Nile, which flows in the direction of Judea. I saw here and there on the way people clipping the hedges, transporting rafters, and laboring in deep ditches. It was nearly evening when Jesus approached the city. Both he and the disciples had let down their garments, something that I had never seen them do before reaching their destination. Some of the laborers, as Jesus came in sight, broke off branches from the trees, hurried forward to meet him, cast themselves down before him, and presented them to him. After he had taken them in his hand, they stuck them down into the ground along the roadside. I know not how they recognized Jesus. Perhaps they knew by his garments that he was a Jew. They had been waiting and hoping for his coming, that he would free them. I saw others, however, who appeared indignant, and who ran back to the city. About twenty men surrounded Jesus as he went to the city, before which stood many trees. Before entering, Jesus paused near a tree that was lying over on one side in such a way that its roots were being torn out of the earth, and around them was a large puddle of black water. This puddle was enclosed by a high iron grating, the bars of which were so close that one could not put his hand through. In this place an idol had sunk at the time of Mary and Joseph's flight with the child Jesus into Egypt, on which occasion the tree, too, had been uprooted. The people conducted Jesus into the city. Before it lay a large, four-cornered, perfectly flat stone, on which, among other names, was inscribed one that bore reference to the city and that ended in the syllable "polis." Inside the city I saw a very large temple surrounded by two courts, several high columns tapering toward the top and ornamented with numerous figures, and a great many huge dogs with human heads, all in a recumbent posture.

The city showed evident signs of decay. The people led Jesus under the projection of a thick wall opposite the temple, and called to several of the citizens of the neighborhood. Then came together many Jews, young and old, among the latter some very aged men with long beards. Among the women there was one, tall and advanced in years, who pleased me especially. All welcomed Jesus respectfully, for they had been friends of the holy family at the time of their sojourn here. In the back of the projecting wall was a space, now ornamented in festal style, in which Joseph had prepared an abode for the holy family. The men who had in their childhood lived in this neighborhood with Jesus, introduced him to it. The apartment was lighted by hanging lamps.

That evening Jesus was escorted by a very aged Jew to the school, which was very ably conducted. The women took their stand back on a grated gallery, where they had a lamp to themselves. Jesus prayed and taught, for they reverently yielded precedence to him.

1/3 On the following day, I saw Jesus again teaching in the synagogue. The inhabitants of this city wore white bands around their heads, their tunics were short, and only a part of their shoulders and breast was covered. The edifices were extraordinarily broad and massive, built of immense blocks of stone upon which numerous figures were carved. I saw also great figures that bore prodigious stones, some upon their neck, others on their head. The people of this country practiced the most extravagant idolatry. Everywhere were to be met idols in the form of oxen, recumbent dogs with human heads, and other animals held in peculiar veneration in special places.

1/4 When Jesus, escorted by many of the inhabitants, left Heliopolis, he took with him a young man belonging to the city, and who now made his fifth disciple. His name was Deodatus, and that of his mother was Mira. She was that tall old lady who had, on the first evening of Jesus's arrival, been among those that welcomed him under the portico. During Mary's sojourn in Heliopolis, Mira was childless; but on the prayer of the blessed Virgin, this son was afterward given her. He was tall and slender, and appeared to be about eighteen years old. When his escort had returned to the city, I saw Jesus journeying through the desert with his five disciples. He took a direction more to the east than that taken by the holy family on their flight into Egypt. The city in which Jesus had just been was called Eliopolis (Heliopolis). The E and the L were joined back to back, something that I had never before seen, on which account I thought there was an X in the word.

1/5 Toward evening, Jesus and his disciples reached a little city in the wilderness inhabited by three different kinds of people: Jews, who dwelt in solid houses; Arabs, who lived in huts built of branches covered with skins; and still another kind. These people had drifted hither when Antiochus ravaged Jerusalem and expelled many of its inhabitants. I saw the whole affair. A pious old priest slew a Jew who had gone forward to sacrifice to the idol, overturned the altar, called all good people together and, like a hero, maintained the Law and testament of God. It was during this persecution that these good people had fled hither. I saw also the place at which they first lived. The Arabs, having joined them, were likewise expelled with them. At a still later period they, the Arabs, fell again into idolatry. As usual the Lord went to the fountain, where he was welcomed by some of the people and conducted to one of their houses.

1/6 In this house Jesus taught, for they had no school. He told them that the time was at hand when he should return to the Father, that the Jews would maltreat him, and he spoke as he had everywhere done on this journey. They could scarcely believe what they heard, and they wanted very much to retain him with them.

When he left this place, two new disciples followed him, the descendants of Mathathias.† The travelers now plunged deeper into the wilderness and hurried onward day and night with but short intervals of rest.

1/7 I saw them in a lovely spot of beautiful balsam hedges taking some rest at that fountain which had gushed forth for the holy family on their flight into Egypt, and with whose waters Mary had refreshed herself and bathed her child. The road by which Jesus had returned from Egypt here crossed the circuitous byway that Mary had taken on her flight thither. Mary had come by an indirect route on the west side of the desert, but Jesus had taken the eastern one which was more direct. On his journey from Arabia to Egypt, Jesus could descry on his right Mount Sinai lying off in the distance.

1/8 *Jesus and the seven young disciples continued their journey. This* **MAP 38** *evening, they arrived at the town of Beersheba where, at the town well, Jesus was received in a friendly way.*

1/9 When Jesus reached Beersheba, he taught in the synagogue. He formally declared his identity, and spoke of his approaching end. From this place also he took with him on his departure some young men. It was about four day's journey from Beersheba to Jacob's well near Shechem, the spot appointed for Jesus and the apostles to meet again. Before the beginning of the sabbath Jesus reached a place in the valley of Mamre [Bethain]‡ where he celebrated the sabbath in the synagogue and taught.

---

† One was about twenty years old, and the other scarcely more than twelve.

‡ Not far from Abraham's grave in the cave of Machpelah, east of Mamre.

1/10 He likewise visited the homes of the inhabitants [of Bethain] and healed their sick. From this place to Jacob's well it may have been twenty hours at most.

1/11–12 Jesus now traveled more by night, in order that the news of his return to Judea might not be the occasion of some sudden rising among the people. He took the route through the shepherd valleys near Jericho to Jacob's well, at which he arrived during the evening twilight.

1/13 He had now sixteen companions, since some other youths had followed him from the valley of Mamre. In the neighborhood of the well was an inn where, in a locked place, was stored all that was necessary to contribute to the traveler's comfort when he stopped to rest. A man had the care of opening both the inn and the well. The country stretching out from Jericho to Samaria was one of indescribable loveliness. Almost the whole road was bordered by trees, the fields and meadows were green, and the brooks flowed sweetly along. Jacob's well was surrounded by beautiful grass plots and shade trees. The apostles Peter, Andrew, John, James, and Philip were here awaiting Jesus. They wept for joy at seeing him again, and washed his and the disciples' feet.†

1/14 *Jesus was very grave. He spoke of the approach of his Passion, of the ingratitude of the Jews, and of the judgment in store for them. It was now only three months before his Passion. I have always seen that the Feast of Easter falls at the right time when it happens late in the season.*

1/15 *Early this morning, Jesus arranged to meet with the apostles and disciples at the sabbath in Shechem. Then he went with the sixteen young disciples to the settlement of the parents of the three shepherd youths—Eliud, Silas, and Eremenzear—a few hours away.*

Jesus taught here and there in the settlement among the shepherds and instructed the new disciples. He wished them to stay there for the time being.

Jesus in Shechem, Ephron, and Jericho

1/16 AS Jesus was journeying with the new disciples from the shepherd village, where he remained only a few hours, to Shechem, I often saw him standing still and giving them animated instructions. He ordered

---

† Beholding their arrival, Anne Catherine suddenly called out in ecstasy: "O, he has arrived! How joyful they are to see him! He is at Jacob's well. They are weeping for joy. They are washing his feet and also the feet of the young disciples with him. There are about twelve of them, shepherd sons, who were with him as he went to Kedar—also Peter, Andrew, John, James, Philip, and one other. They were expecting him here."

Eliud, Silas, and Eremenzear to disclose to no one where they had gone with him nor what had befallen them on that journey, and he told them some of the reasons for silence on those subjects. I saw Eremenzear holding the sleeve of Jesus's robe and begging to be allowed to write down something about it. Jesus replied that he might do so after his death, but ordered him at the same time to leave the writing with John. I cannot help thinking that a part of that writing is still in existence somewhere.

Peter and John came forward to meet the Lord on his way, and outside the gate of the city were waiting six of the other apostles. They conducted him and the disciples to a house, the master of which, though he had never before seen Jesus, gave him a cordial reception. Jesus, however, appeared not to wish to make himself publicly known, but rather to be confounded with the apostles. The feet of the newly arrived were washed, and when the sabbath began, the lamps were lighted. Jesus and his companions put on long, white garments and girdles, and after prayers went to the school, which was built on a little eminence. After that they partook of a meal prepared by their host, at which some Jews with long beards were present. The eldest of them was clothed as a priest of superior rank, and was led by attendants. Neither in the school nor at table did Jesus make himself known. The host had a false look, and it seemed to me that he was a Pharisee.

1/17 The meal over, Jesus demanded that the synagogue should be opened for him. He had, he said, listened to their teaching, but now he too would teach. He spoke of signs and miracles, which are of no avail when in spite of them people forget their own sinfulness and want of love for God. Preaching was for them more necessary than miracles. Even before the meal the apostles had besought Jesus to express himself more clearly, for they did not yet understand him. He was always talking of his approaching end, they said, but he might before it go once more to Nazareth, there to show forth his power and by miracles proclaim his mission. At this juncture also Jesus replied that miracles were useless if people were not converted by him, if after witnessing them they remained what they were before. What, he demanded, had he gained by signs and miracles, by the feeding of the five thousand, by the raising of Lazarus, since even they themselves were hankering after more. Peter and John were of one mind with their Master, but the others were dissatisfied. On the way to Shechem, Jesus had explained to Eliud, Silas, and Eremenzear why he had wrought no signs and wonders on his last journey. It was, he said, because the apostles and disciples should confirm his doctrine by miracles, of which they would perform even more than he himself had done. Jesus was displeased at the apostles' wanting to find out from the three youths where he had been and what he had done. They were very much vexed at the youths' silence on being questioned. Jesus announced to them that he was going to Jerusalem and would preach in the temple. I saw that the Jews of Shechem sent messengers to report in Jerusalem that Jesus had again appeared, for the Pharisees of Shechem were among the most dissatisfied.

1/18 *The Pharisees at Shechem threatened to take Jesus into custody and deliver him to Jerusalem. Jesus replied that his time had not yet come. He said that he would go to Jerusalem of his own accord, and that he had spoken not for their benefit, but for that of his followers. Then he left Shechem, dismissing the apostles and disciples, keeping only the three "silent disciples"—Eremenzear, Eliud, and Silas—with him. Jesus and the three youths proceeded in a southeasterly direction toward Ephron. Meanwhile, his mother, the holy Virgin, who was with her friends in Bethany, had received the news of Jesus's return to Israel. Jesus sent a messenger to her requesting her to meet him at an inn southwest of Ephron.*

1/19 Jesus had previously announced to them his return by the parents of the three disciples. On the journey from Shechem to Ephron it was very foggy, and quantities of rain fell. Jesus did not confine himself to the straight route. He went to different localities, different towns and houses, consoling the inhabitants, healing the sick, and exhorting all to follow him. The apostles and disciples likewise did not take the direct road to the places to which they were sent, but turned off into the farms and houses lying along their way in order to announce Jesus's coming. It was as if all who sighed after salvation were to be again stirred up, as if the sheep that had strayed in the forest because their shepherd had gone away were, now that he had come back, to be gathered again by the shepherd servants into one herd. When, toward evening, Jesus with the three disciples arrived at Ephron, he went into the houses, cured the sick, and called upon all to follow him to the school. This place had a large synagogue, consisting of two halls, one above and the other below.[†] A crowd of people, men and women, some from Ephron and some from neighboring places, flocked to the instruction. The synagogue was crowded. Jesus directed a chair to be placed in the center of the hall whence he

---

† At the large synagogue in Ephron, Jesus then taught concerning his near end. He spoke of the punishment that would come upon those who refused to believe. Meanwhile, in the evening, the holy Virgin Mary, Mary Magdalene, Martha, Peter's wife and stepdaughter, Andrew's wife, Zacchaeus's wife and daughter, and two other holy women arrived at the inn they had rented between Jericho and Ephron.

taught first the men and then the women. The latter were standing back, but the men gave place to them. Jesus taught upon the necessity of following him, upon his approaching end, and upon the chastisement that would fall on all that would not believe. Murmuring arose in the crowd, for there were many wicked souls among them.

1/20 From Ephron Jesus dispatched the three trusty disciples to meet the holy women who, to the number of ten, had reached the rented inn near Jericho. They were the blessed Virgin, Magdalene, Martha, and two others, Peter's wife and stepdaughter, Andrew's wife, and Zacchaeus's wife and daughter. The last-mentioned was married to a very deserving disciple named Annadias, a shepherd and a relative of Silas's mother. Peter, Andrew, and John met Jesus on the road, and with them he went on to Jericho. The blessed Virgin, Magdalene, Martha, and others awaited his coming near a certain well. It was two hours before sundown when he came up with them. The women cast themselves on their knees before him and kissed his hand. Mary also kissed his hand, and when she arose, Jesus kissed hers. Magdalene stood somewhat back. At the well, the disciples washed Jesus's feet, also those of the apostles, after which all partook of a repast. The women ate alone and, when their meal was over, took their places at the lower end of the dining hall to listen to Jesus's words. He did not remain at the inn, but went with the three apostles to Jericho, where the rest of the apostles and disciples along with numerous sick were assembled. The women followed him. I saw him going into many of the houses and curing the sick, after which he himself unlocked the school and ordered a chair to be placed in the center of the hall. The holy women were present in a retired part. They had a lamp to themselves. Mary was with them. After the instruction, the holy women went back to their inn and on the following morning returned to their homes.

1/21 Crowds were gathered at Jericho, for Jesus's coming had been announced by the disciples. During his teaching and healing on the following day, the pressing and murmuring of the Pharisees were very great, and they sent messengers to Jerusalem to report. Jesus next went to the place of baptism on the Jordan where were lying numbers of sick in expectation of his coming. They had heard of his reappearance and had begged his aid. There were little huts and tents around, under which they could descend into the water. I saw too the basin in the little island in which he had been baptized. Sometimes it was full, but again, the water was allowed to run off. They came from all parts for this water, from Samaria, Judea, Galilee, and even from Syria. They loaded asses with large leathern sacks of it. The sacks hung on either side of the beast, and were kept together over the animal's back by hoops. Jesus cured numbers. Only John, Andrew, and James the Less were with him.

No baptisms took place at this time, only ablutions and healing. Even the baptism of John had in it more of a sacramental character than the ablutions on this occasion. The last time that Jesus was in Jericho, many persons were healed at a bath in the city, but it was not baptism. There was at this part of the Jordan a bathing place much resorted to, which John had merely enlarged. In the middle of the well on the island in which Jesus was baptized, the pole on which he had leaned was still standing. Jesus cured many without application of water, though he poured it over the heads of the leprous, and the disciples wiped them dry.

Baptism proper came into use only after Pentecost. Jesus never baptized. The Mother of God was baptized alone at the pool of Bethesda by John after Pentecost. Before the ceremony he celebrated Holy Mass, that is, he consecrated and recited some prayers as they were accustomed to do at that time.

When the crowd became too great, Jesus went with the three apostles to Bethel, where the patriarch Jacob saw on a hill the ladder reaching from earth to heaven. It was already dark when they arrived and approached a house wherein trusty friends were awaiting them: Lazarus and his sisters, Nicodemus, and John Mark, who had come hither from Jerusalem secretly. The master of the house had a wife and four children. The house was surrounded by a courtyard in which was a fountain. Attended by two of his children, the master opened the door to the guests, whom he conducted at once to the fountain and washed their feet. As Jesus was sitting on the edge of the fountain, Magdalene came forth from the house and poured over his hair a little flat flask of perfume. She did it standing at his back, as she had often done before. I wondered at her boldness. Jesus pressed to his heart Lazarus, who was still pale and haggard. His hair was very black. A meal was spread, consisting of fruit, rolls, honeycomb, and green herbs, the usual fare in Judea. There were little cups on the table. Jesus cured the sick who were lying in a building belonging to the house. The women ate alone and afterward ranged in the lower part of the hall to hear Jesus's preaching.

1/22 Next morning Lazarus returned to Jerusalem with his companions, while Jesus with the three apostles went by a very circuitous route to the house of a son of Andrew's half-brother, whose daughter lay ill. They reached the well belonging to the house about noon. The master of the house, a robust man engaged in the manufacture of wicker screens, washed their feet and led them to his home. He had a great many children, some of them still quite small. Two grown sons from sixteen to eighteen years of age were not at home but at the fishery on the Sea of Galilee, in Andrew's dwelling place. Andrew had sent messengers to tell them that Jesus had returned, and to come to meet him at a certain place.

After a repast, the man led Jesus and the apostles to his sick daughter, a girl about twelve years old. For a long time she had been lying upon her bed perfectly pale and motionless. She had anemia, and she was also a simpleton. Jesus commanded her to arise. Then with Andrew he led her by the hand to the well, where he poured water over her head. After that, at the Lord's command, she took a bath under a tent, and returned to the house cured. She was a tall child. When Jesus with the apostles left the place, the father escorted him a part of the way.

1/23 Having made a detour, before the hour of the sabbath Jesus reached a little city. He took up his quarters at an inn in the city wall, and then went at once with his followers to celebrate the sabbath in the synagogue.

1/24 Next morning he went again to the synagogue, where he prayed and delivered a short instruction. I saw a great crowd around him. They brought to him numbers of sick of diverse kinds, and he healed them. I saw that all the people of this place honored Jesus and pressed around him. The concourse was great. The apostles also cured and blessed; even the priests led the sick forward.

I saw Jesus cure in this place a leper who had often been carried and set down on the road he was to travel, but whom he had always passed by. They had, just before Jesus's coming, brought the poor creature from a distant quarter of the city, where he dwelt in a little abode built in the wall. They brought him to Jesus sitting on a couch in a kind of litter shut in by hangings. No one went near the sick man excepting Jesus, who raised the curtain, touched the invalid, and directed that he should be taken to the bath near the city wall. When this order was executed, the scales of leprosy fell from him. He had been afflicted by a double leprosy, for that of impurity was added to the ordinary disease. The Lord healed likewise many women of an issue of blood. When he was healing in the court outside the synagogue, the crowd was so great that the people tore down the barriers and climbed upon the roof.

On leaving this place, Jesus journeyed on with the three apostles and reached a strong castle (Alexandrium) surrounded by moats, or ponds with discharging channels attached. It seemed that there were baths here, and I saw all kinds of vaults and massive walls. When Jesus manifested his intention to enter this castle, the apostles made objections to his doing so. He might, they said, rouse indignation and give occasion for scandal. Jesus rejoined that if they did not want to accompany him, they should suffer him to enter alone, and so he went in. It contained all sorts of people, some of whom appeared to be prisoners, others sick and infirm. Guards were standing at the gates, for the inmates dared not go out alone. Several always went together and attended by a guard. They were obliged to work in the country around the castle, clearing the fields and digging trenches. When Jesus with the apostles attempted to pass through the gate, the guards stopped them, but at a word from him, they respectfully allowed him to enter. The inmates assembled around him in the courtyard, where he spoke with them and separated several from the rest. From the city, which was not far off, Jesus summoned two men who appeared to be officers of the law, for they had little metallic badges hanging on straps from their shoulders. Jesus spoke with them, and it looked as if he were giving bail for those that he had separated from the rest of the inmates. Later on, I saw him leaving the castle with five and twenty of those people, and with them and the apostles traveling up the Jordan the whole night.

1/25 This hurried march brought him to a little city in which he   MAP 39 restored to their wives and children several of the prisoners lately freed. Others crossed the Jordan higher up, and then turned to the east. They were from the country of Kedar where Jesus had taught so long before his journey to the star worshippers. Jesus sent the apostles away on this road. When journeying through the valleys near Tiberias and past the well of Jacob, the three silent disciples—Silas, Eliud, and Eremenzear— and the other companions of his visit to the pagans joined Jesus.

1/26 They continued their journey a part of the night, rested only a few hours under a shed, and toward evening of the next day arrived in Capernaum. Here a young man called Sela, or Selam, was presented to Jesus. He was a cousin of the bridegroom of Kedar to whom Jesus had given the house and vineyard on the occasion of his journey to the star worshippers. It was the bridegroom who had sent Sela to Jesus, and he had been in Andrew's house awaiting his coming. He threw himself on his knees before Jesus, who imposed hands upon his shoulders and admitted him to the number of his disciples. Jesus made use of him at once, sending him to the superintendent of the school to demand the key and the roll of scriptures that had been found in the temple during the seven years that it had stood dilapidated and deprived of divine service. The last time Jesus taught here he had made use of the same roll of scriptures, which were from Isaiah. When the youth returned, Jesus and his companions went into the school and lighted the lamps. Jesus directed a space to be cleared and a pulpit with a flight of steps to be placed in it. A great

crowd was gathered, and Jesus taught a long time from the roll of scriptures. The excitement in Capernaum was very great. The people assembled on the streets, and I heard the cry: "There is Joseph's son again!"

1/27 Jesus left Capernaum before daylight next morning, and I saw him
going into Nazareth with the disciples and several of the apostles who
had joined him. I saw on this occasion that Anne's house had passed into
other hands. Jesus went also to Joseph's old home, now closed and unoccupied. Thence he proceeded straight to the synagogue. His appearance
was the signal for great excitement among the people, who ran out in
crowds. One possessed, who had a mute devil, suddenly began to shout
after him: "There is Joseph's son! There is the rebel! Seize him! Imprison
him!" Jesus commanded him to be silent. The man obeyed, but Jesus did
not drive the devil out of him.

In the school Jesus ordered room to be made and a teacher's chair to
be set for him. On this journey he acted with perfect freedom and taught
openly as one having a right to do so, which proceeding greatly incensed
the Jews against him. After teaching, Jesus and those with him went to
an inn and stayed the night there.

1/28 Jesus visited many of the houses in the neighborhood of Joseph's
old home, and healed and blessed the children; whereupon the Jews
who during the instruction had been tolerably quiet became extremely
indignant. Jesus soon left the city, telling the apostles to meet him on the
mount of the multiplication of the loaves, whither he went accompanied
by the disciples only.

When they reached the mountain, it was already night, and fires were
kindled on its summit. Jesus stood in the center, the apostles ranged
around him, the disciples forming an outer circle. A considerable crowd
had gathered. Jesus taught the whole night and until almost morning.
He indicated to the apostles, pointing with his finger here and there,
whither they should go on their mission of healing and teaching. It
looked as if he were giving them orders as to their journeys and labors
for the time just about to follow. They and many of the disciples took
leave of him here, and at dawn he turned his steps southward.

1/29 On this journey Jesus was implored by a father and mother to go
into their house and cure their daughter who was a lunatic, pale and sick.
He commanded her to arise, and she was cured.

An hour's distance from Thanat-Shiloh all the apostles, bearing green
branches, came to meet Jesus. They prostrated before him and he took
one of the branches in his hand. Then they washed his feet. I think this
ceremony took place because they were all again reunited, and because
Jesus once more appeared openly as their Master and was about to preach

again everywhere. Accompanied by the apostles and disciples he went to the city, where the blessed Virgin, Magdalene, Martha, and the other holy women, except Peter's wife and step-daughter and Andrew's wife, who were still at Bethsaida, received him outside an inn. Mary had come from the region of Jericho and had here awaited Jesus. The other women also had come hither by different routes. They prepared a meal of which fifty guests partook, after which Jesus, having ordered the key to be brought, repaired to the school. The holy women and a great many people listened to his instruction.

Jesus Goes to Bethany

1/30 NEXT morning Jesus cured many sick of the city, although he passed before a number of houses without performing any cures. He healed also at the inn. After that he dismissed the apostles, sending some to Capernaum, and others to the place of the multiplication of the loaves. The holy women went to Bethany. Jesus himself took the same direction, and celebrated the sabbath at an inn with all the disciples whom he had brought back with him from his great journey. They hung a lamp in the middle of the hall, laid a red cover on the table and over it a white one, put on their white sabbath garments, and ranged round Jesus in the order observed at prayer. He prayed from a roll of writings. The whole party numbered about twenty.

1/31 The sabbath lamp burned the whole day, and Jesus alternately prayed and instructed the disciples in their duties. There was present a new disciple named Silvanus, whom Jesus had received in the last city. He was already thirty years old and of the tribe of Aaron. Jesus had known him from early youth, and looked upon him as his future disciple at the children's feast given by holy mother Anne when, as a boy of twelve, he returned from his teaching in the temple. It was at the same feast that he had chosen the future bridegroom of Cana.

2/1 On the way to Bethany, Jesus, to continue his instructions for the benefit of the new disciples, explained to them the Lord's Prayer, spoke to them of fidelity in his service, and told them that he would now teach awhile in Jerusalem, after which he would soon return to his heavenly Father. He told them also that one would abandon him, for treason was already in his heart. All these new disciples remained faithful. On this journey, Jesus healed several lepers who had been brought out on the road. One hour from Bethany, they entered the inn at which Jesus had taught so long before Lazarus's resurrection and to which Magdalene had come forth to meet him. The blessed Virgin also was at the inn with other women, likewise five of the apostles: Judas, Thomas, Simon, James the Less, Thaddeus, John Mark, and some others. Lazarus was not there. The apostles came out a part of the way to meet the Lord at a well, where they saluted him and washed his feet, after which he gave an instruction which was followed by a meal. The women then went on to Bethany while Jesus remained at the inn with the rest of the party.

2/2 Next day, instead of going straight to Bethany, he made a circuit around the adjacent country with the three silent disciples. The rest of the apostles and disciples separated into two bands, headed respectively by Thaddeus and James, and went around curing the sick. I saw them effecting cures in many different ways: by the imposition of hands, by breathing upon or leaning over the sick person, or in the case of children, by taking them on their knees, resting them on their breast and breathing upon them.

On this journey, Jesus cured a man possessed by the devil. The parents of the young man ran after Jesus just as he was entering a little village of scattered houses. He followed them into the court of their house, where he found their possessed son who, at the Lord's approach, became furious, leaping about and dashing against the walls. His friends wanted to bind him, but they could not do it, as he grew more and more rabid, flinging right and left those that approached him. Thereupon Jesus commanded all present to withdraw and leave him alone with the possessed. When they obeyed, Jesus called to the possessed to come to him. But he, heeding not the call, began to put out his tongue and to make horrible grimaces at Jesus. Jesus called him again. He came not, but, with his head twisted over his shoulder, he looked at him. Then Jesus raised his eyes to heaven and prayed.

When Jesus again commanded the possessed to come to him, he did so and cast himself full length at his feet. Jesus passed over him twice first one foot and then the other, as if treading him underfoot, and I saw rising from the open mouth of the possessed a black spiral vapor which disappeared in the air. In this rising exhalation I remarked three knots, the last of which was the darkest and strongest. These three knots were connected together by one strong thread and many finer ones. I can compare the whole thing to nothing better than to three censers one above the other, whose clouds of smoke, issuing from different openings, at last united with one another.

The possessed now lay like one dead at Jesus's feet. Jesus made over him the sign of the cross and commanded him to rise. The poor creature stood up. Jesus led him to his parents at the gate of the courtyard, and said to them: "I give you back your son cured, but I shall demand him again of you. Sin no more against him." They had sinned against him, and it was on that account that he had fallen into so miserable a condition.

Jesus now went to Bethany. The man just delivered and many others went thither also, some before Jesus, others after him. Many of those that had been cured by the apostles were likewise present in the city, and a great tumult arose when the cured everywhere proclaimed their happiness. I saw some priests go to meet Jesus and conduct him into the synagogue, where they laid before him a book of Moses from which they desired him to teach. There were many people in the school, and the holy women were in the place allotted to females.

They went afterward to the house of Simon of Bethany, the healed leper, where the women had prepared a repast in the rented hall. Lazarus was not there. Jesus and the three silent disciples spent the night at the inn near the synagogue, the apostles and other disciples at that outside Bethany; Mary and the other women stayed with Martha and Magdalene. The house in which Lazarus formerly dwelt was toward the Jerusalem side of the city. It was like a castle, surrounded by moats and bridges.

2/3–4 The next morning Jesus again taught in the school where among the many disciples present were Saturnin, Nathaniel Chased, and Zacchaeus. Many sick had been brought to Bethany. In the house of Simon, the healed leper, a meal was again prepared, at which Jesus distributed all the servings to the poor and invited them to partake with the other guests. This gave rise to the report among the Pharisees and in Jerusalem that Jesus was a spendthrift who lavished upon the mob all that he could lay hands on.

While Jesus was teaching in the school, the crowds of sick, all men, were ranged in a double row of tents from the school to Simon's house. There were no lepers among them, for they showed themselves only in retired places. When Jesus approached the tents, three disciples followed him like Levites, two on either side, but a little behind him, and the third directly behind him. There was no crowd. Jesus went up along one row of tents and down by the other, curing in various ways. He merely passed by some of the sick, and exhorted others without curing them. He told them that they should change their manner of life. Some he took by the hand and commanded to rise, while others he merely touched. One man affected with edema he stroked over the head and body with his hand, and the swelling immediately went down. The water poured from his whole person in a stream of perspiration. Many of the cured threw themselves prostrate at Jesus's feet. His companions raised them and led them away. When the Lord returned to the school, he caused the cured to be seated near him, and then he taught.

2/5 I saw Jesus today sending out the disciples two by two from Bethany into the country to teach and to heal. Some he told to return to Bethany, and others to Bethphage. He himself with the three silent disciples journeyed a couple of hours southward from Bethany to a little village where he healed the sick. Here I saw him going into the house of a man whom he had once cured of muteness, but who having sinned again, had now become paralyzed. His hands and fingers were quite distorted. Jesus addressed to him some words of exhortation and touched him. The man arose. He healed likewise several girls who were lying pale and sick. Sometimes they lay unconscious as if dead, and again they alternately wept and laughed heartily. They were lunatics.

2/6 When, before the sabbath, Jesus again returned to Bethany and went to the school, I heard the Jews boasting against him that he could not yet do what God had done for the children of Israel when he rained down manna for them in the desert. They were indignant against Jesus. Jesus passed the night this time not in Bethany, but outside in the disciples' inn.

2/7 *Jesus taught in the synagogue.*

2/8 While at this inn, three men came to him from Jerusalem: Obed, the son of the old man Simeon, a temple servant and a disciple in secret; the second, a relative of Veronica; and the third, a relative of Johanna Chusa. This last-mentioned became, later on, bishop of Kedar. For a time also he lived as a hermit near the date trees that, on her flight into Egypt, had bent down their fruit to Mary that she might partake of it. These disciples asked why he had so long abandoned them, why he had in other places done so much of which they knew nothing. In his answer to these questions, Jesus spoke of tapestry and other precious things which looked new and beautiful to one that had not seen them for some time. He said also that if the sower sowed his seed all at once and in one place, the whole might be destroyed by a hailstorm, and that just so the instructions and cures that were scattered far and wide would not soon be forgotten. Jesus's answers were something like the above.

These disciples brought the news that the high priests and Pharisees were going to station spies in the places round Jerusalem in order to seize him as soon as he appeared. Hearing this, Jesus took with him only his two latest disciples, Selam of Kedar and Silvanus, and traveled the whole night with them to Lazarus's estate near Ginea, where Lazarus himself was then stopping. Two days previously he was in the little city between Bethany and Bethlehem, in the neighborhood of which the three kings had rested on their journey to the latter place; but on receiving a message from Jesus, he had left and gone to his estate. Jesus knew very well that the three disciples would bring him this news from Jerusalem and that he himself would leave Bethany, therefore it was that he had already passed two nights not in Bethany, but in the disciples' inn outside.

2/9 Jesus arrived before dawn (it was still dark) at Lazarus's estate [south of Alexandrium] and knocked at the gate of the courtyard. It was opened by Lazarus himself who, with a light, conducted him into a large hall where were assembled Nicodemus, Joseph of Arimathea, John Mark, and Jairus, the younger brother of Obed. They ate a meal together.

2/10–14 I saw Jesus afterward with the two young disciples again in Bethabara, where he celebrated the sabbath.

2/15 Jesus and the two young disciples went from Bethabara to Ephron. Andrew, Judas, Thomas, James the Less, Thaddeus, Zacchaeus, and seven other disciples were also present, having come hither from Bethany to meet Jesus. When Judas was about leaving Bethany, I saw the blessed Virgin earnestly exhorting him to be more moderate, to watch over himself, and not interfere in affairs as he did. In Ephron, Jesus healed the blind, the lame, the deaf and mute, who had been brought thither for that purpose. He delivered one possessed also from the power of the devil.

2/16 On leaving Ephron, he went to a place north of Jericho where there was an asylum for the sick and the poor. Here he restored sight to an old blind man whom once before, when engaged in healing, he had sent away, although at the same time he had restored sight to two others by anointing their eyes with salve made of clay mixed with spittle. He now cured this man by his word alone. The village was situated on his way.

2/17–18 From this last place Jesus returned to Lazarus's estate near Alexandrium, and thence went with Lazarus to Bethany, whither the holy women came to meet him.

Jesus Traveling Between Towns

The Passion and
Death of Jesus Christ

The Last Weeks before the
Passion • Jesus's Discourse in the Temple

2/19 IN the morning, Jesus, accompanied by Lazarus, left Alexandrium and went to Bethany. He repaired to the temple to teach, and his most holy mother accompanied him a part of the way. He was preparing her for his approaching Passion, and he told her that the time for the fulfillment of Simeon's prophecy, that a sword would pierce her soul, was near at hand. They would, he said, cruelly betray him, take him prisoner, maltreat him, put him to death as a malefactor, and all would take place under her eyes. Jesus spoke long upon this subject, and Mary was grievously troubled.

Jesus put up at the house of Mary Mark, mother of John Mark, about a quarter of an hour from the temple and, so to say, outside the city.

2/20 Next day, after the Jews had left the temple, Jesus began to teach in it openly and very earnestly. All the apostles were in Jerusalem, but they went to the temple separately and by different directions. Jesus taught in the circular hall [the portico of Solomon] in which he had spoken in his twelfth year. Chairs and steps had been brought for the audience, and a very great concourse of people was gathered. Jesus's Passion, properly speaking, was now begun, for he was undergoing an interior martyrdom from his bitter sorrow over humanity's corruption.

2/21–22 On this and the following day he lodged in the house outside the Bethlehem gate where Mary had put up when she brought him as a child to present in the temple. The lodgings consisted of several apartments adjoining one another, and a man acted as superintendent. When Jesus went to the temple, he was accompanied by Peter, James the Greater, and John; the others came singly. The apostles and disciples lodged with Lazarus in Bethany.

2/23 On the next day, after teaching in the temple from morn till noon, the Pharisees having been present at his instructions, Jesus returned to Bethany, where he again spoke with his mother of his approaching Passion. They talked standing in an open bower in the courtyard of the house. Nicodemus, Joseph of Arimathea, Simeon's sons, and other secret disciples did not appear openly in the temple during Jesus's discourses. When the Pharisees were not present, these disciples listened to Jesus from distant corners.

2/24 In the morning, Jesus made his way back to Jerusalem after visiting a little place, Bethphage, on the outskirts of the city.

2/25–26 In his instruction on this day, Jesus repeated the parable of the field overgrown with weeds. It was to be worked cautiously that with the weeds the good grain, which was to be allowed to ripen, might not be rooted up also. Jesus presented this truth to the Pharisees in words so striking that, though full of wrath, they could not stifle a feeling of secret satisfaction.

2/27 Today Jesus was in Bethany and spoke at length with his mother, the holy Virgin, about his approaching suffering. This evening he went to the temple in Jerusalem for the onset of the sabbath. At a later instruction, their vexation led the Pharisees to close the entrance to the hall so that the listeners might not increase. Jesus taught on this day till late into the night

2/28 Jesus made no violent gestures in preaching, but turned sometimes to this side, sometimes to that. He said that he had come for three sorts of people, and saying this, he turned to three different sides of the temple, indicating three different regions of the world, wherein were all the elect comprised. Before this, on his way to the temple, he had said to the apostles with him that when he should have departed from them, they should seek him in the noonday. Peter, always so bold, asked what that meant, "in the noonday." Then I heard Jesus saying: "At noon the sun is directly above us and there is no shadow. At morn and eve shadows follow the light, and at midnight darkness prevails. Seek me, therefore, in the full noonday light. And you shall find me in your own heart, provided no shadow obscures its light." These words bore some allusion also to different parts of the world, though I cannot now recall it.

3/1 The Jews had become still more insolent. They closed the railing around the teacher's chair and even shut in the chair itself. But when Jesus, with the disciples, again entered the hall, he grasped the railing and it opened of itself, and the chair was freed by the touch of his hand. I recall that many of John the Baptist's disciples and some secret partisans of Jesus were present, and that he began by speaking of John and asking what they thought of him and what they thought of himself. He desired that they should declare themselves boldly, but they were afraid to speak out. He introduced into this discourse the parable of a father and two sons. The latter were directed by their parent to dig up and weed a certain field. One of them said "Yes," but obeyed not. The other replied "No," but repenting, went and executed the order. Jesus dwelt long upon this parable. Later on, after his solemn entrance into Jerusalem, he again taught upon it.

3/2 Still in Bethany, Jesus visited the holy women and taught them. He went again to the temple and taught in parables.

3/3 Today the disciples proceeded ahead of Jesus to Jerusalem and opened the temple. He taught in the temple in parables, as he had done yesterday, dined again at the home of Mary Mark, and stayed the night in Bethany.

3/4 Next day when Jesus was going from Bethany to the temple, whither his disciples had preceded him to make ready the lecture hall, a blind man cried after him on the road and implored him to cure him, but Jesus passed him by. The disciples were dissatisfied at this. In his discourse, Jesus referred to the incident, and gave his reasons for acting as he did. The man, he said, was blinder in his soul than in the eyes of his body. His words were very earnest. He said that there were many present who did not believe in him and who ran after him only through curiosity. They would abandon him in the critical hour of trial. They were like those that followed him as long as he fed them with the bread of the body, but when that was over, they scattered in different directions. Those present, he added, should now decide. During this speech I saw many going away, and only some few over a hundred remaining around the Lord. I saw Jesus weeping over this defection on his return to Bethany.

3/5 It was toward evening on the following day when Jesus left Bethany to go to the temple. He was accompanied by six of his apostles, who walked behind him. He himself, on entering the hall, put the seats out of the way and arranged them in order, to the great astonishment of the disciples. In his instruction he touched upon his reason for so doing, and said that he was now soon to leave them.

3/6 This afternoon Jesus came from Bethany to Jerusalem before the onset of the sabbath. He ate at the home of John Mark. The holy women and Lazarus were also present. But Lazarus did not go with Jesus to the temple when the sabbath began. Later, Jesus returned to Bethany.

3/7 On the next sabbath Jesus taught in the temple from morning till evening, part of the time in a retired apartment in presence of the apostles and disciples only, and another part in the lecture hall where the lurking Pharisees and other Jews could hear him. He foretold to the apostles and disciples, though in general terms, much of what was to happen to them in the future. Only at noon did he pause for awhile. He spoke of adulterated virtues: of a love wherein self-love and covetousness predominate; of a humility mixed up with vanity; and he showed how easily evil glides into all things. He said that many believed it was an earthly kingdom and some post of honor in it that they were to expect; and that they hoped by his means to become elevated without pain or trouble on their own part, just as even the pious mother of the sons of Zebedee had petitioned him for a distinguished place for her children. He forbade them to heap up perishable treasures, and he inveighed against avarice. I felt that this was aimed at Judas. He spoke also of mortification, of prayer, of fasting, and of hypocrisy which influences many in these holy practices; and here he made mention of the wrath of the Pharisees against the disciples when the latter, one year before, had stripped some ears of corn. He repeated many of his former instructions, and gave some general explanations upon his own manner of acting in the past. He spoke of his recent absence from them, praised the conduct of the disciples during it, made mention of those that had accompanied him, commending their discretion and docility and recalling in what peace the journey with them had been made. Jesus spoke with much emotion. Then he touched upon the near fulfillment of his mission, his Passion, and the speedy approach of his own end, before which, however, he would make a solemn entrance into Jerusalem. He alluded to the merciless treatment he would undergo, but added that he must suffer, and suffer exceedingly, in order to satisfy divine Justice. He spoke of his blessed Mother, recounting what she too was to suffer with him, and in what manner it would be effected. He exposed the deep corruption and guilt of humankind, and explained that without his Passion no man could be justified. The Jews stormed and jeered when Jesus spoke of his sufferings and their power to satisfy for sin, and some of them left the hall to report to the mob whom they had appointed to spy Jesus. But Jesus addressed his own followers, telling them not to be troubled, that his time was not yet come, and that this also was a part of his Passion.

In this instruction he made some allusion, though without naming it particularly, to the Cenacle, to the house in which the Last Supper was to be eaten and in which later on they were to receive the Holy Spirit. He spoke of their assembling in it and of their partaking of a strengthening and life-giving food in which he himself would remain with them forever. There was some mention made also of his secret disciples, the sons of Simeon, and others. He excused them before the open disciples and designated their caution as necessary, for, as he said, they had a different vocation. As some people from Nazareth had come to the temple out of curiosity to hear him, he said, in a way for them to understand, that they were not in earnest.

When the apostles and disciples alone were standing around Jesus, he touched upon many things that would take place after his return to the Father. To Peter he said that he would have much to suffer, but he should not fear, he should stand firm at the head of the community, which would increase wonderfully. For three years he should with John and James the Less remain with the faithful in Jerusalem. Then he spoke of the youth who was to be first to shed his blood for him, but without mentioning Stephen by name, and of the conversion of his persecutor, who would afterward do more in his service than many others. Here too, he forbore giving Paul's name. Jesus's hearers could not readily comprehend his last words.

He predicted the persecutions that would arise against Lazarus and the holy women, and told the apostles whither they should retire during the first six months after his death: Peter, John, and James the Less were to remain in Jerusalem; Zacchaeus was to go to the region of Gilead; Philip and Bartholomew, to Gessur on the confines of Syria. At these words, I saw in a vision the four apostles crossing the Jordan near Jericho, and then proceeding northward. I saw Philip healing a woman in Gessur where at first he was greatly beloved, though later on he was persecuted. Not far from Gessur was Bartholomew's birthplace. He was descended from a king of the city, a relative of David. His refined manners distinguished him among the other apostles. These four apostles did not remain together; they worked in different parts of the country. Gilead, whither Andrew and Zacchaeus went, was at no great distance from Pella, where Judas had passed his early years.

James the Greater and one of the disciples were sent to the pagan regions north of Capernaum. Thomas and Matthew were dispatched to Ephesus, in order to prepare the country where at a future day Jesus's mother and many of those that believed in him were to dwell. They wondered greatly at the fact of Mary's going to live there. Thaddeus and Simon were to go first to Samaria, though none cared to go there. All preferred cities entirely pagan.

Jesus told them that they would all meet twice in Jerusalem before going to preach the Gospel in distant pagan lands. He spoke of a man between Samaria and Jericho, who would, like himself, perform many miracles, though by the power of the devil. He would manifest a desire of conversion, and they must kindly receive him, for even the devil should contribute to his glory. Simon Magus was meant by these words of Jesus. During this instruction the apostles, as in a familiar conference, questioned Jesus upon whatever they could not understand, and he explained to them as far as was necessary. Everything was perfectly natural.

Three years after the crucifixion all the apostles met in Jerusalem, after which Peter and John left the city and Mary accompanied the latter to Ephesus. Then arose in Jerusalem the persecution against Lazarus, Martha, and Magdalene. The last-named had up to that time been doing penance in the desert, in the cave to which Elizabeth had escaped with John during the Massacre of the Innocents. The apostles, in that first reunion, brought together all that belonged to the body of the church. When half of the time of Mary's life after Christ's Ascension had flown, about the sixth year after that event, the apostles were again assembled in Jerusalem. It was then they drew up the Creed, made rules, relinquished all that they possessed, distributed it to the poor, and divided the church into dioceses, after which they separated and went into far-off pagan countries. At Mary's death they all met again for the last time. When they again separated for distant countries, it was until death.

When Jesus left the temple after this discourse, the enraged Pharisees lay in wait for him both at the gate and on the way, for they intended to stone him. But Jesus avoided them, proceeded to Bethany, and for three days went no more to the temple.

3/8 Jesus wanted to give the apostles and disciples time to think over what they had heard. Meantime they referred to him for further explanations upon many points. Jesus ordered them to commit to writing what he had said relative to the future. I saw that Nathaniel the bridegroom, who was very skillful with the pen, did it, and I wondered that it was not John, but a disciple who recorded the predictions. Nathaniel at that time had no other name. It was only at baptism that he received a second.

3/9–10 During these days, three young men came to Lazarus at Bethany from the Chaldean city of Sikdor, and he procured them quarters at the disciples' inn. These youths were very tall and slight, very handsome and active, and much nobler in figure than the Jews. Jesus spoke only a few words to them. He directed them to the centurion of Capernaum, who had been a pagan like themselves, and would instruct them. Then I saw the youths with the centurion, who was relating to them the cure of his servant. He told them that through shame of the idols that were in his house, and because it was just the time at which the pagan carnival was celebrated, he had begged Jesus, the Son of God, not to enter into his idolatrous household. Five weeks before the Jewish Feast of Easter, the pagans celebrated their carnival, during which they gave themselves up to all kinds of infamous practices. The centurion Cornelius after his conversion gave all his metallic idols in alms to the poor, or to make sacred vessels for the temple. The three Chaldeans returned from Capernaum to Bethany and thence back to Sikdor, where they gathered together the other converts, and with them and their treasures went to join King Mensor.

3/11 Up to this time Jesus had gone to the temple with only three companions; but now he began to go thither escorted by his whole company of apostles and disciples. I saw the Pharisees retiring from Jesus's chair into the surrounding halls, and peering at him through the arches when he began to preach and to predict his Passion to the disciples.

In the wall of one of the forecourts just in front of the entrance of the temple, seven or eight vendors had taken up their quarters to sell eatables and some kind of red beverage in little flasks. They were like sutlers, and I know not whether they were very devout or not, but I often saw the Pharisees sneaking around to them.

3/12 *Today, Jesus taught again in the temple and stayed in Jerusalem overnight.*
3/13 When Jesus, who had passed the night in Jerusalem, went next morning to the temple and reached the hall in which these vendors were, he ordered them to be off instantly with all their goods. As they hesitated to obey, he put his own hand to the work, gathered their things together, and had them removed. When he afterwards entered the temple, he found the teacher's chair occupied by others, but they retired as hurriedly as if he had chased them away.

On the following sabbath, after the Jews had finished their sacred services, Jesus again taught in the temple and prolonged his instruction late into the night. In it he made frequent allusions to his journey among the pagans, so that it could be easily understood how good they were and how willing to receive his teachings. In support of his words, he appealed to the recent arrival of the three Chaldeans. They had not seen Jesus when he was in Sikdor, but they had heard of his doctrine, and were so impressed by it that they had journeyed to Bethany for more instruction.

3/14 On the following day Jesus caused three arches in the lecture hall to be closed, that he might instruct his apostles and disciples in private. He repeated on this occasion his early instructions upon his own fast in the desert. He alluded also to many events connected with his own past life, and said why and how he had chosen the apostles. During this last part of his discourse, he placed the apostles in pairs before him. With Judas, however, he spoke but few words. Treason was already in his heart. He was becoming furious, and had had an interview with the Pharisees. After finishing with the apostles, Jesus turned to the disciples, and spoke of their vocation also.

3/15 I saw that all were very sad. Jesus's Passion was near.†

3/16 Jesus's last instruction in the temple before Palm Sunday lasted four long hours. The temple was full, and all who wanted to hear him could do so. Many women listened from a space separated by a grating. He again explained many things from his former instructions and his own actions. He spoke of the cure of the man at the pool of Bethesda, and said why he had healed him just at that time; of the raising of the son of

† Jesus taught again in the temple concerning his approaching suffering (Matthew 20:17–19).

the widow of Nain, also that of the daughter of Jairus, and said why the former had immediately followed him, but the latter not. Then he referred to what was soon about to happen, and said that he should be abandoned by his own. At first he would with splendor and openly, as in triumph, enter the temple, and the lips of the suckling that had never yet spoken would announce his entrance. Many would break off branches from the trees and strew them before him, while others would spread their mantles in his way. The first, he explained, namely those that strewed branches before him, would not renounce for him what they possessed, and would not remain faithful to him; but they that spread their garments on the way would detach themselves from what they had, would put on the new man, and would remain faithful to him. Jesus did not say that he was going to enter Jerusalem on an ass; consequently, many thought that he would celebrate his entrance with splendor and magnificence, with horses and camels in his train. His words gave rise to a great whispering in the crowd. They did not take his expression, *"fifteen days,"* literally. They understood it to mean a longer time; therefore, Jesus repeated significantly: "Three times five days!"

3/17 This instruction greatly worried the scribes and Pharisees. They held a meeting in Caiaphas's house, and issued a prohibition against anyone's harboring Jesus and his disciples. They also set spies at the gates to watch for him, but he remained concealed in Bethany with Lazarus.

Jesus's Solemn Entrance into Jerusalem

3/18 JESUS along with Peter, John, James, and Lazarus, and the blessed Virgin with six of the holy women, remained hidden at Lazarus's. They were in the same subterranean apartments in which Lazarus lay concealed during the persecution that had risen against him. These apartments were under the rear of the building, and were comfortably fitted up with carpets and seats. Jesus, along with the three apostles and Lazarus, was in a large hall supported by pillars and lighted by lamps, while the holy women were in a three-cornered apartment shut in by gratings. Some of the other apostles and disciples were at the disciples' near Bethany, and the rest in other places. Jesus told the apostles that next morning would usher in the day of his entrance into Jerusalem, and he directed all the absent apostles to be summoned. They came, and he had a long interview with them. They were very sad. Toward the traitor Judas, Jesus was gracious in manner, and it was to him that he entrusted the commission to summon the disciples. Judas was very fond of such commissions, for he was desirous to pass for a person of some consequence and importance.

After that, Jesus propounded to the holy women and Lazarus a great parable, which he explained. He began his instruction by speaking of Paradise, the fall of Adam and Eve, the Promise of a Redeemer, the progress of evil, and the small number of faithful laborers in the garden of God. From this, he went on to the parable of a king who owned a magnificent garden. A splendidly dressed lady came to him, and pointed out near his own a garden of aromatic shrubs, which belonged to a good, devout man. She said to the king: "Since this man has left the country, you should purchase his garden and plant it with aromatic shrubs." But the king wanted to plant garlic and similar strong-smelling herbs in the poor man's garden, although the owner looked upon it as a sacred spot in which he desired to see only the finest aromatics. The king caused the good man to be called, and proposed that he should remove from the place or sell his garden to him. Then I saw the good man in his garden. I saw that he cultivated it carefully and was desirous of keeping it. But he had to suffer great persecutions. His enemies went even so far as to attempt to stone him in his own garden, and he fell quite sick. But at last the king with all his glory came to naught, while the good man, his garden, and all belonging to him prospered and increased. I saw this blessing spreading out like the branches of a tree, and filling all parts of the world. I saw the whole parable while Jesus was relating it. It passed before me in tableaux and looked like a true history. The flourishing of the good man's garden was shown me under the figure of gain, of growth, of the development of all kinds of shrubs, also as a watering by means of far-flowing streams, as overflowing fountains of light, and as floating clouds dissolving in rain and dew. The blessing arose from these sources and spread around and abroad even to the ends of the earth. Jesus explained this parable as having reference to Paradise, the Fall of Man, Redemption, the kingdom of this world, and the Lord's vineyard in it. This vineyard, Jesus said, would be attacked by the prince of the world, who would ill-treat in it the Son of God, to whom the Father had entrusted its care. The parable signified also that as sin and death had begun in a garden, so the Passion of him who had taken upon himself the sins of the world would begin in a garden, and that after satisfying for the same, the victory over death would be gained by his resurrection in a garden.

This instruction was followed by a short repast, after which Jesus continued to speak with the disciples, who as soon as it grew dark had gathered in the neighboring houses.

3/19 Early next morning Jesus sent Eremenzear and Silas to Jerusalem, not by the direct route, but by a road that ran through the enclosed gardens and fields near Bethphage. They were commissioned to make that road passable by opening the hedges and removing the barriers. He told them that in the meadow near the inn outside Bethphage (through which ran the road) they would find a she-ass with her foal; they should fasten the ass to the hedge, and, if questioned as to why they did that, they should answer that the Lord would have it so. Then they should remove every obstruction from the road leading to the temple, which done, they were to return to him.

I saw the two setting out on their journey, opening the hedges, and removing all obstructions from the way. The large public house, near which asses were grazing in a meadow, had a courtyard and fountain. The asses belonged to some strangers who, on going to the temple, had left their beasts here. The disciples bound the she-ass, as directed, and let the foal run at large. Then I saw them continuing their journey to the temple and on the way putting to one side whatever might prove an obstruction. The vendors of foodstuffs, whom Jesus had recently dispersed, had again taken up their stand at a corner near the entrance to the temple. The two disciples went to them and bade them retire, because the Lord was about to make his solemn entrance. After they had thus executed all points of their commission, they returned to Bethphage by the direct route, the other side of the Mount of Olives.

Meanwhile Jesus had sent a band of the eldest disciples to Jerusalem by the usual route with orders to go, some to the house of Mary Mark, others to that of Veronica, to Nicodemus, to the sons of Simeon, and to friends like them, and notify them of his approaching entrance. After that, he himself with all the apostles and the rest of the disciples set out for Bethphage. The holy women, headed by the blessed Virgin, followed at some distance. When the party reached a certain house on the road surrounded by gardens, courtyards, and porticos, they paused for a considerable time. Jesus sent two of the disciples to Bethphage with covers and mantles which they had brought with them from Bethany, in order to prepare the ass of which they had been directed to say that the Lord had need. Meantime he instructed the immense crowd of people that had gathered under the open portico. The latter was supported by polished pillars, between which the holy women took up a place to listen to him. Jesus stood on an elevated platform; the disciples and the crowd filled the courtyard. The portico was ornamented with foliage and garlands. The walls were entirely covered with them, and from the ceiling depended very fine and delicate festoons. Jesus spoke of foresight and of the necessity of using one's own wits, for the disciples had questioned him upon his taking that by-route. He answered that it was in order to shun unnecessary dangers. One should protect himself, he said, and take care not to leave things to chance; therefore he had beforehand ordered the ass to be bound.

And now Jesus arranged his procession. The apostles he ordered to proceed, two by two, before him, saying that from this moment and after his death, they should everywhere head the community (*the Church*). Peter went first, followed by those that were to bear the Gospel to the most distant regions, while John and James the Less immediately preceded Jesus. All carried palm branches. As soon as the two disciples that were waiting near Bethphage spied the procession coming, they hurried forward to meet it, taking with them the two animals. The she-ass was covered with trappings that hung to its feet, the head and tail alone being visible.

Jesus now put on the beautiful festal robe of fine white wool which one of the disciples had brought with him for that purpose. It was long and flowing with a train. The broad girdle that confined it at the waist bore an inscription in letters. He then put around his neck a wide stole that reached to the knees, on the two ends of which something like shields was embroidered in brown. The two disciples assisted Jesus to mount the cross-seat on the ass. The animal had no bridle, but around its neck was a narrow strip of stuff that hung down loose. I know not whether Jesus rode on the she-ass or on its foal, for they were of the same size. The riderless animal ran by the other's side. Eliud and Silas walked on either side of the Lord, and Eremenzear behind him; then followed the disciples most recently received, some of whom he had brought back with him from his last great journey, and others that had been received still later. When the procession was ranged in order, the holy women, two by two, brought up the rear. The blessed Virgin, who up to this time had always stayed in the background, now went at their head. As the procession moved forward, all began to sing, and the people of Bethphage, who had gathered around the two disciples while they were awaiting Jesus's coming, followed after like a swarm. Jesus reminded the disciples of what he had previously told them to notice, namely, those that would spread their garments in his path, those that would break off branches from the trees, and those that would render him the double honor, for these last would devote themselves and their worldly goods to his service.

From Bethany to Jerusalem, the traveler in those days met Bethphage to the right and rather more in the direction of Bethlehem. The Mount of Olives separated the two roads. It lay on low, swampy ground, and was a poor little place consisting of only a row of houses on either side of the road. The house near which the asses were grazing stood some distance from the road in a beautiful meadow between Bethphage and

Jerusalem. On this side the road ascended, but on the other it sank into the valley between the Mount of Olives and the hills of Jerusalem. Jesus had tarried awhile between Bethany and Bethphage, and it was on the road beyond the latter place that the two disciples were waiting for him with the ass.

In Jerusalem the vendors and people whom Eremenzear and Silas had that morning told to clear the temple because the Lord was coming, began straightaway and most joyfully to adorn the road. They tore up the pavement and planted trees, the top branches of which they bound together to form an arch, and then hung them with all kinds of yellow fruit like very large apples. The disciples that Jesus had sent on to Jerusalem, innumerable friends who had gone up to the city for the approaching feast (the roads were swarming with travelers), and many of the Jews that had been present at Jesus's last discourse crowded to that side of the city by which he was expected to enter. There were also many strangers in Jerusalem. They had heard of the raising of Lazarus, and they wished to see Jesus. Then when the news spread that he was approaching, they too went out to meet him.

The road from Bethphage to Jerusalem ran through the lower part of the valley of the Mount of Olives, which was not so elevated as the plateau upon which the temple stood. Going up from Bethphage to the Mount of Olives, one could see, through the high hills that bordered the route on either side, the temple standing opposite. From this point to Jerusalem the road was delightful, full of little gardens and trees.

Crowds came pouring out of the city to meet the apostles and disciples, who were approaching with songs and canticles. At this juncture, several aged priests in the insignia of their office stepped out into the road and brought the procession to a standstill. The unexpected movement silenced the singing. The priests called upon Jesus to say what he meant by such proceedings on the part of his followers, and why he did not prohibit this noise and excitement. Jesus answered that if his followers were silent, the stones on the road would cry out. At these words, the priests retired.

Then the high priests took counsel together, and ordered to be called before them all the husbands and relatives of the women that had gone out of Jerusalem with the children to meet Jesus. When they made their appearance in answer to the summons, they were all shut up in the great court, and emissaries were sent out to spy what was going on.

Many among the crowd that followed Jesus to the temple not only broke off branches from the trees and strewed them in the way, but snatched off their mantles and spread them down, singing and shouting all the while. I saw many that had quite despoiled themselves of their upper garments for that purpose. The children had rushed from the schools, and now ran rejoicing with the crowd. Veronica, who had two children by her, threw her own veil in the way and, snatching another from one of the children, spread that down also. She and the other women joined the holy women, who were in the rear of the procession. There were about seventeen of them. The road was so thickly covered with branches, garments, and carpets that the procession moved on quite softly through the numerous triumphal arches that spanned the space between the walls on either side.

Jesus wept, as did the apostles also, when he told them that many who were now shouting acclamations of joy would soon deride him, and that a certain one would even betray him. He looked upon the city, and wept over its approaching destruction. When he entered the gate, the cries of joy became still greater. Many sick of all kinds had been led or carried thither, consequently Jesus frequently halted, dismounted, and cured all without distinction. Many of his enemies had mingled with the crowd, and they now uttered cries with a view to raise an insurrection.

The nearer to the temple, the more magnificent was the ornamentation of the road. On either side hedges had been put up to form enclosures, in which little animals with long necks, kids, and sheep, all adorned with garlands and wreaths around their neck, were skipping about as if in little gardens. The background of these enclosures was formed of bushes. In this part of the city there were always, and especially toward the Passover feast, chosen animals for sale, pure and spotless, destined for sacrifice. To move from the city gate to the temple, although a distance of about half an hour only, the procession took three hours.

By this time the Jews had ordered all the houses, as well as the city gate, to be closed, so that when Jesus dismounted before the temple, and the disciples wanted to take the ass back to where they had found it, they were obliged to wait inside the gate till evening. In the temple were the holy women and crowds of people. All had to remain the whole day without food, for this part of the city had been barricaded. Magdalene was especially troubled by the thought that Jesus had taken no nourishment.

When toward evening the gate was again opened, the holy women went back to Bethany, and Jesus followed later with the apostles. Magdalene, worried because Jesus and his followers had had no refreshment in Jerusalem, now prepared a meal for them herself. It was already dark when Jesus entered the courtyard of Lazarus's dwelling. Magdalene brought him a basin of water, washed his feet, and dried them with a towel that was hanging over her shoulder. The food that she had prepared did not amount to a regular meal, it was merely a luncheon. While the Lord was partaking of it, she approached and poured balm over his head. I saw Judas, who passed her at this moment, muttering his dissatis-faction, but she replied to his murmurs by saying that she could never thank the Lord sufficiently for what he had done for her and her brother. After that Jesus went to the public house of Simon the leper, where sev-eral of the disciples were gathered, and taught a little while. From there he went out to the disciples' inn, where he spoke for some time, and then returned to the house of Simon the leper.

3/20 As Jesus next day was going to Jerusalem with the apostles, he was hungry, but it seemed to me that it was after the conversion of the Jews and the accomplishment of his own mission. He sighed for the hour when his Passion would be over, for he knew its immensity and dreaded it in advance. He went to a fig tree on the road and looked up at it. When he saw no fruit, but only leaves upon it, he cursed it that it should wither and never more bear fruit. And thus, did he say, would it happen to those that would not acknowledge him. I understood that the fig tree signified the Old Law; the vine, the New. On the way to the temple, I saw a heap of branches and garlands from yesterday's triumph. In the outer portico of the temple, many vendors had again established themselves. Some of them had on their backs cases, or boxes, which they could unfold and which they placed on a pedestal. The latter they carried along with them. When folded, it was like a walking stick. I saw lying on the tables heaps of pence, bound together in different ways by little chains, hooks, and cords, so as to form various figures. Some were yellow; others, white, brown, and variegated. I think they were pieces of money intended for ornamental pendants. I saw also numbers of cages with birds, standing one above another and, in one of the porticos, there were calves and other cattle. Jesus ordered the dealers to be off, and as they hesitated to obey, he doubled up a cincture like a whip and drove them from side to side and beyond the precincts of the temple.

While Jesus was teaching, some strangers of distinction from Greece dispatched their servants from the inn to ask Philip how they could con-verse with the Lord without mingling with the crowd. Philip passed the word to Andrew, who in turn transmitted it to the Lord. Jesus replied that he would meet them on the road between the city gate and the house of John Mark when he should have left the temple to return to Bethany. After this interruption, Jesus continued his discourse. He was very much troubled and when, with folded hands, he raised his eyes to heaven, I saw a flash of light descend upon him from a resplendent cloud, and heard a loud report. The people glanced up frightened, and began to whisper to

The Greeks Ask to See Jesus

The Ointment of Magdalene

one another, but Jesus went on speaking. This was repeated several times, after which I saw Jesus come down from the teacher's chair, mingle with the disciples in the crowd, and leave the temple.

When Jesus taught, the disciples threw around him a white mantle of ceremony which they always carried with them; and when he left the teacher's chair, they took it off so that, clothed like the others, he could more easily escape the notice of the crowd. Around the teacher's chair were three platforms, one above the other, each enclosed by a balustrade, which was ornamented with carving and, I think, molding. There were all sorts of brown heads and knobs on them. I saw no carved images in the temple, although there were various kinds of ornamentation: vines, grapes, animals for sacrifice, and figures like swathed infants, such as I used to see Mary embroidering.

It was still bright daylight when Jesus and his followers reached the neighborhood of John Mark's house. Here the Greeks stepped up, and Jesus spoke to them some minutes. The strangers had some women with them, but they remained standing back. These people were converted. They were among the first to join the disciples at Pentecost and to receive baptism.

MAGDALENE REPEATS HER ANOINTING OF JESUS

FULL of trouble, Jesus went back with the apostles to Bethany for the sabbath. While he was teaching in the temple, the Jews had been ordered to keep their houses closed, and it was forbidden to offer him or his disciples any refreshment. On reaching Bethany, they went to the public house of Simon, the healed leper, where a meal awaited them. Magdalene, filled with compassion for Jesus's fatiguing exertions, met the Lord at the door. She was clothed in a penitential robe and girdle, her flowing hair concealed by a black veil. She cast herself at his feet and with her hair wiped from them the dust, just as one would clean the shoes of another. She did it openly before all, and many were scandalized at her conduct.

After Jesus and the disciples had prepared themselves for the sabbath, that is, put on the garments prescribed and prayed under the lamp, they stretched themselves at table for the meal. Toward the end of it, Magdalene, urged by love, gratitude, contrition, and anxiety, again made her appearance. She went behind the Lord's couch, broke a little flask of precious balm over his head and poured some of it upon his feet, which she again wiped with her hair. That done, she left the dining hall. Several of those present were scandalized, especially Judas, who excited Matthew,

Thomas, and John Mark to displeasure. But Jesus excused her, on account of the love she bore him. She often anointed him in this way. Many of the facts mentioned only once in the Gospels happened frequently.

The meal was followed by prayer, after which the apostles and disciples separated. Judas, full of chagrin, hurried back to Jerusalem that night. I saw him, torn by envy and avarice, running in the darkness over the Mount of Olives, and it seemed as if a sinister glare surrounded him, as if the devil were lighting his steps. He hurried to the house of Caiaphas, and spoke a few words at the door. He could not stay long in any one place. Thence he ran to the house of John Mark. The disciples were wont to lodge there, so Judas pretended that he had come from Bethany for that purpose. This was the first definite step in his treacherous course.

3/21 When, on the following morning, Jesus was going from Bethany to Jerusalem with some of his disciples, they found the fig tree that Jesus had cursed entirely withered, and the disciples wondered at it. I saw John and Peter halting on the roadside near the tree. When Peter showed his astonishment, Jesus said to them: "If ye believe, ye shall do still more wonderful things. Yea, at your word mountains will cast themselves into the sea" (Mark 11:20–25). He continued his instruction on this object, and said something about the signification of the fig tree.

A great many strangers were gathered in Jerusalem, and both morning and evening, preaching and divine service went on in the temple. Jesus taught in the interim. He stood when preaching, but if anyone wanted to put a question to him, he sat down while the questioner rose.

During his discourse today, some priests and scribes stepped up to him and inquired by what right he acted as he did. Jesus answered: "I too shall ask you something; and when you answer me, I shall tell you by what authority I do these things" (Matthew 21:23–32). Then he asked them by what authority John had baptized, and when they would not answer him, he replied that neither would he tell them by what authority he acted.

In his afternoon instruction, Jesus introduced the similitude of the vine dresser, also that of the cornerstone rejected by the builders (Matthew 21:33–46). In the former, he explained that the murdered vine dresser typified himself, and the murderers, the Pharisees. Thereupon these last-named became so exasperated that they would willingly have arrested him then and there but they dared not, as they saw how all the people clung to him. They determined, however, to set five of their confidential followers, who were relatives of some of the disciples, to spy on him, and they gave them orders to try to catch him by captious questions. These five men were some of them followers of the Pharisees; others, servants of Herod.

As Jesus was returning toward evening to Bethany, some kindhearted people approached him on the road and offered him something to drink. He passed the night at the disciples' inn near Bethany.

3/22 Next day Jesus taught for three hours in the temple upon the parable of the royal wedding feast (Matthew 22:1–14), the spies of the Pharisees being present. Jesus returned early to Bethany, where he again taught.

3/23 As he mounted the teacher's chair next day in the circular hall of the temple, the five men appointed by the Pharisees pressed up through the aisle that ran from the door to the chair, the space all around being filled by the audience, and asked him whether they ought to pay tribute to Caesar. Jesus replied by telling them to show him the coin of the tribute; whereupon one of them drew from his breast pocket a yellow coin about the size of a Prussian dollar [or a US quarter] and pointed to the image of the Emperor. Then Jesus told them that they should render to Caesar the things that are Caesar's.

After that Jesus spoke of the kingdom of God, which he likened to a man who cultivated a plant that never ceased to grow and spread its branches. To the Jews, it would come not again; but those Jews that would be converted would attain the kingdom of God. That kingdom would go to the pagans, and a time would come when in the East all would be darkness, but in the West, perfect day. He told them also that they should perform their good works in secret, as he himself had done, and that he would receive his reward at noonday. He spoke too of a murderer's being preferred to himself.

Later in the day, seven of the Sadducees went to Jesus and questioned him upon the resurrection of the dead. They brought forward something about a woman that had already had seven husbands. Jesus answered that after the resurrection there would be no longer any sex or any marrying, and that God is a God of the living and not of the dead. I saw that his hearers were astounded at his teaching. The Pharisees left their seats and conferred together. One of them, named Manasseh, who held an office in the temple, very modestly asked Jesus which of the commandments was the greatest. Jesus answered the question, whereupon Manasseh heartily praised him. Then Jesus responded that the kingdom of God was not far from him, and he closed his discourse by some words on Christ (the Messiah) and David.

All were dumbfounded; they had nothing to reply. When Jesus left the temple, a disciple asked him: "What mean the words that thou didst say to Manasseh, 'Thou art not far from the kingdom of God'?" The Lord answered that Manasseh would believe and follow him, but that they (the disciples) should be silent on that head. From that hour Manasseh took no part against Jesus. He lived in retirement till the Ascension, when he declared himself for him and joined the disciples. He was between forty and fifty years old.

That evening Jesus went to Bethany, ate with the apostles at Lazarus's, then visited the inn where the women were assembled, taught them until after nightfall, and lodged at the disciples' inn.

While Jesus was teaching in Jerusalem, I saw the holy women frequently praying together in the arbor in which Magdalene was sitting when Martha called her to welcome Jesus before the raising of Lazarus. They observed a certain order at prayer: sometimes they stood together, sometimes they knelt, or again they sat apart.

3/24 On the next day Jesus taught about six hours in the temple. The disciples, impressed by his instruction of the preceding day, asked what was meant by the words: "Thy kingdom come to us!" Jesus gave them a long explanation, and added that he and the Father were one, and that he was going to the Father. Then they asked, if he and the Father were one, why was it necessary for him to go to the Father. Thereupon he spoke to them of his mission, saying that he would withdraw from the humanity, from the flesh, and that whoever separated from his own fallen nature, to go *by him to him*, went at the same time to the Father. Jesus's words on this head were so touching that the apostles, ravished with joy and transported out of themselves, started up and exclaimed: "Lord, we will spread thy kingdom to the end of the world!" But Jesus responded: "Whoever talks in that way accomplishes nothing." At this the apostles became sad. Jesus said again: "You must not say, 'I have cast out devils in thy name, I have done this and that in thy name,' nor should ye do your good works in public." And then he told them that the last time he had left them, he had done many things in secret, but that they had at the same time insisted that he should go to his own city (Nazareth) although the Jews, on account of the raising of Lazarus, wanted to kill him! But how then would all things have been accomplished? The apostles then asked how could his kingdom become known if they had to keep all things secret. But I do not remember what answer Jesus gave them. They again grew quite dejected. Toward noon the disciples left the temple, but Jesus and the apostles remained. Some of the former returned soon after with a refreshing drink for Jesus.

After midday, the scribes and Pharisees crowded in such numbers around Jesus that the disciples were pushed to some distance from him.

He spoke very severely against the Pharisees, and I heard him say once during this stern lecture: "You shall not now arrest me, because my hour has not yet come."[†]

INSTRUCTION AT LAZARUS'S •
PETER RECEIVES A SEVERE REPRIMAND

3/25 JESUS spent the whole of this day at Lazarus's with the holy women and the twelve apostles. In the morning he instructed the holy women in the disciples' inn. Toward three o'clock in the afternoon, a great repast was served in the subterranean dining hall. The women waited at table, and afterward withdrew to the grated, three-cornered apartment, to listen to the instruction. In the course of it, Jesus told them that they would not now be together long, they would not again eat at Lazarus's, though they would do so once more at Simon's, but on that last occasion they would not be so tranquil as they now were. He invited them all to be perfectly free with him, and to ask him whatever they wanted to know. On hearing this, they began to ask numerous questions, especially Thomas, who had a great many doubts. John, too, frequently put a question, but softly and gently.

After the meal, as Jesus was speaking of the approach of the time when the Son of Man would be treacherously betrayed, Peter stepped forward eagerly and asked why he always spoke as if they were going to betray him. Now, though he could believe that one of the others (the disciples) might be guilty of such a thing, yet he would answer for the twelve that they would not betray him! Peter spoke boldly, as if his honor had been attacked. Jesus replied with more warmth than I ever before saw in him, more even than had appeared when he said to Peter: "Get thee behind me, Satan!" He said that without his grace, without prayer, they would all fall away, that the hour would come in which they would all abandon him. There was only one among them, he continued, who wavered not, and yet he too would flee, though he would come back again. By these words Jesus meant John who, at the moment of Jesus's arrest, fled, leaving his mantle behind him. All became very much troubled, excepting Judas who, while Jesus was talking, put on a friendly, smiling, and insinuating air.

When they asked Jesus about the kingdom that was to come to them, his answer was inexpressibly kind. He told them that another Spirit

---

† At this, the Pharisees left the temple. It was already dark when Jesus made his way back to Bethany.

would come upon them and then only would they understand all things. He had to go to the Father and send them the Spirit which proceeded from the Father and himself. I distinctly remember his saying this. He said something more, but I cannot repeat it clearly. It was to this effect, that he had come in the flesh in order to redeem man, that there was something material in his influence upon them, that the body works in a corporeal manner, and it was for that reason they could not understand him. But he would send the Spirit, who would open their understanding. Then he spoke of troublous times to come, when all would have to suffer like a woman in the pains of childbirth, of the beauty of the human soul created to the likeness of God, and he showed how glorious a thing it is to save a soul and lead it home to heaven. He recalled to them how many times they had misunderstood him, and his own forbearance with them; in like manner should they, he said, treat with sinners after his departure. When Peter reminded him that he had himself been sometimes full of fire and zeal, Jesus explained the difference between true and false zeal.

This instruction lasted until late into the night, when Nicodemus and one of Simeon's sons came to Jesus secretly. It was past midnight before they retired to rest. Jesus told them to sleep now in peace, for the time would soon come when, anxious and troubled, they would be without sleep; this would be followed by another time when, in the midst of persecution, a stone under their head, they would sleep as sweetly as Jacob at the foot of the ladder that reached to heaven. When Jesus concluded his discourse, all exclaimed: "Lord, how short was this meal! How short this evening!"

THE WIDOW'S MITE

3/26 VERY early the next morning, Jesus repaired to the temple—not, however, to the common lecture hall, but to another in which Mary had made her offering. In the center of the hall, or rather, nearer to the entrance, stood the money box, an angular pillar, about half the height of a man, in which were three funnel-shaped openings to receive the money offerings, and at its foot was a little door. The box was covered with a red cloth over which hung a white transparent one. To the left was the seat for the priest who maintained order, and a table upon which could be laid doves and other objects brought as offerings. To the right and left of the entrance stood the seats for the women and the men, respectively. The rear of the hall was cut off by a grating, behind which the altar had been put up when Mary presented the child Jesus in the temple.

Jesus today took the seat by the money box. It was an offering day for all that desired to purify themselves for the Passover feast. The Pharisees, on coming later, were greatly put out at finding Jesus there, but they declined his offer to yield to them his place. The apostles stood near him, two by two. The men came first to the money box, then the women, and after making their offering, they went out by another door to the left. The crowd stood without awaiting their turn, only five being allowed to enter at a time. Jesus sat there three hours. Toward midday, as a general thing, the offerings ended, but Jesus remained much longer, to the discontent of the Pharisees. This was the hall in which he had acquitted the woman taken in adultery. The temple was like three churches, one behind the other, each standing under an immense arch. In the first was the circular lecture hall. The place of offering in which Jesus was, lay to the right of this hall, a little toward the sanctuary. A long corridor led to it. The last offering was made by a poor, timid widow. No one could see how much the offering was, but Jesus knew what she had given and he told his disciples that she had given more than all the rest, for she had put into the money box all that she had left to buy herself food for that day. He sent her word to wait for him near the house of John Mark.

In the afternoon, Jesus taught again in the customary place, that is, in the portico of the temple. The circular lecture hall was just opposite the door, and right and left were steps leading to the sanctuary, from which again another flight conducted to the Holy of Holies. As the Pharisees approached Jesus, he alluded to their not daring to arrest him the day before as they had intended, although he had given them a chance to do so. But his hour had not yet come, and it was not in their power to advance it; still, it would come in its own time. The Pharisees, he went on to say, should not hope to celebrate as peaceful a Passover as in former years, for they would not know where to hide themselves; the blood of the prophets whom they had murdered should fall upon their heads. The prophets themselves would rise from their graves, and the earth would be moved. In spite of these signs, however, the Pharisees would remain obstinate. Then he mentioned the poor widow's offering. When toward evening he left the temple, he spoke to her on the way and told her that her son would follow him. His words greatly rejoiced the poor mother. Her son joined the disciples even before the crucifixion. The widow was very devout and strongly attached to the Jewish observances, though simpleminded and upright.

JESUS SPEAKS OF THE DESTRUCTION OF THE TEMPLE

AS Jesus was walking along with his disciples, one of them pointed to the temple and made some remark on its beauty. Jesus replied that one stone of it would not remain upon another. They were going to the Mount of Olives, upon one side of which was a kind of pleasure garden containing a chair for instruction and seats cut in the mossy banks. The priests were accustomed to come hither to rest at evening after a long day's work. Jesus seated himself in the chair, and some of the apostles asked when the destruction of the temple would take place. It was then that Jesus recounted the evils that were to fall upon the city, and ended with the words: "But he that shall persevere to the end, he shall be saved." He remained scarcely a quarter of an hour in this place.

From this point of view the temple looked indescribably beautiful. It glistened so brightly under the rays of the setting sun that one could scarcely fix his eyes upon it. The walls were tessellated and built of beautiful sparkling stones, dark red and yellow. Solomon's temple had more gold in it, but this one abounded in glittering stones.

The Pharisees were very greatly exasperated on Jesus's account. They held a council in the night and dispatched spies to watch him. They said, if Judas would only come to them again, otherwise they did not well know how to proceed in the affair. Judas had not been with them since that first evening.

3/27 Early on the following day Jesus returned to the resting place on the Mount of Olives, and again spoke of the destruction of Jerusalem, illustrating with the similitude of a fig tree that was there standing. He said that he had already been betrayed, though the traitor had not yet mentioned his name, and had merely made the offer to betray him. The Pharisees desired to see the traitor again, but he, Jesus, wanted him to be converted, to repent, and not to despair. Jesus said all this in vague, general terms, to which Judas listened with a smile.

Jesus exhorted the apostles not to give way to their natural fears upon what he had said to them, namely, that they would all be dispersed; they should not forget their neighbor and should not allow one sentiment to veil, to stifle another; and here he made use of the similitude of a mantle. In general terms he reproached some of them for murmuring at Magdalene's anointing. Jesus probably said this in reference to Judas's first definitive step toward his betrayal, which had been taken just after that action of hers—also, as a gentle warning to him for the future, since it would be after Magdalene's last anointing that he would carry out his treacherous design. That some others were scandalized at Magdalene's prodigal expression of love arose from their erroneous severity and parsimony. They regarded this anointing as a luxury so often abused at worldly feasts, while overlooking the fact that such an action performed on the Holy of Holies was worthy of the highest praise.

Jesus told them, moreover, that he would only twice again teach in public. Then speaking of the end of the world and the destruction of Jerusalem, he gave them the signs by which they should know that the hour of his departure was near. There would be, he said, a strife among them as to which should be the greatest, and that would be a sign that he was about to leave them. He signified to them also that one of them would deny him, and he told them that he said all these things to them that they might be humble and watch over themselves. He spoke with extraordinary love and patience.

About noon Jesus taught in the temple, his subject being the ten virgins, the talents entrusted, and he again inveighed severely against the Pharisees. He repeated the words of the murdered prophets, and several times up-braided the Pharisees for their wicked designs.

He afterward told the apostles and disciples that even where there was no longer hope of improvement, words of warning must not be withheld.

When Jesus left the temple, a great number of pagans from distant parts approached him. They had not, indeed, heard his teaching in the temple, since they had not dared to set foot therein; but through the sight of his miracles, his triumphal entrance on Palm Sun. and all the other wonders that they had heard of him, they wanted to be converted. Among them were some Greeks. Jesus directed them to the disciples, a few of whom he took with him to the Mount of Olives where, in a public inn formerly used by strangers only, they lodged for the night.

3/28 Next morning, when the rest of the apostles and disciples came thither, Jesus instructed them upon many points. He said that he would be with them at two meals more, that he was longing to celebrate with them the last Love Feast in which he would bestow upon them all that humanly he could give. After that he went with them to the temple, where he spoke of his return to his Father and said that he was the Father's will, but this last expression I did not understand. He called himself in plain terms the salvation of humankind, said that it was he who was to put an end to the power of sin over the human race, and explained why the fallen angels were not redeemed, as well as man. The Pharisees took turns, two at a time, to spy. Jesus said that he had come to put an end to the domination of sin over man. Sin began in a garden, and in a garden it should end, for it would be in a garden that his enemies would seize him. He reproached his hearers with the fact of their already wanting to kill him after the raising of Lazarus, and said that he had kept himself at a distance, that all things might be fulfilled. He divided his journey into three parts, but I no longer recollect whether it was into thrice four, or five, or six weeks. He told them also how they would treat him and put him to death with assassins, and yet they would not be satisfied, they would not be able to effect anything against him after his death. He once more made mention of the murdered just who would arise again; yes, he even pointed out the spot in which their resurrection would take place. But as for the Pharisees, he continued, in fear and anguish they would see their designs against him frustrated.

Jesus spoke likewise of Eve, through whom sin had come upon the earth; therefore it was that woman was condemned to suffer and that she dared not enter into the sanctuary. But it was also through a woman that the cure of sin had come into the world, consequently she was freed from slavery, though not from dependence.

Jesus again took up quarters in the inn at the foot of the Mount of Olives. A lamp was lighted, and the sabbath exercises were performed.

JESUS IN BETHANY

3/29 NEXT morning, Jesus went with his followers across the brook Kidron, and then northward by a row of houses between which were little grass plots on which sheep were grazing. Here was situated John Mark's house. Jesus then turned off to Gethsemane, a little village as large as Bethphage, built on either side of the brook Kidron. John Mark's house stood a quarter of an hour outside the gate through which the cattle were led to the cattle market on the north side of the temple. It was built upon a high hill which, at a later period, was covered with houses. It was from here to Gethsemane one-half hour; and from Gethsemane across the Mount of Olives to Bethany, something less than an hour. The last-named place lay almost in a straight line east of the temple and, by the direct route, it may have been only one hour from Jerusalem. From certain points of the temple and from the castles in the rear, one could descry Bethany. Bethphage, however, was not in sight, as it lay low; and the view was, besides, up to the point at which the temple could be seen through a defile of the mountain road, obstructed by the Mount of Olives. As Jesus was going over the brook Kidron to Gethsemane with the disciples, he said to the apostles as they were entering a hollow of the Mount of Olives: "Here will ye abandon me! Here shall I be taken prisoner!" He was very much troubled. He proceeded afterward to Lazarus's, in Bethany, thence to the disciples' inn, after which he went with some of them around the environs of the city consoling the inhabitants, like one bidding farewell.

That evening there was a supper at Lazarus's, at which the holy women assisted in the grated apartment. At the close of the meal Jesus told them all that they could have one night more of peaceful sleep.

Jesus's Last Discourse in the Temple

3/30 EARLY the next morning, Jesus went with the disciples to Jerusalem. Having crossed the Kidron in front of the temple, he continued his course outside the city toward the south, till he came to a little gate, by which he entered, and, crossing a stone bridge that spanned a deep abyss, he reached the foot of Mount Zion. There were caverns also under the temple. Here Jesus turned from the south side of the temple and proceeded through a long vaulted corridor, which was lighted only from above, into the women's portico.

Here, turning toward the east, he passed through the doorway allotted to women condemned on account of their sterility, crossed the hall in which offerings were made, and proceeded to the teacher's chair in the outer hall of the temple. This door always stood open, although at Jesus's instructions, all the other entrances to the temple were often closed by the Pharisees. They said: "Let the sin-door always remain open to the sinner!"

In words admirable and deeply significant, Jesus taught upon union and separation. He made use of the similitude of fire and water, which are opposed to each other, one of which extinguishes the other, though if the latter does not get the better of the former, the flames become wilder and more powerful. He next spoke of persecution and martyrdom. Under the figure of fire, Jesus alluded to those disciples that would remain true to him; and under that of water, to those that would separate from him and seek the abyss. He called water the martyr of fire. He spoke also of the mingling of water and milk, naming it an intimate commingling that no one could separate. Jesus wished under this figure to designate his own union with his followers, and he dwelt upon the mild and nutritive properties of milk. From this he passed to the subject of marriage and its union, as the disciples had questioned him upon the reunion after death of friends and married people. Jesus said that there was a twofold union in marriage: the union of flesh and blood, which death cuts asunder, and they that were so bound would not find themselves together after death; and the union of soul, which would outlive death. They should not, he continued, be disquieted as to whether they would be alone or together in the other world. They that had been united in union of soul in this life, would form but one body in the next. He spoke also of the Bridegroom and named the church his affianced. Of the martyrdom of the body, he said that it was not to be feared, since that of the soul was the more frightful.

As the apostles and disciples did not comprehend all that he said, Jesus directed them to write down what they failed to understand. Then I saw John, James the Less, and another making signs from time to time on a little tablet that they held before them resting on a support. They wrote upon little rolls of parchment with a colored liquid, which they carried with them in a kind of horn. They drew the little rolls out of their breast pockets, and wrote only in the beginning of the instruction.

Jesus spoke likewise of his own union with them, which would be accomplished at the Last Supper and could by nothing be dissolved.

The obligation of perfect continence, Jesus exposed to the apostles by way of interrogation. He asked, for instance, "Could you do such and such a thing at the same time?" and he spoke of a sacrifice that had to be offered, all which led to perfect continence as a conclusion. He adduced as examples Abraham and the other patriarchs who, before offering sacrifice, always purified themselves and observed a long continence.

When he spoke of baptism and the other sacraments, he said that he would send to them the Holy Spirit who, by his baptism, would make them all children of Redemption. They should after his death baptize at the pool of Bethesda all that would come and ask for it. If a great number presented themselves, they should lay their hands upon their shoulders, two by two, and baptize them there under the stream of the pump, or jet. As formerly the angel, so now would the Holy Spirit come upon the baptized as soon as his blood should have been shed, and even before they themselves had received the Holy Spirit.

Peter, who had been appointed by Jesus chief over the others, asked as such whether they were always to act in this manner without first proving and instructing the people. Jesus answered that the people would be wearied out with waiting for feast days and pining meantime in aridity; therefore they, the apostles, should not delay to do as he had just told them. When they should have received the Holy Spirit, then they would always know what they should do. He addressed some words to Peter on the subject of penance and absolution, and afterward spoke to them all about the end of the world and of the signs that would precede it. A man enlightened by God would have visions on that subject. By these words, Jesus referred to John's revelations, and he himself made use of several similar illustrations. He spoke, for instance, of those that would be marked with the sign on their forehead, and said that the fountain of living water which flowed from Golgotha's mount would at the end of the world appear to be almost entirely poisoned, though all the good waters would finally be gathered into the valley of Jehosaphat. It seemed to me that he said also that all water was to become once more baptismal water. No Pharisees were present at any part of this instruction. That evening Jesus returned to Lazarus's, in Bethany.

3/31 The whole of the next day Jesus taught undisturbed in the temple. He spoke of truth and the necessity of acting out what they, the apostles, taught. He himself, he said, was now about to fulfill it. It is not enough to believe, one must practice one's faith. No one, not even the Pharisees themselves, could reproach him with the least error in his teaching, and now by returning to his Father he would fulfill the truth he had taught. But before going he would give over to them, would leave to them, all that he possessed. Money and property he had not, but he would bequeath to them his strength and power. He would establish with them a union which should be still more intimate than that which now united them to him, and which should last till the end of time. He would also bind them to one another as the members of one body. Jesus spoke of so many things that he would still do with them that Peter, conceiving new hope that he would remain longer on earth, said to him that if he were to fulfill all those things, he would have to abide with them till the end of the world. Jesus then spoke of the essence and effects of the Last Supper, without, however, mentioning it by name. He said also that he was about to celebrate his last Passover. Peter asked where he intended to do so. Jesus answered that he would tell him in good time, and after that last Passover he would go to his Father. Peter again asked whether he would take with him his mother, whom they all loved and reverenced so much. Jesus answered that she should remain with them some years longer. He mentioned the number, and in it there was a five. I think he named fifteen years, and then said many things in connection with her.

In his instruction upon the power and effects of his Last Supper, Jesus made some allusion to Noah, who had once become intoxicated with wine; to the children of Israel, who had lost their taste for the manna sent them from heaven; and to the bitterness they tasted in it. As for himself, he was going to prepare the bread of life before his return home, but it was not yet ready, was not yet baked, not yet cooked.

He had, he continued, so long taught them the truth, so long communicated with them; and yet they had always doubted, indeed they doubted still! He felt that in his corporeal presence he could no longer be useful to them, therefore he would give them all that he had, he would retain only what was absolutely necessary to cover his naked body. These words of Jesus the apostles did not understand. They were under the impression that he would die, or perhaps vanish from their sight. As late as the preceding day, when he was speaking of the persecution of the Jews against him, Peter said that he might again withdraw from these parts and they would accompany him. He had gone away once before after the raising of Lazarus, he could now go again.

When toward evening Jesus left the temple, he spoke of taking leave of it, saying that he would never again enter it in the body. This scene was so touching that all the apostles and disciples cast themselves on the ground crying aloud and weeping. Jesus wept also. Judas shed no tear, though he was anxious and nervous, as he had been during the past days. Yesterday Jesus said no word in allusion to him.

In the court of the temple some pagans were waiting, many of whom wanted to give themselves to Jesus. They saw the tears of the apostles. On learning their desire, Jesus told them that there was no time now, but that they should later on have recourse to his apostles and disciples, to whom he gave power similar to his own. Then taking the way by which he had entered on Palm Sunday and frequently turning with sad and earnest words to gaze upon the temple, he left the city, went to the public inn at the foot of the Mount of Olives, and after nightfall back to Bethany.

Here Jesus taught at Lazarus's, continuing his instructions during the evening meal, at which the women, who now kept themselves less aloof, served. Jesus gave orders for a plentiful meal to be prepared at Simon's public house the following day.

It was very quiet in Jerusalem all this day. The Pharisees did not go to the temple, but assembled in council. They were very anxious on account of Judas's non-appearance. Many good people of the city were in great distress at Jesus's predictions, which they had heard from the disciples. I saw Nicodemus, Joseph of Arimathea, Simeon's sons, and others looking very troubled and anxious, though they had not yet withdrawn from the rest of the Jews. They were still mixing with them in the affairs of every-day life. I saw Veronica also, going about her house sad and wringing her hands. Her husband inquired the cause of her affliction. Her house was situated in Jerusalem between the temple and Mount Calvary. Seventy-six of the disciples lodged in the halls surrounding the Cenacle.

Magdalene's Last Anointing

4/1 NEXT morning, Jesus instructed a large number of the disciples, more than sixty, in the court before Lazarus's house. In the afternoon, about three o'clock, tables were laid for them in the court, and during their meal Jesus and the apostles served. I saw Jesus going from table to table handing something to this one, something to that, and teaching all the time. Judas was not present. He was away making purchases for the entertainment to be given at Simon's. Magdalene also had gone to Jerusalem, to buy precious ointment. The blessed Virgin, to whom Jesus had that morning announced his approaching death, was inexpressibly sad. Her niece, Mary Cleophas, was always around her, consoling her. Full of grief, they went together to the disciples' inn.

Meantime, Jesus conversed with the disciples upon his approaching death and the events that would follow it. One, he said, that had been on intimate terms with him, one that owed him a great debt of gratitude, was about to sell him to the Pharisees. He would not even set a price upon him, but would merely ask: "What will ye give me for him?" If the Pharisees were buying a slave, it would be at a fixed price, but he would be sold for whatever they chose to give. The traitor would sell him for less than the cost of a slave! The disciples wept bitterly, and became so afflicted that they had to cease eating, but Jesus pressed them graciously. I have often noticed that the disciples were much more affectionate toward Jesus than were the apostles. I think as they were not so much with him, they were on that account more humble.

This morning Jesus spoke of many things with his apostles. As they did not understand everything, he commanded them to write down what they could not comprehend, saying that when he would send his Spirit to them, they would recall those points and be able to seize their meaning. I saw John and some of the others taking notes. Jesus dwelt long upon their flight, when he himself would be delivered up to the Pharisees. They could not think that such a thing would ever happen to them, and yet they really did take to flight. He predicted many things that were to follow that event, and told them how they should conduct themselves.

At last he spoke of his holy mother. He said that through compassion, she would suffer with him all the cruel torture of his death, that with him she would die his bitter death, and still would have to survive him fifteen years.

Jesus indicated to the disciples whither they should betake themselves: some to Arimathea, some to Sichar, and others to Kedar. The three that had accompanied him on his last journey were not to return home. Since their ideas and sentiments had undergone so great a change, it would not be well for them to return to their country, otherwise they might give scandal or, on account of the opposition of friends, run the risk of falling back into their former way of acting. Eliud and Eremenzear went, I think, to Sichar, but Silas remained where he was. And thus Jesus went on instructing his followers with extraordinary love, counselling them on everything. I saw many of them dispersing toward evening.

It was during this instruction that Magdalene came back from Jerusalem with the ointment she had brought. She had gone to Veronica's and stayed there while Veronica saw to the purchase of the ointment, which was of three kinds, the most precious that could be procured. Magdalene had expended upon it all the money she had left. One was a flask of the oil of spikenard. She bought the flasks together with their contents. The former were of a clear, whitish, though not transparent material, almost like mother-of-pearl, though not mother-of-pearl. They were in shape like little urns, the swelling base ornamented with knobs, and they had screw-tops. Magdalene carried the vessels under her mantle in a pocket which hung on her breast suspended by a cord that passed over one shoulder and back across the back. John Mark's mother went back with her to Bethany, and Veronica accompanied them a part of the way. As they were going through Bethany, they met Judas who, concealing his indignation, spoke to Magdalene. Magdalene had heard from Veronica that the Pharisees had resolved to arrest Jesus and put him to death, but not yet, on account of the crowds of strangers and especially the numerous pagans that followed him. This news Magdalene imparted to the other women.

The women were at Simon's helping to prepare for the entertainment, for which Judas had purchased everything necessary. He had entirely emptied the purse today, secretly thinking that he would get all back again in the evening. From a man who kept a garden in Bethany, he bought vegetables, two lambs, fruit, fish, honey, etc. The dining hall used at Simon's today was different from that in which Jesus and his friends had dined once before, that is, on the day after the triumphal entrance into the temple. Today they dined in an open hall at the back of the house, and which looked out upon the courtyard. It had been ornamented for the occasion. In the ceiling was an opening which was covered with a transparent veil and which looked like a little cupola. On either side of this cupola hung verdant pyramids of a brownish-green, succulent plant with small round leaves. The pyramids were green likewise at the base, and it seemed to me that they always remained green and fresh. Under this ceiling ornamentation stood the seat for Jesus. One side of the table, that toward the open colonnade through which the servings of food were brought across the courtyard, was left free. Simon, who served, alone had his place on that side. There too on the floor, under the table, stood three water jugs, tall and flat.

The guests reclined during this repast on low cross-benches, which in the back had a support, and in front an arm upon which to lean. The benches stood in pairs, and they were sufficiently wide to admit of the guests' sitting two by two, facing each other. Jesus reclined at the middle of the table upon a seat to himself. On this occasion the women ate in an open hall to the left. Looking obliquely across the courtyard, they could see the men at table.

When all was prepared, Simon and his servant, in festal robes, went to conduct Jesus, the apostles, and Lazarus. Simon wore a long robe, a girdle embroidered in figures, and on his arm a long fur-lined maniple. The servant wore a sleeveless jacket. Simon escorted Jesus; the servant, the apostles. They did not traverse the street to Simon's, but went in their festal robes back through the garden into the hall. There were numbers of people in Bethany, and the crowds of strangers who had come through a desire to see Lazarus raised somewhat of a tumult. It was also a cause of surprise and dissatisfaction to the people that Simon, whose house formerly stood open, had purchased so large a supply of provisions and closed his establishment. They became in a short time angry and inquisitive, and almost scaled the walls during the meal. I do not remember having seen any foot-washing going on, but only some little purification before entering the hall.

Several large drinking glasses stood on the table, and beside each, two smaller ones. There were three kinds of beverages: one greenish, another red, and the third yellow. I think it was some kind of pear juice. The lamb was served first. It lay stretched out on an oval dish, the head resting on the forefeet. The dish was placed with the head toward Jesus. Jesus took a white knife, like bone or stone, inserted it into the back of the lamb, and cut, first to one side of the neck and then to the other. After that he drew the knife down, making a cut from the head along the whole back. The lines of this cut at once reminded me of the cross. He then laid the slices thus detached before John, Peter and himself, and directed Simon, the host, to carve the lamb down the sides, and lay the pieces right and left before the apostles and Lazarus as they sat in order.

The holy women were seated around their own table. Magdalene, who was in tears all the time, sat opposite the blessed Virgin. There were seven or nine present. They too had a little lamb. It was smaller than that of the other table and lay stretched out flat in the dish, the head toward the Mother of God. She it was who carved it.

The lamb was followed by three large fish and several small ones. The large ones lay in the dish as if swimming in a stiff, white sauce. Then came pastry, little rolls in the shape of lambs, birds with outstretched wings, honeycombs, green herbs like lettuce, and a sauce in which the last-named were steeped. I think it was oil. This course was followed by another of fruit that looked like pears. In the center of the dish was something like a gourd upon which other fruit, like grapes, were stuck by their stems. The dishes used throughout the meal were partly white, the inside partly yellow; and they were deep or shallow according to their contents.

Jesus taught during the whole meal. It was nearing the close of his discourse; the apostles were stretched forward in breathless attention. Simon, whose services were no longer needed, sat motionless, listening to every word, when Magdalene rose quietly from her seat among the holy women. She had around her a thin, bluish-white mantle, something like the material worn by the three holy kings, and her flowing hair was covered with a veil. Laying the ointment in a fold of her mantle, she passed through the walk that was planted with shrubbery, entered the hall, went up behind Jesus, and cast herself down at his feet, weeping bitterly. She bent her face low over the foot that was resting on the couch, while Jesus himself raised to her the other that was hanging a little toward the floor. Magdalene loosened the sandals and anointed Jesus's feet on the soles and upon the upper part. Then with both hands drawing her flowing hair from beneath her veil, she wiped the Lord's anointed feet, and replaced the sandals. Magdalene's action caused some interruption in Jesus's discourse. He had observed her approach, but the others were taken by surprise. Jesus said: "Be not scandalized at this woman!" and then addressed some words softly to her. She now arose, stepped behind him and poured over his head some costly water, and that so plentifully that it ran down upon his garments. Then with her hand she spread some of the ointment from the crown down the hind part of his head. The hall was filled with the delicious fragrance. The apostles whispered together and muttered their displeasure—even Peter was vexed at the interruption. Magdalene, weeping and veiled, withdrew around behind the table. When she was about to pass before Judas, he stretched forth his hand to stay her while he indignantly addressed to her some words on her extravagance, saying that the purchase money might have been given to the poor. Magdalene made no reply. She was weeping bitterly. Then Jesus spoke, bidding them let her pass, and saying that she had anointed him for his death, for later she would not be able to do it, and that wherever this Gospel would be preached, her action and their murmuring would also be recounted.

Magdalene retired, her heart full of sorrow. The rest of the meal was disturbed by the displeasure of the apostles and the reproaches of Jesus. When it was over, all returned to Lazarus's. Judas, full of wrath and avarice, thought within himself that he could no longer put up with such things. But concealing his feelings, he laid aside his festal garment, and pretended that he had to go back to the public house to see that what remained of the meal was given to the poor. Instead of doing that, however, he ran full speed to Jerusalem. I saw the devil with him all the time, red, thin-bodied, and angular. He was before him and behind him, as if lighting the way for him. Judas saw through the darkness. He stumbled not, but ran along in perfect safety. I saw him in Jerusalem running into the house in which, later on, Jesus was exposed to scorn and derision. The Pharisees and high priests were still together, but Judas did not enter their assembly. Two of them went out and spoke with him below in the courtyard. When he told them that he was ready to deliver Jesus and asked what they would give for him, they showed great joy, and returned to announce it to the rest of the council. After awhile, one came out again and made an offer of thirty pieces of silver. Judas wanted to receive them at once, but they would not give them to him. They said that he had once before been there, and then had absented himself for so long, that he should do his duty, and then they would pay him. I saw them offering hands as a pledge of the contract, and on both sides tearing something from their clothing. The Pharisees wanted Judas to stay awhile and tell them when and how the bargain would be completed. But he insisted upon going, that suspicion might not be excited. He said that he had yet to find things out more precisely, that next day he could act without attracting attention. I saw the devil the whole time between Judas and the Pharisees. On leaving Jerusalem, Judas ran back again to Bethany, where he changed his garments and joined the other apostles.

Jesus remained at Lazarus's, while his followers withdrew to their own inn. That night Nicodemus came from Jerusalem, and on his return Lazarus accompanied him a part of the way.

Holy Thursday

The Last Passover Supper

4/2 BEFORE break of day, Jesus, calling Peter and John, spoke to them at some length upon what they should order, what preparations they should make in Jerusalem for the eating of the paschal lamb. The disciples had questioned Jesus the day before upon where this supper was to be held. Jesus told the two apostles that they would, when ascending Mount Zion, meet a man carrying a water pitcher, one whom they already knew, as he was the same that had attended to the Passover meal for Jesus the year before at Bethany. They were to follow him into the house and say to him: "The Master bids us say to thee that his time is near at hand. He desires to celebrate Passover at thy house." They should then ask to see the supper room, which they would find prepared, and there they should make ready all that was needed.

I saw the two apostles going up to Jerusalem through a ravine that ran south of the temple and north of Zion. On the south side of the mount upon which the temple stood there were some rows of houses opposite which a rapid stream flowed down the height; on the other side of this stream ran the road by which the apostles ascended. On reaching a point of Zion higher than the temple mount, they turned toward the south and met the man designated by Jesus on a somewhat rising open space, and in the neighborhood of an old building surrounded by courts. They followed him and, when near the house, delivered to him Jesus's message. He showed great pleasure at seeing them and learning their errand. He told them that he had already been ordered to prepare a supper (probably by Nicodemus), though he knew not for whom, but now he greatly rejoiced that it was for Jesus. This man was Heli, the brother-in-law of Zechariah of Hebron, the same in whose house at Hebron Jesus had, after a certain sabbath of the preceding year, announced to the family the death of John. He had five unmarried daughters, but only one son, who was a Levite and who had been a friend of Luke before the latter joined the Lord. Heli went with his servants every year to the feast, hired a supper room, and prepared the Passover meal for people that had no friends in the city. On this occasion Heli had hired the dining hall of a spacious old house belonging to Nicodemus and Joseph of Arimathea.

ON the south side of Mount Zion, not far from the citadel of David and from the market, which was on the eastern ascent to the same, this old house stood in an open court surrounded by courtyards with massive walls, and between rows of shade trees.

To the right and left of the entrance and just inside the walls stood a couple of smaller buildings. In one of these the blessed Virgin and the other holy women celebrated the Passover supper, and there too after the crucifixion they frequently retired. The large building, that is, the principal one which contained the dining hall rented by Heli, stood a little back of the center of the court. It was in this house, in King David's time, that his valiant heroes and generals exercised themselves in arms; here too, before the building of the temple, had the Ark of the Covenant been deposited for a long time. Traces of its presence were still to be found in an underground apartment. I have seen also the prophet Malachi hidden in this vault. There it was that he wrote his prophecies of the most blessed sacrament and the Sacrifice of the New Law. Solomon also held this house in honor, and performed in it some symbolical action, but I now forget what. When a great part of Jerusalem was destroyed by the Babylonians, this house was spared. It was now the property of Nicodemus and Joseph of Arimathea, who arranged the principal building in a very suitable manner and let it as a guest house for strangers coming to Jerusalem for Passover. Moreover, the house and its dependencies served during the year as warehouses for tombstones, building stones, and as a place for stone-cutting in general, for Joseph of Arimathea owned an excellent quarry in his own country. He traded in monuments, architectural ornaments, and columns, which were here sculpted under his own eye. Nicodemus also was engaged in building, and devoted many of his leisure hours to sculpting. Excepting at the time of festivals, he often worked here either in the hall, or in the vault below, sculpting statues. It was owing to this art that he had formed a friendship for Joseph of Arimathea, and many of their transactions were undertaken together.

The principal edifice, the Cenacle proper, was a long, four-cornered building surrounded by a low colonnade, which could be thrown open and thus made one with the lofty hall beyond. The whole building rested on columns, or pillars, and was so constructed as to allow the gaze to penetrate in all directions, that is, when the portable screens generally in use were removed. The light fell through apertures near the top of the walls. In front (and this was the narrow side of the building), there was an anteroom, into which three entrances led. From it one stepped into the lofty and beautifully paved inner hall from whose roof several lamps were hanging. The halls had been decorated for the feast. They were hung half-way up with beautiful matting, or tapestry, and the aperture that had been opened in the ceiling was covered with blue gauze, shining and transparent. The rear end of the hall was cut off by a curtain of the same kind of gauze. The Cenacle, separated from the rest of the room, owing to this division into three parts, bore some resemblance to the temple, as it had a forecourt, a sanctuary, and the holy of holies. On either side in the last division were deposited dresses and other things necessary for the feast. In the center stood a kind of altar. Projecting from the wall and raised on three steps was a stone bench in form like a right-angled triangle whose sharp corner was fitted into the wall.

It must have been the upper side of the oven used for roasting the paschal lamb, for at the meal of today it was quite hot around the steps. On one side of this apartment there was an exit that led into the hall behind that projection, and from that hall there was a descent to the subterranean vaults and cellars, where it was warm. On the projection, or altar, lay different things in preparation for the feast, like chests, or drawers, that could be drawn out. On top were openings like a grating and a place for making a fire, as well as one for extinguishing it. I cannot describe it in detail. It appeared to be a kind of hearth for baking Passover bread and other kinds of pastry, for burning frankincense, or, at certain festivals, for consuming what remained of the sacrifice. It was like a paschal kitchen. Above this hearth, or altar, there was a kind of niche formed of projecting rafters and surmounted by a valve, probably for the escape of smoke. Suspended from the ceiling above the niche and hanging in front of it, I saw the figure of a paschal lamb. A knife was sticking in its throat, and its blood appeared to be dropping on the altar. I no longer remember exactly how this last was effected. In the back of the niche there were three little compartments, or cupboards, that turned like our tabernacles for opening or closing. In them I saw all kinds of vessels for Passover and deep oval dishes. Later on, the most blessed sacrament was kept there. In the side halls of the Cenacle here and there were built inclined couches, upon which lay heavy coverlets rolled together. These were the sleeping places. Fine cellars extended under the whole building. The resting place of the Ark of the Covenant was once in the back part, directly under the spot upon which the paschal hearth now stood. Below the cellars ran five gutters, which served to carry off the refuse to the slope of the hill on the top of which the house stood. At different times, I saw Jesus teaching and performing cures here. The disciples often lodged for the night in the side halls.

While Peter and John were speaking with Heli, I saw Nicodemus in one of the buildings in the courtyard, whither the blocks of stone from the vicinity of the supper hall had been removed. For eight days previously I saw people busy cleaning the court and arranging the hall for the Passover feast. Some of the disciples themselves were among the workers.

WHEN Peter and John finished speaking with Heli, the latter passed through the courtyard and into the house. The two apostles, however, turned off to the right, went down the north side of the mountain through Zion, crossed a brook, proceeded by a path between hedges to the other side of the ravine that lay before the temple, and to the row of houses south of it. Here stood the house of old Simeon, now occupied by his sons, who were disciples in secret. The apostles entered and spoke with Obed, the elder, who served in the temple. Then they went with a tall, dark-complexioned man by the east side of the temple, through that part of Ophel by which Jesus on Palm Sunday entered Jerusalem, and thence to the cattle market in the city north of the temple. Here, on the south side of the market, I saw enclosures like little gardens, in which beautiful lambs were gamboling on the grass. On the occasion of Jesus's triumphal entrance I imagined these arrangements made in honor of that event, but now I found out that these were the paschal lambs here exposed for sale. I saw Simeon's son enter one of these enclosures, and the lambs leaping about him and butting him with their heads, as if they recognized him. He singled out four, which he took with him to the Cenacle, and that afternoon I again saw him there taking part in the preparation of the paschal lambs.

I still saw Peter and John traversing the city in all directions and giving orders for many things. I saw them also outside the door of a house to the north of Mount Calvary. It was the inn, on the northwest side of the city, in which many of the disciples were staying. This was the disciples' inn outside Jerusalem. It was under the care of Veronica, whose former name was Seraphia. From this inn, I saw them go to Veronica's own house, for they had many directions to give her. Veronica's husband was a member of the council. He was generally away from home attending to his business, and when he was in the house, his wife saw little of him. She was a woman of about the same age as the blessed Virgin. She had long known the holy family, for when the boy Jesus remained in Jerusalem after the feast, she it was who supplied him with food.

The two apostles got from Veronica all kinds of table service, which was carried by the disciples in covered baskets to the Cenacle. They took from here also the chalice of which Jesus made use in the institution of the blessed sacrament.

THIS chalice was a very wonderful and mysterious vessel that had lain in the temple for a long time among other old and precious things, whose use and origin even had been forgotten, just as with us many ancient, holy treasures have through the lapse of time fallen into oblivion. Frequently at the temple ancient vessels and precious ornaments whose use was no longer known were reset, made over anew, or sold. It was in this way, and by God's permission, that that holy vessel (whose unknown material prevented its being melted down, although frequent attempts had been made to do so) had been found by the young priests in the treasury of the temple. It was stowed away in a chest along with other objects no longer of use, and when discovered was sold to some antiquaries. The chalice and all the vessels belonging to it were afterward bought by Veronica. It had several times been made use of by Jesus in the celebration of festivals, and from today it became the exclusive possession of the holy community of Jesus Christ. It was not always the same as when used at the Last Supper. I no longer remember when the parts that composed it were put together; perhaps it was on the occasion of the Lord's using it at the Last Supper. It was now, however, along with all that was necessary for the institution of the blessed sacrament, put up in one portable case.

On a flat surface out of which a little board, or tablet, could be drawn, stood the large chalice surrounded by six small beakers. The chalice itself contained another smaller vase. I cannot remember whether the tablet held the holy thing or not. A little plate was laid upon the chalice, and over the whole was a convex cover. In the foot of the chalice was a place for keeping a spoon, which could be easily drawn out. All these vessels in fine linen coverings were protected by a cap, or case of leather, I think, which had a knob on top. The large chalice consisted of the cup and the foot, which latter must have been added at a later period, for it was of different material. The cup was pear-shaped, and of a brownish, highly polished metal, overlaid with gold. It had two small handles, by which it could be raised when its contents rendered it tolerably heavy. The foot was elaborately wrought of dark virgin gold, the edge encircled by a serpent. It was ornamented with a little bunch of grapes, and enriched with precious stones. The small spoon was concealed in the foot.

The large chalice was left to the church of Jerusalem under the care of James the Less. I see it still carefully preserved somewhere. It will again come to light as it did once before. The smaller cups that stood around it were distributed among the other churches: one to Antioch, another to Ephesus. These vessels enriched seven churches. The small beakers once belonged to the patriarchs, who drank some mysterious beverage out of them when they received or imparted the Blessing, as I have seen and already explained.

The large chalice once belonged to Abraham. Melchizedek brought it from the land of Semiramis, where it was lying neglected, to the land of Canaan, when he began to mark off settlements on the site afterward occupied by Jerusalem. He had used it at the sacrifice of bread and wine offered in Abraham's presence, and he afterward gave it to him. This same chalice was even in Noah's possession. It stood in the upper part of the ark. Moses also had it in his keeping. The cup was massive like a bell. It looked as if it had been shaped by nature, not formed by art. I have seen clear through it. Jesus alone knew of what it was made.

In the morning, while the two apostles in Jerusalem were engaged in the preparations for the Passover feast, Jesus took an affecting leave of the holy women, Lazarus, and his mother in Bethany, and gave them some final instructions and admonitions.

I saw him speaking alone with his blessed Mother, and I remember some of the words that passed between them. He had, he said, sent Peter the believing and John the loving to Jerusalem in order to prepare for Passover. Of Magdalene, who was quite out of herself from grief, he said: "She loves unspeakably, but her love is still encompassed by the body, therefore has she become like one quite out of her mind with pain." He spoke also of the treacherous scheming of Judas, and the blessed Virgin implored mercy for him.

Judas, under pretense of attending to different affairs and of discharging certain debts, had again left Bethany and hurried to Jerusalem. Jesus, although he well knew what he was after, questioned the nine apostles about him.

Judas spent the whole day in running around among the Pharisees and concerting his plans with them. The soldiers that were to apprehend Jesus were even shown him, and he so arranged his journey to and fro as to be able to account for his absence. Just before it was time for the Passover supper, he returned to the Lord. I have seen all his thoughts and plans. When Jesus spoke about him to Mary, I saw many things connected with his character and behavior. He was active and obliging, but full of avarice, ambition, and envy, which passions he struggled not to control. He had even performed miracles and, in Jesus's absence, healed the sick. When Jesus made known to the blessed Virgin what was about to happen to him, she besought him in touching terms to let her die with him. But he exhorted her to bear her grief more calmly than the other women, telling her at the same time that he would rise again, and he named the spot upon which he would appear to her. This time she did not shed so many tears, though she was sad beyond expression and there was something awe-inspiring in her deep gravity. Like a devoted Son, Jesus thanked her for all her love. He embraced her with his right arm and pressed her to his breast. He told her that he would celebrate his Last Supper with her in spirit, and named the hour at which she should receive his body and blood. He afterward took a very affecting leave of them all, and gave them instructions on many points.

Toward noon, Jesus and the nine apostles set out from Bethany for Jerusalem, followed by a band of seven disciples who, with the exception of Nathaniel and Silas, were principally from Jerusalem and its neighborhood. I remember that John Mark and the son of the poor widow who on the Thursday before, that is, just eight days ago, had offered her mite when Jesus was teaching by the alms box in the temple, were among them. Jesus had received the youth into the number of his disciples a few days previously. The holy women followed later.

Jesus and his companions walked here and there around the Mount of Olives, through the valley of Jehosaphat, and even as far as Mount Calvary. During the whole walk, Jesus gave uninterrupted instructions. Among other things he told the apostles that until now he had given them his bread and his wine, but that today he would give them his flesh and his blood. He would bestow upon them, he would make over to them, all that he had. While uttering these words, the countenance of the Lord wore a touching expression, as if he were pouring his whole soul out, as if he were languishing with love to give himself to man. His disciples did not comprehend his words—they thought that he was speaking of the paschal lamb. No words can say how affectionate, how patient Jesus was in his last instructions both at Bethany and on his way to Jerusalem. The holy women arrived later at the house of Mary Mark.

The seven disciples who had followed the Lord to Jerusalem did not make the journey with him. They carried in bundles to the Cenacle the robes necessary for the Passover ceremonies. After depositing them in the anteroom, they proceeded to the house of Mary Mark.

When Peter and John reached the Cenacle with the chalice, which they had brought from Seraphia's [that is, from Veronica's], the mantles of ceremony were already lying in the anteroom whither they had been carried by the seven disciples and some of their companions. They had also draped the walls of the supper room, opened the apertures in the roof, and prepared three hanging lamps. This done, Peter and John went out to the valley of Jehosaphat and summoned the Lord and the nine apostles. The disciples and friends who were also to eat their Passover feast in the Cenacle came later.

JESUS and his followers ate the paschal lamb in the Cenacle in three separate groups of twelve, each presided over by one who acted as host. Jesus and the twelve apostles ate in the hall itself; Nathaniel with as many of the oldest disciples, in one of the side rooms; and in another with twelve more sat Heliachim, son of Cleophas and Mary Heli, and the brother of Mary Cleophas. He had been a disciple of John the Baptist. In one of the side buildings near the entrance into the court of the Cenacle, the holy women took their meal.

Three lambs had been immolated and sprinkled for them in the temple. But the fourth was slaughtered and sprinkled in the Cenacle, and it was this that Jesus ate with the twelve. Judas was not aware of this circumstance. He had been engaged in various business affairs, among which was the plot to betray the Lord, and consequently had arrived only a few moments before the repast, and after the immolation of the lamb had taken place.

The slaughter of the lamb for Jesus and the apostles presented a scene most touching. It took place in the anteroom of the Cenacle, Simeon's son, the Levite, assisting at it. The apostles and disciples were present chanting the 118th Psalm. Jesus spoke of a new period then beginning, and said that the sacrifice of Moses and the signification of the paschal lamb were about to be fulfilled, that on this account the lamb was to be immolated as formerly in Egypt, and that now in reality were they to go forth from the house of bondage.

All the necessary vessels and instruments were now prepared. Then a beautiful little lamb was brought in, around its neck a garland which was taken off and sent to the blessed Virgin, who was at some distance with the other women. The lamb was then bound, its back to a little board, with a cord passed around the body. It reminded me of Jesus bound to the pillar. Simeon's son held the lamb's head up, and Jesus stuck it in the neck with a knife, which he then handed to Simeon's son that he might complete the slaughter. Jesus appeared timid in wounding the lamb, as if it cost him pain. His movement was quick, his manner grave. The blood was caught in a basin, and the attendants brought a branch of hyssop, which Jesus dipped into it. Then stepping to the door of the hall, he signed the two posts and the lock with the blood, and stuck the bloody branch above the lintel. He then uttered some solemn words, saying among other things: "The destroying angel shall pass by here. Without fear or anxiety, ye shall adore in this place when I, the true Paschal Lamb, shall have been immolated. A new era, a new sacrifice are now about to begin, and they shall last till the end of the world."

They then proceeded to the Passover hearth at the end of the hall where formerly the Ark of the Covenant reposed. There they found a fire already lighted. Jesus sprinkled the hearth with blood, and consecrated it as an altar. The rest of the blood, along with the fat, was thrown into the fire under the altar, after which, followed by the apostles, Jesus walked around the Cenacle singing psalms, and consecrated it as a new temple. During this ceremony, the doors were closed.

Meanwhile Simeon's son had prepared the lamb. It was fixed upon a spit, the forelegs fastened to a crosspiece, and the hind ones to the spit. Ah! It looked so much like Jesus on the cross! It was then, along with the three others that had been slaughtered in the temple, placed in the oven to be roasted.

All the paschal lambs of the Jews were immolated in the forecourt of the temple, in one of three different places, according as their owners were rich, or poor, or strangers.[†] That of Jesus was not slaughtered in the temple, though he observed all other points of the Law most strictly. That lamb was only a figure. Jesus himself would on the next day become the true Paschal Lamb.

Jesus next gave the apostles an instruction upon the paschal lamb and the fulfillment of what it symbolized, and as the time was drawing near and Judas had returned, they began to prepare the tables. After that they put on the traveling dresses of ceremony, which were in the anteroom, and changed their shoes. The dress consisted of a white tunic like a shirt, and over it a mantle, shorter in front than in the back. The tunic was tucked up into the girdle, and the wide sleeves were turned up. Thus equipped, each set went to its own table: the two bands of disciples into the side halls, Jesus and the apostles into the Cenacle proper. Each took a staff in his hand, and then they walked in pairs to the table at which each stood in his place, his arms raised, and the staff resting upon one. Jesus stood in the center of the table. He had two small staves that the master of the feast had presented to him. They were somewhat crooked on top, and looked like short shepherd crooks. On one side they had a hook, like a cut-off branch. Jesus stuck them into his girdle crosswise on his breast, and when praying, supported his raised arms on the hooks. It was a most touching sight to see Jesus leaning on these staves as he moved. It was as if he had the cross, whose weight he would soon take upon his shoulders, now supporting him under the arms. Meanwhile all were chanting, "Blessed be the Lord God of Israel," "Praised be the Lord," etc. When the prayer was ended, Jesus gave one of the staves to Peter, the other to John. They put them aside, or passed them from hand to hand among the other apostles, but what this signified, I cannot now recall.

The table was narrow and only high enough to reach one-half foot above the knee of a man standing by it. In form it was like a horseshoe; and opposite Jesus, in the inner part of the half-circle, there was a space left free for the serving of the dishes. As far as I can remember, John, James the Greater, and James the Less stood on Jesus's right; then came Bartholomew, still on the right, but more toward the narrow end of the table; and round the corner at the inner side stood Thomas, and next to him Judas Iscariot. On Jesus's left were Peter, Andrew, and Thaddeus; then as on the opposite side, came Simon; and round at the inner side, Matthew and Philip.

† Anne Catherine here explained the manner in which the families assembled together, and in what numbers, but Clemens Brentano says he had forgotten her words.

Peter and John See the Man Bearing a Pitcher

The Last Supper

The Last Passover Supper

In the center of the table lay the paschal lamb on a dish, its head resting on the crossed forefeet, the hind feet stretched out at full length. All around the edge of the dish were little bunches of garlic. Nearby was another dish with the Passover roast meat, and on either side a plate of green herbs. These latter were arranged in an upright position and so closely together that they looked as if they were growing. There was another plate with little bunches of bitter herbs that looked like aromatic herbs. Directly in front of Jesus's place stood a bowl of yellowish-green herbs, and another with some kind of a brownish sauce. Small round loaves served the guests for plates, and they made use of bone knives.

After the prayer, the master of the feast laid on the table in front of Jesus the knife for carving the paschal lamb, placed a cup of wine before him, and from a jug filled six other cups, each of which he set between two of the apostles. Jesus blessed the wine and drank, the apostles drinking two by two from one cup. The Lord cut up the paschal lamb. The apostles in turn reached for their little loaves on some kind of an instrument that held them fast, and received each one a share. They ate it in haste, separating the flesh from the bone with their ivory knives, and the bones were afterward burned. They ate also, and that very quickly, the garlic and green herbs, first dipping them into the sauce. They ate the paschal lamb standing, leaning a little on the back of the seats. Jesus then broke one of the loaves of unleavened bread, covered up one part of it, and divided the other among the apostles. After that they ate the little loaves that had served as plates. Another cup of wine was brought. Jesus gave thanks, but drank not of it. He said: "Take this wine and divide it among you, for I shall henceforth drink no more wine, until the kingdom of God cometh." After the apostles had drunk, two by two, they chanted, and Jesus prayed and taught. After that they again washed their hands, and then reclined on the seats. During the preceding ceremony, they had been standing, or at least supporting themselves somewhat, and everything was done in haste. Jesus had also cut up another lamb, which was carried to the holy women in the side building where they were taking their meal. The apostles partook of the herbs, the salad, and the sauce. Jesus was exceedingly serene and recollected, more so than I ever before saw him. He bade the apostles forget their cares. Even the blessed Virgin was bright and cheerful as she sat at table with the women. It was very touching to see her turning so simply to the other women when, at times, they approached her and drew her attention by a little pull at her veil.

While the apostles were eating the herbs, Jesus continued to converse with them still quite lovingly, though he afterward became grave and sad. He said: "One among you will betray me—one whose hand is with me in the dish." He was at that moment distributing one of the vegetables, namely, the lettuce of which there was only one dish. He was passing it down his own side, and he had directed Judas, who was sitting crosswise from him, to distribute it on the other side. As Jesus made mention of a traitor, the apostles became very much alarmed. Then he repeated: "One whose hand is with me at table, or whose hand dips with me into the dish," which was as much as to say: "One of the twelve who are eating and drinking with me—one with whom I am breaking my bread." By these words, Jesus did not betray Judas to the others, for "to dip into the same dish" was a common expression significant of the most intimate friendship. Still Jesus intended by it to warn Judas, for he really was dipping his hand with him into the dish while distributing the lettuce. Later on, he said: "The Son of Man indeed goeth as it is written of him, but woe to that man by whom the Son of Man shall be betrayed! It were better for him had he never been born."

At these words the apostles became very much troubled, and asked in turn: "Lord, is it I?" for all knew well that they did not understand him perfectly. Peter meantime, leaning behind Jesus toward John, motioned to him to ask the Lord who it was, for having often received reproofs from Jesus, he was anxious lest it might be himself. Now, John was reclining at Jesus's right, and as all were leaning on the left arm in order to eat with the right hand, John lay with his head close to Jesus's breast. At the sign from Peter, John approached his head to Jesus's breast, and asked: "Lord, who is it?"—at which word he was interiorly admonished that Jesus referred to Judas. I did not see Jesus saying with his lips: "He to whom I shall give the morsel dipped," and I cannot say whether or not he said it softly to John. But John understood it when Jesus, having dipped into the sauce the morsel of bread folded in lettuce, offered it affectionately to Judas, who too was asking, "Lord, is it I?" Jesus looked at him lovingly and answered in general terms. To give bread dipped was a mark of love and confidence, and Jesus did it with heartfelt love, to warn Judas and to ward off the suspicions of the others. But Judas was interiorly inflamed with rage. During the whole meal I saw sitting at his feet a little monster, which frequently rose to his heart. I did not see John repeating to Peter what he had learned from Jesus, though I saw him setting his mind at rest by a glance.

The Washing of the Feet

THEY arose from table and, while putting on and arranging their robes, as was the custom before solemn prayer, the master of the feast with two servants came in to take away the table and put back the seats. While this was being done, Jesus ordered some water to be brought him in the ante-room, and the master again left the hall with his servants.

Jesus, standing in the midst of the apostles, spoke to them long and solemnly. But I have seen and heard so many things that it is not possible for me to give the Lord's discourse exactly. I remember that he spoke of his kingdom, of his going to his Father, and he told them that he would, before leaving them, give over to them all that he possessed. Then he gave them instructions upon penance, the knowledge and confession of sin, contrition, and justification. I felt that this bore some reference to the washing of the feet, and I saw that all, with the exception of Judas, acknowledged their sins with sorrow. This discourse was long and solemn. When it was ended, Jesus sent John and James the Less to bring the water from the anteroom, and directed the others to place the seats in a half-circle. Meantime, he himself retired to the anteroom to lay aside his mantle, gird up his robe, and tie around him a towel, one end of which he allowed to hang.

While these preparations were being made, the apostles got into a kind of dispute as to who among them should have the first place, for as the Lord had expressly announced that he was about to leave them and that his kingdom was near, they were strengthened anew in their idea that he had somewhere a secret force in reserve, and that he would achieve some earthly triumph at the very last moment.

Jesus, still in the anteroom, commanded John to take a basin, and James the Less a leathern bottle of water. The latter carried the bottle before his breast, the spout resting on his arm. After he had poured some water from the bottle into the basin, Jesus bade the two follow him into the hall in the center of which the master of the feast had set another large, empty basin.

Entering the hall in this order, Jesus in a few words reproved the apostles for the strife that had arisen among them. He said among other things that he himself was their servant, and that they should take their places on the seats for him to wash their feet. They obeyed, observing the same order as at table. They sat on the backs of the seats, which were arranged in a half-circle, and rested their naked feet upon the seat itself. Jesus went from one to another and, from the basin held under them by John, with his hand scooped up water over the feet presented to him. Then taking in both hands the long end of the towel with which he was girded, he passed it over the feet to dry them, and then moved on with James to the next. John emptied the water after each one into the large basin in the center of the room, and then returned to the Lord with the empty one. Then Jesus again poured water from the bottle held by James over the feet of the next, and so on.

During the whole of the Passover Supper, the Lord's demeanor was most touching and gracious, and at this humble washing of his apostles' feet, he was full of love. He did not perform it as if it were a mere ceremony, but like a sacred act of love springing straight from the heart. By it he wanted to give expression to the love that burned within.

When he came to Peter, the latter, through humility, objected. He said: "Lord, dost thou wash my feet?" And the Lord answered: "What I do, thou knowest not now, but thou shalt know hereafter." And it appeared to me that he said to him in private: "Simon, thou hast deserved that my Father should reveal to thee who I am, whence I came, and whither I go. Thou alone hast known and confessed it, therefore I will build my church upon thee, and the gates of hell shall not prevail against it. My power shall continue with thy successors till the end of the world." Here Jesus pointed to Peter while saying to the others: "Peter shall be my representative with you when I shall have gone from among you. He shall direct you and make known to you your mission." Then said Peter: "Never shalt thou wash my feet!" And the Lord replied: "If I wash thee not, thou shalt have no part with me!" Thereupon, Peter exclaimed: "Lord, wash me—not only my feet, but also my hands and my head!" To which Jesus replied: "He that is washed needeth not but to wash his feet, but is clean wholly. And you are clean, but not all." At these last words, Jesus was thinking of Judas.

In his instruction, Jesus had spoken of the washing of the feet as of a purification from daily faults, because the feet, coming in continual contact with the earth in walking, are constantly liable to become soiled. This was a spiritual foot-washing, a kind of absolution. Peter, however, in his zeal, looked upon it as too great a humiliation for his Master. He knew not that to save him, Jesus would the next day humble himself for love of him to the shameful death of the cross.

When Jesus washed Judas's feet, it was in the most touching and loving manner. He pressed them to his cheek and in a low tone bade him enter into himself, for that he had been unfaithful and a traitor for the past year. But Judas appeared not to notice, and addressed some words to John. This roused Peter's anger, and he exclaimed: "Judas, the Master is speaking to thee!" Then Judas made some vague, evasive remark, such as: "Lord, far be it from me!" Jesus's words to Judas had passed unremarked by the other apostles, for he spoke softly, and they did not hear. They were, besides, busy putting on their sandals. Judas's treachery caused Jesus more pain than any other part of his Passion. Jesus then washed the feet of John and James; first those of the latter while Peter held the water bottle; then the former, for whom James held the basin.

Jesus next delivered an instruction upon humiliation. He told them that he who was the greatest among them should be the servant, and that for the future they should in humility wash one another's feet. Many other things he said bearing reference to their dispute as to who should be the greatest, as is recorded in the Gospel. Jesus now resumed the garments that he had laid aside, and the apostles let down theirs that had been girded up for the eating of the paschal lamb.

The Institution of the Most Blessed Sacrament

AT the command of the Lord, the master of the feast again set out the table, which he raised a little higher. It was placed in the middle of the room and covered with a cloth, over which two others were spread, one red, and the other white and transparent. Then the master set two jugs, one of water, the other of wine, under the table.

Peter and John now brought from the back part of the hall, where was the paschal hearth, the chalice they had brought from Veronica's house. They carried it between them in its case, holding it on their hands, and it looked as if they were carrying a tabernacle. They placed the case on the table before Jesus. The plate with the ribbed Passover loaves, thin and whitish, stood near under a cover, and the other half of the loaf that had been cut at the Passover supper was also on the table. There was a wine and water vessel, also three boxes, one with thick oil, another with liquid oil, and a third empty. A spatula, or flat knife, lay near.

The breaking and distributing of bread and drinking out of the same cup were customary in olden times at feasts of welcome and farewell. They were used as signs of brotherly love and friendship. I think there must be something about it in the scriptures. Today Jesus elevated this custom to the dignity of the most holy Sacrament, for until now it was only a typical ceremony. One of the charges brought before Caiaphas on the occasion of Judas's treason was that Jesus had introduced something new into the Passover cere-monies, but Nicodemus proved from scrip-ture that this was an ancient practice at farewell feasts.

Jesus's place was between Peter and John. The doors were closed, for everything was conducted with secrecy and solemnity. When the cover of the chalice had been removed and taken back to the recess in the rear of the Cenacle, Jesus prayed and uttered some very solemn words. I saw that he was explaining the Last Supper to the apostles, as also the ceremonies that were to accompany it. It reminded me of a priest teaching others the Holy Mass.

Jesus then drew from the flat board upon which the vessels stood a kind of shelf, took the white linen that was hanging over the chalice, and spread it on the shelf. I saw him next take a round, flat plate from the chalice and place it on the covered shelf. Then taking the loaves from the covered plate nearby, he laid them on the one before him. The loaves were four-cornered and oblong, in length sufficient to extend beyond the edge of the plate, though narrow enough to allow it to be seen at the sides.

Then he drew the chalice somewhat nearer to himself, took from it the little cup that it contained, and set to the right and left the six smaller vessels that stood around it.

He next blessed the Passover loaves and, I think, the oil also that was standing near, elevated the plate of bread with both hands, raised his eyes toward heaven, prayed, offered, set it down on the table, and again covered it. Then taking the chalice, he received into it wine and water, the former poured by Peter, and the latter by John. The water he blessed before it was poured into the chalice. He then added a little more water from the small spoon, blessed the chalice, raised it on high, praying and offering, and set it down again.

After that Jesus held his hands over the plate upon which the loaves had lain, while at his bidding Peter and John poured water on them; then with the spoon that he had taken from the foot of the chalice, he scooped up some of the water that had flowed over his own hands, and poured it upon theirs. Lastly, that same plate was passed around, and all the apostles washed their hands in it. I do not know whether these ceremonies were performed in this precise order, but these and all the others that reminded me so much of the Holy Mass, I looked upon with deep emotion.

During all this time Jesus was becoming more and more recollected. He said to the apostles that he was now about to give them all that he possessed, even his very self. He seemed to be pouring out his whole being in love, and I saw him becoming perfectly transparent. He looked like a luminous apparition.

In profound recollection and prayer, Jesus next broke the bread into several morsels and laid them one over another on the plate. With the tip of his finger he broke off a scrap from the first morsel and let it fall into the chalice, and at the same moment I saw, as it seemed to me, the blessed Virgin receiving the blessed sacrament, although she was not present in the Cenacle. It seemed to me that I saw her enter at the door and come before the Lord to receive the blessed sacrament, after which I saw her no more.

Again Jesus prayed and taught. His words, glowing with fire and light, came forth from his mouth and entered into all the apostles, excepting Judas. He took the plate with the morsels of bread (I do not remember whether he had placed it on the chalice or not) and said, "Take and eat. This is my body which is given for you." While saying these words, he stretched forth his right hand over it, as if giving a blessing, and as he did so, a brilliant light emanated from him. His words were luminous as also the bread, which as a body of light entered the mouth of the apostles. It was as if Jesus himself flowed into them. I saw all of them penetrated with light, bathed in light. Judas alone was in darkness. Jesus presented the bread first to Peter, then to John, and next made a sign to Judas, who was sitting diagonally from him, to approach. Thus Judas was the third to whom Jesus presented the blessed sacrament, but it seemed as if the word of the Lord turned back from the mouth of the traitor. I was so terrified at the sight that I cannot describe my feelings. Jesus said to Judas: "What thou art about to do, do quickly." The Lord then administered the blessed sacrament to the rest of the apostles, who came up two by two, each one holding for his neighbor a little, stiff cover with an ornamental edge that had lain over the chalice.

Jesus next raised the chalice by its two handles to a level with his face, and pronounced into it the words of consecration. While doing so, he was wholly transfigured and, as it were, transparent. He was as if passing over into what he was giving. He caused Peter and John to drink from the chalice while yet in his hands, and then he set it down. With the little spoon, John removed some of the sacred blood from the chalice to the small cups, which Peter handed to the apostles who, two by two, drank from the same cup. Judas also (though of this I am not quite certain) partook of the chalice, but he did not return to his place, for he immediately left the Cenacle. The others thought that Jesus had given him some commission to execute. He left without prayer or thanksgiving. And here we may see what an evil it is to fail to give thanks for our daily bread and for the Bread that endures to life eternal. During the whole meal I saw a little red monster with one foot like a bare bone sitting at Judas's feet and often rising up to his heart, but when outside the door, I saw three devils pressing around him. One entered into his mouth, one urged him on, and the third ran in front of him. It was night. They seemed to be lighting him as he hurried on like a madman.

The remains of the sacred blood in the chalice, the Lord poured into the small cup that fitted into it; then holding his fingers over the chalice, he bade Peter and John pour water and wine upon them. This ablution he gave to the two to drink from the chalice and, pouring what remained into the smaller cups, passed it down among the rest of the apostles. After that Jesus wiped out the chalice, put into it the little cup with what was left of the sacred blood, laid upon it the plate with the remains of the consecrated Passover bread, re-placed the cover, wrapped the whole in the linen cloth, and deposited it in its case among the smaller cups. After the resurrection, I saw the apostles partaking of communion from this bread and wine consecrated by Jesus.

I do not remember having seen the Lord himself receive the sacred species. I must have let that pass unnoticed. When he administered his body and blood to the apostles, it appeared to me as if he emptied himself, as if he poured himself out in tender love. It is inexpressible. Neither did I see Melchizedek, when sacrificing bread and wine, receive it himself. It was given me to know why priests partake of the sacrifice, although Jesus did not.

(While uttering these words, Anne Catherine glanced quickly around, as if listening to someone. She received an explanation on the above, but was able to communicate the following only:

Had angels been deputed to administer the Holy Eucharist, they would not receive it, but if priests did not partake of it, it would long since have been lost. It is by their participation that the sacrament is preserved.

Jesus's movements during the institution of the most blessed sacrament were measured and solemn, preceded and followed by explanations and instructions. I saw the apostles after each noting down some things in the little parchment rolls that they carried about them. Jesus's turning to the right and left was full of gravity, as he always was when engaged in prayer. Every action indicated the institution of the Holy Mass. I saw the apostles, when approaching one another and in other parts of it, bowing as priests are wont to do.)

Private Instructions and Consecrations

JESUS now gave to the apostles an instruction full of mystery. He told them how they were to preserve the blessed sacrament in memory of him until the end of the world, taught them the necessary forms for making use of and communicating it, and in what manner they were by degrees to teach and make known the mystery. He told them likewise when they were to receive what remained of the consecrated species, when to give some to the blessed Virgin, and how to consecrate it themselves after he should have sent them the Comforter. Then he instructed them upon the priest-hood, the sacred unction, and the preparation of the Chrism and the Holy Oils.[†] Three boxes, two with a mixture of balsam and oil, also some raw cotton, stood near the chalice case. They were so formed as to admit being placed one on the other. Jesus taught many secret things concerning them: how to mix the ointment, what parts of the body to anoint, and upon what occasions. I remember among other things Jesus's mentioning a certain case in which the blessed sacrament could not be administered. Perhaps it was something bearing reference to extreme unction, though I do not now know clearly. He spoke of different kinds of anointing, among them that of kings. He said that even wicked kings who were anointed possessed a certain interior and mysterious power that was wanting to others. Then Jesus put some of the viscous ointment and oil into the empty box and mixed them together, but I cannot say whether it was at this moment or at the consecration of the bread and wine that the Lord blessed the oil.

After that I saw Jesus anointing Peter and John, on whose hands, at the institution of the blessed sacrament, he had poured the water that had flowed over his own, and who had drunk from the chalice in his hand.

From the center of the table, where he was standing, Jesus stepped a little to one side and imposed hands upon Peter and John, first on their shoulders and then on their head. During this action they joined their hands and crossed their thumbs. As they bowed low before him (and I am not sure that they did not kneel) the Lord anointed the thumb and forefinger of each of their hands with Chrism, and made the sign of the cross with it on their head. He told them that this anointing would remain with them to the end of the world. James the Less, Andrew, James the Greater, and Bartholomew, were likewise consecrated. I saw too that the Lord twisted crosswise over Peter's breast the narrow scarf that he wore around his neck, but that on the others he drew it across the breast over the right shoulder and under the left arm. Still I do not remember clearly whether this took place at the institution of the blessed sacrament, or not till the anointing.

Then I saw—but how, I cannot say—that Jesus at this anointing com-

† Earlier editions include at this point the following note: "It was not without surprise that the editor, some years after these things had been related by Anne Catherine, read, in the Latin edition of the Roman Catechism (Mayence, Muller), in reference to the sacrament of confirmation, that, according to the tradition of the holy Pope Fabian, Jesus taught his apostles in what manner they were to prepare the Holy Chrism, after the institution of the blessed sacrament. The Pope says this expressly, in the 54th paragraph of his *Second Epistle to the Bishops of the East*: 'Our predecessors received from the apostles and delivered to us that our Savior Jesus Christ, after having made the Last Supper with his apostles and washed their feet, taught them how to prepare the Holy Chrism.'"

municated to the apostles something essential, something supernatural. He told them also that after they should have received the Holy Spirit they were to consecrate bread and wine for the first time, and anoint the other apostles. At these words of Jesus, I saw at a glance Peter and John, on the day of Pentecost and before the great baptism, imposing hands upon the other apostles, and eight days later upon several of the disciples. I saw also that John, after the resurrection, gave the most blessed sacrament to the blessed Virgin for the first time. This event used to be commemorated by the apostles as a feast. The church no longer keeps it, but in the Church Triumphant I see the day still celebrated. In the first days after Pentecost, I saw only Peter and John consecrating the most blessed sacrament; but later the others also consecrated.

The Lord blessed fire in a brass vessel. It burned ever after, even during the long absence of the apostles. It was kept near the spot in which the blessed sacrament was deposited, in one division of the ancient paschal hearth whence it was always removed for religious purposes.

All that Jesus did at the institution of the blessed Eucharist and the anointing of the apostles was done very secretly, and was later on taught as a mystery. It has to this day remained essentially in the church, though she has, under the inspiration of the Holy Spirit, developed it according to her needs.

During the preparing and consecrating of the Holy Chrism, the apostles lent their aid, and when Jesus anointed and imposed hands upon them, it was done with ceremony.

Whether Peter and John were both consecrated bishops, or Peter alone as bishop and John as priest, and what dignity the four others received, Sister Emmerich forgot to state. But the different way in which the Lord arranged the narrow scarf on Peter and the others seems to indicate different degrees of consecration.

When these holy ceremonies were concluded, the chalice, near which stood the consecrated Chrism, was recovered, and the blessed sacrament carried by Peter and John into the back part of the room. This portion of the hall was cut off from the rest by a curtain that opened in the middle, and it now became the Holy of Holies. The blessed sacrament was deposited back of and a little above the paschal oven. Joseph of Arimathea and Nicodemus always took care of the sanctuary and the Cenacle in the apostles' absence.

Jesus again delivered a long instruction and prayed several times with deep recollection. He often appeared to be conversing with his heavenly Father, and to be overflowing with love and enthusiasm. The apostles also were full of joy and zeal. They asked questions about different things, all of which Jesus answered. Of all this, I think many things are recorded in the holy scriptures. During this discourse Jesus addressed some words in private to Peter and John, who were sitting next to him, in reference to some of his earlier instructions. They were to communicate them to the other apostles, and these in turn to the disciples and holy women, according to the capacity of each for such knowledge. He spoke for some time to John alone. Of this I remember only that Jesus told him that his life would be longer than that of the others, and that he said something about seven churches, something about crowns and angels and similar significant symbols by which, as well as I know, he designated certain epochs. The other apostles felt slightly jealous at this special communication to John. Jesus alluded several times to his traitor, saying, "Now he is doing this, now he is doing that," and as he spoke, I saw Judas doing just what he said. When Peter vehemently protested that he would certainly remain faithful to him, Jesus said to him: "Simon, Simon! Behold Satan hath desired to have you that he may sift you as wheat. But I have prayed for you that your faith fail not; and you, being once converted, confirm your brethren." When Jesus said that whither he was going they could not follow, Peter again exclaimed that he would follow him even unto death. Jesus replied: "Amen, amen, I say to thee, before the cock crows twice, thou wilt deny me thrice!" When revealing to the apostles the trying times they were to encounter, Jesus asked, "When I sent you without purse or scrip or shoes, did you want any thing?" They answered: "No!" Then he replied: "But now he that hath a purse, let him take it, and likewise a scrip; and he that hath not, let him sell his coat and buy a sword. For I say to you, that this that is written must yet be fulfilled in me: And with the wicked was he reckoned. For the things concerning me have an end."

The apostles understood these words in a carnal sense, and Peter showed him two swords, short and broad like cleavers.

Jesus said: "It is enough. Let us go hence!" Then they recited the hymn of thanksgiving, put aside the table, and went into the anteroom.

Here Jesus met his mother, Mary Cleophas, and Magdalene, who besought him imploringly not to go to the Mount of Olives, for it was reported that he would there be arrested. Jesus comforted them in a few words, and stepped quickly past them. *It was then about nine o'clock.* They went in haste down the road by which Peter and John had come up that morning to the Cenacle, and directed their steps to the Mount of Olives.

I have indeed always seen the Passover supper and the institution of the blessed sacrament take place as just related. But I have always been so deeply affected by it that I could remember only some part of the ceremony; now, however, I have seen it more distinctly. Such a sight exhausts beyond the power of words to say; for in it one beholds the recesses of hearts, one sees the love, the constancy of the Lord, and knows at the same time all that is to befall him. It is altogether impossible under such circumstances to observe external actions closely. One is dissolved in admiration, thanksgiving, and love. One cannot comprehend the errors of others, while the ingratitude of humankind and the thought of one's own sins weigh heavily. The eating of the paschal lamb was performed by Jesus in haste and in perfect conformity to the Law. The Pharisees interspersed the ceremony with some observances of their own.

Jesus on the Mount of Olives

AS described by Anne Catherine, the moon was not quite full as Jesus, accompanied by the eleven apostles, walked through the valley of Jehosaphat up to the Mount of Olives. She recounted in detail the experiences undergone by Jesus in the Garden of Gethsemane, where his suffering began. Here he lived through, in his soul, all the future suffering of the apostles, disciples, and friends of the early church; and he also underwent the temptation which he overcame with the words: "Not my will, but thine, be done" (Luke 22:42). Around midnight Judas arrived at the Garden of Gethsemane accompanied by twenty soldiers and six officials. Judas went up to Jesus and kissed him, saying: "Hail, Master!" Jesus replied: "Judas, would you betray the Son of Man with a kiss?" (Luke 22:47–48).

There then took place the capture of Jesus. Thus began Good Friday, the last day in the earthly life of Jesus Christ. Jesus was disrobed for the crucifixion—at noon a reddish darkening appeared before the sun; Jesus was nailed to the cross at about 12:15 PM; then the cross was raised up; and at 12:30 PM the trumpets sounded forth from the temple announcing the slaying of the Passover lambs; the two criminals were crucified—the repentant one to Jesus's right and the unrepentant one to his left; dice were cast for Jesus's clothes; Jesus, after being mocked, spoke the words: "Father, forgive them, for they know not what they do!"; shortly after 12:30 PM, a darkening of the sun took place, and the heavens grew darker and darker; the repentant criminal said: "Lord, let me come to a place where you may save me; remember me when you come into your kingdom," to which Jesus replied: "Truly, I say to you, today you will be with me in paradise!"; Jesus spoke the words to his mother, Mary, "Woman, behold, this is your son; he will be more your son than if you had given birth to him," and to John he said, "Behold! This is your mother!"; toward three o'clock that afternoon Jesus called out in a loud voice:

"Eli, Eli, lama sabachtani!" which means: "My God, my God, why hast thou *forsaken me!"; Jesus spoke the words: "I thirst!"; the soldier Abenadar reached a sponge soaked in vinegar up to Jesus's mouth; Jesus spoke the words: "It is fulfilled!" followed by the words: "Father, into thy hands I commend my spirit!"; at these words Jesus died—it was just after three o'clock on that Good Friday afternoon, and an earthquake rent a gaping hole in the rock between Jesus's cross and that of the criminal to his left; the heavens were still darkened, and the radiant being of Jesus Christ descended into the gaping hole in the ground—thus began his descent into hell.*

At the resurrection at dawn on Easter Sunday, April 5, AD 33 (Nisan 16), exactly 33 ½ years less 1⅓ days had elapsed since the birth of Jesus just before midnight on Saturday/Sunday, December 6/7, 2 BC.

WHEN Jesus left the Cenacle with the eleven, his soul was already troubled and his sadness on the increase. He led the eleven to the Mount of Olives by an unfrequented path through the valley of Jehosaphat. As they left the house, I saw the moon, which was not yet quite full, rising above the mountain. While walking in the valley of Jehosaphat with the apostles the Lord said that he would one day return hither, though not poor and powerless as he then was, to judge the world. Then would men tremble with fear and cry out: "Ye mountains, cover us!" But the disciples understood him not. They thought, as several times before during the evening, that from weakness and exhaustion he was wandering in speech. Sometimes they walked on, at others stood still talking to him. He said to them: "All of you shall be scandalized in me this night. For it is written: 'I will strike the shepherd, and the sheep of the flock will be dispersed.' But after I shall be risen again, I will go before you into Galilee."

The apostles were still full of the enthusiasm and devotion inspired by the reception of the most holy Sacrament, and the loving, solemn discourse of Jesus afterward. They crowded eagerly around him and expressed their love in different ways, protesting that they never could, they never would, abandon him. But as Jesus continued to speak in the same strain, Peter exclaimed: "Although all should be scandalized in thee, I will never be scandalized in thee!" The Lord replied: "Amen, I say to thee that in this night before the cock crows, thou wilt deny me thrice." "Yea, though I should die with thee, I will not deny thee." And so said all the others. They walked and paused alternately, and Jesus's sadness continued to increase. The apostles tried to dissipate it by human arguments, assuring him that just the opposite of what he dreaded would take place. But finding their efforts vain, they grew weary, and began already to doubt and fall into temptation.

They crossed the brook Kidron, but not by the bridge over which later on Jesus was led bound, for they had taken a byway. Gethsemane on the Mount of Olives, whither they were going, was in a direct line one-half hour from the Cenacle, for it was fifteen minutes from the Cenacle to the valley of Jehosaphat, and the same distance from the latter to Gethsemane. This spot, in which during his last days Jesus had sometimes passed the night with his apostles and instructed them, consisted of a large pleasure garden surrounded by a hedge. It contained some magnificent shrubbery and a great many fruit trees. Outside the garden were a few deserted houses, open for any that might wish to lodge there. Several persons, as well as the apostles, had keys to this garden, which was used both as a place of recreation and prayer. Oftentimes, too, people that had no gardens of their own gave there their feasts and entertainments. There were in it several arbors formed of dense foliage. The Garden of Olives was separated by a road from that of Gethsemane and was higher up the mountain. It was open, being surrounded by only a rampart of earth. It was smaller than the pleasure garden of Gethsemane, a retired corner of the mountain full of grottoes, terraces, and olive trees. One side of it was kept in better order. There were seats and benches and roomy caverns, cheerful and cool. Whoever wished, might find here a place suited to prayer and meditation. The spot chosen by Jesus was the wildest.

It was about nine o'clock when Jesus reached Gethsemane with the disciples. Darkness had fallen upon the earth, but the moon was lighting up the sky. Jesus was very sad. He announced to the apostles the approach of danger, and they became uneasy. Jesus bade eight of them to remain in the Garden of Gethsemane, where there was a kind of summerhouse built of branches and foliage. "Remain here," he said, "while I go to my own place to pray." He took Peter, John, and James the Greater with him, crossed the road, and went on for a few minutes, until he reached the Garden of Olives farther up the mountain. He was inexpressibly sad, for he felt his approaching agony and temptation. John asked how he, who had always consoled them, could now be so dejected. He replied: "My soul is sorrowful even unto death." He glanced around and on all sides saw anguish and temptation gathering about him like dense clouds filled with frightful pictures. It was at that moment he said to the three apostles: "Remain here and watch with me. Pray lest ye enter into temptation!" and they stayed in that place. Jesus went a few steps forward. But the frightful visions pressed around him to such a degree that, filled with alarm, he turned to the left from the apostles and plunged down into a grotto formed by an overhanging rock. The apostles remained in a hollow to the right above. The grotto in which Jesus concealed himself was about six feet deep. The earth sank gently toward the back, and plants and shrubs hanging from the rocks towering over the entrance made it a place into which no eye could penetrate.

When Jesus left the apostles, I saw a great number of frightful figures surrounding him in an ever-narrowing circle. His sorrow and anguish increased. He withdrew tremblingly into the back of the cave, like one seeking shelter from a violent tempest, and there he prayed. I saw the awful visions following him into the grotto, and becoming ever more and more distinct. Ah! It was as if that narrow cave encompassed the horrible, the agonizing vision of all the sins, with their delights and their punishments, committed from the Fall of our first parents till the end of the world; for it was here on the Mount of Olives that Adam and Eve, driven from Paradise, had first descended upon the inhospitable earth, and in that very grotto had they in fear and alarm bewailed their misery. I felt in a most lively manner that Jesus, in resigning himself to the sufferings that awaited him and sacrificing himself to divine Justice in satisfaction for the sins of the world, caused in a certain manner his divinity to return into the most holy Trinity. This he did in order—out of infinite love, in his most pure and sensitive, his most innocent and true humanity, supported by the love of his human heart alone—to devote himself to endure for the sins of the world the greatest excess of agony and pain. To make satisfaction for the origin and development of all kinds of sin and guilty pleasures, the most merciful Jesus, through love for us sinners, received into his own heart the root of all expiatory reconciliation and saving pains. He allowed those infinite sufferings in satisfaction for endless sins, like a thousand-branched tree of pain, to pierce through, to extend through all the members of his sacred body, all the faculties of his holy soul. Thus entirely given up to his humanity, he fell on his face, calling upon God in unspeakable sorrow and anguish. He saw in countless forms all the sins of the world with their innate hideousness. He took all upon himself and offered himself in his prayer to satisfy the justice of his heavenly Father for all that guilt by his own sufferings. But Satan who, under a frightful form and with furious mockery, moved around among all this abomination, became at each moment more violently enraged against him. He evoked before the eyes of his soul visions of the sins of men, one more frightful than the other, and constantly addressed to the sacred humanity of Jesus such words as, "What! Wilt thou take this also upon thyself? Art thou ready to endure its penalty? How canst thou satisfy for this?"

From that point in the heavens in which the sun appears between ten and eleven in the morning, a narrow path of light streamed toward Jesus, and on it I saw a file of angels coming down to him. They imparted to him fresh strength and vigor. The rest of the grotto was filled with the frightful and horrible visions of sin, and with the evil spirits mocking and tempting. Jesus took all upon himself. In the midst of this confusion of abomination, his heart, the only one that loved God and man perfectly, shrank in terror and anguish from the horror, the burden of all those sins. Ah, I saw there so many things! A whole year would not suffice to relate them!

When now this enormous mass of sin and iniquity had passed before the soul of Jesus in an ocean of horrible visions and he had offered himself as the expiatory sacrifice for all, had implored that all their punishment and chastisement might fall upon him, Satan, as once before in the desert, brought forward innumerable temptations; yes, he even dared to allege a crowd of accusations against the innocent Savior himself. "What!" said he to him, "wilt thou take all this upon thee, and thou art not pure thyself? See, here and here and here!" and he unfolded all kinds of forged bonds and notes before him, and with infernal impudence held them up under his eyes. He reproached him with all the faults of his disciples, all the scandal they had given, all the disturbances and disorder he had caused in the world by abolishing ancient customs. Satan acted like the most crafty and subtle Pharisee. He reproached Jesus with causing Herod's massacre of the Holy Innocents, with exposing his parents to want and danger in Egypt, with not having rescued John the Baptist from death, with bringing about disunion in many families, with having protected degraded people, refusing to cure certain sick persons, with injuring the Gergeseans by permitting the possessed to overturn their vats and their swine to rush into the sea. He accused him of the guilt of Mary Magdalene, since he had not prevented her relapse into sin; of neglecting his own family; of squandering the goods of others; and, in one word, all that the tempter would at the hour of death have brought to bear upon an ordinary mortal who, without a high and holy intention, had been mixed up in such affairs, Satan now suggested to the trembling soul of Jesus with the view of causing him to waver. It was hidden from him that Jesus was the Son of God, and he tempted him as merely the most righteous of men.

Yes, our divine Redeemer permitted, in a certain measure, his most holy humanity to veil his divinity, that he might endure those temptations that come upon the holiest souls at the hour of death respecting the intrinsic merit of their good works. That he might drain the chalice of suffering, he permitted the tempter, from whom his divinity was hidden, to upbraid him with his works of beneficence as so many sins incurring penalty and not yet blotted out by the grace of God. The tempter reproached him likewise for desiring to atone for the sins of others, although he was himself without merit and had not yet made satisfaction to God for the grace of many a so-called good work. The divinity of Jesus allowed the wicked fiend to tempt his sacred humanity just as he would tempt a man who might have ascribed his good works to some special merit of their own, independent of that which they can acquire by being united with the merits of the saving death of our Lord and Savior. Thus the tempter called up before Jesus all the works of his love as not only without merit for himself, but as so many crimes against God; and as their value was, in a certain measure, derived from the merits of his Passion not yet perfected and of whose worth Satan was ignorant, therefore for the grace by which he effected them he had not yet made satisfaction. For all his good works, Satan showed Jesus written bonds, telling him as he pointed to them: "For this action and for this also, hast thou incurred indebtedness." At last he unrolled before him a note that he had received from Lazarus for the sale of Magdalene's property in Magdalum, and the proceeds of which he had expended. Satan accompanied the action with these words: "How darest thou squander the property of others and thereby injure the family?" I saw in vision all those things for which the Lord offered himself in atonement, and with him I bore the burden of many of the accusations that the tempter made against him; for among those visions of the sins of the world that the Savior took upon himself I saw my own numerous transgressions. From the cloud of temptations that encircled Jesus, I saw a stream flow toward myself, and in it were shown me, to my great consternation, all my defects of omission and commission. Still, I kept my eyes turned toward my Lord, I struggled and prayed with him, and with him I turned to the consoling angels. Ah! The Lord writhed like a worm under the weight of his sorrow and agony.

It was with the greatest difficulty that I restrained myself while all these charges were brought against the innocent Savior. I was so enraged against Satan. But when he exhibited the note holding Jesus amenable for distributing the proceeds of Magdalene's property, I could no longer subdue my anger, and I exclaimed: "How canst thou charge Jesus with the sale of Magdalene's property as with a crime? I saw myself how the Lord devoted that sum received from Lazarus to works of mercy, how he released with it twenty-seven poor, abandoned creatures held prisoners for debt at Thirza."

At first Jesus knelt calmly in prayer, but after awhile his soul shrank in affright from the multitude and heinousness of man's sins and ingratitude against God. So overpowering was the sadness, the agony of heart which fell upon him that, trembling and shuddering, he prayed imploringly: "Abba, Father, if it be possible, remove this chalice from me! My Father, all things are possible to thee. Take this chalice from me!" Then recovering himself, he added: "But not what I will, but what thou wilt." His will and the Father's were one. But now that through love he had delivered himself up to the weakness of his human nature, he shuddered at the thought of death.

I saw the grotto around him filled with frightful figures. I saw the sins, the wickedness, the vices, the torments, the ingratitude of men torturing and crushing him, and the horror of death, the terror that he experienced as man at the greatness of the expiatory sufferings soon to come upon him. I saw pressing around him and assailing him under the form of the most hideous specters. Wringing his hands, he swayed from side to side, and the sweat of agony covered him. He trembled and shuddered. He arose, but his trembling knees could scarcely support him. His countenance was quite disfigured and almost unrecognizable. His lips were white, and his hair stood on end. *It was about half-past ten o'clock* when he staggered to his feet and, bathed in sweat and often falling, tottered rather than walked to where the three disciples were awaiting him. He ascended to the left of the grotto and up to a terrace upon which they were resting near one another supported on their arm, the back of one turned toward the breast of his neighbor. Exhausted with fatigue, sorrow, and anxiety under temptation, they had fallen asleep. Jesus went to them like a man overwhelmed with sorrow whom terror drives to the company of his friends, and also like a faithful shepherd who, though himself trembling to the utmost, looks after his herd which he knows to be in danger, for he knew that they too were in anguish and temptation. All along this short distance, I saw that the frightful forms never left him. When he found the apostles sleeping, he clasped his hands and, sinking down by them from grief and exhaustion, he said: "Simon, sleepest thou?" At these words, they awoke and raised him up. In his spiritual dereliction, he said: "What! Could ye not watch one hour with me?" When they found him so terrified and disfigured, so pale, trembling, and saturated with sweat, shuddering and shaking, his voice feeble and stammering, they were altogether at a loss what to think. Had he not appeared surrounded by the light so well known to them, they would not have recognized him as Jesus. John said to him: "Master! What has befallen thee? Shall I call the other disciples? Shall we take to flight?" Jesus answered: "Were I to live, teach, and work miracles for thirty-three years longer, it would not suffice for the accomplishment of what I have to fulfill before this time tomorrow. Do not call the eight! I have left them where they are because they could not see me in this suffering state without being scandalized at

You Could Not Watch with Me for One Hour

The Grotto of the Agony

me. They would fall into temptation, forget many things that I have said to them, and lose confidence in me. But you who have seen the Son of Man transfigured, may also see him in this hour of darkness and complete dereliction of soul; nevertheless watch and pray, lest ye fall into temptation, for the spirit is willing, but the flesh is weak." These last words referred both to himself and to the apostles. Jesus wished by them to exhort his followers to perseverance, and to make known to them the struggle of his human nature against death, together with the cause of his weakness. In his overpowering sorrow, he said many other things to them, and remained with them about a quarter of an hour.

Jesus returned to the grotto, his anguish on the increase. The apostles, seeing him leave them thus, stretched out their hands after him, wept, threw themselves into one another's arms, and asked: "What does this mean? What is the matter with him? He is perfectly desolate!" And then covering their heads, they began in great anxiety to pray. All thus far related occupied about one hour and a half counting from Jesus's entrance into the Garden of Olives. In the scripture it does, indeed, say: "Could you not watch one hour with me?" But these words are not to be taken according to our measure of time. The three apostles who were with Jesus had prayed at first and then slept, for, owing to distrusted speeches, they had fallen into temptation. The eight however, who had remained at the entrance, did not sleep. The anxiety that marked all of Jesus's last actions on that evening greatly disquieted them, and they wandered around the Mount of Olives seeking a hiding place for themselves.

There was little bustle in Jerusalem on this evening. The Jews were in their homes busied with preparations for the feast. The lodgings for the Passover guests were not in the neighborhood of the Mount of Olives. As I went to and fro on the road, I saw here and there friends and disciples of Jesus walking together and conversing. They appeared to be uneasy and in expectation of something. The mother of the Lord, with Magdalene, Martha, Mary Cleophas, Mary Salome, and Salome had gone from the Cenacle to the house of Mary Mark. Alarmed at the reports that she had heard, Mary and her friends went on toward the city to get some news of Jesus. Here they were met by Lazarus, Nicodemus, Joseph of Arimathea, and some relatives from Hebron, who sought to comfort Mary in her great anxiety. These friends knew of Jesus's earnest discourse in the Cenacle, some from being themselves present in the side buildings, others from having been informed of it by the disciples; but although they questioned some Pharisees of their acquaintance, yet they heard of no immediate steps against our Lord. They said, therefore, "The danger is not so great. And besides, the enemies of Jesus would make no attempt against him so near to the feast." They did not know of Judas's treachery. Mary told them how restless he had been during the past few days, and of his sudden departure from the Cenacle. He had certainly gone with treacherous intentions, for, as she said, she had often warned him that he was a son of perdition. The holy women returned to the house of Mary Mark.

When Jesus went back into the grotto carrying his load of sadness with him, he cast himself face downward on the ground, his arms extended, and prayed to his heavenly Father. And now began for his soul a new struggle, which lasted three quarters of an hour. Angels came and showed him in a long series of visions and in all its extent what he would have to endure for the atonement of sin. They showed the beauty and excellence of man, the image of God, before the Fall, along with his deformity and corruption after the Fall. They showed how every sin originates from that first sin; they pointed out the essence and significat- ion of concupiscence, its terrible effects upon the powers of the soul, as well as upon the physical well-being of man; also the essence and signification of all the sufferings entailed as chastisements by that same lusting after pleasure. They showed him, in the expiatory sufferings that awaited him, first a suffering that would reach to both body and soul, a punishment that would comprehend in its intensity all the penalty due to divine Justice for all the sins of the whole human race. Secondly, they showed him a suffering which, in order to be satisfactory, should chastise the crimes of the whole human race in that humanity which alone was sinless—namely, the most sacred humanity of the Son of God. That sacred humanity, through love, assumed all the guilt of humankind with the penalty due to it; consequently, it had also to gain the victory over man's abhorrence of pain and death. All this the angels showed Jesus, sometimes appearing in whole choirs and exhibiting row after row of pictures, and sometimes displaying only the principal features of his suf- fering. I saw them pointing with raised finger to the visions as they appeared, and without hearing any voice, I understood what they said.

No tongue can express the horror, the anguish that overwhelmed the soul of Jesus at the sight of these visions of expiatory suffering. He under- stood not only the consequence of every species of concupiscence, but also its own peculiar expiatory chastisement, the significance of all the instruments of torture connected with it; so that not only the thought of the instrument made him shudder, but also the sinful rage of him that invented it, the fury and wickedness of all that had ever used it, and the impatience of all, whether innocent or guilty, who had been tortured with it. All these tortures and afflictions Jesus perceived in an interior contemplation, and the sight filled him with such horror that a bloody sweat started from the pores of his sacred body.

While the humanity of Christ so worthy of adoration was thus agonizing and writhing under this excess of suffering, I saw among the angels a feeling of compassion for him. There seemed to be a pause, in which they appeared desirous of giving him consolation, and I saw them praying to that effect before the throne of God. For an instant, there seemed to be a struggle between the mercy and the justice of God and that love which was sacrificing itself. I had also a vision of God not as before seated upon his throne, but in a less clearly defined, though luminous, figure. I saw the divine nature of the Son in the Person of the Father and, as it were, withdrawn into his bosom. The Person of the Holy Spirit was proceeding from the Father and the Son. He was, as it were, between them, and yet there was only one God. But who can speak of such things? I had more an interior perception of all this than a vision under human forms. In it I was shown that the divine will of Christ withdrew more into the Father in order to permit his most sacred humanity to suffer all those things for whose mitigation and warding off the human will struggled and prayed in agony; so that the Godhead of Christ being one with the Father, all that for whose removal his manhood prayed to the Father, should weigh upon his humanity alone. I saw all this at the instant of the angels' sympathetic emotion, when they conceived the desire to console Jesus, who did in fact, at that same moment, receive some alleviation. But now these visions disappeared, and the angels with their soothing compassion retired from the Lord, to whose soul a new sphere of agony more violent even than the last opened up.

When the Redeemer on the Mount of Olives, as a true and real human being, delivered himself to the temptation of human abhorrence against suffering and death; when he took upon himself also the vanquishing of that abhorrence the endurance of which forms a part of every suffering, the tempter was permitted to do to him what he does to every mortal who desires to offer himself a sacrifice in any holy cause. In the first part of the Lord's agony, Satan with furious mockery set before him the immensity of the debt that he was about assuming, and he carried the temptation so far as to represent the actions of the Redeemer himself as not free from faults. After that, in this second agony, there was displayed before Jesus in all its greatness and intrinsic bitterness the expiatory suffering necessary to discharge that immense debt. This was shown him by the angels, for it belongs not to Satan to show that expiation is possible. The Father of lies and despair never exhibits to men the works of divine mercy. But when Jesus, with heartfelt abandonment to the will of his heavenly Father, had victoriously resisted these assaults, a succession of new and terrifying visions passed before his soul. He experienced that uneasiness felt by every human heart on the point of making some great sacrifice. The questioning doubt: What advantage, what return shall I reap from this sacrifice? arose in the soul of the Lord, and the sight of the awful future overwhelmed his loving heart.

Upon the first man God sent a deep sleep, opened his side, took out one of his ribs, formed from it Eve, the first woman, the mother of all the living, and conducted her to Adam. Receiving her from God, Adam exclaimed: "This now is bone of my bones and flesh of my flesh. The man shall leave father and mother, and shall cleave to his wife; and they shall be two in one flesh." This is the marriage of which it is written: "This is a great sacrament, I speak in Christ and in the church." Christ, the new Adam, was pleased to permit a sleep, the sleep of death, to come upon him on the cross. He permitted, likewise, his side to be opened that the new Eve, his virginal Bride, the Church, the Mother of all the living, might be formed from it. He willed to give her the blood of Redemption, the water of purification, and his own Spirit, the three that render testimony upon earth. He willed to bestow upon her the holy Sacraments in order that she should be a Bride pure, holy, and undefiled. He willed to be her head and we the members, bone of his bone and flesh of his flesh. In taking human nature and willing to suffer death for us, he too left Father and Mother to cleave to his Bride, the Church. He has become one flesh with her, nourishing her with the most holy Sacrament of the Altar, in which he unceasingly espouses us. He wills to remain on earth with his Bride, the Church, until we shall all in her be united to him in heaven. He has said: "The gates of hell shall not prevail against her." To exercise this immeasurable love for sinners, the Lord became man and the brother of sinners, that he might thus take upon himself the punishment of all their guilt. He had indeed contemplated with anguish the immensity of that guilt and the greatness of the expiatory sufferings due to them, but at the same time he had offered himself joyfully as a victim of expiation to the will of his heavenly Father. Now, however, he beheld the sufferings, temptations, and wounds of the future Church, his Bride, which he had purchased at so dear a price, that of his own blood, and he saw the ingratitude of man.

Before the soul of the Lord there passed in review all the future sufferings of his apostles, disciples, and friends, and the small number of the primitive church. As her numbers increased, he saw heresies and schisms entering her fold, and the sin of Adam repeated by pride and disobedience in all forms of vanity and delusive self-righteousness. The tepidity, the malice, the wickedness of innumerable Christians; the manifold lies, the deceptive subtlety of all proud teachers; the sacrilegious crimes of all wicked priests with their frightful consequences; the abomination of desolation in the kingdom of God upon earth, in the sanctuary of the thankless human race whom, amid inexpressible sufferings, he was about to redeem with his blood and his life.

The scandals of the ages down to our own day and even to the end of the world, I saw pass before Jesus's soul in an immense succession of visions: all forms of error, proud fallacies, mad fanaticism, false prophecies, obstinate heresies, all kinds of wickedness. The apostates, the self-righteous, the teachers of error, the pretended reformers, the corrupters and the corrupted of all ages, mocked and tormented him for not having been crucified according to their ideas, for not having died comfortably on the cross according to their desires, according to their fancy or caprice. They tore and divided the seamless robe of the church. Each wanted to have a Redeemer other than he who had delivered himself through love. Countless numbers ill-treated him, mocked him, disowned him. He saw countless others who, disdainfully shrugging their shoulders and wagging their heads at him, avoided his arms stretched out to save them and hurried on to the abyss which swallowed them up. He saw innumerable others who dared not openly deny him, but who turned away in disgust from the wounds of his church, which they themselves had helped to inflict. They were like the Levite passing by the poor man that had fallen among robbers. Jesus saw them abandoning his wounded Bride like cowardly, faithless children who forsake their mother in the dead of night at the approach of the thieves and murderers to whom they themselves had opened the door. He saw them hastening after the booty that had been conveyed into the wilderness, the golden vessels and the broken necklaces. He saw them pitching their tents under the wild offshoots, far away from the true vine. He saw them like wandering sheep becoming the prey of wolves, and led into unwholesome pasturage by base hirelings, instead of going into the sheepfold of the Good Shepherd who gave his life for his sheep. He saw them straying homeless, willfully closing their eyes to his city placed high upon a mountain, and which could not remain hid. He saw them scattered in the desert, driven hither and thither by changing winds among the sand drifts; but they would not see the house of his Bride, the Church, built upon a rock, with which he had promised to abide till the end of time, and against which the gates of hell shall never prevail. They would not enter through the narrow gate, because they were not willing to bend their neck. He saw them following leaders who would conduct them anywhere and everywhere, but not to the true door.

They built upon the sand perishable huts of all kinds, without altar or sacrifice, the roofs surmounted by weathercocks, according to which their doctrines were ever changing; consequently they were ever in opposition to one another, they understood not one another, they had no fixed state. He saw them, time and again, pulling down their huts and hurling the fragments against the cornerstone of the church which, however, stood unshaken. He saw many among them, although darkness reigned in their dwellings, neglecting to go to the light that was placed on the candlestick in the house of the Bride. They wandered with closed eyes around the enclosed gardens of the church by whose perfumes alone they still lived. They stretched out their arms after shadowy forms and followed wandering stars that guided them to wells without water. When on the very brink of the precipice, they heeded not the voice of the Bride calling them and, though dying with hunger, proudly and pityingly derided the servants and messengers sent to invite them to the marriage feast. They would not enter the garden, for they feared the thorns of the hedge. The Lord saw them hungering and thirsting, but without wheat or wine. They were intoxicated with self-esteem and blinded by their own lights, wherefore they persisted in declaring that the church of the Word made flesh is invisible. Jesus beheld all, grieved over all, and longed to suffer for all, even for those that do not see him, that do not carry their cross after him in his Bride, to whom he gives himself in the most holy Sacrament; in his city built upon a mountain, and which cannot remain hidden; in his church founded upon a rock and against which the gates of hell cannot prevail.

All these innumerable visions upon the ingratitude of men and their abuse of the atoning death of my Lord I saw passing before his agonized soul, sometimes in changing pictures, and again in painful reproductions of the same. I saw Satan under many frightful forms, dragging away and strangling under the eyes of the Lord men redeemed by his blood; yes, even those anointed by his Sacrament. Jesus beheld with bitter anguish all the ingratitude, the corruption of Christendom past, present, and future. While these visions were passing before him, the voice of the tempter of his humanity was constantly heard whispering: "See! Canst thou undergo such sufferings in the sight of such ingratitude?" These words, added to the mockery and the abominations that he beheld in the rapidly changing visions, pressed with such violence upon him that his most sacred humanity was crushed under a weight of unspeakable agony. Christ, the Son of Man, writhed in anguish and wrung his hands. As if overwhelmed, he fell repeatedly on his knees, while so violent a struggle went on between his human will and his repugnance to suffer so much for so thankless a race, that the sweat poured from him in a stream of heavy drops of blood to the ground. Yes, he was so oppressed that he glanced around as if seeking help, as if calling upon heaven and earth and the stars of the firmament to witness his anguish. It seemed to me that I heard him crying out: "Ah, is it possible that such ingratitude can be endured! Witness ye my extreme affliction!"

At that moment, the moon and the stars appeared suddenly to draw nearer to the earth, and I felt in that same moment that the night became brighter. I noticed on the moon what I had not seen before. It looked quite different. It was not yet quite full, though it appeared to be larger than it does to us. In its center, I saw a dark spot. It looked like a flat disc lying before it. In the center of this disc, there appeared to be an opening through which streamed light to the moon not yet full. The dark spot was like a mountain, and all around the moon was a circle of light like a rainbow.

In his sore distress, Jesus raised his voice for some instants in loud cries of anguish. I saw that the three apostles sprang up in fright. With raised hands, they listened to Jesus's cries and were on the point of hastening to him. But Peter stopped James and John, saying: "Stay here! I will go to him." And I saw him hurrying forward and entering the grotto. "Master," he cried, "what has happened to thee?"—but he paused in terror at the sight of Jesus bathed in blood and trembling with fear. Jesus made no answer, and appeared not to notice Peter. Then Peter returned to the other two, and reported that Jesus had answered him only by sighs and groans. This news increased the sorrow and anxiety of the apostles. They covered their heads and sat weeping and praying with many tears.

I turned again to my Lord in his bitter agony. The frightful visions of the ingratitude and the misdeeds of future generations whose debt he was taking upon himself, whose chastisement he was about to endure, overwhelmed him with their ever-increasing multitude and horror. His struggle against the repugnance of his human nature for suffering continued, and several times I heard him cry out: "Father, is it possible to endure all this? O Father, if this chalice cannot pass from me, may thy will be done!"

Among this throng of apparitions typical of the outrages offered to divine Mercy, I saw Satan under various abominable forms, each bearing reference to the kind of guilt then exhibited. Sometimes he appeared as a great black figure in human shape, and again as a tiger, a fox, a wolf, a dragon, a serpent; not that he really took any of these forms, but he displayed the chief characteristics of their nature joined to other hideous appearances. There was nothing in them that perfectly resembled any creature. They were symbols of discord, of abomination, of contradiction, of horror, of sin—in a word, they were diabolical shapes. And by these hellish forms, Jesus beheld innumerable multitudes of men urged on, seduced, strangled, and torn to pieces—men for whose redemption from the power of Satan he was about to enter upon the way that led to the bitter death of the cross. At first I saw the serpent but seldom, but toward the last I beheld it in gigantic form, a crown upon its head. With terrible might and leading after it immense legions of human beings from every condition of life and of every race, it prepared to attack Jesus. Armed with all kinds of engines and destructive weapons, they struggled for some moments among themselves, and then with frightful fury turned the attack upon Jesus. It was an awful spectacle. Their weapons, their swords and spears, rose and fell like flails on a boundless threshing floor, and they raged against the heavenly grain of wheat that had come upon earth to die in order to feed humankind eternally with the bread of life.

I saw Jesus in the midst of these raging multitudes, many of whom appeared to me blind. He was as much affected by the sight as if their weapons really descended upon him. I saw him staggering from side to side, sometimes standing upright, and then falling to the ground. The serpent formed the central figure in this army, which it constantly led forward to new attacks. It lashed its tail around on all sides, and all whom it felled to the earth or enveloped in its coils it strangled, tore to pieces, or devoured. Upon this I received an instruction that these multitudes that were thus tearing Jesus to pieces represented the countless number of those that in diverse ways ill-treat him who, in his divinity and humanity, body and soul, flesh and blood under the forms of bread and wine in the most blessed sacrament, dwells ever present in that mystery as their Redeemer. Among these enemies of Jesus, I recognized the offences of all kinds committed against the blessed sacrament, that living pledge of his uninterrupted personal presence with the Catholic church. I saw with horror all the outrages springing from neglect, irreverence, and omission, as also those of abuse and the most awful sacrilege. I saw those that arose from the worship of the gods of this world, from spiritual darkness and false, superficial knowledge, from error, incredulity, fanaticism, hatred, and bloody persecution. I saw all kinds of people among these enemies: the blind and the lame, the deaf and the mute, and children. There were blind who would not see the truth; the lame through sloth, who would not follow it; the deaf who would not listen to its warnings or its threats; the mute who would never, with the sword of the word, take up their Lord's defense; and in fine, children spoiled by following worldly-minded and God-forgetting parents and teachers, who were fed on earthly pleasure, who were intoxicated with empty knowledge, and who loathed divine things, though starving without them. Among these children (the sight of whom grieved me especially, because Jesus so loved children), I noticed in particular many badly instructed, badly reared, and irreverent acolytes who do not honor Christ in the Holy Mass. Their guilt falls partly upon their teachers and the careless sacristans. But with terror I saw that many of the priests themselves, both of high and low degree, yes, even some that esteem themselves full of faith and piety—contribute their share toward outraging Jesus in the blessed sacrament. Of the many whom, to my great sorrow, I thus saw, I shall say a word of warning to one class only, and it is this: I saw numbers that believe, adore, and teach the presence of the living God in the most blessed sacrament, yet who do not sufficiently take it to heart. They forget, they neglect, the palace, the throne, the canopy, the seat, and the royal adornments of the king of heaven and earth, that is, the church, the altar, the tabernacle, the chalice, the monstrance of the living God, along with all the vessels, the furniture, the decorations, the festal robes, and all that is used in his worship, or the adornment of his house. All things were ignominiously covered with dust and rust, mouldering away and, through long years of neglect, falling to ruin. The service of the living God was shamefully neglected, and where it was not inwardly profaned, it was outwardly dishonored. Nor did all this arise from real poverty, but from indifference and sloth, from following old customs, from preoccupation of mind with vain, worldly affairs, and often too from self-seeking and spiritual death. I saw neglect of this kind in rich churches and in others tolerably well-off. Yes, I saw many in which worldly love of splendor and tinseled finery had replaced the magnificent and appropriate adornments of a more devout age. What the rich in ostentatious arrogance do, the poor foolishly aim at in their poverty and simplicity. This recalls to me our poor convent chapel in which the beautiful old stone altar had been covered with wood veined to imitate marble, a fact that always gave me sorrow.

These visions of the outrages offered to Jesus in the blessed sacrament I saw multiplied by innumerable church wardens who were totally deficient in their sense of equity, who failed to share at least what they had with their Redeemer present upon the altar, although he had delivered himself to death for them, although he remains for them hidden in the Sacrament. Even the poorest creatures are often better off than the Lord of heaven and earth in his churches. Ah, how deeply did the inhospitality of men trouble Jesus, who had given himself to them as food!

The Passion and Death of Jesus Christ

Truly, riches are not necessary to entertain him who rewards a thousand-fold the glass of cold water given to the thirsty! And how great is his thirst for us! Ought he not to complain when water swarming with worms is offered him in impure glasses? By such neglect I saw the weak scandalized, the sanctuary profaned, the churches abandoned, the ministers of religion despised. This state of impurity and negligence sometimes extended even to the souls of the faithful. They kept not the tabernacle of their hearts purer to receive therein the living God than was the tabernacle of the altar. For the fawning eye-service of princes and lords of the world, and to indulge their caprice and worldly designs, I saw every means carefully and actively resorted to by these unenlightened ecclesiastics, while the king of heaven and earth lay like another Lazarus outside the gate, vainly sighing after the crumbs of love denied him. He has nothing but the wounds which we have inflicted upon him and which the dogs lick, namely, ever-relapsing sinners who like dogs vomit and return to their food.

Were I to talk a whole year, it would not suffice to recount the different outrages committed against Jesus Christ in the blessed sacrament made known to me in this way. I saw the offenders in immense crowds with weapons corresponding to the varieties of crime perpetrated by them, assaulting the Lord and striking him to the ground. I saw irreverent sacristans of all centuries, light-minded, sinful, worthless priests offering the holy Sacrifice and distributing the blessed sacrament, and multitudes of tepid and unworthy communicants. I saw countless numbers to whom the source of all blessing, the mystery of the living God, had become an oath or a curse expressive of anger, and furious soldiers and servants of the devil who profaned the sacred vessels, who threw away the most blessed sacrament, who horribly outraged it, or who dishonored it in their frightful, hellish worship of false gods. Side by side with these hideous, barbarous cruelties, I saw innumerable other forms of godlessness more refined and subtle, but not less atrocious. I saw many souls, owing to bad example and perfidious teachers, losing their faith in Jesus's promises to remain always in the blessed sacrament, and no longer humbly adoring their Savior therein present. I saw in this multitude a great many sinful teachers who became teachers of error. They first struggled against one another, and then united against Jesus in the blessed sacrament of his church. I saw a great crowd of these apostate heresiarchs disdainfully rejecting the priesthood of the church, attacking and denying Jesus Christ's presence in the mystery of the blessed sacrament in the manner in which he himself gave this mystery to the church, which has truly preserved It. By their seductive words, they tore from the heart of Jesus countless numbers for whom he had shed his blood. Ah! It was fearful to look upon! For I saw the church as the body of Jesus, its scattered members all knitted together by him in his bitter Passion. I saw all those people, all those families with their descendants that had separated from the church, torn away from Jesus like entire pieces mangled and most painfully rent from his living flesh. Ah! He glanced at them so pitifully, he moaned so gently! He who, in order to unite to the body of his church, to the body of his bride, men so separated, so divided from one another, had given himself in the blessed sacrament to be their food, saw himself in this, his bride's body, torn and lacerated through the wicked fruit of the tree of disunion. The table of union in the blessed sacrament, Jesus's highest work of love, that in which he willed to remain forever among men, became through false teachers the boundary line of separation. And where alone it is good and beneficial that many should become one, namely, at the holy table, whereon the living God is himself the food, there must his children separate from infidels and heretics in order not to render themselves guilty of similar sins. I saw whole nations torn in this way from the heart of Jesus and deprived of participation in the treasures of grace left to the church. It was frightful to behold how at first only a few separated from Christ's church; and when, having increased to whole nations, they returned to her, they again attacked her and warred against one another on the question of what was holiest in her worship, namely, the blessed sacrament. But finally, I saw all who had separated from the church plunging into infidelity, superstition, heresy, darkness, and the false philosophy of the world. Perplexed and enraged, they united in large bodies to vent their anger against the church. They were urged on and destroyed by the serpent in the midst of them. Ah! It was as if Jesus felt himself torn into countless shreds. The Lord saw and felt in this distressing vision the whole weight of the poisonous tree of disunion with all its branches and fruits, which will continue to rend itself asunder until the end of time when the wheat will be gathered into the barn and the chaff cast into the fire.

The terror that I felt in beholding all this was so great, so dreadful, that our Lord appeared to me, and mercifully laying his hand on my breast, he said: "No one has ever before seen these things, and thy heart would break with fright, did I not sustain it."

I now saw the blood in thick, dark drops trickling down the pale face of the Lord. His once smoothly parted hair was matted with blood, tangled and bristling on his head, and his beard was bloody and torn. It was after that last vision, in which the armed bands had lacerated his flesh, that he turned as if fleeing out of the grotto, and went again to his disci-

ples. But his step was far from secure. He walked bowed like one tottering under a great burden. He was covered with wounds, and he fell at
every step. When he reached the three apostles, he did not, as on the first
occasion, find them lying on their side asleep; they had sunk back on
their knees with covered head, as I have often seen the people of that
country sitting when in sorrow or in prayer. Worn out with grief, anxiety, and fatigue, they had fallen asleep; but when Jesus approached, trembling and groaning, they awoke. They gazed upon him with their weary
eyes, but did not at once recognize him, for he was changed beyond the
power of words to express. He was standing before them in the moonlight, his breast sunken, his form bent, his face pale and bloodstained, his
hair in disorder, and his arms stretched out to them. He stood wringing
his hands. The apostles sprang up, grasped him under the arms, and supported him tenderly. Then he spoke to them in deep affliction. On the
morrow, he said, he was going to die. *In another hour*, his enemies would
seize him, drag him before the courts of justice, abuse him, deride him,
scourge him, and put him to death in the most horrible manner. He
begged them to console his mother. He recounted to them in bitter
anguish all that he would have to suffer until the evening of the next day,
and again begged them to comfort his mother and Magdalene. He stood
thus speaking for some moments, but the apostles kept silence, not
knowing what to reply. They were so filled with grief and consternation
at his words and appearance that they knew not what to say; indeed,
they even thought that his mind was wandering. When he wanted to
return to the grotto, he had not the power to do so. I saw that John and
James had to lead him. When he entered it, the apostles left him and
went back to their own place. *It was then a quarter past eleven.*

During this agony of Jesus, I saw the blessed Virgin overwhelmed with
sorrow and anguish in the house of Mary Mark. She was with Magdalene and Mary Mark in a garden adjoining the house. She had sunk on
her knees on a stone slab. She was perfectly absorbed in her own interior, quite diverted in thought from everything around her, seeing only,
feeling only the sufferings of her divine Son. She had sent messengers to
obtain news of him, but unable to await their coming, in her anguish of
heart she went with Magdalene and Salome out into the valley of Jehosaphat. I saw her walking along veiled, her arms often outstretched
toward the Mount of Olives, where she saw in spirit Jesus agonizing and
sweating blood. It seemed as if she would with her outstretched hands
wipe his sacred face. In answer to these interior and vehement movements of her soul toward her Son, I saw that Jesus was stirred with
thoughts of her. He turned his eyes in her direction as if seeking help

from her. I saw this mutual sympathy under the appearance of rays of light passing to and fro between them. The Lord thought also of Magdalene and felt for her in her distress. He glanced toward her, and his soul was touched at sight of her. He therefore ordered the disciples to console her, for he knew that her love for him, after that of his mother, was greater than that of anyone else. He saw what she would have to suffer for him in the future, and also that she would never more offend him.

About this time, *perhaps a quarter after eleven*, the eight apostles were again in the arbor in the Garden of Gethsemane. They spoke together for awhile and then fell asleep. They were unusually faint-hearted, discouraged, and in sore temptation. Each had been looking out for a place of safety and anxiously asking: "What shall we do when he is dead? We have abandoned our friends, we have given up everything, we have become poor and objects of scorn to the world, we have devoted ourselves entirely to his service—and now, behold him crushed and helpless, with power to afford us no consolation!" The other disciples, after wandering about in various directions and hearing the reports of the awful prophecies to which Jesus had given utterance, nearly all retired to Bethphage.

Again I saw Jesus praying in the grotto. He had conquered the natural repugnance to suffer. Exhausted and trembling, he exclaimed: "My Father, if it be thy will, remove this chalice from me! Nevertheless, not my will but thine be done!"

And now the abyss opened before him and, as if on a pathway of light, he saw a long flight of steps leading down to Limbo. There he beheld Adam and Eve, all the patriarchs and prophets, the just of the Old Law, his mother's parents, and John the Baptist. They were with longing so intense awaiting his coming into that nether world that at the sight his loving heart grew strong and courageous. His death was to open heaven to these languishing captives! He was to deliver them from prison! For him they were sighing!

After Jesus had with deep emotion gazed upon those citizens of heaven belonging to former ages, the angels pointed out to him the multitudes of future saints who, joining their labors to the merits of his Passion, would through him be united to the heavenly Father. This vision was unspeakably beautiful and consoling. All passed before the Lord in their number, their race, and various degrees of dignity—all adorned with their sufferings and good works. Then did he behold the hidden and inexhaustible streams of salvation and sanctification that were to spring from the death that awaited him as Redeemer of humankind. The apostles, the disciples, virgins and holy women, martyrs, con-

The Passion and Death of Jesus Christ

fessors, and hermits, popes and bishops, the future multitudes of religious men and women—in a word, the immense army of the blessed passed before him. All were adorned with crowns of victory won over passion and suffering. The flowers of their crowns differed in form, color, perfume, and vigor in accordance with the various sufferings, labors, and victories in which they had gloriously struggled. Their whole lives and actions, the peculiar worth and power of their combats and victories, as well as all the light, all the colors that symbolized their triumphs, came solely from their union with the merits of Jesus Christ. The reciprocal influence and relation of all these saints upon one another, their drinking out of one same fountain, namely, the most blessed sacrament and the Passion of the Lord, was a spectacle unspeakably wonderful and touching. Nothing connected with them happened by accident: their works and omissions, their martyrdom and victories, their apparel and appearance, though all so different, yet acted upon one another in unending unity and harmony. And this perfect unity in the most striking diversity sprang from the rays of light and sparkling colors of one single Sun, from the Passion of the Lord, the Word made flesh, in whom was life, the light of men, which shone in darkness, but which the darkness did not comprehend.

It was the army of future saints that passed before the soul of the Lord. Thus stood the Lord and Savior between the ardent desires of the patriarchs and the triumphant host of future saints, which reciprocally filling up and completing one another, so to say, surrounded the loving heart of the Redeemer like an immense crown of victory. This unspeakably touching spectacle afforded the soul of the Lord, who had allowed all kinds of human suffering to pass over him, some strength and consolation. Ah, he so dearly loved his brethren, his creatures, that willingly he would have suffered all for the purchase of one soul! As these visions referred to the future, they appeared hovering above the earth.

But now these consoling pictures disappeared, and the angels displayed before his eyes all the scenes of his approaching Passion. They appeared quite close to the earth, for the time was near at hand. There were many angelic actors in these scenes. I beheld everyone close to Jesus, from the kiss of Judas to his own last words upon the cross. I saw all, all there again, as I am accustomed to see it in my meditations upon the Passion. The treason of Judas, the flight of the disciples, the mockery and sufferings before Annas and Caiaphas, Peter's denial, Pilate's tribunal, Herod's derision, the scourging and crowning with thorns, the condemnation to death, the sinking under the weight of the cross, the meeting with the blessed Virgin and her swooning, the jeers of the

HOLY THURSDAY, APRIL 2, AD 33

executioners against her, Veronica's handkerchief, the cruel nailing to the cross and the raising of the same, the insults of the Pharisees, the sorrows of Mary, of Magdalene, and of John, and the piercing of his side—in a word, all, all, clearly, significantly, and in their minutest details passed before him. All the gestures, all the sentiments, and words of his future tormentors, I saw that the Lord beheld and heard in alarm and anguish of soul. He willingly accepted all, he willingly submitted to all through love for man. He was most painfully troubled at his shameful stripping on the cross, which he endured to atone for the immodesty of men, and he implored that he might retain a girdle at least upon the cross, but even this was not allowed him. I saw, however, that he was to receive help, not from the executioners, but from a certain good person.

Jesus saw and felt also his blessed Mother's sorrow and anguish of heart. With two holy women in the valley of Jehosaphat, she was in uninterrupted union with him by her interior participation in his sufferings and agony on the Mount of Olives.

At the close of these visions of the Passion, Jesus sank prostrate on his face like one in the throes of death. The angels and the visions disappeared, and the bloody sweat poured from him more copiously than before. I saw it soaking his yellowish garment and moistening the earth around. It was now dark in the grotto.

And now I saw an angel sweeping down toward him. In stature he was taller, in figure more distinct and more like a human being than any I had yet seen. He appeared in long, flowing robes, like those of a priest, ornamented with fringe. He carried in his hands, and before his breast, a small vessel shaped like the chalice used at the Last Supper. Just above it floated a small oval morsel, about the size of a bean, which glowed with a reddish light. The angel hovered over the place where Jesus was lying and stretched forth his hand to him. When Jesus arose, he placed the shining morsel in his mouth and gave him to drink from the little luminous chalice. After that he disappeared.

Jesus had now voluntarily accepted the chalice of his Passion, and he received new strength. He remained in the grotto for a few minutes longer, absorbed in prayer and thanksgiving. He was indeed still under the pressure of mental suffering, but supernaturally strengthened to such a degree that, without fear or anxiety, he was able to walk with a firm step to his disciples. Though pale and exhausted, his bearing was erect and resolute. He had wiped his face with a linen cloth and with it smoothed down his hair which, moist with the blood and sweat of his agony, hung down in matted strands.

As he left the grotto, I saw the moon still with the remarkable-looking spot upon it and the circle around it; but its light, as well as that of the stars, was different from that which they gave forth during that great agony of Jesus. It seemed now to be more natural.

When Jesus returned to the disciples, he found them, as at first, lying on their side near the wall of the terrace, their heads covered, and asleep. The Lord said to them: "This is not the time to sleep. Ye should arise and pray, for behold the hour is at hand, and the Son of Man shall be betrayed into the hands of sinners. Arise, let us go! Behold, the traitor is approaching! Oh, it were better for him had he never been born!" The apostles sprang up affrighted and looked around anxiously. They had scarcely recovered themselves, when Peter exclaimed vehemently: "Master, I will call the others, that we may defend thee!" But Jesus pointed out to them at some distance in the valley, though still on the other side of the brook Kidron, a band of armed men approaching with torches. He told the apostles that one of that band had betrayed him. This they looked upon as impossible. Jesus repeated this and several other things with calm composure, again exhorted them to console his mother, and said: "Let us go to meet them! I shall deliver myself without resistance into the hands of my enemies." With these words, he left the Garden of Olives with the three apostles and went out to meet the soldiers on the road that separated it from the Garden of Gethsemane.

The blessed Virgin, Magdalene, and Salome, accompanied by some of the disciples who had seen the approach of the soldiers, left the valley of Jehosaphat and returned to the house of Mary Mark. Jesus's enemies came by a shorter route than that by which he had come from the Cenacle.

The grotto in which Jesus prayed that night was not the one in which he usually prayed on the Mount of Olives. The latter was a more distant cavern of the mountain. It was there that he prayed on the day upon which he cursed the fig tree. He was then in great affliction of spirit, and he prayed with outstretched arms, leaning upon a rock. The impression of his form and hands remained upon the stone, and later on became objects of veneration, although it was not clearly known upon what occasion the marks were made. I have frequently beheld such impressions left upon stone by the prophets of the Old Law, by Jesus, Mary, some of the apostles, the body of St. Catherine of Alexandria on Mount Sinai, and by some other saints. They did not appear to be deep, nor were the lines very clearly defined. They resembled the marks that might be made by pressing upon a piece of solid dough.

HOLY THURSDAY, APRIL 2, AD 33

Judas and His Band • The Wood of the Cross

AT the beginning of his treasonable career, Judas had really never looked forward to the result that followed upon it. He wanted to obtain the traitor's reward and please the Pharisees by pretending to deliver Jesus into their hands, but he had never counted on things going so far, he never dreamed of Jesus's being brought to judgment and crucified. He was thinking only of the money, and he had for a long time been in communication with some sneaking, spying Pharisees and Sadducees who by flattery were inciting him to treason. He was tired of the fatiguing, wandering, and persecuted life led by the apostles. For several months past he had begun this downward course by stealing the alms committed to his care; and his avarice, excited by Magdalene's lavish anointing of Jesus, urged him on to extremes. He had always counted upon Jesus's establishing a temporal kingdom in which he hoped for some brilliant and lucrative post. But as this was not forthcoming, he turned his thoughts to amassing a fortune. He saw that hardships and persecution were on the increase; and so he thought that before things came to the worst he would ingratiate himself with some of the powerful and distinguished among Jesus's enemies. He saw that Jesus did not become a king, whereas the high priests and prominent men of the temple were people very attractive in his eyes. And so he allowed himself to be drawn into closer communication with their agents, who flattered him in every way and told him in the greatest confidence that under any circumstances an end would soon be put to Jesus's career. During the last few days they followed him to Bethany, and thus he continued to sink deeper and deeper into depravity. He almost ran his legs off to induce the high priests to come to some conclusion. But they would not come to terms and treated him with great contempt. They told him that the time now intervening before the feast was too short. If any action were taken now, it would create trouble and disturbance on the feast. The Sanhedrin alone paid some degree of attention to his proposals. After his sacrilegious reception of the sacrament, Satan took entire possession of him and he went off at once to complete his horrible crime. He first sought those agents who had until now constantly flattered him and received him with apparent friendship. Some others joined the party, among them Caiaphas and Annas, but the last-named treated him very rudely and scornfully. They were irresolute and mistrustful of the consequences, nor did they appear to place any confidence in Judas.

I saw the kingdom of hell divided against itself. Satan desired the crime of the Jews by the death of the most innocent; he longed for the death of

The Passion and Death of Jesus Christ

Jesus, the converter of sinners, the holy teacher, the Savior, the just one, whom he hated. But at the same time he experienced a sentiment of fear at the thought of the guiltless death of Jesus, who would make no effort to conceal himself, who would not save himself; he envied him the power of suffering innocently. And so I saw the adversary on the one side stimulating the hatred and fury of Jesus's enemies assembled around the traitor; and on the other, insinuating to some of their number that Judas was a scamp, a knave, that the sentence could not be pronounced before the festival, nor could the requisite number of witnesses against Jesus be brought together.

They expressed opposite views upon the means to lay hold of Jesus, and some of them questioned Judas, saying, "Shall we be able to capture him? Has he not an armed band with him?" The base traitor answered: "No! He is alone with eleven disciples. He himself is greatly dejected and the eleven are quite faint-hearted." He told them also that now was their time to apprehend Jesus, now or never, for later he might not have it in his power to deliver him into their hands, and perhaps he would never return to them. For several days past, he said, and especially on that present day, the other disciples and Jesus himself aimed at him in their words; they appeared to divine what he was about, and if he returned to them again they would certainly murder him. He added that, if they did not seize Jesus now, he would slip away and, returning with a large army of followers, would cause himself to be proclaimed king. By such threats as these, Judas at last succeeded. They yielded to his proposals to seize Jesus according to his directions, and he received the thirty pieces of silver, the price of his treason. These thirty pieces were of silver in plates, in shape like a tongue. In one end they were pierced with a hole, through which they were strung together with rings into a kind of chain. Each piece bore some impression.

Judas could not help feeling the marked and contemptuous mistrust with which the Pharisees were treating him. Pride and ostentation therefore urged him to present to them as an offering for the temple the money he had just received. By so doing, he thought to appear before them as an upright, disinterested man. But they rejected it as the price of blood, which could not be offered in the temple. Judas felt the cutting contempt, and he was filled with smothered rage. He had not expected such treatment. The consequences of his treachery were already assailing him even before his evil design was accomplished; but he was now too much entangled with his employers, he was in their hands and could not free himself. They watched him closely and would not allow him to leave their sight until he had laid before them the whole plan to be followed in apprehending Jesus. After that, three of the Pharisees went with the traitor down into a hall in which were the soldiers of the temple. None of them were of pure Jewish origin; they were of other and mixed nationalities. When all was agreed upon and the requisite number of soldiers gathered together, Judas, accompanied by a servant of the Pharisees, ran first to the Cenacle in order to see whether Jesus was still there; for if such were the case, they could easily have taken him by setting guards at the door. This information Judas had agreed to send the Pharisees by a messenger.

A short time before, after Judas had received the price of his treason, a Pharisee had gone down and dispatched seven slaves to procure the wood and get Christ's cross ready at once in case he should be judged, for next day, on account of the Passover feast, there would be no time to attend to it. They brought the wood from a distance of about three-quarters of an hour, where it lay near a long, high wall with a quantity of other wood belonging to the temple, and dragged it to a square behind the tribunal of Caiaphas. The trunk of the cross belonged to a tree that once grew in the valley of Jehosaphat near the brook Kidron. Having fallen across the stream, it had long served as a bridge. When Nehemiah hid the sacred fire and the holy vessels in the pool of Bethesda, with other pieces of wood it had been used as a covering; later on, it was again removed and thrown on the side of another wood pile. Partly with the view of deriding the royalty of Jesus, partly by apparent chance—but in reality because such was the design of God—the cross was formed in a very peculiar way. Together with the inscription, it consisted of five different pieces. I have seen many facts, many different meanings in connection with the cross, but with the exception of what I have related, I have forgotten all.

Judas returned and reported that Jesus was no longer in the Cenacle. He must therefore be in his accustomed place of prayer on the Mount of Olives. Judas urged that only a small number of soldiers might be sent with him, lest the disciples, who were everywhere on the watch, should perceive something unusual and raise a protest. Three hundred men were to be stationed at the gates and in the streets of Ophel, a part of the city to the south of the temple, and along the valley of Millo as far as the house of Annas on Zion. They were to be in readiness to send reinforcements if necessary, for, as Judas reminded the Pharisees, Jesus counted all the rabble of Ophel among his followers. The infamous traitor told them also how careful they must be that he might not escape them, and recalled the fact of his often, by some mysterious means, suddenly becoming invisible and concealing himself in the mountains from his companions. He recommended them, moreover, to bind him with a chain and to make use of certain magical means to prevent his breaking his bonds. The Jews rejected his advice with scorn, saying: "We are not to be dictated to by you. When we get him, we shall hold him fast."

Judas arranged with the soldiers that he would enter the garden before them, kiss and salute Jesus as a friend and disciple coming to him on some business; then they were to step forward and take him into custody. He wanted to behave as if their coming coincided accidentally with his own, for he thought that after the betrayal he would take to flight like the other disciples and be heard of no more. He likewise thought that perhaps a tumult would ensue in which the apostles would defend themselves and Jesus would disappear as he had often done before. These thoughts especially occupied him now that he was thoroughly vexed at the contemptuous and distrustful manner of Jesus's enemies toward him, but not because his evil deed caused him remorse or the thought of Jesus touched him, for he had wholly given himself over to Satan.

He was very desirous also that the soldiers immediately following him should not carry chains and fetters, or that any notoriously infamous characters should appear in the party. The soldiers pretended to accede to his wishes, though in reality they regarded him as a dishonorable traitor of whom they had need, but who was not to be trusted and who was to be cast off when no longer of use. They had received special instructions to keep a close watch on him, and not to let him out of their sight and custody until they had taken Jesus and bound him; for he had received his pay and it was feared that the rascal would run off with the money and in the darkness of night they would either not capture Jesus at all, or else take another instead of him. In this case, nothing would come of their undertaking but disturbance and excitement on the Passover feast. The band that had been chosen for Jesus's apprehension was composed of about twenty soldiers, some of whom belonged to the temple guard, and others were in the employ of Annas and Caiaphas. Their dress was almost like that of the Roman soldiers. They wore helmets, and from their doublets hung leathern straps around their hips just like the Romans. The principal difference between them, however, was in their beard, for the Roman soldiers in Jerusalem wore whiskers only, their chin and upper lip being shaved. All of the twenty carried swords, and only a few were armed with spears also. Some bore lanterns mounted on long poles, while others carried torches of sticks smeared with pitch, but when they approached, only one of the lanterns was lighted. The Pharisees had intended sending a larger band with Judas, but he objected that so large a crowd would attract notice, since the

Mount of Olives commanded a view of the whole valley. The greater part of them, therefore, remained in Ophel. Sentinels were stationed around here and there on the byroads, as well as in the city, in order to prevent a tumult or any attempt at rescue.

Judas went forward with the twenty soldiers, followed at some distance by four common executioners of the lowest grade, who carried ropes and fetters. Some steps behind these came those six agents with whom Judas had for a short time past been in communication. Of these one was a priest, a confidential friend of Annas; another was devoted to Caiaphas; the third and fourth were Pharisees; and the remaining two were agents of the Sadducees and at the same time Herodians. All were spies, sneaking fellows, cringing eye-servants of Annas and Caiaphas, and in secret the most malicious enemies of the Savior. The twenty soldiers accompanied Judas in a friendly manner until they reached the place where the road divided between the Garden of Gethsemane and that of Olives. Here they refused to allow him to advance alone. They adopted quite another tone, and acted toward him insolently and saucily.

The Arrest of the Lord

WHEN Jesus with the three apostles went out upon the road between Gethsemane and the Garden of Olives, there appeared at the entrance, about twenty paces ahead, Judas and the band of soldiers, between whom a quarrel had arisen. Judas wanted to separate from the soldiers and go forward alone to Jesus, as if he were a friend returning after an absence. They were to follow, and act in such a way as to make it appear that their coming was altogether unknown to him. But they would not agree to his proposal. They held him fast, exclaiming: "Not so, friend! Thou shalt not escape us, until we have the Galilean!" And when they caught sight of the eight apostles, who at sound of the noise came forth from the Garden of Gethsemane, they called up four of the soldiers to their assistance. But this Judas by no means assented to, and a lively dispute arose between him and the soldiers. When Jesus and the three apostles, by the light of the torches, distinguished the armed and wrangling band, Peter wished to repel them by force. He exclaimed: "Lord, the eight from Gethsemane are close at hand. Let us make an attack on the soldiers!" But Jesus told him to hold his peace, and took a few steps with them back on the road to a green plot. Judas, seeing his plans quite upset, was filled with rage and spite. Just at this moment, four of the disciples issued from the Garden of Gethsemane and inquired what was going on. Judas began to exchange words with them, and would fain have cleared himself by a lie, but the guards would not allow him to go on. These four last-comers were James the Less, Philip, Thomas, and Nathaniel. The last-named, who was a son of the aged Simeon, had along with several others been sent by Jesus's friends to the eight apostles in the Garden of Gethsemane to find out what was going on. They were actuated as much by anxiety as by curiosity.

With the exception of these four, all the disciples were straggling around in the distance, furtively on the lookout to discover what they could.

Jesus took some steps toward the band and said in a loud, distinct voice: "Whom seek ye?" The leaders answered: "Jesus of Nazareth," whereupon Jesus replied: "I am he." But scarcely had he uttered the words when, as if suddenly attacked by convulsions, they crowded back and fell to the ground one upon another. Judas, who was still standing by them, became more and more embarrassed. He looked as if desirous of approaching Jesus; consequently the Lord extended his hand, saying: "Friend, whereto art thou come?" Judas, confused and perplexed, stammered out something about a commission he had executed. Jesus in reply uttered some words like the following: "Oh, how much better it would have been for thee hadst thou never been born!"—I cannot remember the words distinctly. Meanwhile the soldiers had risen and approached the Lord and his apostles, awaiting the traitor's sign, the kiss.

Peter and the other disciples gathered around Judas, calling him a thief and a traitor. He tried to free himself by all kinds of excuses, but just at that moment up came the soldiers with offers of protection, thus openly witnessing against him.

Jesus again inquired: "Whom seek ye?" Turning toward him, they again answered: "Jesus of Nazareth." Jesus again replied: "I am he. I have already told you that I am he. If you seek me, let these go." At the words, "I am he," the soldiers fell to the ground a second time. They writhed as if struck with epilepsy, and Judas was again surrounded by the other apostles, for they were exasperated to a degree against him. Jesus now called out to the soldiers: "Arise"—and they arose, full of terror. Judas was still struggling with the apostles, who were pressing up against the guards. The latter turned upon them and freed the traitor, urging him anew to give them the sign agreed upon. They had been ordered to seize no one but him whom Judas would kiss. Judas now approached Jesus, embraced him and kissed him with the words: "Hail, Rabbi!" Jesus said: "Judas, dost thou betray the Son of Man with a kiss?" The soldiers instantly formed a circle around Jesus, and, drawing near, laid hands upon him. Judas wanted at once to flee, but the apostles would not allow

The Guards Falling Backward

The Healiing of Malchus

him. They rushed upon the soldiers, crying out: "Lord, shall we strike with the sword?" Peter, more impetuous than the rest, seized the sword and struck at Malchus, the servant of the high priest, who was trying to drive them back, and cut off a piece of his ear. Malchus fell to the ground, thereby increasing the confusion.

At the moment of Peter's impetuous movement, the actors in the scene were situated as follows: Jesus was in the hands of the guard, who were about to bind him, and forming a circle around him at some little distance were the soldiers, one of whose number, Malchus, had been laid low by Peter. The other soldiers were engaged, some in driving back the disciples that were approaching too near, and some in pursuing those that had taken to flight. Four of the disciples were wandering around, timidly showing themselves only here and there in the distance. The soldiers were still too much alarmed by their late fall, and too much afraid of weakening the circle around Jesus, to make any very active pursuit. Judas, who immediately after his traitorous kiss wanted to make his escape, was met on his way by some of the disciples, who overwhelmed him with reproaches. Six official functionaries hastened to his rescue, while the four guards were busy around Jesus with cords and bands, being on the point of binding him.

This was the state of affairs when Peter struck down Malchus, and Jesus said: "Peter, put up thy sword, for whoever takes the sword shall perish by the sword. Thinkest thou that I cannot ask my Father to send me more than twelve legions of angels? Shall I not drink the chalice that my Father has given me? How will the scriptures be fulfilled if it shall not thus be done?" Then he added: "Suffer me to heal the man!" And going to Malchus, he touched his ear and prayed, and at the same moment it was healed. The guard, the executioners, and the six officers surrounded Jesus. They mocked him, saying to the crowd: "He has dealings with the devil. It was by witchcraft that the ear appeared to be cut off, and now by witchcraft it appears to be healed."

Then Jesus addressed them: "Ye are come out with spears and clubs to apprehend me as if I were a murderer. I have daily taught among you in the temple, and ye dared not lay hands upon me; but this is your hour and the hour of darkness." They ordered him to be bound still more securely, and said to him deridingly: "Thou couldst not overthrow us by thy sorcery!" And the executioners said: "We shall deprive thee of thy skill!" Jesus made some reply that I cannot recall, and the disciples fled on all sides. The four executioners and the six Pharisees did not fall to the ground, nor did they in consequence rise again. The reason of this was revealed to me. They were in the same rank as Judas, that is, entirely in the power of Satan. Judas did not fall at the words of Jesus, although he was standing among the soldiers. All those that fell and rose up again were afterward converted and became Christians. Their falling and rising were symbolical of their conversion. They had not laid hands upon Jesus; they merely stood around him. Malchus was, after his healing, already converted to such a degree that he only kept up appearances in respect to the service he owed the high priest; and during the following hours, those of Jesus's Passion, he ran backward and forward to Mary and the other friends, giving them news of all that was taking place.

The executioners bound Jesus with the greatest rudeness and barbarous brutality, the Pharisees meanwhile uttering insolent and scornful words. The executioners were pagans of the very lowest class. Their necks, legs, and arms were naked; their loins were girded with a sort of bandage, and they wore a short jerkin without sleeves, fastened at the sides with straps. They were short, stout, very active, with a brownish-red complexion like the Egyptian slaves.

They bound Jesus's hands upon his breast in a cruel manner. With sharp new cords, they pitilessly fastened the wrist of the right hand to the left forearm just below the elbow and that of the left hand to the right forearm. They put around his waist a broad girdle armed with sharp points, and bound his hands again with links of willow, or osier, which were fixed to the girdle. Around his neck they laid a collar in which were points and other instruments to wound, and from it depended two straps, which like a stole were crossed over the breast and bound down to the girdle so tightly that the neck was not free to move. At four points of this girdle were fastened four long ropes, by means of which the executioners could drag our Lord hither and thither according to their wicked will. All the fetters were perfectly new. They appeared to have been especially prepared, when the plan was formed of apprehending Jesus, for the purpose to which they were now being put.

And now, after several more torches had been lighted, the pitiable procession was set in motion. First went ten of the guard, then followed the executioners dragging Jesus by the ropes; next came the scoffing Pharisees, and the ten other soldiers closed the procession. The disciples were still straying about wailing and lamenting, as if bereft of their senses. John, however, was following rather closely behind the last of the guards. The Pharisees, seeing him, ordered him to be seized. At this command, some of the guard turned and hurried after him. But he fled from them, and when they laid hold of the linen scarf he wore around his neck, he loosened it quickly and thus effected his escape. He had laid aside his mantle, retaining nothing but a short, sleeveless undergarment, that he might be able to flee more easily. Around his neck, head, and arms, however, he was enveloped in that long, narrow scarf which the Jews were accustomed to wear.

The executioners dragged and ill-used Jesus in the most cruel manner. They exercised upon him all kinds of malice, and this principally from a base deference and desire to please the six officials, who were full of rage and venom against him. They led him along the roughest roads, over ruts and stones and mire, keeping the long ropes stretched while they themselves sought good paths. In this way Jesus had to go wherever the ropes would allow him. His tormentors carried in their hands knotted cords with which they struck him, as a butcher might do the animal he was leading to slaughter. All this they accompanied with mockery and insult so low and indecent that the repetition of it would be revolting.

Jesus was barefoot. Besides the usual undergarment, he wore a seamless, woollen shirt, or blouse, and over that an outside robe. The undergarment of the disciples, like that of the Jews in general, consisted of a scapular that fell before and behind over the breast and shoulders. It was made of two pieces fastened together on the shoulder by straps, but open at the sides. The lower part of the body was covered with a girdle from which hung four lappets which, after being wound around the loins, formed a sort of trousers. I must not forget to say that, at the apprehension of the Lord, I saw no written order. His enemies went to work as if he were an outlaw, a person beyond the pale of the law.

The procession moved on at a hurried pace. When it left the road between the Garden of Olives and the pleasure garden of Gethsemane, it turned for a short distance to the right on the west side of Gethsemane, until it reached a bridge that there crossed the brook Kidron. When Jesus was coming with the apostles to the Mount of Olives, he did not cross that bridge. He took a round-about way through the valley of Jehosaphat and crossed the brook over a bridge farther to the south. That over which he was now led in fetters was very long, since it spanned not only the Kidron, which flowed here close to the mount, but also a part of the uneven heights of the valley, thus forming a paved highway for transportation. Even before the procession reached the bridge, I saw Jesus fall to the earth twice, owing to the pitiless manner in which he was dragged along and the jerking of the executioners at the ropes. But when they reached the middle of the bridge, they exercised their villainy upon him with still greater malice. The executioners pushed poor, fettered Jesus, whom they held fast with ropes, from the bridge into the brook Kidron, about the height of a man below, accompanying their brutality with abusive words, as for instance: "Now he can drink his fill!" Were it not for divine assistance, Jesus would have been killed by the fall. He fell first on his knees and then on his face, so that he would have been severely wounded on the stony bed of the brook, which was here very shallow, if he had not saved himself a little by stretching out his previously tightly bound hands. They had been loosened from the girdle, I know not whether by divine help or whether by the executioners before they thrust him down. The marks of his knees, feet, elbows, and fingers were, by God's will, impressed upon the places that they touched, which later on became objects of veneration. Such things are no longer believed, but similar impressions in stone, made by the feet, the hands, and the knees of the patriarchs and prophets, made by Jesus, the blessed Virgin, and some of the saints, have often been shown me in historical visions. The rocks were softer and more believing than the hearts of men; they bore witness at this terrible moment to the divine Truth that had thus impressed them.

I had not seen Jesus take anything to drink in the vehement thirst that consumed him after his awful agony in the Garden of Olives. But when pushed into the Kidron, I saw him drinking with difficulty and, at the same time, I heard him murmuring that thereby was fulfilled a prophetic verse from the Psalms, which bore reference to drinking from the torrent by the way (Ps. cviii).

Meanwhile the executioners relaxed not their hold on the long ropes that bound Jesus; and since it would have been difficult for them to draw him up again, and a wall on the opposite shore rendered it impossible for them to allow him to wade across, they dragged him by means of the ropes back through the Kidron. Then they went down themselves and hauled him up backwards over the high bank. And now, amid mocking and cursing, kicking and striking, those miserable wretches dragged poor Jesus forward with the ropes, a second time over the long bridge. His long, woollen garment, heavy with water, clung so closely around his limbs that he could scarcely walk; and when he reached the opposite end of the bridge, he sank once more to the earth. They pulled him up again, striking him with the cords and, with shameful and mocking words, tucked up his wet garment into the girdle. They said, for example, something about his girding himself for the eating of the paschal lamb, and similar mockery.

It was not yet midnight when I saw the four executioners dragging Jesus over a rugged, narrow road, along which ran only an uneven footpath. They dragged him over sharp stones and fragments of rocks, through thorns and thistles, inhumanly hurrying him on with curses and blows. The six brutal Pharisees were, wherever the road permitted it, always in his vicinity. Each carried in his hand a different kind of torturing stick, with which he tormented him, thrusting him, goading him on, or beating him with it.

While the executioners were dragging Jesus, his naked feet bleeding, over sharp stones, thorns, and thistles, the scornful satirical speeches of the six Pharisees were piercing his loving heart. It was at these moments they made use of such mockery as: "His precursor, the Baptist, did not prepare a good way for him here!" or: "Why does he not raise John from the dead that he may prepare the way for him?" Such were the taunts uttered by these ignominious creatures and received with rude shouts of laughter. They were caught up in turn by the executioners, who were incited thus to load poor Jesus with fresh ill-usage.

After the soldiers had driven the Lord forward for some time, they noticed several persons lurking around here and there in the distance. They were disciples who, upon the report of Jesus's arrest, had come from Bethphage and other hiding places, to spy around and see how it was faring with their Master. At sight of them, Jesus's enemies became anxious, lest they should make a sudden attack and rescue him; therefore they signalled by a call to Ophel, a little place in the environs of Jerusalem, to send a reinforcement, as had been agreed upon.

The procession was still distant some minutes from the entrance which, to the south of the temple, led through Ophel to Mount Zion, upon which Annas and Caiaphas dwelt, when I saw a band of fifty soldiers issuing from the gate, in order to reinforce their companions. They came forward in three groups: the first was ten strong; the last, fifteen, for I counted them; and the middle group, five and twenty. They bore several torches. They were bold and wanton in their bearing, and they shouted and hurrahed as they came along, as if to announce themselves to the approaching band and to congratulate them on their success. Their coming was a noisy one. At the moment in which the foremost band joined Jesus's escort, a slight confusion arose, and I saw Malchus and several others drop out of the rear and slip off in the direction of the Mount of Olives.

When this shouting band hurried from Ophel by torchlight to meet the approaching procession, the disciples lurking around dispersed in all directions. I saw that the blessed Virgin, in her trouble and anguish, with Martha, Magdalene, Mary Cleophas, Mary Salome, Mary Mark, Susanna, Johanna Chusa, Veronica, and Salome, again directed her steps to the valley of Jehosaphat. They were to the south of Gethsemane, opposite that part of the Mount of Olives where was another grotto in which Jesus had formerly been accustomed to pray. I saw Lazarus, John Mark,

The Passion and Death of Jesus Christ

Veronica's son, and Simeon's son with them. The last-named, along with Nathaniel, had been in Gethsemane with the eight apostles, and had fled across when the tumult began. They brought news to the blessed Virgin. Meanwhile they heard the cries and saw the torches of the two bands as they met. The blessed Virgin was in uninterrupted contemplation of Jesus's torments and sympathetic suffering with her divine Son. She allowed the holy women to lead her back part of the way so that, when the tumultuous procession should have passed, she might again return to the house of Mary Mark.

The fifty soldiers belonged to a company of three hundred men who had been sent at once to guard the gates and streets of Ophel and its surroundings, for Judas the traitor had drawn the high priest's attention to the fact that the inhabitants of Ophel, who were mostly poor artisans, day laborers, and carriers of wood and water to the temple, were the most attached partisans of Jesus. It might easily be feared therefore that some attempt would be made to free him as he passed through. The traitor knew very well that Jesus had here bestowed upon many of the poor laborers consolation, instruction, healing, and alms. It was also here in Ophel that Jesus had tarried when, after the murder of John the Baptist in Machaerus, he was journeying back from Bethany to Hebron. He had paused awhile to console John's friends, and he had healed many of the poor day laborers and brick carriers who had been wounded at the overthrow of the great building and the tower of Siloam. Most of these people, after the descent of the Holy Spirit, joined the Christian community, and when the separation of the Christians from the Jews took place and several settlements of the former were erected, they pitched their tents and built their huts across the valley as far as the Mount of Olives. Stephen resided there at that time. Ophel was on a hill south of the temple. It was surrounded by walls and inhabited principally by day laborers. It appeared to me to be not much smaller than Dulmen.[†]

The good inhabitants of Ophel were roused by the shouts of the garrison as their companions entered. They hurried from their houses and pressed to the streets and gates held by the soldiers, asking the cause of the uproar. But here they met with a rough reception. The military rabble, made up of a mixture of low, insolent slaves, roughly and jeeringly drove them back to their dwellings. But as here and there they heard such remarks as these: "Jesus, the evildoer, your false prophet, is about to be led in a prisoner. The high priests will put an end to his proceedings. He will have to pay the penalty of the cross," the whole place was roused

† A small town in Westphalia, where Anne Catherine lived at this time.

from sleep by the loud cries and lamentations of the people. The poor creatures, men and women, ran about wailing or, with outstretched arms, cast themselves on their knees, crying to heaven and lauding Jesus's good deeds. The soldiers, thrusting them and dealing blows on all sides, drove them back to their homes, at the same time insulting Jesus, and saying: "Here is an evident proof that he is an agitator of the people!" They were, however, a little cautious in acting with the populace, through fear of rousing them by greater violence to open insurrection; consequently, they aimed only at clearing the streets by which the procession was to pass through Ophel.

Meanwhile the ill-used Jesus and his barbarous escort came nearer and nearer to the gates of Ophel. Our Lord had repeatedly fallen to the earth, and he now appeared utterly unable to proceed farther. Taking advantage of this, a compassionate soldier said: "You see for yourselves that the poor man can go no farther. If we are to take him alive before the high priests, we must loosen the cords that bind his hands, that he may be able to support himself when he falls." While the procession halted for the executioners to loosen the cords, another good-hearted soldier brought him a drink of water from a neighboring well. He scooped it up in a vessel made of bark formed into the shape of a cone, such as soldiers and travelers carried about them in that country as drinking vessels. When Jesus said to this man a few words of acknowledgment, uttering at the same time some prophetic expressions about "drinking from living fountains," and "the streams of living waters," the Pharisees mocked and reviled him, accusing him of vain boasting and blasphemy. He ought, they said, to give up his empty talk. He should never again give drink to a beast, much less to a human being. It was shown me that the two compassionate soldiers, through whose intervention his bands had been loosened and he had received a drink, were suddenly illuminated by grace. After Jesus's death they were converted, and later on joined the community in the capacity of disciples. I once knew their names, also those that they afterward bore as disciples, and their whole history, but it would be impossible to remember all that. It is too much.

The procession again started forward, Jesus being ill-treated as before, and crossed a height up to the gates of Ophel. Here it was received by the heartrending cries and lamentations of the inhabitants, who were bound to Jesus by a debt of gratitude. Only with great difficulty could the soldiers keep back the crowds of men and women pressing from all sides. They rushed forward wringing their hands, falling on their knees and, with outstretched arms, crying aloud: "Release unto us this man! Who will help us? Who will heal us? Who will console us? Release unto us this man!" It was a heartrending spectacle—Jesus pale, bruised, and disfigured, his hair torn, his robe wet and soiled, tucked up into his girdle, he himself dragged with ropes, urged on with blows, like a poor, fainting animal driven to sacrifice by insolent, half-naked executioners and overbearing soldiers. The latter were busy keeping off the crowd of lamenting and grateful people who were making their way to see Jesus, who were stretching out to him hands that he had cured of lameness, who were crying after him in supplicating tones with tongues that he had loosened from muteness, who were gazing after him with eyes to which he had restored vision and which were now streaming with tears.

Already in the Valley of Kidron numbers of filthy, ragged creatures from the lowest classes, excited by the soldiers and urged on by the followers of Annas, Caiaphas, and other enemies of Jesus, joined the procession with cries of mockery and derision. These newcomers now added their share of jeers and insults against the good people of Ophel. Ophel was built on a hill, for I saw in thecenter of it the highest point. It was an open place, and on it were all kinds of beams and rafters for building, like piles of wood in a carpenter yard. The procession now reached another gate in the wall through which it wound somewhat downward.

The people were prevented from following it beyond the city limits. The road now led somewhat into a valley. On the right stood a large building, I think the remains of Solomon's works, and to the left lay the pool of Bethesda.

After passing these, they kept on in a westerly direction down a steep street called Millo and then, turning a little to the south, they ascended a flight of high steps to the Mount of Zion, upon which was the house of Annas. Along the way our Lord was abused and reviled, while the rabble that kept pouring from the city incited his vile custodians to multiplied cruelties. From the Mount of Olives to this point, Jesus fell to the ground seven times.

The inhabitants of Ophel were still full of terror and distress when a new scene excited their compassion. The blessed Mother was, by the holy women and their friends, led through Ophel from the Valley of Kidron to the house of Mary Mark, which stood at the foot of Mount Zion. When the good people recognized her, their compassion was aroused and they sent up a wail of anguish. So great a crowd pressed around Mary and her companions that the mother of Jesus was almost carried in their arms.

Mary was speechless with grief. She did not open her lips after she reached the house of Mary Mark until the arrival of John. Then she began to ask questions and to give vent to her grief. John related to her everything that he had seen happen to Jesus from the moment that they left the Cenacle up to the present. A little later she was conducted to Martha's house near that of Lazarus at the west side of the city. They led her along unfrequented routes, in order to shun those by which Jesus was being dragged, and thus spare her the anguish of a meeting with him.

Peter and John, who were following the procession at some distance, ran hurriedly when it entered the city to some of the good acquaintances whom John had among the servants of the high priests, to find in some way an opportunity of entering the judgment hall into which their Master would soon be brought. These acquaintances of John were messengers attached to the court. They had now to scour the whole town in order to awaken the ancients of different ranks and many other personages, and call them to the council. They desired very much to please the two apostles, but could think of no other means of doing so than by supplying them with mantles such as they themselves wore and letting hem assist in calling the members of the council; then under cover of the mantle they might enter with them into the judgment hall of Caiaphas, from which all were to be excluded but the bribed rabble, the soldiers, and false witnesses. Nicodemus, Joseph of Arimathea, and other well-disposed individuals belonged to the council, so that the apostles were able to deliver the summons to their Master's friends, the only ones whom the Pharisees had perhaps designedly omitted from the list of the invited. Judas meanwhile, the devil at his side, like a frantic malefactor was wandering around the steep, wild precipices south of Jerusalem where all the filth of the city was thrown.

Means Taken by Jesus's Enemies for Carrying Out Their Designs

AS soon as Jesus was taken into custody, Annas and Caiaphas were informed of the fact and they began actively to arrange their plans. The courts were lighted up and all the entrances provided with guards. Messengers were dispatched to all parts of the city to summon the members of the council, the scribes, and all those that had anything to do with the trial. Many of them, however, as soon as the compact with Judas was completed, had already assembled at the house of Caiaphas and were there awaiting the result. The ancients from the three classes of citizens were also called; and as the Pharisees, the Sadducees and the Herodians from all parts of the country had been for some days gathered in Jerusalem for the feast, they discussed among themselves and before the High Council the design of seizing Jesus. The high priests now selected from the lists in their possession those whom they knew to be his most bitter enemies. These they summoned with the command to gather up, each in his own circle, all the evidence and proofs against Jesus they possibly could, and to bring them to the judgment court. Just at this time, all the Pharisees and Sadducees and other wicked people from Nazareth, Capernaum, Thirza, Gabara, Jotopata, Shiloh, and other places, whom Jesus had so often, by exposing the truth, put to shame before the people, were assembled in Jerusalem. They were filled with rage and vengeance. Each hunted up some scoundrel among the Passover guests from his own country, and bribed him with money to cry out against and calumniate Jesus. These guests were gathered in bands, according to their respective districts. But with the exception of some evident lies and bitter invectives, nothing could be brought forward but those accusations upon which in their own synagogues Jesus had so often silenced them.

All these now gathered, one after another, in the judgment hall of Caiaphas. There, too, assembled the mass of Jesus's enemies from among the haughty Pharisees and scribes, along with their suborned witnesses from Jerusalem itself. Many of those exasperated vendors whom he had driven from the temple; many a puffed-up doctor whom he had there silenced before the people; and perhaps many a one who had not yet forgotten that he had been instructed and put to shame by him when, as a boy of twelve, he had taught for the first time in the temple, were now here arrayed against him. Among his enemies were also impenitent sinners whom he had refused to heal; relapsing sinners who had again become sick; conceited youths whom he would not receive as disciples; wicked avaricious persons who were exasperated at his distributing to the poor the money that they were in hopes of getting for themselves; rascals whose companions he had converted; debauchees and adulterers whose victims he had won over to virtue; covetous heirs who had been disappointed in their expectations by the cure of those from whom they expected to inherit; and many venal time-servers ever ready to pander to wickedness. These emissaries of Satan were brimful of rage against everything holy, and consequently against the Holy of Holies. This scum of the Jewish people assembled for the feast, urged on by the chief enemies of Jesus, pressed forward from all sides and rushed in a continuous stream to the palace of Caiaphas in order falsely to accuse the true Paschal Lamb of God, the spotless one, who had taken upon himself the sins of the world; and to cast upon him their foul consequences which, indeed, he had really assumed, which he was then enduring, and for which he was atoning.

While this miserable Jewish rabble was seeking after some way by which to sully the pure Savior, many devout souls and friends of Jesus were going around in trouble and anguish of heart (for they were ignorant of the mystery about to be accomplished), sighing and listening to all that they could hear. If they uttered a word, they were repulsed by the bystanders; and if they kept silence, they were regarded as disaffected. Many well-meaning, but weak, simple-minded people were scandalized at what they saw and heard. They yielded to temptation and fell away from their faith. The number of those that persevered was not great. Things were then as they are now. Many a one was willing to bear the semblance of a good Christian so long as no inconvenience resulted from it, but became ashamed of the cross when they saw it held in contempt. Still, many in the beginning of these unfounded, these unjust proceedings whose fury and base cruelty cried to heaven for vengeance, seeing the uncomplaining patience of the Savior, were touched at heart, and they walked away silent and dejected.

Glance at Jerusalem at this Hour

THE LARGE and densely populated city, now increased in extent by the numerous camps of the Passover guests stretching out around it, was, after the multiplied private and public prayers, religious exercises, and other preparations for the feast, sunk in sleep, when the news of the arrest roused alike the foes and friends of the Lord. Numbers immediately responded to the summons of the high priests, and the various points of the city began to present a lively scene. They hurried, some by moonlight, others with torches, through the streets—which in Jerusalem were generally dismal and desolate at night, for the windows and doors of most of the houses opened into their inner courts. All turned their steps in the direction of Zion, from whose height glimmered the light of torches. The report of what had just taken place soon spread around, and here and there might be heard knocking at courtyard gates to rouse the sleepers within. Bustle, talking, and confusion were going on in many sections of the city. Servants and newsmongers were hurrying to and fro in search of news, which they hastened to report to those by whom they had been sent. Heavy bars and bolts were shoved with a clang before many a gate, for the people were full of anxiety and in dread of a revolt. Here and there they stepped to the doors and called out to some acquaintance who was passing for news; or the latter, as he hurried by, shouted the desired information. Then were heard malicious speeches, such as are made nowadays on similar occasions. They said: "Now will Lazarus and his sisters see with whom they have been dealing. Johanna

Chusa, Susanna, Mary Mark, and Salome will now regret their conduct, but too late! And how humbled will Sirach's wife Seraphia [Veronica] appear before her husband, who so often forbade her having anything to do with the Galilean! The followers of this seditious leader, this visionary, always looked with pity upon those that entertained views other than their own—and now many a one of them will not know where to hide his head. Who would now be seen strewing palm branches and spreading mantles and veils under the feet of the animal he rides? Those hypocrites, who always wanted to be better than others, will now receive their due. They too will be brought up to trial, for they are all implicated in the affairs of the Galilean. The matter is more deeply rooted than is generally thought. I am anxious to see how Nicodemus and Joseph of Arimathea will comport themselves. They have long been looked upon with a mistrustful eye, for they make common cause with Lazarus, but they are very cunning. Now all will come to light." Many were heard to speak in this way. They were persons embittered against certain families, and especially against those women who up till now had borne public witness to Jesus and his followers. In other places, the news was received in a very different way. Some were frightened at it, some bewailed it in private, while others timidly hunted up a friend in sympathy with themselves in order to pour out their heart. But only a few ventured to express such sympathy openly and decidedly.

All quarters of the city, however, were not aroused, only those parts to which the messengers had brought the invitation to the trial and those in which the Pharisees sought their false witnesses. The streets in the direction of Zion were of all others the most alive. It seemed as if one saw in different parts of Jerusalem sparks of hatred and fury bursting forth, flames rushing along the streets, uniting with others, becoming stronger and more powerful until at last, like a whirlwind of lurid fire, they flashed up Mount Zion and into the judgment hall of Caiaphas. In some quarters all was still at peace, but there too, by degrees, things became stirring.

The Roman soldiers took no part in what was going on, but their posts were strengthened and their cohorts drawn up together. They kept a sharp lookout on all sides. This indeed they always did at the Passover time, on account of the great multitude come together to the feast. They were quiet, and self-possessed, but at the same time very much on their guard. The people who were now hurrying forward shunned the points at which the sentinels were stationed, for it was always vexatious to the Pharisaical Jews to be accosted by them. The high priests had sent a message to Pilate telling him why they had stationed soldiers around

Ophel and one quarter of Zion, but he and they were full of mutual distrust. Pilate slept not. He passed the night listening to reports and issuing orders. His wife, however, lay stretched upon her couch. Her sleep, though heavy, was disturbed. She sighed and wept as if in troubled dreams.

In no part of the city was sympathy with Jesus so touching as in Ophel among the poor temple slaves and day laborers who dwelt on that hill. Terror came upon them so suddenly in the stillness of the night, and the violence of the proceedings roused them from sleep. There they saw their holy teacher, their benefactor, who had healed and nourished them, torn and ill-used, passing like a fearful vision before them. Their sympathy and grief gathered fresh strength upon beholding his afflicted mother wandering about with her friends. Ah, what a sad sight to see that mother pierced with anguish hurrying through the streets at midnight with the holy women, the friends of Jesus, from one acquaintance's house to another, their hearts beating with fear at being out at so unusual an hour! They were often obliged to hide in corners from some rude band that was passing; frequently were they insulted as women of bad character; more than once they heard bitter, malicious speeches against Jesus, and rarely a compassionate word. Reaching at last their place of refuge, they sank down completely exhausted, shedding tears and wringing their hands. They were all equally distressed; and yet each tried to support her fainting neighbor in her arms, or else sat apart in deep affliction, her head enveloped and resting on her knees. And now came a knock at the door. The women heard it anxiously. The rap was gentle and timid. No enemy raps in that manner. The holy women open the door, though not without some feeling of dread, and welcome a friend or the servant of some friend of their Lord and Master. They gather round him with questions, and hear what fills them with fresh sorrow. They can no longer remain quiet, and so they again hurry out into the streets to seek for news of Jesus, though soon to return with renewed grief.

Most of the apostles and disciples were now timidly wandering in the valleys near and around Jerusalem, and hiding in the caves on the Mount of Olives. They started at one another's approach, asked in low tones for news, and the sound of every footstep interrupted their anxious communications. They often changed their place of concealment, and some of them ventured to approach the city. Others stole away to the camps of the Passover guests, there to inquire for news from acquaintances belonging to their own part of the country, or to send scouts into the city for a similar purpose. Others again climbed to the top of Mount Zion and gazed anxiously at the torches moving to and fro on Zion, listened to the distant sounds, formed a thousand conjectures as to the cause, and then hurried down into the valley with the hope of getting some certain intelligence.

The stillness of the night began to be more and more interrupted by the din and bustle around the court of Caiaphas. This quarter was brilliantly lighted up with torches and burning pitch lamps, while from all around the city sounded the bellowing of the numerous beasts of burden and animals for sacrifice belonging to the multitudes of strangers now in the Passover quarters. Ah, how touching was the sound of the bleating of the gentle, innocent, helpless lambs! It was heard throughout the night from countless little victims which were next morning to be slaughtered in the temple. One alone was offered because he himself willed it. Like a sheep led to the slaughter, he opened not his mouth; and like a lamb mute before the shearers, he opened not his mouth. That pure, spotless Paschal Lamb was Jesus Christ!

Above these scenes on earth was spread a sky whose appearance was strikingly dark and lowering. The moon sailed on with a threatening aspect, red, her disc covered with spots. She appeared, as it were, sick and in dread, as if shuddering at the prospect of becoming full, for then it was that Jesus was to be put to death. Outside the city to the south, in the steep, wild, and dismal Valley of Hinnom, wandering companionless through accursed, swampy places filled with ordure and refuse, lashed by his guilty conscience, fleeing from his own shadow, hunted by Satan, was Judas Iscariot, the traitor—while thousands of evil spirits were hurrying around on all sides urging men on to wickedness and entangling them in sin. Hell was let loose, and everywhere were its inmates tempting humankind to evil. The burden of the Lamb grew heavier, and the fury of Satan, taking a twofold increase, became blind and insane in its effects. The Lamb took all the burden upon himself, but Satan wills the sin. And although the righteous one sins not, although this vainly tempted one falls not, yet let his enemies perish in their own sin.

The angels were wavering between grief and joy. They were longing to entreat at the throne of God for help to be sent down to Jesus, but at the same time they were able only to adore in deepest amazement that wonder of divine justice and mercy which the Holy of Holies in the heights of heaven had contemplated from all eternity, and which was now about to be accomplished in time upon earth, for the angels believe in God the Father, the almighty Creator of heaven and earth, and in Jesus Christ, his only Son, our Lord, who was conceived by the Holy Spirit, born of the Virgin Mary, who began that night to suffer under Pontius Pilate, who would the next morning be crucified, who would die, and who would be buried; who would descend into hell, and who would rise from the dead on the third day; who would ascend into heaven, there to sit at the right hand of God, the Father almighty, whence he should come to judge the living and the dead. They believe too in the Holy Spirit, the holy Catholic church, the communion of saints, the forgiveness of sins, the resurrection of the body, and life everlasting. Amen!

All this is only a small portion of the impression which must fill even to bursting a poor sinful heart with anguish, contrition, consolation, and compassion, if, seeking some relief as it were from these terrible scenes, it turns its gaze for a few minutes from the cruel arrest of our Savior and glances over Jerusalem at that solemn midnight of time created, and looks into that hour in which the everlasting justice and infinite mercy of God meeting, embracing, and penetrating each other, began the most holy work of divine and human love, to chastise the sins of men assumed by the God-Man, and to atone for them by that same God-Man. Such was the aspect of Jerusalem when the dear Savior was led to Annas.

Good Friday

Jesus before Annas

IT *was toward midnight* when Jesus was led through the brilliantly lit courtyard into the palace of Annas. He was conducted to a hall as large as a small church. At the upper end opposite the entrance on a high gallery, or platform, under which people could come and go, sat Annas surrounded by twenty-eight counselors. A flight of steps broken here and there by landings, or resting places, led up to the front of his tribunal, or judgment seat, which was entered from behind, thus communicating with the inner part of the building.

Jesus, still surrounded by a body of the soldiers by whom he had been arrested, was dragged forward several steps by the executioners that held the cords. The hall was crowded with soldiers, the rabble, the slandering Jews, the servants of Annas, and some of the witnesses whom Annas had gathered together, and who later on made their appearance at the house of Caiaphas.

Annas could scarcely wait for the arrival of the poor Savior. He was beaming with mischievous joy; cunning and mockery were in his glance. He was at this time the president of a certain tribunal, and he sat here with his committee authorized to examine into false doctrines and to hand over the accused to the high priest.

Jesus stood before Annas pale, exhausted, silent, his head bowed, his garments wet and spattered with mud, his hands fettered, his waist bound by ropes the ends of which the executioners held. Annas, that lean, old villain, with a scraggy beard, was full of irony and freezing Jewish pride. He put on a half-laughing appearance, as if he knew nothing at all of what had taken place, and as if he were greatly surprised to find Jesus in the person of the prisoner brought before him. His address to him, which, however, I cannot reproduce in his own words, was in sense something like the following: "Ha, look there! Jesus of Nazareth! It is thou! Where now are thy disciples, thy crowds of followers? Where is thy kingdom? It appears that things have taken another turn with thee! Thy slanders have come to an end! People have had quite enough of thy blasphemy, thy calumny against priests, and thy sabbath-breaking. Who are thy disciples? Where are they? Now, art thou silent? Speak, seditious man! Speak, seducer! Didst thou not eat the paschal lamb in an unlawful place? Thou dost wish to introduce a new doctrine. Who has given thee authority to teach? Where hast thou studied? Speak! What is thy doctrine which throws everything into confusion? Speak! Speak! What is thy doctrine?"

At these words, Jesus raised his weary head, looked at Annas, and replied: "I have spoken openly before all the world where the Jews were gathered together. In secret I have spoken nothing. Why questionest thou me? Ask those that have heard what I have spoken unto them. Behold! They know what I have said."

The countenance of Annas during this reply of Jesus betrayed rage and scorn. A base menial standing near Jesus remarked this, and the villain struck the Lord with his open, mailed hand. The blow fell full upon the mouth and cheek of the Lord, while the scoundrel uttered the words: "Answerest thou the high priest so?" Jesus, trembling under the violence of the blow and jerked at the same time by the executioners, one pulling this way, another that, fell sideways on the steps, the blood flowing from his face. The hall resounded with jeers and laughter, mockery, muttering, and abusive words. With renewed ill-usage, they dragged Jesus up. He said quietly: "If I have spoken evil, give testimony of the evil; but if well, why strikest thou me?"

Annas, still more enraged by Jesus's calm demeanor, summoned the witnesses (because Jesus himself so willed it) to come forward and declare whatever they had heard him say. Thereupon the rabble set up a storm of cries and abuse. "He has said," they cried, "that he is a king, that God is his Father, that the Pharisees are adulterers. He stirs up the people, he heals on the sabbath day and by the power of the devil. The inhabitants of Ophel have gone crazy over him, calling him their deliverer, their prophet. He allows himself to be called the Son of God. He speaks of himself as one sent by God. He cries woe to Jerusalem, and alludes in his instructions to the destruction of the city. He observes not the fasts. He goes about with a crowd of followers. He eats with the unclean, with pagans, publicans, and sinners, and saunters around with adulteresses and women of bad character. Just now, outside the gate of Ophel, he said to a man who gave him a drink that he would give to him the waters of eternal life and that he should never thirst again. He seduces the people with words of double meaning. He squanders the money and property of others. He tells people all kinds of lies about his kingdom and such like things."

These accusations were brought forward against the Lord without regard to order or propriety. The witnesses stepped up to him and made their charges, derisively gesticulating in his face, while the executioners jerked him first to one side, then to the other, saying: "Speak! Answer!" Annas and his counselors, laughing scornfully, insulted him during the pauses made by the witnesses; for instance, they would exclaim: "Now, there! We hear the fine doctrine! What hast thou to answer? That, also, would be public teaching. The whole country is full of it! Canst thou produce nothing here? Why dost thou not issue some command, O King thou Son of God—show now thy mission!"

These expressions on the part of the judges were followed by pulling, pushing, and mocking on that of the executioners and bystanders, who would all have been glad to imitate the insolent fellow that struck Jesus in the face.

Jesus staggered from side to side. With freezing irony, Annas again addressed him: "Who art thou? What kind of a king art thou? What kind of an envoy art thou? I think that thou art only an obscure carpenter's son. Or art thou Elijah who was taken up to heaven in a fiery chariot? They say that he is still living. Thou too canst render thyself invisible, for thou hast often disappeared. Or perhaps thou art Malachi? Thou hast always vaunted thyself upon this prophet, and thou didst love to apply his words to thyself. It is also reported of him that he had no father, that he was an angel, and that he is not yet dead. What a fine opportunity for an imposter to give himself out for him! Say, what kind of a king art thou? Thou art greater than Solomon! That too is one of thy speeches. Come on! I shall not longer withhold from thee the title of thy kingdom!"

Annas now called for writing materials. Taking a strip of parchment about three feet long and three fingers in breadth, he laid it upon a table before him, and with a reed pen wrote a list of words in large letters, each of which contained some accusation against the Lord. Then he rolled the parchment and stuck it into a little hollow gourd, which he closed with a stopper. This he next fastened to a reed and, sending the mock scepter to

Jesus, scornfully addressed him in such words as the following: "Here, take the scepter of thy kingdom! In it are enclosed all thy titles, thy rights, and thy honors. Carry them hence to the high priest, that he may recognize thy mission and thy kingdom, and treat thee accordingly." Then turning to the soldiers, he said: "Bind his hands and conduct this king to the high priest."

Some time previously they had loosened Jesus's hands. They now bound them again crosswise on his breast after they had fastened in them the accusations of Annas against him, and thus amid shouts of laughter, mocking cries, and all kinds of ill-usage, Jesus was dragged from the tribunal of Annas to that of Caiaphas.

Jesus Led from Annas to Caiaphas

WHEN Jesus was being led to Annas, he had passed the house of Caiaphas. He was now conducted back to it by a road that ran diagonally between the two. They were scarcely three hundred paces apart. The road, which ran between high walls and rows of small houses belonging to the judgment hall of Caiaphas, was lighted up by torches and lanterns, and filled with clamoring, boisterous Jews. It was with difficulty that the soldiers could keep back the crowd. Those that had outraged Jesus before Annas continued their jibes and jests and ill-treatment before the crowd, abusing and ill-treating him the whole way. I saw armed men of all kinds belonging to the tribunal driving away little parties of wailing people who were compassionate toward Jesus, while to some that had distinguished themselves by reviling and accusing him, they gave money, and admitted them with their companions into the court of Caiaphas.

To reach the judgment hall of Caiaphas, one had to pass through a gateway into a spacious exterior court, then through a second gateway into another which, with its walls, surrounded the whole house. (This we shall call the inner court.) A kind of open vestibule surrounded on three sides by a covered colonnade formed the front of the house, which was more than twice as long as it was broad and before which was a level, open square. This vestibule, or forecourt, was called the atrium, into which entrances led from the three sides, the principal one being from the rear, that is, from the house itself. Entering from this side, one proceeded to the left under the open sky to a pit lined with masonry, wherein fire was kept burning; then turning to the right, he would come upon a covered space back of a row of columns higher than any yet described. This formed the fourth side of the atrium and was about half its size. Here upon a semicircular platform up to which led several steps, were the seats for the members of the council. That of the high priest was elevated and in the center. The prisoner, surrounded by the guard, stood for trial in the middle of the semicircle. Upon either side and behind him down into the atrium were places for the witnesses and accusers. Three doors at the back of the judges' seats led into a large, circular hall, around whose wall seats were ranged. This room was used for secret consultations. On leaving the judges' seats and coming out into this hall, one found doors right and left. They opened upon flights of several steps, leading down into the inner court which here following the shape of the house, ran off into a circular form. On leaving the hall by the door on the right and turning to the left in the court, one found himself at the entrance of a dark, subterranean vault containing prison cells. They lay under the rear halls which, like the open tribunal, were higher than the atrium, and consequently afforded space for underground vaults. There were many prisons in this round part of the court. In one of them after Pentecost, I saw John and Peter sitting a whole night. This was when they were imprisoned after Peter had cured the lame man at the Beautiful Gate of the temple.

In and around the building were numberless lamps and torches. All was as bright as day. In the center of the atrium, besides, shone the great pit of fire. It was like a furnace sunk in the earth, but open on top. The fuel was, I think, peat, and it was thrown in from above. Rising from the sides to above the height of a man were pipes in the shape of horns for carrying off the smoke. In the center, however, one could see the fire. Soldiers, servants, the rabble, most of whom were bribed witnesses, were crowding around the fire. There were some females among them, girls of doubtful fame, who sold to the soldiers a reddish beverage by the glass and, on receipt of a trifling sum, baked cakes for them. This scene of disorder and merriment reminded me of carnival time.

Most of those that had been summoned were already assembled around the high priest Caiaphas on the semicircular platform, while here and there others were coming in. The accusers and false witnesses almost filled the atrium; others were trying to force their way in, and it was only with difficulty that they were kept back.

Shortly before the arrival of the procession with Jesus, Peter and John, still enveloped in the messenger mantles, entered the outer court of the house. Through the influence of one of the servants known to him, John was fortunate enough to make his way through the gate of the inner court which, however, on account of the great crowd, was at once closed behind him. When Peter, who had been kept back a little by the crowd, reached the closed gate, the maidservant in charge would not let him

pass. John interposed, but Peter would not have got in had not Nicodemus and Joseph of Arimathea, who just then sought admittance, said a
good word for him. Once inside they laid off the mantles, which they
gave back to the servants, and then took their place to the right among
the crowd in the atrium where they could see the judges' seats. Caiaphas
was already seated in his elevated tribunal in the center of the raised
semicircular platform, and around him were sitting about seventy members of the Sanhedrin. Public officers, the scribes, and the ancients were
sitting or standing on either side, and around them ranged many of the
witnesses and rabble. Guards were stationed below the platform, under
the entrance colonnade, and through the atrium as far as the door by
which the procession was expected. This door was not the one directly
opposite the tribunal, but that to the left of the atrium.

Caiaphas was a man of great gravity, his countenance florid and fierce.
He wore a long, dull red mantle ornamented with golden flowers and
tassels. It was fastened on the shoulders, the breast, and down the front
with shining buckles of various form. On his head was a cap, the top of
which resembled a low episcopal miter. The pieces front and back were
bent so as to meet on top, thus leaving openings at the side, from which
hung ribbons. From either side of the head lappets fell upon the shoulders. Caiaphas and his counselors were already a long time assembled;
many of them had even remained since the departure of Judas and his
gang. The rage and impatience of Caiaphas had reached such a pitch
that, magnificently attired as he was, he descended from his lofty tribunal and went into the outer court asking angrily whether Jesus would
soon come. At last the procession was seen approaching, and Caiaphas
returned to his seat.

Jesus before Caiaphas

AMID frantic cries of mockery, with pushing and dragging and casting of
mud, Jesus was led into the atrium, where, instead of the unbridled rage
of the mob, were heard the dull muttering and whispering of restrained
rage. Turning to the right on entering, the procession faced the tribunal.
When Jesus passed Peter and John, he glanced at them lovingly, though
without turning his head, for fear of betraying them. Scarcely had he
passed through the colonnaded entrance and appeared before the council, when Caiaphas cried out to him: "Hast thou come, thou blasphemer
of God, thou that dost disturb this our sacred night!" The tube containing
Annas's accusations against Jesus was now drawn from the mock scepter.
When the writing which it contained was read, Caiaphas poured forth a

stream of reproaches and abusive epithets against Jesus, while the soldiers and wretches standing near dragged and pulled him about. They had in their hands little iron rods, some of them capped with sharp goads, others with pear-shaped knobs, with which they drove him from side to side, crying: "Answer! Open thy mouth! Canst thou not speak!" All this went on while Caiaphas, even more enraged than Annas, hurled question after question to Jesus who, calm and suffering, kept his eyes lowered, not even glancing at him. The wretches, in their efforts to force him to speak, struck him on the neck and sides, hit him with their fists, and goaded him with their puncheons. And more than this, a cruel lad, with his thumb, pressed Jesus's underlip upon his teeth, saying: "Here, now, bite!"

And now came the interrogation of the witnesses. It consisted of nothing but the disorderly cries, the enraged shouts of the bribed populace, or the deposition of some of Jesus's enemies belonging to the exasperated Pharisees and Sadducees. A certain number of them had been selected as representatives of their party on this feast. They brought forward all those points that Jesus had answered a hundred times before: for instance, they said that he wrought cures and drove out devils through the devil himself; that he violated the sabbath, kept not the prescribed fasts; that his disciples ate with unwashed hands; that he incited the people, called the Pharisees a brood of vipers and an adulterous generation; predicted the destruction of Jerusalem; and associated with pagans, publicans, sinners, and women of ill-repute; that he went around with a great crowd of followers, gave himself out as a king, a prophet, yes, even as the Son of God; and that he was constantly talking about his kingdom. They advanced, moreover, that he attacked the liberty of divorce, that he had cried woe upon Jerusalem, that he called himself the bread of life and put forward the unheard-of doctrine that whoever did not eat his flesh and drink his blood would not have eternal life.

In this way were all his words, his instructions, and his parables misrepresented and perverted, mixed up with words of abuse and outrage, and attributed to him as crimes. The witnesses, however, contradicted and confused one another. One said: "He gives himself out for a king"; another cried, "No! He only allows himself to be so styled, for when they wanted to proclaim him king, he fled." Then one of them shouted: "He says he is the Son of God," to which someone else retorted: "No, that's not so! He calls himself a son only because he fulfills his father's will." Some declared that those whom he had healed fell sick again, so that his healing power was nothing but the effect of magic. On the charge of sorcery principally, many accusations were lodged against him, and numbers of witnesses came forward. The cure of the man at the pool of Bethesda was brought up in a distorted light and falsely represented. The Pharisees of Sepphoris, with whom Jesus had once disputed upon the subject of divorce, accused him now of teaching false doctrine, and that young man of Nazareth whom he had refused to receive as a disciple was base enough to step forward and witness against him. They accused him also of acquitting at the temple the woman taken in adultery, of taxing the Pharisees with crime, and of many other things.

Notwithstanding all their efforts, they were unable to prove any one of their charges. The crowd of witnesses seemed to come forward more for the purpose of deriding Jesus to his face than to render testimony. They contended hotly among themselves, while Caiaphas and some of the counselors ceased not their raillery and taunting expressions. They cried out: "What a king thou art! Show thy power! Call the angelic legions of which thou spokest in the Garden of Olives! Where hast thou hidden the money thou didst receive from widows and simpletons? Thou hast squandered whole estates, and what hast thou to show for it? Answer! Speak! Now that thou shouldst speak before the judges, thou art mute; but where it would have been better to be silent, that is, before the mob and female rabble, thou didst have words enough," etc.

All these speeches were accompanied by renewed ill-usage from the servants, who tried with cuffs and blows to force Jesus to answer. Through God's help alone was he enabled longer to live, that he might bear the sins of the world. Some of the vile witnesses declared the Lord to be an illegitimate son, which charge others contradicted with the words: "That is false! His mother was a pious virgin belonging to the temple, and we were present at her marriage to a most God-fearing man." And then followed a hot dispute among these last witnesses.

They next accused Jesus and his disciples of not offering sacrifice in the temple. True it is that I never saw Jesus or the apostles, after they began to follow him, bringing any sacrifice to the temple excepting the paschal lamb, though Joseph and Anne frequently during their lifetime offered sacrifice for Jesus. But these accusations were of no account, for the Essenes never offered sacrifice, and no one thought of subjecting them to punishment for the omission. The charge of sorcery was frequently repeated, and more than once Caiaphas declared that the confusion of the witnesses in their statements was due to witchcraft.

Some now said that Jesus had, contrary to the law, eaten the paschal lamb on the previous day, and that the year before he had sanctioned other irregularities at the same feast. This testimony gave rise to new expressions of rage and derision from the vile crowd. But the witnesses had so perplexed and contradicted one another that, mortified and exasperated, Caiaphas and the assembled counselors found that not one of the accusations against Jesus could be substantiated. Nicodemus and Joseph of Arimathea were then called up to explain how it happened that they had allowed Jesus to eat the paschal lamb in a supper room belonging to the last-named. Having taken their places before Caiaphas, they proved from written documents that the Galileans, according to an ancient custom, were permitted to eat the paschal lamb one day earlier than the other Jews. They added that everything else pertaining to the ceremony had been carefully observed, for that persons belonging to the temple were present at it. This last assertion greatly puzzled the witnesses, and the enemies of Jesus were particularly exasperated when Nicodemus sent for the writings and pointed out the passages containing this right of the Galileans. Besides several other reasons for this privilege, which I have forgotten, there was this: the immense crowds congregated at the same time and for the same purpose in the temple rendered it impossible for all to get through the ceremonies at a given hour; and again, if all were to return home at the same time, the roads would be so thronged as to render them impassable. Now, although the Galileans did not always make use of their privilege, yet Nicodemus incontestably proved its existence from written documents. The rage of the Pharisees against Nicodemus became still greater when the latter closed his remarks by saying that the members of the council must feel greatly aggrieved at being called upon to preside over a trial instituted by prejudice so evident, carried on with haste so violent on the night preceding the most solemn of their festivals; and that the gross contradictions of all the witnesses in their presence and before the assembled multitude were to them a positive insult. The Pharisees glanced wrathfully at Nicodemus and, with barefaced insolence, hurriedly continued to question the base witnesses. After much shameful, perverse, lying evidence, two witnesses at last came forward and said: "Jesus declared that he would destroy the temple made by hands, and in three days build up another not made by human hands." But these two also wrangled over their words. One said: "Jesus was going to build up a new temple; therefore it was that he had celebrated a new Passover in another building, for he was going to destroy the old temple." The other retorted: "The building in which he ate the paschal lamb was built by human hands, consequently he did not mean that."

Caiaphas was now thoroughly exasperated, for the ill-treatment bestowed upon Jesus, the contradictory statements of the witnesses, and the incomprehensibly silent patience of the accused were beginning to make a very deep impression upon many of those present, and some of

The Passion and Death of Jesus Christ

the witnesses were laughed to scorn. The silence of Jesus roused the conscience of many, and about ten of the soldiers were so touched by it that, under pretext of indisposition, they left the court. As they passed Peter and John, they said to them: "The silence of Jesus the Galilean in the midst of treatment so shameful is heart-rending. It is a wonder the earth does not swallow his persecutors alive. But tell us, whither shall we go?" The two apostles, however, perhaps because they did not trust the soldiers or feared to be recognized by them or the bystanders as Jesus's disciples, answered sadly and in general terms: "If truth calls you, follow it; the rest will take care of itself." Thereupon these men left the outer court of Caiaphas's house, and hurried from the city. They met some persons who directed them to caves on the other side of Mount Zion to the south of Jerusalem. Here they found hidden several of the apostles, who at first shrank from them in alarm. But their fears were dispelled on receiving news of Jesus and upon hearing that the soldiers were themselves in danger. They soon after separated and scattered to different places.

Caiaphas, infuriated by the wrangling of the last two witnesses, rose from his seat, went down a couple of steps to Jesus, and said: "Answerest thou nothing to this testimony against thee?" He was vexed that Jesus would not look at him. At this the executioners pulled our Lord's head back by the hair, and with their fist gave him blows under his chin. But his glance was still downcast. Caiaphas angrily raised his hands and said in a tone full of rage: "I adjure thee by the living God that thou tell us whether thou be Christ, the Messiah, the Son of the most blessed God."

A solemn silence fell upon the clamoring crowd. Jesus, strengthened by God, said in a voice inexpressibly majestic, a voice that struck awe into all hearts, the voice of the Eternal Word: "I am! Thou sayest it! And I say to you, soon you shall see the Son of Man sitting on the right hand of the power of God, and coming in the clouds of heaven!"

While Jesus was pronouncing these words, I saw him shining with light. The heavens were open above him and, in an inexpressible manner, I saw God, the Father almighty. I saw the angels and the prayers of the just crying, as it were, and pleading for Jesus. I saw, besides, the divinity as if speaking from the Father and from Jesus at the same time: "If it were possible for me to suffer, I would do so, but because I am merciful, I have taken flesh in the Person of my Son, in order that the Son of Man may suffer. I am just—but behold! He is carrying the sins of these men, the sins of the whole world!"

I saw yawning below Caiaphas the whole abyss of hell, a lurid, fiery sphere full of horrible shapes. I saw Caiaphas standing above it, separated from it by only a thin crust. I saw him penetrated with diabolical rage.

GOOD FRIDAY, APRIL 3, AD 33

The whole house now appeared to be one with the open abyss of hell below. When the Lord solemnly declared that he was Christ, the Son of God, it was as if hell grew terror-stricken before him, as if it launched the whole force of its rage against him by means of those gathered in the tribunal of Caiaphas.

As all these things were shown me in forms and pictures, I saw hell's despair and fury in numberless horrible shapes coming up in many places out of the earth. Among them I remember to have seen crowds of little, dark figures like dogs with short paws and great, long claws, but I do not now recall what species of wickedness was symbolized in them. I remember only the figures. I saw frightful-looking shadows similar to those moving among most of those present, or sitting upon the head or shoulders of many. The assembly was full of them, and they excited the people to fury and wickedness. I saw also at this moment, from the graves on the other side of Zion, hideous figures hurriedly rising. I think they were evil spirits. In the vicinity of the temple, likewise, I saw many apparitions rising out of the earth. Some of them appeared to be captives, for they moved along slowly in fetters. I do not now know whether these last were demons, or souls banished to certain places on the earth and who were perhaps now going to Purgatory, which the Lord was about to open to them by his condemnation to death. One can never fully express such things for fear of scandalizing the ignorant, but when one sees these things, one feels them, and they make the hair stand on end. This moment was full of horror. I think that John too must have seen something of it, for I heard him afterward speaking about it. The few who were not entirely abandoned to evil felt with deep dismay the horror of this moment, but the wicked experienced only a wild outburst of rage.

Caiaphas, as if inspired by hell, seized the hem of his magnificent mantle, clipped it with a knife and, with a whizzing noise, tore it as he exclaimed in a loud voice: "He has blasphemed! What need have we of further witnesses? Behold now ye have heard the blasphemy, what think ye?" At these words, the whole assembly rose and cried out in a horrid voice: "He is guilty of death! He is guilty of death!"

During these shouts, that sinister rage of hell was most frightful in the house of Caiaphas. Jesus's enemies appeared to be possessed by Satan, as did also their partisans and fawning servants. It was as if the powers of darkness were proclaiming their triumph over light. Such a sense of horror fell upon all present in whom there was still some little connection with good, that many of them drew their mantles closer around them and slipped away. The witnesses belonging to the better classes, as their presence was no longer necessary, also left the judgment hall, their conscience racked by remorse. The rabble, however, gathered around the fire in the forecourt where, having received the price of their perfidy, they ate and drank to excess.

The high priest, addressing the executioners, said: "I deliver this king to you. Render to the blasphemer the honors due him!" After these words, he retired with his council to the round hall back of the tribunal, into which no one could see from the vestibule.

John, in his deep affection, thought only of the blessed Virgin. He feared that the dreadful news might be communicated to her suddenly by some enemy; so casting at Jesus, the Holy of Holies, a glance that said: "Master, thou knowest well why I am going," he hurried from the judgment hall to seek the blessed Virgin as sent to her by Jesus himself. Peter, quite consumed by anxiety and pain and, on account of his bodily exhaustion, feeling keenly the sensible chilliness of the coming morning, concealed his deep trouble as well as he could, and timidly approached the fire in the atrium, around which all kinds of low-lived wretches were warming themselves. He knew not what he was doing, but he could not leave his Master.

Jesus Mocked and Insulted

AS soon as Caiaphas, having delivered Jesus to the soldiers, left the judgment hall with his council, the very scum of the miscreants present fell like a swarm of infuriated wasps upon our Lord, who until then had been held fast by two of the four executioners that guided the ropes with which he was bound. Two of them had retired before the sentence, in order to make their escape with the others. Even during the trial, the executioners and other wretches had cruelly torn whole handfuls of hair from the head and beard of Jesus. Some good persons secretly picked up the locks of hair from the ground and slipped away with them, but after a little while it disappeared from their possession. During the trial also the miscreants had spat upon Jesus, struck him again and again with their fists, goaded him with cudgels whose rounded ends were armed with sharp points, and had even run needles into his body. But now they exercised their villainy upon him in a manner altogether frantic and irrational. They put upon him, one after the other, several crowns of straw and bark plaited in various ludicrous forms which, with wicked words of mockery, they afterward struck from his head. Sometimes they cried: "Behold the Son of David crowned with the crown of his Father!" Or again: "Behold, here is more than Solomon!" Or: "This is the king who is preparing a marriage feast for his son!" And thus they turned to ridicule all the eternal truths which, for the salvation of humankind, he had in truth and parables taught. They struck him with their fists and sticks, threw him from side to side, and spat upon him. At last they plaited a crown of coarse wheat straw, such as grows in that country, put upon him a high cap, almost similar to the high miters of the present day; and, after stripping him of his knitted robe, placed over the miter the straw crown. There, now, stood poor Jesus clothed only in his nether-bandage and the scapular that fell on his breast and back; but this last they soon tore from him, and he never recovered it. They threw around him an old, tattered mantle too short in front to cover the knees, and put around his neck a long iron chain which, like a stole, hung from the shoulders across the breast and down to the knees. The ends of the chain were furnished with two great, heavy rings studded with sharp points which, as he walked, struck against his knees and wounded them severely. They pinioned anew his hands upon his breast, placed in them a reed, and covered his disfigured countenance with the spittle of their impure mouths. His torn hair and beard, his breast, and the whole of the upper part of the mantle of derision were laden with filth in every degree of loathsomeness. They tied a rag across his eyes, struck him with their fists and sticks, and cried out: "Great prophet! Prophesy, who has struck thee?" But Jesus answered not. He prayed interiorly, sighed, and bore their blows. Thus ill-used, blindfolded, and covered with filth, they dragged him by the chain into the rear council hall. They kicked him and drove him forward with their clubs, while uttering such derisive cries as, "Forward, O king of straw! He must show himself to the council in the regal insignia which we have bestowed upon him!" When they entered the council hall wherein many of the members were still sitting with Caiaphas on the elevated, semicircular platform, a new scene of outrage began; and with an utterly base meaning and purely sacrilegious violation, sacred customs and ceremonies were imitated. As, for instance, when they covered Jesus with mud and spittle, the vile miscreants exclaimed: "Here now is thy royal unction, thy prophetic unction!" It was thus they mockingly alluded to Magdalene's anointing and to baptism. "What!" they cried jeeringly, "art thou going to appear before the Sanhedrin in this unclean trim? Thou wast wont to purify others, and yet thou art not clean thyself. But we will now purify thee." Thereupon, they brought a basin full of foul, muddy water in which lay a coarse rag; and amid pushes, jests, and mockery mingled with ironical bows and salutations, with sticking out the tongue at him or turning up to him their hinder parts, they passed the wet smeary rag over his face and shoulders as if cleansing him, though in reality rendering him more filthy than before. Finally, they poured the whole contents of the basin over his face with the mocking words: "There, now, is precious balm for thee! There now, thou hast had water at a cost of three hundred pence! Now, thou hast thy baptism of the pool of Bethesda!"

This last outrage showed forth, though without their intending it, the likeness between Jesus and the paschal lamb, for on this day the lambs slaughtered for sacrifice were first washed in the pond near the sheep gate and then in the pool of Bethesda to the south of the temple. They were then solemnly sprinkled with water before being slaughtered in the temple for the Passover. The enemies of Jesus were alluding to the paralytic who for thirty-eight years had been sick, and who had been cured by him at the pool of Bethesda, for I afterward saw that same man washed or baptized in its waters. I say "washed or baptized," because at this moment the action with its circumstances does not recur clearly to my mind.

Now they dragged and pulled Jesus around with kicks and blows in the circle formed by the members of the council, all of whom greeted him with raillery and abuse. I saw the whole assembly filled with raging, diabolical figures. It was a scene of horrible gloom and confusion. But around the ill-treated Jesus, since the moment in which he said that he was the Son of God, I frequently saw a glory, a splendor. Many of those present seemed to have an interior perception of the same, some more, others less; they experienced, at least, a feeling of dread upon seeing that, in spite of the scorn and ignominy with which he was laden, the indescribable majesty of his bearing remained unchanged. The halo around him seemed to incite his enemies to a higher degree of fury. But to me that glory appeared so remarkable that I am of opinion that they veiled Jesus's countenance on that account, because since the words: "I am he," the high priest could no longer endure his glance.

Peter's Denial

WHEN Jesus solemnly uttered the words: "I am he," and Caiaphas rent his garments crying out: "He is guilty of death"—when the hall resounded with the mocking cries and furious shouts of the rabble—when the heavens opened above Jesus—when hell gave free vent to its rage—when the graves gave up their captive spirits—when all was horror and consternation—then were Peter and John, who had suffered much from having to witness silently and passively the frightful abuse to which Jesus was subjected, no longer able to remain. John went out with many of the crowd and some of the witnesses who were leaving the hall, and hurried off to the mother of Jesus, who was staying at Martha's, not far from the corner gate, where Lazarus owned a beautiful house in Jerusalem. But Peter could not go—he loved Jesus too much. He could scarcely contain himself. He wept bitterly, though trying to hide his tears as well as he could.

He could not remain standing any longer in the judgment hall, for his deep emotion would have betrayed him, nor could he leave without attracting notice. So, he retired to the atrium and took a place in the corner near the fire, around which soldiers and people of all kinds were standing in groups. They went out occasionally to mock Jesus and then came back to make their low, vulgar remarks upon what they had done. Peter kept silence; but already the interest he manifested in the proceedings, joined to the expression of deep grief depicted on his countenance, drew upon him the attention of Jesus's enemies. Just at this moment, the portress approached the fire; and as all were prating and jesting at Jesus's expense and that of his disciples, she, like a bold woman, saucily put in her word and, fixing her eyes upon Peter, said: "Thou too art one of the Galilean's disciples!" Peter, startled and alarmed, and fearing rough treatment from the rude crowd, answered: "Woman, I know him not! I know not what thou meanest. I do not understand thee!" With these words, wishing to free himself from further remark, he arose and left the atrium. *At that moment, a cock somewhere outside the city crowed.* I do not remember having *heard* it, but I *felt* that it was crowing outside the city. As Peter was making his way out, another maidservant caught sight of him, and said to the bystanders: "This man, also, was with Jesus of Nazareth." They at once questioned him: "Art thou not also one of his disciples?" Peter, greatly troubled and perplexed, answered with an oath: "Truly, I am not! I do not even know the man!" And he hurried through the inner to the exterior court, to warn some of his acquaintances whom he saw looking over the wall. He was weeping and so full of grief and anxiety on Jesus's account that he hardly gave his denial a thought. In the other court were many people, among them some of Jesus's friends, who not being able to get nearer to the scene of action had climbed on the wall to be better able to hear. Peter, being allowed to go out, found among them a number of disciples whom anxiety had forced hither from their caves on Mount Hinnom. They went straight up to Peter, and with many tears questioned him about Jesus. But he was so excited and so fearful of betraying himself that he advised them in a few words to go away, as there was danger for them where they were. Then he turned off and wandered gloomily about, while they, acting on his word, hastened to leave the city. I recognized about sixteen of the first disciples, among them: Bartholomew,

Nathaniel, Saturnin, Joseph Barsabbas, Simeon (later on, bishop of Jerusalem), Zacchaeus, and Manahem, the youth endowed with the gift of prophecy but born blind, to whom Jesus had restored sight.

Peter could not rest anywhere. His love for Jesus drove him back into the inner court that surrounded the house. They let him in again, on account of Nicodemus and Joseph of Arimathea, who had in the first instance procured his admittance. He did not, however, return to the court of the judgment hall, but turning went along to the right until he reached the entrance of the circular hall back of the tribunal. In that hall Jesus was being dragged about and abused by the vile rabble. Peter drew near trembling, and although he felt himself an object of remark, yet his anxiety for Jesus drove him through the doorway, which was beset by the crowd watching the outrages heaped upon Jesus. Just then they were dragging him, crowned with straw, around the circle. Jesus cast a glance full of earnest warning upon Peter, a glance that pierced him to the soul. But when, still struggling with fear, he heard from some of the bystanders the words: "What fellow is that?" He re-entered the court. There, sad and distracted with compassion for Jesus and anxiety for his own safety, he wandered about with loitering steps. At last seeing that he was attracting notice upon himself, he went again into the atrium and took a seat by the fire. He had sat there a considerable time when some that had seen him outside and noticed his preoccupied and excited manner re-entered and again directed their attention to him, while referring in slighting terms to Jesus and his affairs. One of them said: "Truly, thou also dost belong to his adherents! Thou art a Galilean. Thy speech betrays thee." Peter began to evade the remark and to make his way out of the hall, when a brother of Malchus stepped up to him and said: "What! Did I not see thee with him in the Garden of Olives? Didst thou not wound my brother's ear?"

Peter became like one beside himself with terror. While trying to free himself, he began in his impetuous way to curse and swear that he knew not the man, and ended by running out of the atrium into the court that surrounded the house. *The cock again crowed.* Just at that moment, Jesus was being led from the circular hall and across this court down into a prison under it. He turned toward Peter and cast upon him a glance of mingled pity and sadness. Forcibly and with a terrifying power, the word of Jesus fell upon his heart: "Before the cock crows twice, thou wilt deny me thrice!" Worn out with grief and anxiety, Peter had entirely forgotten his presumptuous protestation on the Mount of Olives, rather to die with his Master than to deny him, as also the warning he had then received from Jesus. But at that glance, the enormity of his fault rose up before him and well-nigh broke his heart. He had sinned. He had sinned against his ill-treated, unjustly condemned Savior, who was silently enduring the most horrible outrages, who had so truly warned him to be on his guard. Filled with remorse and sorrow, he covered his head with his mantle and hurried into the other court, weeping bitterly. He no longer feared being accosted. To everyone he met he would willingly have proclaimed who he was, and how great was the crime that rested on him. Who would presume to say that in such danger, affliction, anxiety, and perplexity, in such a struggle between love and fear, worn out with fatigue, consumed by watching, pursued by dread, half-crazed from pain of mind caused by the overwhelming sorrows of this most pitiful night, with a temperament at once so childlike and so ardent, he would have been stronger than Peter? The Lord left Peter to his own strength, therefore did he become so weak, just as they always do that lose sight of the words: "Pray and watch, that ye enter not into temptation."

Mary in the Judgment Hall of Caiaphas

THE BLESSED Virgin, united in constant, interior compassion with Jesus, knew and experienced in her soul all that happened to him. She suffered everything with him in spiritual contemplation, and like him she was absorbed in continual prayer for his executioners. But at the same time, her mother-heart cried uninterruptedly to God that He might not suffer these crimes to be enacted, that He might ward off these sufferings from her most blessed Son, and she irresistibly longed to be near her poor, outraged Jesus. When then John, after the frightful cry: "He is guilty of death!" left the court of Caiaphas and went to her at Lazarus's in Jerusalem, not far from the corner gate; and when, by his account of the terrible sufferings of her Son, he confirmed what she already well knew from interior contemplation, she ardently desired to be conducted together with Magdalene (who was almost crazed from grief), and some others of the holy women, to where she might be near her suffering Jesus. John, who had left the presence of his divine Master only to console her who was next to Jesus with him, accompanied the blessed Virgin when led by the holy women from the house. Magdalene, wringing her hands, staggered with the others along the moonlit streets, which were alive with people returning to their homes. The holy women were veiled. But their little party, closely clinging to one another, their occasional sobs and expressions of grief, which could not be restrained, drew upon them the notice of the passersby, many of whom were Jesus's enemies; and the bitter, abusive words which they heard uttered against the

Lord added to their pain. The most afflicted mother suffered in constant, interior contemplation the torments of Jesus, which, however, like all other things, she quietly kept in her heart; for, like him, she suffered with him in silence. The holy women supported her in their arms. When passing under an arched gateway of the inner city, through which their way led, they were met by some well-disposed people returning from Caiaphas's judgment hall and lamenting the scenes they had witnessed. They approached the holy women and, recognizing the mother of Jesus, paused a moment to salute her with heartfelt compassion: "O thou most unhappy mother! Thou most afflicted mother! O thou most distressed mother of the Holy One of Israel!" Mary thanked them earnestly, and the holy women with hurried steps continued their sorrowful way.

As they drew near to Caiaphas's, the route led to the side opposite the entrance where there was only one surrounding wall, while on the side of the entrance itself, it ran through two courts. Here a fresh and bitter sorrow was in store for the mother of Jesus and her companions. They had to pass a high, level place upon which, under a light awning, the cross of Christ was being constructed by torchlight. The enemies of Jesus had already, as soon as Judas went out to betray him, commanded the cross to be prepared for him just as soon as he should be seized, for then Pilate would have no cause for delay. They thought they would deliver the Lord very early to him for sentence of death; they did not expect it to be so long delayed. The Romans had already prepared the crosses for the two robbers. The workmen, full of chagrin at being obliged to labor during the night, uttered horrible curses and abusive epithets which, with every stroke of the hammer, pierced the heart of the most afflicted mother. Still she prayed for those blind wretches who, cursing and swearing, were putting together the instrument for their own redemption, and the cruel martyrdom of her Son.

When now they reached the outer court of the house, Mary, in the midst of the holy women and accompanied by John, withdrew into a corner under the gateway leading into the inner court. Her soul, filled with inexpressible sufferings, was with Jesus. She sighed for the door to be opened, and hoped, through John's intervention, to be allowed admittance. She felt that this door alone separated her from her Son *who, at the second crowing of the cock,* was to be led out of the house and into the prison below. At last the door opened and Peter, weeping bitterly, his head covered and his hands outstretched, rushed to meet the crowd issuing forth. The glare of the torches, added to the light shed by the moon, enabled him at once to recognize John and the blessed Virgin. It seemed to him that conscience, which the glance of the Son had roused and terrified, stood before him in the person of the mother. Oh, how the soul of poor Peter quivered when Mary accosted him with: "O Simon, what about my Son, what about Jesus?" Unable to speak or to support the glance of Mary's eyes, Peter turned away wringing his hands. But Mary would not desist. She approached him and said in a voice full of emotion: "O Simon, son of Cephas, thou answerest me not?" Thereupon in the deepest woe, Peter exclaimed: "O Mother, speak not to me! Thy Son is suffering cruelly. Speak not to me! They have condemned him to death, and I have shamefully denied him thrice!" And when John drew near to speak to him, Peter, like one crazed by grief, hurried out of the court and fled from the city. He paused not until he reached that cave on the Mount of Olives upon whose stones were impressed the marks of Jesus's hands while he prayed. In that same cave our first father Adam did penance, for it was here that he first reached the curse-laden earth.

The blessed Virgin, in compassion for Jesus in this new pain, that of being denied by the disciple who had been the first to acknowledge him the Son of the Living God, at these words of Peter sank down upon the stone pavement upon which she was standing by the pillar of the gateway. The marks of her hand or foot remained impressed upon the stone, which is still in existence, though I do not now remember where I have seen it. Most of the crowd had dispersed after Jesus was imprisoned, and the gate of the court was still standing open. Rising from where she had fallen and longing to be nearer her beloved Son, John conducted the blessed Virgin and the holy women to the front of the Lord's prison. Mary was indeed with Jesus in spirit and knew all that was happening to him, and he too was with her. But this most faithful mother wished to hear with her bodily ears the sighs of her Son. She could in her present position hear both the sighs of Jesus and the insults heaped upon him. The little group could not here remain long unobserved. Magdalene was too greatly agitated to conquer the vehemence of her grief, and though the blessed Virgin by a special grace appeared wonderfully dignified and venerable in her exterior manifestation of her exceedingly great suffering, yet even while going this short distance she was obliged to listen to words of bitter import, such as: "Is not this the Galilean's mother? Her Son will certainly be crucified, though not before the festival, unless indeed he is the greatest of criminals." The blessed Virgin turned and, guided by the Spirit that enlightened her interiorly, went to the fireplace in the atrium where only a few of the rabble were still standing. Her companions followed in speechless grief. In this place of horror, where Jesus had declared that he was the Son of God and where the brood of Satan had cried out: "He is guilty of death," the most afflicted mother's anguish was so great that she appeared more like a dying than a living person. John and the holy women led her away from the spot. The lookers-on became silent, as if stupefied. The effect produced by Mary's presence was what might be caused by a pure spirit passing through hell.

The little party proceeded along a way that ran back of the house and passed that mournful spot upon which the cross was being prepared. As it was found difficult to pronounce sentence upon Jesus, so was it hard to get ready his cross. The workmen were obliged frequently to bring fresh wood, because this or that piece proved a misfit or broke under their hands. It was in this way that the various kinds of wood were employed that God willed to be used. I have had many visions on this subject, and I have seen the angels hindering the laborers in their work until they recommenced and finished it as God would have it done. But as I do not clearly remember the several circumstances, I shall pass them over.

Jesus Imprisoned

THE PRISON cell into which Jesus was introduced lay under the judgment hall of Caiaphas. It was a small, circular vault. A part of it I see in existence even now. Only two of the four executioners remained with Jesus. After a short interval they exchanged places with two others, and these again were soon relieved. They had not given the Lord his own garments again. He was clothed with only the filthy mantle of mockery, and his hands were still bound.

When the Lord entered the prison, he prayed his heavenly Father to accept all the scorn and ill-treatment that he had endured up to that moment and all that he had still to suffer in atonement for the sins of his executioners and for all those that, in future ages, might be in danger of sinning through impatience and anger.

Even in this prison the executioners allowed Jesus no rest. They bound him to a low pillar that stood in the center of the prison, though they would not permit him to lean against it. He was obliged to stagger from side to side on his tired feet, which were wounded and swollen from frequent falls and the strokes of the chain that hung to his knees. They ceased not to mock and outrage him, and when the two executioners in charge were wearied, two others replaced them, and new scenes of villainy were enacted.

It is not possible for me to repeat all the acts of wickedness performed against the purest and the holiest. I am too sick. I am almost dying from compassion. Ah, how ashamed we should be that through effeminacy and fastidiousness we cannot bear to talk of or listen to the details of all

GOOD FRIDAY, APRIL 3, AD 33

that the innocent Redeemer patiently suffered for us. Horror seizes upon us on such occasions, similar to that of a murderer forced to lay his hands upon the wounds of his victim. Jesus endured all without opening his lips; and it was man, sinful man, who thus raged against his Brother, his Redeemer, and his God. I too am a poor, sinful creature, and it was for my sake that all this suffering fell upon him. On the Day of Judgment all things will be laid open. Then shall we see how, in the ill-treatment of the Son of God, when as the Son of Man he appeared in time, we have had a share by the sins we so frequently commit, and which are indeed a kind of continuation of and participation in the outrages offered to Jesus by those diabolical miscreants. Ah! If we rightly reflected upon this, we should more earnestly than ever repeat the words found in so many of our prayer books: "Lord, let me rather die than ever outrage thee again by sin!"

Standing in his prison, Jesus prayed uninterruptedly for his tormentors. When at last they grew tired of their cruel sport and became somewhat quiet, I saw Jesus leaning against the pillar and surrounded by light. *Day was dawning*, the day of his infinite sufferings and atonement. The day of our Redemption glanced faintly through an opening overhead in the prison wall and shone upon our holy, ill-used Paschal Lamb, who had taken upon himself all the sins of the world. Jesus raised his manacled hands to greet the dawning light and clearly and audibly pronounced a most touching prayer to his Father in heaven. In it he thanked him for sending this day after which the patriarchs had sighed, after which he too, since his coming upon earth, had longed so ardently as to break forth into the cry: "I have a baptism wherewith I am to be baptized, and how am I straitened until it be accomplished!" How touchingly the Lord thanked for this day, which was to accomplish the aim of his life, our salvation; which was to unlock heaven, subdue hell, open the source of blessings to humankind, and fulfill the will of his Father!

I repeated that prayer after Jesus, but I cannot now recall it. I was so sick from compassion, and I had to weep over his pains. As he continued to thank for all the terrible sufferings which he bore for me, I desisted not from imploring: "Ah, give me, give me thy pains! They are mine by right, they are all for my crimes!"

In streamed the light, and Jesus greeted the day in a prayer of thanksgiving so touching that, quite overcome with love and compassion, I repeated his words after him like a child. It was a scene indescribably sad, sacred, and solemn, a scene full of love—to see Jesus after the horrible turmoil of the night standing radiant with light by that low pillar in the center of his narrow prison cell, and *hailing with thanksgiving the first ray of dawn* on that great day of his propitiatory sacrifice. Ah! That ray of light came to Jesus as a judge might visit a criminal in prison to be reconciled to him before the execution of the sentence. Jesus thanked it so lovingly. The executioners, worn out, appeared to be dozing. Suddenly they looked up in wonder, but did not disturb Jesus. They appeared frightened and amazed. *Jesus may have been something over an hour in this prison.*

Judas at the Judgment Hall

WHILE Jesus was in prison, Judas, who until then—like one in despair and driven by the demon—was wandering around the Valley of Hinnom, on the steep southern side of Jerusalem, where lay naught but refuse, bones, and carrion, approached the precincts of Caiaphas's judgment hall. He stole around with the bundle of silver pieces, the price of his treachery, still hanging to the girdle at his side. The pieces were linked together by a little chain. All was silent. Judas, unrecognized, asked the guard what was going to happen to the Galilean. They replied: "He has been condemned to death, and he will be crucified." He heard some persons telling one another how dreadfully Jesus had been treated and how patient he was, while others said that at daybreak he was to appear again before the High Council to receive solemn condemnation. While the traitor, in order to escape recognition, gathered up this news here and there, day dawned and things began to be astir both in and around the hall. Judas, to escape being seen, slipped off behind the house. Like Cain, he fled the sight of men. Despair was taking possession of his soul. But what did he meet here? This was the place where the cross had been put together.

The several pieces lay in order side by side, and the workmen, wrapped in their mantles, were lying asleep. The sky glistened with a white light above the Mount of Olives, as if shuddering at sight of the instrument of our Redemption. Judas glanced at it in horror, and fled. He had seen the gibbet to which he had sold the Lord! He fled from the spot and hid, resolved to await the result of the morning trial.

The Morning Trial

AS soon as it was clear daylight, Caiaphas, Annas, the ancients and scribes assembled in the great hall to hold a trial perfectly lawful. Trial by night was not legal. That of the preceding night had been held only because time pressed on account of the feast, and that some of the preparatory attestations might be taken. Most of the members had passed the rest of the night in side chambers in Caiaphas's house, or on couches prepared for them above the judgment hall; but many, such as Nicodemus and Joseph of Arimathea, went away and *returned at daybreak*. It was a large assembly, and business was conducted in a very hurried manner. When now they held council against Jesus in order to condemn him to death, Nicodemus, Joseph of Arimathea, and a few others opposed his enemies. They demanded that the case should be postponed till after the festival in order not to give rise to a tumult among the people. They argued also that no just sentence could be rendered upon the charges as yet brought forward, since all the witnesses had contradicted one another. The high priests and their large party became exasperated by this opposition, and they told their opponents in plain terms that they understood clearly why this trial was so repugnant to them since, perhaps, they themselves were not quite innocent of having taken part in the doctrines of the Galilean.

The high priests even went so far as to exclude from the council all those that were in any way well-disposed toward Jesus. These members protested against taking any part in its proceedings, left the judgment hall, and betook themselves to the temple. From that time forward they never sat in the council. Caiaphas now ordered poor, abused Jesus, who was consumed from want of rest, to be brought from the prison and presented before the council, so that after the sentence he might without delay be taken to Pilate. The servants hurried tumultuously into the prison, overwhelmed Jesus with words of abuse, loosened his hands, dragged the old tattered mantle from his shoulders, put on him his own long, woven robe, which was still covered with all kinds of filth, fastened the ropes again around his waist, and led him forth from the prison. All this was accompanied with blows, by way of hastening the operation, for now as before all took place with violent hurry and horrible barbarity. Like a poor animal for sacrifice, with blows and mockery, Jesus was dragged by the executioners into the judgment hall through the rows of soldiers assembled in front of the house. And as through ill-treatment and exhaustion he presented so unsightly an appearance, his only covering being his torn and soiled undergarment, the disgust of his enemies filled them with still greater rage. Compassion found no place in any one of those hardened hearts.

Caiaphas, full of scorn and fury for Jesus standing before him in so miserable a plight, thus addressed him: "If thou be the anointed of the Lord, the Messiah, tell us!" Then Jesus raised his head and with divine forbearance and solemn dignity said: "If I shall tell you, you will not believe me. And if I shall also ask you, you will not answer me, nor let me go. But hereafter the Son of Man shall be sitting on the right hand of the power of

God." The members of the council glanced from one to another and, smiling scornfully, said to Jesus with disdain: "So then, thou! *Thou* art the Son of God?" With the voice of eternal truth, Jesus answered: "Yes, it is as ye say. I am he!" At this word of the Lord all looked at one another, saying: "What need we any further testimony? For we ourselves have heard it from his own mouth."

Then all rose up with abusive words against Jesus, "the poor, wandering, miserable, destitute creature of low degree, who was their Messiah, and who would one day sit upon the right hand of God!" They ordered the executioners to bind him anew, to place the chain around his neck, and to lead him as a condemned criminal to Pilate. A messenger had already been dispatched to notify Pilate to hold himself in readiness to judge a malefactor at an early hour, because on account of the coming festival there was no time to be lost. Some words of dissatisfaction passed among them with regard to the Roman governor; they were vexed at having to send Jesus first to him. But they dared not themselves pronounce sentence of death in cases that concerned other than their religious laws and those of the temple; and as they wanted to bring Jesus to death with a greater appearance of justice, they desired that he should be judged as an offender against the Emperor, and that the condemnation should come principally from the Roman governor. Soldiers were ranged in the outer court and in front of the house, and many of Jesus's enemies and others of the rabble were already gathered outside. The high priest and some other members of the council walked first, then followed the poor Savior among the executioners and a crowd of soldiers, and lastly came the mob. In this order they descended Zion into the lower city, and proceeded to Pilate's palace. Many of the priests that had assisted at the late trial now went to the temple, where there was much to be done today.

The Despair of Judas

JUDAS, the traitor, lurking at no great distance, heard the noise of the advancing procession, and words such as these dropped by stragglers hurrying after it: "They are taking him to Pilate. The Sanhedrin has condemned the Galilean to death. He has to die on the cross. He cannot live much longer, for they have already handled him shockingly. He is patient as one beside himself with horror. He speaks not, excepting to say that he is the Messiah and that he will one day sit at the right hand of God. That is all that he says, therefore he must be crucified. If he had not said that, they could have brought no cause of death against him, but now he

Good Friday Morning: Jesus in Prison

The Morning Judgment

must hang on the cross. The wretch that sold him was one of his own disciples and he had only a short time previously eaten the paschal lamb with him. I should not like to have a share in that deed. Whatever the Galilean may be, he has never delivered a friend to death for money. In truth, the wretch that sold him deserves to hang!" Then anguish, despair, and remorse began to struggle in the soul of Judas, but all too late. Satan instigated him to flee. The bag of silver pieces hanging from his girdle under his mantle was for him like a hellish spur. He grasped it tightly in his hand, to prevent its rattling and striking him at every step. On he ran at full speed, not after the procession, not to cast himself in Jesus's path to implore mercy and forgiveness, not to die with Jesus. No, not to confess with contrition before God his awful crime, but to disburden himself of his guilt and the price of his treachery before men. Like one bereft of his senses, he rushed into the temple, whither several of the council, as superintendents of the priests whose duty it was to serve, also some of the elders, had gone directly after the condemnation of Jesus. They glanced wonderingly at one another, and then fixed their gaze with a proud and scornful smile upon Judas, who stood before them, his countenance distorted by despairing grief. He tore the bag of silver pieces from his girdle and held it toward them with the right hand, while in a voice of agony he cried: "Take back your money! By it ye have led me to betray the just one. Take back your money! Release Jesus! I recall my contract. I have sinned grievously by betraying innocent blood!" The priests poured out upon him the whole measure of their contempt. Raising their hands, they stepped back before the offered silver, as if to preserve themselves from pollution, and said: "What is it to us that thou hast sinned? Thinkest thou to have sold innocent blood? Look thou to it! It is thine own affair! We know what we have bought from thee, and we find him deserving of death. Thou hast thy money. We want none of it!" With these and similar words spoken quickly and in the manner of men that have business on hand and that wish to get away from an importunate visitor, they turned from Judas. Their treatment inspired him with such rage and despair that he became like one insane. His hair stood on end, with both hands he rent asunder the chain that held the silver pieces together, scattered them in the temple, and fled from the city.

I saw him again running like a maniac in the Valley of Hinnom with Satan under a horrible form at his side. The evil one, to drive him to despair, was whispering into his ear all the curses the prophets had ever invoked upon this valley, wherein the Jews had once sacrificed their own children to idols. It seemed to him that all those maledictions were directed against himself; as, for instance, "They shall go forth, and behold the carcasses of those that have sinned against me, whose worm dieth not, and whose fire shall never be extinguished." Then sounded again in his ears: "Cain, where is Abel, thy brother? What hast thou done? His blood cries to me. Cursed be thou upon the earth, a wanderer and a fugitive!" And when, reaching the brook Kidron, he gazed over at the Mount of Olives, he shuddered and turned his eyes away, while in his ears rang the words: "Friend, whereto hast thou come? Judas, dost thou betray the Son of Man with a kiss?"

Oh, then horror filled his soul! His mind began to wander, and the fiend again whispered into his ear: "It was here that David crossed the Kidron when fleeing from Absalom. Absalom died hanging on a tree. David also sang of thee when he said: 'And they repaid me evil for good. May he have a hard judge! May Satan stand at his right hand, and may every tribunal of justice condemn him! Let his days be few, and his bishopric let another take! May the iniquity of his father be remembered in the sight of the Lord, and let not the sin of his mother be blotted out, because he persecuted the poor without mercy and put to death the broken in heart! He has loved cursing, and it shall come unto him. And he put on cursing like a garment, and like water it went into his entrails, like oil into his bones. May it be unto him like a garment which covereth him, and like a girdle may it enclose him forever!' Amid these frightful torments of conscience, Judas reached a desolate spot full of rubbish, refuse, and swampy water southeast of Jerusalem, at the foot of the Mount of Scandals where no one could see him. From the city came repeated sounds of noisy tumult, and Satan whispered again: "Now he is being led to death! Thou hast sold him! Knowest thou not how the law runs: 'he who sells a soul among his brethren, and receives the price of it, let him die the death'? Put an end to thyself, thou wretched one! Put an end to thyself!" Overcome by despair, Judas took his girdle and hung himself on a tree. The tree was one that consisted of several trunks, and rose out of a hollow in the ground. As he hung, his body burst asunder, and his bowels poured out upon the earth.

Jesus is Taken to Pilate

THE INHUMAN crowd that conducted Jesus from Caiaphas to Pilate passed through the most populous part of the city, which was now swarming with Passover guests and countless strangers from all parts of the country.

The procession moved northward from Mount Zion, down a closely-built street that crossed the valley, then through a section of the city

called Acre, along the west side of the temple to the palace and tribunal
of Pilate, which stood at the northwest corner of the temple opposite the
great forum, or market.

Caiaphas and Annas, with a large number of the chief council in robes
of state, stalked on in advance of the procession. After them were carried
rolls of writing. They were followed by numerous scribes and other Jews,
among them all the false witnesses and the exasperated Pharisees who
had been particularly active at the preceding accusation of the Lord.
Then after a short intervening distance, surrounded by a crowd of soldiers and those six functionaries who had been present at the capture,
came our dear Lord Jesus bound as before with ropes which were held
by the executioners. The mob came streaming from all sides and joined
the procession with shouts and cries of mockery. Crowds of people were
standing along the way.

Jesus was now clothed in his woven undergarment, which was covered with dirt and mud. From his neck hung the heavy, rough chain that
struck his knees painfully as he walked. His hands were fettered as on the
day before, and the four executioners dragged him again by the cords
fastened to his girdle. By the frightful ill-treatment of the preceding
night, he was perfectly disfigured. He tottered along, a picture of utter
misery—haggard, his hair and beard torn, his face livid and swollen with
blows. Amid fresh outrage and mockery he was driven onward. Many of
the mob had been instigated by those in power to scoff in this procession
at Jesus's royal entrance into Jerusalem on Palm Sunday. They saluted
him in mockery with all kinds of regal titles; cast on the road at his feet
stones, clubs, pieces of wood, and filthy rags; and in all kinds of satirical
songs and shouts reproached him with his solemn entrance. The executioners pushed him and dragged him by the cords over the objects that
impeded his path, so that the whole way was one of uninterrupted maltreatment.

Not very far from the house of Caiaphas, crowded together in the corner of a building, and waiting for the coming procession, were the blessed
and afflicted mother of Jesus, Magdalene, and John. Mary's soul was
always with Jesus, but wherever she could approach him in body also, her
love gave her no rest. It drove her out upon his path and into his footsteps.
After her midnight visit to Caiaphas's tribunal, she had in speechless grief
tarried only a short time in the Cenacle; for scarcely was Jesus led forth
from prison for the morning trial when she too arose. Enveloped in mantle and veil, and taking the lead of John and Magdalene, she said: "Let us
follow my Son to Pilate. My eyes must again behold him." Taking a
bypath, they got in advance of the procession, and here the blessed Virgin

stood and waited along with the others. The mother of Jesus knew how things were going with her Son. Her soul had him always before her eyes, but that interior view could never have depicted him so disfigured and maltreated as he really was by the wickedness of human creatures. She did, in truth, see constantly his frightful sufferings, but all aglow with the light of his love and his sanctity, with the glory of that patient endurance with which he was accomplishing his sacrifice. But now passed before her gaze the frightful reality in all its ignoble significance. The proud and enraged enemies of Jesus, the high priests of the true God, in their robes of ceremony, full of malice, fraud, falsehood, and blasphemy, passed before her, revolving deicidal designs. The priests of God had become priests of Satan. Oh, terrible spectacle! And then that uproar, those cries of the populace! And lastly, Jesus, the Son of God, the Son of Man, Mary's own Son, disfigured and maltreated, fettered and covered with blows, driven along by the executioners, tottering rather than walking, jerked forward by the barbarous executioners who held the ropes that bound him, and overwhelmed by a storm of mockery and malediction! Ah! Had he not been the most wretched, the most miserable in that tempest of hell unchained, had he not been the only one calm and in loving prayer, Mary would never have known him, so terribly was he disfigured. He had, besides, only his undergarment on, and that had been covered with dirt by the malicious executioners. As he approached her, she lamented as any mother might have done: "Alas! Is this my Son? Ah! Is this my Son! O Jesus, my Jesus!" The procession hurried by. Jesus cast upon his mother a side glance full of emotion. She became unconscious of all around, and John and Magdalene bore her away. But scarcely had she somewhat recovered herself when she requested John to accompany her again to Pilate's palace.

That friends abandon us in our hour of need, Jesus likewise experienced on this journey, for the inhabitants of Ophel were all assembled at a certain point on the way. But when they beheld Jesus so despised and disfigured, led forward in the midst of the executioners, they too wavered in their faith. They could not imagine that the king, the prophet, the Messiah, the Son of God could possibly be in such a situation. They heard their attachment to Jesus jeered at by the Pharisees as they passed. "There, look at your fine king!" they cried. "Salute him! Ah, now you hang your head when he is going to his coronation, when he will so soon mount his throne! It is all over with his prodigies. The high priest has put an end to his witchcraft." The poor people, who had received so many cures and favors from Jesus, were shaken in their faith by the frightful spectacle exhibited before them by the most venerable personages of the land, the high priest and the members of the Sanhedrin. The best of them turned away in doubt, while the viciously inclined, with scoffs and jeers, joined the procession wherever they could, for the avenues of approach were here and there occupied by guards appointed by the Pharisees in order to prevent a tumult.

The Palace of Pilate and its Surroundings

AT the foot of the northwestern corner of the temple mount stood the palace of Pilate, the Roman governor. It was on somewhat of an elevation, and was reached by a long flight of marble steps. It overlooked a spacious square surrounded by a colonnade under which vendors sat to sell their wares. A guardhouse and four entrances on the north, south, east, and west sides, respectively, broke the uniformity of the colonnade enclosing the square, which was called the forum, and which on the east stretched over the northwest corner of the temple mount. From this end of the forum, one could see as far as Mount Zion. Pilate's palace lay to the south. The forum was somewhat higher than the surrounding streets, which sloped down from it. On the outer side of the colonnade the houses of the neighboring streets adjoined it in some places. Pilate's palace did not adjoin the forum—a spacious court separated the two. On the eastern side of this court was a high arched gateway, which opened into a street that led to the sheep gate on the road to the Mount of Olives. On the western side was another gateway like the first, which led to the west of the city through the section Acre and up to Zion.

From Pilate's steps one could see across the court and into the forum, which lay to the north, and whose entrance at that point was furnished with columns and stone seats, the latter resting against the courtyard wall. As far as these seats and no farther would the Jewish priests approach the judgment hall of Pilate in order not to incur defilement; a line was even drawn across the pavement of the court to indicate the precise boundary. Near the western gateway of the court was erected in the precincts of the square a large guardhouse, which extending to the forum on the north, and on the south connecting by means of the gateway with the praetorium of Pilate, formed a forecourt and an atrium from the forum to the praetorium. That part of Pilate's palace used as a judgment hall was called the praetorium. The guardhouse was surrounded by columns. It had an open court in the center, under which were the prisons in which the two robbers were confined. This court was alive with Roman soldiers. In the forum, not far from this guardhouse and near the colonnade that surrounded it, stood the whipping pillar. Several others were standing in the enclosure of the square. The nearest were used for corporal punishment; to the most distant were fastened the beasts for sale. On the forum in front of the guardhouse was a terrace, level and beautiful, something like a place of execution, furnished with stone seats and reached by a flight of stone steps. From this place, which was called Gabbatha, Pilate was accustomed to pronounce solemn sentence. The marble steps that gave access to Pilate's palace led to an open terrace from which the governor listened to the plaintiffs, who sat opposite on the stone benches next the entrance to the forum. By speaking in a loud voice from the terrace, one could easily be heard in the forum.

Back of Pilate's palace rose still higher terraces with gardens and summerhouses. By these gardens, the palace was connected with the dwelling of Pilate's wife, whose name was Claudia Procula. A moat separated these buildings from the mountain on which the temple was built.

Adjoining the eastern side of Pilate's palace was that council house or judgment hall of Herod the Elder, in whose inner court many innocent children were once upon a time murdered. Its appearance was now somewhat changed, owing to the addition of new buildings; the entrance was from the eastern side, although there was still one from Pilate's hall.

Four streets ran hither from the eastern section of the city, three toward Pilate's palace and the forum; the fourth passed the northern side of the latter toward the gate that led to Bethzur. Near this gate and on this street stood the beautiful house owned by Lazarus in Jerusalem, and not far from it a dwelling belonging to Martha.

Of these four streets, the one that was nearest to the temple extended from the sheep gate. On entering the latter, one found on his right the Probatica, or pool in which the sheep were washed. It was built so close to the wall that the arches above it were constructed in that same wall. It had a drain outside the wall down into the valley of Jehosaphat, on which account this place, just before the gate, was marshy. Some buildings surrounded the pool. The paschal lambs were, before being taken to the temple, washed here for the first time; but at the pool of Bethesda, south of the temple, they afterward received a more solemn purification. In the second street stood a house and courtyard that once belonged to Mary's mother, St. Anne. She and her family used to put up there with their cattle for sacrifice when they went to Jerusalem for the festival days. In this house also, if I remember rightly, Joseph and Mary's wedding was celebrated.

The forum, as I have said, stood higher than the surrounding streets, through which ran gutters down to the sheep pool. On Mount Zion, opposite the ancient citadel of David, stood a similar forum; to the southeast and in its vicinity lay the Cenacle; and to the north were the judgment halls of Annas and Caiaphas. The citadel of David was now a deserted, dilapidated fortress full of empty courts, stables, and chambers, which were hired as resting places to caravans and travelers with their beasts of burden. This building had already long lain deserted. Even at the birth of Christ, I saw it in its present condition. The retinue of the three holy kings with its numerous beasts of burden put up at it.

Jesus before Pilate

ACCORDING to our reckoning of time, it was *about six in the morning* when the procession of the high priests and Pharisees, with the frightfully maltreated Savior, reached the palace of Pilate. Between the large square and the entrance into the praetorium were seats on either side of the road where Annas, Caiaphas, and the members of the council that had accompanied them placed themselves. Jesus, however, still bound by cords, was dragged forward by the executioners to the foot of the steps that led up to Pilate's judgment seat. At the moment of their arrival, Pilate was reclining on a kind of easy-chair upon the projecting terrace. A small, three-legged table was standing by him, upon which lay the insignia of his office and some other things, which I do not now recall. Officers and soldiers surrounded him, and they too wore badges indicative of Roman dominion.

The high priests and Jews kept far from the tribunal because, according to their Law, to approach it would have defiled them. They would not step over a certain boundary line.

When Pilate saw the mob hurrying forward with great tumult and clamor, and the maltreated Jesus led to the foot of his steps, he arose and addressed them with a scornful air. His manner was something like that of a haughty French marshal treating with the deputies of a poor little city. "What have you come about so early? Why have you handled the poor man so roughly? You began early to flay him, to slaughter him." But they cried out to the executioners: "Onward with him into the judgment hall!" Then turning to Pilate, they said: "Listen to our accusation against this malefactor. We cannot, for fear of defilement, enter the judgment hall."

Scarcely had this outcry died away when a tall, powerful, venerable-looking man from the crowd, pressing behind in the forum, cried out: "True, indeed, ye dare not enter that judgment hall, for it has been consecrated with innocent blood! Only he dares enter! Only he among all the Jews is pure as the Innocents!" After uttering these words with great emotion, he disappeared in the crowd. His name was Zadoch. He was a wealthy man and a cousin of the husband of Seraphia, who was afterward called Veronica. Two of his little boys had, at Herod's command, been slaughtered among the innocent children in the court of the judgment hall. Since that time he had entirely withdrawn from the world and, like an Essene, lived with his wife in continency. He had once seen Jesus at Lazarus's and listened to his teaching. At this moment, in which he beheld the innocent Jesus dragged in so pitiable a manner up the steps, the painful recollection of his murdered babes tore his heart, and he uttered that cry as a testimony to the Lord's innocence. The enemies of Jesus were, however, too urgent in their demands and too exasperated at Pilate's manner toward them and their own humbled position before him, to pay particular attention to the cry.

Jesus was dragged by the executioners up the lofty flight of marble steps and placed in the rear of the terrace, from which Pilate could speak with his accusers below. When Pilate beheld before him Jesus, of whom he had heard so many reports, so shockingly abused and disfigured, and still with that dignity of bearing which no ill-treatment could change, his loathing contempt for the Jewish priests and council increased. These latter had sent word to him at an early hour that they were going to hand over to him Jesus of Nazareth, who was guilty of death, that he might pronounce sentence upon him. Pilate, however, let them see that he was not going to condemn him without some well-proved accusation. In an imperious and scornful manner, therefore, he addressed the high priests: "What accusation do you bring against this man?" To which they answered angrily: "If we did not know him to be a malefactor, we should not have delivered him to you." "Take him," replied Pilate, "and judge him according to your Law." "Thou knowest," they retorted, "that it is not lawful for us to condemn any man to death."

The enemies of Jesus were full of rage and fury. Their whole desire seemed to be to put an end to him before the legal festival, that they might then slaughter the paschal lamb. For this end they wished to proceed in the most violent hurry. They knew not that he was the true Paschal Lamb, he whom they themselves had dragged before the tribunal of an idolatrous judge, over whose threshold they did not dare to pass for fear of defiling themselves and thus being unable to eat the typical paschal lamb.

As the governor summoned them to bring forward their accusations, this they now proceeded to do. They laid three principal charges against him, for each of which they produced ten witnesses. They worded them in such a way that Jesus might be made to appear as an offender against the Emperor, and Pilate be forced to condemn him. It was only in cases pertaining to the laws of religion and the temple that they had a right to take things into their own hands. The first charge they alleged was: "Jesus is a seducer of the people, a disturber of the peace, an agitator," and then they brought forth some witnesses to substantiate the charge. Next they said: "He goes about holding great meetings, breaking the sabbath, and healing on the sabbath." Here Pilate interrupted them scornfully: "It is easily seen that none of you were sick, else you would not be scandalized at healing on the sabbath." They continued: "He seduces the people by horrible teaching, for he says that to have eternal life, they must eat his flesh and blood." Pilate was provoked at the furious hate with which they uttered this charge. He glanced at his officers and with a smile said sharply to the Jews: "It would almost appear that you yourselves are following his teaching and are aiming at eternal life, since you, too, seem so desirous of eating his flesh and his blood."

Their second accusation was: "Jesus stirs up the people not to pay tribute to the Emperor." Here Pilate interrupted them angrily. As one whose office it was to know about such things, he retorted with emphasis: "That is a great lie! I know better than that!" Then the Jews shouted out their third accusation: "Let it be so! This man of low, obscure, and doubtful origin, puts himself at the head of a large party and cries woe to Jerusalem. He scatters also among the people parables of double meaning of a king who is preparing a wedding feast for his son. The people gathered in great crowds around him on a mountain, and once they wanted to make him king; but it was sooner than he wished, and so he hid himself. During the last few days he came forward more boldly. He made a tumultuous entrance into Jerusalem, causing regal honors to be shown him, while the people, by his orders, cried: 'Hosanna to the son of David! Blessed be the reign of our father David which is now come!' Besides this, he teaches that he is the Christ, the anointed of the Lord, the Messiah, the promised king of the Jews, and allows himself so to be called." This third charge, like the two preceding, was supported by ten witnesses.

At the word that Jesus caused himself to be called the Christ, the king of the Jews, Pilate became somewhat thoughtful. He went from the open terrace into the adjoining apartment, casting as he passed him a scrutinizing glance upon Jesus, and ordered the guard to bring the Lord into the judgment chamber.

PILATE was a fickle, weak-minded, superstitious pagan. He had all kinds of dark forebodings concerning the sons of his gods who had lived upon earth, and he was not ignorant of the fact that the Jewish prophets had long ago foretold one who was to be the anointed of God, a redeemer, a deliverer, a king, and that many of the Jews were looking for his coming. He knew also that kings from the East had come to Herod the Elder, inquiring after a newborn king, that they might honor him; and that after this many children were put to death at Herod's order. He knew indeed the traditions relating to a Messiah, a king of the Jews; but zealous idolater that he was, he put no faith in them, he could not fancy what kind of a king was meant. Most likely he thought with the liberal-minded Jews and Herodians of his day, who dreamed but of a powerful, victorious ruler. So the accusation that Jesus, standing before him so poor, so miserable, so disfigured, should give himself out for that anointed of the Lord, for that king, appeared to him truly ridiculous. But because the enemies of Jesus had brought forward the charge as injurious to the rights of the Emperor, Pilate caused the Savior to be conducted to his presence for an examination.

Pilate regarded Jesus with astonishment as he addressed him: "Art thou the king of the Jews?" And Jesus made answer: "Sayest thou this thing of thyself, or have others told it thee of me?" Pilate, a little offended that Jesus should esteem him so foolish as, of his own accord, to ask so poor and miserable a creature whether he was a king, answered evasively something to this effect: "Am I a Jew, that I should know about things so nonsensical? Thy people and their priests have delivered thee to me for condemnation as one deserving of death. Tell me, what hast thou done?" Jesus answered solemnly: "My kingdom is not of this world. If my kingdom were of this world, I should certainly have servants who would combat for me, that I should not be delivered to the Jews. But my kingdom is not here below." Pilate heard these earnest words of Jesus with a kind of shudder, and said to him thoughtfully: "Art thou then indeed a king?" And Jesus answered: "As thou sayest! Yes, I am the king. I was born, and I came into this world, to bear witness to the truth. Everyone that is of the truth, heareth my voice." Pilate cast a glance on him and, rising, said: "Truth! What is truth?" Some other words were then exchanged, whose purport I do not now remember.

Pilate went out again to the terrace. He could not comprehend Jesus, but knew this much about him, that he was not a king who would prove mischievous to the Emperor, and that he laid no claim to any kingdom of this world. As to a kingdom belonging to another world, the Emperor troubled himself little about that. Pilate therefore called down from the terrace to the high priests below: "I find no kind of crime in this man!"

Thereupon the enemies of Jesus were seized with new fury. They launched out into a torrent of accusations against him, while Jesus stood in silence praying for the poor creatures. Pilate turned to him and asked: "Hast thou nothing to say to all these charges?" But Jesus answered not a word. Pilate regarded him in amazement as he said: "I see plainly that they are acting falsely against thee!" (He used some expression for the word lie that I cannot remember.) But the accusers, whose rage was on the increase, cried out: "What! Thou findest no guilt in him? Is it no crime to stir up the people? He has spread his doctrine throughout the whole country, from Galilee up to these parts."

When Pilate caught the word *Galilee*, he reflected a moment and then called down: "Is this man from Galilee a subject of Herod?" The accusers answered: "Yes. His parents once lived in Nazareth, and now his own dwelling is near Capernaum." Pilate then said: "Since he is a Galilean and subject to Herod, take him to Herod. He is here for the feast, and can judge him at once." He then caused Jesus to be taken from the judgment chamber and led down again to his enemies, while at the same time he sent an officer to inform Herod that one of his subjects, a Galilean, Jesus of Nazareth, was being brought to him to be judged. Pilate was rejoiced to be able in this way to escape passing sentence on Jesus, for the whole affair made him feel uncomfortable. At the same time, he had a motive of policy in showing this act of courtesy to Herod, between whom and himself there was an estrangement, for he knew that Herod was very desirous of seeing Jesus.

Jesus's enemies were in the highest degree exasperated at being thus dismissed before the populace, at being thus obliged to lead Jesus away to another tribunal; consequently, they vented their rage upon him. With renewed fury they surrounded him, bound him anew and, along with the clamoring soldiers, drove him in furious haste with cuffs and blows across the crowded forum and through the street that led to the palace of Herod not far off. Some Roman soldiers accompanied them.

Claudia Procula, the lawful wife of Pilate, had while Pilate was treating with the Jews sent a servant to tell her husband that she was very anxious to speak with him. As Jesus was now being led to Herod, she stood concealed upon an elevated balcony, and with deep anxiety and trouble of mind watched him being led across the forum.

Origin of the Devotion of the "Holy Way of the Cross"

THE BLESSED Virgin, standing with Magdalene and John in a corner of the forum hall, had with unspeakable pain beheld the whole of the dreadful scene just described, had heard the clamorous shouts and cries. And now when Jesus was taken to Herod, she begged to be conducted by John and Magdalene back over the whole way of suffering trodden by her divine Son since his arrest the preceding evening. They went over the whole route—to the judgment hall of Caiaphas, to the palace of Annas, and thence through Ophel to Gethsemane on the Mount of Olives. On many places where Jesus had suffered outrage and injury, they paused in heartfelt grief and compassion, and wherever he had fallen to the ground the blessed Mother fell on her knees and kissed the earth. Magdalene wrung her hands, while John in tears assisted the afflicted mother to rise, and led her on further. This was the origin of that devotion of the church, the Holy Way of the Cross, the origin of that sympathetic meditation upon the bitter Passion of our divine Redeemer even before it was fully accomplished by him. Even then, when Jesus was traversing that most painful way of suffering, did his pure and immaculate mother, in her undying, holy love, seek to share the inward and outward pains of her Son and her God, venerate and weep over his footsteps as he went to die for us, and offer all to the heavenly Father for the salvation of the world.

Thus, at every step of the blessed Redeemer, did she gather the infinite merits that he acquired for us, and lay them up in her most holy and compassionate heart, that unique and venerable treasury of all the gifts of salvation, out of which and through which, according to the eternal degree of the triune God, every fruit and effect of the mystery of Redemption perfected in the fullness of time should be bestowed upon fallen man. From the most pure blood of this most holy heart was formed by the Holy Spirit that body which today was, from a thousand wounds, pouring forth Its precious blood as the price of our Redemption. For nine months had Jesus dwelt under that heart full of grace. As a virgin inviolate had Mary brought him forth, cared for him, watched over him, and nourished him at her breast, in order to give him over today for us to the most cruel death on the tree of the cross. Just as the Eternal Father spared not his Only-Begotten Son, but delivered him up for us, so the blessed Mother, the Mother of God, spared not the blessed Fruit of her womb, but consented that he, as the true Paschal Lamb, should be sacrificed for us upon the cross. And so Mary is, in her Son and next to him, the concurrent cause of our salvation, our redemption, our mediatrix and powerful advocate with God, the Mother of grace and of mercy.

All the just of olden times from our penitent first parents down to the last soul that had entered into Abraham's bosom, lamented, prayed, and offered sacrifice on this day in the holy heart of the divine Mother, the queen of patriarchs and prophets. So too, till the end of time, will it belong only to a childlike love for Mary to practice the devotion of the Holy

Way of the Cross, a devotion originated by her and by her bequeathed to
the church. By this devotion so rich in blessings, so pleasing to God, will
the soul advance in faith and in love to the most holy Redeemer. It is an
extremely significant fact, though unfortunately one too little appreciated, that wherever the love of Mary grows cold and devotion to the mysteries of the rosary becomes extinct, there too dies out the devotion of the
Holy Way of the Cross yes, even faith in the infinite value of the precious
blood is lost.

Magdalene in her grief was like an insane person. Immeasurable as her
love was her repentance. When, in her love, she longed to pour out her
soul at the feet of Jesus, as once the precious balm upon his head, full of
horror she descried between her and the Redeemer the abyss of her
crimes; then was the pain of repentance in all its bitterness renewed in her
heart. When, in her gratitude, she longed to send up like a cloud of
incense her thanksgiving for forgiveness received, she saw him, full of
pains and torments, led to death. With unspeakable grief she comprehended that Jesus was undergoing all this on account of her sins, which he
had taken upon himself in order to atone for them with his own blood.
This thought plunged her deeper and deeper into an abyss of repentant
sorrow. Her soul was, as it were, dissolved in gratitude and love, in sorrow and bitterness, in sadness and lamentation, for she saw and felt the
ingratitude, the capital crime of her nation, in delivering its Savior to the
ignominious death of the cross. All this was expressed in her whole
appearance, in her words and gestures.

John suffered and loved not less than Magdalene, but the untroubled
innocence of his pure heart lent a higher degree of peace to his soul.

Pilate and his Wife

WHILE Jesus was being taken to Herod and while he was enduring
mockery at his tribunal, I saw Pilate going to his wife, Claudia Procula.
They met at a summerhouse in a terraced garden behind Pilate's palace.
Claudia was trembling and agitated. She was a tall, fine-looking woman,
though rather pale. She wore a veil that fell gracefully in the back, but
without concealing her hair, which was wound round her head and
adorned with ornaments. She wore earrings and necklace, and her long,
plaited robe was fastened on her bosom by a clasp. She conversed long
with Pilate and conjured him by all that was sacred to him not to injure
Jesus, the prophet, the Holy of Holies, and then she related some things
from the dreams, or visions, which she had had of Jesus the night before.

I remember that she saw the annunciation to Mary, the birth of Christ, the adoration of the shepherds and the kings, the prophecies of Simeon and Anna, the flight into Egypt, the massacre of the Holy Innocents, the temptation in the desert, and other scenes from the holy life of Jesus. She saw him always environed with light, while the malice and wickedness of his enemies appeared under the most terrible pictures. She saw the sanctity and anguish of his mother and his own infinite sufferings under symbols of unchanging love and patience. She endured unspeakable anguish and sadness, for these visions, besides being something very unusual for her, were irresistibly impressive and convincing. Some of them, as for instance, the massacre of the Innocents and Simeon's prophecy in the temple, she beheld as taking place even in the neighborhood of her own house.

When next morning, alarmed by the uproar of the tumultuous mob, she looked out upon the forum, she recognized in the Lord the one shown her in vision the night before. She saw him now the object of all kinds of abuse and ill-treatment, while being led by his enemies across the forum to Herod. In terrible anguish, she sent at once for Pilate to whom, frightened and anxious, she related the visions she had seen in her dreams as far as she could make herself understood. She entreated and implored, and clung to Pilate in the most touching manner.

Pilate was greatly astonished, and somewhat troubled at what she related. He compared it with all that he had heard of Jesus, with the fury of the Jews, with Jesus's silence, and with his dignified and wonderful answers to all the questions he had put to him. He wavered uneasily in his own mind, but soon yielded to his wife's representations and said: "I have already declared that I find no guilt in Jesus. I shall not condemn him, for I know the utter wickedness of the Jews." He spoke at length of Jesus's bearing toward himself, quieted his wife's fears, and even went so far as to give her a pledge of assurance that he would not condemn him. I do not remember what kind of a jewel, whether a ring or a seal, Pilate gave as a sign of his promise. With this understanding they parted.

I saw Pilate as a crack-brained, covetous, proud, vacillating man, with a great fund of meanness in his character. He was deterred by no high fear of God from working out his own ends, could give himself to the meanest actions, and at the same time practiced the lowest, the most dastardly kind of superstitious idolatry and divination when he found himself in any difficulty. So now, off he hurried to his gods, before whom in a retired apartment of his house he burned incense and demanded of them all kinds of signs. He afterward watched the sacred chickens eating, and Satan whispered to him sometimes one thing, sometimes another. At one time he thought that Jesus ought to be released as innocent;

again, he feared that his own gods would take vengeance on him if he saved the life of a man who exercised so singular an influence upon him that he believed him some kind of demigod, for Jesus might do much harm to his divinities. "Perhaps," thought he, "he is indeed a kind of Jewish god. There are so many prophecies that point to a king of the Jews who shall conquer all things. Kings from the star worshippers of the East have already been here seeking such a king in this country. He might, perhaps, elevate himself above my gods and my Emperor, and so I should have much to answer for, if he does not die. Perhaps his death would be a triumph for my gods." Then came before him the remembrance of the wonderful dreams of his wife, who had never seen Jesus, and this remembrance weighed heavily in favor of Jesus's release in the wavering scales held by Pilate. It looked now as if he were resolved to release him. He wanted to be just, but he attained not his aim for the same reason that he had not waited for an answer from Jesus to his own question, "What is truth?"

Jesus before Herod

ON the forum and in the streets through which Jesus was led to Herod, a constantly increasing crowd was gathered, composed of the inhabitants from the neighboring places and the whole country around, come up for the feast. The most hostile Pharisees in the whole land had taken their places with their own people in order to stir up the fickle mob against Jesus. Before the Roman guardhouse near Pilate's palace, the Roman soldiers were drawn up in strong numbers, and many other important points of the city were occupied by them.

Herod's palace was situated in the new city to the north of the forum, not far from that of Pilate. An escort of Roman soldiers from the country between Switzerland and Italy joined the procession. Jesus's enemies were greatly enraged at this going backward and forward, and they ceased not to insult him and encourage the executioners to drag him and push him about. Pilate's messenger had announced the coming procession, consequently Herod was awaiting it. He was seated in a large hall on a cushioned throne, surrounded by courtiers and soldiers. The high priests went in through the colonnade and ranged on either side, while Jesus stood in the entrance. Herod was very much flattered that Pilate had openly, before the high priests, accorded to him the right of judgment upon a Galilean; so he put on a very arrogant air and made a great show of business. He was well-pleased also at seeing Jesus before him in so sorry a plight, since he had always disdained to appear in his presence.

The Passion and Death of Jesus Christ

John had spoken of Jesus in terms so solemn, and he had heard so much
of him from his spies and tale-bearers, that Herod was exceedingly curi-
ous about him. He was in an extraordinarily good humor at the thought
of being able to institute, before his courtiers and the high priests, a
grand judicial inquiry concerning Jesus, in which he might show off his
knowledge before both parties. He had also been informed that Pilate
could find no guilt in Jesus, and that was to his cringing mind a hint that
he was to treat the accusers with some reserve, a proceeding that only
increased their fury. As soon as they entered his presence, they began to
vociferate their complaints. Herod however looked inquisitively at Jesus,
and when he saw him so miserable, so ill-treated, his garments bespat-
tered with filth, his hair torn and dishevelled, his face covered with blood
and dirt, a feeling of loathsome compassion stole over the effeminate,
voluptuous king. He uttered God's name (it was something like "Jeho-
vah"), turned his face away with an air of disgust and said to the priests:
"Take him away! Clean him! How could you bring before my eyes so
unclean, so maltreated a creature!" At these words the servants led Jesus
into the vestibule, brought a basin of water and an old rag with which
they removed some of the dirt, ill-treating him all the while. Their rough
manner of acting opened the wounds on his disfigured face. Herod
meantime reproached the priests with their brutality. He appeared to
wish to imitate Pilate's manner of acting toward them, for he said: "It is
very evident that he has fallen into the hands of butchers. You are beginning your work today before the time." The high priests replied only by
vehemently alleging their complaints and accusations. When Jesus was
again led in, Herod, who wanted to play the agreeable toward him,
ordered a glass of wine to be brought to him that he might regain a little
strength. But Jesus shook his head, and would not accept the drink.

Herod was very affable to Jesus; he even flattered him and repeated all
that he knew of him. At first he asked him several questions, and wanted
to see a sign from him. But Jesus answered not a syllable, and quietly
kept his eyes cast down. Herod became very much vexed and ashamed
before those present. Wishing, however, to conceal his embarrassment,
he poured forth a torrent of questions and empty words. "I am very
sorry," he said, "to see thee so gravely accused. I have heard many things
of thee. Dost thou know that thou didst offend me in Thirza when, without my permission, thou didst release the prisoners whom I had confined there? But perhaps thy intentions were good. Thou hast now been
delivered to me by the Roman governor that I may judge thee. What sayest thou to all these charges? Thou art silent? They have often told me of
thy great wisdom in speaking and teaching—I should like to hear thee

refute thy accusers. What sayest thou? Is it true that thou art the king of the Jews? Art thou the Son of God? Who art thou? I hear that thou hast performed great miracles. Prove it to me by giving me some sign. It belongs to me to release thee. Is it true that thou hast given sight to men born blind? Didst thou raise Lazarus from the dead? Didst thou feed several thousand people with a few loaves? Why dost thou not answer! I conjure thee to perform one of thy miracles! It will be to thy own advantage." But Jesus was silent. Herod, with increasing volubility, went on: "Who art thou? What is the matter with thee? Who has given thee power? Why canst thou no longer exercise it? Art thou he of whose birth things so extraordinary are told? Once some kings came from the East to my father, to inquire after a newborn king of the Jews, to whom they wanted to do homage. Now, they say that this child is no other than thyself. Is this true? Didst thou escape the death which at that time fell upon so many children? How did that happen? Why didst thou remain so long in retirement? Or do they relate those events of thee only in order to make thee a king? Answer me! What kind of a king art thou? Truly, I see nothing royal about thee! They have, as I have heard, celebrated for thee lately a triumphant procession, to the temple. What does that mean? Speak! How comes it that such popularity ends in this way?" To all these questions Herod received no answer from Jesus. It was revealed to me that Jesus would not speak with him because, by his adulterous connection with Herodias and the murder of the Baptist, Herod was under excommunication.

Annas and Caiaphas took advantage of Herod's displeasure at Jesus's silence in order to renew their charges. Among others, they brought forward the following: Jesus had called Herod a fox, and for a long time he had been laboring to overthrow his whole family; he wanted to establish a new religion, and he had already eaten the Passover yesterday. This last accusation had been lodged with Caiaphas at the time of Judas's treason, but some of Jesus's friends had brought forth writings to show that that was allowed under certain circumstances.

Herod, although greatly vexed at Jesus's silence, did not permit himself to lose sight of his political ends. He did not wish to condemn Jesus, partly because of his own secret fear of him and the remorse he felt for John's murder, and partly again because the high priests were odious to him, because they would never palliate his adultery and on account of it had excluded him from the sacrifices. But the chief reason for Herod's not condemning Jesus was that he would not pass sentence on one whom Pilate had declared to be without guilt. He had political views also in thus acting; he wanted to show Pilate an act of courtesy in presence of the

The Passion and Death of Jesus Christ

high priests. He ended by overwhelming Jesus with words of scorn and contempt, and said to his servants and bodyguard (of whom there were about two hundred in his palace): "Take this fool away, and show the honor due to so ridiculous a king. He is more fool than malefactor!"

The Savior was now led out into a large court and treated with unspeakable outrage and mockery. The court was surrounded by the wings of the palace, and Herod, standing on a flat roof, gazed for a considerable time upon the ill-treatment offered to Jesus. Annas and Caiaphas were at his back, trying by all means in their power to induce him to pass sentence upon Jesus. Herod, however, would not yield. He replied in a tone loud enough to be heard by the Roman soldiers: "It would be for me the greatest sin, did I condemn him." He meant probably the greatest sin against Pilate's decision, who had been so gracious as to send Jesus to him.

When the high priests and enemies of Jesus saw that Herod would in no way comply with their wishes, they dispatched some of their number with money to Acre, a section of the city where at present many Pharisees were stopping. The messengers were directed to summon them to be in attendance at once with all their people in the vicinity of Pilate's palace. A large sum of money was put into the hands of these Pharisees for distribution among the people as bribes, that with furious and vehement clamoring they might demand Jesus's death. Other messengers were sent to spread among the people threats of God's vengeance if they did not insist upon the death of the blasphemer. They gave out the report also that if Jesus were not put to death, he would go over to the Romans, that this was what he meant by the kingdom of which he had so constantly spoken. Then, indeed, would the Jews be utterly ruined. On other sides they spread the report that Herod had condemned Jesus, but that the people must express their will on the subject; that his followers were to be feared, for if Jesus were freed in any way, the feast would be altogether upset, and then would the Romans and his followers unite in taking vengeance. Thus were scattered abroad confused and alarming rumors in order to rouse and exasperate the populace. At the same time, Jesus's enemies caused money to be distributed among Herod's soldiers, that they might grossly maltreat Jesus, yes, even hasten his death, for they would rather see him die in that way than live to be freed by Pilate's sentence.

From this insolent, godless rabble, our Lord had to suffer the most shameful mockery, the most barbarous ill-treatment. When they led him out into the court, a soldier brought from the lodge at the gate a large white sack in which cotton had been packed. They cut a hole in the bottom of the sack and, amid shouts of derisive laughter from all present,

242   GOOD FRIDAY, APRIL 3, AD 33

threw it over Jesus's head. It hung in wide folds over his feet. Another soldier laid a red rag like a collar around his neck. And now they bowed before him, pushed him here and there, insulted him, spat upon him, struck him in the face because he had refused to answer their king, and rendered him a thousand acts of mock homage. They threw filth upon him, pulled him about as if he were dancing, forced him in the wide, trailing mantle of derision to fall to the earth, and dragged him through a gutter which ran around the court the whole length of the buildings, so that his sacred head struck against the pillars and stones at the corners. Then they jerked him to his feet and set up fresh shouting, began new outrages. Among the two hundred soldiers and servants of Herod's court were people from regions most widely separated, and every wicked miscreant in that crowd wanted, by some special, infamous act toward Jesus, to do honor to himself and his province. They carried on their brutality with violent haste and mocking shouts. Those that had received money from the Pharisees took advantage of the confusion to strike the sacred head of Jesus with their clubs. He looked at them with compassion, sighed and groaned from pain. But they, in whining voices, mocked his moaning, and at every fresh outrage broke out into derisive shouts of laughter. There was not one to pity Jesus. I saw the blood running down from his head in the most pitiable manner, and three times did I see him sink to the earth under the blows from their clubs. At the same time, I saw weeping angels hovering over him, anointing his head. It was made known to me that these blows would have proved fatal, were it not for the divine assistance. The Philistines who, in the racecourse at Gaza, hunted blind Samson to death, were not so violent and cruel as these wretches.

But time pressed. The high priests must soon appear in the temple and, as they had received the assurance that all their instructions would be attended to, they made one more effort to obtain Jesus's condemnation from Herod. But he was deaf to their prayers. He still turned his thoughts toward Pilate alone, to whom he now sent back Jesus in his garment of derision.

Jesus Taken from Herod to Pilate

WITH renewed irritation, the high priests and the enemies of Jesus made their way back with him from Herod to Pilate. They were mortified at being forced to return, without his condemnation, to a tribunal at which he had already been pronounced innocent. They took therefore another and longer route in order to exhibit him in his ignominy to another por-

The Passion and Death of Jesus Christ

tion of the city, also that they might have longer to abuse him, and give their emissaries more time to stir up the populace against him.

The way they now took was very rough and uneven. The executioners by whom Jesus was led left him no moment of peace, and the long garment impeded his steps. It trailed in the mud and sometimes threw him down, on which occasions he was, with blows on the head and kicks, dragged up again by the cords. He was on this journey subjected to indescribable scorn and outrage both from his conductors and the populace, but he prayed the while that he might not die until he had consummated his Passion for us.

It was a quarter after eight in the morning when the procession with the maltreated Jesus again crossed the forum (though from another side, probably the eastern) to Pilate's palace. The crowd was very great. The people were standing in groups, those from the same places and regions together. The Pharisees were running around among them, stirring them up. Remembering the insurrection of the Galilean zealots at the last Passover, Pilate had assembled upwards of a thousand men whom he distributed in the praetorium and its surroundings, and at the various entrances of the forum, and his own palace.

The blessed Virgin, her elder sister Mary Heli with her daughter Mary Cleophas, Magdalene, and several other holy women—in all about twenty—were, while the following events were taking place, standing in a hall from which they could hear everything, and where they could slip in and out. John was with them in the beginning.

Jesus, in his garments of derision, was led through the jeering crowd. The most audacious were everywhere pushed forward by the Pharisees, surpassing the others in mockery and insults. One of Herod's court officers, who had reached the place before the procession, announced to Pilate how very much he appreciated his attention, but that he found the Galilean, so famed for his wisdom, nothing better than a silent fool, that he had treated him as such and sent him back to him. Pilate was very glad that Herod had not acted in opposition to himself and condemned Jesus. He sent his salutations to him in return, and thus they today were made friends who, since the fall of the aqueduct, had been enemies.

Jesus was led again through the street before Pilate's house and up the steps to the elevated platform. The executioners dragged him in the most brutal manner, the long garment tripped him, and he fell so often on the white marble steps that they were stained with blood from his sacred head. His enemies, who had retaken their seats on the side of the forum, and the rude mob, broke out into jeers and laughter at his every fall, while the executioners drove him up with kicks.

244   GOOD FRIDAY, APRIL 3, AD 33

Pilate was reclining on a chair something like a small couch, a little table by his side. As on the preceding occasion, he was attended by officers and men holding rolls of written parchment. Stepping out upon the terrace from which he was accustomed to address the multitude, he thus spoke to Jesus's accusers: "You have presented unto me this man as one that perverteth the people, and behold I, having examined him before you, find no cause in him in those things wherein you accuse him. No, nor Herod neither. For I sent you to him and behold, nothing worthy of death is brought against him. I will chastise him therefore and let him go." At these words, loud murmurs and shouts of disapprobation arose among the Pharisees, who began still more energetically to stir up the people and distribute money among them. Pilate treated them with the utmost contempt. Among other cutting remarks, he let fall the following sarcastic words: "You will not see enough innocent blood flow at the slaughtering today without this man's!"

It was customary for the people to go to Pilate just before Passover and, according to an ancient custom, demand the release of some one prisoner. It was now time for this. The Pharisees, while at Herod's palace, had dispatched emissaries to Acre—a section of the city west of the temple—to bribe the assembled multitude to demand, not Jesus's liberation, but his crucifixion. Pilate was hoping that the people would ask that Jesus should be released, and he thought by proposing along with him a miserable miscreant, who had already been condemned to death, he was leaving to them no choice. That notorious malefactor was called Barabbas, and was hated by the whole nation. He had in an insurrection committed murder; and besides that, I saw all kinds of horrible things connected with him. He was given to sorcery and, in its practice, had even cut open the womb of pregnant women.

And now there arose a stir among the people in the forum. A crowd pressed forward, their speaker at their head. Raising their voice so as to be heard on Pilate's terrace, they cried out: "Pilate, grant us what is customary on this feast!" For this demand Pilate had been waiting, so he at once addressed them. "It is your custom that I should deliver to you one prisoner on your festival day. Whom will you that I release to you, Barabbas or Jesus, the king of the Jews—Jesus, the anointed of the Lord?"

Pilate was quite perplexed concerning Jesus. He called him the "king of Jews," partly in character of an arrogant Roman who despised the Jews for having so miserable a king, between whom and a murderer the choice rested; and partly from a kind of conviction that he might really be that wonderful king promised to the Jews, the anointed of the Lord, the Messiah. His presentiment of the truth was also half-feigned. He mentioned these titles of the Lord because he felt that envy was the principal motive that excited the high priests against Jesus, whom he himself esteemed innocent.

A moment of hesitation and deliberation on the part of the populace followed upon Pilate's question, and then only a few voices shouted loudly: "Barabbas!" At that instant, Pilate was called for by one of his wife's servants, who showed him the pledge he had given her that morning, and said: "Claudia Procula bids thee remember thy promise." The Pharisees and high priests were greatly excited. They ran among the crowd, threatening and commanding. They had, however, no great trouble in making the mob carry out their wishes.

Mary, Magdalene, John, and the holy women, trembling and weeping, were standing in a corner of the hall. Although the mother of Jesus knew that there was no help for humankind excepting by his death, yet she was, as the mother of the most holy Son, full of anxiety, full of longing for the preservation of his life. Jesus had become man voluntarily to undergo crucifixion; still, when led to death, though innocent, he suffered all the pangs and torments of his frightful ill-treatment just as any human being would have suffered. And in the same way did Mary suffer all the affliction and anguish of an ordinary mother whose most innocent child should have to endure such things from the thankless multitude. She trembled, she shuddered with fear, and still she hoped. John went frequently to a little distance in the hope of being able to bring back some good news. Mary prayed that so great a crime might not be perpetrated. She prayed like Jesus on the Mount of Olives: "If it be possible, let this chalice pass!" And thus the loving mother continued to hope, for while the words and efforts of the Pharisees to stir up the people ran from mouth to mouth, the rumor also reached her that Pilate was trying to release Jesus. Not far from her stood a group of people from Capernaum, and among them many whom Jesus had healed and taught. They feigned not to recognize John and the veiled women standing so sorrowfully apart, and cast toward them furtive glances. Mary, like all the rest, thought they would surely not choose Barabbas in preference to their benefactor and Savior, but in this she was disappointed.

Pilate had returned to his wife, as a sign that his promise still held good, the pledge he had given her early that morning. He again went out on the terrace and seated himself on the chair by the little table. The high priests also were seated. Pilate called out again: "Which of the two shall I release unto you?" Thereupon arose from the whole forum and from all sides one unanimous shout: "Away with this man! Give us Barabbas!" Pilate again cried: "But what shall I do with Jesus, the Christ, the king of the Jews?" With tumultuous violence, all yelled: "Crucify him! Crucify him!" Pilate asked for the third time: "Why, what evil hath he done? I find not the least cause of death in him. I will scourge him and then let him go." But the shout: "Crucify him! Crucify him!" burst from the crowd like a roar from hell, while the high priests and Pharisees, frantic with rage, were vociferating violently. Then poor, irresolute Pilate freed the wretch Barabbas and condemned Jesus to be scourged!

The Scourging of Jesus

PILATE, the base, pusillanimous judge, had several times repeated the cowardly words: "I find no guilt in him, therefore will I chastise him and let him go!" To which the Jews shouted no other response than, "Crucify him! Crucify him!" But Pilate, still hoping to carry out his first resolve not to condemn Jesus to death, commanded him to be scourged after the manner of the Romans. Then the executioners, striking and pushing Jesus with their short staves, led him through the raging multitude on the forum to the whipping pillar, which stood in front of one of the halls that surrounded the great square to the north of Pilate's palace and not far from the guardhouse.

And now there came forward to meet Jesus the executioners' servants with their whips, rods, and cords, which they threw down near the pillar. There were six of them, swarthy men all somewhat shorter than Jesus, with coarse, crisp hair, to whom nature had denied a beard other than a thin, short growth like stubble. Their loins were girded and the rest of their clothing consisted of a jacket of leather, or some other wretched stuff, open at the sides, and covering the upper part of the body rather like a scapular. Their arms were naked, and their feet encased in tattered sandals. They were vile malefactors from the frontiers of Egypt who, as slaves and culprits, were here employed on buildings and canals. The most wicked, the most abject among them were always chosen for the punishment of criminals in the praetorium.

These barbarous men had often scourged poor offenders to death at this same pillar. There was something beastly, even devilish, in their appearance, and they were half-intoxicated. Although the Lord was offering no resistance whatever, yet they struck him with their fists and ropes and with frantic rage dragged him to the pillar, which stood alone and did not serve as a support to any part of the building. It was not very high, for a tall man with outstretched arms could reach the top, which was provided with an iron ring. Toward the middle of it on one side were other rings, or hooks. It is impossible to express the barbarity with which those furious hounds outraged Jesus on that short walk to the pillar. They tore from him Herod's mantle of derision, and almost threw the poor Savior to the ground.

Jesus trembled and shuddered before the pillar. With his own hands, swollen and bloody from the tight cords, and in tremulous haste, he laid aside his garments, while the executioners struck and abused him. He prayed and implored so touchingly and, for one instant, turned his head toward his most afflicted mother, who was standing with the holy women in a corner of one of the porches around the square, not far from the scourging place. Turning to the pillar, as if to cover himself by it, Jesus said: "Turn thine eyes from me!" I know not whether he said these words vocally or mentally, but I saw how Mary took them, for at the same moment, I beheld her turning away and sinking into the arms of the holy women who surrounded her, closely veiled.

And now Jesus clasped the pillar in his arms. The executioners, with horrible imprecations and barbarous pulling, fastened his sacred, upraised hands, by means of a wooden peg, behind the iron ring on top. In thus doing, they so stretched his whole body, that his feet, tightly bound below at the base, scarcely touched the ground. There stood the Holy of Holies, divested of clothing, laden with untold anguish and ignominy, stretched upon the pillar of criminals, while two of the bloodhounds, with sanguinary rage, began to tear with their whips the sacred back from head to foot. The first rods, or scourges, that they used looked as if made of flexible white wood, or they might have been bunches of ox sinews, or strips of hard, white leather.

Our Lord and Savior, the Son of God, true God and true Man, quivered and writhed like a poor worm under the strokes of the criminals' rods. He cried in a suppressed voice, and a clear, sweet-sounding wailing, like a loving prayer under excruciating torture, formed a touching accompaniment to the hissing strokes of his tormentors. Now and then the cries of the populace and the Pharisees mingled with those pitiful, holy, blessed, plaintive tones like frightful peals of thunder from an angry storm cloud. Many voices cried out together: "Away with him! Crucify him!" for Pilate was still negotiating with the people. The uproar was so great that, when he wanted to utter a few words, silence had to be enforced by the flourish of a trumpet. At such moments could be heard the strokes of the rods, the moans of Jesus, the blasphemy of the executioners, and the bleating of the paschal lambs, which were being washed in the pool near the sheep gate to the east. After this first purification, that they might not again soil themselves, their jaws were muzzled and they were carried by their owners along the clean road to the temple.

They were then driven around toward the western side, where they were subjected to another ceremonial washing. The helpless bleating of the lambs had in it something indescribably touching. They were the only sounds in unison with the Savior's sighs.

The Jewish mob kept at some distance, about the breadth of a street, from the place of scourging. Roman soldiers were standing here and there, but chiefly around the guardhouse. All kinds of loungers were loitering near the pillar itself, some in silence, others with expressions of contempt. I saw many of them suddenly roused to sympathy, and at such moments it seemed as if a sudden ray of light shot from Jesus to them.

I saw infamous, scantily clad youths at one side of the guardhouse preparing fresh rods, and others going off to seek thorn branches. Some executioners of the high priests went up to the scourgers and slipped them money, and a large jug of thick, red juice was brought to them, from which they guzzled until they became perfectly furious from intoxication. *They had been at work about a quarter of an hour* when they ceased to strike, and joined two of the others in drinking. Jesus's body was livid, brown, blue, and red, and entirely covered with swollen cuts. His sacred blood was running down on the ground. He trembled and shuddered. Derision and mockery assailed him on all sides.

The night before had been cold. All the morning until now the sky was overcast, and a shower of hail had for a few moments fallen on the wondering multitude. Toward noon, however, the sky cleared and the sun shone out.

The second pair of scourgers now fell upon Jesus with fresh fury. They made use of different rods, rough, as if set with thorns, and here and there provided with knots and splinters. Under their furious blows, the swollen welts on Jesus's sacred body were torn and rent; his blood spurted around so that the arms of his tormentors were sprinkled with it. Jesus moaned and prayed and shuddered in his agony.

Just at this time, a numerous band of strangers on camels were riding past the forum. They gazed with fright and horror while some of the bystanders explained to them what was going on. They were travelers, some of whom had received baptism, and others had been present at Jesus's Sermon on the Mount. The shouts and uproar of the populace became still greater in the vicinity of Pilate's palace.

The last two scourgers struck Jesus with whips consisting of small chains, or straps, fastened to an iron handle, the ends furnished with iron points, or hooks. They tore off whole pieces of skin and flesh from his ribs. Oh, who can describe the awful barbarity of that spectacle!

But those monsters had not yet satiated their cruelty. They loosened the cords that bound Jesus and turned his back to the pillar and, because he was so exhausted as to be no longer able to stand, they bound him to it with fine cords passed under his arms across his breast, and below the knees. His hands they fastened to the ring in the middle of the opposite side. Only blood and wounds, only barbarously mangled flesh could be seen on the most sacred, most venerable body of the Son of God. Like furious bloodhounds raged the scourgers with their strokes. One held a slender rod in his left hand, and with it struck the face of Jesus. There was no longer a sound spot on the Lord's body. He glanced, with eyes swimming in blood, at his torturers, and sued for mercy; but they became only the more enraged. He moaned in fainting tones: "Woe! Woe!"

The terrible scourging had lasted fully three-quarters of an hour when an obscure man, a stranger and relative of that blind Ctesiphon whom Jesus had restored to sight, rushed indignantly to the back of the pillar, a sickle-shaped knife in his hand, and cried out: "Hold on! Do not beat the innocent man to death!" The drunken executioners, startled for a moment, paused, while with one stroke the stranger quickly cut the cords that bound Jesus. They were all knotted together, and fastened to a great iron nail at the back of the pillar. The man then fled back and disappeared in the crowd. Jesus sank, covered with blood and wounds, at the foot of the pillar and lay unconscious in his own blood. The executioners left him lying there and went to drink and call to their villainous companions, who were weaving the crown of thorns.

Jesus quivered in agony as, with bleeding wounds, he lay at the foot of the pillar. I saw just then some bold girls passing by. They paused in silence before him, holding one another by the hand, and looked at him in feminine disgust, which renewed the pain of all his wounds. He raised his bleeding head, and turned his sorrowful face in pity toward them. They passed on, while the executioners and soldiers laughed and shouted some scandalous expressions after them.

Several times during the scourging I saw weeping angels around Jesus and, during the whole of that bitter, ignominious punishment that fell upon him like a shower of hail, I heard him offering his prayer to his Father for the sins of humankind. But now, as he lay in his own blood at the foot of the pillar, I saw an angel strengthening him. It seemed as if the angel gave him a luminous morsel.

The executioners again drew near and, pushing Jesus with their feet, bade him rise, for they had not yet finished with the king. They struck at him while he crept after his linen band, which the infamous wretches kicked with shouts of derision from side to side, so that Jesus, in this his dire necessity, had most painfully to crawl around the ground in his own blood like a worm trodden underfoot, in order to reach his girdle and with it cover his lacerated loins. Then with blows and kicks they forced him to his tottering feet, but allowed him no time to put on his robe, which they threw about him with the sleeves over his shoulders. They hurried him to the guardhouse by a roundabout way, all along which he wiped the blood from his face with his robe. They were able to proceed quickly from the place of scourging because the porches around the building were open toward the forum; one could see through to the covered way under which the robbers and Barabbas lay imprisoned. As Jesus was led past the seats of the high priests, the latter cried out: "Away with him! Away with him!" and in disgust turned from him into the inner court of the guardhouse. There were no soldiers in it when Jesus entered, but all kinds of slaves, executioners, and vagrants, the very scum of the populace.

As the mob had become so excited, Pilate had sent to the fortress Antonia for a reinforcement of Roman guards, and these he now ordered to surround the guardhouse. They were permitted to talk and laugh and ridicule Jesus, though they had to keep their ranks. Pilate wanted thus to restrain the people and keep them in awe. There were upwards of a thousand men assembled.

Mary during the Scourging of Jesus

I SAW the blessed Virgin, during the scourging of our Redeemer, in a state of uninterrupted ecstasy. She saw and suffered in an indescribable manner all that her Son was enduring. Her punishment, her martyrdom, was as inconceivably great as her most holy love. Low moans frequently burst from her lips, and her eyes were inflamed with weeping. Mary Heli, her elder and very aged sister, who bore a great resemblance to St. Anne, supported her in her arms. Mary Cleophas, Mary Heli's daughter, was likewise present, and she too for the most part leaned on her mother's arm. The other holy women were trembling with sorrow and anxiety. They were pressing with low cries of grief around the blessed Virgin, as if expecting their own sentence of death. Mary wore a long robe, almost sky-blue, and over it a long, white, woollen mantle, and a veil of creamy white. Magdalene was very much disturbed, indeed quite distracted by grief; her hair hung loose under her veil.

When, after the scourging, Jesus fell at the foot of the pillar, I saw that Claudia Procula, Pilate's wife, sent to the Mother of God a bundle of large linen cloths. I do not now know whether she thought that Jesus would be released, and then the mother of the Lord could bind up his wounds with them, or whether the compassionate pagan sent the linens for the use to which the blessed Virgin afterward put them.

Mary saw her lacerated Son driven past her by the executioners. With his garment he wiped the blood from his eyes in order to see his mother. She raised her hands in agony toward him and gazed upon his blood-stained footprints. Then, as the mob moved over to another side, I saw the blessed Virgin and Magdalene approaching the place of scourging. Surrounded and hidden by the other holy women and some well-disposed people standing by, they cast themselves on their knees and soaked up the sacred blood of Jesus with the linens until not a trace of it could be found.

The holy women were about twenty in number, but I did not see John with them at that time. Simeon's son Obed, Veronica's son, and Aram and Themeni, the two nephews of Joseph of Arimathea were, though sad and full of sorrow, busied in the temple.

It was about nine o'clock in the morning when the scourging was over.

Personal Appearance
of Mary and of Magdalene

I SAW the blessed Virgin with cheeks pale and haggard, her nose pinched and long, her eyes almost bloodshot from weeping. It is astonishing, as well as indescribable, how plain, straightforward, and simple she was in appearance. Although since yesterday evening and even during the whole night, she had in fright, in anguish, and in tears, been wandering through the valley of Jehosaphat and the crowded streets of Jerusalem, still was her dress in perfect order, her whole appearance marked by extreme propriety. There was not even a fold of her garments that did not bespeak sanctity. Everything about her was so upright and simple, so dignified, so pure, and so innocent. Her look as she gazed around was so noble, and as she turned her head a little, her veil fell in soft and graceful folds. Her movements were not eager and, though under the influence of the most grievous anguish, all her actions were performed simply and gently. Her garments were damp with the dew of the night and her own innumerable tears, but they were spotless and in perfect order. Her beauty was indescribable and altogether superhuman, for beauty in her was made up of immaculate purity, truth, simplicity, dignity, and holiness.

Magdalene, on the contrary, was just the reverse. She was taller and, both in figure and carriage, exhibited much more style. Her beauty, however, was now destroyed, owing to her violent repentance and intense grief. She was, if not decidedly ugly, at least painful to look upon, on account of the unrestrained fury of her passions. Her garments, wet and stained with mud, hung torn and disordered around her; her long hair floated loose and dishevelled under her wet, tossed veil. She was perfectly changed in appearance. She thought of nothing but her grief, and looked almost like one bereft of sense. There were many people here from Magdalum and the surrounding country who had known her in her early splendor, who had seen her in her wasting life of sin, and who had lost sight of her in her long retirement. Now they pointed her out with the finger and mocked at her forlorn appearance. Yes, there were some from Magdalum base enough even to throw mud at her as she passed along. But she did not notice it, so absorbed was she in her own sorrow.

Jesus Crowned
with Thorns and Mocked

WHILE Jesus was being scourged, Pilate had several times addressed the multitude, and again had the shout gone up: "He shall be executed, even if we die for it!" And when Jesus was led to the crowning, they cried again: "Away with him! Away!" New bands of Jews were constantly arriving, and as they came, they were instigated by the runners of the high priests to raise that cry.

Now followed a short interval of rest. Pilate gave some orders to his soldiers. The high priests and council meanwhile, seated on elevated benches on either side of the street in front of Pilate's terrace, shaded by trees and awnings, ordered food and drink to be brought them by their servants. I saw Pilate again perplexed and doubting. Yielding to his superstition, he retired alone to burn incense before his gods and to busy himself in all kinds of divination.

I saw the blessed Virgin and her companions, when they had dried up Jesus's blood after the scourging, leaving the forum. I saw them with the bloody linens in a small house built in a wall in the neighborhood. I do not now recall to whom it belonged, nor do I remember having seen John at the scourging.

The crowning and mocking of Jesus took place in the inner court of the guardhouse, which stood in the forum over the prisons. It was surrounded with pillars, and the entrance was open. There were about fifty low-lived wretches belonging to the army, jailer's servants, executioners, lads, slaves, and whipping servants, who took an active part in this maltreatment of Jesus. The mob at first crowded in eagerly, but was soon displaced by the thousand Roman soldiers who surrounded the building.

They stood in rank and order, jeering and laughing, thereby giving to Jesus's tormentors new inducement to multiply his sufferings. Their jokes and laughter encouraged them as applause does the actor.

There was a hole in the middle of the court, and to this they had rolled the base of an old column, which may once have stood there. On that base they placed a low, round stool with an upright at the back by which to raise it, and maliciously covered it with sharp stones and potsherds.

Once more they tore Jesus's clothing from his wounded body, and threw over him instead an old red military cloak tattered and so short that it did not reach to the knees. Shreds of yellow tassels hung on it here and there. It was kept in a corner of the executioners' room and used to throw around criminals after their scourging, either to dry the blood or to turn them into derision. Now they dragged Jesus to the stool covered with stones and potsherds, and violently forced his wounded, naked body down upon them. Then they put upon him the crown of thorns. It was two hands high, thick, and skillfully plaited, with a projecting edge on top. They laid it like a binder round his brow and fastened it tightly in the back, thus forming it into a crown. It was woven from thorn branches three fingers thick, the thorns of which grew straight out. In plaiting the crown, as many of them as possible had been designedly pressed inward. There were three kinds of thorns, such as with us are called buckthorn, blackthorn, and hawthorn. The projecting edge on top was formed of one kind, which we call blackberry, and it was by this the torturer fastened it on and moved it in order to produce new sufferings. I have seen the spot whence the miscreants brought the thorns.

Next they placed in Jesus's hand a thick reed with a tufted top. All this was done with mock solemnity, as if they were really crowning him king. Then they snatched the reed from his hand and with it struck the crown violently, until his eyes filled with blood. They bent the knee before him, stuck out their tongue at him, struck and spat in his face, and cried out: "Hail, king of the Jews!" With shouts of mocking laughter, they upset him along with the stool, in order to force him violently down upon it again.

I am not able to repeat all the base inventions employed by those wretches to insult the poor Savior. Ah! His thirst was horrible, for he was consumed with the fever of his wounds, the laceration caused by the inhuman scourging. He quivered. The flesh on his sides was in many places torn even to the ribs. His tongue contracted convulsively. Only the sacred blood trickling down from his head laved, as it were in pity, his parched lips which hung languishingly open. Those horrible monsters, seeing this, turned his mouth into a receptacle for their own disgusting filth. Jesus underwent this maltreatment for ab*out half an hour*, during which time the cohort surrounding the praetorium in rank and order kept up an uninterrupted jeering and laughing.[†]

"Ecce Homo!"

AND now they again led Jeus, the crown of thorns upon his head, the mock scepter in his fettered hands, the purple mantle thrown around him, into Pilate's palace. He was unrecognizable on account of the blood that filled his eyes and ran down into his mouth and beard. His body, covered with swollen welts and wounds, resembled a cloth dipped in blood, and his gait was bowed down and tottering. The mantle was so short that he had to stoop in order to cover himself with it, for at the crowning they had again torn off all his clothing. When he reached the lowest step of the flight that led up to Pilate, even that hard-hearted being was seized with a shudder of compassion and disgust. He leaned on one of his officers, and as the priests and the people kept up their shouts and mockery, he exclaimed: "If the devil were as cruel as the Jews, one could not live with him in hell!" Jesus was wearily dragged up the steps, and while he stood a little back, Pilate stepped to the front of the balcony. The trumpet sounded to command attention, for Pilate was going to speak. Addressing the high priests and the people, he said: "Behold! I bring him forth to you, that you may know that I find no cause in him!"

Then Jesus was led forward by the executioners to the front of the balcony where Pilate was standing, so that he could be seen by all the people in the forum. Oh, what a terrible, heart-rending spectacle! Silence, awful and gloomy, fell upon the multitude as the inhumanly treated Jesus, the sacred, martyrized figure of the Son of God, covered with blood and wounds, wearing the frightful crown of thorns, appeared and,

---

[†] These meditations on the sufferings of Jesus filled Anne Catherine with such feelings of compassion that she begged of God to allow her to suffer as he had done. She instantly became feverish and parched with thirst, and, by morning, was speechless from the contraction of her tongue and of her lips. She was in this state when her friend came to her in the morning, and she looked like a victim that had just been sacrificed. Those around succeeded, with some difficulty, in moistening her mouth with a little water, but it was long before she could give any further details concerning her meditations on the Passion. Even then, she was so exhausted that it was not without great difficulty, and after many intervals of rest, that she narrated all which our Lord suffered in this crowning with thorns. She was scarcely able to speak, because she herself felt every sensation which she described in this account.

from his eyes swimming in blood, cast a glance upon the surging crowd! Nearby stood Pilate, pointing to him with his finger and crying to the Jews: "Behold the man!"

While Jesus, the scarlet cloak of derision thrown around his lacerated body, his pierced head sinking under the weight of the thorny crown, his fettered hands holding the mock scepter, was standing thus before Pilate's palace, in infinite sadness and benignity, pain and love, like a bloody phantom, exposed to the raging cries of both priests and people, a band of strangers, men and women, their garments girded, crossed the forum and went down to the sheep pool. They were going to help in the washing of the paschal lambs, whose gentle bleating was still mingling with the sanguinary shouts of the multitude, as if wishing to bear witness to the silent truth. Now it was that the true Paschal Lamb of God, the revealed though unrecognized mystery of this holy day, fulfilled the prophecies and stretched himself in silence on the slaughtering bench.

The high priests and judges were perfectly infuriated at the sight of Jesus, the dread mirror of their own conscience, and they vociferated: "Away with him! Crucify him!" Pilate called out: "Are you not yet satisfied? He has been handled so roughly that he will never more want to be a king." But they and all the people, as if beside themselves with fury, cried out violently: "Away with him! To the cross with him!" Again did Pilate order the trumpet to be sounded, and again did he cry out: "Take him you and crucify him, for I find no cause in him!" To this the high priests shouted: "We have a law, and according to it he must die, for he has made himself the Son of God!" Pilate responded: "If you have such a law, that a man like this one must die, then may I never be a Jew!" The words, however, "He has made himself the Son of God," renewed Pilate's anxiety, aroused again his superstitious fears. He caused Jesus therefore to be brought before him into the judgment hall, where he spoke to him alone. He began by asking: "Whence art thou?" But Jesus gave him no answer. "Dost thou not answer me?" said Pilate. "Knowest thou not that I have power to crucify thee and power to release thee?" "Thou shouldst not have any power," answered Jesus, "unless it were given thee from above; therefore he that hath delivered me to thee hath the greater sin."

Just at this moment, Claudia Procula, Pilate's wife, anxious at seeing his irresolution, sent again to him, directing the messenger to show him once more the pledge he had given her of his promise. But he returned a vague, superstitious reply in which he appealed to his gods.

Undecided and perplexed as before, Pilate again went forth and addressed the people, telling them that he could find no guilt in Jesus. They meanwhile had been stirred up by the report spread by the high priests and Pharisees, namely, that "Jesus's followers had bribed Pilate's wife; that if Jesus were set free, he would unite with the Romans and then they would all be put to death." This so roused the multitude that they clamored more vehemently than ever for his death. Pilate, desirous of obtaining in some way an answer to his questions, went back again to Jesus in the judgment hall. When alone with him, he glanced at him almost in fear, and thought in a confused sort of a way: "What if this man should indeed be a god?" And then with an oath he at once began adjuring Jesus to say whether he was a god and not a human being, whether he was that king promised to the Jews. How far did his kingdom extend? To what rank did his divinity belong? and ended by declaring that, if Jesus would answer his questions, he would set him free. What Jesus said to Pilate in answer, I can repeat only in substance, not in words. The Lord spoke words of terrible import. He gave Pilate to understand what kind of a king he was, over what kind of a kingdom he reigned, and what was the truth, for he told him the truth. He laid before him the abominable state of his own conscience, foretold the fate in store for him—exile in misery and a horrible end. He told him, moreover, that he would one day come to pass sentence upon him in just judgment.

Frightened and vexed at Jesus's words, Pilate again went out upon the balcony and proclaimed his intention of freeing Jesus. Then arose the cry: "If thou release this man, thou art not Caesar's friend, for whosoever maketh himself a king, speaketh against Caesar!" Others shouted: "We will denounce thee to Caesar as a disturber of our feast. Make up thy mind at once, for under pain of punishment we must be in the temple by ten tonight." And the cry: "To the cross with him! Away with him!" resounded furiously on all sides, even from the flat roofs of the houses near the forum, upon which some of the mob had clambered.

Pilate now saw that he could do nothing with the raging multitude. There was something truly frightful in the confusion and uproar. The whole mass of people collected before the palace was in such a state of rage and excitement that a violent insurrection was to be feared. Then Pilate called for water. The servant that brought it poured it from a vase over his hands before the people, while Pilate called down from the balcony: "I am innocent of the blood of this just man! Look ye to it!" Then went up from the assembled multitude, among whom were people from all parts of Palestine, the horrible, the unanimous cry: "His blood be upon us and upon our children!"

The Passion and Death of Jesus Christ

Jesus Condemned
to the Death of the Cross

PILATE, who was not seeking the truth but a way out of difficulty, now became more undecided than ever. His conscience reproached him: "Jesus is innocent." His wife said: "Jesus is holy." His superstition whispered: "He is an enemy of thy gods." His cowardice cried out: "He is himself a god, and he will avenge himself." Then did he again anxiously and solemnly question Jesus, and then did Jesus make known to him his secret transgressions, his future career and miserable end, and warned him that he would come one day sitting on the clouds to pronounce a just sentence upon him. And now came a new weight to be cast into the false scales of his justice against Jesus's release. He was offended at having to stand before Jesus, whom he could not fathom, with his ignominious conscience unveiled under his gaze; and that the man whom he had caused to be scourged and whom he had power to crucify, should predict for him a miserable end; yes, that the lips to which no lie had ever been imputed, which had uttered no word of self justification, should, even in this moment of dire distress, summon him on that day to a just judgment. All this roused his pride. But as no one sentiment ruled supreme in this miserable, irresolute creature, he was seized with anxiety at the remembrance of the Lord's warning, and so he determined to make a last effort to free him. At the threats of the Jews, however, to denounce him to the Emperor, another cowardly fear took possession of Pilate. The fear of an earthly sovereign overruled the fear of the king whose kingdom was not of this world. The cowardly, irresolute wretch thought: "If he dies, so die with him also what he knows of me and what he has predicted of me." At the threat of the Emperor, Pilate yielded to the will of the multitude, although against the promise he had pledged to his wife, against right and justice and his own conscience. Through fear of the Emperor, he delivered to the Jews the blood of Jesus; for his own conscience he had naught but the water which he ordered to be poured over his hands while he cried out: "I am innocent of the blood of this just man. Look ye to it!" No, Pilate! But do thou thyself look to it! Thou knowest him to be just, and yet thou dost shed his blood! Thou art an unjust, an unprincipled judge! And that same blood, which Pilate sought to wash from his hands and which he could not wash from his soul, the bloodthirsty Jews invoked as a malediction upon themselves and upon their children. The blood of Jesus, which cries for pardon for us, they invoke as vengeance upon themselves: They cry: "His blood be upon us and our children!"

258 GOOD FRIDAY, APRIL 3, AD 33

While this terrible cry was resounding on all sides, Pilate ordered preparations to be made for pronouncing the sentence. His robes of ceremony were brought to him. A crown, in which sparkled a precious stone, was placed on his head, another mantle was thrown around him, and a staff was borne before him. A number of soldiers surrounded him, officers of the tribunal went before him carrying something, and scribes with parchment rolls and little tablets followed him. The whole party was preceded by a man sounding a trumpet. Thus did Pilate leave his palace and proceed to the forum where, opposite the scourging place, there was a high, beautifully constructed judgment seat. Only when delivered from that seat had the sentence full weight. It was called Gabbatha. It consisted of a circular balcony, and up to it there were several flights of steps. It contained a seat for Pilate, and behind it a bench for others connected with the tribunal. The balcony was surrounded and the steps occupied by soldiers. Many of the Pharisees had already left the palace and gone to the temple. Only Annas, Caiaphas, and about twenty-eight others went at once to the judgment seat in the forum, while Pilate was putting on his robes of ceremony. The two thieves had been taken thither when Pilate presented the Lord to the people with the words, "*Ecce Homo.*" Pilate's seat was covered with red, and on it lay a blue cushion bordered with yellow.

And now Jesus in the scarlet cloak, the crown of thorns upon his head, his hands bound, was led by the soldiers and executioners through the mocking crowd and placed between the two thieves in front of the judgment seat. From this seat of state Pilate once more said aloud to the enemies of Jesus: "Behold there your king!" But they yelled: "Away, away with this man! Crucify him!" "Shall I crucify your king?" said Pilate. "We have no king but Caesar!" responded the high priests.

From that moment Pilate spoke no word for nor with Jesus. He began the sentence of condemnation. The two thieves had been already sentenced to the cross, but their execution, at the request of the high priests, had been postponed till today. They thought to outrage Jesus the more by having him crucified with two infamous murderers. The crosses of the thieves were already lying near them, brought by the executioners' assistants. Our Lord's was not yet there, probably because his death sentence had not yet been pronounced.

The blessed Virgin, who had withdrawn to some distance when Pilate presented Jesus to the Jews and when he was greeted by them with that bloodthirsty cry, now, surrounded by several women, again pressed through the crowd to be present at the death sentence of her Son and her God. Jesus, encircled by the executioners and greeted with rage and deri-

sive laughter by his enemies, was standing at the foot of the steps before
Pilate. The trumpet commanded silence, and with dastardly rage Pilate
pronounced the sentence of death.

The sight of that base double-tongued wretch; the triumph of the
bloodthirsty but now satisfied Pharisees who had so cruelly hunted down
their prey; the innumerable sufferings of the most blessed Savior; the
inexpressible affliction and anguish of his blessed Mother and the holy
women; the eager listening of the furious Jews; the cold, proud demeanor
of the soldiers; and the apparitions of all those horrible, diabolical forms
among the crowd, quite overpowered me. Ah! I felt that I should have
been standing there instead of my beloved Lord. Then truly would the
sentence have been just!

Pilate first spoke some words in which, with high-sounding titles, he
named the Emperor Claudius Tiberius. Then he set forth the accusation
against Jesus; that, as a seditious character, a disturber and violator of the
Jewish laws, who had allowed himself to be called the Son of God and
the king of the Jews, he had been sentenced to death by the high priests,
and by the unanimous voice of the people given over to be crucified. Fur-
thermore Pilate, that iniquitous judge, who had in these last hours so frequently and publicly asserted the innocence of Jesus, now proclaimed
that he found the sentence of the high priests just, and ended with the
words: "I also condemn Jesus of Nazareth, king of the Jews, to be nailed
to the cross." Then he ordered the executioners to bring the cross. I have
also some indistinct recollection of his taking a long stick, the center of
which was full of pith, breaking it, and throwing the pieces at Jesus's feet.

The most afflicted mother of Jesus, the Son of God, on hearing Pilate's
words became like one in a dying state, for now was the cruel, frightful,
ignominious death of her holy and beloved Son and Savior certain. John
and the holy women took her away from the scene, that the blinded multitude might not render themselves still more guilty by jeering at the sorrow of the mother of their Savior. But Mary could not rest. She longed to
visit every spot marked by Jesus's sufferings. Her companions had once
more to accompany her from place to place, for the mystical sacrifice
that she was offering to God by her most holy compassion urged her to
pour out the sacrifice of her tears wherever the Redeemer born of her
had suffered for the sins of humankind, his brethren. And so the mother
of the Lord, by the consecration of her tears, took possession of all the
sacred places upon earth for the future veneration of the church, the
mother of us all, just as Jacob set up the memorial stone and consecrated
it with oil that it should witness to the promise made him.

Pilate next seated himself upon the seat of judgment and wrote out the

The Judgment on the Gabbatha

Jesus Bearing the Cross

sentence, which was copied by several officials standing behind him. Messengers were dispatched with the copies, for some of them had to be signed by others. I do not know whether this formality was requisite for the sentence, or whether it included other commissions, but some of the writings were certainly sent to certain distant places. Pilate's written condemnation against Jesus clearly showed his deceit, for its purport was altogether different from that which he had pronounced orally. I saw that he was writing against his will, in painful perplexity of mind, and as if an angel of wrath were guiding his hand. The written sentence was about as follows:

"Urged by the high priests, and the Sanhedrin, and fearing an insurrection of the people who accuse Jesus of Nazareth of sedition, blasphemy, and infraction of the laws, and who demand that he should be put to death, I have (though indeed without being able to substantiate their accusations) delivered him to be crucified along with two other condemned criminals whose execution was postponed through the influence of the high priests because they wanted Jesus to suffer with them. I have condemned Jesus because I do not wish to be accused to the Emperor as an unjust judge of the Jews and as an abettor of insurrections; and I have condemned him as a criminal who has acted against the laws, and whose death has been violently demanded by the Jews."

Pilate caused many copies of this sentence to be made and sent to different places. The high priests, however, were not at all satisfied with the written sentence, especially because Pilate wrote that they had requested the crucifixion of the thieves to be postponed in order that Jesus might be executed with them. They quarrelled with Pilate about it at the judgment seat. And when with varnish he wrote on a little dark brown board the three lines of the inscription for the cross, they disputed again with him concerning the title, and demanded that it should not be "king of the Jews," but "He called himself the king of the Jews." Pilate, however, had become quite impatient and insulting, and he replied roughly: "What I have written, I have written!"

They wanted likewise the cross of Jesus not to rise higher above his head than those of the two thieves. But it had to be so, for it was at first too short to allow the title written by Pilate to be placed over Jesus's head. They consequently opposed its being made higher by an addition, thus hoping to prevent the title so ignominious to themselves from being put up. But Pilate would not yield. They had to raise the height by fastening on the trunk a piece upon which the title could be placed. And it was thus the cross received that form so full of significance, in which I have always seen it.

The Passion and Death of Jesus Christ

Claudia Procula sent back to Pilate his pledge and declared herself released from him. I saw her that same evening secretly leaving his palace and fleeing to the holy women, by whom she was concealed in Lazarus's house. Later on, she followed Paul and became his special friend. On a greenish stone in the rear side of Gabbatha, I afterward saw a man engraving two lines with a sharp iron instrument. In them were the words, *Judex injustus*, "Unjust judge," and also the name of Claudia Procula. I see this stone still in existence, though unknown, in the foundation of a building that occupies the site upon which Gabbatha once stood.

After the proclamation of the sentence, the most holy Redeemer again fell a prey to the savage executioners. They brought him his own clothes, which had been taken from him at the mocking before Caiaphas. They had been safely kept and, I think, some compassionate people must have washed them, for they were clean. It was also, I think, customary among the Romans thus to lead the condemned to execution. Now was Jesus again stripped by the infamous ruffians, who loosened his hands that they might be able to clothe him anew. They dragged the red woollen mantle of derision from his lacerated body, and in so doing tore open many of his wounds. Tremblingly, he himself put on the undergarment about his loins, after which they threw his woollen scapular over his neck. But as they could not put on over the broad crown of thorns the brown, seamless tunic which his blessed Mother had woven, they snatched the crown from his head, causing the blood to gush anew from all the wounds with unspeakable pain. When they had put the woven tunic upon his wounded body, they threw over it his loose white, woollen robe, his broad girdle, and lastly his mantle. Then they bound around his waist the fetter girdle, by whose long cords they led him. All this took place with horrible barbarity, amid kicks and blows.

The two thieves were standing on the right and left of Jesus, their hands bound. When before the tribunal, they had, like Jesus, a chain hanging around their neck. They had a covering around their loins, and a kind of sleeveless scapular jacket made of some old stuff and open at the sides. On their head was a cap of twisted straw around which was a roll, or pad, shaped almost like the hats worn by children. The thieves were of a dirty brown complexion, and were covered with the welts left by their scourging. The one that was afterward converted was now quiet and recollected in himself, but the other was furious and insolent. He joined the executioners in cursing and deriding Jesus who, sighing for their salvation, cast upon them looks of love and bore all his sufferings for them. The executioners meanwhile were busy gathering together their tools. All things were made ready for this, the saddest, the most cruel journey, upon which the loving, the most sorely afflicted Redeemer was to carry for us ingrates the burden of our sins, and at the end of which he was to pour out from the chalice of his body, pierced by the outcasts of the human race, the atoning torrent of his precious blood.

At last Annas and Caiaphas, angry and wrangling, finished with Pilate. Taking with them the couple of long, narrow scrolls, or parchment rolls, that they had received, copies of the sentence, they hurried off to the temple. They had need of haste to arrive in time.

Here the high priests parted from the true Paschal Lamb. They hurried to the temple of stone, to slaughter and eat the type, while allowing its realization, the true Lamb of God, to be led to the altar of the cross by infamous executioners. Here did the way divide—one road leading to the veiled, the other to the accomplished sacrifice. They delivered the pure, expiating Paschal Lamb of God, whom they had outwardly attacked with their atrocious barbarity, whom they had striven to defile, to impure and inhuman executioners, while they themselves hastened to the stone temple, there to sacrifice the lambs that had been washed, purified, and blessed. They had, with timid care, provided against contracting outward legal impurity themselves, while sullying their soul with inward wickedness, which was boiling over in rage, envy, and scorn. "His blood be upon us and upon our children!" With these words they had fulfilled the ceremony, had laid the hand of the sacrificer upon the head of the victim. Here again, the road branched into two: the one to the Altar of the Law, the other to the Altar of Grace. But Pilate, that proud, irresolute pagan, who trembled in the presence of the true God and who nevertheless paid worship to his idols and courted the favor of the world—Pilate, a slave of death, ruling for a short time and on his way to the ignominious term of eternal death—goes with his assistants, and surrounded by his guard, along a path running between those two roads of his own palace, preceded by his trumpeters. *The unjust sentence was pronounced at about ten o'clock in the morning according to our time.*

Jesus Carries
His Cross to Golgotha

WHEN Pilate left the judgment seat, part of the soldiers followed him and drew up in file before the palace. A small band remained near the condemned. Twenty-eight armed Pharisees, among them those six furious enemies of Jesus who had assisted at his arrest on the Mount of Olives, came on horseback to the forum in order to accompany the procession. The executioners led Jesus in to the center. Several slaves, dragging the wood of the cross, entered through the gate on the western side, and threw it down noisily at his feet. The two arms, which were lighter and provided with tenons, were bound with cords to the trunk, which was broader and heavier. The wedges, the little foot-block, and the board just finished for the inscription were carried along with other things by boys who were learning the executioners' trade.

As soon as the cross was thrown on the ground before him, Jesus fell on his knees, put his arms around it, and kissed it three times while softly uttering a prayer of thanksgiving to his heavenly Father for the redemption of humankind now begun. Pagan priests were accustomed to embrace a newly erected altar, and in like manner the Lord embraced his cross, the eternal altar of the bloody sacrifice of expiation. But the executioners dragged Jesus up to a kneeling posture; and with difficulty and little help (and that of the most barbarous kind) he was forced to take the heavy beams upon his right shoulder and hold them fast with his right arm. I saw invisible angels helping him, otherwise he would have been unable to lift the cross from the ground. As he knelt, he bent under the weight. While Jesus was praying, some of the other executioners placed on the back of the two thieves the arms of their crosses (not yet fastened to the trunk), and tied their upraised hands upon them by means of a stick around which they twisted the cord. These crosspieces were not quite straight, but somewhat curved. At the moment of crucifixion they were fastened to the upper end of the trunk, which trunk—along with the other implements of execution—was carried after the condemned by slaves. Pilate's horsemen were now ready to start, and the trumpet sounded. Just then one of the mounted Pharisees approached Jesus, who was still kneeling under his load, and exclaimed: "It is all over with fine speeches now! Hurry up, that we may get rid of him! Forward! Forward!" They jerked him to his feet, and then fell upon his shoulder the whole weight of the cross, of that cross which, according to his own sacred words of eternal truth, we must carry after him. And now that blessed triumphal procession of the king of kings, so ignominious upon earth, so glorious in the sight of heaven, began. Two cords were tied to the end of the cross, and by them two of the executioners held it up, so that it could not be dragged on the ground. Around Jesus, though at some distance, walked the four executioners holding the cords fastened to the fetter-girdle that bound his waist. His mantle was tied up under his arms. Jesus, with the wood of the cross bound on his shoulder, reminded me in a striking manner of Isaac carrying the wood for his own sacrifice on the mountain. Pilate's trumpeter gave the signal for starting, for Pilate himself with a detachment of soldiers intended to go into the city, in order to prevent the possibility of an insurrection. He was armed and on horseback, surrounded by his officers and a troop of cavalry. A company of about three hundred foot soldiers followed, all from the frontier between Switzerland and Italy.

The procession of the crucifixion was headed by a trumpeter, who sounded his trumpet at every street corner and proclaimed the execution. Some paces behind him came a crowd of boys and other rude fellows, carrying drink, cords, nails, wedges, and baskets of tools of all kinds, while sturdy servant men bore poles, ladders, and the trunks belonging to the crosses of the thieves. The ladders consisted of mere poles, through which long wooden pegs were run. Then followed some of the mounted Pharisees, after whom came a lad bearing on his breast the inscription Pilate had written for the cross. The crown of thorns, which it was impossible to leave on during the carriage of the cross, was taken from Christ's head and placed on the end of a pole, which this lad now carried over his shoulder. This boy was not very wicked.

And next came our Lord and Redeemer, bowed down under the heavy weight of the cross, bruised, torn with scourges, exhausted, and tottering. Since the Last Supper of the preceding evening, without food, drink, and sleep, under continual ill-treatment that might of itself have ended in death, consumed by loss of blood, wounds, fever, thirst, and unutterable interior pain and horror, Jesus walked with tottering steps, his back bent low, his feet naked and bleeding. With his right hand he grasped the heavy load on his right shoulder, and with the left he wearily tried to raise the flowing garment constantly impeding his uncertain steps. The four executioners held at some distance the cords fastened to his fetter girdle. The two in front dragged him forward, while the two behind urged him on. In this way he was not sure of one step, and the tugging cords constantly prevented his lifting his robe. His hands were bruised and swollen from the cords that had tightly bound them, his face was covered with blood and swellings, his hair and beard were torn and matted with blood, the burden he carried and the fetters pressed the coarse woollen garment into the wounds of his body and the wool stuck fast to those that had been reopened by the tearing off of his clothes. Jeers and malicious words resounded on all sides. He looked unspeakably wretched and tormented, though lovingly resigned. His lips moved in prayer, his glance was supplicating, forgiving, and suffering. The two executioners behind him, who held up the end of the cross by means of ropes fastened to it, increased the toil of Jesus, for they jerked the ropes or let them lie slack, thus moving his burden from side to side. The procession was flanked by soldiers bearing lances.

GOOD FRIDAY, APRIL 3, AD 33

The Passion and Death of Jesus Christ

Then came the two thieves, each led by two executioners holding cords fastened to their girdles. They had the curved crosspieces belonging to the trunk of their crosses fastened on their backs, with their outstretched arms bound to the ends of them. They wore only a short tunic around their loins; the upper part of their body was covered with a loose, sleeveless jacket open at the sides, and on their head was the cap of twisted straw. They were partly intoxicated by the drink that had been given them. The good thief, however, was very quiet; but the bad one was insolent and furious, and he cursed continually. The executioners were dark complexioned, short, thickset fellows, with short, black hair, crisp and scrubby. Their beard was sparse, a few little tufts scattered over the chin. The shape of their face was not Jewish. They were canal laborers, and belonged to a race of Egyptian slaves. They wore only a short tunic like an apron, and on their breast was a leathern covering without sleeves. They were, in every sense of the word, beastly. Behind the thieves rode one-half of the Pharisees, closing the procession. Sometimes they rode together, and again singly along the whole line of the procession, urging them on and keeping order. Among the mob that led the way, carrying the implements of execution, were some low-born Jewish lads who, of their own accord, had pushed themselves into the crowd.

At a considerable distance followed Pilate, his party preceded by a trumpeter on horseback. Pilate, in military costume, rode among his officers followed by a troop of cavalry and three hundred foot soldiers. His train crossed the forum, and then passed out into a broad street.

The procession formed for Jesus wound through a very narrow back street, in order not to obstruct the way of the people going to the temple, as well as to prove no hindrance to Pilate and his escort.

Most of the people had dispersed immediately after the sentence was pronounced, either to return to their own homes or to go to the temple. *They had already lost a great part of the morning,* and so they had to hurry their preparations for the slaughtering of the paschal lamb. The crowd of loiterers was nevertheless very great. It was a mixed company consisting of strangers, slaves, workmen, boys, women, and all kinds of rough people. They rushed headlong through the streets and byways, in order here and there to catch a glimpse of the mournful procession. The Roman soldiers in the rear kept them from swelling its numbers, and they were obliged consequently to plunge down the next bystreet and head off the procession again. Most of them, however, made straight for Golgotha. The narrow alley through which Jesus was first conducted was scarcely two paces wide, and it was full of filth thrown from the gates of the

268

GOOD FRIDAY, APRIL 3, AD 33

houses on either side. He had much to suffer here. The executioners were brought into closer contact with him and from the gates and windows the servants and slaves there employed threw after him mud and kitchen refuse. Malicious rascals poured black, filthy, bad-smelling water on him; yes, even children, running out of their houses, were incited by the rabble to gather stones in their aprons and, darting through the crowd, throw them at his feet with words of mockery and reviling. Thus did children do unto him who had pronounced the children beloved, blessed, and happy.

Jesus's First Fall under the Cross

TOWARD the end of that narrow street or alley, the way turned again to the left, becoming broader and somewhat steep. Under it was a subterranean aqueduct extending from Mount Zion. I think it ran along the forum, where flowed a covered gutter down to the sheep pool near the sheep gate. I could hear the gurgling and rippling of the water in the pipes. Just here where the street begins to ascend, there was a hollow place often filled, after a rain, with mud and water. In it, as in many such places in the streets of Jerusalem, lay a large stone to facilitate crossing. Poor Jesus, on reaching this spot with his heavy burden, could go no farther. The executioners pulled him by the cords and pushed him unmercifully. Then did the divine cross-bearer fall full length on the ground by the projecting stone, his burden at his side. The drivers, with curses, pulled him and kicked him. This brought the procession to a halt, and a tumult arose around Jesus. In vain did he stretch out his hand for someone to help him. "Ah! It will soon be over!" He exclaimed, and continued to pray. The Pharisees yelled: "Up! Raise him up! Otherwise he'll die in our hands." Here and there on the wayside weeping women might be seen, and children whimpering from fear. With the aid of supernatural help, Jesus raised his head, and the terrible, the diabolical wretches, instead of alleviating his sufferings, put the crown of thorns again upon him. When at last, with all kinds of ill-treatment, they dragged him up again, they laid the cross once more upon his shoulder. And now with the greatest difficulty he had to hang his poor head, racked with thorns, to one side in order to be able to carry his heavy load on his shoulder, for the crown was broad. Thus Jesus tottered, with increased torture, up the steep and gradually widening street.

Jesus, Carrying His Cross, Meets His Most Holy and Afflicted Mother • His Second Fall under the Cross

THE BLESSED Mother of Jesus, who shared every suffering of her Son, had about an hour previously—when the unjust sentence was pronounced upon him—left the forum with John and the holy women to venerate the places consecrated by his cruel suffering. But now when the running crowd, the sounding trumpets, and the approach of the soldiers and Pilate's cavalcade announced the commencement of the bitter Way of the Cross, Mary could no longer remain at a distance. She must behold her divine Son in his sufferings, and she begged John to take her to some place that Jesus would pass. They left, in consequence, the vicinity of Zion, passed the judgment seat, and went through gates and shady walks which were open just now to the people streaming hither and thither, to the western side of a palace which had an arched gateway on the street into which the procession turned after Jesus's first fall. The palace was the residence of Caiaphas; the house on Zion was his official tribunal. John obtained from the compassionate porter the privilege of passing through and of opening the opposite gate. I was terrified when I saw the blessed Virgin so pale, her eyes red with weeping, wrapped from head to foot in a bluish-green mantle, trembling and shuddering, going through this house with the holy women, John, and one of the nephews of Joseph of Arimathea. They could already distinguish the tumult and uproar of the approaching multitude only some houses off, the sound of the trumpet and the proclamation at the corners that a criminal was being led to execution. When the servant opened the gate, the noise became more distinct and alarming. Mary was in prayer. She said to John: "Shall I stay to behold it, or shall I hurry away? Oh, how shall I be able to endure it?" John replied: "If thou dost not remain, it will always be to thee a cruel regret." They stepped out under the gateway and looked to the right down the street, which was here somewhat rising, but which became level again at the spot upon which Mary was standing. The procession at this moment may not have been more than eighty paces distant from them. It was preceded by none of the rabble, though they were still following on the side and in the rear. Many of them, as I have said, were running through the neighboring street, to get other places from which they could obtain a look.

And now came on the executioner's servants, insolent and triumphant, with their instruments of torture, at sight of which the blessed Mother trembled, sobbed, and wrung her hands. One of the men said to the bystanders: "Who is that woman in such distress?" And someone answered: "She is the mother of the Galilean." When the miscreants heard this, they jeered at the sorrowing mother in words of scorn, pointed at her with their fingers; and one of the base wretches, snatching up the nails intended for the crucifixion, held them up mockingly before her face. Wringing her hands, she gazed upon Jesus and, in her anguish, leaned for support against one of the pillars of the gate. She was pale as a corpse, her lips livid. The Pharisees came riding forward, then came the boy with the inscription—and oh! a couple of steps behind him, the Son of God, her own Son, the Holy One, the Redeemer! Tottering, bowed down, his thorn-crowned head painfully bent over to one shoulder on account of the heavy cross he was carrying, Jesus staggered on. The executioners pulled him forward with the ropes. His face was pale, wounded, and bloodstained, his beard pointed and matted with blood. From his sunken eyes full of blood he cast, from under the tangled and twisted thorns of his crown, frightful to behold, a look full of earnest tenderness upon his afflicted mother, and for the second time tottered under the weight of the cross and sank on his hands and knees to the ground. The most sorrowful mother, in vehemence of her love and anguish, saw neither soldiers nor executioners—saw only her beloved, suffering, maltreated Son. Wringing her hands, she sprang over the couple of steps between the gateway and the executioners in advance, and rushing to Jesus, fell on her knees with her arms around him. I heard, but I know not whether spoken with the lips or in spirit, the words: "My Son!"—"My Mother!"

The executioners insulted and mocked. One of them said: "Woman, what dost thou want here? If thou hadst reared him better, he would not now be in our hands." I perceived, however, that some of the soldiers were touched. They obliged the blessed Virgin to retire, but not one of them laid a finger on her. John and the women led her away, and she sank, like one paralyzed in the knees by pain, on one of the cornerstones that supported the wall near the gateway. Her back was turned toward the procession, and her hands came in contact with the obliquely projecting stone upon which she sank. It was a green veined stone. Where Mary's knees touched it, shallow hollow places were left, and where her hands rested, the impression remained. They were not very distinct impressions, but such as might be made by a stroke upon a surface like dough, for the stone was very hard. I saw that, under Bishop James the Less, it was removed into the first Catholic church, the church near the pool of Bethesda. As I have before said, I have more than once seen similar impressions in stone made by the touch of holy persons on great and remarkable occasions. This verifies the saying: "It would move the heart of a stone," and this other: "This makes an impression." The Eternal Wisdom, in his mercy, needed not the art of printing in order to leave to posterity a witness to holy things.

When the soldiers flanking the procession drove it forward with their lances, John took the blessed Mother in through the gate, which was then closed.

The executioners meanwhile had dragged our Lord up again, and laid the cross upon his shoulder in another position. The arms of the cross had become loose from the trunk to which they had at first been bound, and one had slipped down and become entangled in the ropes. Jesus now took them in his arms, and the trunk dragged behind a little more on the ground.

Here and there among the rabble following the procession with jeers and laughter, I saw the veiled figures of weeping women moving along with uneven steps.

Simon of Cyrene •
Jesus's Third Fall under the Cross

AFTER going some distance up the broad street, the procession passed through a gateway in an old inner wall of the city. In front of this gate was a wide open space at which three streets met. There was a large stepping stone here, over which Jesus staggered and fell, the cross by his side. He lay on the ground, leaning against the stone, unable to rise. Just at this instant, a crowd of well-dressed people came along on their way to the temple. They cried out in compassion: "Alas! The poor creature is dying!" Confusion arose among the rabble, for they could not succeed in making Jesus rise. The Pharisees leading the procession cried out to the soldiers: "We shall not get him to Golgotha alive. You must hunt up someone to help him carry the cross." Just then appeared, coming straight down the middle of the street, Simon of Cyrene, a pagan, followed by his three sons. He was carrying a bundle of sprigs under his arm, for he was a gardener, and he had been working in the gardens toward the eastern wall of the city. Every year about the time of the feast, he was accustomed to come up to Jerusalem with his wife and children, to trim the hedges. Many other laborers used to come for the same purpose. The crowd was so great that he could not escape, and as soon as the soldiers saw by his dress that he was a poor pagan laborer, they laid hold on him and dragged him forward to help carry the Galilean's cross. He resisted and showed great unwillingness, but they forcibly constrained him. His little boys screamed and cried, and some women that knew the man took charge of them. Simon was filled with disgust and repugnance for the task imposed upon him. Poor Jesus looked so horribly miserable, so awfully disfigured, and his garments were covered with mud; but he was weeping, and he cast upon Simon a glance that roused his compassion. He had to help him up. Then the executioners tied one arm of the cross toward the end of the trunk, made a loop of the cords, and passed it over Simon's shoulder. He walked close behind Jesus, thus greatly lightening his burden. They rearranged the crown of thorns, and at last the dolorous procession resumed its march.

Simon was a vigorous man of forty years. He had no covering on his head. He wore a short, close-fitting jacket; his loins were bound with lappets, his legs with leathern straps, and his sandals turned up in sharp beaks at the toes. His little boys were dressed in tunics of colored stripes. Two of them were almost grown. They were named Rufus and Alexander, and later on they joined the disciples. The third was younger, and I have seen him still as a child with Stephen. Simon had not borne the cross long after Jesus when he felt his heart deeply touched.

Veronica and her Veil

THE STREET through which Jesus was now going was long and somewhat winding, and into it several side streets ran. From all quarters respectable-looking people were on their way to the temple. They stepped back, some from a pharisaical fear of becoming legally impure, others moved by a feeling of compassion. Simon had assisted the Lord with his burden almost two hundred paces when, from a handsome house on the left side of the street, up to whose forecourt (which was enclosed by a low, broad wall surmounted by a railing of some kind of shining metal) a flight of terraced steps led, there issued a tall, elegant-looking woman, holding a little girl by the hand, and rushed forward to meet the procession. It was Seraphia, the wife of Sirach, one of the members of the council belonging to the temple. Owing to her action of this day, she received the name of Veronica from *vera* (true) and *icon* (picture, or image).

Seraphia had prepared some costly spiced wine with the pious design of refreshing the Lord on his dolorous journey. She had been waiting in anxious expectation and had already hurried out once before to meet the procession. I saw her veiled, a little girl (whom she had adopted as her own child) by the hand, hurrying forward at the moment in which Jesus met his blessed Mother. But in the disturbance that followed, she found no opportunity to carry out her design, and so she hastened back to her house to await the Lord's coming.

As the procession drew near, she stepped out into the street veiled, a linen cloth hanging over her shoulder. The little girl, who was about nine years old, was standing by her with a mug of wine hidden under her little mantle. Those at the head of the procession tried in vain to keep her back. Transported with love and compassion, with the child holding fast to her dress, she pressed through the mob running at the side of the procession, in through the soldiers and executioners, stepped before Jesus, fell on her knees, and held up to him the outspread end of the linen kerchief, with these words of entreaty: "Permit me to wipe the face of my Lord!" Jesus seized the kerchief with his left hand and, with the flat, open palm, pressed it against his bloodstained face. Then passing it still with the left hand toward the right, which was grasping the arm of the cross, he pressed it between both palms and handed it back to Seraphia with thanks. She kissed it, hid it beneath her mantle, where she pressed it to her heart, and arose to her feet. Then the little girl timidly held up the mug of wine, but the brutal soldiers and executioners would not permit her to refresh Jesus with it. This sudden and daring act of Seraphia caused a stoppage in the procession of hardly two minutes, of which she made use to present the kerchief. The mounted Pharisees, as well as the executioners, were enraged at the delay, and still more at this public homage rendered to the Lord. They began, in consequence, to beat and pull Jesus. Veronica meanwhile fled back with the child to her house.

Scarcely had she reached her own apartment when, laying the kerchief on a table, she sank down unconscious. The little girl, still holding the mug of wine, knelt whimpering by her. A friend of the family, entering the room, found her in this condition. She glanced at the outspread kerchief and beheld upon it the bloody face of Jesus frightfully, but with wonderful distinctness, impressed. It looked like the face of a corpse. She roused Seraphia and showed her the Lord's image. It filled her with grief and consolation, and casting herself on her knees before the kerchief, she exclaimed: "Now will I leave all, for the Lord has given to me a memento!"

This kerchief was a strip of fine fabric about three times as long as wide. It was usually worn around the neck, and sometimes a second was thrown over the shoulder. It was customary upon meeting one in sorrow, in tears, in misery, in sickness, or in fatigue, to present it to wipe the face. It was a sign of mourning and sympathy. In hot countries, friends presented them to one another. Seraphia ever after kept this kerchief hanging at the head of her bed. After her death, it was given by the holy women to the Mother of God, and through the apostles at last came into the possession of the church.

Seraphia was a cousin of John the Baptist, her father being the son of Zechariah's brother. She was from Jerusalem. When Mary, a little girl of four years, was placed among the young girls at the temple, I saw Joachim, Anne, and some that had accompanied them going into Zechariah's paternal house not far from the fish market. A very old relative of the family now occupied it, Zechariah's uncle, perhaps, and Seraphia's grandfather. At the time of Mary's espousals with Joseph, I saw that Seraphia was older than the blessed Virgin. She was related also to the aged Simeon who had prophesied at Jesus's presentation in the temple, and from early youth she was brought up with his sons. Simeon had inspired these young people with a longing after the Messiah. This waiting for salvation was, for a long time, like a secret affection among many good people; others at that time had no idea of such things. When Jesus at the age of twelve remained behind in Jerusalem to teach in the temple, I saw Seraphia older than the mother of Jesus and still unmarried. She sent Jesus food to a little inn outside of Jerusalem, where he put up when he was not in the temple. It was at this same inn, a quarter of an hour from Jerusalem and on the road to Bethlehem, that Mary and Joseph, when going to present Jesus in the temple after his birth, spent one day and two nights with the two old people. They were Essenes, and the wife was related to Johanna Chusa. They were acquainted with the holy family and Jesus. Their inn was an establishment for the poor. Jesus and the disciples often took shelter there; and in his last days, when he was preaching in the temple, I often saw food sent thither by Seraphia. But at that time there were other occupants in it. Seraphia married late in life. Her husband Sirach, a descendant of the chaste Susanna, was a member of the council belonging to the temple. He was at first very much opposed to Jesus, and Seraphia, on account of her intimate connection with Jesus and the holy women, had much to suffer from him. He had even on several different occasions confined her for a long time in a prison cell. Converted at last by Joseph of Arimathea and Nicodemus, he became more lenient, and allowed his wife to follow Jesus. At Jesus's trial before Caiaphas, both last night and this morning, he had, in company with Nicodemus, Joseph of Arimathea, and all well-disposed people, declared himself for our Lord, and with them left the Sanhedrin. Seraphia was still a beautiful, majestic woman, although she must have been over fifty years old. At the triumphant entrance of Jesus into Jerusalem, which we celebrate on Palm Sunday, I saw her among the other women with a child on her arm. She took her veil from her head and spread it joyfully and reverently in the Lord's path. It was this same veil with which she now went forward to meet the Lord in his dolorous, but victorious and triumphant procession, and remove in part the traces of his sufferings—this same veil that gave to its possessor the new and triumphant name of Veronica, and this same veil that is now held in public veneration by the church.

In the third year after Christ's ascension, the Roman Emperor sent officials to Jerusalem to collect proofs of the rumors afloat in connection with Jesus's death and resurrection. One of these officials took back with him to Rome Nicodemus, Seraphia, and a relative of Johanna Chusa, the disciple Epaphras. This last-named was merely a simple servant of the disciples, having formerly been engaged in the temple as a servant and messenger of the priests. He was with the apostles in the Cenacle during the first days after Jesus's resurrection, when he saw Jesus as he frequently did afterward. I saw Veronica with the Emperor, who was sick. His couch was elevated a couple of steps, and concealed by a large curtain. The room was four-cornered, and not very large. I saw no window in it, but light entered from the roof in which there were valves that could be opened or closed by means of hanging cords. The Emperor was alone, his attendants in the antechamber. I saw that Veronica had brought with her, besides the veil, one of the linens from Jesus's tomb. She unfolded the former before the Emperor. It was a long, narrow strip of stuff, which she had once worn as a veil around her head and neck. The impression of Jesus's face was on one end of it, and when she held it up before the Emperor, she grasped the whole length of the veil in one hand. The face of Jesus was not a clean, distinct portrait, for it was impressed on the veil in blood; it was also broader than a painted likeness would have been, for Jesus had pressed the veil all around his face. On the other cloth that Veronica had with her, I saw the impression of Jesus's scourged body. I think it was one of the cloths upon which Jesus had been washed for burial. I did not see that these cloths made any impression on the Emperor, or that he touched them, but he was cured by merely looking upon them. He wanted to keep Veronica in Rome, and to give her as a reward a house, goods, and faithful servants, but she longed for nothing but to return to Jerusalem and to die where Jesus had died. I saw that she did return, with the companions of her journey. I saw in the persecution of the Christians in Jerusalem, when Lazarus and his sisters were driven into exile, that Seraphia fled with some other women. But being overtaken, she was cast into prison where, as a martyr for the truth, for Jesus, whom she had so often fed with earthly bread, and who with his own flesh and blood had nourished her to eternal life, she died of starvation.

The Weeping Daughters of Jerusalem
•Jesus's Fourth and Fifth Falls beneath the Cross

THE PROCESSION had still a good distance to go before reaching the gate, and the street in that direction was somewhat declining. The gate was strong and high. To reach it, one had to go first through a vaulted arch, then across a bridge, then through another archway. The gate opened in a southwesterly direction. The city wall at this point of egress ran for a short distance, perhaps for some minutes, southward, then turned a little toward the west, and, finally, took a southerly direction once more around Mount Zion. On the right of the gate, the wall extended northward to the corner gate, and then turned eastward along the northern side of Jerusalem.

As the procession neared the gate, the executioners pressed on more violently. Close to the gate there was a large puddle of muddy water in the uneven road, cut up by vehicles. The barbarous executioners jerked Jesus forward; the crowd pressed. Simon of Cyrene tried to step sideways for the sake of convenience, thereby moving the cross out of its place, and poor Jesus for the fourth time fell so heavily under his burden into the muddy pool that Simon could scarcely support the cross. Jesus then, in a voice interrupted by sighs, though still high and clear, cried out: "Woe! Woe, Jerusalem! How often would I have gathered together thy children as the hen doth gather her chickens under her wings, and thou dost cast me so cruelly out of thy gate!" The Lord was troubled and in sorrow. The Pharisees turned toward him and said mockingly: "The disturber of the peace has not yet had enough. He still holds forth in unintelligible speeches," etc. They beat him and pushed him, and raising him to his feet, dragged him out of the rut. Simon of Cyrene meanwhile had become very much exasperated at the barbarity of the executioners, and he exclaimed: "If you do not cease your villainy, I will throw down this cross even if you kill me also!"

Just outside the gate there branched from the highroad northward to Golgotha a rough, narrow road several minutes in length. Some distance farther, the highroad itself divided in three directions: on the left to the southwest through the Valley of Gihon toward Bethlehem; westward toward Emmaus and Joppa; and on the right, off to the northwest and running around Mount Calvary toward the corner gate which led to Bethzur. Through this gate by which Jesus was led out, one could see off toward the southwest and to the left the Bethlehem gate. These two gates of Jerusalem were next to each other.

In the center of the highroad and opposite the gate where the way branched off to Mount Calvary, stood a post supporting a board upon which, in white raised letters that looked as if they were done in haste, was written the death sentence of our Savior and the two thieves. Not far from this spot, at the corner of the road, a large number of women might be seen weeping and lamenting. Some were young maidens, others poor married women, who had run out from Jerusalem to meet the procession; others were from Bethlehem, Hebron, and the neighboring places, who, coming up for the feast, had here joined the women of Jerusalem.

Jesus again sank fainting. He did not fall to the ground, because Simon, resting the end of the cross upon the earth, drew nearer and supported his bowed form. The Lord leaned on him. This was the fifth fall of Jesus while carrying his cross. At sight of his countenance so utterly wretched, the women raised a loud cry of sorrow and pity and, after the Jewish manner of showing compassion, extended toward him kerchiefs with which to wipe off the perspiration. At this Jesus turned to them and said: "Daughters of Jerusalem" (which meant, also, people from other Jewish cities), "weep not over me, but weep for yourselves and for your children. For behold, the days shall come wherein they will say: 'Blessed are the barren and the wombs that have not borne, and the paps that have not given suck!' Then shall they begin to say to the mountains: 'Fall upon us!' and to the hills: 'Cover us!' For if in the green wood they do these things, what shall be done in the dry?" Jesus said some other beautiful words to the women, but I have forgotten them. Among them, however, I remember these: "Your tears shall be rewarded. Henceforth, ye shall tread another path," etc.

There was a pause here, for the procession halted awhile. The rabble bearing the instruments of torture went on ahead to Mount Calvary, followed by a hundred Roman soldiers detached from Pilate's corps. He himself had, at some distance, accompanied the procession as far as the gateway, but there he turned back into the city.

Jesus on Golgotha • The Sixth and Seventh Falls of Jesus • His Imprisonment

THE PROCESSION again moved onward. With blows and violent jerking at the cords that bound him, Jesus was driven up the rough, uneven path between the city wall and Mount Calvary toward the north. At a spot where the winding path in its ascent turned toward the south, poor Jesus fell again for the sixth time. But his tormentors beat him and drove him on more rudely than ever until he reached the top of the rock, the place of execution, when with the cross he fell heavily to the earth for the seventh time.

Simon of Cyrene, himself fatigued and ill-treated, was altogether worn out with indignation and compassion. He wanted to help poor Jesus up again, but the executioners with cuffs and insults drove him down the path. He soon after joined the disciples. All the lads and workmen that had come up with the procession, but whose presence was no longer necessary, were driven down also. The mounted Pharisees had ridden up by the smooth and easy winding path on the western side of Mount Calvary, from whose top one could see even over the city wall.

The place of execution, which was on the level top of the mount, was circular, and of a size that could be enclosed in the cemetery of our own parish church. It was like a tolerably large riding ground, and was surrounded by a low wall of earth, through which five pathways were cut. Five paths, or entrances, of this kind seemed to be peculiar to this country in the laying out of different places; for instance, bathing places, baptismal pools, and the pool of Bethesda. Many of the cities also were built with five gates. This arrangement is found in all designs belonging to the olden times, and also in those of more modern date built in the spirit of pious imitation. As with all other things in the Holy Land, it breathed a deeply prophetic signification, which on this day received its realization in the opening of those five ways to salvation, the five sacred wounds of Jesus.

The Pharisees on horseback drew up on the western side beyond the circle, where the mountain sloped gently; that toward the city, up which the criminals were brought, was steep and rough. About one hundred Roman soldiers from the confines of Switzerland were stationed, some on the mountain, some around the circular wall of the place of execution. Some, too, were standing on guard around the two thieves. As space was needed, they were not at once brought up to the top of the mount, but with their arms still bound to the crosspieces were left lying on a slope where the road turned off to the south, and at some distance below the place of execution. A great crowd, mostly of the vulgar class, who had no fear of defilement, strangers, servants, slaves, pagans, and numbers of women, were standing around the circle. Some were on the neighboring heights, and these were being constantly joined by others on their way to the city. Toward evening there had gathered on Mount Gihon a whole encampment of Passover guests, many of whom gazed from a distance at the scene on Mount Calvary, and at times pressed nearer to get a better view.

It was about a quarter to twelve when Jesus, laden with the cross, was dragged into the place of execution, thrown on the ground, and Simon driven off. The executioners then pulled Jesus up by the cords, took the sections of the cross apart, and put them together again in proper form. Ah! How sad and miserable, what a terribly lacerated, pale and blood-stained figure was that of poor Jesus as he stood on that place of martyr-dom! The executioners threw him down again with words of mockery such as these: "We must take the measure of thy throne for thee, O king!" But Jesus laid himself willingly upon the cross. Had it been possible for him, in his state of exhaustion, to do it more quickly, they would have had no necessity to drag him down. Then they stretched him out and marked the length for his hands and feet. The Pharisees were standing around, jeering and mocking. The executioners now dragged Jesus up again and led him, bound, about seventysteps northward down to a cave cut in the rock. It looked as if intended for a cellar, or cistern. They raised the door and pushed him down so unmercifully that, without a miracle, his knees would have been crushed on the rough stone floor. I heard his loud, sharp cries of pain. The executioners closed the door above him, and set guards before it. I accompanied Jesus on those seventy steps, and I think that I saw angels helping him, supporting him a little, that his knees should not be crushed. The stone under them became soft.

And now the executioners began their preparations. In the center of the place of execution, the highest point of Golgotha's rocky height, was a circular elevation, about two feet high, with a few steps leading to it. After taking the measure of the lower part of each of the three crosses, the executioners chiselled out holes in that little elevation to receive them. Those for the thieves were raised to the right and left of the emi-nence. Their trunks were rough, shorter than that of Jesus, and sawed off obliquely at the upper end. The crosspieces, to which their hands were still fastened, were at the moment of crucifixion attached tightly to the upper end of the cross. The executioners next laid Christ's cross on the spot upon which they intended to crucify him, so that it could be conve-niently raised and deposited in the hole made to receive it. They fitted the tenons of the two arms into the mortises made for them in the trunk, nailed on the foot-block, bored the holes for the nails and also for the title written by Pilate, hammered in the wedges under the mortised arms, and made hollow places here and there down the trunk. These were intended to receive the crown of thorns and Jesus's back, so that his body might rather stand than hang, thus preventing the hands from being torn by the weight and hastening death. In the earth behind the lit-tle eminence they sank a post with a crossbeam around which the ropes for raising the cross could be wound. They made several other prepara-tions of a similar nature.

Mary and the
Holy Women Go to Golgotha

AFTER that most painful meeting with her divine Son carrying his cross before the dwelling of Caiaphas, the most afflicted mother was conducted by John and the holy women, Johanna Chusa, Susanna, and Salome, to the house of Nazareth in the vicinity of the corner gate.

Here the other holy women, in tears and lamentations, were gathered around Magdalene and Martha. Some children were with them. They now went all together, in number seventeen, with the blessed Virgin, careless of the jeers of the mob, grave and resolute, and by their tears awe-inspiring, across the forum, where they kissed the spot upon which Jesus had taken up the burden of the cross. Thence they proceeded along the whole of the sorrowful way trodden by him and venerated the places marked by special sufferings. The blessed Virgin saw and recognized the footprints of her divine Son, she numbered his steps, pointed out to the holy women all the places consecrated by his sufferings, regulated their halting and going forward on this Way of the Cross, which with all its details was deeply imprinted in her soul.

In this manner, that most touching devotion of the early church, first written by the sword of Simeon's prophecy on the loving mother-heart of Mary, was transmitted from her lips to the companions of her sorrows, and from them passed down to us. It is the sacred gift of God to the heart of the Mother whence it has descended from heart to heart among her children. Thus is the tradition of the church propagated. If people could see as I do, such gifts would appear to them more replete with life and holiness than any other. To the Jews, all places in which holy events, events dear to the heart happened, were thenceforth sacred. They forgot no spot remarkable for some great occurrence. They raised upon it a monument of stones, and went thither at times to pray. And so arose the devotion of the Holy Way of the Cross, not from any afterthought, but from the nature of man himself and the designs of God over his people, and from the truest mother-love which, so to speak, first trod that way under the very feet of Jesus himself.

The holy band of mourners now arrived at Veronica's dwelling, which they entered, for Pilate with his riders and two hundred soldiers, having turned back at the city gate, was coming along the street. Here with tears and expressions of sorrow, the holy women gazed upon the face of Jesus impressed upon Veronica's veil, and glorified his goodness toward his faithful friend. Taking the vessel of aromatic wine which Veronica had not been permitted to present to Jesus, they went to the gate nearby and out to Golgotha. Their number was increased on the way by the addition of many well-disposed people who traversed the streets with a demeanor at once orderly and deeply impressed. This procession was almost greater than that which followed Jesus, inclusive of the rabble running after it.

The sufferings of the most afflicted Mother of Sorrows on this journey, at the sight of the place of execution and her ascent to it, cannot be expressed. They were twofold: the pains of Jesus suffered interiorly and the sense of being left behind. Magdalene was perfectly distracted, intoxicated and reeling, as it were, with grief, precipitated from agony to agony. From silence long maintained she fell to lamenting, from listlessness to wringing her hands, from moaning to threatening the authors of her misery. She had to be continually supported, protected, admonished to silence, and concealed by the other women.

They went up the hill by the gently sloping western side and stood in three groups, one behind the other, outside the wall enclosing the circle. The mother of Jesus, her niece Mary Cleophas, Salome, and John stood close to the circle. Martha, Mary Heli, Veronica, Johanna Chusa, Susanna, and Mary Mark stood a little distance back around Magdalene, who could no longer restrain herself. Still farther back were about seven others, and between these groups were some well-disposed individuals who carried messages backward and forward. The mounted Pharisees were stationed in groups at various points around the circle, and the five entrances were guarded by Roman soldiers.

What a spectacle for Mary! The place of execution, the hill of crucifixion, the terrible cross outstretched before her, the hammers, the ropes, the dreadful nails! And all around, the brutal, drunken executioners, with curses completing their preparations! The crucifixion stakes of the thieves were already raised, and to facilitate ascent, plugs were stuck in the holes bored to receive them. The absence of Jesus intensified the mother's martyrdom. She knew that he was still alive, she longed to see him, and yet she shuddered at the thought, for when she should again behold him it would be in suffering unutterable.

Toward ten in the morning, when the sentence had been pronounced, a little hail fell at intervals. At the time of Jesus's journey to Golgotha, the sky cleared and the sun shone out, but toward twelve it was partially obscured by a lurid, reddish fog.

Jesus Stripped for Crucifixion and Drenched with Vinegar

FOUR executioners now went to the prison cave, seventy steps northward, and dragged Jesus out. He was imploring God for strength and offering himself once more for the sins of his enemies. They dragged him with pushes, blows, and insults over these last steps of his Passion. The people stared and jeered; the soldiers, cold and grave, stood proudly erect keeping order; the executioners furiously snatched him from the hands of his guards and dragged him violently into the circle.

The holy women gave a man some money to take to the executioners together with the vessel of spiced wine and beg them to allow Jesus to drink it. The wretches took the wine but, instead of giving it to Jesus, they drank it themselves. There were two brown jugs standing near.

In one was a mixture of vinegar and gall, and in the other, a kind of vinegar yeast. It may have been wine mingled with wormwood and myrrh. Some of this last-mentioned they held in a brown cup to the lips of the Savior, who was still bound in fetters. He tasted it, but would not drink. There were eighteen executioners in the circle: the six scourgers, the four that led Jesus, the two that held the ropes, and six crucifiers. Some were busied around Jesus, some with the thieves, and they worked and drank alternately. They were short, powerfully built fellows, filthy in appearance, cruel and beastly. Their features denoted foreign origin; their hair was bushy, their beard scrubby. They served the Romans and Jews for pay.

The sight of all this was rendered still more frightful to me, since I saw what others did not see, namely, the evil one in his proper form. I saw, too, great, frightful-looking demons at work among those barbarous men, handing them what they needed, making suggestions, and helping them in every way. Besides these, I saw numberless little figures of toads, serpents, clawed dragons, and noxious insects, which entered into the mouth of some, darted into the bosom of others, and sat on the shoulders of others. They upon whom I saw these evil spirits were those that indulged in wicked thoughts of rage, or that uttered words of mockery and malediction. But above the Lord I frequently saw during the crucifixion great figures of weeping angels and, in a halo of glory, little angelic faces. I saw similar angels of compassion and consolation hovering above the blessed Virgin and all others well-disposed to Jesus, strengthening and supporting them.

And now the executioners tore from our Lord the mantle they had flung around his shoulders. They next removed the fetter-girdle along with his own, and dragged the white woollen tunic over his head. Down the breast it had a slit bound with leather. When they wanted to remove the brown, seamless robe that his blessed Mother had knit for him, they could not draw it over his head, on account of the projecting crown of thorns. They consequently tore the crown again from his head, opening all the wounds afresh, tucked up the woven tunic and, with words of imprecation and insult, pulled it over his wounded and bleeding head.

There stood the Son of Man, trembling in every limb, covered with blood and welts; covered with wounds, some closed, some bleeding; covered with scars and bruises! He still retained the short woollen scapular over his breast and back, and the tunic about his loins. The wool of the scapular was dried fast in his wounds and cemented with blood into the new and deep one made by the heavy cross upon his shoulder. This last wound caused Jesus unspeakable suffering. The scapular was now torn ruthlessly from his frightfully lacerated and swollen breast. His shoulder and back were torn to the bone, the white wool of the scapular adhering to the crusts of his wounds and the dried blood on his breast. At last, they tore off his girdle and Jesus, our sweetest Savior, our inexpressibly mal-treated Savior, bent over as if trying to hide himself. As he appeared about to swoon in their hands, they set him upon a stone that had been rolled nearby, thrust the crown of thorns again upon his head, and offered him a drink from that other vessel of gall and vinegar. But Jesus turned his head away in silence. And now, when the executioners seized him by the arms and raised him in order to throw him upon the cross, a cry of indig-nation, loud murmurs and lamentations arose from all his friends. His blessed Mother prayed earnestly, and was on the point of tearing off her veil and reaching it to him for a covering. God heard her prayer. At that same instant a man, who had run from the city gate and up through the crowd thronging the way, rushed breathless, his garments girded, into the circle among the executioners, and handed Jesus a strip of linen, which he accepted with thanks and wound around himself.

There was something authoritative in the impetuosity of this benefac-tor of his Redeemer, obtained from God by the prayer of the blessed Vir-gin. With an imperious wave of the hand toward the executioners, he said only the words: "Allow the poor man to cover himself with this!" and, without further word to any other, hurried away as quickly as he came. It was Jonadab, the nephew of Joseph, from the region of Bethle-hem. He was the son of that brother to whom, after the birth of Christ, Joseph had pawned the ass that was no longer necessary. He was not one of Jesus's courageous followers, and today he had been keeping at a distance and spying around everywhere. Already, on hearing of the stripping for the scourging, he was filled with sorrow; and when the time for the crucifixion was drawing near, he was seized in the temple by extraordinary anxiety. While the blessed Mother on Golgotha was crying to God, a sudden and irresistible impulse took possession of Jonadab, drove him out of the temple, and up to Mount Calvary. He indignantly felt in his soul the ignominy of Ham, who mocked at his father Noah intoxicated with wine, and like another Shem, he hurried to cover his blessed Redeemer. The executioners who crucified Jesus were Hamites, that is, descendants of Ham. Jesus was treading the bloody wine press of the new wine of Redemption when Jonadab covered him. Jonadab's action was the fulfillment of a prefiguring type, and it was rewarded.

Jesus Nailed to the Cross

JESUS was now stretched on the cross by the executioners. He had lain himself upon it; but they pushed him lower down into the hollow places, rudely drew his right hand to the hole for the nail in the right arm of the cross, and tied his wrist fast. One knelt on his sacred breast and another held the closing hand flat; another placed the long, thick nail, which had been filed to a sharp point, upon the palm of his sacred hand, and struck furious blows with the iron hammer. A sweet, clear, spasmodic cry of anguish broke from the Lord's lips, and his blood spurted out upon the arms of the executioners. The muscles and ligaments of the hand had been torn and, by the three-edged nail, driven into the narrow hole. I counted the strokes of the hammer, but my anguish made me forget their number. The blessed Virgin sobbed in a low voice, but Magdalene was perfectly crazed.

The hand auger was a large piece of iron like a Latin T, and there was no wood at all about it. The large hammer also was, handle and all, of one piece of iron, and almost of the same shape as the wooden mallet we see used by a joiner when striking on a chisel.

The nails, at the sight of which Jesus shuddered, were so long that when the executioners grasped them in their fists, they projected about an inch at either end. The head consisted of a little plate with a knob, and it covered as much of the palm of the hand as a crown-piece would do. They were three-edged, thick near the head as a moderate sized thumb, then tapered to the thickness of a little finger, and lastly were filed to a point. When hammered in, the point could be seen projecting a little on the opposite side of the cross.

After nailing our Lord's right hand, the crucifiers found that his left, which also was fastened to the cross-piece, did not reach to the hole made for the nail, for they had bored a good two inches from the finger-tips. They consequently unbound Jesus's arm from the cross, wound cords around it and, with their feet supported firmly against the cross, pulled it forward until the hand reached the hole. Now, kneeling on the arm and breast of the Lord, they fastened the arm again on the beam, and hammered the second nail through the left hand. The blood spurted up and Jesus's sweet, clear cry of agony sounded above the strokes of the heavy hammer. Both arms had been torn from their sockets, the shoulders were distended and hollow, and at the elbows one could see the disjointed bones. Jesus's breast heaved, and his legs were drawn up doubled to his body. His arms were stretched out in so straight a line that they no longer covered the obliquely rising crosspieces. One could see through the space thus made between them and his armpits.

The blessed Virgin endured all this torture with Jesus. She was pale as a corpse, and low moans of agony sounded from her lips. The Pharisees were mocking and jesting at the side of the low wall by which she was standing, therefore John led her to the other holy women at a still greater distance from the circle. Magdalene was like one out of her mind. She tore her face with her fingernails, till her eyes and cheeks were covered with blood.

About a third of its height from below, there was fixed to the cross by an immense spike a projecting block to which Jesus's feet were to be nailed, so that he should be rather standing than hanging; otherwise his hands would have been torn, and his feet could not have been nailed without breaking the bones. A hole for the nail had been bored in the block, and a little hollow place was made for his heels. Similar cavities had been made all down the trunk of the cross, in order to prolong his sufferings, for without them the hands would have been torn open and the body would have fallen violently by its own weight.

The whole body of our blessed Redeemer had been contracted by the violent stretching of the arms to the holes for the nails, and his knees were forcibly drawn up. The executioners now fell furiously upon them and, winding ropes around them, fastened them down to the cross; but on account of the mistake made in the holes in the crosspiece, the sacred feet of Jesus did not reach even to the block. When the executioners saw this, they gave vent to curses and insults. Some thought they would have to bore new holes in the transverse arm, for that would be far less difficult than moving the footblock. Others with horrible scoffing cried out: "He will not stretch himself out, but we will help him!" Then they tied ropes around the right leg and, with horrible violence and terrible torture to Jesus, pulled the foot down to the block, and tied the leg fast with cords.

Jesus's body was thus most horribly distended. His chest gave way with a cracking sound, and he moaned aloud: "O God! O God!" They had tied down his arms and his breast also that his hands might not be torn away from the nails. The abdomen was entirely displaced, and it seemed as if the ribs broke away from the breastbone. The suffering was horrible.

With similar violence the left foot was drawn and fastened tightly with cords over the right; and because it did not rest firmly enough over the right one for nailing, the instep was bored with a fine, flathead piercer, much finer than the one used for the hands. It was like an auger with a puncher attached. Then seizing the most frightful-looking nail of all, which was much longer than the others, they drove it with great effort through the wounded instep of the left foot and that of the right foot resting below. With a cracking sound, it passed through Jesus's feet into the hole prepared for it in the footblock, and through that again back into the trunk of the cross. I have seen, when standing at the side of the cross, one nail passing through both feet.

The nailing of the feet was the most horrible of all, on account of the distension of the whole body. I counted thirty-six strokes of the hammer amid the poor Redeemer's moans, which sounded to me so sweet, so pure, so clear.

The blessed Virgin had returned to the place of execution. At the sound of the tearing and cracking and moaning that accompanied the nailing of the feet, in her most holy compassion she became like one dying, and the holy women, supporting her in their arms, led her again from the circle just as the jeering Pharisees were drawing nearer. During the nailing and the raising of the cross which followed, there arose here and there, especially among the women, such cries of compassion as: "Oh, that the earth would swallow those wretches! Oh, that fire from heaven would consume them!" But these expressions of love were answered with scorn and insult by Jesus's enemies.

Jesus's moans were purely cries of pain. Mingled with them were uninterrupted prayers, passages from the Psalms and Prophecies, whose predictions he was now fulfilling. During the whole time of his bitter Passion and until the moment of death, he was engaged in this kind of prayer, and in the uninterrupted fulfillment of the prophecies. I heard all the passages he made use of and repeated them with him, and when I say the Psalms, I always remember the verses that Jesus used. But now I am so crushed by the tortures of my Lord that I cannot recall them. I saw weeping angels hovering over Jesus during this terrible torture.

At the beginning of the crucifixion, the commander of the Roman guard ordered the title written by Pilate to be fastened on its tablet at the head of the cross. This irritated the Pharisees, for the Romans laughed loudly at the words: "King of the Jews." After consulting as to what measures they should take to procure a new title, some of the Pharisees rode back to the city, once more to beg Pilate for another inscription.

While the work of crucifixion was going on, some of the executioners were still chiselling at the hole on the little elevation into which the cross was to be raised, for it was too small and the rock very hard. Some others, having drunk the spiced wine which they had received from the holy women, but which they had not given to Jesus, became quite intoxicated, and they felt such a burning and griping in their intestines that they became like men insane. They called Jesus a sorcerer, railed furiously at his patience, and ran more than once down the mount to gulp down asses' milk. Near the encampment of the Passover guests were women with she-asses, whose milk they sold.

The position of the sun at the time of Jesus's crucifixion showed it to be about a quarter past twelve, and at the moment the cross was lifted, the trumpet of the temple resounded. The paschal lamb had been slaughtered.

The Raising of the Cross

AFTER the crucifixion of our Lord, the executioners passed ropes through a ring at the back of the cross, and drew it by the upper part to the elevation in the center of the circle. Then they threw the ropes over the transverse beam, or derrick, raised on the opposite side. Several of the executioners, by means of these ropes, lifted the cross upright, while others supported it with blocks around the trunk, and guided the foot to the hole prepared for it. They shoved the top somewhat forward, until it came into a perpendicular line, and its whole weight with a tremulous thud shot down into the hole. The cross vibrated under the shock. Jesus moaned aloud. The weight of the outstretched body fell lower, the wounds were opened wider, the blood ran more profusely, and the dislocated bones struck against one another. The executioners now shook the cross again in their efforts to steady it, and hammered five wedges into the hole around it: one in front, one to the right, another to the left, and two at the back, which was somewhat rounded.

A feeling of terror and, at the same time, one akin to deep emotion, was felt by Jesus's friends on beholding the cross swaying in the air and, at last, plunging into place with a heavy crash, amid the jeering shouts of the executioners, the Pharisees, and the distant crowd, whom Jesus could now see. But along with those shouts of derision, there arose other sounds at that dreadful moment—sounds of love and compassion from his devout followers. In touching expressions of pity, the holiest voices on earth, that of his afflicted mother, of the holy women, the beloved disciple, and all the pure of heart, saluted the "Eternal Word made flesh" elevated upon the cross. Loving hands were anxiously stretched forth as if to help the Holy of Holies, the Bridegroom of souls, nailed alive to the cross, quivering on high in the hands of raging sinners. But when the upraised cross fell with a loud crash into the hole prepared for it, a moment of deep silence ensued. It seemed as if a new feeling, one never before experienced, fell upon every heart. Hell itself felt with terror the shock of the falling cross and, with cries of rage and blasphemy, rose up again against the Lord in its instruments, the cruel executioners and Pharisees. Among the poor souls and in Limbo, there arose the joy of anxious expectation about to be realized. They listened to that crash with longing hope. It sounded to them like the rap of the coming victor at the door of redemption. For the first time, the holy cross stood erect upon the earth, like another tree of life in Paradise, and from the wounds of Jesus, enlarged by the shock, trickled four sacred streams down upon the earth, to wash away the curse resting upon it and to make it bear for himself, the new Adam, fruits of salvation.

While our Savior was thus standing upright upon the cross, and the cries of derision had for a few minutes been reduced to sudden silence, the flourish of trumpets and trombones sounded from the temple. It announced that the slaughter of the types, the paschal lambs, had begun; and at the same time, with solemn foreboding, it broke in upon the shouts of mockery and the loud cries of lamentation around the true, slaughtered Lamb of God. Many a hard heart shuddered and thought of the Baptist's words: "Behold the Lamb of God, who hath taken upon himself the sins of the world!"

The little eminence upon which the cross was raised was about two feet high. When the foot of the cross was placed near the hole, the feet of Jesus were about the height of a man above the ground; but when it was sunk into it, his friends could embrace and kiss his feet. A sloping path led up to it. Jesus's face was turned toward the northwest.

The Crucifixion of the Thieves

WHILE Jesus was being nailed to the cross, the thieves were still lying on the eastern side of the mount, their hands bound to the crosspiece fastened on their shoulders, and guards keeping watch over them. Both were suspected of the murder of a Jewish woman who, with her children, was traveling from Jerusalem to Joppa. They were arrested under the disguise of wealthy merchants at a castle in that neighborhood. Pilate often made this castle his stopping place when he was engaged in military affairs. The thieves had been imprisoned a long time before being brought to trial and condemnation, but I have forgotten the details. The one commonly called "the left thief" was older than the other and a great miscreant. He was the master and seducer of the converted one. They are usually called Dismas and Gesmas. I have forgotten their right names, so I shall call them the good Dismas and the bad Gesmas.

Both belonged to that band of robbers on the Egyptian frontiers from whom the holy family, on the flight to Egypt with the child Jesus, received shelter for the night. Dismas was that leprous boy who, on Mary's advice, was washed by his mother in the water used for bathing the child Jesus and instantly healed by it. The charity and protection which his mother, in spite of her companions, then bestowed upon the holy family, was rewarded by that outward, symbolical purification, which received its realization at the time of the crucifixion when, through the blood of Jesus, her son was inwardly cleansed from sin. Dismas had gone to ruin and he knew not Jesus; still he was not utterly bad, and the patience of the Lord had touched him. While lying on the mount, he spoke constantly of Jesus to his companion, Gesmas. He said: "They are dealing frightfully with the Galilean. The evil he has done by his new laws must be much greater than ours. But he has great patience, as well as great power, above all men." To which Gesmas responded: "Come now, what kind of power has he? Were he as powerful as they say, he could help us and himself too." And thus they bandied words. When Jesus's cross was raised, the executioners dragged the thieves up to it with the words: "Now it's your turn." They unbound them from the crosspiece and proceeded with great hurry, for the sun was clouding over and all things betokened a storm.

The executioners placed ladders against the upright trunks and fastened the curved crosspieces to the top of them. Two ladders were now placed against each of the two crosses, and executioners mounted them. Meanwhile the mixture of myrrh and vinegar was given them to drink, their old doublets were taken off, and by means of ropes passed under their arms and thrown up over those of the cross, they were drawn up to their places. Their ascent was rendered the more painful by the shocks they received and the striking against the wooden pegs that were stuck through the holes in the trunk of the cross. On the crossbeam and the trunk, ropes of twisted bark were knotted. The arms of the thieves were bent and twisted over the crosspieces; and around the wrists and elbows, the knees and ankles, cords were wound and twisted so tightly by means

The Raising of the Cross

The Garments Divided by Cast Lots

of those long wooden pegs that blood burst from the veins and the joints cracked. The poor creatures uttered frightful shrieks of pain. The good thief Dismas said to the executioners as they were drawing him up the cross: "Had you treated us as you did the poor Galilean, this trouble would have been spared you."

The Executioners
Cast Lots for Jesus's Garments

AT the place outside the circle upon which the thieves had lain, the crucifiers had meanwhile gathered Jesus's garments and divided them into several parts, in order to cast lots for them. The mantle was narrow at the top and wide at the bottom. It had several folds, and the breast was lined, thus forming pockets. The executioners tore it up into long strips, which they distributed among themselves. They did the same to the long white garment, which was closed at the opening on the breast with straps. Then they divided the long linen scarf, the girdle, the breast scapular, and the linen that was worn around the loins, all of which were soaked with the Lord's blood. But because they could not agree concerning the brown woven robe, which would have been useless to them if torn up, they brought out a board with numbers on it and some bean-shaped stones marked with certain signs. They threw the stones on the board in order to decide by lot whose the robe should be. Just at this point of the proceedings a messenger, sent by Nicodemus and Joseph of Arimathea, came running toward them to say that a purchaser had been found for the clothes of Jesus. So they bundled them up, ran down the mount, and sold them. It was in this way that these sacred relics came into the possession of the Christians.

Jesus Crucified • The Two Thieves

THE TERRIBLE concussion caused by the shock when the cross was let fall into the hole prepared for it drove the precious blood in rich streams from Jesus's thorn-crowned head, and from the wounds of his sacred feet and hands. The executioners now mounted ladders and loosened the cords with which they had bound the sacred body to the trunk of the cross, in order to prevent its tearing away from the nails when raised. The blood, whose circulation had been checked by the tightly bound cords and the horizontal position of the body, now with new force, owing to the loosening of the cords and the upright position, resumed its course. Jesus's torments were, in consequence, redoubled. For seven minutes he hung in silence as if dead, sunk in an abyss of untold pain, and for some moments unbroken stillness reigned around the cross. Under the weight of the thorny crown, the sacred head had sunk upon the breast, and from its countless wounds the trickling blood had filled the eyes, the hair, the beard, and the mouth—open, parched, and languishing. The sacred face, on account of the immense crown, could be uplifted only with unspeakable pain. The breast was widely distended and violently torn upward; the shoulders were hollow and frightfully stretched; the elbows and wrists, dislocated; and the blood was streaming down the arms from the now enlarged wounds of the hands. Below the contracted breast there was a deep hollow place, and the entire abdomen was sunken and collapsed, as if shrunken away from the frame. Like the arms, the loins and legs were most horribly disjointed. Jesus's limbs had been so violently distended, his muscles and the torn skin so pitifully stretched, that his bones could be counted one by one. The blood trickled down the cross from under the terrible nail that pierced his sacred feet. The whole of the sacred body was covered with wounds, red swellings and scars, with bruises and boils, blue, brown and yellow, and with bloody places from which the skin had been peeled. All these wounds had been reopened by the violent tension of the cords, and were again pouring forth red blood. Later the stream became whitish and watery, and the sacred body paler. When the crusts fell off, the wounds looked like flesh drained of blood. In spite of its frightful disfigurement, our Lord's sacred body presented upon the cross an appearance at once noble and touching. Yes, the Son of God, the Eternal sacrificing himself in time, was beautiful, holy, and pure in the shattered body of the dying Paschal Lamb laden with the sins of the whole human race.

Mary's complexion was a beautiful bright olive tinged with red; and such, also, was that of her divine Son. By the journeys and fatigue of his later years, his cheeks below the eyes and the bridge of his nose were somewhat tanned. His chest, high and broad, was free from hair, unlike that of John the Baptist, which was like a skin quite covered with hair. Jesus had broad shoulders and strong, muscular arms. His thighs also were provided with powerful, well-marked sinews, and his knees were large and strong, like those of a man that had traveled much on foot and knelt long in prayer. His limbs were long, the muscles of the calves strongly developed by frequent journeying and climbing of mountains. His feet were very beautiful and perfect in form, though from walking barefoot over rough roads the soles were covered with great welts. His hands, too, were beautiful, his fingers long and tapering. Though not effeminate, they were not like those of a man accustomed to hard work.

His neck was not short, though firm and muscular. His head was beautifully proportioned and not too large, his forehead high and frank, his whole face a pure and perfect oval. His hair, not exceedingly thick, and of a golden brown, was parted in the middle and fell in soft tresses down his neck. His beard, which was rather short, was pointed and parted on his chin.

But now his hair was almost all torn off, and what was left was matted with blood, his body was wound upon wound, his breast was crushed and there was a cavity visible below it. His body had been stretched asunder, and the ribs appeared here and there through the torn skin. Over the projecting bones of the pelvis the sacred body was so stretched in length that it did not entirely cover the beam of the cross.

The cross was somewhat rounded in the back, but flat in front, and hollowed out in the necessary places. The trunk was about as wide as it was thick. The several pieces of which the cross was formed were of different colored wood: some brown, some yellow, the trunk darker than the rest, like wood that had lain a long time in water.

The crosses of the thieves were rougher. They stood on the edge of the little eminence, to the right and left of Jesus's cross, and far enough from it for a man to ride on horseback between them. They were somewhat turned toward each other, and not so high as the Lord's. The thieves looked up to Jesus, one praying, the other jeering, and Jesus said something down from his cross to Dismas. The aspect of the thieves on the cross was hideous, especially that of the one to the left, who was a ferocious, drunken reprobate. They hung there distorted, shattered, swollen, and bound fast with cords. Their faces were livid, their lips brown from drink and confined blood, their eyes red, swollen, and starting from their sockets. They yelled and shrieked under the pressure of the cords. Gesmas cursed and reviled. The nails in the crosspiece forced their heads forward. They writhed convulsively, and in spite of the hard twisting around the wooden peg of the cords that bound their legs, one of them worked his foot up so that the bent knee stood out.

Jesus Mocked •
His First Saying on the Cross

AFTER the crucifixion of the thieves and the distribution of the Lord's garments, the executioners gathered up their tools, addressed some mocking and insulting words to Jesus, and went their way. The Pharisees still present spurred up their horses, rode around the circle in front of Jesus, outraged him in many abusive words, and then rode off. The hundred Roman soldiers with their commander also descended the mount and left the neighborhood, for fifty others had come up to take their place. The captain of this new detachment was Abenadar, an Arab by birth, who was later on baptized as Ctesiphon. The subaltern officer was Cassius. He was a kind of petty agent of Pilate, and at a subsequent period he received the name of Longinus. Twelve Pharisees, twelve Sadducees, twelve scribes, and some of the Ancients likewise rode up the mount. Among the last-named were those Jews that had in vain requested of Pilate another inscription for the title of the cross. They were furious, for Pilate would not allow them even to appear in his presence. They rode around the circle and drove away the blessed Virgin, calling her a dissolute woman. John took her to the women who were standing back. Magdalene and Martha supported her in their arms.

When the Pharisees and their companions, in making the rounds of the circle, came before Jesus, they wagged their heads contemptuously, saying: "Fie upon thee, liar! How dost thou destroy the temple, and buildest it again in three days?" "He always wanted to help others, and he cannot help himself! Art thou the Son of God? Then, come down from the cross!" "Is he the king of Israel? Then let him come down from the cross, and we will believe in him." "He trusted in God. Let him help him now!" The soldiers, in like manner, mocked and said: "If thou art the king of the Jews, help thyself now!"

At the sight of the Redeemer's silently abandoning himself to the full of his immeasurable sufferings, the thief on the left exclaimed: "His demon has now deserted him"; and a soldier stuck a sponge filled with vinegar on a stick and held it before Jesus's face. He appeared to suck a little of it. The mocking went on, and the soldier said: "If thou art the king of the Jews, help thyself!" All this took place while the first detachment of soldiers was being relieved by that under Abenadar.

And now Jesus, raising his head a little, exclaimed: "Father, forgive them, for they know not what they do!" and then he prayed in a low tone. Gesmas cried out: "If thou art the Christ, help thyself and us!" The mocking continued. Dismas, the thief on the right, was deeply touched at hearing Jesus pray for his enemies. When Mary heard the voice of her child, she could no longer be restrained, but pressed forward into the circle, followed by John, Salome, and Mary Cleophas. The captain of the guard did not prevent her.

Dismas, the thief on the right, received by virtue of Jesus's prayer an interior enlightenment. When the blessed Virgin came hurrying forward, he suddenly remembered that Jesus and his mother had helped him when a child. He raised his voice and cried in a clear and commanding tone: "How is it possible that ye can revile him when he is praying for you! He has kept silence and patience, he prays for you, and you outrage him! He is a prophet! He is our king! He is the Son of God!" At this unexpected reproof out of the mouth of the murderer hanging there in misery, a tumult arose among the scoffers. They picked up stones to stone him on the cross. The centurion Abenadar, however, repulsed their attack, caused them to be dispersed, and restored order and quiet.

The blessed Virgin felt herself strengthened by that prayer of Jesus. Gesmas was again crying to Jesus: "If thou be the Christ, help thyself and us!" when Dismas thus addressed him: "Neither dost thou fear God, seeing thou art under the same condemnation. And we indeed justly, for we receive the due reward of our deeds, but this man had done no evil. Oh, bethink thee of thy sins, and change thy sentiments!" Thoroughly enlightened and touched, he then confessed his crime to Jesus, saying: "Lord, if thou dost condemn me, it will be just. But have mercy on me!" Jesus replied: "Thou shalt experience my mercy." At these words Dismas received the grace of deep contrition, *which he indulged for the next quarter of an hour.*

All the foregoing incidents took place, either simultaneously or one after the other, between twelve and half-past, as indicated by the sun, and a few moments after the raising of the cross. A great change was rapidly taking place in the souls of most of the spectators, for even while the penitent thief was speaking, fearful signs were beheld in nature, and all present were filled with anxiety.

The Sun Obscured • The Second and the Third Sayings of Jesus on the Cross

UNTIL ten that morning at which hour Pilate pronounced the sentence, hail had fallen at intervals, but from that time until twelve o'clock the sky was clear and the sun shone. *At twelve, however, the sun became obscured by a murky red fog. About the sixth hour (but, as I saw, about half-past by the sun, for the Jewish mode of reckoning varied from the sun) that luminary began to be obscured in a manner altogether wonderful.* I saw the celestial bodies, the stars and the planets, circling in their orbits and passing one another. I descried the moon on the opposite side of the earth and then, by a sudden run or bound, looking like a hanging globe of fire, it flashed up full and pale above the Mount of Olives. The sun was enveloped in fog, and the moon came sweeping up before it from the east. At first, I saw to the east of the sun something like a dark mountain, which soon entirely hid it. The center appeared pale yellow, and around it was a red circle like a ring of fire. The sky became perfectly dark, and the stars shone out with a reddish gleam. Terror seized upon man and beast. The cattle bellowed and ran wildly about; the birds sought their hiding places, and lighted in flocks on the hills around Mount Calvary. One could catch them in his hands. The scoffers were silenced, while the Pharisees tried to explain these signs as natural phenomena, but they succeeded badly, and soon they, too, were seized with terror. All eyes were raised to the sky. Many beat their breast, wrung their hands, and cried: "His blood be upon his murderers!" Others far and near fell on their knees and implored Jesus's forgiveness, and Jesus, notwithstanding his agony, turned his eyes toward them. While the darkness was on the increase, the spectators gazing up at the sky and the cross deserted by all excepting Jesus's mother and his nearest friends, Dismas, in deepest contrition and humble hope, raised his head to Jesus and said: "Lord, let me go to some place whence thou mayest rescue me! Remember me when thou shalt come into thy kingdom!" Jesus replied to him: "Amen, I say to thee, this day thou shalt be with me in Paradise!"

The mother of Jesus, Mary Cleophas, Mary Magdalene, and John were standing around Jesus's cross, between it and those of the thieves, and looking up at the Lord. The blessed Virgin, overcome by maternal love, was in her heart fervently imploring Jesus to let her die with him. At that moment, the Lord cast an earnest and compassionate glance down upon his mother and, turning his eyes toward John, said to her: "Woman, behold, this is thy son! He will be thy son more truly than if thou hadst given him birth."

Then he praised John, and said: "He has always been innocent and full of simple faith. He was never scandalized, excepting when his mother wanted to have him elevated to a high position." To John, he said: "Behold, this is thy mother!" and John reverently and like a filial son embraced beneath the cross of the dying Redeemer Jesus's mother, who had now become his mother also. After this solemn bequest of her dying Son, the blessed Virgin was so deeply affected by her own sorrow and the gravity of the scene that the holy women, supporting her in their arms, seated her for a few moments on the earthen rampart opposite the cross, and then took her away from the circle to the rest of the holy women.

I do not know whether Jesus spoke all those words aloud with his sacred lips or not, but I perceived them interiorly when, before his death, he gave his blessed Mother to John as his mother and John to her as a son. In such contemplations many things are understood that are not set down in writing, and one can relate the least part of them only in ordinary language. What is seen in such visions is so clear that one believes and understands it at once, but it is impossible to clothe it in intelligible words. So on such an occasion one is not at all surprised to hear Jesus addressing the blessed Virgin, not as "Mother," but as "Woman"; for one feels that in this hour in which, by the sacrificial death of the Son of Man, her own Son, the Promise was realized. Mary stood in her dignity as the Woman who was to crush the serpent's head. Nor is one then surprised that Jesus gave to her, whom the angel saluted: "Hail, full of grace!" John as a son, for everyone knows that his name is a name of grace, for there, all are what they are called. John was become a child of God and Christ lived in him. I felt that by these words Jesus gave to Mary, as to their mother, all those that, like John, receiving him and believing in his name, become the sons of God, and who are born not of blood, nor of the will of the flesh, nor of the will of man, but of God. I felt that the purest, the humblest, the most obedient of creatures, she who said to the angel: "Behold the handmaid of the Lord! Be it done to me according to thy word!"—she who had become the Mother of the Eternal Word Incarnate, now that she understood from her dying Son that she was to be the spiritual mother of another son, in the midst of her grief at parting and still humbly obedient, again pronounced, though in her heart, the words: "Behold the handmaid of the Lord! Be it done to me according to thy word!" I felt that she took at that moment for her own children all the children of God, all the brethren of Jesus. These things appear in vision so simple, so necessarily following as a consequence, though out of vision so manifold and complex, that they are more easily felt by the grace of God than expressed in words.

Fear Felt by the Inhabitants of Jerusalem

IT *was about half-past one o'clock* when I was taken into Jerusalem to see what was going on there. Fear and consternation filled Jerusalem. Fog and gloomy darkness hung over its streets. Many lay with covered heads in corners, striking their breasts. Others, standing on the roofs of the houses, gazed up at the sky and uttered lamentations. Animals were bellowing and hiding, birds were flying low and falling to the ground. Pilate had made a visit to Herod, and both were now looking in terror at the sky from that terrace upon which Herod had that morning, with so much state, watched Jesus insulted and maltreated by the mob. "This is not natural," they said. "Too much has certainly been done to Jesus." Then they went across the forum to Pilate's palace. Both were very uneasy, and they walked with rapid strides surrounded by their guards. Pilate turned away his head from Gabbatha, the judgment seat, from which he had sentenced Jesus to death. The forum was deserted. The people had hurried to their homes, though some few were still running about with mournful cries, and several small groups were gathered in the public places. Pilate sent for some of the Jewish elders to come to his palace, and asked them what they thought the darkness meant. As for himself, he said, he looked upon it as a sign of wrath. Their God appeared to be angry at their desiring to put the Galilean to so violent a death, for he certainly was a prophet and a king, but that he himself washed his hands, etc. But the elders, hardened in their obstinacy, explained it as a natural phenomenon not at all uncommon. Many were converted, also those soldiers that, at the arrest of Jesus on the Mount of Olives, had fallen and again risen.

By degrees a crowd gathered before Pilate's palace. On the same spot upon which they had in the morning cried: "Crucify him! Away with him!" they now cried: "Unjust judge! His blood be upon his murderers!" Pilate had to surround himself with soldiers. That Zadoch who, in the morning, when Jesus was taken into the judgment hall, had loudly proclaimed his innocence, cried and shouted in such a way that Pilate was on the point of arresting him. Pilate sternly reproached the Jews. He had, he said, no part whatever in the affair. Jesus was their king, their prophet, their holy one whom they, and not he, had put to death. It was nothing to him (Pilate), for they themselves had brought about his death.

Anxiety and terror reached their height in the temple. The slaughtering of the paschal lamb had just begun when the darkness of night suddenly fell upon Jerusalem. All were filled with consternation, while here and there broke forth loud cries of woe. The high priests did all they could to maintain peace and order. The lamps were lighted, making the sacred precincts as bright as day, but the consternation became only the greater. Annas, terribly tormented, ran from corner to corner in his desire to hide himself. The screens and lattices before the windows of the houses were shaken, and yet there was no storm. The darkness was on the increase. In distant quarters of the city, the northwest section toward the walls, where there were numerous gardens and sepulchers, some of the latter fell in, as if the ground were shaken.

Jesus Abandoned •
His Fourth Saying on the Cross

AFTER Jesus's third word to his blessed Mother and John, an interval of gloomy silence reigned upon Golgotha, and many of the onlookers fled back to the city. The malicious revilings of the Pharisees ceased. The horses and asses of the riders huddled close to one another and drooped their heads. Vapor and fog hung over everything.

Jesus, in unspeakable torture, endured on the cross extreme abandonment and desolation of soul. He prayed to his heavenly Father in those passages of the Psalms that were now being fulfilled in himself. I saw around him angelic figures. He endured in infinite torment all that a poor, crushed, tortured creature, in the greatest abandonment, without consolation human or divine, suffers when faith, hope, and love stand alone in the desert of tribulation, without prospect of return, without taste or sentiment, without a ray of light, left there to live alone. No words can express this pain. By this suffering Jesus gained for us the strength, by uniting our abandonment to the merits of his own upon the cross, victoriously to conquer at our last hour, when all ties and relations with this life and mode of existence, with this world and its laws, cease; and when therefore the ideas which we form in this life of the other world also cease. He gained for us merit to stand firm in our own last struggle when we too shall feel ourselves entirely abandoned. He offered his misery, his poverty, his pains, his desolation for us miserable sinners, so that whoever is united with Jesus in the body of the church must not despair at that last hour even if, light and consolation being withdrawn, he is left in darkness. Into this desert of interior night we are no longer necessitated to plunge alone and exposed to danger. Jesus has let down into the abyss of the bitter sea of desolation his own interior and exterior abandonment upon the cross, thus leaving the Christian not alone in the dereliction of death, when the light of heavenly consolation burns dim. For the Christian in that last hour of peril, there is no longer any dark and unknown region, any loneliness, any abandonment, any despair; for Jesus, the Light, the Truth, and the Way, blessed the dark way by traversing it himself, and by planting his cross upon it, chased from it all that is frightful.

Jesus wholly abandoned, wholly deprived of all things, and utterly helpless, sacrificed himself in infinite love. Yes, he turned his abandonment itself into a rich treasure by offering to his heavenly Father his life, labors, love, and sufferings, along with the bitter sense of our ingratitude that thereby he might strengthen our weakness and enrich our poverty. He made before God his last testament, by which he gave over all his merits to the church and to sinners. He thought of everyone. In his abandonment he was with every single soul until the end of time. He prayed too for those heretics who believe that being God, he did not feel his sufferings, and that as man he felt them only a little, or at least far less than another would have done. But while I was sharing in and sympathizing with Jesus's prayer, I heard these words as if coming from his lips: "We

The Passion and Death of Jesus Christ

should, by all means, teach the people that Jesus, more keenly than any human being can conceive, endured this pain of utter abandonment, because he was hypostatically united with the divinity, because he was truly God and man. Being in his sacred humanity wholly abandoned by the Father, he felt most perfectly that bereavement, he drained to the dregs the bitter cup of dereliction, he experienced for the time what a soul endures that has lost its God forever.

And so when in his agony he cried out with a loud voice, he meant not only to make known his dereliction, but also to publish to all afflicted souls who acknowledge God as their Father that the privilege of recurring to him in filial confidence he merited for them then and there. Toward the third hour, Jesus cried in a loud voice: "Eli, Eli, lama sabachthani!" which means: "My God! My God! Why hast thou forsaken me!"

When this clear cry of our Lord broke the fearful stillness around the cross, the scoffers turned toward it and one said: "He is calling Elijah"; and another: "Let us see whether Elijah will come to deliver him." When the most afflicted mother heard the voice of her Son, she could no longer restrain herself. She again pressed forward to the cross, followed by John, Mary Cleophas, Magdalene, and Salome.

While the people around were lamenting and trembling with fear, a troop of about thirty distinguished men from Judea and the neighborhood of Joppa came riding up on horseback. They were on their way to Jerusalem for the celebration of the feast. When they beheld the frightful treatment to which Jesus had been subjected and the threatening appearances in nature, they expressed their horror aloud and cried out: "Were it not that the temple of God is in it, this cruel city should be burned to the ground for having charged itself with such a crime."

Such expressions from strangers evidently of high rank encouraged the people. Loud murmurs and cries of grief resounded everywhere, and many of those similarly impressed retired together from the scene. The remaining spectators were now divided into two parties: one gave utterance to sorrow and indignation; the other continued to insult Jesus and rage against him. The Pharisees, however, were disheartened. They feared a rising of the populace, since great disturbance was even then prevailing in Jerusalem. They deliberated with the centurion Abenadar, whereupon an order was given to close the city gate in the neighborhood of Mount Calvary, that communication with the city might thus be cut off. A messenger was sent to Pilate and Herod for a bodyguard of five hundred men to prevent an insurrection. In the meantime, the centurion Abenadar did all in his power to secure peace and order. He forbade the Pharisees to insult Jesus, lest the people might be infuriated.

Soon after three o'clock the sky brightened a little, and the moon began to recede from the sun in an opposite direction. The sun, red and rayless, appeared surrounded by a mist, and the moon sank suddenly as if falling to the opposite side. By degrees the sunbeams shone out again, and the stars disappeared, but the sky still looked lowering. With returning light, the scoffers on Golgotha again became bold and triumphant. Then it was that they said: "He is calling Elijah." Abenadar commanded quiet and order.

The Death of Jesus • Fifth, Sixth, and Seventh Sayings on the Cross

AS it grew light, the body of Jesus could be seen on the cross, pale, weak, perfectly exhausted, becoming whiter from the great loss of blood. He said, I know not whether praying in voice audible to me alone, or half-aloud: "I am pressed like the wine which was once trodden here in the wine press. I must pour out all my blood until water cometh, and the shell becometh white, but wine shall here be made no more." I afterward had a vision relating to these words, and in it I saw Japhet making wine in this place.†

Jesus was now completely exhausted. With his parched tongue he uttered the words: "I thirst!" And when his friends looked up at him sadly, he said to them: "Could you not have given me a drink of water?" He meant that during the darkness no one would have prevented their doing so. John was troubled at Jesus's words, and he replied: "O Lord, we forgot it!" Jesus continued to speak in words such as these: "My nearest friends must forget me and offer me no drink, that the scriptures may be fulfilled." This forgetfulness was very bitter to him. Hearing Jesus's complaint, his friends begged the soldiers and offered them money if they

---

† Of this vision, Anne Catherine related what follows: I saw on Mount Calvary after the Deluge the patriarch Japhet, a tall, dark-skinned old man, encamping with numerous flocks and descendants. Their huts were sunk in the earth, the roofs covered with sods upon which plants and flowers were growing. Grapevines were everywhere flourishing, and wine was made on Mount Calvary in a new way, over which Japhet himself presided. I saw also the various ways in which wine was formerly prepared and used, and many circumstances connected with the wine itself, of which I remember only the following: at first, the grapes were merely eaten; later on, they were pressed in stone troughs by means of wooden blocks, and lastly huge wooden cylinders and pestles were employed for the same end. But in the time of Japhet, I saw that a new kind of press was invented, in form very like the holy cross. The trunk of a tree, hollow and large in diameter, was placed upright, and in it were suspended the grapes in a sack through which the juice could run.

would reach to him a drink of water. They would not do it, but instead they dipped a pear-shaped sponge into vinegar, a little bark keg of which was standing near, and poured upon it some drops of gall. But the centurion Abenadar, whose heart was touched by Jesus, took the sponge from the soldiers, pressed it out, and filled it with pure vinegar. Then he stuck into it a sprig of hyssop, which served as a mouthpiece for sucking, and fastened the whole to the point of his lance. He raised it in such a way that the tube should incline to Jesus's mouth and through it he might be able to suck the vinegar from the sponge.

Of some of the words that I heard the Lord speaking in admonition to the people, I remember only that he said: "And when I shall no longer have voice, the mouth of the dead shall speak"; whereupon some of the bystanders cried out: "He still blasphemes!" But Abenadar commanded peace.

Upon the sack pressed a pestle and block. On either side of the hollow trunk and directed toward the sack were arms which, on being worked up and down, crushed the grapes. The juice thus expressed flowed through five holes bored in the hollow trunk down into a vat cut in the rock. From this it ran into a vessel formed of two pieces of bark, each taken from a tree cut in half from top to bottom. The two halves, being put together, were then overlaid with thin wooden rods, and the cracks cemented with pitch. From this last vessel, the grape juice flowed into that rocky cellar-like cave into which the Lord Jesus was thrust before his crucifixion. At the time of Japhet it was a pure cistern. I saw that the cracks of the wooden vat were covered with sods and stones for greater protection. At the foot of the press and that of the stone vat, haircloth was laid before an opening in one of the cracks, to catch the skins which were always disposed of on that side. When the press was ready to receive them, the workmen filled the sack with grapes (which until wanted were stored away in the cistern), hung it in the hollow upright, nailed it fast, placed the heavy pestle with its block in the open mouth of the sack, and began to work the levers in and out, thus making them strike against the sack of grapes, from which the wine flowed. I saw another workman busy at the top of the press, keeping the contents of the sack from making their way up above the block. These particulars reminded me of Jesus's crucifixion, on account of the striking similarity between the press and the cross. They had also a long tube with a prickly head, like a hedgehog (perhaps it was a large thistlehead), and this they pushed through the crack and the upright press whenever they became stopped up. This tube recalled the lance and sponge. I saw, standing around, leathern bottles and vessels of bark smeared with pitch. I saw many youths and boys, with girdles such as Jesus used to wear, working here. Japhet was very old. He was clothed in the skins of beasts and wore a long beard. He regarded the new wine press with great satisfaction. There was celebrated a festival, and on a stone altar animals that had been allowed to run in the vineyard, young asses, goats, and sheep, were sacrificed.

The hour of the Lord was now come. He was struggling with death, and a cold sweat burst out on every limb. John was standing by the cross and wiping Jesus's feet with his handkerchief. Magdalene, utterly crushed with grief, was leaning at the back of the cross. The blessed Virgin, supported in the arms of Mary Cleophas and Salome, was standing between Jesus and the cross of the good thief, her gaze fixed upon her dying Son. Jesus spoke: "It is consummated!" and raising his head he cried with a loud voice: "Father, into thy hands I commend my Spirit!" The sweet, loud cry rang through heaven and earth. Then he bowed his head and gave up the spirit. I saw his soul like a luminous phantom descending through the earth near the cross down to the sphere of Limbo. John and the holy women sank, face downward, prostrate on the earth.

Abenadar the centurion, an Arab by birth, and a disciple baptized later on as Ctesiphon, had, since the moment in which he had given Jesus the vinegar to drink, remained seated on his horse close to the eminence upon which the cross was raised, the forefeet of the animal planted near it and, consequently, higher than the hindfeet. Deeply affected, he gazed long, earnestly and fixedly into the thorn-crowned countenance of Jesus. The horse hung his head as if in fear, and Abenadar, whose pride was humbled, let the reins hang loose. When the Lord in a clear, strong voice uttered those last words, when he died with that loud cry that rang through heaven, earth, and hell, the earth quaked and the rock between him and the thief on his left was rent asunder with a crashing sound. That loud cry, that witness of God, resounded like a warning, arousing terror and shuddering in mourning nature. It was consummated! The soul of our Lord had left the body! The death cry of the dying Redeemer had roused all that heard it; even the earth, by its undulations, seemed to recognize the Savior, and a sharp sword of sorrow pierced the hearts of those that loved him. Then it was that grace penetrated the soul of Abenadar. The horse trembled under his rider, who was reeling with emotion; then it was that grace conquered that proud mind, hard as the rock of Golgotha. He threw his lance to the ground and, with his great clenched fist, struck his breast vigorous blows, crying aloud in the voice of a changed man: "Blessed be God the almighty, the God of Abraham and Jacob! This was a just man! Truly, he is the Son of God!" And many of the soldiers, deeply affected by his words, followed his example.

Abenadar, who was now a changed being, a man redeemed, after his public homage to the Son of God would no longer remain in the service of his enemies. He turned his horse toward Cassius, the subaltern officer, known under the name of Longinus, dismounted, picked up his lance, presented it to him and addressed a few words both to him and the soldiers. Cassius mounted the horse and assumed the command. Abenadar next hurried down Mount Calvary and through the Valley of Gihon to the caves in the Valley of Hinnom, where he announced to the disciples hidden therein the death of the Lord, after which he hastened into the city and went straight to Pilate.

Terror fell upon all at the sound of Jesus's death cry, when the earth quaked and the rock beneath the cross was split asunder. A feeling of dread pervaded the whole universe. The veil of the temple was on the instant rent in twain, the dead arose from their graves, the walls in the temple fell, while mountains and buildings were overturned in many parts of the world.

Abenadar rendered public testimony to his belief in Jesus, and his example was followed by many of the soldiers. Numbers of those present, and some of the Pharisees last come to the scene, were converted. Many struck their breast, wept, and returned home, while others rent their garments and sprinkled their head with dust. All were filled with fear and dread.

John at last arose. Some of the holy women, who until then were standing at a distance, now pressed into the circle, raised the mother of Jesus and her companions, and led them away.

When the loving Lord of life, by a death full of torture, paid for sinners their debt, as man he commended his soul to his God and Father, and gave his body over to the tomb. Then the pale, chill pallor of death overspread that sacred vessel now so terribly bruised and quivering with pain. It became perfectly white, and the streams of blood running down from the numerous wounds grew darker and more perceptible. His face was elongated, his cheeks sunken, his nose sharp and pinched. His underjaw fell, and his eyes, which had been closed and full of blood, opened halfway. For a few instants he raised his thorn-crowned head for the last time and then let it sink on his breast under the burden of pain. His lips, blue and parted, disclosed the bloody tongue in his open mouth. His fingers, which had been contracted around the heads of the nails, now relaxed and fell a little forward while the arms stretched out to their natural size. His back straightened itself against the cross, and the whole weight of his sacred body fell upon the feet. His knees bent and fell to one side, and his feet twisted a little around the nail that pierced them.

When Jesus's hands became stiff, his mother's eyes grew dim, the paleness of death overspread her countenance, her feet tottered, and she sank to the earth. Magdalene, John, and the others, yielding to their grief, fell also with veiled faces.

When that most loving, that most afflicted mother arose from the ground, she beheld the sacred body of her Son, whom she had conceived by the Holy Spirit, the flesh of her flesh, the bone of her bone, the heart of her heart, the holy vessel formed by the divine overshadowing in her own blessed womb, now deprived of all its beauty and comeliness and even of its most holy soul, given up to the laws of that nature which he had himself created and which man had by sin abused and disfigured. She beheld that beloved Son crushed, maltreated, disfigured, and put to death by the hands of those whom he had come in the flesh to restore to grace and life. Ah! She beheld that sacred body thrust from among men, despised, derided, emptied, as it were, of all that was beautiful, truthful, and lovely, hanging like a leper, mangled on the cross between two murderers! Who can conceive the sorrow of the mother of Jesus, of the queen of martyrs!

The sun was still obscured by fog. During the earthquake the air was close and oppressive, but afterward there was a sensible decrease in temperature. The appearance of our Lord's corpse on the cross was exceedingly awful and impressive. The thieves were hanging in frightful contortions, and seemingly intoxicated with liquor. At last both became silent. Dismas was in prayer.

It was just after three o'clock when Jesus expired. When the first alarm produced by the earthquake was over, some of the Pharisees grew bolder. They approached the chasm made by it in the rock of Golgotha, threw stones into it, fastened ropes together, and let them down; but as they could not reach the bottom of the abyss, they became a little more thoughtful and, comprehending in some degree why people were lamenting and beating their breast, they rode off from the scene. Some were entirely changed in their ideas. The people soon dispersed and went in fear and anxiety through the valley in the direction of the city, many of them being converted. Part of the band of fifty Roman soldiers strengthened the guard at the city gate until the arrival of the five hundred that had been asked for. The gate was locked. Other posts around were occupied by soldiers, to prevent a concourse of people and confusion. Cassius (Longinus) and about five of his soldiers remained inside the circle and lying around on the rampart. Jesus's relatives were near the cross. They sat in front of it, lamenting and weeping. Several of the holy women had returned to the city. All was lonely, still, and sad. Off in the distance, here and there, in the valley and on the remote heights, a disciple might be descried peering timidly and inquiringly toward the cross, and retiring quickly on the approach of anyone.

The Earthquake •
Apparitions of the Dead in Jerusalem

WHEN Jesus with a loud cry gave up his spirit into the hands of his heavenly Father, I saw his soul, like a luminous figure, penetrating the earth at the foot of the cross, accompanied by a band of luminous angels, among whom was Gabriel. I saw a great multitude of evil spirits driven by those angels from the earth into the abyss.

Jesus sent many souls from Limbo to re-enter their body, in order to frighten and warn such impenitents, as well as to bear witness to himself.

By the earthquake at Jesus's death, when the rock of Golgotha was split, many portions of the earth were upheaved while others sank, and this was especially the case in Palestine and Jerusalem. In the temple and throughout the city, the inhabitants were just recovering somewhat from the fright caused by the darkness when the heaving of the earth, the crash of falling buildings in many quarters, gave rise to still more general consternation; and, to crown their terror, the trembling and wailing crowd, hurrying hither and thither in dire confusion, encountered here and there the corpses raised from the dead, as they walked about uttering their warnings in hollow voices.

The high priests in the temple had recommenced the slaughtering of the lambs, which had been interrupted by the frightful darkness. They were rejoicing triumphantly over the returning light when suddenly the ground began to quake, a hollow rumbling was heard, and the crash of toppling walls, accompanied by the hissing noise made by the rending of the veil, produced for the moment in the vast assemblage speechless terror broken only by an occasional cry of woe. But the crowd was so well-ordered, the immense edifice so full, the going and coming of the great number engaged in slaughtering so perfectly regulated—the act of slaughtering, the draining of blood, the sprinkling of the altars with it by the long row of countless priests amid the sound of canticles and trumpets—all this was done with so great accord, so great harmony of action, that the fright did not lead to general confusion and dispersion. The temple was so large, there were so many different halls and apartments, that the sacrifices went on quietly in some, while fright and horror were pervading others, and in others still the priests managed to keep order. It was not till the dead made their appearance in different parts of the temple that the ceremonies were entirely interrupted and the sacrifices discontinued, as if the temple had become polluted. Still even this did not come so suddenly upon the multitude as to cause them in their flight to rush preci-pitously down the numerous steps of the temple. They dispersed by degrees, hurrying down one group at a time, while in some quarters of the building the priests were able to bring back the frightened worshippers and keep them together. Still, however, the anxiety, the fright of all, though different in degree, was something quite indescribable.

The appearance of the temple at this moment may be pictured to oneself by comparing it to a great anthill in full and well-ordered activity. Let a stone be thrown into it or a stick introduced among the little creatures here and there, and confusion will reign around the immediate scene of disturbance, though activity may continue uninterruptedly in other groups, and soon the damaged places are covered and repaired.

The high priest Caiaphas and his followers, owing to their desperate insolence, did not lose presence of mind. Like the sagacious magistrate of a seditious city, by threats, by the separation of parties, by persuasion, and all kinds of deceitful arguments, Caiaphas warded off the danger. By his demoniacal obstinacy especially, and his own apparent calmness, he prevented not only a general panic, so destructive in its consequences, but likewise hindered the people from construing those frightful warnings into a testimony of the innocent death of Jesus. The Roman garrison on the fortress Antonia did all that could be done to maintain order, and although the confusion and consternation were great and caused a discontinuance of the festal ceremonies, yet there was no insurrection. The blaze was reduced to a glimmering spark of anxiety, which the people, separating by degrees, carried with them to their homes, and which was there for the most part by the activity of the Pharisees finally extinguished.

And so it was in general. I remember the following striking incidents: The two great columns at the entrance of the Holy of Holies in the temple, between which hung a magnificent curtain, fell in opposite directions, the left-hand one to the south, the right-hand to the north. The beam which they supported gave way and the great curtain was, with a hissing noise, rent from top to bottom so that, opening on either side, it fell. This curtain was red, blue, white, and yellow. Many celestial spheres were described upon it, also figures like the brazen serpent. The people could now see into the Holy of Holies. In the northern wall near it was the little cell in which Simeon used to pray. A great stone was hurled upon it, and the roof fell in. In some of the halls the floor sank here and there, beams were displaced, and pillars gave way.

In the Holy of Holies, between the porch and the altar, an apparition of the murdered high priest Zechariah was seen. He uttered threatening words, spoke of the death of the other Zechariah,[†] also that of John, denominating the high priests the murderers of the prophets. He came from the opening made by the falling stone near Simeon's place of prayer, and addressed the priests in the Holy of Holies. Simon Justus was a pious high priest, an ancestor of the aged priest Simeon who had prophesied on the occasion of Jesus's presentation in the temple. His two prematurely deceased sons now appeared as tall phantoms near the principal chair of instruction, and in menacing terms spoke of the murder of the prophets, of the sacrifice of the Old Law, which was now at an end, and admonished all present to embrace the doctrine of the crucified.

Jeremiah appeared at the altar and uttered words of denunciation. The sacrifice of the Old Law was ended, he said, and a new one had begun. These speeches and apparitions in places to which Caiaphas or the priests alone had access were hushed up and denied. It was forbidden to speak of them under penalty of excommunication. And now there arose a great clamor, the doors of the sanctuary sprang open, a voice cried out: "Let us go hence!" and I saw the angels departing from the temple. The altar of incense was elevated to some height and a vessel of incense tilted over. The shelf that held the rolls of scripture fell in, and the rolls were scattered around. The confusion increased to such a degree that the time of day was forgotten. Nicodemus, Joseph of Arimathea, and many others left the temple and went away. Corpses were lying here and there, others were wandering through the halls and uttering warning words to the people. At the sound of the voice of the angels fleeing from the temple, the dead returned to their graves. The teacher's chair in the outer porch fell to pieces. Many of the thirty-two Pharisees who had ridden to Golgotha just before Jesus expired, returned in the midst of this confusion to the temple. As they had been converted at the foot of the cross, they looked upon all these signs with still greater consternation and, addressing some stern reproaches to Annas and Caiaphas, they quickly retired.

Annas, who was really, though in secret, Jesus's principal enemy, who for a long time had headed all the hidden intrigues against him and the disciples, and who had also instructed the false witnesses as to what they were to say, was so terrified that he became like one bereft of reason. He fled from corner to corner through the most retired apartments of the temple. I saw him moaning and crying, his muscles contracted as if in convulsions, conveyed to a secret room where he was surrounded by sev-

---

[†] The Zechariah here referred to was the father of John the Baptist, who was tortured and afterwards put to death by Herod because he would not betray John into the hands of the tyrant. He was buried by his friends within the temple precincts.

GOOD FRIDAY, APRIL 3, AD 33

eral of his followers. Once Caiaphas clasped him tightly in his arms in order to raise his courage, but in vain. The apparition of the dead cast him into utter despair. Caiaphas, although excessively alarmed, had in him so proud and obstinate a devil that he would not allow his terror to be seen. He bade defiance to all and, with a bold front, set his rage and pride against the warning signs of God and his own secret fright. But as he could no longer continue the sacred ceremonies, he hid and commanded others to hide all the events and apparitions not already known to the people. He gave out, and caused others to do the same, that these apparitions, indicative of God's anger, were due to the followers of the crucified Galilean, for their coming to the temple had polluted it. Only the enemies of the sacred Law, he said, which Jesus had tried to overturn, had experienced any alarm, and many of the things that had happened could be ascribed to the witchcraft of the Galilean who, in death as in life, had disturbed the peace of the temple. And so it came to pass that he silenced some by such words, and frightened others with threats. Many, however, were deeply impressed, though they concealed their sentiments. The feast was postponed until the temple could be purified. Many of the lambs were not slaughtered, and the people dispersed by degrees.

The tomb of Zechariah under the temple wall was sunken and destroyed, and in consequence, some stones fell out of the wall. Zechariah left it, but did not again return to it. I know not where he again laid off his body. Simon Justus's sons, who had arisen from their graves, laid theirs down again in the vault under the temple mount, when Jesus's body was being prepared for burial.

While all these things were going on in the temple, a similar panic was experienced in many other quarters of Jerusalem. *Just after three o'clock*, many tombs were violently shattered, especially in the northwestern section of the city where there were numerous gardens. I saw here and there the dead lying in their winding sheets. In other places, there were only masses of rottenness, in others skeletons, and from many proceeded an intolerable stench.

At Caiaphas's tribunal, the steps upon which Jesus stood when exposed to the mockery of the rabble were overturned, also a portion of the fireplace in the hall in which Peter's first denial took place. The destruction here was so great that a new entrance had to be made. It was in this place that the corpse of the high priest Simon Justus appeared, to whose race belonged Simeon who had prophesied at Jesus's presentation in the temple. His apparition uttered some menacing words upon the unjust sentence that had here been pronounced. Several members of the Sanhedrin were present. The individuals that on the preceding night had given entrance to Peter and John, were converted. They fled to the caves in which the disciples were concealed. At Pilate's palace, the stone was shattered and the whole place upon which Pilate had exhibited Jesus to the multitude fell in. All things reeled under the powerful shaking-up they got, and in the court of the neighboring judgment hall the place in which the bodies of the innocents murdered by Herod's orders were interred fell in. In many other parts of the city walls were overturned and others cracked, but no edifices were entirely destroyed. Pilate, perplexed and superstitious, was in the greatest consternation and wholly incapable of discharging the duties of his charge. The earthquake shook his palace. It rocked and trembled under him as he fled from room to room. The dead from the court below proclaimed to him his false judgment and contradictory sentence. He thought that those voices proceeded from the gods of Jesus the prophet, so he locked himself up in a secret corner of his palace, where he burned incense and sacrificed to his own deities, to whom he also made a vow, that they might render those of the Galilean innocuous to him. Herod too was in his own palace and, like one crazed from fear, he ordered every entrance to be bolted and barred.

There were about one hundred deceased belonging to all periods of time who arose in body from their shattered tombs both in Jerusalem and its environs. They went mostly in couples to certain parts of the city, encountering the frightened inhabitants in their flight, and testifying to Jesus in denunciatory words, few but vigorous. Most of the sepulchers stood solitary in the valleys, though there were many in the newly laid out portions of the city, especially among the gardens toward the northwest, between the corner gate and that leading to the place of crucifixion. There were besides, around and under the temple, many secret graves long since forgotten.

Not all the dead whose corpses were exposed to view by the falling of their tombs arose. Many a one became merely visible, because the graves were in common. But many others, whose souls Jesus sent to earth from Limbo, arose, threw off the covering from their face and went, not walking, but as if floating, along the streets of Jerusalem to their friends and relatives. They entered the houses of their posterity, and rebuked them severely for the part they had taken in the murder of Jesus. I saw some of them meeting, as if they were friends or relatives, and going in couples through the streets of the city. I could see no movement of their feet under their long winding sheets. They passed along as if lightly hovering above the ground. The hands of some were enfolded in broad bands of linen, others hung down under the large sleeves that bound the arms. The covering of the face was thrown up over the head, and the pale, yellow countenance with its long beard looked dried and withered. Their voices sounded strange and unearthly, and these voices, joined to their incessant moving from place to place, unconcerned about all around, was their only external expression; indeed they seemed almost nothing but voice. They were clothed somewhat differently, each according to the custom at the time of his death, his position in society, and his age. On the crossways upon which Jesus's punishment was trumpeted as the procession moved on to Golgotha, they stood still and proclaimed glory to Jesus and woe to his murderers. The people standing afar hearkened, shuddered, and fled, as the dead floated toward them. I heard them on the forum in front of Pilate's palace crying aloud in threatening terms. I remember the words: "Cruel Judge!" The people fled into the most secret corners of their houses and hid. Intense fear pervaded the whole city. About four o'clock, the dead returned to their graves. Many other spirits appeared in different quarters after Christ's resurrection. The sacrifice was interrupted and everything thrown into confusion. Only a very few of the people ate the paschal lamb that evening.

Among the dead who arose on this occasion in and around Jerusalem (and there were at least one hundred), no relative of Jesus was found. The tombs in the northwestern section of Jerusalem were once beyond the precincts of the city, but when it was enlarged they were included in its limits. I had also a glimpse of other deceased persons who arose here and there in different parts of the Holy Land, appeared to their relatives, and bore witness to Jesus Christ's mission. I saw, for instance, Zadoch, a very pious man, who divided all his wealth between the poor and the temple and founded an Essene community near Hebron. He was one of the last prophets before Christ. He had waited very earnestly for the appearance of the Messiah, he had many revelations upon the same, and communication with the ancestors of the holy family. This Zadoch, who lived about one hundred years before Jesus, I saw arise and appear to several persons in the region of Hebron. I saw once that his soul was among the first to return to his body, and then I saw all those souls walking around with Jesus, as if they had again laid their body down. I saw also various deceased persons appearing to the disciples of the Lord in their hiding places, and addressing to them words of admonition.

I saw that the darkness and earthquake were not confined to Jerusalem and its environs. They extended throughout other regions of the country, yes, even in far distant places they spread terror and destruction. In Thirza, the towers of the prison from which Jesus had released the captives were overthrown, as well as other buildings. In the land of Cabul I saw that a great many places suffered injury. Throughout Galilee, where chiefly Jesus had journeyed, I saw isolated buildings in many places, and especially numerous houses belonging to the Pharisees who had persecuted the Lord most violently, toppling down over wife and child, while they themselves were away at the feast. The destruction around the Sea of Galilee was very remarkable. In Capernaum many buildings were overturned. The place between Tiberias and the garden of Zorobabel, the centurion of Capernaum, was almost demolished. The entire rocky projection belonging to the centurion's beautiful gardens near Capernaum was torn away. The lake rushed into the valley and its waters flowed near to Capernaum, which, before that, was fully half an hour's distance from it. Peter's house and the dwelling of the blessed Virgin outside Capernaum and toward the lake remained unharmed.

The Sea of Galilee was greatly disturbed. In some places its banks caved in, and in others they seemed to be pushed out, its shape thereby being notably changed. It began to assume that which it has at the present day, and, especially in its near surroundings, it can no longer be readily recognized. The change was particularly great at the southwest end of the sea, just below Tarichea, where the long dike of black stone which separated the marsh from the sea and gave a fixed direction to the course of the Jordan entirely gave way and occasioned great destruction.

On the eastern side of the sea, where the swine of the Gerasens plunged into the marsh, many places sank in; the same happened likewise in Gergesa, Gerasa, and throughout the entire district of Chorazin. The mountain upon which Jesus had twice multiplied the loaves sustained a great shaking, and the stone upon which the bread was multiplied was rent in twain. In and around Paneas, many things were overturned. In the Decapolis half of the cities sank, and many places in Asia sustained severe damage: for instance, Nicaea, but chiefly many situated east and northeast of Paneas. In Upper Galilee too I saw great destruction. Most of the Pharisees found, on their return from the feast, dire distress in their homes, and news of it reached others while yet in Jerusalem. It was on this account that the enemies of Jesus were so dejected, and that they ventured not until Pentecost to molest his followers in any notable way.

On Mount Garizim I saw many objects belonging to the temple tumbling down. Above a well, which was protected by a little temple, stood an idol. Both idol and roof were precipitated into the well. At Nazareth, one half of the synagogue out of which his enemies had thrust Jesus, fell; and that part of the mountain down which they wanted to cast him was torn away.

Many a mountain, valley, and city sustained great damage, and several changes were made in the bed of the Jordan. By the shocks upon the seashore and the inflowing of little streams, obstacles arose against the rushing water, so that the course of the river was in many places considerably turned aside. In Machaerus and the other cities under Herod's jurisdiction, the earthquake was not felt. They were situated outside the circle of warning and repentance, like those men who did not fall in the Garden of Olives and who consequently did not rise again.

In many regions, the sojourn of evil spirits, I saw those spirits falling in great crowds with the toppling buildings and mountains. The quaking of the earth reminded me then of the convulsions of the possessed when the evil one felt that he had to depart. When, near Gerasa, a portion of that mountain from which the demon with the herd of swine had plunged into the swamp by the seashore rolled down into that same swamp, I saw rushing with it into the abyss, like an angry cloud, an immense multitude of evil spirits.

I think it was in Nicaea that I saw something of which I still remember, although imperfectly, the details. I saw a harbor in which lay many ships, and nearby a house from which rose a great tower. I saw there a man, a pagan, the custodian of the ships. It was his duty to climb up into the tower from time to time and gaze out over the sea, to find out whether ships were coming or if any assistance was needed. Hearing a roaring noise among the ships in the harbor, he became apprehensive of an enemy's approach. Hurrying quickly up into the watchtower, and looking out upon the ships, he beheld floating over them numerous dark figures that cried out to him in mournful tones: "If you desire to save these ships, steer them away from here, for we have to go into the abyss! Great Pan is dead." These are the only words that I distinctly remember of the apparitions. But they told him other things, and gave him many directions as to where and how, on a voyage which he was destined to take, he should make known what they now imparted to him. They exhorted him also when messengers would come and announce the doctrine of him who had just died, to receive them well.

Through the power of the Lord, the evil spirits were forced to warn that good man and proclaim their own disgrace. Then a violent storm arose, but the ships had already been secured. I saw at the same time the devils plunging with loud bellowing into the sea, and one half of the city swallowed up by the earthquake. The good man's house remained standing. Soon after that he sailed around in his ship for a long time, executing his commissions and making known the death of "The great Pan," as they called the Lord. Later on he went to Rome, where his statements excited intense wonder. I saw many other things connected with this man, but I have forgotten them. Among other things, I saw that one of the narratives of his travels became in repetition mixed up with what I had seen, and it was very far-spread, but I do not clearly recollect how they were connected. I think the man's name sounded like Thamus, or Tramus.

Joseph of Arimathea
Requests the Body of Jesus from Pilate

QUIET was scarcely restored to Jerusalem after all those frightful events, when Pilate, already so terrified, was assailed on all sides with accounts of what had occurred. The council of the Jews also, as they had determined to do that morning, sent to him for permission to break the legs of the crucified, and thus put an end to their life, for they wanted to take them down from the cross, that they might not hang thereon upon the sabbath. Pilate dispatched some executioners to Golgotha for this purpose.

Just after that I saw Joseph of Arimathea, a member of the council, going to Pilate. He had already heard of Jesus's death, and with Nicodemus had concluded to bury the Lord's body in the new sepulcher hewn out of a rock in his own garden, not very far from Golgotha. I think I saw him outside the gate as if examining, or reconnoitering, the premises. Some few of his servants were already in the garden, cleaning it and arranging things inside the sepulcher. Nicodemus had gone to buy linen and spices for preparing the body for burial, and he was now waiting for Joseph.

Joseph found Pilate very anxious and perplexed. He begged openly and fearlessly that he might be allowed to take the body of Jesus, the king of the Jews, down from the cross, as he wanted to lay it in his own sepulcher. Pilate's anxiety increased on beholding so distinguished a man begging so earnestly to be permitted to honor the body of Jesus, whom he himself had caused to be ignominiously crucified. The innocence of Jesus recurred to him, making him still more uneasy, but he overcame himself, and asked: "Is he, then, already dead?" for only a few moments had elapsed since he sent executioners out to break the bones of the crucified, and thus end their life. He summoned the centurion Abenadar, who was returned from the caves where he had spoken with some of the disciples, and asked him whether the king of the Jews was already dead. Abenadar in reply related to him the death of the Lord about three o'clock, his last words, and his loud cry, the quaking of the earth and the rending of the rock. Outwardly Pilate appeared merely to be surprised, since the crucified generally lived longer, but inwardly he was filled with trouble and alarm at the coincidence of those signs with Jesus's death. He wished perhaps to palliate in some measure his cruelty by at once expediting an order for Joseph of Arimathea, by which he gave him the body of the king of the Jews with permission to take it down from the cross and bury it. He was glad by so doing to be able to annoy the high priests, who would rather have had Jesus dishonorably buried along with the two thieves. It was probably Abenadar himself whom Pilate dispatched to see the order executed, for I saw him present at the taking down of Jesus from the cross.

Joseph of Arimathea took leave of Pilate and went to meet Nicodemus, who was awaiting him at the house of a well-disposed woman. She lived on the broad street near that narrow alley in which our Lord, just at the commencement of his bitter Way of the Cross, was made to endure such ignominy. Nicodemus had purchased here a lot of aromatic plants and herbs for the embalming, for the woman was a vendor of such things. She procured elsewhere many kinds of spices that she herself did not have, also linen and bandages for the same purpose, all of which she rolled together into a package that could be easily carried. Joseph of Arimathea went himself and bought a winding sheet of cotton, very fine and beautiful, six ells long and several wide. His servants collected under a shed near the house of Nicodemus ladders, hammers, strong iron nails, water bottles, vessels, sponges, and all that was necessary for the work before them. The smaller objects they packed on a light litter, or handbarrow, almost like that upon which the disciples carried the body of John the Baptist from Herod's citadel of Machaerus.

The Side of Jesus Opened •
The Legs of the Thieves Broken

MEANWHILE all was silent and mournful on Gol-gotha. The crowd had timidly dispersed to their homes. The mother of Jesus, John, Magdalene, Mary Cleophas, and Salome were standing or sitting with veiled heads and in deep sadness opposite the cross. Some soldiers were seated on the earthen wall, their spears stuck in the ground near them. Cassius was riding around, and the soldiers were interchanging words with their companions posted at some distance below. The sky was lowering; all nature appeared to be in mourning. Things were in this position when six executioners were seen ascending the mount with ladders, spades, ropes, and heavy, triangular iron bars used for breaking the bones of malefactors.

When they entered the circle, the friends of Jesus drew back a little. New fear seized upon the heart of the blessed Virgin lest the body of Jesus was to be still further outraged, for the executioners mounted up the cross, roughly felt the sacred body, and declared that he was pretending to be dead. Although they felt that he was quite cold and stiff, yet they were not convinced that he was already dead. John, at the entreaty of the blessed Virgin, turned to the soldiers, to draw them off for a while from the body of the Lord. The executioners next mounted the ladders to the crosses of the thieves. Two of them with their sharp clubs broke the bones of their arms above and below the elbows, while a third did the same above the knees and ankles. Gesmas roared frightfully, consequently the executioner finished him by three blows of the club on the breast. Dismas moaned feebly, and expired under the torture. He was the first mortal to look again upon his Redeemer. The executioners untwisted the cords and allowed the bodies to fall heavily to the earth. Then tying ropes around them, they dragged them down into the valley between the mount and the city wall, and there buried them.

The executioners appeared still to have some doubts as to the death of the Lord, and his friends, after witnessing the terrible scene just described, were more anxious than ever for them to withdraw. Cassius, the subaltern officer, afterward known as Longinus, a somewhat hasty, impetuous man of twenty-five, whose airs of importance and officiousness joined to his weak, squinting eyes often exposed him to the ridicule of his inferiors, was suddenly seized by wonderful ardor. The barbarity, the base fury of the executioners, the anguish of the blessed Virgin, and the grace accorded him in that sudden and supernatural impulse of zeal, all combined to make of him the fulfiller of a prophecy. His lance, which was shortened by having one section run into another, he drew out to its full length, stuck the point upon it, turned his horse's head, and drove him boldly up to the narrow space on top of the eminence upon which the cross was planted. There was scarcely room for the animal to turn, and I saw Cassius reining him up in front of the chasm made by the cleft rock. He halted between Jesus's cross and that of the good thief, on the right of our Savior's body, grasped the lance with both hands, and drove it upward with such violence into the hollow, distended right side of the sacred body, through the entrails and the heart, that its point opened a little wound in the left breast. When with all his force he drew the blessed lance from the wide wound it had made in the right side of Jesus, a copious stream of blood and water rushed forth and flowed over his upraised face, bedewing him with grace and salvation. He sprang quickly from his horse, fell upon his knees, struck his breast, and before all present proclaimed aloud his belief in Jesus.

The blessed Virgin, John, and the holy women, whose eyes were riveted upon Jesus, witnessed with terror the sudden action, accompanied the thrust of the lance with a cry of woe, and rushed up to the cross. Mary, as if the thrust had transfixed her own heart, felt the sharp point piercing her through and through. She sank into the arms of her friends, while Cassius, still on his knees, was loudly confessing the Lord and joyfully praising God. He was enlightened; he now saw plainly and distinctly. The eyes of his body, like those of his soul, were healed and opened. All were seized with a sentiment of the deepest reverence at sight of the Redeemer's blood which, mixed with water, fell in a foamy stream into a hollow in the rock at the foot of the cross. Mary, Cassius, the holy women, and John scooped it up in the drinking cups they had with them, poured it into flasks, and dried the hollow with linen cloths.[†]

Cassius was entirely changed, deeply touched and humbled. He had received perfect sight. The soldiers present, touched also by the miracle they had witnessed, fell on their knees, striking their breast and confessing Jesus, from the wide opening of whose right side blood and water were copiously streaming. It fell upon the clean stone, and lay there foaming and bubbling. The friends of Jesus gathered it up with loving care, Mary and Magdalene mingling with it their tears. The executioners who meanwhile had received Pilate's order not to touch the body of Jesus, as he had given it to Joseph of Arimathea for burial, did not return.

The lance of Cassius was in several sections that slipped one into the other. When not drawn out, it looked like a stout staff of moderate length. The part that inflicted a wound was of iron, smooth and pear-shaped, on the top of which a point could be stuck, and from the lower part two sharp, curved blades could be drawn when needed.

All the above took place around the cross of Jesus soon after four o'clock, while Joseph of Arimathea and Nicodemus were making the purchase necessary for the burial of Christ. When the friends of Jesus on Golgotha were informed by Joseph of Arimathea's servants, who were come from cleaning and arranging the sepulcher, that their master had Pilate's permission to take down the sacred body and lay it in his own new tomb, John and the holy women returned at once to the city, to the quarter on

---

† Anne Catherine added: "Cassius was baptized by the name of Longinus; and was ordained deacon, and preached the faith. He always kept some of the blood of Christ—it dried up, but was found in his coffin in Italy. He was buried in a town at no great distance from the locality where St. Clare passed her life. There is a lake with an island upon it near this town, and the body of Longinus must have been taken there." Anne Catherine appears to designate Mantua by this description, and there is a tradition preserved in that town to the effect. I do not know which St. Clare lived in the neighborhood.

Mount Zion, that the blessed Virgin might take a little rest. They wanted also to get some things still necessary for the burial. The blessed Virgin had a little dwelling among the buildings belonging to the Cenacle. They did not go by the nearest gate, for that was closed and guarded on the other side by the soldiers that the Pharisees had called for when they feared an uprising of the populace. They went by one more to the south, the one that led to Bethlehem.

Some Localities of Ancient Jerusalem

ON the eastern side of Jerusalem was the first gate south of the southeast angle of the temple, which led into that quarter of the city called Ophel. The one to the north of the northeast corner was the sheep gate. Between these two gates was a third (though not as yet long in existence) that led to some streets which ran one above another on the east side of the temple mount, and in which principally stonecutters and other laborers resided. Their dwellings adjoined the foundation walls of the temple. Almost all the houses of these two streets belonged to Nicodemus, who had had them built. The stonecutters that occupied them either paid him rent or worked for him, for they had business relations with him and his friend, Joseph of Arimathea. The last-named owned large quarries in his native place, and carried on an active trade in marble. Nicodemus had not long before built a beautiful new gate for these streets; it is now called the gate of Moriah. As it was just finished, Jesus was the first to pass through it on Palm Sunday. He went through Nicodemus's new gate, through which no one before him had passed, and he was buried in Joseph of Arimathea's new sepulcher, in which before him no one had rested. Later on, this gate was walled up, and there is a saying that the Christians will once again enter the city through it. Even in the present day, there is a walled-up gate in this region, called by the Turks "the Golden Gate."

If there were no walls to obstruct the course, a straight road from the sheep gate toward the west would strike almost between the northwest end of Mount Zion and through the center of Golgotha. From this gate to Golgotha in a straight line the distance was perhaps three-quarters of an hour, but from Pilate's house to Golgotha it was in a straight line about five-eighths of an hour. The fortress Antonia rose from a projecting rock on the northwest of the temple mount. When one turned to the left from Pilate's palace and passed westward through the arch, the fortress lay on his left. On one of its walls was an elevated platform that overlooked the forum, and from it Pilate was accustomed to address the populace, to publish new laws, for instance. When Jesus was carrying his cross inside the city, he often had Mount Calvary on his right. (Jesus's journey must have been made partly in a southwesterly direction). It led through the gate of an inner wall which ran off toward Zion, which quarter of the city stood very high. Beyond this wall and to the west there was another quarter that contained more gardens than houses. Toward the outer wall of the city there were magnificent sepulchers with beautifully sculptured entrances, and above many of them pretty little gardens. In this quarter stood the house owned by Lazarus. It has beautiful gardens that extended toward where the outer western wall turned off to the south. There was, I think, near the great sheep gate a little private entrance through the city wall into those gardens. Jesus and his disciples, with Lazarus's permission, often made use of it in coming and going. The gate on the northwest corner opened in the direction of Bethzur, which lay more to the north than Emmaus and Joppa. Several royal tombs stood to the north of the outer wall. This western and sparsely built portion of the city was the lowest of all. It sloped gently toward the city wall and then as gently rose again before reaching it. This second slope was covered with beautiful gardens and vineyards. Back of this ran a broad paved road inside the walls with paths leading to them and to the towers. The latter were not like ours, which have their stairs inside. On the other side of the wall outside the city there was a declivity toward the valley, so that the walls around this lower quarter looked as if built on a raised terrace. Here too were found gardens and vineyards. Jesus's way to Golgotha did not run through these gardens, for the quarter in which they were lay at the end of his journey northward to the right. It was thence Simon of Cyrene was coming when he met Jesus. The gate through which Jesus was led out of the city was not directly toward the west, but rather facing the southwest. On passing out of that gate and turning to the left, one found the city wall running southward for a short distance when it made a sharp turn to the west, and then ran again to the south around Mount Zion. On this left side of the wall and on the way to Zion rose a very strong tower like a fortress. On this same side and very near the gate that led to the place of execution, opened another. Of all the city gates, these two were nearest each other. The distance between them was not greater than that between the castle gate and Luding's gate here in Dulmen. This last-mentioned gate of Jerusalem opened westward into the valley, and from it the road ran to the left and a little southward toward Bethlehem. Somewhat beyond the gate of execution the road turned northward and ran straight to Golgotha, which faced the city on the east and was very steep, but which on the west sloped gradually. Looking from this side toward the west, one could see for some distance along the road leading to Emmaus.

There was a field on the roadside, and there I saw Luke gathering herbs when, after the resurrection, he and Cleophas on their way to Emmaus were met by Jesus. Toward ten o'clock on the morning of the crucifixion, Jesus's face was turned to the northwest, that is, in the direction of the cross erected for him on Golgotha. When hanging on the cross, if he turned his head to the right, he could catch a glimpse of the fortress Antonia. All along the city wall, both north and east of Golgotha, lay gardens, vineyards, and sepulchers. The cross of Jesus was buried on the northeast side and at the foot of Mount Calvary. Opposite the spot upon which the crosses were afterward discovered and to the northeast there were beautiful terraces covered with vines. Looking southward from the point upon which the cross stood on Golgotha, one could see the house of Caiaphas away below the fortress of David.

Garden and Tomb
Belonging to Joseph of Arimathea

THE GARDEN of Joseph of Arimathea was at least seven minute's distance from Mount Calvary, near the Bethlehem gate, and on the height that sloped down to the city wall. It was very beautiful with its tall trees, its seats, and its shady nooks. On one side it extended up to the height upon which rose the city wall. A person coming down into the valley from the northern side would perceive on entering the garden that the ground rose on his left up to the city wall. To the right and at the end of the garden lay a detached rock, in which was the sepulcher. Turning to the right, he would come to the entrance of the grotto which was facing the east, on rising ground and against the city wall. In either end of the same rock, north and south, there were two smaller grottoes with low entrances. A narrow pathway ran around its western side. The ground in front of the grotto was higher than that of the entrance itself, so that to reach the door, one had to descend some steps, just as in another little tomb on the eastern side of the rock. The outer entrance was closed with lattice-work. The space inside the grotto was sufficiently great for four men to stand against the wall to the right and as many to the left, and yet permit the body to be carried between them by the bearers. The walls of the grotto rounded at the western side until they formed, just opposite the door, a broad but not very high niche. The rocky wall here formed an arching roof over the tomb, which was about two feet above the level of the ground, with space hollowed out on top to receive a corpse in its winding sheet. The tomb projected like an altar, being connected with the rock only on one side. There was room for one person to stand at the head, another at the foot, and still a third before the tomb even when the doors of the niche were closed. The doors were of copper, or some other metal, and opened to both sides, where there was space for them against the walls. They did not stand perpendicularly, but lay a little obliquely before the niche, and reached low enough to the ground for a stone laid against them to prevent their being opened. The stone intended for this purpose was now lying outside the entrance of the grotto. After the burial of the Lord it was brought in for the first time and laid before the closed doors of the tomb. It was large and somewhat rounded on the side that was to lie next the doors, because the wall near them was not at right angles. To open the doors, the immense stone was not first rolled out of the vault, for that, owing to the confined space, would have been attended with the greatest difficulty. But a chain let down from the roof was fastened to rings fixed in the stone. Then the chain being drawn up by the aid of several men exerting all their strength, the stone was swung to one side of the grotto, leaving the doors of the tomb free.

In the garden opposite the entrance to the grotto there was a stone bench. If one mounted to the roof of the grotto, which was covered with grass, he could descry the heights of Zion and some of the towers above the city walls. The Bethlehem gate, an aqueduct, and the well of Gihon also could be seen from here. The rock inside was white veined with red and brown. The grotto was finished very neatly.

We must here remark that, in the four years during which Anne Catherine related her visions, she described many changes connected with the holy places profaned and laid waste, yet always venerated either secretly or openly. She herself venerated them in vision. She saw many stones and fragments of rock, the witnesses of the Passion and Resurrection of the Lord, placed by St. Helena, after her discovery of the holy places, in the Church of the Holy Sepulcher built by her. They were placed in a narrow space near one another, and put under the protection of the city. Anne Catherine honored in vision the Church of the Crucifixion, that of the Holy Sepulcher, and several parts of the Sepulcher itself over which chapels are now raised. But sometimes, when she venerated not so much the tomb itself as the site upon which the sepulcher stood, it seemed to her that she saw it in the vicinity, though still somewhat removed from the spot upon which the cross had stood.

The Descent from the Cross

WHILE there were only a few guards around the cross, I saw about five men coming through the valley from Bethany. They drew near the place of execution, looked up to the cross, and then stole away again. I think they must have been disciples. Three times I saw two men in the vicinity as if making examinations and anxiously deliberating together. They were Joseph of Arimathea and Nicodemus. The first time was during the crucifixion. (Perhaps it was then that they sent to buy Jesus's garments from the soldiers). The second was when they came to see whether the crowd had dispersed. After looking around, they went to the tomb to make some preparations. The third time was when they returned from the tomb. They went right up to the cross, looked up and all around, as if watching for a good opportunity, consulted as to the best plan of action for the task before them, and then went back to the city.

And now began the transport to Golgotha of all that was necessary for the embalming. Besides the instruments to be used in taking the sacred body down from the cross, the servants took with them two ladders from a shed near Nicodemus's dwelling. Each of these ladders consisted of a single pole in which pieces of thick plank were so fitted as to form steps. They were provided with hooks, which could be hung higher or lower at pleasure, either to steady the ladder itself in some particular position or to hang on it the tools and other articles necessary for the work that was being done.

The good women from whom they had received the spices for the embalming packed everything nicely for them. Nicodemus had brought one hundred pounds of spices, equal to thirty-seven pounds of our weight, as has more than once been explained to me. They carried these spices around the neck in little kegs made of bark. One of the kegs contained some kind of powder. In bags made of parchment, or leather, were bunches of aromatic herbs. Joseph had with him also a box of ointment. Of what the box was composed I know not, but it was red with a blue rim. The servants, as already mentioned, carried in a handbarrow various kinds of vessels, leathern bottles, sponges, and tools. They took with them likewise fire in a closed lantern.

The servants left the city before their master and by another gate (I think the Bethlehem Gate) and went out to Golgotha. On their way through the city, they passed a house to which the blessed Virgin with the other women and John had retired, in order to make some preparations for the Lord's burial. They joined the servants, whom they followed at a little distance. There were about five women, some of whom carried

The Descent from the Cross

325

The Holy Virgin Kisses the Face of Jesus on the Anointing Stone

large bundles of linen under their mantles. It was a custom among the women, whenever they went out toward evening or upon any secret mission of piety, to envelop their whole person in a long strip of linen at least a yard in width. This they did very skillfully. They began with one arm, and then wound the linen so closely about the lower limbs that they could not take a long step. I have seen them entirely enveloped in this way, the linen brought up cleverly around the other arm and even enveloping the head. On this occasion there was something striking in the dress, for it looked to me like a robe of mourning.

Joseph and Nicodemus also were in mourning attire: false sleeves, maniples, and wide girdles of black, and their long and flowing mantles which they had drawn over their head were of a dark gray color. Their wide mantles covered all that they were carrying. Both directed their steps toward the gate of execution.

The streets were quiet and lonely. General terror kept the inhabitants in their homes. Many were prostrate in penance, and only a few were observing the prescriptions for the festival. When Joseph and Nicodemus arrived at the gate, they found it closed, and the streets and walls around beset by soldiers. *They were those for whom the Pharisees asked after two o'clock when they were fearing a tumult,* and they had not yet been remanded. Joseph presented them Pilate's written order to be allowed to pass. The soldiers expressed their readiness to comply with it, but explained at the same time that they had already vainly tried to open the gate, that probably it had received some damage from the earthquake shock, and that the executioners sent out to break the bones of the crucified had to return through the corner gate. But as soon as Joseph and Nicodemus grasped the bolt, the gate opened of itself with perfect ease.

It was still cloudy and foggy when they reached Golgotha, where they found their servants and the holy women, the latter sitting in front of the cross and in tears. Cassius and several converted soldiers stood like changed men, timidly and reverently, at some distance. Joseph and Nicodemus told the holy women and John of all that they had done to save Jesus from the ignominious death inflicted upon the thieves, and heard from them in return with what difficulty they had warded off the breaking of the Lord's bones, and how the prophecy had been fulfilled. They told also of how Cassius had pierced the sacred body with his lance. As soon as the centurion Abenadar arrived, they began sadly and reverently that most holy labor of love, the taking down from the cross and preparing for burial of the sacred body of their Master, their Lord, their Redeemer.

The most holy Virgin and Magdalene were seated upon the right side of the little mound between the cross of Dismas and that of Jesus. The other women were busied arranging the spices and linens, the water, the sponges, and the vessels. Cassius also drew near when he saw Abenadar approaching, and imparted to him the miracle wrought on his eyes. All were extremely touched. Their movements were marked by an air of solemn sadness and gravity. They worked with hearts full of love, but without many words. Sometimes the silence in which the sacred duties were quickly and carefully being rendered was broken by a deep sigh or a vehement exclamation of woe. Magdalene gave way unrestrainedly to her grief. Her emotion was violent. No consideration, not even the presence of so many around her, could make her repress it.

Nicodemus and Joseph placed the ladders behind the cross and mounted, carrying with them a very long strip of linen, to which three broad straps were fastened. They bound the body of Jesus under the arms and knees to the trunk of the cross, and the arms they fastened in the same way at the wrists. Then by striking upon strong pegs fixed against the points of the nails at the back of the cross, they forced out the nails from Jesus's hands, which were not very much shaken by the blows. The nails fell easily out of the wounds, for they had been enlarged by the weight of the body which, supported now by means of the linen band, no longer rested upon them. The lower part of the body, which in death had sunk down on the knees, rested now in a sitting posture upon a linen band that was bound up around the hands on the arms of the cross. While Joseph was striking out the left nail and allowing the left arm to sink down gently on the body, Nicodemus was binding the right arm in the same way to the cross, also the thorn-crowned head, which had fallen upon the right shoulder. The right nail was then forced out, and the arm allowed to sink into the band that supported the body. Abenadar the centurion had meanwhile, though with great effort, been driving out the enormous nail from the feet.

Cassius reverently picked up the nails as they fell out, and laid them down together by the blessed Virgin. Next, removing the ladders to the front of the cross and close to the sacred body, they loosened the upper band from the trunk of the cross, and hung it on one of the hooks of the ladder. They did the same to the two other bands, which they hung on two of the lower hooks. Thus with the gently lowered bands, the sacred body sank by degrees to where the centurion Abenadar, mounted on portable steps, was waiting to receive it. He clasped the limbs below the knees in his arms and descended slowly, while Nicodemus and Joseph, holding the upper part in their arms, gently and cautiously, as if carrying a beloved and very severely wounded friend, came down the ladders step by step. In this way did that most sacred, that most terribly maltreated body of the Redeemer reach the ground.

This taking down of Jesus from the cross was inexpressibly touching. Everything was done with so much precaution, so much tenderness, as if fearing to cause the Lord pain. Those engaged in it were penetrated with all the love and reverence for the sacred body that they had felt for the Holy of Holies during his life. All were looking up with eyes riveted, and accompanying every movement with raising of hands, tears, and gestures of pain and grief. But no word was uttered. When the men engaged in the sacred task gave expression to their reverent emotion it was as if involuntary, as if they were performing some solemn function; and when necessary to communicate directions to one another, they did it in few words and a low tone. When the blows of the hammer by which the nails were driven out resounded, Mary and Magdalene, as well as all that had been present at the crucifixion, were pierced with fresh grief, for the sound reminded them of that most cruel nailing of Jesus to the cross. They shuddered, as if expecting again to hear his piercing cries, and grieved anew over his death proclaimed by the silence of those blessed lips. As soon as the sacred body was taken down, the men wrapped it in linen from the knees to the waist and laid it on a sheet in his mother's arms which, in anguish of heart and ardent longing, were stretched out to receive it.

The Body of Jesus Prepared for Burial

THE BLESSED Virgin was seated upon a large cover spread upon the ground, her right knee raised a little, and her back supported by a kind of cushion made, perhaps, of mantles rolled together. There sat the poor mother, exhausted by grief and fatigue, in the position best suited for rendering love's last, sad duties to the remains of her murdered Son. The men laid the sacred body on a sheet spread upon the mother's lap. The venerable head of Jesus rested upon her slightly raised knee, and his body lay outstretched upon the sheet. Love and grief in equal degrees struggled in the breast of the blessed Mother. She held in her arms the body of her beloved Son, whose long martyrdom she had been able to soothe by no loving ministrations; and at the same time she beheld the frightful maltreatment exercised upon it, she gazed upon its wounds now close under her eyes. She pressed her lips to his bloodstained cheeks, while Magdalene knelt with her face bowed upon his feet.

The men meanwhile had retired to a little cave that lay deep on the southwestern side of the mount. There they completed their preparations for the burial and set all things in order. Cassius and a number of soldiers who had been converted to the Lord remained standing at a respectful distance. All the ill-disposed had returned to the city, and those now present served as a guard to prevent the approach of anyone likely to interrupt the last honors being shown to Jesus. Some of them, when called upon, rendered assistance here and there by handing different articles.

The holy women helped in various ways, presenting when necessary vessels of water, sponges, towels, ointments, and spices. When not so engaged, they remained at a little distance attentively watching what was going on. Among them were Mary Cleophas, Salome, and Veronica, but Magdalene was always busied around the sacred body. Mary Heli, the blessed Virgin's elder sister, who was already an aged matron, was sitting apart on the earthwall of the circle, silently looking on. John lent constant assistance to the blessed Virgin. He went to and fro between the women and the men, now helping the former in their task of love, and afterward assisting the latter in every way to prepare all things for the burial. Everything was thought of. The women had leathern water bottles, which they opened, and pressed the sides together to pour out their contents, also a vessel nearby on burning coals. They gave Mary and Magdalene clear water and fresh sponges as required, squeezing into leathern bottles those that had been used. I think the round lumps that I saw them squeezing out must have been sponges.

The blessed Virgin's courage and fortitude, in the midst of her inexpressible anguish, were unshaken. Her sorrow was not such as could cause her to permit the marks of outrage and torture to remain upon the sacred body, and so she immediately began earnestly and carefully to wash and purify it from every trace of ill-usage. With great care she opened the crown of thorns in the back and, with the assistance of others, removed it from Jesus's head. Some of the thorns had penetrated deeply, and that the removal of the crown might not by disturbing them enlarge the wounds, they had first to be cut off. The crown was deposited near the nails. Then with a pair of round, yellow pincers,† Mary drew from the wounds the long splinters and sharp thorns still sunken in the Lord's head, and showed them sadly to the compassionate friends

---

† Anne Catherine said that the shape of these pincers reminded her of the scissors with which Samson's hair was cut off. In her visions of the third year of the public life of Jesus she had seen our Lord keep the sabbath-day at Misael—a town belonging to the Levites, of the tribe of Asher—and as a portion of the Book of Judges was read in the synagogue, had beheld upon that occasion the life of Samson.

standing around. The thorns were laid by the crown, though some of them may have been kept as tokens of remembrance.

The face of the Lord was hardly recognizable, so greatly was it disfigured by blood and wounds. The torn hair of the head and beard was clotted with blood. Mary washed the head and face and soaked the dried blood from the hair with sponges. As the washing proceeded, the awful cruelties to which Jesus had been subjected became more apparent, and roused emotions of compassion, sorrow, and tenderness as she went from wound to wound. With a sponge and a little linen over the fingers of her right hand, she washed the blood from the wounds of the head, from the broken eyes, the nostrils, and the ears. With the little piece of linen on the forefinger, she purified the half-opened mouth, the tongue, the teeth, and the lips. She divided into three parts the little that remained of his hair. One part fell on either side of the head, and the third over the back. The front hair, after disengaging and cleansing it, she smoothed behind his ears.†

When the sacred head had been thoroughly cleansed, the blessed Virgin kissed the cheeks and covered it. Her care was next directed to the neck, the shoulders, the breast, and the back of the sacred body, the arms and the torn hands filled with blood. Ah, then was the terrible condition to which it had been reduced displayed in all its horror! The bones of the breast, as well as all the nerves, were dislocated and strained and thereby become stiff and inflexible. The shoulder upon which Jesus had borne the heavy cross was so lacerated that it had become one great wound,

---

† Anne Catherine was accustomed, when speaking of persons of historical importance, to explain how they divided their hair. "Eve," she said, "divided her hair in two parts, but Mary into three." And she appeared to attach importance to these words. No opportunity presented itself for her to give any explanation upon the subject, which probably would have shown what was done with the hair in sacrifices, funerals, consecrations, or vows, etc. She once said of Samson: "His fair hair, which was long and thick, was gathered up on his head in seven tresses, like a helmet, and the ends of these tresses were fastened upon his forehead and temples. His hair was not in itself the source of his strength, but only as the witness to the vow which he had made to let it grow in God's honor. The powers that depended upon these seven tresses were the seven gifts of the Holy Spirit. He must have already broken his vows and lost many graces, when he allowed this sign of being a Nazarene to be cut off. I did not see Delilah cut off all his hair, and I think one lock remained on his forehead. He retained the grace to do penance and of that repentance by which he recovered strength sufficient to destroy his enemies. The life of Samson is figurative and prophetic."

and the whole of the upper part of the body was full of welts and cuts from the scourges. There was a small wound in the left breast where the point of Cassius's lance had come out, and in the right side was opened that great, wide wound made by the lance, which had pierced his heart through and through. Mary washed and purified all these wounds, while Magdalene, kneeling before her, frequently lent assistance, though for the most part she remained at Jesus's feet, bathing them for the last time, more with her tears than with water, and wiping them with her hair.

The head, the upper part of the body, and the feet of the Lord had now been cleansed from blood. The sacred body still lay in Mary's lap, bluish white, glistening like flesh drained of blood, with here and there brown stains of coagulated blood that looked like red moles, and red places where the skin had been torn off. The blessed Virgin covered the parts as they were washed, and began to embalm the wounds, commencing with those of the head. The holy women knelt by her in turn, presenting to her a box from which, with the forefinger and thumb of the right hand, she took out something like salve, or precious ointment, with which she filled and anointed all the wounds. She put some upon the hair also, and I saw her taking the hands of Jesus in her own left hand, reverently kissing them, and then filling the wide wounds made by the nails with the ointment, or sweet spices. The ears, nostrils, and wound of Jesus's side, she likewise filled with the same. Magdalene was busied principally with the feet of Jesus. She repeatedly wiped and anointed them, but only to bedew them again with her tears, and she often knelt long with her face pressed upon them.

I saw that the water used was not thrown away, but poured into the leathern bottles into which the sponges had been squeezed. More than once I saw fresh water brought by some of the men, Cassius or some other soldier, in the leathern bottles and jugs that the women had brought with them. They procured it at the well of Gihon, which was so near that it could be seen from the garden of the sepulcher.

When the blessed Virgin had anointed all the wounds, she bound up the sacred head in linen, but the covering for the face, attached to that of the head, she did not as yet draw down. With a gentle pressure, she closed the half-broken eyes of Jesus, and kept her hand upon them for a little while. Then she closed the mouth, embraced the sacred body of her Son, and weeping bitter tears, allowed her face to rest upon his. Magdalene's reverence for Jesus did not permit her to approach her face to his. She pressed it to his feet only.

Joseph and Nicodemus had already been standing awhile at some distance waiting, when John drew near the blessed Virgin with the request that she would permit them to take the body of Jesus, that they might proceed in their preparations for the burial, as the sabbath was near. Once more Mary closely embraced Jesus, and in touching words took leave of him. The men raised the most sacred body in the sheet upon which it was resting in the lap of his mother, and carried it down to the place where the burial preparations were to be made. Mary's grief, which had been somewhat assuaged by her loving ministrations to Jesus, now burst forth anew, and, quite overcome, she rested with covered head in the arms of the women. Magdalene, as if fearing that they wanted to rob her of her Beloved, with outstretched hands ran some steps after the sacred body, but soon she turned back again to the blessed Virgin.

They carried the body of Jesus a little distance down from Golgotha's summit to a cave on the side of the mount in which there was a beautiful flat rock. It was here that the men had prepared the place for embalming. I saw first a linen cloth, open-worked something like a net. It looked as if it had been pierced with a sharp instrument, and was like the large so-called hunger cloth (*Hungertuch*) that is hung up in our churches during Lent. When as a child I saw that cloth hanging up, I used to think it was the same that I had seen at the preparations for the Lord's burial. Perhaps it was pierced like a net in order to allow the water used in washing to flow through it. I saw another large cloth opened out. They laid the body of the Lord on the open-worked one, and some of them held the other over it. Nicodemus and Joseph knelt down and, under cover of this upper cloth, loosened from the lower part of Jesus's body the bandage that they had bound around it from the knees to the hips when taken down from the cross. They removed likewise that other covering which Jonadab, the nephew of his foster father Joseph, had given him before the crucifixion. Thus with great regard to modesty, they sponged, under cover of the sheet held over it, the lower part of the Lord's body.

Then, linen bands being stretched under the upper part of the sacred body and the knees, it was raised, still under cover of the sheet, and the back treated in the same way without turning the body over. They washed it until the water squeezed from the sponges ran clean and clear. After that they poured water of myrrh over the whole body, and I saw them laying it down and reverently, with their hands, stretching it out at full length, for it had stiffened in the position in which, when in death it had sunk down upon the cross, the knees bent. Under the hips they laid a linen strip, four feet in width and about twelve feet in length, almost filled the lap with bunches of herbs and fine, crisp threadlike plants, like saffron, and then sprinkled over all a powder, which Nicodemus had brought with him in a box. The bunches of herbs were such as I have often seen on the celestial tables laid upon little green and gold plates with blue rims. Next they tightly bound the linen strip around the whole, drew the end up between the sacred limbs, and stuck it under the band that encircled the waist, thus fastening it securely. After this they anointed the wounds of the thighs, scattered sweet spices over them, laid bunches of herbs between the limbs all the way down to the feet, and bound the whole in linen from the feet up.

John once more conducted the blessed Virgin and the other holy women to the sacred remains of Jesus. Mary knelt down by Jesus's head, took a fine linen scarf that hung around her neck under her mantle and which she had received from Claudia Procula, Pilate's wife, and laid it under the head of her Son. Then she and the other holy women filled in the spaces between the shoulders and the head, around the whole neck and up as far as the cheeks with herbs, some of those fine threadlike plants, and the costly powder mentioned before, all of which the blessed Virgin bound up carefully in the fine linen scarf. Magdalene poured the entire contents of a little flask of precious balm into the wound of Jesus's side, while the holy women placed aromatic herbs in the hands and all around and under the feet. Then the men covered the pit of the stomach and filled up the armpits and all other parts of the body with sweet spices, crossed the stiffened arms over the bosom, and closely wrapped the whole in the large white sheet as far as the breast, just as a child is swathed. Then, having fastened under one of the armpits the end of a broad linen band, they wound it round the arms, the hands, the head, and down again around the whole of the sacred body until it presented the appearance of a mummy. Lastly, they laid the Lord's body on the large sheet, twelve feet long, that Joseph of Arimathea had bought, and wrapped it closely around it. The sacred body was laid on it crosswise. Then one corner was drawn up from the feet to the breast, the opposite one was folded down over the head and shoulders, and the sides were doubled round the whole person.

While all were kneeling around the Lord's body, taking leave of it with many tears, a touching miracle was exhibited before their eyes: the entire form of Jesus's sacred body with all its wounds appeared, as if drawn in brown and reddish colors, on the cloth that covered it. It was as if he wished gratefully to reward their loving care of him, gratefully to acknowledge their sorrow, and leave to them an image of himself imprinted through all the coverings that enveloped him. Weeping and lamenting, they embraced the sacred body, and reverently kissed the miraculous portrait. Their astonishment was so great that they opened the outside wrapping, and it became still greater when they found all the linen bands around the sacred body white as before and only the upper-most cloth marked with the Lord's figure.

The cloth on the side upon which the body lay received the imprint of the whole back of the Lord; the ends that covered it were marked with the front likeness. The parts of this latter, to produce the perfect form, had to be laid together, because the corners of the cloth were all crossed over the body in front. The picture was not a mere impression formed by bleeding wounds, for the whole body had been tightly wrapped in spices and numerous linen bands. It was a miraculous picture, a witness to the creative Godhead in the body of Jesus.

I have seen many things connected with the subsequent history of this holy winding sheet, but I cannot recall them in their precise order. After the resurrection it, along with the other linens, came into the possession of Jesus's friends. Once I saw a man carrying it off with him under his arm when he was starting on a journey. I saw it a second time in the hands of the Jews, and I saw it long in veneration among the Christians of different places. Once a dispute arose about it, and for its settlement, the holy winding sheet was thrown into the fire; but rising miraculously above the flames, it flew into the hands of the Christians.

At the prayer of holy men, three impressions of the holy image were taken off, both the back and the picture formed on the folds of the front. These impressions were consecrated by contact with the original and the solemn intention of the church. They have even effected great miracles. I have seen the original, somewhat damaged, somewhat torn, held in ven-eration by some non-Catholic Christians of Asia. I have forgotten the name of the city, but it is situated in a large country near the home of the three kings. In those visions I also saw something connected with Turin and France and Pope Clement I, as well as something about the Emperor Tiberius, who died five years after the death of Christ, but I have forgotten it.

The Sepulcher

THE MEN now laid the sacred body on the leathern litter, placed over it a brown cover, and ran two poles along the sides. I thought right away of the Ark of the Covenant. Nicodemus and Joseph carried the front ends on their shoulders; Abenadar and John, the others. There followed the blessed Virgin, her elder sister Mary Heli, Magdalene, and Mary Cleo-phas. Then the group of women that had been seated at some distance; Veronica, Johanna Chusa, Mary Mark; Salome, the wife of Zebedee; Mary Salome, Salome of Jerusalem, Susanna, and Anna, a niece of Joseph. She was the daughter of one of his brothers, and had been reared in Jerusalem. Cassius and his soldiers closed the procession. The other women, namely, Maroni of Nain, Dinah the Samaritan, and Mara the Suphanite were at the time with Martha and Lazarus in Bethany.

Two soldiers with twisted torches walked on ahead, for light was needed in the grotto of the sepulcher. The procession moved on for a distance of about seven minutes singing Psalms in a low, plaintive tone, through the valley to the garden of the tomb. I saw on a hill on the other side of the valley James the Greater, the brother of John, looking at the procession, and then going off to tell the other disciples, who were hiding in the caves.

The garden of the sepulcher was not laid out with any view to regularity. The rock in which the sepulcher was cut lay at one end, entirely overgrown with verdure. The front of the garden was protected by a quickset hedge, inside of which at the entrance was a little enclosure formed of stakes, upon which rested long poles held in place by iron pegs. Outside the garden and also to the right of the sepulcher stood some palm trees; the other vegetation consisted chiefly of bushes, flowers, and aromatic plants.

I saw the procession halt at the entrance of the garden. It was opened by removing some of the poles, which were afterward used as levers for rolling away the stone from the door of the grotto. Before reaching the rock, they took the cover from the litter, raised the sacred body, and placed it upon a narrow board which had previously been covered with a linen cloth. Nicodemus and Joseph took one end of the board; the other two, the upper end, which was covered. The grotto, which was perfectly new, had been cleaned out and fumigated by Nicodemus's servants. It was very neat inside and was ornamented by a beautifully carved coping. The funereal couch was broader at the head than at the foot. It was cut out in the form of a body swathed in its bands and winding sheet, and slightly elevated at the head and foot.

The holy women sat down upon a seat opposite the entrance of the grotto. The four men carried the Lord's body down into it, set it down, strewed the stone couch with sweet spices, spread over it a linen cloth, and deposited the sacred remains upon it. The cloth hung down over the couch. Then, having with tears and embraces given expression to their love for Jesus, they left the cave. The blessed Virgin now went in, and I saw her sitting on the head of the tomb, which was about two feet from the ground. She was bending low over the corpse of her child and weeping. When she left the cave, Magdalene hurried in with flowers and branches, which she had gathered in the garden and which she now scattered over the sacred body. She wrung her hands, and with tears and sighs embraced the feet of Jesus. When the men outside gave warning that it was time to close the doors, she went back to where the women were sitting. The men raised the cloth that was hanging over the side of the tomb, folded it around the sacred body, and then threw the brown cover over the whole. Lastly, they closed the brown doors, probably of copper or bronze, which had a perpendicular bar on the outside crossed by a transverse one. It looked like a cross.

The great stone, intended for securing the doors and which was still lying outside the cave, was in shape almost like a chest[†] or tomb, and was large enough for a man to lie at full length upon it. It was very heavy. By means of the poles brought from the garden entrance, the men rolled it into place before the closed doors of the tomb. The outside entrance was secured by a light door of wickerwork.

All that took place in the grotto was by torchlight, for it was dark in there. I saw during the burial several men lurking around in the neighborhood of the garden and of Mount Calvary. They looked timid and sorrowful. I think they were disciples who, in consequence of Abenadar's account of what was going on, had ventured forth from their caves and come hither. They now appeared to be returning.

The Return from the Burial • The Sabbath

IT was now the hour at which the sabbath began. Nicodemus and Joseph returned to the city by a little private gate which, by special permission I think, Joseph had been allowed to make in the city wall near the garden. They had previously informed the blessed Virgin, Magdalene, John, and some of the women, who wanted to return to Golgotha to pray and to get some things they had left there, that this gate, as well as that of the Cenacle, would be opened to them whenever they would knock. Mary Heli, the blessed Virgin's aged sister, was conducted back to the city by Mary Mark and some other women. The servants of Nicodemus and Joseph went back to Golgotha for the tools and things they had left here.

The soldiers went to join the guard at the gate of execution, while Cassius rode to Pilate with the lance. He related all that had happened to him, and promised to bring him an exact account of all that might still

† Apparently Anne Catherine here spoke of the ancient cases in which her poor countrymen keep their clothes. The lower part of these cases is smaller than the upper, and this gives them some likeness to a tomb. She had one of these cases, which she called her chest. She often described the stone by this comparison, but her descriptions have not, nevertheless, given us a very clear idea of its shape.

take place, if he would give him command of the guard which the Jews, as had already been reported, would not fail to ask of him. Pilate listened with secret dismay, but treated Cassius as an enthusiast, and impelled by disgust and superstition, ordered him to put the lance outside the door.

When the blessed Virgin and her companions were returning with their vessels and other things from Golgotha, where they had again poured out their tears and prayers, they espied coming toward them a troop of soldiers headed by a torchbearer. The women halted on both sides of the road until the crowd passed. The soldiers were going up to Golgotha, perhaps to take away and bury the crosses before the sabbath. When they had passed, the holy women continued their way to the little private gate.

Peter, James the Greater, and James the Less met Joseph and Nicodemus in the city. All wept. Peter was especially vehement in his expressions of grief. He embraced Joseph and Nicodemus with tears, accused himself, lamented that he had not been present at the death of the Lord, and thanked them for bestowing upon him a tomb. All were quite beside themselves with sorrow. They agreed that the door of the Cenacle should be opened upon their knocking, and then separated, in order to seek the other disciples who were scattered in various directions.

Later I saw the blessed Virgin and her companions knocking at the Cenacle and being admitted, then Abenadar, and by degrees most of the apostles and several of the disciples entered. The holy women retired to the apartments occupied by the blessed Virgin. They took some refreshment and spent some moments in tears and mourning, relating to one another all that had happened. The men changed their garments, and I saw them standing under the lamp celebrating the sabbath. Then they ate lambs at the different tables around the Cenacle, but without any ceremony. It was not the paschal lamb. They had already eaten that yesterday. All were in great trouble and sadness. The holy women also prayed with Mary under a lamp. Later, when it had grown quite dark, Lazarus, Martha, the widow Maroni of Nain, Dinah the Samaritan, and Mara the Suphanite were admitted. They were come from Bethany to keep the sabbath. Once more was sorrow renewed by the narrations of each.

The Imprisonment of Joseph of Arimathea • The Holy Sepulcher Guarded

JOSEPH of Arimathea left the Cenacle *at a late hour* and, with some of the disciples and holy women, started for his home. They were proceeding sadly and timidly along the streets of Zion when an armed band dashed suddenly from their place of concealment in the neighborhood of Caiaphas's judgment hall and laid hands upon Joseph of Arimathea. His companions fled with cries of terror. I saw that they imprisoned the good Joseph in a tower of the city wall not very far from the judgment hall. Caiaphas had committed the care of this seizure to pagan soldiers, who celebrated no sabbath. The intention was to let Joseph die of starvation, and to keep his disappearance secret.

On the night between Friday and Saturday, Caiaphas and some of the chief men among the Jews held a consultation upon what ought to be done with regard to the extraordinary events that had just taken place, and their effect upon the people. *It was far in the night* when they went to Pilate to tell him that as that seducer said, while he was still alive, "After three days I will rise again," it would be right "to command the sepulcher to be guarded until the third day; otherwise his disciples might come and steal him away, and say to the people, 'He is risen from the dead,' and the last error would be worse than the first."

Pilate wanted to have nothing more to do with the affair, so he said to them: "You have a guard. Go, guard it as you know." He, however, appointed Cassius to keep watch and give him an account of all that he observed. Thereupon *I saw twelve men leaving the city before sunrise*. They were accompanied by soldiers not dressed in the Roman uniform. They were temple soldiers, and looked to me like halbadiers, or life-guardsmen. They took with them lanterns on long poles, in order to be able to distinguish things clearly in the dark, and also to have light in the gloomy sepulcher.

When, on their arrival, they assured themselves that the sacred body was safe, they fastened a string across the doors of the tomb proper and another from that to the stone lying before them. Then they sealed the two together with a seal in the form of a half-moon. The twelve men returned afterward to the city, and the guard took up a position opposite the outer door of the sepulcher. Five or six took turns in watching, while some others presented themselves occasionally with provisions from the city. Cassius never left his post. He remained most of the time in the sepulcher itself, sitting or standing before the entrance to the tomb, and in such a position that he could see that side at which rested the feet of the Lord. He had received great interior graces and had been admitted to the clear understanding of many mysteries. As such a condition, being almost all the time in a state of wonderful interior enlightenment, was something so new to him, he was, as it were, transported out of himself, wholly regardless of external things. He here became entirely changed, a new man. He spent the day in penance, thanksgiving, and adoration.

Holy Saturday

The Friends of Jesus on Holy Saturday

AS I have said, I saw yesterday evening the men in the Cenacle celebrating the sabbath and then taking a repast. They were about twenty in number. They were clothed in long white garments girdled at the waist, and were gathered together under a hanging lamp. When they separated after the repast, some went to take their rest in adjoining apartments, others to their own homes. *Today* I saw most of them remaining quietly in the house, assembling at intervals for prayer and reading, and occasionally admitting some newcomer.

In the house occupied by the blessed Virgin there was a large hall with several little recesses cut off by hangings and movable partitions. These were private sleeping places. When the holy women returned from the sepulcher, they put everything they brought back again into its place, and lighted the lamp that was hanging from the center of the ceiling. Then they gathered under it around the blessed Virgin, and took turns in praying most devoutly. They were all in deep sorrow. After that they partook of some refreshment, and were soon joined by Martha, Maroni, Dinah, and Mary who, after celebrating the sabbath in Bethany, had come hither with Lazarus. The last-named went to the men in the Cenacle. When, with tears on both sides, the death and burial of the Lord had been recounted to the newly arrived, and *the hour was far advanced*, some of the men, among them Joseph of Arimathea, left the supper room, called for the women that wanted to return to their homes in the city, and took their leave. It was on the way that that armed band seized Joseph near the judgment hall of Caiaphas, and cast him into the tower.

The women who had remained with the blessed Virgin now retired, each to her own screened sleeping place. They veiled their heads in long linen scarves, and sat for a little while in silent grief on the ground, leaning on the sleeping covers that were rolled up against the wall. After some moments, they arose, spread out the covers, laid aside their sandals, girdles, and some articles of dress, enveloped themselves from head to foot, as they were accustomed to do on retiring to rest, and lay down on their couches for a short sleep. *At midnight* they rose again, dressed, folded the couch together, assembled once more under the lamp around the blessed Virgin, and prayed in turn.

When the blessed Virgin and the holy women, notwithstanding their great suffering, had discharged this duty of nocturnal prayer (which I have frequently seen practiced since by the faithful children of God and holy persons, either urged thereto by special grace, or in obedience to a rule laid down by God and his church), John and some of the disciples knocked at the door of the women's hall. He and the other men had previously prayed, like the women, under the lamp in the Cenacle. The holy women at once enveloped themselves in their mantles and, along with the blessed Virgin, followed them to the temple.

It was about the same time that *the tomb was sealed, that is, about three o'clock in the morning,* that I saw the blessed Virgin with the other holy women, John, and several of the disciples, going to the temple. It was customary among many of the Jews to visit the temple at daybreak the morning after the eating of the paschal lamb. It was in consequence opened about midnight, because the sacrifices on that morning began very early. But today, on account of the disturbance of the feast and the defilement of the temple, everything had been neglected, and it seemed to me as if the blessed Virgin, with her friends, wanted to take leave of it. It was there that she had been reared, there she had adored the holy mystery, until she herself bore in her womb that same holy mystery, that holy one who, as the true Paschal Lamb, had been so barbarously immolated the day before. The temple was, according to the custom of this day, open, the lamps lighted, and even the vestibule of the priests (a privilege granted to this day) was thrown open to the people. But the sacred edifice, with the exception of a few guards and servants, was quite deserted; marks of yesterday's disorder and confusion lay everywhere around. It had been defiled by the presence of the dead, and at the sight of it, the thought arose in my mind: "How will it ever be restored?"

Simeon's sons and Joseph of Arimathea's nephews, the latter of whom were very much grieved at the news of their uncle's arrest, welcomed the blessed Virgin and her companions and conducted them everywhere, for they had the care of the temple. Silently they gazed, with mingled feelings of awe and adoration, at the work of destruction, the visible marks of God's anger. Only here and there were a few words spoken, to recount the events of the preceding day.

Yesterday's destruction was evidenced in many different ways, for no attempt at repair had yet been made. Where the vestibule joined the sanctuary, the wall had so given way that a person could easily creep through the fissure, and the whole threatened to fall. The beam above the rent curtain before the sanctuary had sunk; the pillars that supported it had declined from each other at the top; and the curtain, torn in two, hung down at the sides. So great an opening was made in the wall of the vestibule by the huge stone that had been precipitated from the north side of the temple near Simeon's oratory upon the spot on which Zechariah appeared, that the blessed Virgin could pass through without difficulty. This brought her to the great teacher's chair, from which the boy Jesus had taught, and from this spot she could see through the torn curtain into the Holy of Holies, something that would not have been possible before. Here and there, likewise, walls were cracked, portions of the floor sunk in, beams displaced, and pillars leaning out of their proper direction.

The blessed Virgin visited with her companions all places rendered sacred to her by the presence of Jesus. Kneeling down, she kissed them, recalling with tears and in a few touching words the particular remembrances connected with each. Her companions imitated her example, kneeling and kissing the hallowed spots.

The Jews regarded with extraordinary reverence all places in which anything held sacred by them had happened. They touched and kissed them, prostrating with their faces upon them, and I could never feel surprised at such manifestations. When one knows, believes, and feels that the God of Abraham, Isaac, and Jacob is a living God, who dwelt among his people in his temple, his house, at Jerusalem, the wonder would be if they did not venerate such places. Whoever believes in a living God, in a Father and Redeemer and Sanctifier of humankind, His children, wonders not that, impelled by love, He is still living among the living. He feels that he owes to Him and to everything connected with him more love, honor, and reverence than to earthly parents, friends, teachers, superiors, and princes. The temple and holy places were to the Jews what the most blessed sacrament is to Christians. But there were among them some blind and some enlightened, just as there are amongst us some that, adoring not the living God in our midst, are fallen into the superstitious service of the gods of the world. They reflect not upon these words of Jesus: "Whoever denies me before men, him also will I deny before my heavenly Father." People that unceasingly serve the spirit and falsehood of the world in thoughts and words and works, that cast aside all exterior worship of God, say indeed, if perchance they have not cast off God himself as altogether too exterior for them: "We adore God in spirit and in truth." But they do not know that these words mean in the Holy Spirit and in the Son, who took flesh from Mary, the Virgin, and who bore witness to the truth; who lived amongst us, who died for us on earth, and who will be with his church in the blessed sacrament until the end of time.

The blessed Virgin and her companions thus reverently visited many parts of the temple. She showed them where, as a little girl, she had first entered the sacred edifice, and where on the south side she had been educated until her espousals with Joseph. She pointed out to them the scene of her marriage, that of Jesus's presentation, and that of Simeon's and Anna's prophecies. At this point she wept bitterly, for the prophecy had been fulfilled, the sword had pierced her soul. She showed where she had found Jesus when a boy teaching in the temple, and she reverently kissed the teacher's chair. They went also to the offering box into which the widow had put her mite, and to the spot upon which the Lord forgave the woman taken in adultery. After they had thus with reverential touching, tears, prayers, and recalling of reminiscences, honored all the places rendered venerable by Jesus's presence, they returned to Zion.

The blessed Virgin did not leave the temple without many tears and deep grief, for its ruins and its desolate aspect on that day, once so sacred, bore witness to the sins of her people. She thought of Jesus weeping over it, and of his prophecy: "Destroy this temple, and in three days I will build it up again." She thought of how the enemies of Jesus had destroyed the temple of his body, and she longed for the third day upon which that word of Eternal Truth would be fulfilled.

Returned to the Cenacle on Zion at daybreak, the blessed Virgin retired with her companions to her own dwelling on the right of the courtyard. At the entrance John left them and joined the men in the Cenacle, upwards of twenty in number, who spent the whole sabbath in the supper room, mourning the death of their Master and praying by turns under the lamp. I saw them occasionally and very cautiously admitting newcomers, and conferring with them in tears. All experienced an inward reverence for John and a feeling of confusion in his presence, since he had been at the death of the Lord. But John was full of love and sympathy toward them, and, simple and ingenuous as a child, he gave place to everyone. Once I saw them eating. They remained very silently together, and the house was closed. They were safe from attack, for the house belonged to Nicodemus, and they had hired it for the Passover supper.

Again *I saw the holy women assembled until evening* in the hall which was lighted by a lamp, the doors being closed and the windows covered. Sometimes they ranged round the blessed Virgin under the lamp for prayer; or sometimes they retired alone to their several recesses, enveloped their heads in mourning veils, and sat on flat boxes strewn with ashes (the sign of grief), or prayed with the face turned to the wall. Before they assembled under the lamp for prayer, they always laid aside their mourning veils and left them in the little recesses. I saw also that the weak among them took a little nourishment, but the others fasted.

More than once my gaze was directed to the holy women, and I always saw them as just described, praying or mourning in a darkened hall. When my meditation turned to the blessed Virgin dwelling in thought upon our Savior, I sometimes saw the holy tomb and about seven guards sitting or standing opposite the entrance. Close to the doors of the rocky cave, in which was the real tomb, the tomb proper, stood Cassius. He moved not from the spot, he was silent and recollected. I saw the closed doors of the tomb and the stone lying before them. But through the doors, I could see the body of the Lord lying just as it had been left. It was environed with light and splendor, and rested between two adoring angels, one at the head, the other at the foot. When my thoughts turned to the holy soul of our Redeemer, there was vouchsafed me a vision of his descent into hell so great, so extended, that I have been able to retain only a very small portion. I shall, however, relate what I can of it.

Some Words on Christ's Descent into Hell

WHEN Jesus with a loud cry gave up his most holy soul, I saw it as a luminous figure surrounded by angels, among them Gabriel, penetrating the earth at the foot of the holy cross. I saw his divinity united with his soul, while at the same time, it remained united to his body hanging on the cross. I cannot express how this was. I saw the place whither the soul of Jesus went. It seemed to be divided into three parts. It was like three worlds, and I had a feeling that it was round, and that each one of those places was a kind of locality, a sphere separated from the others.

Just in front of Limbo, there was a bright, cheerful tract of country clothed in verdure. It is into this that I always see the souls released from Purgatory entering before being conducted to heaven. The Limbo in which were the souls awaiting Redemption was encompassed by a gray, foggy atmosphere, and divided into different circles. The Savior, resplendent and conducted in triumph by angels, pressed on between two of these circles. The one on the left contained the souls of the leaders of the people down to Abraham, that on the right, the souls from Abraham to John the Baptist. Jesus went on between these two circles. They knew him not, but all were filled with joy and ardent desire. It was as if this place of anxious, distressed longing was suddenly enlarged. The Redeemer passed through them like a refreshing breeze, like light, like dew, quickly like the sighing of the wind. The Lord passed quickly between these two circles to a dimly lighted place in which were our first parents, Adam and Eve. He addressed them, and they adored him in unspeakable rapture. The procession of the Lord, accompanied by the first human beings, now turned to the left, to the Limbo of the leaders of God's people before the time of Abraham. This was a species of Purgatory, for here and there were evil spirits, who in manifold ways worried and distressed some of those souls. The angels knocked and demanded admittance. There was an entrance, because there was a *going in*; a gate, because there was an *unlocking*; and a *knocking*, because the one that was coming had to be announced. It seemed to me that I heard the angel call out: "Open the gates! Open the doors!" Jesus entered in triumph, while the wicked spirits retired, crying out: "What hast thou to do with us? What dost thou want here? Art thou now going to crucify us?" and so on. The angels bound them and drove them before them. The souls in this place had only a vague idea of Jesus, they knew him only slightly; but when he told them clearly who he was, they broke forth into songs of praise and thanksgiving. And now the soul of the Lord turned to the circle on the right, to Limbo proper. There he met the soul of the good thief going under the escort of angels into Abraham's bosom, while the bad thief, encompassed by demons, was being dragged down into hell. The soul of Jesus addressed some words to both and then, accompanied by a multitude of angels, of the redeemed, and by those demons that were driven out of the first circle, went likewise into the bosom of Abraham.

This space, or circle, appeared to me to lie higher than the other. It was as if a person climbed from the earth under the churchyard up into the church itself. The evil spirits struggled in their chains, and wanted not to enter, but the angels forced them on. In this second circle were all the holy Israelites to the left, the patriarchs, Moses, the judges, the kings; on the right, the prophets and all the ancestors of Jesus, as also his relatives down to Joachim, Anne, Joseph, Zechariah, Elizabeth, and John. There were no demons in this circle, no pain nor torment, only the ardent longing for the fulfillment of the Promise now realized. Unspeakable felicity and rapture inundated these souls as they saluted and adored the Redeemer, and the demons in their fetters were forced to confess before them their ignominious defeat. Many of the souls were sent up to resuscitate their bodies from the tomb and in them to render visible testimony to the Lord. This was the moment in which so many dead came forth from their tombs in Jerusalem. They looked to me like walking corpses. They laid their bodies again upon the earth, just as a messenger of justice lays aside his mantle of office after having fulfilled his superior's commands.

I now saw the Savior's triumphant procession entering another sphere lower than the last. It was the abiding place of pious pagans who, having had some presentiment of truth, had ardently sighed after it. It was a kind of Purgatory, a place of purification. There were evil spirits here, for I saw some idols. I saw the evil spirits compelled to confess the deception they had practiced. I saw the blessed spirits rendering homage to the Savior with touching expressions of joy. Here, too, the demons were chained by the angels and driven forward before them.

And thus I saw the Redeemer passing rapidly through these numerous abodes and freeing the souls therein confined. He did a great many other things, but in my present miserable state I am unable to relate them.

At last I saw him, his countenance grave and severe, approaching the center of the abyss, namely, hell itself. In shape it looked to me like an immeasurably vast, frightful, black stone building that shone with a metallic luster. Its entrance was guarded by immense, awful-looking doors, black like the rest of the building, and furnished with bolts and locks that inspired feelings of terror. Roaring and yelling most horrible could plainly be heard, and when the doors were pushed open, a frightful, gloomy world was disclosed to view.

As I am accustomed to see the Heavenly Jerusalem under the form of a city, and the abodes of the blessed therein under various kinds of palaces and gardens full of wonderful fruits and flowers, all according to the different degrees of glory, so here I saw everything under the appearance of a world whose buildings, open spaces, and various regions were all closely connected. But all proceeded from the opposite of happiness, all was pain and torment. As in the sojourns of the blessed all appears formed upon motives and conditions of infinite peace, eternal harmony and satisfaction, so here are the disorder, the malformation of eternal wrath, disunion, and despair.

As in heaven there are innumerable abodes of joy and worship, unspeakably beautiful in their glittering transparency, so here in hell are gloomy prisons without number, caves of torment, of cursing, and despair. As in heaven there are gardens most wonderful to behold, filled with fruits that afford divine nourishment, so here in hell there are horrible wildernesses and swamps full of torture and pain and of all that can give birth to feelings of detestation, of loathing, and of horror. I saw here temples, altars, palaces, thrones, gardens, lakes, streams, all formed of blasphemy, hatred, cruelty, despair, confusion, pain, and torture, while in heaven all is built up of benedictions, of love, harmony, joy, and delight. *Here* is the rending, eternal disunion of the damned; *there* is the blissful communion of the saints. All the roots of perversity and untruth are here cultivated in countless forms and deeds of punishment and affliction. Nothing here is right, no thought brings peace, for the terrible remembrance of divine justice casts every damned soul into the pain and torment that his own guilt has planted for him. All that is terrible here, both in appearance and reality, is the nature, the form, the fury of sin unmasked, the serpent that now turns against those in whose bosom it was once nourished. I saw there also frightful columns erected for the sole purpose of creating feelings of horror and terror, just as in the kingdom of God they are intended to inspire peace and the sentiment of blissful rest, etc. All this is easily understood, but cannot be expressed in detail.

When the gates were swung open by the angels, one beheld before him a struggling, blaspheming, mocking, howling, and lamenting throng. I saw that Jesus spoke some words to the soul of Judas. Some of the angels forced that multitude of evil spirits to prostrate before Jesus, for all had to acknowledge and adore him. This was for them the most terrible torment. A great number were chained in a circle around others who were in turn bound down by them. In the center was an abyss of darkness. Lucifer was cast into it, chained, and thick black vapor mounted up around him. This took place by the divine decree. I heard that Lucifer (if I do not mistake) will be freed again for awhile fifty or sixty years before the year AD 2000. I have forgotten many other dates that were told me. Some other demons are to be freed before Lucifer, in order to chastise and tempt humankind. I think that some are let loose now in our own day, and others will be freed shortly after our time.

It is impossible for me to relate all that was shown me. It is too much. I cannot reduce it to order, I cannot arrange it. I am also so dreadfully sick. When I try to speak of these things, they rise up before my eyes, and the sight is enough to make one die.

I saw too the redeemed souls in countless numbers leaving the places of their purification, leaving Limbo, and accompanying the soul of the Lord to a place of bliss below the Heavenly Jerusalem. It was there that some time ago I saw a deceased friend of mine. The soul of the good thief entered with the rest and again saw the Lord, according to his promise, in Paradise. I saw prepared here for the delight and refreshment of the souls celestial tables such as were often shown me in visions vouchsafed for my consolation.

I cannot say exactly the time of these events, nor their duration, neither can I repeat all that I saw and heard, because some things were incomprehensible even to myself, and others would be misunderstood. I saw the Lord in many different places, even on the seas. It seemed as if he sanctified and delivered every creature; everywhere the evil spirits fled before him into the abyss. Then I saw the soul of the Lord visiting many places on the earth. I saw him in Adam's tomb under Golgotha. The souls of Adam and Eve came again to him there. He conversed with them, and I saw him as if under the earth, going with them in many directions, visiting tomb after tomb of the prophets. Their souls entered their bodies, and Jesus explained many mysteries to them. Then I saw him with this chosen band, among whom was David, visiting many scenes of his own life and Passion, explaining to them the typical events that had there taken place, and with inexpressible love pointing out to them their fulfillment.

Among other places, I saw him with these souls at that of his baptism, where numerous figurative events had happened. He explained them all and, deeply touched, I beheld the everlasting mercy of Jesus in permitting the grace of his own holy baptism to flow upon them for their greater advantage.

It was unspeakably touching to see the soul of the Lord encompassed by those happy, blessed spirits shining through the dark earth, through rocks, through the water and the air, and lightly floating over the surface of the ground.

These are the few points that I can remember of my meditations, so full, so extended, upon the descent of the Lord into hell after his death, and of his releasing the souls of the just patriarchs of the earliest times. But besides this vision relating to time, I saw one connected with eternity, in which I was shown his mercy toward the poor souls on this day. I saw that, every year on the solemn celebration of this day (Good Friday) by the church, he casts upon Purgatory a glance by which many souls are released. I saw that even today, Holy Saturday, upon which day I had this contemplation, he released from their place of purification some souls that had sinned at the time of his crucifixion. I saw today the release of many souls, some unknown and others known to me, though I cannot name any of them.

(Being in a state of ecstasy today, Sister Emmerich related what follows):

The first descent of Jesus into Limbo was the fulfillment of early types, and in itself a type whose fulfillment is effected by today's releasing of the poor souls. The descent into hell that I saw was a vision of time past, but the freeing of the souls today is a lasting truth. The descent of Jesus into hell was the planting of the tree of grace, the tree of his own sacred merits, for the poor souls; and the constant recurrence of today's releasing of those souls is the fruit brought forth by that tree of grace in the spiritual garden of the ecclesiastical year. The Church Militant must cultivate the tree and gather the fruits, in which the Church Suffering must be allowed to share, since it can do nothing for itself. So it is with all the merits of the Lord. We must labor with him, in order to share in them. We must eat our bread in the sweat of our brow. All that Jesus did for us in time brings forth fruit for eternity, but we must in time cultivate and gather that fruit, otherwise we shall not enjoy it in eternity. The church is a most provident mother. Her year is in time the most complete garden of fruits for eternity. Her year contains a supply sufficient for the wants of all. Woe to the slothful and faithless laborers in that garden who, in any way, allow to go to waste a grace that might have restored health to the sick, strength to the weak, or furnished food to the hungry! On the Day of Judgment, the Master of the garden will demand an account of even the least blade of grass.

Resurrection • Ascension • Descent of the Holy Spirit

The Eve of the Holy Resurrection

AT *the close of the sabbath,* John, Peter, and James the Greater visited the holy women, to mourn with them and to console them. On their departure, the holy women enveloped themselves again in their mourning mantles, and retired to pray in the recesses strewn with ashes.

I saw an angel appear to the blessed Virgin. He announced to her that the Lord was near, and bade her to go out to the little gate belonging to Nicodemus. At these words, Mary's heart was filled with joy. Without saying a word to the holy women, wrapped in her mantle, she hastened to the gate in the city wall through which she had come on her return from the garden of the tomb.

It may have been *almost nine o'clock* when, in a solitary place near the gate, I saw the blessed Virgin suddenly halt in her hurried walk. She gazed as if ravished with joyous longing up at the top of the wall. Floating down toward her in the midst of a great multitude of the souls of the ancient patriarchs, I saw the most holy soul of Jesus, resplendent with light and without trace of wound. Turning to the patriarchs and pointing to the blessed Virgin, he uttered the words: "Mary, my mother!" and appeared to embrace her. Then he vanished. The blessed Virgin sank on her knees and kissed the ground upon which he had stood. She left the impress of her knees and feet upon the stone. Inexpressibly consoled, she hurried back to the women, whom she found busied preparing ointment and spices on a table. She did not tell them what had happened, but she consoled and strengthened them in faith.

The table at which the holy women were standing had an undersupport with crossed feet, something like a dresser, and it was covered with a cloth that hung down to the floor. I saw lying on it bunches of all kinds of herbs mixed and put in order, little flasks of ointment and nard water, and several flowers growing in pots, among which I remember one, a striped iris, or lily. The women packed them all in linen cloths. During Mary's absence, Magdalene, Mary Cleophas, Johanna Chusa, and Mary Salome went to the city to buy all these things. They wanted to go early next morning to scatter them over the body of Jesus in its winding sheet and pour upon it the perfumed water. I saw a part of it brought by the disciples from the dealer and left at the house without their going in to speak to the women.

Joseph of Arimathea Miraculously Set at Large

AFTER that I had a glimpse of Joseph of Arimathea praying in his prison cell. Suddenly the cell shone with light, and Joseph heard his name pronounced. I saw the roof raised just where the cornice joined it to the wall, and a radiant figure letting down a strip of linen that reminded me of one of those in which the body of Jesus had been wrapped. The figure commanded Joseph to climb up by holding on to it. Then I saw Joseph grasp the linen with both hands and, supporting his feet on the projecting stones of the wall, climb to the opening, a distance of about twelve feet. The roof immediately resumed its position when Joseph reached it, and the apparition disappeared. I do not know whether it was the Lord himself or an angel that released him.

I saw him running unnoticed a short distance along the city wall to the neighborhood of the Cenacle, which was situated near the south wall of Zion. He climbed down and knocked at the door. The disciples were assembled with closed doors. They were very sorrowful over Joseph's disappearance, for they credited the report that he had been thrown into a sewer. When they opened the door and he entered, their joy was as great as that which they experienced later on when Peter, freed from his prison, appeared before them. Joseph told them all about the apparition he had had. They were greatly rejoiced and consoled by his account; they gave him food and thanked God. *He left Jerusalem that night* and fled to Arimathea, his native place, where he remained until he received news that he might return to Jerusalem without fear of danger.

After the close of the sabbath, I saw Caiaphas and some other high priests in the house of Nicodemus, to whom, with an air of assumed benevolence, they were putting many questions. I do not now remember what subject they were discussing, but Nicodemus remained true and firm in his defense of the Lord, and so they parted.

The Night of Resurrection

ALL was quiet and silent around the holy sepulcher. About seven guards were in front and around it, some sitting, others standing. The whole day long Cassius maintained his stand inside the sepulcher at the entrance of the tomb proper, leaving it scarcely for a few moments. He was still absorbed in recollection. He was in expectation of something that he knew was going to happen, for extraordinary grace and light had been vouchsafed to him. *It was night*; the lanterns before the tomb shed a dazzling light. I saw the sacred body wrapped in its winding sheet just as it had been laid on the stone couch. It was surrounded by a brilliant light and, since the burial, two angels had in rapt adoration guarded the sacred remains, one at the head, the other at the foot. They looked like priests. Their whole attitude, their arms crossed on their breast, reminded me of the cherubim on the Ark of the Covenant, excepting that they had no wings. The whole tomb, and especially the resting place of the Lord, reminded me in a striking manner of the Ark of the Covenant at different periods of its history. The light and the presence of the angels may have been in some degree visible to Cassius, and it may have been on that account that he stood gazing so fixedly at the closed doors of the tomb, like one adoring the most blessed sacrament.

Now I saw the blessed soul of Jesus floating with the released spirits of the ancient patriarchs through the rock into the tomb, and showing them all the marks of ill-treatment upon his martyred body. The linen bands and winding sheet seemed to have been removed, for I saw the sacred body full of wounds; and it seemed as if in some mysterious way the indwelling divinity displayed before the souls the blessed body in the whole extent of its cruel laceration and martyrdom. It appeared to me perfectly transparent, its inmost parts disclosed to the eye. Its wounds, its sufferings, its pains could be seen to their very depths. The souls gazed in mute reverence; they appeared to be sobbing and weeping with compassion.

My next vision was so mysterious that I cannot relate the whole of it in an intelligible manner. It was as if the soul of Jesus, though without restoring the sacred body to life by a perfect union with it, was transported in and with the body from the tomb. The two adoring angels raised the tortured body, not in an upright position, but just as it lay in the tomb, and floated with it up to heaven. The rock trembled as they passed through. Then it seemed to me that Jesus, between countless choirs of adoring angels ranged on either hand, presented his wounded body before the throne of his heavenly Father. Jesus's body seemed to have been resuscitated in a manner similar to that in which those of many of the prophets had been assumed by their souls after the death of

Jesus and taken into the temple. They were not really alive, nor did they have again to die, for they were laid down by their souls without any forcible separation from each other. I saw that the souls of the ancient patriarchs did not accompany the Lord's body to heaven.

I remarked a trembling in the rock of the sepulcher. Four of the guards had gone to the city to get something; the three others fell to the ground unconscious. They ascribed the shock to an earthquake, but knew nothing of the cause. Cassius, however, was very much agitated and frightened, for he had a clear view of what had happened without fully understanding it. He kept to his post, and with great devotion awaited what would next take place. Meanwhile the absent soldiers returned.

When the spices were prepared and packed in linen cloths ready to be taken to the tomb, the holy women again retired to their recesses and lay down on their couches to rest, because *they wanted to start before daylight* for Jesus's tomb. They had more than once expressed their anxiety as to the success of their design. They were full of dread lest the enemies of Jesus might waylay them when they went out. But the blessed Virgin consoled them. She bade them take some rest and then go courageously to the tomb, for no harm would befall them. And so they went to rest.

It was about eleven o'clock at night when the blessed Virgin, moved by love and ardent desire, could no longer remain in the house. She rose, wrapped herself in a gray mantle, and went out alone. I thought: Ah! How can they allow that blessed Mother, so full of sorrow and alarm, to go out alone under such circumstances. I saw her going sadly to the house of Caiaphas and then to Pilate's palace, which was a long way back into the city. And thus she walked alone the whole way passed over by Jesus bearing his cross. She went through the deserted streets, pausing at every spot upon which some special suffering or outrage had befallen the Lord. She looked like one seeking something lost. She frequently knelt down, felt around on the stones with her hand, and touched her lips to them, as if reverently touching and kissing something sacred, namely, the blood of Jesus. She beheld around her everything sanctified by contact with Jesus bright and shining, and her soul was entirely lost in love and adoration.

She went on until she approached Mount Calvary, when she stood quite still. It was as if the apparition of Jesus with his sacred, martyred body stepped before her. One angel preceded him, the two adoring angels of the tomb were at his side, and a multitude of released souls followed him. He seemed not to walk, but looked like a corpse floating along, environed with light. I heard a voice proceeding from him, which related to his mother what he had done in Limbo. Now, he continued, he was about to come forth from the tomb alive, in a glorified body, and he bade her await him near Mount Calvary, on the stone upon which he had fallen. Then I saw the apparition going to the city, and the blessed Virgin kneeling and praying on the spot indicated by the Lord. *It may now have been past twelve o'clock*, for Mary had spent a considerable time in the Way of the Cross.

Then I saw the Lord's procession going over the whole of the same dolorous way. In a mysterious manner the angels gathered up all the sacred substance, the flesh and blood, that had been torn from Jesus during his Passion. I saw that the nailing to the cross, the raising of the same, the opening of the sacred side, the taking down from the cross, and the preparing of the holy body for burial, were shown to the souls in Jesus's train. The blessed Virgin also saw it all in spirit. She loved and adored.

Afterward it was as if the Lord's body rested again in the holy sepulcher. With it was all that had been torn from it during the Passion and replaced in an incomprehensible manner by the angels. I saw it as before, wrapped in the funereal bands and winding sheet, environed with dazzling splendor, the two adoring angels at the head and the foot of the tomb.

When the morning sky began to clear with a streak of white light, I saw Magdalene, Mary Cleophas, Johanna Chusa, and Salome, enveloped in mantles, leaving their abode near the Cenacle. They carried the spices packed in linen cloths, and one of them had a lighted lantern. They kept all hidden under their mantles. The spices consisted of fresh flowers for strewing over the sacred body, and also of expressed sap, essences, and oils for pouring over it. The holy women walked anxiously to the little gate belonging to Nicodemus.

The Resurrection of the Lord

THE BLESSED soul of Jesus in dazzling splendor, between two warrior angels and surrounded by a multitude of resplendent figures, came floating down through the rocky roof of the tomb upon the sacred body. It seemed to incline over it and melt, as it were, into one with it. I saw the sacred limbs moving beneath the swathing bands, and the dazzling, living body of the Lord with his soul and his divinity coming forth from the side of the winding sheet as if from the wounded side. The sight reminded me of Eve coming forth from Adam's side. The whole place was resplendent with light and glory.

And now I had another vision. I saw the apparition of a dragon with a human head coiling itself up out of the abyss, as if right under the tomb upon which the Lord had been lying. It lashed its tail, and turned its head angrily toward the Lord. The risen Redeemer held in his hand a delicate white staff, on whose top floated a little standard. He placed one foot upon the dragon's head, and struck three blows of the staff upon its tail. At each stroke the monster seemed to contract, and at last sank into the earth, first the body, then the head, the human face still turned upward. I saw a similar serpent lurking around at the moment of Christ's conception. It reminded me of the serpent in Paradise and, I think, this vision bore reference to the Promise: "The seed of the woman shall crush the serpent's head." The whole vision appeared to me symbolical of victory over death, for as I watched the crushing of the serpent's head, the tomb of the Lord vanished from my sight.

Now I saw the Lord floating in glory up through the rock. The earth trembled, and an angel in warrior garb shot like lightning from heaven down to the tomb, rolled the stone to one side, and seated himself upon it. The trembling of the earth was so great that the lanterns swung from side to side, and the flames flashed around. The guards fell stunned to the ground and lay there stiff and contorted, as if dead. Cassius saw indeed the glory that environed the holy sepulcher, the rolling away of the stone by the angel, and his seating himself upon it, but he did not see the risen Savior himself. He recovered himself quickly, stepped to the stone couch, felt among the empty linens, and left the sepulcher, outside of which, full of eager desire, he tarried awhile to become the witness of a new and wonderful apparition. At the instant the angel shot down to the tomb and the earth quaked, I saw the risen Lord appearing to his blessed Mother on Mount Calvary. He was transcendently beautiful and glorious, his manner full of earnestness. His garment, which was like a white mantle thrown about his limbs, floated in the breeze behind him as he walked. It glistened blue and white, like smoke curling in the sunshine. His wounds were very large and sparkling; in those of his hands, one could easily insert a finger. The lips of the wounds formed the sides of an equilateral triangle which met, as it were, in the center of a circle, and from the palm of the hand shot rays of light toward the fingers.

The souls of the early patriarchs bowed low before the blessed Mother, to whom Jesus said something about seeing her again. He showed her his wounds, and when she fell on her knees to kiss his feet, he grasped her hand, raised her up, and disappeared.

When I was at some distance from the sepulcher I saw fresh lights burning there, and I likewise beheld a large luminous spot in the sky immediately above Jerusalem.

The Holy Women at the Sepulcher

THE HOLY women, when the Lord arose from the dead, were near the little gate belonging to Nicodemus. They knew nothing of the prodigies that were taking place; they did not know even of the guard at the sepulcher, for they had remained shut up in their house the whole of the preceding day, the sabbath. They anxiously inquired of one another: "Who will roll away for us the stone from the doors?" Full of longing desire to show the last honors to the sacred body in the tomb, they had entirely lost sight of the stone. They wanted to pour nard water and precious balm over the sacred body and scatter their flowers and aromatic shrubs upon it; for to the spices of yesterday's embalming, which Nicodemus alone had procured, they had contributed nothing. They wished therefore to offer now to the body of their Lord and Master the most precious that could be obtained.

Salome had shared with Magdalene in defraying most of the cost. She was not the mother of John, but another Salome, a rich lady of Jerusalem, a relative of Joseph. At last the holy women concluded to set the spices on the stone before the tomb and to wait till some disciple would come who would open it for them. And so they went on toward the garden.

Outside the tomb the stone was rolled to the right, so that the doors, which were merely lying to, could now be easily opened. The linens in which the sacred body had been enveloped were on the tomb in the following order: the large winding sheet in which it had been wrapped lay undisturbed, only empty and fallen together, containing nothing but the aromatic herbs; the long bandage that had been wound around it was still lying twisted and at full length just as it had been drawn off, on the outer edge of the tomb; but the linen scarf with which Mary had enveloped Jesus's head lay to the right at the head of the tomb. It looked as if the head of Jesus was still in it, excepting that the covering for the face was raised.

When, as they approached, the holy women noticed the lanterns of the guard and the soldiers lying around, they became frightened, and went a short distance past the garden toward Golgotha. Magdalene, however, forgetful of danger, hurried into the garden. Salome followed her at some distance, and the other two waited outside.

Magdalene, seeing the guard, stepped back at first a few steps toward Salome, then both made their way together through the soldiers lying around and into the sepulcher. They found the stone rolled away, but the doors closed, probably by Cassius. Magdalene anxiously opened one of them, peered in at the tomb, and saw the linens lying empty and apart. The whole place was resplendent with light, and an angel was sitting at the right of the tomb. Magdalene was exceedingly troubled. She hurried out of the garden of the sepulcher, off through the gate belonging to Nicodemus, and back to the apostles. Salome, too, who only now entered the sepulcher, ran at once after Magdalene, rushed in fright to the women waiting outside the garden, and told them of what had happened. Though amazed and rejoiced at what they heard from Salome, they could not resolve to enter the garden. It was not until Cassius told them in a few words what he had seen, and exhorted them to go see for themselves, that they took courage to enter. Cassius was hurrying into the city to acquaint Pilate of all that had taken place. He went through the gate of execution. When with beating heart the women entered the sepulcher and drew near the holy tomb, they beheld standing before them the two angels of the tomb in priestly robes, white and shining. The women pressed close to one another in terror and, covering their faces with their hands, bowed tremblingly almost to the ground. One of the angels addressed them. They must not fear, he said, nor must they look for the crucified here. He was alive, he had arisen, he was no longer among the dead. Then the angel pointed out to them the empty tomb, and ordered them to tell the disciples what they had seen and heard, and that Jesus would go before them into Galilee. They should, continued the angel, remember what the Lord had said to them in Galilee, namely, "The Son of Man will be delivered into the hands of sinners. He will be crucified and, on the third day, he will rise again." The holy women, shaking and trembling with fear, though still full of joy, tearfully gazed at the tomb and the linens, and departed, taking the road toward the gate of execution. They were still very much frightened. They did not hurry, but paused from time to time and looked around from the distance, to see whether they might not possibly behold the Lord, or whether Magdalene was returning.

Meanwhile Magdalene reached the Cenacle like one beside herself, and knocked violently at the door. Some of the disciples were still asleep on their couches around the walls, while several others had risen and were talking together. Peter and John opened the door. Magdalene, without entering, merely uttered the words: "They have taken the Lord from the tomb! We know not where"—and ran back in great haste to the garden of the sepulcher. Peter and John followed her, but John outstripped Peter.

Magdalene was quite wet with dew when she again reached the garden and ran to the tomb. Her mantle had slipped from her head down on her shoulders, and her long hair had fallen around loose. As she was alone, she was afraid to enter the sepulcher at once, so she waited out on the

Mary Magdalene and the Holy Women at the Tomb

Noli Me Tangere: *Touch Me Not*

step at the entrance. She stooped down, trying to see through the low doors into the cave and even as far as the stone couch. Her long hair fell forward as she stooped, and she was trying to keep it back with her hands, when she saw the two angels in white priestly garments sitting at the head and the foot of the tomb, and heard the words: "Woman, why weepest thou?" She cried out in her grief: "They have taken my Lord away! I know not where they have laid him!" Saying this and seeing nothing but the linens, she turned weeping, like one seeking something, and as if she must find him. She had a dim presentiment that Jesus was near, and even the apparition of the angels could not turn her from her one idea. She did not appear conscious of the fact that it was an angel that spoke to her. She thought only of Jesus; her only thought was: "Jesus is not here! Where is Jesus?" I saw her running a few steps from the sepulcher and then returning like one half-distracted and in quest of something. Her long hair fell on her shoulders. Once she drew the whole mass on the right shoulder through both hands, then flung it back and gazed around.

About ten steps from the sepulcher and toward the east, where the garden rose in the direction of the city, she spied in the gray light of dawn, standing among the bushes behind a palm tree, a figure clothed in a long, white garment. Rushing toward it, she heard once more the words: "Woman, why weepest thou? Whom seekest thou?" She thought it was the gardener. I saw that he had a spade in his hand and on his head a flat hat, which had a piece of something like bark standing out in front, as a protection from the sun. It was just like that I had seen on the gardener in the parable which Jesus, shortly before his Passion, had related to the women in Bethany. The apparition was not resplendent. It looked like a person clad in long, white garments and seen at twilight. At the words: "Whom seekest thou?" Magdalene at once answered: "Sir, if thou hast taken him hence, show me where thou hast laid him! I will take him away!" And she again glanced around, as if to see whether he had not laid him someplace near. Then Jesus, in his well-known voice, said: "Mary!" Recognizing the voice, and forgetting the crucifixion, death, and burial now that he was alive, she turned quickly and, as once before, exclaimed: "Rabboni!" (Master!). She fell on her knees before him and stretched out her arms toward his feet. But Jesus raised his hand to keep her off, saying: "Do not touch me, for I am not yet ascended to my Father. But go to my brethren, and say to them: I ascend to my Father and to your Father, to my God and to your God." At these words the Lord vanished. It was explained to me why Jesus said: "Do not touch me," but I have only an indistinct remembrance of it. I think he said it because Magdalene was so impetuous. She seemed possessed of the idea that Jesus was alive just as he was before, and that everything was as it used to be. Upon Jesus's words that he had not yet ascended to his Father, I was told that he had not yet, since his resurrection, presented himself to his heavenly Father, had not yet thanked him for his victory over death and for redemption. I understood by those words that the first fruits of joy belong to God. It was as if Jesus had said that Magdalene should recollect herself and thank God for the mystery of redemption just accomplished and his conquest over death. After the disappearance of the Lord, Magdalene rose up quickly and again, as if in a dream, ran to the tomb. She saw the two angels, she saw the empty linens, and hurried, now certain of the miracle, back to her companions.

It may have been about half-past three o'clock when Jesus appeared to Magdalene. Scarcely had she left the garden when John approached, followed by Peter. John stood outside the entrance of the cave and stooped down to look, through the outer doors of the sepulcher, at the half-opened doors of the tomb, where he saw the linens lying. Then came Peter. He stepped down into the sepulcher and went to the tomb, in the center of which he saw the winding sheet lying. It was rolled together from both sides toward the middle, and the spices were wrapped in it. The bandages were folded around it, as women are accustomed to roll together such linens when putting them away. The linen that had covered the sacred face was lying to the right next to the wall. It too was folded. John now followed Peter to the tomb, saw the same things, and believed in the resurrection. All that the Lord had said, all that was written in the scriptures, was now clear to them. They had had only an imperfect comprehension of it before. Peter took the linens with him under his mantle. Both again went back by the little gate belonging to Nicodemus, and John once more got ahead of Peter.

As long as the sacred body lay in the tomb, the two angels sat one at the head, the other at the foot, and when Magdalene and the two apostles came, they were still there. It seems to me that Peter did not see them. I heard John afterward saying to the disciples of Emmaus that, on looking into the tomb, he saw one angel. Perhaps it was through humility that he forbore to mention it in his Gospel, that he might not appear to have seen more than Peter.

Now, for the first time, I saw the guards arise from where they were lying on the ground. They took their lances, also the lanterns that were hanging on poles at the door of the entrance and shedding their light into the cave, and hurried in evident fear and trepidation to the gate of execution and into the city.

Meanwhile, Magdalene had reached the holy women and told them of the Lord's apparition. Then she too hurried on to the city through the neighboring gate of the execution, but the others went again to the garden, outside of which Jesus appeared to them in a white flowing garment that concealed even his hands. He said: "All hail!" They trembled and fell at his feet. Jesus waved his hand in a certain direction while addressing to them some words, and vanished. The holy women then hastened through the Bethlehem gate on Zion, to tell the disciples in the Cenacle that they had seen the Lord and what he had said to them. But the disciples would not at first credit Magdalene's report, and, until the return of Peter and John, they looked upon the whole affair as the effect of women's imagination.

John and Peter, whom amazement at what they had seen had rendered silent and thoughtful, met on their way back James the Less and Thaddeus, who had set out after them for the tomb. They too were very much agitated, for the Lord had appeared to them near the Cenacle. Once I saw Peter, as they went along, suddenly start and tremble, as if he had just got a glimpse of the risen Savior.

The Guards' Statements

ABOUT *an hour after the resurrection,* Cassius went to Pilate, who was resting on his couch. Full of emotion, Cassius related all that had passed, the trembling of the rock, the descent of the angel, the rolling away of the stone, the empty winding sheet. Jesus, he said, was certainly the Messiah, certainly the Son of God. He was risen, he was no longer in the tomb. Pilate heard every detail with secret terror but, letting nothing appear, he said to Cassius: "Thou art a visionary! Thou didst act very unwisely by standing in the tomb of the Galilean. His gods have thereby acquired full power over thee, and it was they who conjured up all kinds of magic pictures before thee. I advise thee to say nothing of all this to the high priest, else it will be worse for thee." He pretended to believe that Jesus had been stolen away by the disciples, and that the guards had reported what they did in order to hide their own negligence; or because they were bribed, or even perhaps because they too had been bewitched. When Cassius left, Pilate again offered sacrifice to his gods.

Four of the soldiers returned from the tomb and went directly to Pilate with the same report. But he would listen to nothing more, and sent them to Caiaphas. The other guards went to a large court near the temple in which a number of aged Jews were gathered. These latter consulted together and came to the conclusion that they would, with money and threats, force the guards to report that the disciples had stolen the body of Jesus. But when the guards objected that their companions, who had informed Pilate of the whole affair, would contradict them, the Pharisees promised to make it all right with Pilate. Meanwhile the four guards who had been dismissed by Pilate arrived, but they adhered strictly to the account they had given to the governor. The report of Joseph of Arimathea's deliverance, in some unaccountable way, through the closed prison doors was already noised abroad and when the Pharisees, wishing to cast upon the soldiers the suspicion of having had an understanding with the disciples for the carrying off of Jesus's body, threatened them with severe punishment if they did not forthwith produce it, the men replied that they could no more do that than could the guard in Joseph of Arimathea's prison bring him back after he had disappeared. They defended themselves stoutly, and by no species of bribery could they be reduced to silence. Yes, they spoke even freely and openly of Friday's iniquitous judgment, and declared that it was on that account the Passover ceremonies had been interrupted. The four soldiers were seized and imprisoned. Jesus's enemies spread the report that his body had been stolen by the disciples; and the Pharisees, Sadducees, and Herodians caused the lie to be everywhere propagated, to be published in every synagogue in the whole world, accompanying it with slanderous abuse of Jesus. Their lies profited them little, for after Jesus's resurrection, many souls of holy deceased Jews appeared here and there to those of their descendants still susceptible of grace and holy impressions, and frightened their hearts to conversion. To many of the disciples also who, shaken in faith and disheartened, were dispersed throughout the country, similar apparitions appeared to console and strengthen them in faith.

The rising of the dead bodies from their tombs after the death of Jesus had no similarity whatever with the Lord's resurrection. Jesus arose in his renewed, glorified body, walked for some days alive upon the earth, and, in that same body, ascended into heaven in the sight of his friends. But those other bodies were only corpses given to the souls merely as so many coverings. They were again laid down by them to await with us all the resurrection of the last day. Lazarus was raised from the dead, but he really lived and afterward died for the second time.

I saw the Jews beginning to purify, to wash and scour the temple. They strewed aromatic herbs, also ashes from the bones of the dead, and offered expiatory sacrifices. They cleared away the rubbish, covered the marks of the earthquake with boards and tapestry, and finished the Passover solemnities interrupted on the day of the feast.

With threats of punishment and excommunication, they tried to suppress all remarks and murmurs. They explained the disturbance of the feast and the damage done the temple as effects of the earthquake and the presence of the unclean at the sacrifices. They brought forward something from a vision of Ezekiel upon the risen dead, but I do not now remember how they applied it. Thus they quieted the people, for many had taken part in the crime. But it was only the great crowd of the obstinate and the incorrigible; all the better disposed were converted. They kept silence until Pentecost, when they proclaimed aloud their faith, later also in their native places through the teaching of the apostles. The high priests consequently began to lose courage. As early as the time of Stephen's ministry as deacon, Ophel and the eastern quarter of Zion could no longer contain the multitude of believers, so that they had to extend their huts and tents beyond the city, across the valley of Kidron to Bethany.

Annas was like one possessed. He was obliged to be confined, and he never again appeared in public. Caiaphas became like a madman consumed by secret rage. Simon of Cyrene went to the apostles after the sabbath, asking to be received among the baptized followers of Jesus.

The First Love Feast
(Agape) after the Resurrection

IN the open entrance hall outside that of the holy Last Supper, Nicodemus prepared a repast for the apostles, the holy women, and the disciples. Thomas was not present at it. He kept himself in absolute retirement. All that took place at this feast was in strict accordance with Jesus's directions. During the holy Last Supper, he had given Peter and John, who were sitting by him and whom he ordained priests, detailed instructions relative to the blessed sacrament, with the command to impart the same to the other apostles, along with some points of his early teachings.

I saw first Peter and then John communicating to the eight other apostles, who were standing around them in a circle, what the Lord had entrusted to them, and teaching them the way in which he wished this sacrament to be dispensed and the disciples instructed. All that Peter taught was repeated in the selfsame manner by John. The apostles had put on their festal garments. Peter and John had, besides, a stole crossed on their breast and fastened with a clasp. The eight apostles wore a stole over one shoulder and across the breast and back. It fastened under the arm with a clasp crosswise. Peter and John had been ordained priests by Jesus; the others looked still like deacons.

After that instruction, the holy women, nine in number, entered the

hall. Peter addressed them in some words of instruction. I saw John at
the door receiving into the house of the master of the feast seventeen
(as I counted) of the most trusty disciples, those that had been longest
with the Lord. Zacchaeus, Nathaniel, Matthew, Barsabbas, and others
were there. John served them while they were washing their feet and
putting on festal garments, long white robes and girdles. Matthew was
sent back to Bethany after Peter's discourse, in order there to reproduce,
at a similar repast given in the house of Lazarus, the instructions just
heard and the ceremonies witnessed. There were many disciples present
at this feast.

And now a table was prepared in the entrance hall. It was so long that
the seats of some of the disciples extended beyond the hall and into the
courtyard, planted with trees, that surrounded the Cenacle. Three avenues were left open to the tables, in order to approach them with the
servings of food. The holy women now sat together at one end of the
same table with the men. They too wore long white garments. They
were veiled, but without their faces being concealed. They sat cross-
legged on little stools that had a kind of upright at the backs. Peter and
John sat opposite each other at the center of the table. They closed the
men's row, and then began the women's. The couches used at this feast
were not like those at the Last Supper. They were low cushions. They
looked as if they were woven, and were scarcely long enough to receive
the upper part of the body, for they hardly reached below the knees.
Each had before him a cushion raised upon two higher feet, which were
fastened into cross-uprights. It stood in an oblique direction. All reclined
near the table, the feet of one at his neighbor's back. At Simon's house
and at the Last Supper, the guests reclined on stools of a different kind,
the feet turned entirely out.

The meal was conducted with ceremony. The guests prayed standing
and ate lying, while Peter and John taught. At the end of the meal, a flat,
ribbed loaf was placed before Peter, which he divided into small pieces as
marked by the ribs. These he distributed right and left on two plates. A
large cup was next sent round, and out of it each one drank. Although
Peter blessed the bread, yet it was not a sacrament, only an agape, a love
feast. Peter said that they should all desire to be one as was the bread that
they were eating and the wine they were drinking. After that they sang
psalms, standing.

When the tables were moved aside, the holy women retired to an
apartment in the form of a half-circle at the end of the hall. The disciples
ranged on either side, while the apostles walked up and down teaching
and imparting to these ripe disciples all they could concerning the blessed

sacrament. This was like the first catechetical instruction after Jesus's death. I saw also that they walked around among one another extending hands joyously declaring that they would have all things in common, would resign all things for one another, and would live perfectly united. A feeling of deep emotion stole over them. I saw them flooded with light and, as it were, dissolving into one another. All seemed to resolve into a pyramid of light in which the blessed Virgin appeared to be not only the apex, but the radiant center of all. All graces flowed in streams from Mary down upon the apostles, and from them back again through her to the Lord. This vision was symbolical of their union and the reciprocal relations existing among them.

Matthew, in the court of Lazarus's house, taught a great many more of the disciples who were not so well instructed as the others. They had the same kind of a meal and went through similar ceremonies.

Communion of the Holy Apostles

4/6 EARLY in the morning, Peter and John went with Andrew into the hall of the Last Supper and vested in their priestly robes, while the other apostles entered the antehall. Pushing aside the folds of woven tapestry, the three apostles entered the Holy of Holies, which was curtained in so as to form a little chamber. The ceiling, which was not so high as that of the hall, could be opened by a hanging cord ornamented with tassels, to admit light from the windows in the roof of the hall. The holy communion table stood therein. The chalice with the remains of the wine that Jesus had consecrated and the plate with what was left of the consecrated bread were standing in the compartments formed like a tabernacle in a niche in the wall. A lamp was hanging, one branch of it lighted, before the blessed sacrament. They lighted the lamp of sacrifice that was suspended in the center of the hall, carried the communion table forward into the hall, placed the blessed sacrament on it in its case, and extinguished the lamp in the Holy of Holies. The other apostles, Thomas among them, took their places around the table. Of the bread consecrated by Jesus, the blessed sacrament of his body, there was still a great deal on the little plate, which stood on top of the chalice, the whole concealed under a bell-shaped cover surmounted by a knob. A white veil was thrown over it. Peter drew out the leaf from the base, spread the cover upon it, and placed on it the plate with the blessed sacrament. Andrew and John were standing behind him in prayer. Peter and John, bowing reverently, received the blessed sacrament. Then Peter sent the plate around, and each one communicated himself. Into the chalice, in which there was not so much of the wine consecrated by Jesus, they poured some wine and water, and drank of it. After that they sang psalms and prayed, covered the chalice, and carried it, along with the table, back to its place. This was the first divine service that I saw celebrated.

Thomas went after that to some little place near Samaria with a disciple from that part of the country.

The Disciples Going to Emmaus • Jesus Appears to the Apostles in the Hall of the Last Supper

LUKE had been among the disciples only a short time, but he had, before joining them, received John's baptism. He was present at the love feast and the instruction upon the blessed sacrament delivered by Matthew in the evening at Lazarus's, in Bethany. After the instruction he went, troubled and doubting, to Jerusalem where he spent the night in John Mark's house.

There he met several other disciples, among them Cleophas, a grandson of the paternal uncle of Mary Cleophas. He had been at the instructions and the love feast given in the house of the Last Supper. The disciples were talking about Jesus's resurrection and expressing their doubts. Luke and Cleophas, especially, were wavering in faith. As, moreover, the commands of the high priests were again made known, that no one should harbor the disciples of Jesus or supply them with food, both resolved to go together to Emmaus. They left the assembly. On leaving John Mark's house, one turned to the right and went around out of the city in a northerly direction, and the other took a route on the opposite side, as if not wishing to be seen together. One went straight out of the city, the other made his way between the walls and out by the gate, beyond which they again met upon a hill. They carried each a staff, and a bundle at his side. Luke had a leathern pocket. I saw him frequently stepping aside from the road and gathering herbs.

Luke had not seen the Lord during those last days, and had not been present at his instructions at Lazarus's. He had been more in the disciples' inn at Bethany and with the disciples in Machaerus. He had not long been a declared disciple, though he had always gone around with the rest and was very desirous of knowing what was going on. I felt that both these disciples were anxious and doubting, and that they wanted to talk over all they had heard. They were especially put out at the Lord's being so ignominiously crucified! They could not understand how the Redeemer and Messiah could have been so shamefully ill-treated.

About the middle of their journey, Jesus drew near to them from a side path. As soon as they saw him, they went more slowly, as if wanting to let the stranger go on ahead, as if fearing to be overheard. But Jesus likewise slackened his pace, and stepped out on the road only after they were somewhat in advance. I saw him walking behind them for a little while, then drawing near and asking of what they were talking.

Where the road branched off outside of Emmaus (a pretty, clean little place) Jesus appeared as if he wanted to take that which ran southward to Bethlehem. But the two disciples constrained him to go with them into a house that stood in the second row of the city. There were no women in it, and it appeared to me to be a public house, for it looked as if a feast had lately been held in it. Some signs of it were still to be seen. The room was quadrangular and very neat. The table was covered, and reclining cushions lay around it, of the same kind as those used at the love feast on Easter day. A man put on it a honeycomb in a woven basketlike vessel, a large, four-cornered cake, and a small, thin, almost transparent Passover loaf. This last was set before the Lord as being the guest. The man that put the cake on the table appeared to be good, and he wore an apron, as if he were a cook or a steward. He was not present at the solemn breaking of the bread. The cake was marked by lines, the spaces between them being about two fingers wide. A knife was lying on the table. It was white, as if made of stone or bone, not straight, but bent crooked, and only as large as one of our large blades. Before eating the bread, they notched along the lines with the sharp edge of the knife, which edge was only at the point. For this reason they had to hold it near the point. The morsel previously notched they then broke off.

Jesus reclined at the table with the two disciples and ate with them of the cake and honey. Then taking the small cake, the ribbed one, he broke off a piece that he afterward divided into three with the short, white bone knife. These he laid on the little plate, and blessed. Then he stood up, elevated the plate on high with both hands, raised his eyes, and prayed. The two disciples stood opposite him, both intensely moved, and as it were transported out of themselves. When Jesus broke the little pieces, they opened their mouth and stretched forward toward him. He reached his hand across the table and laid the particle in their mouth. I saw that as he raised his hand with the third morsel to his own mouth, he disappeared. I cannot say that he really received it. The morsels shone with light after he had blessed them. I saw the two disciples standing a little while as if stupefied, and then casting themselves with tears of emotion into each other's arms.

This vision was especially touching on account of the Lord's mild and loving manner, the calm joy of the two disciples even before they knew him, and their rapture as soon as they recognized him and after he had disappeared. Cleophas and Luke hurried back at once to Jerusalem.

On the evening of the same day, many of the disciples and all the apostles excepting Thomas assembled with Nicodemus and Joseph of Arimathea in the hall of the Last Supper, the doors being closed. They stood ranged in a triple circle under the lamp that hung from the center of the ceiling, and prayed. They seemed to be engaged in some after-celebration of mourning or thanksgiving, for the Passover solemnities ended today in Jerusalem. All wore long white garments. Peter, John, and James the Less were vested in robes that distinguished them from the rest, and they held rolls of writing in their hands. Around their white, flowing garment, which was somewhat longer behind than before, they wore a girdle more than a hand in breadth. From it depended to below the knees scalloped strips, black like the girdle, and covered with large white letters. The girdle was knotted in the back, the ends crossing and reaching as low down as the strips in front. The sleeves were very wide, and one served as a pocket in which the prayer rolls could be stuck. Above the elbow of the left arm hung a broad maniple tripped with tassels of the same color and embroidered in the same way as the girdle. Peter wore a stole around his neck. It was broader from the shoulders down than it was around the neck, and was crossed and fastened on the breast with a little blank shield in the form of a heart and ornamented with stones. The two other apostles wore their stoles crossed under the arm, and had shorter strips to their girdles. When in prayer, all laid their hands crosswise on their breast. The apostles occupied the inner circle under the lamp; the two others were formed by the disciples. Peter, between John and James, stood with his back turned to the closed entrance of the house of the Last Supper; two only were behind him, and the circle was not closed in front of him, but open toward the Holy of Holies.

The blessed Virgin was, during the whole celebration, with Mary Cleophas and Magdalene in the hall outside, which opened into the supper room. Peter preached at intervals during the prayers.

I was surprised to see that although Jesus had appeared to Peter, John, and James, yet the greater number of the apostles and disciples would not fully believe in his resurrection. They still felt uneasy, as if his apparition was not a real and corporeal one, only a vision, a phantom, similar to those the prophets had had.

All had ranged again for prayer after Peter's instruction when Luke and Cleophas, hurrying back from Emmaus, knocked at the closed doors of the courtyard and received admittance. The joyful news they related somewhat interrupted the prayer. But scarcely was it again continued when I saw all present radiant with joyful emotion, and glancing in the same direction. Jesus was come in through the closed doors. He was robed in a long white garment simply girded. They did not appear to be really conscious of his approach, until he passed through the circles and stood in their midst under the lamp. Then they became very much amazed and agitated. He showed them his hands and feet and, opening his garment, disclosed the wound in his side. He spoke to them and, seeing that they were very much terrified, he asked for something to eat. I saw rays of light proceeding from his mouth. The apostles and disciples were as if completely ravished.

And now I saw Peter going behind a screen, or hanging tapestry, into a recess of the hall which one might fail to remark, since the screen was like the entire wainscoting. In the center of this recess, on the paschal hearth, stood the blessed sacrament. There was a side compartment into which they had pushed the table, which was one foot high, after they had eaten reclining around it under the lamp. On this table stood a deep oval dish covered with a little white cloth, which Peter took to the Lord. In the dish were a piece of fish and some honey. Jesus gave thanks and blessed the food, ate and gave a portion of it to some, but not to all. To his Holy Mother also and the other women, who were standing in the doorway of the outer hall, he likewise distributed some.

After that I saw him teaching and imparting strength. The circles around him were still triple, the ten apostles forming the inmost. Thomas was not there. It appeared wonderful to me that part of Jesus's words and instructions was heard by the ten apostles only, though I ought not to say *heard*, for I did not see Jesus moving his lips. He was resplendent. Light streamed over them from his hands, his feet, his side, his mouth, as he breathed upon them. It flowed in upon them. They became interiorly recollected, and felt themselves endued with power to forgive sins, to baptize and heal and impose hands; and I saw that, if they drank any poisonous thing, it would be without receiving harm from it. But here I saw no talking with the mouth, no hearing with the ears. I knew not how it was, but I felt that Jesus did not impart these gifts with words, that he spoke not in words, and that all did not hear what he said; but that he infused these gifts substantially, with a substance as it were, with a flashing of light in upon their soul. Still, I do not know whether the apostles felt that they had received them in this way, or whether they thought that they had simply heard the words uttered naturally. I felt, however, that it was only the innermost circle, the apostles, that took or received these gifts. To me it was like an interior speech, but without a whisper, without the softest word.

Jesus explained to the apostles several points of holy scripture relative to himself and the blessed sacrament, and ordered the latter to be venerated at the close of the sabbath solemnities. He spoke of the sacred mystery of the Ark of the Covenant; of the bones and relics of ancestors and their veneration, thus to obtain their intercession; of Abraham, and of the bones of Adam which he had had in his possession and which he had laid on the altar when offering sacrifice. Another point relating to Melchizedek's sacrifice, which I then saw, I have forgotten, although it was very remarkable. Jesus further said that the colored coat which Jacob gave to Joseph was an emblem of his own bloody sweat on the Mount of Olives. At these words, I saw that coat of many colors. It was white with broad red stripes. It had three black cords on the breast, with a yellow ornament in the middle. It was full around the body so that things could be put into it as into a kind of pocket, and girded at the waist. It was narrow below and had slits at the side to afford more room for walking. It reached to the ankles, was longer behind than before, and on the breast, was open down to the girdle. Joseph's ordinary dress reached only to the knee.

Jesus likewise told the disciples that Adam's bones, which had been preserved in the Ark of the Covenant, Jacob gave to Joseph along with the many-colored coat. I saw then that Jacob gave them to Joseph without the latter's knowing what they were. Jacob's love prompted him to bestow them upon Joseph as a means of protection, as a treasure, because he knew that his brothers did not love him. Joseph carried the bones hanging on his breast in a little pouch formed of two leathern tablets, not square, but rounded on top. When his brothers sold him, they took from him only the colored coat and the undergarment, leaving him a bandage round his loins and a scapular on his breast. It was under the latter that the little pouch hung. On going into Egypt, Jacob questioned Joseph about that treasure and revealed to him that it was Adam's bones. Again I saw the bones under Mount Calvary. They were white as snow and still very hard. Some of Joseph's own bones were preserved in the Ark of the Covenant.

Jesus spoke too of the mystery contained in the Ark of the Covenant. He said that that mystery was now his body and blood, which he gave to them forever in the Sacrament. He spoke of his own Passion and of some wonderful things relating to David of which they were ignorant and which he explained. Lastly, he bade them go in a couple of days to the region of Sichar, and there proclaim his resurrection. After that he vanished. I saw the apostles and disciples going around among one another, perfectly intoxicated with joy. They opened the doors, went in and out, and assembled again under the lamp, to sing canticles of praise and thanksgiving.

The Apostles Preaching the Resurrection

4/6–9 ON *that same night* a part of the apostles, at Jesus's bidding, betook themselves to Bethany, while some of them went around Jerusalem, for example, to Veronica. The older disciples remained in Bethany to teach the younger and weaker in the faith, which they did partly at the house of Lazarus and partly in the synagogue. Nicodemus and Joseph of Arimathea were staying at Lazarus's. The holy women were in a neighboring building surrounded by the same moat and courtyard that enclosed Lazarus's house. It had an entrance on the street, and was formerly occupied by Magda-lene and Martha.

The apostles went with a troop of disciples, among them Luke, in the direction of Sichar. Peter said joyfully as they were setting out: "We shall go to the sea and catch fish," by which words he meant souls. They separated and went different ways, teaching at the inns and in the public places of the Passion and Resurrection of Jesus. This was a preparation for the conversions of Pentecost.

They met together again at the inn outside Thanat-Shiloh. Thomas also, with two disciples, joined them as they were gathered at a meal prepared for them by Silvan's father, who had care of the inn. The apostles told Thomas of the apparition of the risen Savior in their midst. But he raised his hands to silence them, and said that he would not believe it until he had touched his wounds. He did the same before the disciples when they declared to him that they had seen the Lord. Thomas had kept a little aloof from the followers of Jesus, and was thereby somewhat weakened in faith.

Peter taught till late at night in the school of Thanat-Shiloh. He spoke out quite freely of how the Jews had dealt with Jesus. He related many things of his last predictions and teachings, of his unspeakable love, of his prayer on the Mount of Olives, and of Judas's treachery and wretched end. The people were very much amazed and troubled at all they heard, for they loved Judas, who in Jesus's absence, had assisted many by his readiness to serve them, and had even wrought miracles. Peter did not spare himself. He recounted his flight and denial with bitter tears. His hearers wept with him. Then with still more vehement expressions of sorrow, he told of how cruelly the Jews had treated Jesus, of his rising again on the third day, of his appearing first to the women, then to some of the others, and lastly to all in general, and he called upon all present that had seen him to witness to his words. Upwards of a hundred hands were raised in answer to his call. Thomas, however, remained silent and responded by no sign. He could not bring himself to believe. Peter then called upon the people to leave all things, to join the new community, and to follow Jesus. He invited the less courageous to go to Jerusalem, where the faithful would share all they had with them. There was, he said, no reason to fear the Jews, for they were now themselves afraid. All were very much impressed by Peter's words, and many were converted. They wanted the apostles to remain longer with them, but Peter said that they must go back to Jerusalem.

The apostles cured many sick persons in Thanat-Shiloh, among whom were some lunatics and some possessed. They went about these cures just as Jesus had done, that is, they breathed upon the sick, they imposed hands while leaning over them. Some of these invalids Jesus had passed without curing on the occasion of his last visit to the place. The inhabitants of Thanat-Shiloh were very friendly toward the apostles. The disciples performed no cures, but they served the others, carrying, lifting, and leading the sick. Luke, who was a physician, now became quite a nurse.

I saw the Mother of God in Bethany. She was quiet and grave, more deeply absorbed in feelings of holy awe than in natural sorrow. Mary Cleophas was remarkably amiable and, of all the women, most like Mary. I often saw her leaning over her gently, consoling her in the most touching way.

Magdalene, in her sorrow and love, was above all fear. She was perfectly heroic and without a thought of danger. She took no rest, but often left the house, hurried through the streets with streaming hair, and wherever she found listeners, whether in their homes or in public places, she accused them as the murderers of the Lord, vehemently recounting all they had done to the Savior, and announcing to them his resurrection. If she found no one to listen to her, she wandered through the gardens and told it to the flowers, the trees, and the fountains. Oftentimes a crowd gathered around her, some offering her compassion, others insulting her on account of her past life. She was little esteemed by the crowd, for she had once given great scandal. I saw that her present violent conduct scandalized some of the Jews, and about five of them wanted to seize her, but she passed straight through them and went on as before. She had lost sight of the whole world, she sighed only after Jesus.

During the dispersion of the disciples and the Passion of the Lord, Martha had a heavy duty to fulfill and she still discharged it. Though torn with grief, she had to see to everything, to lend a helping hand everywhere. She had to feed the dispersed and wandering, attend to their wants, provide nourishment for all. Her assistant in all this, as well as in the cooking, was Johanna Chusa, a widow whose husband had been a servant of Herod.

Simon of Cyrene was now in Bethany with the disciples, among whom he found his two sons. He was a pious man from Cyrene who was accustomed to sojourn in Jerusalem during the Passover time, working for different families that knew him, doing up gardens and cutting hedges. He took his meals sometimes in this house, sometimes in that. He was perfectly silent and upright. His sons were already some time among strangers and with the disciples without his knowing it, as occasionally happens to the children of the poor.

In those days, the emissaries of the high priests went throughout Jerusalem, visiting all the houses whose owners kept up communication with Jesus and the disciples, discharging them from whatever public employments they might happen to hold, and arresting any of Jesus's followers found there. Nicodemus and Joseph of Arimathea had, since Christ's burial, nothing more to do with the Jews. Joseph of Arimathea was something like an elder of a congregation. He always stood among the Jews like a man who, by his unobtrusive merit and multiplied good works modestly performed, had won the esteem of even the wicked. What very much rejoiced me was to see how Veronica's husband conceded to her when she told him that she would rather separate from him than from the crucified Jesus. I saw that he too was discharged from his public office. But I was informed that he bore it more for love of his wife than for love of Jesus. The Jews, moreover, caused the ways and paths to the Holy Sepulcher on Mount Calvary to be obstructed by ditches and hedges, because they had become a resort for many, and diverse moving incidents and miracles took place in them.

Pilate's interior disquietude drove him from Jerusalem. Herod, a couple of days previously, had gone to Machaerus, but finding no rest there, he proceeded to Madian. Here, where they had once refused to receive the Lord, they now opened the gates to the murderer.

I saw Jesus appearing in many places during these days, and lastly in Galilee, in a valley across the Jordan in which was a large school. Many people were standing together, speaking about him and expressing their doubts upon the report of his resurrection. He appeared among them, and vanished again after some words. I saw him appearing in this way in different localities.

The apostles very quickly returned from the region of Sichar. They sent a messenger on ahead to Bethany, to announce their return and to direct several of the disciples to go to Jerusalem for the sabbath. Others were commanded to celebrate it in Bethany, for they already had a certain law and order. The apostles only passed through the different places on the road without stopping. Thaddeus, James the Less, and Eliud went in their traveling dress, and ahead of the rest, to see the blessed Virgin and Mary Cleophas at John Mark's. As they had not seen the newcomers for a considerable time, the holy women were very much rejoiced. I saw that James was carrying on his arm a priestly vestment, a mantle, which the holy women in Bethany had made for Peter, and which he was taking to the house of the Last Supper.

4/10 It was so late when the apostles assembled in the house of the Last Supper that they could not partake of the meal prepared for them. *They had to begin the sabbath solemnities.* They at once put on their robes of ceremony, preceded of course by the customary foot washing. The lamps were lighted, and I already remarked some departure from the Jewish sabbatical ceremonies. First, the curtains were opened in front of the Holy of Holies, and the seat upon which Jesus had reclined at table at the institution of the Holy Eucharist was placed before it. They spread a cover over it, and laid upon it their prayer rolls. Peter knelt before it, John and James a little in the rear, the rest of the apostles behind them, and then came the disciples. When they knelt they bowed their heads to the ground, burying their faces in their hands. The cover was removed from the chalice, but the white linen cloth was still left hanging over it. Only those disciples were present who were already initiated into the mystery of the blessed sacrament, just as those chiefly had been taken on the journey to Sichar who had seen the Lord after his resurrection that they might be able to attest the fact.

Peter, with John and James at his side, delivered a meditation, or prayer, in which the holy Institution of the Lord and also his Passion were considered, and an interior sacrifice of prayer was offered. After that, standing under the lamp, they began the usual ceremonies of the sabbath. When all was over, they took a repast in the outer hall. In the supper hall itself I saw no more eating going on after the institution of the Holy Eucharist, excepting perhaps the taking of bread and wine.

On the occasion of his apparition through the closed doors, Jesus had taught the apostles the addition to the sabbath service that relates to the blessed sacrament.

The blessed Virgin was taken to Jerusalem by Mary Mark; and Veronica, who now went round with her openly, accompanied them, along with Johanna Chusa.

The blessed Virgin liked to be in Jerusalem, for she could there go alone in the twilight and darkness over the Way of Jesus's Passion, pray and meditate on the places upon which he had suffered or had fallen. And as she could not reach them all, on account of the Jews' having hedged some of them in and filled others up, she made the Holy Way at home, also, or in the open air, for she had all the distances and the numbers connected with it deeply engraven in her soul, and thus she constantly revived, in her compassionate contemplations, the whole of that sorrowful journey of her Son.

It is a certainty that after the death of her Son, the blessed Virgin was first to begin the devotion of the Way of the Cross and the practice of meditating upon the bitter Passion, a practice she ever after continued.

The Second Love Feast (Agape) • Thomas Puts his Hand into the Marks of Jesus's Wounds

4/11–13 AFTER *the close of the sabbath*, the apostles having laid aside their robes of ceremony, I saw a great meal spread in the outer hall. It was a love feast, such as had taken place on the preceding Sunday. Thomas must have celebrated the sabbath somewhere in the neighborhood, for I did not see him come in till after the meal, when they had again returned to the Cenacle. It was still early in the evening; the lamps were not yet lighted. Several of the apostles and disciples were in the hall, and I saw others entering. They robed themselves again in long white garments, and prepared for prayer as on the preceding occasion. Peter, John, and James again put on the vestments that distinguished them as priests.

While these preparations were being made, I saw Thomas entering the supper room. He passed through the apostles who were already robed, and put on his own long white garment. As he went along, I saw the apostles accosting him. Some caught him by the sleeve, others gesticulated with the right hand as they spoke, as if emphatically protesting against him. But he behaved like one in a hurry to vest and as if he could not credit the account given him of the wonderful things which had happened in that place. While all this was going on, a man entered the hall. He appeared to be a servant. He wore an apron and had in one hand a little lighted lamp, in the other a rod terminating in a hook. With the latter he drew down the lamp that was suspended from the center of the ceiling, lighted it, and again pushed it up. Then he left the hall! And now I saw the blessed Virgin, Magdalene, and another woman come into the house. The blessed Virgin and Magdalene entered the hall, Peter and John going to meet them. The third woman remained in the antechamber. The entrance hall was opened into the supper room, also some of the side halls. The exterior doors leading into the courtyard, as well as those of the court itself, were shut. A great many disciples were gathered in the side halls.

As soon as Mary and Magdalene entered, the doors were closed and all ranged for prayer. The holy women remained reverently standing on either side of the door, their arms crossed upon their breast. The apostles kneeling before the Holy of Holies, prayed again as before; then standing under the lamp, they sang psalms, in choirs. Peter stood before the lamp, his face toward the Holy of Holies, John and James the Less at his side. Right and left of the lamp were the other apostles. The side toward the Holy of Holies was left free. Peter stood between the two, his back to the door, so that the two holy women were standing behind him at some distance.

After some time there was a pause in the assembly, an intermission of prayer, or as if prayer was at an end, and they began to speak of going to the Sea of Tiberias and of how they would disperse. But soon they assumed an expression of rapt attention, called up by the approach of the Lord. At the same moment, I saw Jesus in the courtyard. He was resplendent with light, clothed in white garments and a white girdle. He directed his steps to the door of the outer hall, which opened of itself before him and closed behind him. The disciples in the outer hall saw the door opening of itself, and fell back on both sides to make room. But Jesus walked quickly through the hall into the supper room and stepped between Peter and John who, like all the other apostles, fell back on either side.

Jesus did not enter walking properly so called, that is, in the usual way of mortals, and yet it was not a floating along, or hovering, as I have seen spirits doing. It reminded me, as I saw them all falling back, of a priest in his alb passing through a crowded congregation. Everything in the hall appeared to become suddenly large and bright. Jesus was environed with light. The apostles had fallen back from the radiant circle, otherwise they would not have been able to see him.

Jesus's first words were: "Peace be to you!" Then he spoke with Peter and John, and rebuked them for something. They had departed a little from his directions, in order to follow their own ideas about something, and consequently they had not met with success. It related to some of the cures they had sought to effect on their return from Sichar and Thanat-Shiloh. They had not followed Jesus's directions to the letter, and therefore had not been entirely successful. They had done something according to their own ideas. Jesus told them that if it happened again, they should act otherwise. Jesus now stepped under the lamp, and the apostles closed around him. Thomas, very much frightened at the sight of the Lord, timidly drew back. But Jesus, grasping his right hand in his

376   AD 33

own right hand, took the forefinger and laid the tip of it in the wound of his left hand; then taking the left hand in his own left, he placed the forefinger in the wound of his right hand; lastly, taking again Thomas's right hand in his own right, he put it, without uncovering his breast, under his garment, and laid the fore and middle fingers in the wound of his right side. He spoke some words as he did this. With the exclamation: "My Lord, and my God!" Thomas sank down like one unconscious, Jesus still holding his hand. The nearest of the apostles supported him, and Jesus raised him up by the hand. That sinking down and rising up had some peculiar signification.

When Jesus grasped Thomas's hand, I saw that his wounds were not like bloody marks, but like little radiant suns. The other disciples were very greatly touched by this scene. They leaned forward, without, however, crowding, to see what the Lord was allowing Thomas to feel. I saw the blessed Virgin during the whole time of Jesus's stay, perfectly motionless, as if absorbed in calm, deep interior recollection. Magdalene appeared more agitated, yet manifesting far less emotion than did the disciples.

Jesus did not disappear immediately after Thomas's declaration of faith. He still continued to speak to the apostles, and asked for something to eat. I saw a little oval dish brought to him again from the partitioned recess in which the table stood. It was not precisely like that presented to him the first time. There was on it something that looked like a fish, of which he ate, then blessed and distributed what was left to those around him, beginning with Thomas.

Jesus then told them why he stood in the midst of them, although they had abandoned him, and why he did not place himself nearer to those that had remained faithful to him. He told them also that he had commissioned Peter to confirm his brethren, and explained why he had given him that charge. Then turning to them all, he told them why he wished to give them Peter for a leader, although he had so recently denied him. He must, he said, be the shepherd of the flock, and he enlarged upon Peter's zeal.

John brought on his arm from the Holy of Holies the large, colored, embroidered mantle that James had received from Mary and on which, in those last days, the holy women had worked at Bethany. Besides that, he brought also a hollow, slender staff, high and bent at the top like a shepherd's crook. It was shining and looked like a long pipe. The mantle was white with broad red stripes; and on it were embroidered, in colors, wheat, grapes, a lamb, and other symbols. It was wide, and long enough to reach to the feet. It was fastened over the breast with a little four-cornered metal shield, and bordered down the front with red stripes crossed by shorter ones on which were letters. It had a collar and a kind of hood, of a sky-blue color, which could be drawn up over the neck and head.

Peter next knelt down before Jesus, who gave him to eat a round morsel, like a little cake. I do not remember seeing any plate, nor do I know where Jesus got the morsel, but I do know that it shone with light. I felt that Peter received with it some special power, and I saw also strength and vigor poured into his soul when Jesus breathed upon him. This action of Jesus was not a simple, ordinary breathing. It was words, a power, something substantial that Peter received, but no merely spoken words. Jesus put his mouth to Peter's mouth, then to his ears, and poured that strength into each of the three. It was not the Holy Spirit himself, but something that the Holy Spirit was to quicken and vivify in Peter at Pentecost. Jesus laid his hands on him, gave him a special kind of strength, and invested him with chief power over the others. Then he placed upon him the mantle that John, who was standing next to him, was holding on his arm, and put the staff into his hand. While performing this action, Jesus said that the mantle would preserve in him all the strength and virtue that he had just imparted to him, and that he should wear it whenever he had to make use of the power with which he had been endued.

Peter addressed the assembly in his new dignity. He had become as it were a new being, a man full of vigor and energy. His hearers were greatly moved; they listened with tears. He consoled them, alluded to many things that Jesus had before told them, and which were now being fulfilled. He told them, as I still remember, that Jesus, during his Passion of eighteen hours, had borne insult and outrage from the whole world. In that discourse mention was made of how much was wanting to the completion of Jesus's thirty-four years. While Peter was speaking, Jesus vanished. No alarm, no exclamations of surprise broke in upon the attention with which Peter's words were received. He appeared to be endowed with strength entirely new. The discourse ended, they sang a psalm of thanksgiving. Jesus addressed neither his blessed Mother nor Magdalene.

Jesus Appears to the
Holy Apostles at the Sea of Galilee

4/14 BEFORE going to the sea, the holy apostles went over the Way of the Cross to Mount Calvary, and thence to Bethany, from which place they took with them some disciples.

They went by different routes and in several companies to the Sea of Galilee. Peter went with John, James the Greater, Thaddeus, Nathaniel, John Mark, and Silas, seven in all, to Tiberias, leaving Samaria to the left.

The Disbelief of Thomas

The Risen One Appears on the Shore of Lake Tiberias

All chose routes remote from cities. They went to a fishery outside Tiberias, which Peter had held on lease, but which was now rented by another man, a widower with two sons. They took a repast with this man, and I heard Peter saying that he had not fished here for three years.

They went aboard two ships, one somewhat larger and better than the other. They gave to Peter the choice of the former, into which he mounted with Nathaniel, Thomas, and one of the fisherman's servants. In the second ship were John, James, John Mark, and Silas. Peter would not suffer another to row. He wanted to do it himself. Although so distinguished by Jesus, he was exceedingly humble and modest, especially before Nathaniel, who was polished and educated.

4/15 *They sailed about the whole night* with torches, casting the nets here and there between the two ships, but always drawing them in empty. At intervals they prayed and sang psalms. *When day was beginning to dawn,* the ships approached the opposite side of the mouth of the Jordan, on the eastern shore of the sea. The apostles were worn out and wanted to cast anchor. They had laid aside their garments while fishing, retaining only a linen bandage and a little mantle. When about resuming their clothing preparatory to taking a little rest, they saw a figure standing behind the reeds on the shore. It was Jesus. He cried out: "Children, have you any meat?" They answered: "No!" Then he cried out again, telling them to cast the net to the west of Peter's ship. They did it, and John had to sail round to the other side of the ship. And now the net was so heavily filled that John recognized Jesus, and called to Peter across the silent deep: "It is the Lord!" At these words Peter instantly girded his coat about him, leaped into the water, and waded through the reeds to the shore where Jesus was standing. But John pushed on in a boat, very light and narrow, that was fastened to his ship.

Two of this kind were hooked together. They pushed one before the other, and crossed over it to land. It held only one man, and was needed only for shallow water near the land.

While the apostles were on the sea fishing, I saw the Savior floating out of the valley of Jehosaphat and surrounded by many souls of the ancient patriarchs whom he had freed from Limbo, also by others that had been banished to different places, caves, swamps, and deserts. During the whole period of these forty days, I saw Jesus, when not among the disciples, with the holy souls. They were principally from Adam and Eve down to Noah, Abraham, and other ancient leaders of the people. He went over all places remarkable in his life, showing them all things, and instructing them upon what he had done and suffered for them, whereby they became indescribably quickened and through gratitude purified. He taught them, in a certain measure at this time, the mysteries of the New Testament, by which they were released from their fetters. I saw him with them in Nazareth, in the crib cave and Bethlehem, and in every place in which anything remarkable had happened to him. One could distinguish, by a certain weakness or vigor in the appearance of the souls, whether they animated men or women when on earth. I saw them in long, narrow garments that fell around them in shining folds, and floated behind in a long train. Their hair did not look like ordinary hair, but like rays of light, each of which signified something. The beards of the men were composed of similar rays. Though not distinguished by any external sign, yet I recognized the kings, and especially the priests that from the time of Moses had anything to do with the Ark of the Covenant. In the journeys of the Savior I always saw them floating around him, so that here too the spirit of order reigned in everything. The movements of these apparitions were exceedingly graceful and dignified. They seemed to float along, not exactly in an upright position, but inclining gently forward. They did not touch the earth like bodies that have weight, but appeared to hover just above the ground.

I saw the Lord arrive at the sea in company with these souls while the apostles were still fishing. Back of a little mound on the shore there was a hollow in which was a covered fireplace, for the use of the shepherds, perhaps. I did not see Jesus kindling a fire, catching a fish, or getting one in any other way. Fire and fish and everything necessary appeared at once in presence of the souls as soon as ever it entered into the Lord's mind that a fish should here be prepared for eating. How it happened, I cannot say.

The spirits of the patriarchs had a share in this fish and in its preparation. It bore some signification relative to the Church Suffering, to the souls undergoing purification. They were in this meal bound to the Church Militant by visible ties. In the eating of this fish, Jesus gave the apostles an idea of the union existing between the Church Suffering and the Church Militant. Jonah in the fish was typical of Jesus's stay in the lower world. Outside the hut was a beam that served for a table.

I saw all this before Jesus crossed the mound and went down to the sea. Peter did not swim, he waded through the water. The bottom could be seen, although the water was tolerably deep. Peter was already standing by Jesus when John came up. Those on the ship now began to cry to them to help draw in the net. Jesus told Peter to go bring in the fish. They drew the net to land, and Peter emptied it on the shore. In it were one hundred and fifty-three different kinds of fishes. This number signified that of the new believers who were to be gained at Thebez.

There were on the ships several people in the employ of the fishermen of Tiberias, and they took charge of the ships and the fish, while the apostles and disciples went with Jesus to the hut whither he invited them to come and eat. When they entered, the spirits of the patriarchs had vanished. The apostles were very much surprised to see the fire and a fish, not of their own catching, also bread and honeycakes. The apostles and disciples reclined by the beam while Jesus played the host. He handed to each on a little roll a portion of the fish from the pan. I did not see that the fish became less. He gave to them also of the honeycakes and then reclined with them at table and ate. All this took place very quietly and solemnly.

Thomas was the third of those that had on the ship a perception of Jesus's presence. But they were all timid and frightened, for Jesus was more spirit-like than before, and the whole meal and the hour had in them something full of mystery. No one dared ask a question. A feeling of holy awe stole over them and gave rise to solemn silence. Jesus was wrapped in a mantle, his wounds not visible.

After the meal, I saw Jesus and the apostles rise from table. They walked up and down the shore, and at last stood still while Jesus solemnly addressed Peter: "Simon, son of John, lovest thou me more than these?" Peter timidly answered. "Yea, Lord, thou knowest that I love thee!" Jesus said to him: "Feed my lambs!" And at the same instant I saw a vision of the church and the Chief Pastor. I saw him teaching and guiding the first Christians, and I saw the baptizing and cleansing of the new Christians, who appeared like so many tender lambs.

After a pause, Jesus again said to Peter: "Simon, son of John, lovest thou me?" (They were walking all the time, Jesus occasionally turning and pausing while they regarded him with attention). Peter very timidly and humbly, for he was thinking of his denial, again answered: "Yea, Lord, thou knowest that I love thee!" Jesus again addressed him solemnly: "Feed my sheep!" Again I had a vision of the rising church and her persecutions. I saw the Chief Bishop gathering together the numerous scattered Christians, protecting them, providing them with shepherds, and governing them.

After another pause and still walking, Jesus said once more: "Simon, son of John, lovest thou me?" I saw that Peter grew troubled at the thought that Jesus asked him so often, as if he doubted his love. It reminded him of his thrice-repeated denial, and he answered: "Lord, thou knowest all things, thou knowest that I love thee!" I saw that John was thinking: "Oh, what love must Jesus have, and what ought a shepherd to have, since he thrice questions Peter, to whom he confides his flock, concerning his love!" Jesus again said: "Feed my sheep! Amen, amen, I say to thee: when thou wast younger, thou didst gird thyself, and didst walk where thou wouldst. But when thou shalt be old, thou shalt stretch forth thy hands, and another shall gird thee, and lead thee whither thou wouldst not. Follow me!"

Jesus turned again to go on. John walked with him, for Jesus was saying something to him alone, but what it was I could not hear. I saw that Peter, noticing this, asked the Lord while pointing to John: "Lord, what will become of this man?" Jesus, to rebuke his curiosity, answered: "If I will have him to remain till I come, what is it to thee? Follow thou me!" And Jesus turning again, they went forward.

When Jesus said for the third time: "Feed my sheep!" and that Peter would in his old age be bound and led away, I had a vision of the spreading church. I saw Peter in Rome bound and crucified, also the martyrdom of the saints. Peter too had a vision of his own martyrdom and of John's future sufferings. While Jesus was predicting his death to Peter, the latter glanced at John and very naturally thought: "Shall not this man whom Jesus loves so dearly be crucified like him?" Putting the question to Jesus, he was answered with a rebuke. I had at this moment a vision of John's death in Ephesus. I saw him stretch himself out in his grave, address some words to his disciples, and die. After his death I saw his body no longer on earth, but in a place as resplendent as the sun off toward the southeast, and it seemed as if John here received something from above that he transmitted to the earth. I became aware also that some understand these words of Jesus falsely and think they mean: "I will that he *so* remain," or "If I will that he *so* remain." But they mean: "If I will that he *remains*." They therefore that heard these words thought that John would not die. But he did die. I had on this occasion, as I have said, a vision of his death and his subsequent sojourn.

The apostles and disciples went on a little farther with Jesus, who was instructing them upon their future conduct. He then vanished before them eastward of the sea toward Gerasa and they returned to Tiberias, though not by a route that would lead them past the place in which Jesus had given them to eat.

Of the fish that the apostles caught, none were used at that meal. When Jesus said that they should bring them ashore, Peter threw them in rows at Jesus's feet, that they might be numbered. By this it was acknowledged that they had caught the fish not by themselves and for themselves, but by his miraculous power and for him. When the fish were deposited on the shore, Jesus said to the apostles: "Come and eat!" and conducted them over the little hill, or mound, where the sea could no longer be seen, to the mud hut over the furnace. Jesus did not at once place himself at table, but went to the pan and brought to each a portion of fish on a piece of bread. He blessed the portions and they shone with light. The honeycakes were not in the pan. They were already prepared, and lay in a pile one above the other. Jesus distributed them, and when all were served, he too ate with them. There was only one fish in the pan, but it was larger than any they had caught. There was some mystery connected with this meal. The presence of the souls of the patriarchs and others, their participation in the preparation of the meal, and the subsequent call of Peter, gave me to understand that in this spiritual meal the Church Suffering, the holy souls, should be committed to Peter's care, should be incorporated with the Church Militant, and the Church Triumphant, in short, that they should occupy a third place in the church as a whole. I cannot explain how this was to be done, but I had in vision this intimate conviction. It was in reference to this also that Jesus closed with the prophecy of Peter's death and John's future.

Jesus next went with the souls of the ancient patriarchs to the country in which he had driven the demons into the swine. There he released some other souls that had been confined in dreary and desolate regions, for there were many possessed in these parts, and innocent people had here been murdered whose souls, according to God's decrees, were here condemned to sojourn.

Jesus went with the souls to Paradise also, which I distinctly saw as beautiful as ever. He explained to them all that their first parents had lost by their fall, and what a happiness it was for them that he could free them from its effects. I saw that the souls sighed indeed after redemption, though ignorant of the way in which it was to be effected, just as men on earth had only vague notions on the same point. Jesus walked with them and instructed them in a manner suited to their peculiar condition, as he had done in his communications with men upon earth. I again understood that man was created to fill up the places of the angelic choirs that had fallen from heaven. If the Fall had not taken place, men would have multiplied only until that number was reached, and then creation would have come to an end. But by the Fall, a dispersing, an arbitrary scattering, a transplanting arose mixed up with impurity and darkness; therefore is the punishment of death a necessary consequence, a real benefit, a real kindness to man. As to what is said of the end of the world, this much is certain: it will not end until all the wheat is separated from the chaff and those choirs of the fallen angels filled up with it.

I saw Jesus with the souls on great battlefields, explaining to them how they had been led to salvation. As he was speaking, I saw visions of the battles and everything connected with them, just as if they were going on under my eyes. I never saw anyone terrified in these ghostlike encounters. It was like a pleasant breeze blowing over the country, and joy abounded in all creatures. Jesus went with the ancient patriarchs to those regions also into which the apostles were first to carry the Gospel, and blessed them with his presence. In this way, he visited the whole world.

When Peter, with the three apostles and the three disciples, *returned that afternoon* to the fisherman Aminadab, who for the last two years had had possession of Peter's fishery, they took a meal with him. Peter related the miracle that they had witnessed, the apparition of the Lord, the meal, and the abundant draught of fish, and gave an instruction on leaving all things and following the Lord. The old fisherman, on seeing the ship approaching laden with fish and hearing from his sons who accompanied it an account of the same miracle, resolved at once to abandon all his worldly goods. The fish were distributed among the poor, the fishery was handed over to another, and he went that night with his two sons, Isaac and Josaphat, to join the disciples. Their route lay for some distance along the west side of the sea, and then turned off inland. The fisherman's intention was not perfectly pure. He thought that by leaving all he had he would get something in return.

4/16 Toward dawn the next morning, the apostles reached a synagogue of considerable size. It stood in an open field, surrounded by inns, and formed the central point of three villages. A great many disciples were here assembled, to whom Peter related the miracle of the draught of fishes and the meal, and repeated the words of Jesus. He taught in the school, taking for his subject the miraculous draught and the following of the Lord. There was a large gathering of people here, among them many sick, also some possessed. Peter was the only one that healed on this occasion, and he did it in the name of Jesus; the other apostles and disciples served and taught. All the good and those best disposed toward Jesus's doctrine were here gathered from the whole country around. Peter spoke also of the Lord's Passion and Resurrection, told how the apostles had seen him, and invited his hearers to follow him. The people were carried away by Peter's words, for his whole deportment had undergone an entire change since the last two apparitions. He was full of inspiration, full of gentleness. He so touched the hearts of these people that all wanted to follow him right away, and he had to command many of them to go back to their homes.

Jesus Appears to the Five Hundred

FROM that last place, which was some hours south of Tiberias, Peter went with the other apostles, the disciples, and many of the people westward to an elevated region which had on the north an extraordinarily fertile valley. Even in the depth of winter, it was covered with beautiful, tall grass, for there was a brook running through it; but in hot weather it was parched. Sometimes the whole valley was inundated by the rains that flowed down the mountains in streams. Up on this plateau they came to a hill, around which lay houses with gardens behind them extending up its sides. The hill was not much higher than the houses themselves. Five pathways planted with hedges and trees ran up the hill, whose summit afforded ample space for about a hundred people to walk about freely. From it the view extended far around the country and over the Galilean sea. It was a very beautiful prospect. At no great distance arose the mountain of the multiplication of the loaves, and it was in this region that Jesus delivered his Sermon on the Mount. The well of Capernaum was at the base of this elevated plateau. The rest of the apostles, many of the disciples, and all the holy women were here, besides the Mother of God and Veronica. Peter's wife and daughter, the wives of Andrew and Matthew were come down from Bethsaida, along with many others. The apostles and disciples knew that they were all to meet here. They scattered around, some under sheds, some in the open air. Peter related to the apostles and the women the miraculous draught of fishes, and then went with them up the mountain, upon which the people had already been ranged by some of the disciples.

There was on it a hollow place in whose center stood a teacher's pillar overgrown with moss. One could mount into it as into a pulpit. The hollow in which the pillar stood was furnished with steps in tiers, so that the numerous audience could see over one another. Peter placed five apostles on the five several pathways that led up the mountain, and they taught the people, because all could not hear him, on account of the crowd. He himself stood on the pillar in the center, the apostles, disciples, and many of the people around him, and spoke of the Passion, the Resurrection, the apparitions of the Lord, and the obligation of following him.

And now I saw Jesus approaching by the same route that Peter had come. He went up the mountain. The holy women, who were standing on one of the paths, prostrated before him, and he spoke to them as he passed. As, resplendent with light, he stepped in through the crowd, many shuddered and became alarmed. These did not remain faithful. Then Jesus went to the pillar on which Peter was standing. Peter resigned his place and took up a position opposite Jesus, who now addressed the multitude. He spoke of abandoning one's relatives, of following him, and of the persecution that they would have to endure. About two hundred of his hearers withdrew when they heard him talking of such things. All these were gone away, said Jesus. He had spoken to them mildly in order not to scandalize the weak. He uttered some very grave words upon the sufferings and persecution of those that would follow him upon earth, and he alluded to their eternal reward. He addressed these remarks to the apostles and disciples, as he had once before done in his last instruction in the temple. He told them that they should at first remain in Jerusalem. When he should have sent them the Spirit, they should baptize in the name of the Father, and of the Son, and of the Holy Spirit, and should at once establish a community. Then he told them how they should disperse, form distant communities, meet together once more, again separate for far-off countries, and receive at last the baptism of blood.

While Jesus was speaking, the spirits of the ancient patriarchs encircled the whole assembly, though invisibly. Jesus vanished. His disappearance was like a light suddenly extinguished in their midst. Many fell prostrate on their face. Peter again taught and prayed. This was Jesus's principal apparition in Galilee, where he taught and gave proof to all of his resurrection. The other apparitions were more secret.

Peter, Thaddeus, Andrew, and James the Less, I saw after that in another place, where they healed many sick whom lately in the region of Sichar they could not cure. Their fault was that, wishing to imitate the great dignity and reserve of Jesus in his demeanor, they did something extraordinary, they assumed an air of importance. They did not give humbly what they had received, but they gave it as coming from themselves, therefore success was not theirs. But now I saw them (and the sight touched me greatly) humbling themselves, kneeling down by the sick, and begging their pardon for failing to assist them. The sick were all cured. There were people even from Kedar among them. The cured went with the apostles to Bethany for the sabbath.

Love Feast (Agape) in Bethany
and in the House of the Last Supper •
The Destruction of the Holy Places by the Jews

I SAW the apostles in Bethany, whither they were followed by about three hundred of the faithful, among them fifty women. They had given over their goods to the community. The blessed Virgin also had come from Jerusalem to Bethany, and was stopping in Martha and Magdalene's house. There was a great Love Feast of bread-breaking and passing round of the cup held in the open hall of Lazarus's court.

Peter afterward gave an instruction before a great multitude. There were some spies among the listeners. When Peter announced that they should leave all and join the community, and that he would give them what they needed, the spies laughed derisively. He had nothing himself, they said. He was only a poor fisherman, a vagrant, who could hardly support his wife at home. Peter still continued to teach, more on the command of Jesus than from any interior, quickening sentiment which the apostles received only with the Holy Spirit. He now spoke in the assemblies, excepting when the crowd was very great, for then he ordered some of the others to teach on various points. Since his reception of the mantle from Jesus and the meal of fish (which indeed was not a natural fish), at which he had received special power, he had become quite another being. All recognized him as the head, the mouth, the hand of the community. At Jesus's prediction on the seashore respecting Peter's death and John's future, at the command, "Feed my lambs!" I felt that Peter, in his successors, was forever to provide for the guiding and feeding of the flocks, while John should stand ever at the source of the water that was to refresh and irrigate the meadow and quicken the sheep. It seemed to me that Peter's influence belonged more to time, more to the exterior condition, and therefore was it divided among his successors; but that John's was more interior, that it consisted more in inspiration, in the sending abroad of inspired messengers. Peter was more like the rock, the edifice; John more like a wind, a cloud, a thunderstorm, a son of thunder, a voice sender. Peter was more like the frame, the cords, and the tone of a harp; John was the sighing of the breeze through its strings. I am unable to express in more significant words what I inwardly perceived.

About fifty soldiers, the same that seized the Lord on the Mount of Olives, came from Jerusalem to Bethany. They were guards belonging to the temple and the high priests. Some deputies also of the Sanhedrin made their appearance at the council house in Bethany, and summoned the apostles before them. Peter, John, and Thomas presented themselves and replied boldly and openly to the charge that they convened assemblies and occasioned disturbance among the people. Soldiers were placed at Lazarus's. The deputies from Jerusalem interrogated the apostles publicly before the council house. The magistrates of Bethany opposed them, saying that if they knew anything against those men, they ought to take them into custody, but that they must not disturb the peace of the place by the presence of soldiers. Peter, in order to avoid giving offense, dismissed one hundred and twenty-three of the assembled faithful. Those from the greatest distance were directed to remain at the dwellings in the neighborhood, for they already had all things in common. The fifty women also withdrew and lived together in separate abodes. Peter gave orders for all to return to Bethany before the day of Christ's ascension.

The apostles, on leaving Bethany, went to the house of the Last Supper near Jerusalem, where they prayed under the lamp before the Holy of Holies. There were about seven disciples with them. They could no longer reach the house of the Last Supper through the city, for the road on that side had been partly destroyed by the Jews. They had to go to the left of the temple, and strike into the road taken by Peter and John on Maundy Thursday. There were numerous inns for the accommodation of strangers on this road, and the people living around these parts were not of pure Jewish origin. The Jews had expelled from their society and from public offices all that declared themselves for Jesus and that fraternized with the disciples. The places upon which Jesus fell during his sorrowful journey to Golgotha, or at which something noteworthy had happened, they cut through with ditches. The ways leading to the sections chiefly inhabited or frequented by the followers of Jesus, they walled up. It appeared to me very strange to see a person caught in such a street as in a blind alley, and have to turn round and come out again. Sometimes the friends of Jesus again opened the ways to Golgotha by night. All places around Jerusalem especially consecrated by the presence or the sufferings of Jesus, and on that account held in particular veneration by his follow-ers, were maliciously laid waste by the Jews. The charming sites upon which Jesus had taught and tarried were rendered impassable and closed in with hedges. In some places they actually dug pitfalls into which the pious pilgrim might fall, but I saw some of those vicious Jews plunging into them themselves. Mount Golgotha was rendered unapproachable by hedges and beams. Its summit was dug up and the earth scattered like manure over the paths, also over the five grassy, heart-shaped plots that were formed by the pathways running up to the place of crucifixion. When they had taken away the mound that encircled the place of crucifixion, there remained a white stone. In it was a four-cornered hole about four feet deep, in which the cross had been planted. I saw the work-men toiling with crowbars, trying to upturn that stone, but the more they tried, the deeper it sank, so they buried it at last under some rubbish. The Holy Sepulcher alone was left unmolested, for that was Nicodemus's property. Christ's head, while in the tomb, lay toward the east. If a person on leaving the cave went around toward the south, he would have the sun directly above him, and the west on his right.

I was interiorly instructed that all demolishers of representations of the

Holy Way of the Cross, of crucifixes, chapels or churches, of ancient devotions, of holy exercises and practices, and in general of all objects that draw us into closer relation with the history of Redemption, whether in building, picture, and writing, or by custom, festival, and prayer, will be judged with the enemies of Jesus's bloody footsteps and as belonging to them.

The Majesty and Dignity of the Blessed Virgin

4/17 *ON the evening of the following day,* I saw the apostles and twenty of the disciples in the hall at prayer under the lamp. The blessed Virgin, all the holy women, Lazarus, Nicodemus, Joseph of Arimathea, and Obed were present. The prayer over, John addressed the apostles, and Peter, the disciples. They spoke in words full of mystery of their relations to the mother of the Lord and what she should be to them. During this instruction of the two apostles, which they based on a communication received from Jesus, I saw the blessed Virgin hovering over the assembly in a shining, outspread mantle whose folds embraced them all, and on her head descended a crown from the most holy Trinity through the open heavens above her. I no longer saw her kneeling outside the hall in prayer, and I had the conviction that Mary was the legitimate head of them all, the temple that enclosed them all. I think this vision was symbolical of what God designed to take place for the church at this moment through the exposition of the apostles upon Mary's dignity.

Toward nine o'clock, I saw a meal set in the outer hall. The guests wore festal robes and Mary her wedding garment. When at prayer, however, she wore a white mantle and veil. She sat between Peter and John at the table of the apostles, who were seated, their back to the court, the door of the hall in view. The other women and disciples were seated right and left at separate tables. Nicodemus and Joseph served. Peter carved the lamb, just as Jesus had done the paschal lamb. At the end of the meal, there was a breaking of bread and a passing around of blessed (not consecrated) bread and wine.

After that I saw the blessed Virgin with the apostles in the supper room. She was standing between Peter and John under the lamp. The Holy of Holies was open, and they were praying on their knees before it. **4/18** *When midnight had sounded,* the blessed Virgin, kneeling, received the blessed sacrament from Peter. He carried the bread that had been consecrated and broken by Jesus on the little plate belonging to the chalice. At that instant I saw Jesus appear to her, though not visible to the others. Mary was penetrated with light and splendor. She was still in prayer. I saw that the holy apostles were very reverent in their manner toward her. Mary next went to the little dwelling on the right of the entrance into the court of the Cenacle, in which she now had her apartment. Here standing she recited the Magnificat, the Canticle of the three youths in the fiery furnace, and the 130th Psalm. *The day was beginning to dawn* when I saw Jesus entering through the closed doors. He spoke long to her, telling her that she was to help the apostles, and explaining what she was to be to them. He gave her power over the whole church, endued her with his strength, his protecting influence, and it was as if his light flowed in upon her, as if he penetrated her through and through. I cannot express it. A covered way of mats across the court to the house of the Last Supper was made for the blessed Virgin, so that she could go from her little room to the Holy of Holies and the choir of the apostles and disciples. John also resided in the little dwelling. When Jesus appeared to Mary in her cell, I saw her head encircled by a crown of stars as it had been at her communion.

It was revealed to me also that as often as the blessed Virgin communicated, the form of the bread remained in her unchanged from one communion to another, so that she always adored in her breast the sacramental presence of the God-Man. During a period of persecution, after the stoning of St. Stephen, the apostles for a time refrained from consecrating. But even then the church was not without the blessed sacrament, for it was preserved in the living tabernacle of Mary's most holy heart. I also learned at the same time that this was a grace entirely special, and that it could be imparted to the blessed Virgin alone.

Increase of the Community

4/19– THE NUMBER of the faithful continued to increase. Many came
5/11 to join them, especially from the Galilean Sea, with asses laden with baggage. It kept some busy procuring them quarters. They generally stopped first at the disciples' inn outside Bethany, where the disciples dwelt in turn to receive the strangers, and give them advice and directions. The newcomers were sent by them to Lazarus, who owned many houses and dwellings. Many of them lived at Jerusalem also, in the quarter of Mount Zion. Only a few poor Jews were scattered around here. There were numerous old walls of extraordinary thickness, and vacant lots on which I saw asses grazing. Strangers who had come for the feast pitched their tents around this quarter. Besides the house of the Last Supper, there was another on Mount Zion, a very large, dilapidated old building (the Citadel of David), and numbers of the faithful found shelter under its surroundings. They dwelt in huts, or in lodgings adjoining

them. I saw that people dwelt below in the massive walls, while on their top were erected tents of coarse tapestry.

The Chaldeans from Sikdor, whom Jesus had directed to the centurion of Capernaum, and who had from there returned to their homes, were now come back again in great numbers with their beasts of burden and baggage. Their beasts and packs were standing in the inner court of the large, dilapidated building. The Jews did not molest them; only the road to the temple mount and to the quarter of the city belonging to it was entirely walled up on the side of Mount Zion near the pool of Bethesda where the Christians were stopping. The community was thereby completely separated, cut off from the Jews.

I saw the newcomers resigning, for the good of the community, quantities of stuffs of fine and coarse, white and yellowish wool, carpets, canvas for tents, all in great rolls. Nicodemus and Joseph managed everything. Garments for religious service and baptism were made out of some, and some was given to the needy, all of whom were cared for.

There was, at the pool of Bethesda, an old synagogue formerly used only by strangers come for the feast. It stood at some elevation above the pool. The apostles now appropriated it to their own use. In it the newcomers assembled to be instructed by some of the apostles. But all these strangers were not at once admitted to the community, much less to the house of the Last Supper. I saw neither the apostles nor the disciples, nor these newly arrived again frequenting the temple. True, the apostles, having received the Holy Spirit, went there after Pentecost, but it was only that they might preach to the assembled multitude. Their temple was the house of the Last Supper that sheltered the blessed sacrament. The mother of all was the blessed Virgin. The apostles consulted with her, and she was for them like an apostle herself.

Peter's wife and daughter, Mark's wife, and other women had now come from Bethsaida to Bethany, where they dwelt under tents. They had no communication whatever with the men. They came into the presence of the apostles only for instruction, and they employed themselves in weaving and twisting long strips of stuff and coarse covers for tents, many of them working at the same time upon one piece. The blessed Virgin also, along with Martha and Magdalene, worked at embroidery, sometimes reclining, sometimes walking about, work in hand. I saw the blessed Virgin embroidering in delicate colors figures something like an apostle, or the Lord himself, on a yellow, brown, or sky-blue ground. The figures were not so enveloped in mantles as formerly. Once they embroidered a representation of the most holy Trinity. It was like God the Father handing the cross to the Son, who looked like a high priest. From both proceeded the Holy Spirit, though not in the form of a dove, for instead of wings there were arms. The figures were arranged more in a triangular form than one below the other. I have seen in the earliest churches of that period vestments that Mary had embroidered.

The apostles themselves lent a hand in preparing the dwellings of the newcomers. They carried to them wood and matting and wicker partitions, and worked hard. The poor were provided with clothing, and even their food was prepared for them, for Lazarus had contributed toward the foundation of a general fund.

The holy women, among whom was the wife of Zacchaeus, busied themselves in helping the newly arrived women. No one had anything of his own. He that brought something with him gave it up, and he that had nothing, received something. The house of Simon the Leper was crowded with disciples. Simon himself no longer dwelt in it, for he had resigned it to the community, and he now lived among the brethren. On the flat roof of the house there was formed, by means of movable wicker partitions, a kind of hall in which was placed an orator's chair. It was reached from outside by steps in the wall. They built everywhere, they put up tents and sheds, they made use of every corner of walls and old buildings. There were also many vacant dwellings both here and in Jerusalem, for numbers of Jews went away after the crucifixion.

The newly converted and the baptized became so numerous after Pentecost that the apostles had to negotiate with the Jewish magistrates for procuring suitable dwelling-places for the newcomers. They sent Nicodemus, Joseph of Arimathea, Nathaniel, and others well known among the Jews, to the magistrates who were assembled, about twenty in number, in a hall over the gate of the women's porch. Three places outside the city and distant from the usual routes were assigned the converts: one to the west of Bethany, between it and Bethphage, where some huts and sheds were already put up; and two others south of Bethany, distant also from the highroads. In exchange for these, the disciples were to vacate the inn on the road outside Bethany, nor should they live permanently or put up at the inn beyond Jerusalem and on the road to Bethlehem, where Mary had stopped before her purification in the temple. I saw the magistrates indicating from the temple the regions named, the deputies carrying back the news to the community, some parties of the faithful going thither, and Peter and John pointing out to them sites for building. Supplies of all kinds were transported on asses, and water in great leathern bottles, to the place between Bethany and Bethphage, where there was no water. But when the Christians began to dig a well, water at once gushed forth. I saw Simon of Bethany, who had had a household of his own and understood domestic economy, under an awning near the pool of Bethesda, and he appeared to be noting down on a roll of parchment the goods and chattels of the people, who had brought with them sheep, goats, doves, and great birds with red beaks and legs. All were distributed to those in need of them, also covers and woollen stuffs for clothing. Admirable order was observed in this distribution. The women received their portion through the hands of women; the men, from men. There were people from the most widely scattered regions, who did not understand one another's language, but who with the greatest love handed over their property for distribution. The apostles alone understood all. Magdalene and Martha gave up their houses at Bethany to the new converts, and Lazarus delivered over all that he owned to the community. Nicodemus and Joseph of Arimathea did the same. They assumed the charge of providing for the community and distributing the alms. But when they were ordained priests, Peter appointed deacons in their place.

The Days Immediately Preceding the Ascension

JESUS communicated with the apostles quite naturally *in those last days*. He ate and prayed with them, walked with them in many directions, and repeated all that he had before told them. He appeared also to Simon of Cyrene as he was working in a garden between Bethphage and Jerusalem. Jesus, resplendent with light, approached him as if floating in the air. Simon fell on his knees and kissed the ground at Jesus's feet, who signed to him with his hand to keep silence, and then vanished. Some others that were working nearby likewise saw Jesus, and they too fell on their knees like Simon. When Jesus was walking with the apostles around Jerusalem, some of the Jews perceived the apparition, and were terrified. They ran to hide themselves, or to shut themselves up in their houses. Even the apostles and disciples accompanied him with a certain degree of timidity, for there was in him something too spiritual for them. Jesus appeared also in other places, Bethlehem and Nazareth for instance, to those especially with whom he and his blessed Mother had formerly had contact. He scattered blessings everywhere, and they that saw him believed and joined the apostles and disciples.

5/12–13 *On the last day but one before the Ascension*, I saw Jesus with five of the apostles approaching Bethany from the east, whither the blessed Virgin also, with other holy women, was coming from Jerusalem. Many of the faithful were gathered around Lazarus's house. They knew that Jesus was soon to leave them, and they wanted to see him once more and bid him goodbye. When Jesus had entered the house, these people were admitted into the spacious courtyard and the gates closed. Jesus took with the apostles and disciples some refreshments standing, and to the latter, who were weeping bitterly, he said: "Why do ye weep, dear brethren? Behold this woman! She is not weeping!" and he pointed to his blessed Mother, who was standing with the holy women at the entrance of the hall. A long table was set in the court for the numerous strangers. Jesus went out to them, blessed little rolls, and distributed them, after which he gave them a sign to retire. And now his blessed Mother humbly approached, to present to him a petition. But Jesus, checking her with a gesture of his hand, told her that he could not grant it. Mary thanked most humbly, and withdrew.

Jesus took a singularly touching leave of Lazarus. He gave him a shining morsel, blessed him, and extended to him his hand. Lazarus, who generally remained hidden in his own house, did not accompany Jesus when he left for Jerusalem with the apostles and disciples. They took the Palm Sunday route, though with many turnings into side ways. They went in four companies, allowing considerable distance to intervene between them. The eleven went on with Jesus; the holy women followed last. I saw Jesus shining with light, a conspicuous figure in their midst. The marks of his wounds were not always visible to me, but when I did see them, they were brilliant as the sun. All were anxious and greatly depressed. Some were in tears; others were talking to one another, saying: "He has often before vanished from us," for they did not want to think that he would really leave them. Peter and John alone appeared more calm, as if they understood the Lord better, for Jesus often spoke to them interiorly and explained to them many things. He often disappeared and then suddenly reappeared in their midst, as if desirous of preparing them for his final departure.

The way ran past charming little gardens where Jews were busy weaving and clipping the hedges, on which lovely bushes covered with flowers were growing in the form of pyramids. The laborers often covered their faces with their hands, fell to the earth, or fled among the shrubbery, I know not whether from fright and terror or from deep emotion. I do not know whether they saw the Lord, or whether they could not see him. Once I heard Jesus saying to the disciples: "After all these places shall have been converted to the faith by your preaching, and after others shall have driven the faithful away and laid all things waste—then shall come a sad time. Ye do not as yet comprehend me, but when ye will for the last time celebrate with me the Last Supper, then ye will understand me better."

Nicodemus and Joseph of Arimathea had prepared a meal, which was served in the entrance hall of the house of the Last Supper. The hall opened on all sides, and a passage ran from the left through the court-yard, which was planted with trees, to the little house with the kitchen hearth built near the surrounding wall. The covered walks on the right were opened into the courtyard, and here were set the tables for the dis-ciples. They consisted of long planks only. The table for Jesus and the eleven was prepared in the entrance hall. On it stood little mugs and a large dish ornamented with delicate foliage, in which lay a fish along with some small rolls. On the disciples' table were fruits and three-cornered dishes containing honeycombs. Flat bone knives were placed around. Near every dish lay three slices of bread, for there was one dish for every three of the guests.

The sun had set and it was beginning to grow dark when Jesus drew near with the apostles. The blessed Virgin, Nicodemus, and Joseph of Ari-mathea received him at the gate. He went with his blessed Mother into her little abode, while the apostles proceeded to the entrance hall. When the disciples and holy women arrived somewhat later, Jesus joined the eleven in the hall. The table, only one long side of which they occupied, was higher than those in general use. The apostles reclined on cross-seats, but Jesus stood. At his side reclined John, who was more cheerful than the others. He was just like a child in disposition, now quickly trou-bled, and again full of consolation and joy. The lamp over the table was lighted. Nicodemus and Joseph served. I saw the blessed Virgin standing at the entrance of the Supper Room. Jesus blessed the fish, the bread, and the herbs, and passed them around with words of earnest instruction. I saw his words like rays of light issuing from his mouth and entering that of the apostles, into some quickly, into others slowly, according to their greater or less desire, their greater or less hunger after the teaching of Jesus. At the end of the meal, Jesus blessed the cup, drank from it, and then passed it around. This, however, was not a consecration.

The love feast over, all assembled outside the hall under the trees. Jesus addressed to them a long instruction, and ended by giving them his bless-ing. To his blessed Mother, who was standing in front of the holy women, he extended his hand. All were very much affected, and I felt that Magda-lene ardently longed to embrace Jesus's feet. But she restrained her desire, for his demeanor was so grave that he inspired holy fear. When he left them, they wept very much. It was not, however, an exterior weep-ing; it was like the weeping of the soul. I did not see the blessed Virgin shedding tears. I never saw her actually weeping excepting when she lost Jesus, a boy of twelve, on her return journey from the Passover festival, and again when she stood under the cross after his death. *The assembly broke up before midnight.*

Jesus's Ascension into Heaven

5/14 *ON the night before* his wonderful ascension, I saw Jesus in the inner hall of the house of the Last Supper with the blessed Virgin and the eleven. The disciples and the holy women were praying in the side halls. In the supper room the communion table was standing under the lighted lamp, and on it the Passover bread and chalice. The apostles were in their robes of ceremony. The blessed Virgin was opposite Jesus who, as on Maundy Thursday, was consecrating bread and wine.

I saw the blessed sacrament entering the mouths of the apostles in the form of a luminous body, and Jesus's words at the consecration of the wine flowing into the chalice like a stream of red light.

During the last days, Magdalene, Martha, and Mary Cleophas received the blessed sacrament.

Toward morning, matins were solemnly recited as usual under the lamp. Jesus again imparted to Peter jurisdiction over the others, again laid upon him the mantle of which I have spoken, and repeated what he had said on the mountain by the Sea of Tiberias. He gave some instructions also on baptism and the blessing of water. During matins and the instructions I saw seventeen of the most confidential disciples standing in the hall behind the blessed Virgin.

Before leaving the house, Jesus presented the blessed Virgin to the apostles and disciples as their Mother, their Mediatrix, and their Advocate, and she bestowed upon Peter and all the rest her blessing, which they received bowing very low. At that instant I beheld Mary raised upon a throne, a sky-blue mantle around her, a crown upon her head. This was symbolical of her dignity as Queen of Mercy.

At dawn of day Jesus left the house of the Last Supper with the eleven. The blessed Virgin followed them closely; the disciples, at some little distance. They passed through the streets of Jerusalem where all was quiet, the inhabitants still buried in sleep. At each moment the Lord became more earnest, more rapid in speech and action. On the preceding evening he appeared to me much more sympathetic in his words to his followers. I recognized the route that they took as that of the Palm Sunday procession. I saw that Jesus went with them over all the paths trodden by him during his Passion, in order to inspire them by his teachings and admonitions with a lively appreciation of the fulfillment of the Promise. In every place in which some scene of his Passion had been enacted, he paused a moment to instruct them upon the accomplishment of the words of the prophets, upon the Promises, and to explain the symbolical relation of the place to the same. On those sites which the

Jews had laid waste, over which they had thrown heaps of stones, through which they had opened ditches, or which they had rendered impassable in other ways in order to prevent their being venerated, Jesus ordered the disciples in his train to go on ahead and clear away all obstructions, which they quickly did. Then, bowing low as he passed, they allowed him to take the lead again while they followed. Just before the gate that led out to Mount Calvary, they turned aside from the road to a delightful spot shaded by trees. It was one of several places of prayer that lay around Jerusalem. Jesus paused to teach and comfort the little flock. *Meanwhile, day dawned brightly*; their hearts grew lighter, and they even began to think that Jesus would still remain with them.

New crowds of believers arrived, but I saw no women among them. Jesus again took the road that led to Mount Calvary and the Holy Sepulcher. But he did not follow it up to those points; he turned off and went around the city to the Mount of Olives. Some of the places on these roads consecrated to prayer and sanctified by Jesus's teaching, and which had been laid waste or hedged in by the Jews, were now restored by the disciples. The tools for their work they found in the gardens on their way. I remember round shovels that looked like our bake-oven shovels.

Jesus paused awhile with the crowd in an exceedingly cool and lovely spot covered with beautiful long grass. I was surprised to see that it was nowhere trodden down. The multitude that here surrounded Jesus was so great that I could no longer count them. Jesus spoke to them a very long time, like one who is about closing his discourse and coming to a conclusion. His hearers divined that the hour of parting was near, and yet they had no idea that the time still intervening was to be so short. The sun was already high, was already far above the horizon. I know not whether I express it rightly, for in that country it seems to me the sun is not so high as it is here. It always appears to me as if it were nearer to one. I do not see it as here, rising like a small globe. It shines there with far more brilliancy. Its rays are, on the whole, not so fine. They often look like a broad pathway of light. Jesus and his followers tarried here fully an hour. By this time the people in Jerusalem were all on the alert, amazed at the crowds of people they descried around the Mount of Olives. Out of the city, too, crowds were pouring in bands. They consisted of all that had gone out to meet Jesus on Palm Sunday. The narrow roads were soon thronged, though around Jesus and his own, the space was left free.

The Lord went only to Gethsemane, and from the Garden of Olives up to the summit of the mount. He did not set foot upon the path on which he had been arrested. The crowd followed as in a procession, ascending by the different paths that encircled the mount. Many even pressed through the fences and garden hedges. Jesus at each instant shone more brightly and his motions became more rapid. The disciples hastened after him, but it was impossible to overtake him. When he reached the top of the mountain, he was resplendent as a beam of white sunlight. A shining circle, glancing in all the colors of the rainbow, fell from heaven around him. The pressing crowd stood in a wide circle outside, as if blending with it. Jesus himself shone still more brightly than the glory about him. He laid the left hand on his breast and, raising the right, turned slowly around, blessing the whole world. The crowd stood motionless. I saw all receive the benediction. Jesus did not impart it with the flat, open hand, like the rabbis, but like the Christian bishops. With great joy I felt his blessing of the whole world.

And now the rays of light from above united with the glory emanating from Jesus, and I saw him disappearing, dissolving as it were in the light from heaven, vanishing as he rose. I lost sight of his head first. It appeared as if one sun was lost in another, as if one flame entered another, as if a spark floated into a flame. It was as if one were gazing into the *full midday* splendors of the sun, though this light was whiter and clearer. Full day compared with this would be dark. First, I lost sight of Jesus's head, then his whole person, and lastly his feet, radiant with light, disappeared in the celestial glory. I saw innumerable souls from all sides going into that light and vanishing on high with the Lord. I cannot say that I saw him becoming apparently smaller and smaller like something flying up in the air, for he disappeared as it were in a cloud of light.

Out of that cloud something like dew, like a shower of light, fell upon all below, and when they could no longer endure the splendor, they were seized with amazement and terror. The apostles and disciples, who were nearest to Jesus, were blinded by the dazzling glare. They were forced to lower their eyes, while many cast themselves prostrate on their faces. The blessed Virgin was standing close behind them and gazing calmly straight ahead.

After some moments, when the splendor began to diminish, the whole assembly in deep silence—their souls swayed by varying emotions— gazed fixedly up at the brightness, which continued visible for a long time. I saw two figures appear in this light. They looked small at first, but seemed to grow larger and larger as they descended. They were clothed in long white garments, and each held a staff in one hand. They looked like prophets. They addressed the multitude, their voices like trumpets resounding loud and clear. It seemed to me that they could surely be heard in Jerusalem. They made no motion, stood perfectly still, and said: "Ye men of Galilee, why stand ye looking up to heaven? This Jesus who is

Feed My Lambs

The Ascension as Seen from Below

taken up from you into heaven shall so come as you have seen him going into heaven." After these words the figures vanished. The brightness remained for a while longer and then disappeared like daylight retiring before the darkness of night. The disciples were quite out of themselves, for they now comprehended what had happened to them. The Lord had left them and gone to his heavenly Father! Many, stunned by grief and amazement, fell to the earth. When the glare had entirely died away, they arose again, and the others gathered around them. They formed groups, the blessed Virgin stepped forward, and so they stood for some time longer recovering themselves, talking together, and gazing upward. At last, the apostles and disciples went back to the house of the Last Supper, and the blessed Virgin followed. Some were weeping like children that refuse to be comforted, others were lost in thought. The blessed Virgin, Peter, and John were very calm and full of consolation. I saw, however, some among the different groups who remained unmoved, unbelieving, and full of doubts. They withdrew from the rest.

On the top of the Mount of Olives, from which Jesus ascended, there was a level rock. On it he stood addressing the multitude before he blessed them and the cloud of light received him. His footsteps remained impressed on the stone, and on another the mark of one hand of the blessed Virgin. It was past noon before the crowd entirely dispersed.

The apostles and disciples now felt themselves alone. They were at first restless and like people forsaken. But by the soothing presence of the blessed Virgin they were comforted, and putting entire confidence in Jesus's words that she would be to them a mediatrix, a mother, and an advocate, they regained peace of soul.

A certain fear stole over the Jews in Jerusalem. I saw many closing doors and windows, others gathering together in groups. During the last days, they had experienced some peculiar feelings of alarm, which today were greatly intensified.

5/15–23 *On the following days* I saw the apostles always together and the blessed Virgin with them in the house of the Last Supper. At the last repast of Jesus, and ever after, I saw Mary when at prayer and the breaking of bread always opposite Peter, who now took the Lord's place in the prayer circle and at meals. I received at the time the impression that Mary now held a position of high importance among the apostles, and that she was placed over the church.

The apostles kept themselves very much aloof. I saw no one out of the great crowd of Jesus's followers going to them into the house of the Last Supper. They guarded more against persecution from the Jews and gave themselves up to more earnest and well-regulated prayer than did the disciples dispersed in bands throughout the other apartments of the same house. The latter went in and out more freely. I saw many of them also very devoutly traversing the way of the Lord by night.

At the election of Matthias to the apostolate, I saw Peter in the house of the Last Supper. He was clothed in his episcopal mantle and was standing in the center of the circle formed by the apostles. The disciples were gathered in the open side halls. Peter proposed Joseph Barsabbas and Matthias both of whom were standing off among the bands of disciples. There were some among these that wanted to be chosen in Judas's place. The two mentioned had never thought of such a thing, and had no desires on the subject. Next day the lots were cast, Barsabbas and Matthias being excluded from the assembly. When it was found that the lot had fallen on Matthias, someone went into the disciples' apartments and led him to the apostles.

The Holy Day of Pentecost

THE whole interior of the Last Supper room was, on the eve of the feast, ornamented with green bushes in whose branches were placed vases of flowers. Garlands of green were looped from side to side. The screens that cut off the side halls and the vestibule were removed; only the gate of the outer court was closed. Peter in his episcopal robe stood at a table covered with red and white under the lamp in front of the curtained Holy of Holies. On the table lay rolls of writing. Opposite him in the doorway leading from the entrance hall stood the blessed Virgin, her face veiled, and behind her in the entrance hall stood the holy women. The apostles stood in two rows turned toward Peter along either side of the hall, and from the side halls the disciples ranged behind the apostles took part in the hymns and prayers. When Peter broke and distributed the bread that he had previously blessed, first to the blessed Virgin, then to the apostles and disciples who stepped forward to receive it, they kissed his hand, the blessed Virgin included. Besides the holy women, there were in the house of the Last Supper and its dependencies one hundred and twenty of Jesus's followers.

5/24 *After midnight* there arose a wonderful movement in all nature. It communicated itself to all present as they stood in deep recollection, their arms crossed on their breast, near the pillars of the supper room and in the side halls, silently praying. Stillness pervaded the house, and silence reigned throughout the whole enclosure.

Toward morning I saw above the Mount of Olives a glittering white cloud of light coming down from heaven and drawing near to the house. In the distance it appeared to me like a round ball borne along on a soft, warm breeze. But coming nearer, it looked larger and floated over the city like a luminous mass of fog until it stood above Zion and the house of the Last Supper. It seemed to contract and to shine with constantly increasing brightness, until at last with a rushing, roaring noise as of wind, it sank like a thunder cloud floating low in the atmosphere. I saw many Jews, who espied the cloud, hurrying in terror to the temple. I myself experienced a childlike anxiety as to where I should hide if the stroke were to follow, for the whole thing was like a storm that had suddenly gathered, that instead of rising from the earth came down from heaven, that was light instead of dark, that instead of thundering came down with a rushing wind. I felt that rushing motion. It was like a warm breeze full of power to refresh and invigorate.

The luminous cloud descended low over the house, and with the increasing sound, the light became brighter. I saw the house and its surroundings more clearly, while the apostles, the disciples, and the women became more and more silent, more deeply recollected. Afterward there shot from the rushing cloud streams of white light down upon the house and its surroundings. The streams intersected one another in sevenfold rays, and below each intersection resolved into fine threads of light and fiery drops. The point at which the seven streams intersected was surrounded by a rainbow light, in which floated a luminous figure with outstretched wings, or rays of light that looked like wings, attached to the shoulders. In that same instant the whole house and its surroundings were penetrated through and through with light. The five-branched lamp no longer shone. The assembled faithful were ravished in ecstasy. Each involuntarily threw back his head and raised his eyes eagerly on high, while into the mouth of every one there flowed a stream of light like a burning tongue of fire. It looked as if they were breathing, as if they were eagerly drinking in the fire, and as if their ardent desire flamed forth from their mouth to meet the entering flame. The sacred fire was poured forth also upon the disciples and the women present in the antechamber, and thus the resplendent cloud gradually dissolved as if in a rain of light. The flames descended on each in different colors and in different degrees of intensity. After that effusion of heavenly light, a joyous courage pervaded the assembly. All were full of emotion, and as if intoxicated with joy and confidence. They gathered around the blessed Virgin who was, I saw, the only one perfectly calm, the only one that retained a quiet, holy self-possession. The apostles embraced one another and, urged by joyous confidence, exclaimed: "What were we? What are we now?" The holy women too embraced. The disciples in the side halls were similarly affected, and the apostles hastened out to them. A new life full of joy, of confidence, and of courage had been infused into all. Their joy found vent in thanksgiving. They ranged for prayer, gave thanks and praised God with great emotion. The light meanwhile vanished. Peter delivered an instruction to the disciples, and sent several of them out to the inns of the Pentecost guests.

Between the house of the Last Supper and the pool of Bethesda there were several sheds and public lodging houses for the accommodation of guests come up for the feast. They were at this time very numerous, and they too received the grace of the Holy Spirit. An extraordinary movement pervaded all nature. Good people were roused interiorly, while the wicked became timid, uneasy, and still more stiff-necked. Most of these strangers had been encamped here since Passover, because the distance from their homes rendered a journey to and fro between that feast and Pentecost altogether impracticable. They were become, by all that they had seen and heard, quite intimate and kindly disposed toward the disciples, so that the latter, intoxicated with joy, announced to them the Promise of the Holy Spirit as fulfilled. Then too did they become conscious of a change within their own souls and, at the summons of the disciples, they gathered around the pool of Bethesda.

In the house of the Last Supper, Peter imposed hands on five of the apostles who were to help to teach and baptize at the pool of Bethesda. They were James the Less, Bartholomew, Matthew, Thomas, and Judas Thaddeus. The last-named had a vision during his ordination. It seemed to him that he was clasping to his breast the body of the Lord.

Before departing for the pool of Bethesda to consecrate the water and administer baptism, they received on their knees the benediction of the blessed Virgin. Before Jesus's ascension, this ceremony was performed standing. On the following days I saw this blessing given whenever the apostles left the house, and also on their return. The blessed Virgin wore on such occasions, and generally when she appeared among the apostles in her post of dignity, a large white mantle, a creamy white veil, and a scarf of sky-blue stuff that hung from her head down both sides to the ground. It was ornamented with embroidery, and was held firmly on the head by a white silken crown.

Baptism at the pool of Bethesda had been arranged by Jesus himself for this day's feast, and the disciples had, in consequence, made all kinds of preparations at the pool, as well as in the old synagogue that they had appropriated for their own use. The walls of the synagogue were hung with tapestry, and from the building down to the pool a covered tent-way was erected.

The apostles and disciples went in solemn procession, two by two, from the house of the Last Supper to the pool. Some of the disciples carried a leathern bottle of holy water and an asperges. The five apostles upon whom Peter had imposed hands separated, each taking one of the five entrances to the pool, and addressed the people with great enthusiasm. Peter stepped upon the teacher's chair that had been prepared for him in the third circle of the pool, counting from the outside one. This terrace was the broadest. The hearers filled all the terraces of the pool. When the apostles spoke, the multitude hearkened in amazement, for everyone listened to what sounded to him his own language. It was owing to this astonishment of the people that Peter lifted up his voice, as is recorded in the Acts of the apostles.

As many presented themselves for baptism, Peter, assisted by John and James the Less, solemnly blessed the water. The holy water, which they had brought in a leathern bottle from the house of the Last Supper, Peter sprinkled in fine streams far over the pool with an asperges. The preparations for baptism and the baptism itself occupied the whole day.

The neophytes approached Peter's chair in bands and by turns, the other apostles preaching and baptizing at the entrances. The blessed Virgin and the holy women were busy in the synagogue near the pool, distributing the white garments to the neophytes. The sleeves of these garments were bound over the hands with black bands, which were taken off after baptism and laid together in a pile. The neophytes leaned upon a railing. The water was scooped up in a basin and then with the hand poured three times over the head. It flowed again through a channel into the pool below. One basin held enough water for about ten couples. Every two baptized gave place to two neophytes upon whom they laid their hands as sponsors. Those baptized here today were they that had received John's baptism only. The holy women too were baptized. The people added to the community today amounted to three thousand. That evening the apostles and disciples returned to the house of the Last Supper, where they took a repast and distributed blessed bread. Then came the evening prayer.

The Jews offered today in the temple little baskets containing two small loaves made of this year's grain. The baskets were deposited one upon another, until they formed high heaps, and they were afterward distributed to the poor. Once I saw that the high priest held a bunch of ears, thick like maize. Something like roots also was offered, and some kind of fruit unknown to me. The strangers under the sheds had asses laden with them, and the people made purchases of them. The bread was of their own baking. The apostles offered only the two loaves through Peter.

5/25–30 On the following days also, preaching and baptizing went on at the pool. Before the apostles and disciples went down for these duties, they received the blessing of the blessed Virgin.

The Church at the Pool of Bethesda

THE pool of Bethesda lay in a ravine of the valley that separated Mount Zion from the temple and the rest of that quarter of the city, and which declined eastward into the valley of Jehosaphat. It seemed to have been constructed in such a way as to cut off the view of the temple on the west, for on one side one could not see all around, as could be done on the others. The way to it was indeed broad enough, but the walls were partly overturned and the road was full of grass and sedge. Just at that point it ran down into a ravine that became greener in proportion to its depth. From the pool could be seen off to the southwest an angle of the Holy of Holies. The sheep pool lay to the north of the temple near the cattle market, and was entirely enclosed by a wall. From the house of the Last Supper, which stood on the eastern height of Mount Zion, the way led to the pool of Bethesda first to the east around the height of Zion, then wound in a half-circle to the north, then turned to the west, and lastly eastward again down into a curve. The whole of this quarter of Zion as far as the pool and across down into the valley of Jehosaphat, presented an appearance of desolation. In the dilapidated buildings were formed dwellings for the poor, on the slopes grew groves of juniper trees, and the hollows were covered with high grass and reeds. The Jews shunned this locality, so the new converts now began to settle in it.

The pool of Bethesda was oval in form and surrounded by five terraces, like an amphitheater. Five flights of steps led down to the pool from these terraces to the little trough-like skiffs in which the sick who were seeking a cure were laid when waiting to be sprinkled by the bubbling waters. There was also in the pool a copper pump, which arose to nearly the height of a man above the surface of the water and was about as large around as a churn. A little wooden bridge with a railing led to it. I saw by the bridge a tube and piston, which were connected with the pump. When the piston was forced down, a valve was opened and a stream of water squirted out of the pump. By changes made in the opening, the stream could be increased or diminished and made to flow in different directions. The top of the pump could be closed also, and from side jets the streams could be made to spurt all around, like water from a watering pot. I often saw the sick in the skiffs rowing up to the pump to receive the streams over them. The entrance to the pool was usually closed. It was opened for the sick only. This pump was out of use, and on the Feast of

Pentecost was not yet repaired, but a few days later I saw it restored. The terrace walls contained little vaulted halls in which were stone benches hollowed out in the form of a trough. They were for the accommodation of the sick. They could from all sides look down upon the pool, to see whether the waters were being stirred or not. The lowest terrace, the one nearest the pool, was provided with little parapets, or bars. The bottom of the pool was covered with shining white sand, through which three springs bubbled up and sometimes jetted above the surface of the water. The blood of the animals offered in sacrifice flowed through pipes under the altar in the temple down into the pool. With its surroundings and the old buildings in its vicinity, the pool covered a very large area. Before reaching it, one had to pass a wall through which there were only three openings. To the east of the pool, the valley made a steep descent, but westward, back of the pool, it was less deep and was spanned by a little bridge. The north side too was steep and overgrown, and on the northeast was a road conducting to the temple. But it was now gone to ruin and altogether impracticable. Little footpaths, however, led into the city, so that one did not have to go by the public gates. Jesus had often made use of these paths.

The whole pool had hitherto been out of use, for it as well as its surroundings had been allowed to fall to decay. Like many old sanctuaries of our own day, it was quite neglected. Only some poor people with lively faith still held it in veneration and visited it. After the healing of the paralytic by Jesus, the pool was again more frequented, though all the more hateful to the Pharisees. The outer walls were in some places quite in ruins, and many parts of the terraces were in a dilapidated condition. But now all was repaired. The fallen walls were partly replaced by movable screens, and from the pool to the synagogue was raised a covered tentway.

The old synagogue, which was now erected into a church, was less hemmed in by buildings than the house of the Last Supper, whose court on one side adjoined a row of houses. I saw the apostles and disciples, after the Feast of Pentecost, working continually at the interior arrangements of the church. Peter, John, Andrew, and James the Less took turns in preaching at three different places around the pool and on the third terrace, upon which was Peter's chair of instruction. A great many of the faithful were always in attendance, and I often saw them prostrate on the ground in ardent prayer. Words cannot say what activity reigned throughout the whole community at all times. Weaving, plaiting, and every kind of work for the new church and for the poor were carried on.

The church was a large, long, quadrangular edifice with real windows high up in the walls. By means of steps in the wall, one could mount up on the outside to the flat roof, which was surrounded by a gallery. On it were three little cupolas that could be opened like draught holes. The inside, on the two lengths and one of the ends, was furnished with stone benches for the congregation, and the building was in all respects turned into a church. At one end was the altar, at such a distance from the wall that sufficient space was left behind for a sacristy, which was formed by wickerwork screens that reached from the altar to the side walls. These screens were covered in front with fine white stuff, on the other side with coarser. The altar was portable. It consisted of a long, four-cornered piece of wood covered, and resting on three steps. On either side, however, there was only a single step, which could be opened to allow carpets to be laid in, and the back of the altar likewise opened to receive the vestments. On it was a bell-shaped tabernacle with a fine white cover closed in front by two little metallic shields. There was a knob on top, by which it could be lifted. On either side of the tabernacle were branched lamps with burning wicks. The whole altar was enclosed by a white curtain with colored stripes, which was supported by a canopy. It hung down only a little below the top of the altar. The canopy itself formed a niche and depended by five straps from the hand of a figure embroidered by the holy women. It represented an old man in the robes of a high priest, a triangular halo around the head. It stood in a bowed posture, as if looking down through an opening in the cover, one hand outstretched as if giving a blessing, the other grasping the five straps of the canopy. The curtain was in one piece at the back, but in front it could be drawn to either side or closed with metal clasps.

From the raised altar down to the pulpit was a space set aside apart for the choir ceremonies of the apostles and disciples. After the holy Resurrection I saw them assembled every day in the Last Supper room for prayer in choir. The apostles stood along either side of the hall facing the Holy of Holies, while the disciples occupied the vestibule thrown open for the occasion. They sang and prayed in choirs. I saw Nicodemus, Joseph of Arimathea, and Obed present also. The blessed Virgin usually stood under the middle entrance of the vestibule, her face turned toward the Holy of Holies. She wore the long white mantle and was veiled. Jesus had himself arranged the choral service, and about the time of the eating of the fish at Tiberias, or perhaps during the meal itself, explained to the apostles the mysterious signification of this religious ceremony. He had repeated the same on the occasion of Thomas's touching his sacred wounds and giving testimony of his faith. Once also I saw that Jesus appeared to them while they were chanting in choir before daybreak.

They daily assembled twice, in the evening till after dark, and before dawn in the morning. Below the pulpit the congregation was cut off from the choir by a grating, through many places of which the blessed sacrament could be reached to them. It was almost like the grating seen in cloisters. On either side of the pulpit there were small doors by which the apostles and disciples could enter the choir. The congregation was arranged in a certain order, the women separate from the men.

I saw the apostles and disciples going in procession with the blessed sacrament from the house of the Last Supper to the new church. Before setting out, Peter, standing in the entrance to the courtyard and surrounded by about twenty of the disciples, delivered a public discourse before many people. He spoke in fiery words. Many Jews ran to hear, and tried to interrupt him by advancing objections, but their efforts were fruitless. The discourse over, the procession wound down to the new church near the pool, Peter bearing in his hands the chalice containing the blessed sacrament. The chalice was covered with a white linen, something like a bag, which was suspended from his neck. The blessed Virgin walked after the apostles with the other women and the disciples. A part of the way was hung with screens of matting, and in the vicinity of the church the road was even covered in with awnings. The blessed sacrament was placed in the new tabernacle on the altar. The tray full of blessed bread had also been brought.

The floor of the church, like that of the house of the Last Supper in these latter days, was covered with colored carpets. The faithful entered barefoot. The blessed sacrament was deposited in a vessel whose cover could be turned to one side. It lay in morsels on a plate that covered the bottom of the vessel and which could be raised by means of a handle, the more conveniently to get at them.

Peter Celebrates the First Holy Mass in the Last Supper Room

5/31 ON *the eighth day after Pentecost,* I saw the apostles busily engaged the whole night in the house of the Last Supper, praying, etc. At *daybreak* they went with many of the disciples into the temple, to which the blessed Virgin and the holy women had preceded them. There appeared to be a feast going on, for in front of the entrance a triumphal arch had been erected upon which stood a figure holding a conqueror's sword. Beneath this arch Peter addressed a great crowd of people in powerful language. He told them openly that no punishment, neither scourging nor crucifixion, should deter them from publicly proclaiming Jesus

Christ. He then entered the temple and preached from the teacher's chair that Jesus had so often occupied. Once I heard all the apostles and disciples interrupting Peter's discourse with a loud "Yes," as if in confirmation of his words. Afterward, when they were engaged in prayer, I saw a cloud of light hovering over the temple, and such rays streaming down upon them that the tiny flames of the lamps looked quite dim and red compared with them.

Toward eight o'clock that morning they left the temple. In the court of the pagans they formed in a long procession, two by two, first the apostles, after them the disciples, then the baptized and the newly converted. They proceeded across the cattle market to the sheep gate, out into the valley of Jehosaphat, and thence up Zion to the house of the Last Supper. The blessed Virgin and the other women had left the temple some time previously, in order to kneel alone before the blessed sacrament and pray. Magdalene prayed in the entrance hall sometimes standing, sometimes kneeling, or again prostrate on the ground, her arms outstretched. The other women had retired into their cells adjoining the church of Bethsaida. There they dwelt two together, occupying their time in washing and preparing the baptismal garments for the neophytes, and with the arrangement of such things for distribution.

When the procession reached the court of the Last Supper house, the new converts were ranged in order by the apostles outside the entrance hall. Peter and John went into the house and escorted the blessed Virgin to the door of the entrance hall. She was clothed in robes of ceremony. She wore the long white mantle with the embroidered facing down the sides, and over her veil the narrow scarf that hung down on either side and was kept in place by a wreath. Peter addressed the new converts and presented them to the blessed Virgin as to their common mother. He led them forward in bands of about twenty, one after another, and they received the benediction of the blessed Virgin.

After that I saw solemn service celebrated in the Last Supper room, into which the side halls and entrance hall were thrown open. In the sanctuary over the altar hung a festal wreath of green leaves and flowers. On either side of the chalice, that used at the Last Supper, were lighted lamps. The chalice was raised on a stand of some kind, and concealed under a little white cover. There was also on the altar a smaller chalice and some bread, both covered, and behind them a plate upon which stood two vessels, one for water, the other for wine. The plate was put aside; then the water vessel was placed at one end of the altar, the wine vessel at the other.

Peter, vested in his episcopal mantle, celebrated holy mass. John and

James the Less served him. I saw all the ceremonies performed just as Jesus had performed them at the institution of the holy eucharist: the offertory, the pouring of wine into the chalice, the washing of the fingers, and the consecration. Wine and water were poured at different sides of the altar, on one end of which were lying the rolls of scripture. They were written in two columns and, by means of pegs placed higher or lower on the desk that supported them, they could be rolled or unrolled. When one leaf was read, it was thrown over the desk. There were many leaves lying one over another. After Peter had communicated, he handed his two assistants the sacrament, the bread and the chalice. Then John handed the sacrament first to the blessed Virgin, then to the apostles and the six disciples, who afterward received priestly ordination, and to many others. The communicants were kneeling, before them a narrow linen cloth, which two held on either side. I did not see the faithful partake of the chalice.

The six disciples who now received ordination were thereby advanced to a rank above the disciples, though below that of the apostles. Mary brought the vestments for them and laid them on the altar. The disciples ordained were Zacchaeus, Nathaniel, Joseph Barsabbas, Barnabas, John Mark, and Eliud, a son of the aged Simeon. They knelt, two by two, before Peter, who addressed them and read prayers from a little roll. John and James held lights in one hand and laid the other on their shoulders, while Peter imposed his on their head. Peter cut some hair from their head and placed it on the altar in the little plate; then he anointed their head and fingers from a box that John was holding. The vestments were next put on, the stole being crossed first under the arm and then in front over the breast. I saw that the ceremonies, though more solemn, were shorter than at the present day. At the close of the solemnity, Peter blessed the faithful with the large chalice of the Last Supper in which reposed the blessed sacrament.

Mary and the other women went after that to the church of the pool of Bethesda. The apostles, disciples, and the neophytes went thither also in procession with singing. Mary prayed there kneeling before the altar in the choir. Peter gave an instruction from the pulpit in reference to the order to be observed in the new community. No one, he said, was to have more than the others. All must share what they had and provide for the poor newcomers. His discourse, moreover, embodied thanks for the Savior's graces, and blessings upon the community.

Baptism was next administered, and several of the apostles were engaged in it. Two laid their hands upon the neophytes who, holding the railing of the little bridge that led to the pump, bowed their head to the stream issuing from it. Peter, who had put on his girdle over his white garment, turned the stream three times with his hand over the head of the neophyte, pronouncing the words at the same moment. I often saw a radiant cloud dissolving over the baptized, or a ray of light falling upon them. I saw that they were marvelously strengthened and, as it were, transfigured, transformed. It was most touching to see people from far-off countries leaving all that belonged to them, and coming hither to form one with the community of Jesus. At the edge of the pool burned a light on a pole, just such a one as those used by the guards at the Holy Sepulcher.

That evening in the entrance hall of the house of the Last Supper a meal was spread during which the blessed Virgin sat at table with the apostles, Joseph of Arimathea, Nicodemus, and Lazarus.

First General Communion of the New Converts • Choice of the Seven Deacons

6/1 ALL the baptized since Pentecost were instructed in the Bethsaida church upon the most blessed sacrament and prepared for its reception by six of the apostles robed in long white garments. They received it at the Holy Mass celebrated by Peter in the Bethsaida church, assisted by two of the apostles. Peter wore over his long, white robe and broad girdle with its flowing ends, a mantle that was taken out from the chest formed in the back of the altar. It was red and shining gold. It was like a large cape, deep in the back and pointed in front; and it fell so low over the shoulders that only the girdle could be seen at the side. It was fastened on the breast with three little shields. On the middle one just in front of the breast was the representation of a figure holding a loaf in one hand. The lowest shield, that nearest the points, or the ends of the mantle, bore on it a cross. On either shoulder was a figure formed of precious stones.

The altar was covered first with a red and over that a white transparent cloth, on which was laid another little white linen cloth like a corporal. On an oval plate lay a little pile of white bread sliced very thin and furrowed with lines for breaking. Beside it stood a white bowl with a foot like a low chalice, or ciborium, in which after being consecrated by Peter the bread broken into morsels was placed for distribution among the faithful. Besides all this, the chalice used at the Last Supper was standing full of wine on the altar. When, during holy mass, Peter uttered the words of consecration over the bread and wine, I saw the bread become luminous, while above the altar, as if issuing from a cloud, appeared a resplendent hand. It accompanied the movements of Peter's hand as he blessed the bread and wine, and did not disappear till all dispersed after receiving communion.

The apostles and disciples were the first to receive the blessed sacrament from Peter after his own communion. When the bowl, or ciborium, was emptied, Peter replenished it from the plate on the altar, and then proceeded with the distribution of the sacred species. The chalice also was handed by him to the apostles and to all the others. The communicants were so numerous that the church could not contain them, and many had to stand outside. The first to receive holy communion left the church in order to allow others to enter. The communicants did not kneel, but while receiving stood reverently bowed.

Before choosing the seven deacons, I saw the apostles gathered around Peter in the Last Supper room, where they assisted him in a solemn ceremony. They accompanied him to the Holy of Holies, where John laid upon him the mantle, another placed the mitre on his head, and another put the crosier into his hand. After all had received communion from Peter, robed in his sacred vestments and surrounded by the apostles, he addressed in the entrance hall a large crowd of disciples and new converts. He said among other things that it was not becoming for the Word of God to be neglected for the care of clothing and nourishment; consequently Lazarus, Nicodemus, and Joseph of Arimathea could not with propriety any longer oversee the temporal interests of the community as they had hitherto done, for they now had become priests. Then he added some words relative to the order observed in the distribution of alms, of household affairs, of widows and orphans. Stephen, a slender, handsome youth, stepped forward and offered himself for the services needed. Among others that did the same, I recognized Parmenas, who was one of the elder disciples. There were among them some Moors, still very young, who had not yet received the Holy Spirit. Peter laid his hands upon them and the stole crossed under their arm. While he did so a light was infused upon those that had not yet received the Holy Spirit. After that the treasures and goods of the community were delivered over to the seven deacons, and for their accommodation was assigned Joseph of Arimathea's house, which was not far from that of John Mark. John Mark helped them. The money was carried on asses, and consisted of bags filled with different kinds of coins. Some were like little stalks twisted into screws, others like stamped plate strung together on a little chain, and others again were in small, oval leaves. Most of the movables consisted of large packs of different stuffs, coverlets, clothing, also numbers of vessels and various kinds of furniture suitable for plain housekeeping.

On the day following the giving over of Joseph of Arimathea's house to the deacons, I saw the apostles dispersing into Judea.

Peter wrought more miracles than all the others. He drove out devils, raised the dead—yes, I even saw an angel going before him to the people and telling them that they should do penance and ask Peter for help.

6/2 I saw the healing of the lame man. It was about three hours after noon when Peter and John went up to the temple with several of the disciples. Mary and some of the holy women went too. A lame man had been brought on a litter and laid at the door of the temple. Peter and John, on their arrival, exchanged some words with him. Then I saw Peter standing under an awning in the open square on the south side of the temple, his back turned to that part of the edifice in which was the altar of sacrifice, and addressing the people in a fiery speech. During his instruction I saw the door of egress beset by soldiers and priests conferring together. And now I saw Peter and John, as they turned again toward the temple, accosted by the lame man and petitioned for alms. He was lying outside the door, a perfect cripple, leaning on the left elbow, while vainly striving to raise something with the crutch in his right hand. Peter said to him: "Look up!" and when the man obeyed, he continued: "I have no silver nor gold, but what I have, I give to thee! In the name of Jesus Christ of Nazareth, arise and walk!" Peter raised him by the right hand, while John grasped him under the shoulder. The man, full of joy and vigor, stood upon his feet, and I saw him leaping about cured, and running with shouts of triumph through the halls of the temple.

Twelve Jewish priests who were there seated on their chairs looked, with outstretched necks, in the direction of the tumult, and as the crowd around the cured man increased at every moment, they left their seats and withdrew. Peter and John went into the forecourt, and I saw the former mounting the teacher's chair from which Jesus had taught as a boy of twelve. The cured man was standing before him encompassed by a multitude of people, some from the city, others strangers from a distance. Peter preached long and in words full of inspiration. It was already dark when I saw him, along with John and the cured man, seized by the temple soldiers and thrown into a prison near the judgment hall in which he had denied the Lord. Next day all three were taken by the soldiers, and with much ill usage, up the same flight of steps upon which Jesus had stood, and there tried by Caiaphas and the other priests. Peter spoke with great warmth, after which they were set free.

The rest of the apostles had passed the night in the house of the Last Supper in continual prayer for the prisoners. When Peter and John returned and told them all that had taken place, their joy burst out into a loud act of thanksgiving, and the whole house shook, as if the Lord wanted to remind them thereby that he was still among them and had heard their prayer. Upon that, James the Less said that Jesus, when he appeared to him alone on the mountain in Galilee, had told him that after Peter and John, on going up to the temple, would be imprisoned and then set free, they should keep themselves somewhat retired for awhile.

On this news, I saw the apostles shutting up everything, and Peter, with the blessed sacrament suspended round his neck in a bag, going with the others to Bethany. They made the journey in three bands. The Mother of God and other women went also. While in Bethany, the apostles preached enthusiastically at the disciples' inn, at Simon's, and at Lazarus's. When they again returned to Jerusalem, they were more enthusiastic, more determined than ever. Peter, when teaching in the house of the Last Supper and in the church at the pool of Bethesda, declared that now was the time to discover who had preserved the Spirit sent by Jesus, now was the time to labor, to suffer persecution, and to give up all things. Whoever did not feel himself strong enough for this should depart. I saw that about a hundred of those that had most recently joined the community withdrew from the great crowd in the Bethsaida church.

When Peter, accompanied by John and seven other apostles, went again to teach in the temple, he found numbers of sick lying on litters under tents in the valley of Jehosaphat. Many others were lying around the temple in the court of the pagans and even up as far as the steps. I saw Peter performing most of the cures. The others did indeed effect some, but they helped Peter more than they cured. Peter cured those only that believed and were desirous of joining the community. In those places in which the sick lay in two rows opposite each other, I saw cured, Peter willing it, those upon whom his shadow fell, while he was busied with the opposite row.

The Life of Mary
After Christ's Ascension

The Blessed Virgin Goes with
John to the Neighborhood of Ephesus

ABOUT one year after the crucifixion of our Lord, Stephen was stoned, though no further persecution of the apostles took place at that time. The rising settlement of new converts around Jerusalem, however, was dissolved, the Christians dispersed, and some were murdered. A few years later, a new storm arose against them. Then it was that the blessed Virgin, who until that time had dwelt in the small house near the Cenacle and in Bethany, allowed herself to be conducted by John to the region of Ephesus, where the Christians had already made settlements. This happened a short time after the imprisonment of Lazarus and his sisters by the Jews and their setting out over the sea. John returned again to Jerusalem, where the other apostles still were. James the Greater was one of the first of the apostles who, after the division of the different countries had been made, left Jerusalem and started for Spain. I saw him on his departure in Bethlehem, where he concealed himself in the crib cave, and then with his companions secretly wandering through the country, for there were spies in search of them with orders to prevent their leaving Palestine. But James had friends in Joppa, and he succeeded in embarking. He sailed first to Ephesus in order to visit Mary, and thence to Spain. Shortly before his death, he visited Mary and John a second time in their home at Ephesus. Here Mary told him that his death would soon take place in Jerusalem. She encouraged and consoled him. James took leave of her and his brother John, and started for Jerusalem. It was at this period that he was brought into contact with Hermogenes and his pupil, both of whom he converted by his miracles. James was several times apprehended and taken before the synagogue. I saw that shortly before Easter, while he was preaching on a hill in an open square of Jerusalem, he was arrested. It must have been about this time, for I saw the customary encampments around the city. James was not imprisoned long. He was sentenced to death in the same place of trial as Jesus. The whole place, however, had undergone a change. Those sites upon which Jesus had trodden were no longer in existence, and I have always thought that none other ever after trod the same. I saw James led out toward Mount Calvary. He continued his preaching all along the way, and thereby made many converts. When they bound his hands, he remarked: "Ye can bind my hands, but ye cannot bind the blessing, ye cannot bind my tongue!" A lame man was sitting by the roadside. He called to James, begging him to extend his hand and help him. James responded: "Come thou to me, and reach out thine hand to me!" The lame man arose, seized the fettered hands of the apostle, and was cured. I saw also the man that had denounced him. He was named Josias. His heart smote him. He hurried to the apostle and begged forgiveness. He declared himself for Christ and was likewise put to death. James asked him whether he desired baptism, and when Josias answered yes, he embraced and kissed him, saying: "Thou wilt be baptized in thy blood!" I saw a woman running with her blind child to James on the place of execution, and imploring its restoration to sight.

James was at first stationed near Josias on an elevated place, and the sentence proclaimed aloud. Then he was laid on a large stone, his hands bound to it, his eyes blindfolded, and his head struck off. This took place in the twelfth year after Jesus's death, or between 46 and 47 after the birth of Christ. I did not see James present at the death of the blessed Virgin in Ephesus. There was another in his place, a relative of the holy family, and one of the first among the seventy-two disciples. Mary died in the year 48 after the birth of Christ, thirteen years and two months after Christ's ascension. This was shown me in numbers, not in writing. First, I saw IV, and then VIII, which denoted the year 48; lastly, I saw XIII, and two full months.

The blessed Virgin's dwelling was not in Ephesus itself, but from three to four hours distant. It stood on a height upon which several Christians from Judea, among them some of the holy women related to her, had taken up their abode. Between this height and Ephesus glided, with many a crooked curve, a little river. The height sloped obliquely toward Ephesus. From the southeast one beheld the city as if lying just before him, at the foot of a mountain, but on nearer approach, he found the latter stretching still further away. From Ephesus, before which I saw great avenues with yellow fruit strewing the ground, narrow footpaths led up to this wild, overgrown height, upon which, to the circumference of about an hour, stretched a very solitary but fertile plain covered with smooth-trunked, wide-spreading trees, and containing clean rocky caves. These latter had, by means of light woodwork, been converted into hermitages by the early Christian settlers who had fled thither for refuge. These abodes, along with others that stood alone scattered here and there over the whole country, gave the region the appearance of a little village. From the top of this elevated plain, which was nearer to the sea than Ephesus, one could see both the city itself and the sea with its numerous islands.

Not very far from the Christian settlement rose a castle whose occupant appeared to be a deposed king. John often visited him and finally converted him. At a later period, this place became a bishopric. Among the Christians settled here, I saw women, children, and some men. Not all of these people had contact with the blessed Virgin. Only some holy women came now and then for a visit, or to render her some assistance, for they saw to her needs. The locality was very retired and seldom visited by anyone, for no highway ran through it. The people of Ephesus did not trouble themselves about the little colony, and so they lived as if forgotten. The soil was fruitful, and the settlers owned some gardens and orchards. The only animals I saw in this place were wild goats.

Before John brought the blessed Virgin to this settlement, he had built for her a dwelling of stone very similar to her own at Nazareth. It stood among trees, and was divided into two apartments by the fireplace in the center. The fire was on the earth opposite the entrance, in a kind of furnace formed by the wall, which rose up on either side like steps to the roof of the house. In it was cut the flue, from which the smoke escaped through a tube that protruded above the flat roof.

The front room of the house was separated from the back by wicker screens placed on either side of the fireplace. Similar screens rested against the walls, right and left, the whole length of the house. They were used to form little apartments when needed, and could be easily put aside when the room was to be used as one. Mary's maidservant used one of them as a sleeping apartment, and the others were occupied by the holy women of the settlement when they happened to come on a visit of some length.

To the right and left on either side of the fireplace, light doors opened through the wicker partition into the two back rooms, whose end walls were rounded and very pleasing to the eye, covered as they were with neatly wrought woodwork. The roof was rounded on the sides, and the beams above it were bound with wainscoting and twisted work, and ornamented with some simple imitation of foliage. In the most remote space of the rounded end Mary had her oratory, before which hung a curtain. Here in a niche in the wall was a kind of closet which, like a certain kind of tabernacle, could be made to open and close by revolving. In it was a crucifix about the length of one's arm. The arms were set into the trunk in an obliquely raised direction like that of Christ. This most simply carved crucifix was, I think, made by the blessed Virgin herself and John. It was constructed of three different kinds of wood: the whitish trunk was cypress wood, one arm of a brownish color was cedar, the other, which was yellowish, was made from wood of the palm tree. The top piece that supported the inscription was of polished yellow olive wood. The foot of the crucifix was set firmly in a stone like Christ's in the rock of Golgotha. At its foot lay a strip of parchment on which were inscribed some words of the Savior. The figure representing the Lord was formed simply of dark-colored lines cut into the cross. On either side of the crucifix stood a pot of flowers. I saw also lying near the cross a little linen, of which I had the intuitive knowledge that it was the one with which the blessed Virgin, after the taking down of the sacred body from the cross, had cleansed the wounds from blood; for as soon as I saw the little cloth, I had a vision of that exercise of her most sacred mother-love, in which she held the little linen in the same way as does the priest at the holy Mass when he is purifying the chalice. Mary had a similar crucifix, though only half as large, in the alcove in which she slept.

On the right of the oratory and against the rounded wall, was the alcove of the blessed Virgin. It was formed of two lightly woven screens of sapwood in its natural color. These stood at the head and the foot of the couch respectively; in front hung two curtains of tapestry that could be drawn and looped to either side. The couch was placed along the wall, which too was hung with tapestry. It was the length and breadth of a small bed, and consisted of a wooden frame about a foot and a half high. Over it a tester was stretched and fastened on the knobs of the four corners. The sides of the frame also were covered with tapestry, which hung down to the floor and was fringed with tassels. A round roll served as a pillow. The cover was of brownish checkered material. The ceiling of this little sleeping apartment was the loftiest in the house. It too was formed of wickerwork and, from the four corners to the center, ran up into a concave dome from which was suspended a branched lamp.

Here, on the last days before her death, I saw the blessed Virgin lying entirely enveloped in a white sleeping sheet; even her arms were wound up in it. The veil over her head was thrown up in crossfolds, but when conversing with men, she lowered it. Even her hands were uncovered only when she was alone. During those last days, I did not see her taking anything excepting the juice of a grapelike fruit with yellow berries, which the maid pressed out for her into a little cup.

By the wall to the left of the oratory and directly opposite the alcove, a recess was formed by means of wicker screens in which clothes and other things were kept. Besides some veils and girdles and the upper garment that Mary always wore when making the holy Way of the Cross, there hung in that recess two long robes, one white, the other sky-blue. The latter was a very delicate blue, and there was likewise a mantle of the same color. This was the robe in which Mary was married to Joseph.

I saw too that Mary kept near her many of the garments of her divine Son, among them his woven tunic.

From that recess to the alcove extended a curtain by which the oratory could be concealed. When at work, Mary used to sit before this curtain and just between the recess and the alcove.

In this most silent and solitary little dwelling,† from which the abodes of the other settlers were distant about a quarter of an hour, lived the blessed Virgin alone with her maid, who procured for her the little that she needed for her support. There was no man in the house, and only at times was Mary visited by John or some other traveling apostle and disciple. Once I saw John entering the house. He was thin and looked older. He wore a long white garment girdled in folds, but which was now tucked up. He laid it aside on entering, and taking out another from under his mantle, put it on instead. There was an inscription in letters on this second one. He laid a maniple on his arm. The blessed Virgin was in a little private room from which the maid conducted her to John. She was enveloped in a white robe and looked very weak. Her face was, as it were, transparent and white as snow. She appeared to be soaring upward on the wings of her ardent desires. Her whole life after her Son's ascension into heaven was stamped by an ever-increasing longing to be freed from earth. She retired with John to her oratory, pulled a band, or strap, upon which the tabernacle in the niche revolved and disclosed the crucifix of the length of one's arm standing between two vases of natural flowers. After

---

† In 1891, after reading Anne Catherine's description of Mary's home at Ephesus, two Lazarite priests from Smyrna set off to search for it. After five days' search in the mountainous area south of Ephesus they were guided by some local people to a ruined building located on the summit of an isolated hill. The site, and also the plan of the house, exactly fit Anne Catherine's description. The priests learned that the place had been venerated down through the ages as Panaya Kapulu ("The House of the Holy Virgin"). Local villagers made annual pilgrimages there each year on August 15, the Festival of the Assumption of the Blessed Virgin Mary. Subsequent archeological investigations have confirmed the authenticity of Panaya Kapulu. The foundations of the original house date back to the first century. In the seventh century the building appears to have been enlarged and converted into a chapel in which Mary's Oratory became the main altar. At that time the entry was added and the fireplace wall removed. In 1898 the original hearthstones were discovered under the existing floor, still containing some ashes, petrified with age. In 1951 the Turkish government built a road up to the Holy Hill and the Society of Panaya, founded by the Archbishop of Smyrna, completely restored the ruins in accordance with the description in Anne Catherine's visions. In 1954 the Little Brothers of Jesus accepted the post of serving at Panaya Kapulu, now known as the Shrine of Our Lady of the Assumption.

Mary and John had prayed long on their knees before the crucifix, the latter arose and took from a metal box a roll of fine woollen stuff. Opening this, he took out a small piece of white bread, in shape four-cornered, that was carefully folded in white linen cloths. It was the most blessed sacrament, which with some words he gave to Mary. He presented to her no cup.

Mary's "Holy Way of the Cross" near Ephesus • She Visits Jerusalem

IN the neighborhood of her dwelling, the blessed Virgin had herself erected the stations of the Holy Way of the Cross. I saw her at first going alone and measuring off all the special points of the bitter Passion according to the number of steps which, after the death of her Son, she had so often counted. At the end of each definite number, she raised a memorial stone in remembrance of the special suffering there endured by her divine Son. I saw her with a sharp instrument, a stylus, recording what there had taken place and how many steps it was to it. If a tree happened to be standing on that particular spot, she marked it as one of the stations, of which there were twelve. The way led to a grove, and there was the Holy Sepulcher represented by a cave in the side of a hill. After all the stations were definitively marked, the blessed Virgin made the Holy Way with her maid in silent meditation. When they reached a station, they sat down, meditated upon the mystery and its signification, and prayed. By degrees, the whole route was improved and more beautifully arranged. John gave orders for regular monuments to be set up. I saw also the cave representing the sepulcher being cleared out and made more suitable for prayer. The memorial stones lay in hollows of greater or less depth, which were covered with grass and flowers and surrounded by a hedge. They were of polished white marble. The thickness of the underlying surface could not be seen, on account of the grass. The faithful, when performing this devotion, carried a cross about a foot in length with a support which they placed in the little hollow on the upper surface of the stone while they were meditating, either kneeling or prostrate on their face. The path that ran in a hollow around the stone was wide enough for two persons to walk side by side. There were twelve such stones. When the devotion was ended, each was covered with a mat. The sides and base of all bore similar inscriptions in Hebrew characters, but the hollow places in which they rested differed, some being larger, others smaller. The first station, or that of the Mount of Olives, was in a little valley. There was a small cave in it, in which several could kneel together. The Mount Golgotha station was the only one not in a hollow. It was on a hill.

For that of the Holy Sepulcher, one had to cross another hill on whose opposite side stood the memorial stone in a hollow. Thence one descended to the foot of the hill and into the tomb itself, in which later on Mary's remains rested. I think this tomb is still in existence under the surface of the earth, and that it will come to light someday.

Whenever I saw Mary making the Holy Way of the Cross, she wore an overgarment that fell in folds down the back as far as the feet. It was laid over the shoulders and was fastened under the collar by a button. It was girded round the waist, thus taking in the brownish underdress. It appeared to be a festal robe, for in accordance with ancient Jewish customs, a similar one had been worn also by Anne. Her hair was concealed under a yellowish cap, which was pointed on the forehead and gathered together in folds at the back of the head. A black veil of soft material hung down far below the waist. In this dress I saw her making the Way of the Cross. She had worn it at the crucifixion under the mantle of prayer, or mourning, which entirely enveloped her, and she wore it now only when performing this devotion. When at work in the house, she laid it aside.

The blessed Virgin was now very advanced in years, but she had in her appearance no other mark of age than that of a great longing, which at length effectuated her glorification. She was inexpressibly grave. I never saw her laugh. The older she grew, the whiter and more transparent became her face. She was thin, but I saw no wrinkle, no sign of decay in her. She was like a spirit.

Once I saw the blessed Virgin and five other women making the Holy Way, along which she went first. She was perfectly white and transparent, indescribably touching to look upon. It seemed to me that she was now making the devotion for the last time. Among the holy women who were praying with her, there were several that had become acquainted with her in the first year of Jesus's teaching. One was a relative of the prophetess Anna, and another was the granddaughter of a maternal aunt of Elizabeth. I saw two of the women making the Way of the Cross by turns every morning and evening.

After Mary had lived three years in the settlement near Ephesus, she conceived a great desire to visit Jerusalem, so John and Peter escorted her thither. Several apostles were there assembled, of whom I remember Thomas. I think it was a council, and Mary assisted the apostles with her advice. On her arrival, I saw her in the evening twilight visiting, before she entered the city, the Mount of Olives, Mount Golgotha, the Holy Sepulcher, and all the Holy Places around Jerusalem. The Mother of God was so sad, so moved by compassion, that she could scarcely walk. Peter and John supported her under the arms.

A year and a half before her death, she made one more journey from Ephesus to Jerusalem, and I saw her again visiting the Holy Places. She was unspeakably sorrowful, and she continually sighed: "O my Son! My Son!" When she came to the back gate of that palace where she had first seen Jesus passing with the cross and where he fell, she was so agitated by the painful remembrance that she too sank to the ground. Her companions thought her dying. They removed her to Zion, upon which the Cenacle was still standing, and in one of whose buildings she took up her abode. For several days she appeared to be so weak and so near death that her friends began to think of preparing her a tomb. She herself made choice of a cave on the Mount of Olives, and the apostles had a beautiful tomb built there by a Christian stonecutter. Many were of the opinion that she would really die; and so the report of her death spread abroad. But she recovered sufficient strength to journey back to Ephesus where, a year and a half later, she did indeed die. The tomb prepared for her on the Mount of Olives was ever after held in reverence, and at a later period a church was built over it. John Damascene, as I was told in vision, wrote from hearsay that the blessed Virgin died in Jerusalem and was buried there. Her death, her assumption into heaven, and the site of her tomb, as I believe, God has allowed to be subjects of uncertain tradition that the pagan sentiments of the time might not penetrate Christianity, for the blessed Virgin might otherwise have been adored as a goddess.

The Apostles Arrive to be Present at the Blessed Virgin's Death

AS the blessed Virgin felt her end approaching, in accordance with the directions of her divine Son, she called the apostles to her by prayer. She was now in her sixty-third year. At the time of Christ's birth she was in her fifteenth. Before his ascension Jesus had made known to his most holy mother what she should say at the end of her earthly career to the apostles and some of the disciples who should be with her. He told her also that she should bless them, and that it would conduce very much to their welfare and eternal salvation. He entrusted to her also certain spiritual labors for the general good, which being accomplished, her longing after heaven was to be realized. Jesus had at the same time made known to Magdalene that she was to live concealed in the wilderness, and that Martha was to establish a community of women. He added that he himself would always be with them.

At the prayer of the blessed Virgin, the apostles received, through angels, an admonition to repair to her at Ephesus. In the various places in which they were, they had erected little churches here and there. Many of them were constructed merely of plaited rods, or branches, covered with clay, but all were of the same form as Mary's house, that is, three-cornered in the back. They were provided with altars for the celebration of holy mass. The journeys of the apostles, so distant, so exceedingly remote, were not made without divine assistance. Although they themselves were perhaps unconscious of it at the time, yet I do not doubt that they passed through many dangers in a supernatural manner. I often saw them walking unnoticed through the midst of a crowd. I have likewise seen that the miracles wrought by them among the various pagan nations were very numerous and of a different kind from those recorded of them in the holy scriptures. They labored everywhere according to the peculiar needs of the people. I saw that they carried about them the bones of the prophets or those of the first Christian martyrs, which relics they placed before them in time of prayer or when offering the holy sacrifice.

When called to Mary, Peter was in the region of Antioch with another apostle. Andrew, who had shortly before been in Jerusalem, but had there been persecuted, was not far from Peter. I saw them both on their way to Ephesus at places not very distant from each other. They passed the nights in those open inns that are met along the roads in hot countries. As Peter was lying one night near a wall, a resplendent youth approached him, took him by the hand, and bade him arise and hasten to Mary. On the way, the youth said, he would meet Andrew. Peter, who had grown stiff from age and fatigue, rose to a sitting posture and, clasping his hands round his knees to support himself, listened to the angel's words. Then he stood up, put on his mantle, girded himself, took his staff, and started on his journey. He soon came up with Andrew, who had been called by the same apparition. After traveling some distance they were met by Thaddeus, who also had received a similar warning. They journeyed together to Mary, with whom they found John.

Judas Thaddeus and Simon were in Persia when they received their summons. Thomas, who was in stature thick and short and had reddish-brown or auburn hair, was of all the apostles the farthest off. He arrived only after Mary's death. When the angel came to call him, he was praying in a hut built of reeds. With one very poor, simple servant, I saw him sailing alone in a little boat far over the waters. Then he journeyed across the country, turning aside from all the cities. A disciple now accompanied him. Thomas was in India when he received the warning. Before receiving it he had determined to go into Tartary, and he could not bring himself to change his plans. He always wanted to do so much, therefore it was that he was often behind time. So off he started northward almost across China, where Russia now is. Here he was called a second time. He obeyed the summons and hurried to Ephesus. The servant with him was a Tartar whom he had baptized. Thomas did not return to Tartary after Mary's death. He was pierced with a lance in India. I have seen that he set up a stone in this last-named country, upon which he knelt in prayer, and upon which the marks of his knees remained impressed. He told the people that when the sea would reach that stone, another would here preach Jesus Christ.

John had shortly before been in Jericho, for he often journeyed to Palestine. He usually abode in Ephesus, however, and the country around. Bartholomew was in Asia east of the Red Sea. He was handsome and very active, his complexion fair and his forehead high. He had large eyes, black curly hair, and a short, crisp beard, black and parted on the chin. He had already converted a king and all the royal family. Paul was not summoned. Those only were called that were related or acquainted with the holy family. Peter, Andrew, and John were the first to reach the blessed Virgin's house. She was already near death. She was lying calmly on her couch in her sleeping place. I saw the maidservant looking very sorrowful in this and that corner of the house, also outdoors, where she prayed prostrate with outstretched arms. I saw also two of Mary's sisters and five disciples coming together to the house. All looked tired and exhausted. They carried staves of various kinds, each according to his rank. They wore, under their hooded mantles of white wool, long albs of the same material fastened all the way down the front with little leather straps slit in the middle over little rolls like buttons. Both mantle and alb were girded high when traveling. Some had a pouch hanging from their girdle at the side. They embraced each other tenderly when they met. Many wept from mingled feelings of joy and sorrow at meeting on such an occasion. On entering the house, they laid aside their mantles, staves, pouches, and girdles; allowed their white robes to fall in broad folds down to their feet, and each put on a wide girdle inscribed with letters, which he had brought with him. Then with deep emotion they drew near Mary's couch to salute her, though she could now say only a few words. I did not see the travelers taking anything on their arrival, excepting some kind of beverage from a little flask, with which each one came provided. They did not sleep in the house, but outside under light awnings, which were put up on posts against the walls, and which were divided off and enclosed by movable screens and wickerwork.

I saw that the first to arrive prepared in the front apartment of the house a place suitable for prayer and offering the holy sacrifice. There was an altar covered with a red and over that a white cloth, and on it stood a crucifix, white like mother-of-pearl, and in shape like a Maltese cross. The cross could be opened. It contained five compartments, likewise cross-shaped. The middle one held the most blessed sacrament, while the others were intended respectively for chrism, oil, cotton, and salt. It was not quite a span, or nine inches, in length. Each of the apostles when traveling carried one like it on his breast. It was in this cross that Peter took to Mary the holy communion, during the reception of which the apostles stood bowing low, ranged in two rows from the altar down to her couch. The altar, before which was a stand with rolls of scripture hanging over it, was not in the center of the front apartment, where the fireplace stood, for that was still in use. It was placed near the wall on the right, and was put up and taken down every day.

When the apostles went all together into Mary's little sleeping chamber in order to take leave of her, they wore their long white albs and broad mantles. The screens that separated the front from the back of the house had been removed. The disciples and holy women remained standing in the front apartment. I saw that Mary sat upright, that the apostles knelt in turn at the side of her couch, and that she prayed over each and blessed him with her hands laid upon him crosswise. She did the same to the disciples and to the women. One of the latter, who stood quite bent in two over Mary, received an embrace from her. When Peter stepped up to the couch, I saw that he had a roll of scriptures in his hand. Mary then addressed them in a body, and did all that Jesus had in Bethany directed her to do. I saw also that she told John what was to be done with her remains, and that he should see that her clothes were divided between her own maidservant and a maiden of the neighborhood who came sometimes to render her service. As she spoke, she pointed to the press, or partition, and I saw the maid going to it, opening and closing it.

Death, Burial, and
Assumption of the Blessed Virgin

8/15 AND now the altar with its covers, one red, the other white, was placed in front of the crucifix of the blessed Virgin's own oratory. Peter here celebrated the Holy Mass with the same ceremonies as I had seen him first observe in the church at the pool of Bethesda. Tapers, not lamps, were burning on the altar. Mary was in a sitting posture on her couch during the whole celebration. Peter was vested in the large mantle and the pallium, whose colors glanced from white to red. These he wore over the white robe. The four apostles assisting him were also vested in festal mantles. After the communion, Peter gave the blessed sacrament to all present. During this Holy Mass, Philip arrived from Egypt. Weeping bitterly, he received the benediction of the blessed Virgin, and after the others the blessed sacrament.

Peter bore the blessed sacrament to Mary in the cross hanging on his breast, and John carried on a shallow dish the chalice containing the most sacred blood. This chalice was white, small as if for pouring, and of the same shape as that used at the Last Supper. Its stem was so short that it could be held with two fingers only. Thaddeus now brought forward a little incense basin. Peter first gave the blessed Virgin the last anointing, just as that sacrament is administered at the present day. Next he administered holy communion, which she received sitting up without support. Then she sank back again on her pillow, and after the apostles had offered a short prayer, she received the chalice from John, but not now in so upright a posture.

After communion, Mary spoke no more. Her countenance, blooming and smiling as in youth, was raised above. I no longer saw the roof of her chamber, and the lamp appeared to be suspended in the open air. A pathway of light arose from Mary up to the Heavenly Jerusalem, up to the throne of the most holy Trinity. On either side of this pathway I saw clouds of light out of which gazed angelic faces. Mary raised her arms to the Heavenly Jerusalem. Her body with all its wrappings was floating so high above the couch that I could see under it. A figure of light, also with upraised arms, appeared to issue from Mary. The two choirs of angels united under this figure and soared up with it, as if separating it from the body, which now sank back upon the couch, the hands crossed upon the breast. Many holy souls, among whom I recognized Joseph, Anne, Joachim, John the Baptist, Zechariah, and Elizabeth, came to meet her. But up she soared, followed by them, to her Son, whose wounds were flashing light far more brilliant than that which surrounded him. He received her and placed in her hand a scepter, pointing at the same time over the whole circumference of the earth. At last I saw—and the sight filled me with joy—a multitude of souls released from Purgatory and soaring up to heaven, and I received the surety that every year on the Feast of Mary's Assumption many of her devout clients are freed from Purgatory. The hour of Mary's death was made known to me as that of None, at which time also Jesus had died on the cross. Peter and John likewise must have seen the glory of Mary's blessed soul, for their faces were turned upward, but the other apostles were kneeling bowed to the ground. The body of the blessed Virgin lay radiant with light upon the couch, the eyes closed, the hands crossed upon the breast. All present knelt, adoring God.

At last the women covered the blessed remains with a sheet, put all the furniture of the house aside and covered it, even covering the fireplace. Then they veiled themselves and prayed together in a space in the front of the house, sometimes kneeling, sometimes sitting. The apostles too enveloped their head with the scarf they wore about their shoulders, and ranged in order for prayer. They took turns, two at a time, to kneel and pray at the head and feet of the blessed remains. I saw them exchanging places with one another four times in the day, and I likewise saw them making the Way of the Cross.

Andrew and Matthew were busy preparing the place of burial, which was the little grotto that Mary and John had arranged at the end of the Way of the Cross, to represent the Holy Sepulcher of Christ. It was not so large as Jesus's tomb, being scarcely as high as a man, and was surrounded by a little garden hedged in by stakes. A pathway ran obliquely down into it, and the stone couch, which was like a narrow altar, was hollowed on top to the shape of a body enveloped in its winding sheet, the head being a trifle higher than the foot. The station of Mount Calvary (the crucifixion) was on a hill nearby. No cross was erected on it, but there was one cut out on the stone. Andrew was especially active in preparing the grotto, and setting up a door firmly in front of the tomb proper.

The blessed body was prepared by the women for burial. Among them I remember having seen a daughter of Veronica and John Mark's mother. They brought spices and pots of fresh herbs, in order to embalm it according to the Jewish custom. They closed the house, and worked by the light of lamps. They opened up the apartment back of the fireplace and removed the screens that enclosed the little alcove used by the blessed Virgin as a sleeping place, in order to have more room for their work of embalming. The wicker screens of the alcove were not again replaced, for immediately after the obsequies they, along with those of the clothes press, were put out of sight by the maid-servant. Only the altar was allowed to remain standing before the crucifix in Mary's sleeping apartment. The whole house had now become like a little chapel in which the apostles prayed and celebrated the most holy and unbloody sacrifice. While the women were preparing the holy body for burial, the apostles prayed in choirs, sometimes in the front apartment, sometimes outside the house. The women went about their task most devoutly and reverently, just as had been done when preparing the most sacred body of Jesus for burial. The body of the blessed Virgin was lifted in the linen of the deathbed and laid in a long basket, which had a lid and which was filled with covers, so that when lying on them, it rose above the edge. The body was of a dry, indescribable whiteness as if shining with light, and of so little weight that, like a mere husk, it could be raised quite easily on the hands. The face was fresh and blooming. The women cut off some locks of hair to keep as relics. They laid bunches of herbs around the neck and throat, under the arms, and in the armpits.

Before the holy body was shrouded in its white garments and enveloped in the winding sheets, Peter celebrated the unbloody sacrifice on the altar of the oratory and gave holy communion to the other apostles. After that Peter and John approached the body in their mantles of ceremony. John carried a vessel of oil, with which Peter anointed, in the form of a cross and with accompanying prayers, the forehead, hands, and feet of the holy body, which was afterward entirely enveloped in linens by the women. They placed on the head a wreath of flowers, white, red, and sky-blue, as a symbol of Mary's virginity, and over the face a transparent veil, through which it could be seen encircled by the wreath. The feet also, which were bound up in aromatic herbs, could be traced through the linens that enveloped them. The arms and hands were bound crosswise on the breast. Thus prepared, the holy body was laid in a coffin of snow-white wood with a tightly fitting, arched cover, which was fastened down at the head, the foot, and in the middle, with gray straps. The coffin was then laid on a litter. Everything was done with the utmost solemnity, and all were penetrated with deep emotion. The sorrow of the mourners was more human and more openly expressed than at Jesus's burial, at which holy awe and reverence predominated.

When it was time to bear the coffin to the grotto, one half-hour distant, Peter and John raised it from the litter and carried it in their hands to the door of the house, outside of which it was again laid on the litter, which Peter and John then raised upon their shoulders. Six of the apostles thus carried it in turn. The coffin hung between the bearers as in a cradle, for the poles of the litter were run through leathern straps, or matting. Some of the apostles walked before the coffin praying, and after it came the women. Lamps, or lanterns on poles, were carried.

Before reaching the grotto, the litter was set down. Four of the apostles bore the coffin in, and placed it in the hollow of the tomb. All went, one by one, into the grotto, where they knelt in prayer before the holy body, honoring it and taking leave of it. Then the tomb was shut in by a wicker screen that extended from the front edge of the tomb to the top of the vaulted wall above. Before the entrance of the grotto they made a trench, which they planted so thickly with blooming flowers and bushes covered with berries that one could gain access to it only from the side, and that only by making his way through the underbrush.

8/15–16 *On the night following the burial* took place the bodily assumption of the blessed Virgin into heaven. I saw on this night several of the apostles and holy women in the little garden, praying and singing psalms before the grotto. I saw a broad pathway of light descend from heaven and rest upon the tomb. In it were circles of glory full of angels, in the midst of whom the resplendent soul of the blessed Virgin came floating down. Before her went her divine Son, the marks of his wounds flashing with light. In the innermost circle, that which surrounded the holy soul of Mary, the angels appeared like the faces of very young children; in the second circle, they were like those of children from six to eight years old; and in the outermost, like the faces of youths, I could clearly distinguish only the face, the rest of the figure consisting of perfectly transparent light. Encircling the head of the blessed Virgin like a crown was a choir of blessed spirits. I know not what those present saw of all this. But I saw that some gazed up in amazement and adoration, while others cast themselves prostrate in fright upon the earth. These apparitions, becoming more and more distinct as they approached nearer, floated over the grotto, and another pathway of light issued from it and arose to the Heavenly Jerusalem. The blessed soul of Mary, floating before Jesus, penetrated through the rock and into the tomb, out of which she again arose radiant with light in her glorified body and, escorted by the entire multitude of celestial spirits, returned in triumph to the Heavenly Jerusalem.

8/16 Next day, when the apostles were engaged in choir service, Thomas made his appearance with two companions. One was a disciple named Jonathan Eleazar, and the other a servant from the most remote country of the three holy kings. Thomas was greatly grieved when he heard that the blessed Virgin was already buried. He wept with an abundance of tears quite astonishing to behold, for he could not forgive himself for coming so late. Weeping bitterly he threw himself, with Jonathan at his side, on the spot upon which the blessed soul of Mary had left her body, and afterward knelt long before the altar. The apostles, who had not interrupted their choir-chanting on account of his coming, now gathered around him, raised him up, embraced him, and set before him and his companions bread, honey, and some kind of beverage in little jugs. After that they accompanied him with lights to the tomb. Two disciples bent the shrubbery to one side. Thomas, Eleazar, and John went in and prayed before the coffin. Then John loosened the three straps that bound it, for it rose high enough above the trough-like couch to admit of being opened. They stood the lid of the coffin on one side and, to their intense astonishment, beheld only the empty winding sheets lying like a husk, or shell, and in perfect order. Only over the face was it drawn apart, and over the breast slightly opened. The swathing bands of the arms and hands lay separate, as if gently drawn off, but in perfect order. The apostles gazed in amazement, their hands raised. John cried out: "She is no longer here!" The others came in quickly, wept, prayed, looking upward with raised arms, and finally cast themselves on the ground, remembering the radiant cloud of the preceding night. Then rising, they took the winding sheet just as it was, all the grave linens, and the coffin to keep as relics, and returned to the house by the Holy Way, praying and singing psalms.

When they entered the house, John laid the folded linens on a little flap-table before the altar. Thomas and the others were in prayer, but Peter went a little apart, as if pondering some mystery. After that I saw him celebrating divine service at the altar before Mary's crucifix, and the apostles standing in order behind him, praying and singing. The women were standing in the doorways and by the walls of the fireplace.

The young servant that had come with Thomas looked quite unlike any of those present. He had small eyes, high cheekbones, forehead and nose remarkably flat, and his complexion was brownish. He was already baptized. He was perfectly innocent, and obeyed orders simply. He did all that he was told, remained standing or sitting wherever they told him to do so, turned his eyes in any direction indicated to see whatever was pointed out to him, and smiled upon everyone. When Thomas wept, he wept also. He always remained with Thomas, and I saw him dragging immense stones when Thomas was building a chapel.

I often saw the apostles and disciples standing together in circles and relating where they had been and giving their experience.

Before the apostles left Mary's house to journey again into distant parts, they rendered the grotto of the tomb wholly inaccessible by raising an embankment of earth before the entrance. At the rear, however, they made a low passage to the back wall of the tomb proper and an opening in the wall, by which one could look down upon it. This passage was known only to the holy women. Above the grotto they built a chapel of wood and wicker-work, and hung it with mats and tapestry. The little altar consisted of a stone slab; the step, too, was of stone. Behind the altar hung a strip of stuff on which was sewed or embroidered quite simply, in the colors of her festal robes, a picture of Mary. The little garden in front of the tomb, and especially the whole of Mary's Way of the Cross, was beautified by them. While engaged in this task of love, they prayed continually and chanted psalms. The apartment of the house in which Mary had had her oratory and sleeping alcove was converted into a little church. Mary's maid continued her abode in the front part of the house, and two of the disciples were left there by Peter for the benefit of the faithful dwelling in that section of the country.

The Life of Mary After Christ's Ascension

The apostles, with tears and embraces, took leave of one another after they had once more celebrated solemn service in Mary's house. An apostle or disciple often returned at different times to pray there. I saw also that here and there, out of devotion and in reverence for the blessed Virgin, churches were built by the faithful in the same style as her house, and that her Way of the Cross and her tomb were for a long time devoutly visited by the Christians. I had a vision of those early times, just after Mary's assumption into heaven: A woman living near Ephesus, who entertained great love for Mary, visited her house. On her return she caused an altar like that she had seen there to be made, and covered it with a very costly cloth of tapestry. The woman was very poor, and had to defray the debt she thereby incurred by the sale of a piece of her property. Finding herself after some time in dire distress, she went, though very sorrowfully, to a married Christian and sold to her the beautiful altar cloth. But when the Feast of Mary's Assumption came round, I saw the poor woman very much troubled at no longer having the cloth with which to adorn her little altar. She went very humbly to the house of the purchaser, who meanwhile had given birth to twins, and begged her to lend her for the feast the cloth she had sold her, that she might adorn with it the altar of the blessed Virgin. But the present owner would not hear of lending it, and her husband repulsed the poor woman with the words: "Mary is dead and needs not the cloth; but my wife who bought it needs it." The poor woman went away sad, and complained to Mary of her want. Next night, I saw the blessed Virgin appear to the sleeping couple. She looked displeased and told them that, as a punishment of their hard and unchristian sentiments toward the poor devout woman, their children would die, and they themselves become poorer than the one whose request they had spurned. The couple awoke, and looked upon it at first as an empty dream. But on finding the twins dead, they recognized their offense with bitter lamentations. With many tears the husband and wife did penance. They received forgiveness from Mary, and the punishment in store for them was averted.

MAPS

Area Around Capernaum During Time of Christ

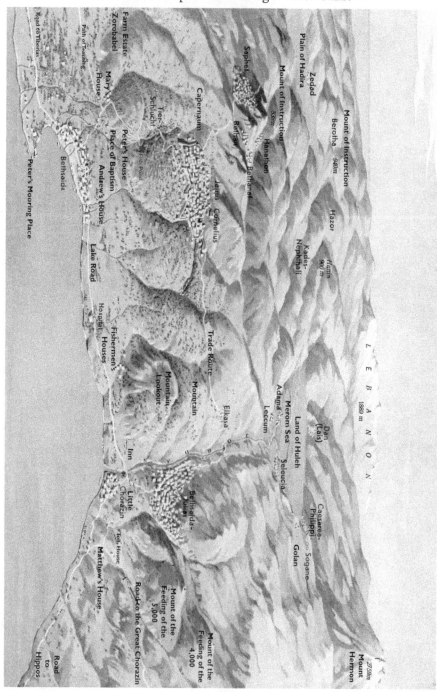

Road to Tiberias

Path of Teaching

Farm Estate
Zorobabel

Mary's
House

Peter's Mooring Place

Bethsaida

Treppe
Schlucht

Capernaum

Peter's House
Place of Baptism

Andrew's House

Lake Road

Hospital
Houses

Fishermen's

Inn

Jairus

Cornelius

Saphet

Zedad
Plain of Hadira

Mount of Instruction
33m

Bethano

Hananiam

Trade Route

Mountain

Mountain
Lookout

Little
Chorazin

Matthew's House

Berotha
94m

Hazor

Kades-
Nephthali

Elkasa

Bethsaida-
Julias

Toll House

Road to the Great Chorazin

Mount of Instruction

Hulin
90 m

Merom Sea
Adama
Leccum

Land of Huleh

Seleucia

Dan
(Lais)

Sogane

Golan

Caesarea-
Philippi

Mount of the
Feeding of the
4,000

Mount of the
Feeding of the
5,000

Road
to
Hippos

L E B A N O N

1869 m

2759m
Mount
Hermon

436

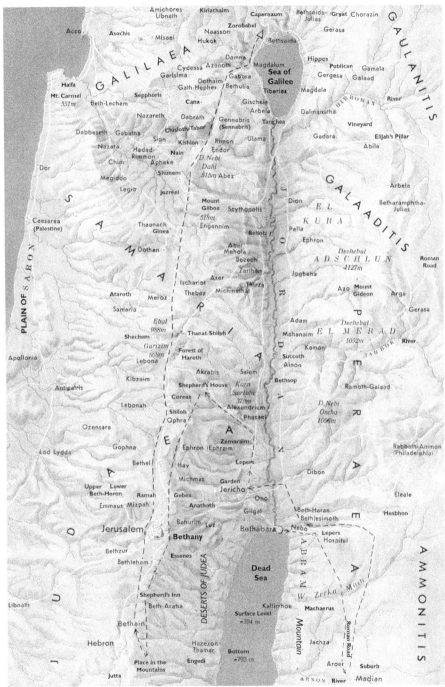

Bethabara—Hospital near Nebo—Suburb of Madian—Bethjesimoth—Jericho
Shepherd's Fields in Southern Samaria—Shepherd's House near Hebron
Place in the Mountains near Jutta—Bethain—Capernaum

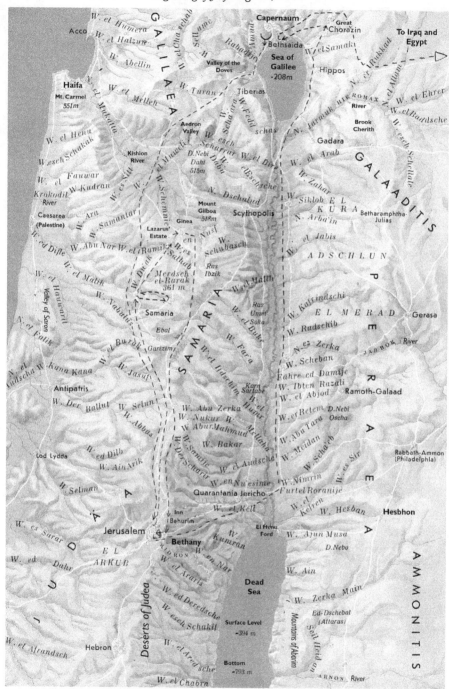

Capernaum—Jerusalem—Places near Samaria—Ginea—Lazarus's Estate near Ginea
Ginea—Inn near Bahurim—Bethany—Jerusalem—Stretch of Land in Perea
Great Chorazin—Bethsaida—In the Direction of Iraq

MAP 37: The Journey to the Kings, to Ur, and to Heliopolis
August 7, AD 32– January, AD 33

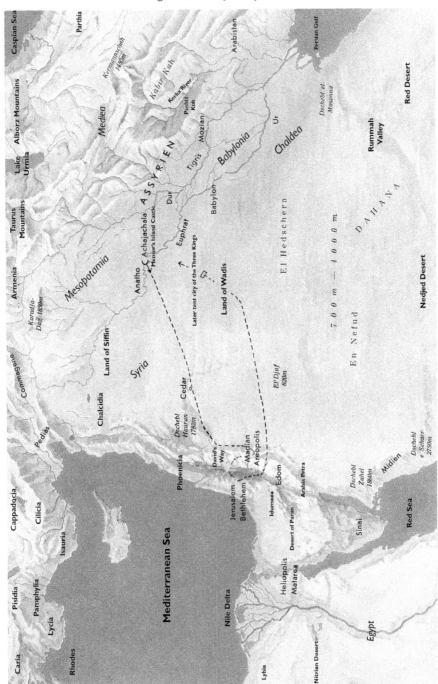

Kedar—Tent City of the Kings—Mozian—Ur—Heliopolis—Beersheba

439

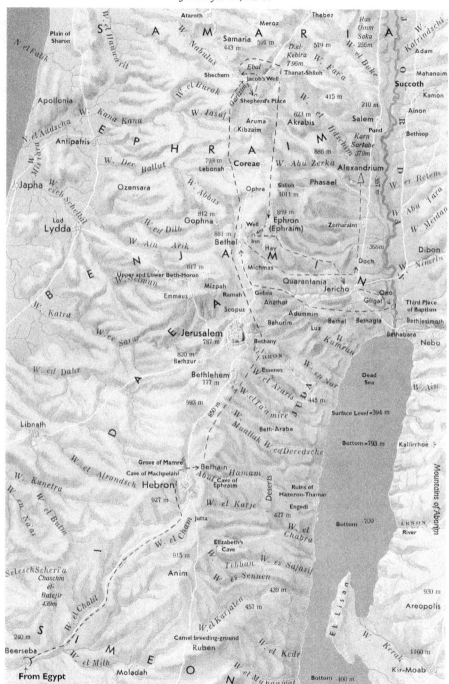

Beersheba—Bethain—Jacob's Well—Shepherd's Place in Samaria—Shechem—Ephron Jericho—Third Place of Baptism—Bethel—Doch—Alexandrium

MAP 39: The Last Journey to Jerusalem
January 24–February 19, AD 33

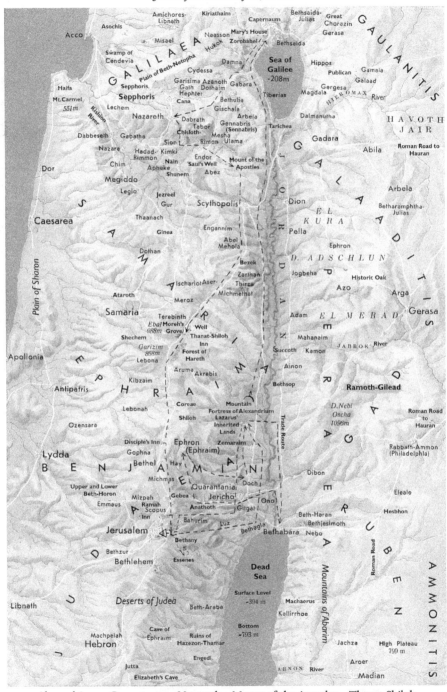

Alexandrium—Capernaum—Nazareth—Mount of the Apostles—Thanat-Shiloh
Bethany—Ensemes—Bethany—Lazarus's Property near Alexandrium—Bethabara
Ephron—Doch—Lazarus's Property near Alexandrium—Bethany—Jerusalem

441

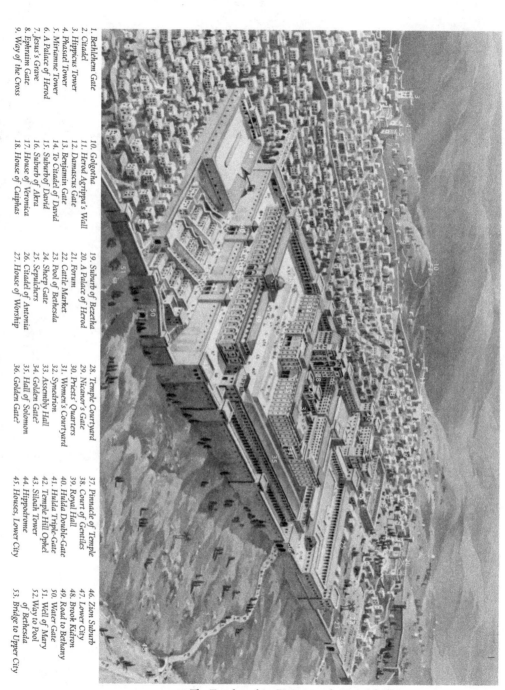

1. Bethlehem Gate
2. Citadel
3. Hippicus Tower
4. Phasael Tower
5. Miriamne Tower
6. A Palace of Herod
7. Jesus's Grave
8. Ephraim Gate
9. Way of the Cross

10. Golgotha
11. Herod Agrippa's Wall
12. Damascus Gate
13. Benjamin Gate
14. To Citadel of David
15. Suburb of David
16. Suburb of Akra
17. House of Veronica
18. House of Caiphas

19. Suburb of Bezetha
20. A Palace of Herod
21. Forum
22. Cattle Market
23. Pool of Bethesda
24. Sheep Gate
25. Sepulchers
26. Citadel of Antonia
27. House of Worship

28. Temple Courtyard
29. Nicanor's Gate
30. Priests' Quarters
31. Women's Courtyard
32. Synedrion
33. Assembly Hall
34. Golden Gate?
35. Hall of Solomon
36. Golden Gate?

37. Pinnacle of Temple
38. Court of Gentiles
39. Royal Hall
40. Hulda Double-Gate
41. Hulda Triple-Gate
42. Temple Hill Ophel
43. Siloah Tower
44. Hippodrome
45. Houses, Lower City

46. Zion Suburb
47. Lower City
48. Brook Kidron
49. Road to Bethany
50. Water Gate
51. Well of Mary
52. Way to Pool
    of Bethesda
53. Bridge to Upper City

The Temple and its Environs at the Time of Christ

442